M000281949

Praise for *My Confederate Kinfolk: A Twenty-First Century Freedwoman Discovers Her Roots*

"What began as a personal desire to unravel her family's racial ancestry became a gripping historical tale that is uniquely, tragically American. . . . Davis willfully provokes a painful but necessary dialogue. . . . This book's gift is to underline a subject that tends to make people uncomfortable—this nation's knotty racial ties."—RENÉE GRAHAM, *The Boston Globe*

"In her engaging new book, Thulani Davis . . . provides a vivid portrait of her African American and white forebears, people who crossed paths in war, in work, in slavery, in freedom, and, finally, in love. . . . The book weaves these disparate, intimate histories into one compelling tale and gives us, at the same time, a detailed and lively rendering of Reconstruction. . . . Readers will joyfully discover that [Davis] really is both a genealogist and a tamer of history."—DENISE NICHOLAS, *The Washington Post*

"This is one of those rare memoirs in which personal history becomes American history. In a profound sense, Thulani Davis's family is the American family, and her book is redemptive."—RUSSELL BANKS, author of *The Sweet Hereafter* and *Affliction*

"[Davis's] very personal story opens poignant perspectives on an American past where identity was both more and less than black-and-white."—THOMAS J. DAVIS, *Library Journal*

"In telling the story of her search for ancestors that began with old letters, the writings of her grandmother and a strange photograph of a black child of the 19th century completely decked out in authentic tartan plaid, Davis also documents the condition of blacks making the transition from bondage to Emancipation as 'freedmen and freedwomen.'"—*Kirkus Reviews*

THE
EMANCIPATION
CIRCUIT

THE EMANCIPATION CIRCUIT

BLACK ACTIVISM FORGING A CULTURE OF FREEDOM

THULANI DAVIS

DUKE UNIVERSITY PRESS *Durham and London* 2022

© 2022 Thulani Davis
All rights reserved
Printed in the United States of America on acid-free paper ∞
Project editor: Lisa Lawley
Designed by Matthew Tauch
Typeset in Adobe Jenson Pro and ITC Franklin Gothic by
Westchester Publishing Services

Library of Congress Cataloging-in-Publication Data
Names: Davis, Thulani, author.
Title: The emancipation circuit : Black activism forging a culture of
freedom / Thulani Davis.
Description: Durham : Duke University Press, 2022. | Includes
bibliographical references and index.
Identifiers: LCCN 2021031830 (print)
LCCN 2021031831 (ebook)
ISBN 9781478015567 (hardcover)
ISBN 9781478018193 (paperback)
ISBN 9781478022800 (ebook)
Subjects: LCSH: African Americans—Politics and government—
19th century. | African Americans—History—1863–1877. |
Reconstruction (U.S. history, 1865–1877) | Freedmen—Political
activity—Southern States—History—19th century. | African
Americans—Civil rights—History—19th century. | BISAC: SOCIAL
SCIENCE / Ethnic Studies / American / African American & Black
Studies | HISTORY / United States / 19th Century
Classification: LCC E185.2.D39 2022 (print) | LCC E185.2 (ebook) |
DDC 973/.0496073009034—dc23
LC record available at https://lccn.loc.gov/2021031830
LC ebook record available at https://lccn.loc.gov/2021031831

Cover art: *Map Showing the Distribution of the Slave Population
of the Southern States of the United States.* Compiled from
the census of 1860. Geography and Map Division, Library
of Congress, Washington, DC.

SUPPORT FOR THIS RESEARCH WAS PROVIDED BY THE
UNIVERSITY OF WISCONSIN-MADISON OFFICE OF THE VICE
CHANCELLOR FOR RESEARCH AND GRADUATE EDUCATION
WITH FUNDING FROM THE WISCONSIN ALUMNI RESEARCH
FOUNDATION.

For

Gerri Hollins
(1947–2012)
Friend, founder of the
Contraband Society

Ntozake Shange
(1948–2018)
Joyous advocate and inspiration

Joseph Jarman
(1937–2019)
Fierce dharma messenger

George Floyd
(1973–2020)
Mighty human being

this little light o' mine

CONTENTS

LIST OF MAPS

LIST OF TABLES

ACKNOWLEDGMENTS

I came into this project as a middle-aged woman and finish as an elder, a person with debts to many, especially mentors who are no longer here, half a dozen of whom made their homecoming while I worked on this book. During the 2020 election, we marked the 150th anniversary of the Fifteenth Amendment, granting Black males the right to vote, an event of great import to this book. We also honored the 100th anniversary of women voting, if only the fifty-fifth anniversary of this right for southern Black women like myself. Events in this book helped make these rights possible and ask us to defend them. Frankly, we do so now at less personal risk and even greater risk to the idea of democracy.

At New York University, friends and advisers not only provided me with incredible training but allowed me to build an interdisciplinary context for work somewhere inside the bounds of Black political theory, history, and cultural theory. For this I owe my deepest thanks to Jennifer Morgan, Nikhil Pal Singh, and Martha Hodes, as well as to theorist George Shulman, who taught me a lot, and Michael Ralph, a gifted interrogator, whose questions on the first manuscript continue to serve my thinking.

I also cannot say enough about those brilliant members of my NYU cohort who read early sections of this manuscript and reacted with such insight and provocative language that for months I checked the notes I took from them: Justin Leroy, Brittany C. Carter, Laura E. Helton, Carmen I. Phillips, Stuart Schrader, Samuel Ng, and A. J. Bauer. I thank Laura in particular for identifying the diverse forms of fugitivity here. In the Department of Social and Cultural Analysis, I want to thank Arlene Davila, Dean Phillip Brian Harper, and Awam Amkpa for important interventions at critical moments, and the department's great support of my sojourn there, especially for the encouragement of the Lerner Prize in American Studies and a Summer Research Fellowship. Other scholars who had a great influence must include the exquisite intellectual guides Cyrus Patell, Ana Dopico, Deborah Willis, and Michele Mitchell. I owe a debt to the NYU Graduate School of Arts and Sciences for a Predoctoral Summer Fellowship, and the Gallatin School of Individualized Study for its personalized mentoring and the help of a Dean's Scholarship and an NYU Gallatin Newington-Cropsey Foundation Fellowship.

I have to reach back and thank my onetime mentor/colleague, Quandra Prettyman, the first African American teacher at Barnard College. She always quietly told me to "do my thing" my way and say what I wanted to say. Thanks also must go to the Veterans Braintrust Award of the Congressional Black Caucus, US House of Representatives for a most surprising honor for working on getting a national monument made at Fort Monroe, Virginia. Readers of this book will see why I was happy to help local organizers in Virginia save that site, which opened in August 2019 to commemorate the four hundredth year since the African arrival there in 1619.

Thanks also to the many librarians who helped me at the NYU Bobst microform collection; the Library of Virginia; the New Orleans Public Library; Special Collections at the Howard-Tilton Library and the Amistad Collection at Tulane University; Special Collections, Miami University, Ohio; Northwestern State University of Louisiana (at Natchitoches); the Mississippi State Archive; the Archives and Special Collections, Blues Manuscript and Special Collections at the University of Mississippi, Oxford, Mississippi; and the Stuart A. Rose Manuscript, Archive and Rare Book Library, Emory University, Atlanta, Georgia. Since I moved to Madison, the librarians at the Wisconsin Historical Society, a very special place, have been of great help.

For making survival way more possible, thanks to Richard Wesley of the Maurice Kanbar Institute of Film and Television; Rita and Burton Goldberg Department of Dramatic Writing at NYU's Tisch School of the Arts; filmmakers Louis Massiah, Orlando Patterson, and Denise Greene; and miniseries producer Faith Childs, who all gave me great projects to work on part-time. Thanks to McArthur Binion for pushing me to see two other important projects to completion during these years—sound and video recording of Joseph Jarman's last full concert and re-publication of his book.

Among those with bottomless wisdom I must name Faith Childs and Christine Clark-Evans. Arnim Johnson, a friend of more than fifty years, provided sage advice and read early twentieth-century legal documents, checked my understanding of Supreme Court cases, and drove the entire state of Mississippi with me a second time, after doing so with me on my last book. They have been through it all with me, and I hope I have been there for them in some way. For matchless hospitality, I thank Carole Oliver and her family in New Orleans, and Joan Thornell, for aid during and after an earthquake on a research trip. And whoever the cooks were who made the fried green tomatoes I ate at every Mississippi Delta roadside diner—may they live long and prosper.

Coming to Wisconsin was a great move thanks to then chair Craig Werner; Dolores Liamba, former department administrator; and all my colleagues in the Department of Afro-American Studies, especially former chair Christina Greene, Brenda Gayle Plummer, Christy Clark-Pujara, Sandy Adell, Michael Thornton, and Anthony Black. I thank them also for nominating me for the Nellie Y. McKay Fellowship, which gave me an invaluable year to work on this book, and for concern that I have leave during a period of terminal illness and bereavement for three loved ones. Tireless support for this study in the way of reading chapters, as part of our writers group, the Fundis (after Ella Baker), was given by Brenda, Christina, Christy, and April Haynes. I am very grateful for support I have also received from other parts of the university, especially for receipt of a Vilas Early Investigators Award, which has supported my new work for two years, and I was fortunate to receive assistance from the College of Letters and Science. Support for this research was provided by the University of Wisconsin–Madison Office of the Vice Chancellor for Research and Graduate Education with funding from the Wisconsin Alumni Research Foundation. Thanks also to Florence Hsia in that office.

Thanks to Alesia Alexander, my graduate research assistant, who pored over data tables, and Dorothea Salo, Distinguished Faculty Associate in the Information School, who digitized some of my archive. The amazing Cartography Lab at UW, headed by Tanya Buckingham, and cartographer Alicia Iverson are owed much gratitude for their care and generosity in translating my handmade maps into much smarter creations. Joe Bucciero gave me invaluable insight on restructuring a massive amount of material and also asked good questions. I am fortunate to work with Duke University Press, especially Ken Wissoker, Elizabeth Ault, Ryan Kendall, and Lisa Lawley as well as copyeditor Susan Ecklund. I feel very fortunate in having had readers who gave generous, thoughtful, and inspirational insights, which I hope I have put to good use.

I miss Ntozake Shange, my friend of fifty-plus years, whose boundless enthusiasm and welcome laughter always answered the question "Should I?" with "Yes." I also miss the matchless grin with which Joseph Jarman always greeted me. My partner of twenty years and friend of forty-five years, he always showed me what he meant by "you have to do it with total commitment": be fully present in doing one's chosen work. This willingness to be in the moment, not knowing what sounds or people may be flying your way, taught me to trust and go where I'm going. My family has stood by my adventurous career with sustained support and celebration. I hope they know how I much I cherish them all. My most long-standing debt for a life chasing African American history and culture is to two people who told tales over crabs in the kitchen or over drinks and cigars on the front porch: my father, Collis P. Huntington Davis (1900–1974), who raised me, and his younger brother Arthur Paul Davis (1904–96), the youngest two of nine whose parents were enslaved as children. They told me what I know about the many slavery survivors who raised them. They did this with great humor and a serenity I hope to acquire before much longer. Nothing in here would have surprised them, except my lateness in doing it. Over that, we all would have had a good laugh.

INTRODUCTION

Black Political Thought as Shaped in the South

The Colored People are crazily fond of organization.
—*American Missionary* 41, no. 2 (April 1887)

In one description of the place in history to be held by the events in the southern civil rights movement, the Reverend Martin Luther King Jr. wrote: "Seen in perspective, the summer of 1963 was historic partly because it witnessed the first offensive in history launched by Negroes along a broad front. The heroic but spasmodic and isolated slave revolts of the antebellum South had fused, more than a century later, into a simultaneous, massive assault against segregation."[1] This magical fusing of slave revolts into the "massive assault" of the 1960s may seem odd now, except that it reveals how little even King and other leading activists of his day were able to really know about the Black past. King was, I believe, at pains to make this connection as his book was published on the one hundredth anniversary of emancipation.

The anniversary was an occasion on which many African American thinkers pondered the connection between the civil rights movement underway and its possible legacy and debt to the enslaved and the first generations to become citizens of this country. James Baldwin weighed the century's meaning as well in *The Fire Next Time*, asking: "How can the American Negro past be used?" He, in turn, evoked W. E. B. Du Bois's identification of the centrality of "the color line" at the outset of the twentieth century.[2] At the time, there was one recently published book covering the broad scope of African American history, published the previous year. I would assume King and Baldwin read it along with millions of us anxious to know about our history because, as a general readership book, it was a first. Lerone Bennett's *Before the Mayflower: A History of Black America, 1619–1962* put into popular parlance the fact that Africans were here before the 1620 settler landing at Plymouth Rock. Malcolm (X) Shabazz probably read it too, as he was known to refer to the Plymouth Rock landing and quip that "we didn't land on Plymouth Rock, the rock was landed on us."[3] I read Du Bois's *Black Reconstruction* in the 1960s, and I would guess King and Shabazz did as well, only because there was so little reliable information (as Du Bois points out) and because it was by Du Bois.[4]

Yet King's conviction that the long civil rights movement of the twentieth century was the first "offensive" on "a broad front" is roughly what many high school students are taught today. Some students I have taught were also under the impression that change was begun and *completed* by the mid-twentieth-century activism. Thanks in part to the work of King and many other Black southerners who built movements and freedom schools across the South, and other movements across the nation, several generations of historians were moved to create a body of work that is filling in the gap King wanted to close between his time and the long past of generations trapped in the slave system. In 1972, Angela Davis made a specific call for scholarship to expose the resistance and rebellion against the slave system obscured in the historiography of the Black past.[5]

The main proposition of my contribution to this lacuna is that the first offensive in history launched by Negroes "along a broad front" was begun by the enslaved during the Civil War, and that its connections to later movements are (1) a heritable oral regime of knowledge on building social and political formations, and (2) the sustained need to access organizing skills and groups due to the continued lack of protections against systemic injustice and routine violence. I argue that in fact King's "Beloved Community" is very old. Those of us who have spent our lives in its demanding, restoring, and empowering embrace in fact inherited it from churches, teachers in segregated schools, and old folks who told stories never written down.

The Emancipation Circuit: Black Activism Forging a Culture of Freedom contributes to the literature of Reconstruction and post-Reconstruction by focusing on grassroots organizing among African Americans and studying activist organizing as a heritable facet of cultural continuity. It proposes further that the study of Black southern resistance is an excavation of geographical circuits at one level and of an intricate infrastructure of social networks at the most local level, tailoring struggle to specific needs. Owing to the military occupation in the South from 1865 to 1877, freedpeople often asked for federal troops to put down violence—with mixed results—and they did what King would later do, appealed to the US Congress and the president of the United States. In making an analysis of Black political drives over the second half of the nineteenth century, this project proposes that the "long arc" of Black movements begins and continues through the nineteenth century, and it lays the groundwork for looking at the continually evolving regional agendas in the Black South that would be marginalized at the turn of the twentieth century by the efforts to form a national civil rights agenda, national unions, and national hierarchies in religious and social institutions.[6]

Along the Eastern Seaboard and the Mississippi Delta, organizing centers began to emerge with the liberation and flight of slaves during the Civil War. The self-liberation, or emancipation by flight, of at least 400,000 enslaved people, followed by the emancipation of the rest of the four million Blacks in the South, produced new social formations within a region already marked by uneven development. For most African Americans, emancipation was begun without assistance and created the need to develop resources from within communities to provide all the benefits and services commonly available in other regions—or in the South, for whites—either by purchase or from municipal agencies: housing, food, clothing, access to water and sewerage, jobs, medical service, education, policing, roads, sites for spiritual practice, and entertainment. I show that Black communities attempted to meet this broad range of community-building needs through a wide array of grassroots organizations and a capacious sense of the political. I believe the diverse efforts by millions of freedpeople to seek safety from the slave system, and later to exercise citizenship rights, constituted the first mass Black movement in the United States and that it was built in active connection with allies across the region and in conscious awareness of acting as a collectivity.[7]

The Emancipation Circuit situates the emergence of African American community organizing in the postemancipation South along a route trafficked by cotton bales and hogsheads of sugar and tobacco, and establishes that a long history of local organizing left progressive veins running through states that remained stubbornly conservative over time. The communities on this route—both urban and rural—were subject to multiple layers of organizing over two or more generations. The circuits in the southern states constituted a network I call the Emancipation Circuit, which was built by community ties among Blacks after the war and elaborated by activists, missionaries, and teachers—circuit riders who moved from one newly free community to another, advocating for constitutional rights, self-reliance, electoral structures, and literacy and petitioning for redress. Starting in the 1880s, the circuit became the route for populist and union organizers, as well as blues singers and preachers moving locally in the Mississippi Delta, and in the 1890s for Black press distribution around the South, and in the early 1900s for Garvey organizers, minstrels, and tent show divas like Ma Rainey and Bessie Smith.

Stephanie Camp's adaptation of Edward Said's term *rival geography* has proved useful in describing the practice of enslaved people redefining local geography as they resisted containment by the slave system. As Camp explains, "The rival geography was not a settled spatial formation, for it included quarters, outbuildings, woods, swamps, and neighboring farms as chance granted them. Where planters' mapping of their farms was defined by fixed places for enslaved residents, the rival geography was characterized by motion: the movement of bodies, objects, and information within and around plantation space."[8] Clearly, *rival geography* could also describe the escape routes used by runaways. Still, it is important to distinguish the Emancipation Circuit from the circuit Blacks built inside the slave system (and the Native American trail system they sometimes used) and the inland routes of the Underground Railroad. The Emancipation Circuit uses much more direct routes between southern places, whereas the others served the desire for secrecy.

The Emancipation Circuit could be described as a system of regional networks built on labor sites and shipping routes with local routes that created ties between communities as well as ties to other networks. Importantly, though, it was a circuit born of abolition. It was made possible by the presence of US military, during the war and after, and by the opportunity fugitive settlements provided for holding meetings and large assemblies, setting up schools, and conducting prayer meetings. The camps in which fugitives first settled became sites of what Katherine McKittrick terms *oppositional spatial practices*, due to the sheer numbers involved, the fact that they were often on contestable ground not owned by slaveholders, and the access to new information. As she points out, "Traditional geographies did, and arguably still do, require black displacement, black placelessness, black labor, and a black population that submissively stays 'in place.'"⁹ The mass movement to camps and spontaneous settlements created the opposite conditions from those in which space for community was usually created. The fugitive settlements and camps set up during the war laid the groundwork for the dissemination of information on citizenship, governance, and collective histories, despite the fact that the military and missionaries were prioritizing all able workers returning to labor. The oppositional practices of the refugees turned the camps into hubs for activists to hear and to share collective notions around blackness that united thousands who had not necessarily been neighbors in the slave system. The tremendous thirst for information and the diverse forms of information needed, from sources of survival to the whereabouts of missing loved ones to literacy, naturally caused meeting agendas to build a capacious sense of community and mobilizations to construct. Finally, because most people were fugitives living in near-combat situations, they created communities and groups highly motivated to move on actionable information.

This work differs from much of the Reconstruction historiography in asserting that such a widespread geographical circuit was created and was a social and political achievement of the four million seeking to define freedom after abolition. The circuit is an achievement that emerged as a product of displacement during the Civil War and emancipation, created by people defined by overt fugitive status, and characterized by the understandings people had of being fugitive, of displacement, and of fugitive status provoking policing and resistance. After emancipation, these understandings persisted and informed how Reconstruction was built on the local level. The circuit was shaped by people seeing freedom through the prism of slavery, flight from slavery, and the conditions of displacement and statelessness that were the first realities of abolition.

I contend that what they built proved durable and renewable. It is apparent that community organizing among freedpeople was social in nature and that social reproduction took place in the creation of institutions supporting newly autonomous families, and in the processes of creating institutions in an environment of policing and opposition that elided differences between the political and criminal, or action regarded as "offensive" to "southern culture." The reproduction of tactics used in hostile environments proved renewable—out of necessity—in later political and social development. The means by which the people on the Emancipation Circuit struggled for citizenship and justice also immediately affected others coming into the country as alternative labor forces, such as Asians and Italians, who raised more new questions of statelessness, citizenship, and belonging. The Thirteenth, Fourteenth, and Fifteenth Amendments, legacies of the first free generation, have spurred voting rights activism ever since. Members of Congress cited the Fifteenth, during the summer of 2021, in objection to recent voter repression measures in states, reading aloud section 1: "The right of citizens of the United States to vote shall not be denied or abridged by the United States or by any State on account of race, color, or previous condition of servitude."[10]

The Emancipation Circuit was a route for the circulation of ideas about citizenship, workers' demands, and contending with racial violence—or cotton prices, political meetings, and revivals—as well as evolving Black views on labor, gender, and the prospects for something better, literally or metaphorically, down the line. The phrase *down the line* encapsulates the view of long-term struggle ignited during the Civil War, if not by the slave system. Many of us have heard the phrase for decades, maybe in church, where it can mean "in the sweet by and by," or in a union hall, but in the late nineteenth century the railroads gave "down the line" a place in the nearer future and in geography. Word no longer just passed down the line of the cotton rows and from quarter to quarter but from depot to flag stop. While the Underground Railroad and its "freedom train" had separated the fortunate from the slavery system, mobility in freedom connected southern African Americans to each other, and "down the line" meant possible futures.

This work focuses on the process by which freedpeople engaged citizenship and built a palimpsest of layers of organizing structures that allowed the continued pursuit of community interests after Reconstruction, often movements that happened across the region. The diverse forms of equality that freedmen and freedwomen sought from emancipation proved elusive and, even in the most successful struggles, transient—such as with the right to vote. The freedoms they strove for proved fugitive in much the same sense that Sheldon Wolin describes democracy: "a mode of being that is conditioned by bitter experience, doomed to succeed only temporarily, but . . . a recurrent possibility as long as the memory of the political survives." The freedoms sought were elusive because they required a full exercise of democracy, a reality hampered by "the peculiarity of democratic liberty that it shields antidemocratic forms of power."[11] We still struggle as a society for the full exercise of democracy that might prevent the constant marginalization of rights gained before, such as the right for all citizens to vote.

In the case of freedpeople, "the memory of the political" that survived was, as one of my students put it to me, "a new knowledge regime." That memory of the political contained the tools for mobilizing communities, tools kept alive in subsequent drives described in this study. In turn, that new knowledge regime created new possible futures, including awareness of the need for freedoms not envisioned by earlier activists and new language with which to call out the contemporary "changing same." Organizing creates new knowledge regimes, which, in turn, unleash new possible futures.[12] The efforts of freedpeople to participate in society as citizens brought antidemocratic forces into full battle mode, despite the exhaustion, deprivation, and suffering among all southerners that had not yet been calculated at the end of the Civil War. Nothing freedpeople hoped to achieve could happen quickly in that unsettled and violent landscape; long-term vision had to be part of their calculation. It meant teaching the next generation to prepare to play a role, which became foundational to political and spiritual teaching in Black communities. A circuit of resistance over time can be a thickly layered manuscript that helps keep alive the memory of the political and lays a groundwork of knowledge that makes efforts at democracy "a recurrent possibility." Freedpeople distinguished themselves by acting as though that possibility could recur. Even in an age of pessimism the codex of Black political theory persists. It is one of the most profound legacies of slavery survivors to the country.

The first intervention in this book is to show ways in which Black political thought developed in sites along this circuit during the war and in the postemancipation era. African Americans on the circuit deployed mass participatory democracy, producing leadership from the laboring class that worked in counterpoint to and in partnership with Black elites. They created organic venues where women voiced their concerns and political agendas were more egalitarian in gender terms than indicated in much of the early scholarship of the period.[13]

The second intervention examines the possibility that the foundational structures for community building and activism of all sorts emerged from a matrix of early benevolent societies and trade associations with overlapping membership and local roots.[14] These associations, more numerous than the churches thought to be the primary basis of Black southern civil rights organizing, seem to have been developed at three different periods. A few burial societies were established by free Blacks in antebellum years in a number of the circuit sites to acquire land for cemeteries, since freedpeople could not be buried in public cemeteries or plantation sites where enslaved people had been buried. After the war, a wave of mutual aid society development occurred in response to local needs, which varied by region in some specifics but always included aid to the poor, access to medical treatment, and building schools. A third stage, representing the fullest period of society development and activity, began after the end of the Freedmen's Bureau operations in the South in 1872 and included popular demands of Black churches to build societies to aid the poor and/or set up loan associations for the purchase of land. By the 1880s and 1890s these entities were widely referred to as "secret societies" by white southerners, but even during Reconstruction in the 1870s, when Black meetings and organizing were suppressed, such groups were secretive by necessity *because* they were political or engaged in labor issues, and because they were *profiled as political* even if they were not. This is the remnant of overt fugitive status and ground-level awareness of the continuation of freedom's fugitive status.

Black political thought in former slave societies begins with the problem of being outside of the body politic. Although, tragically, this remained true in the American South for all but a handful of years until the Civil Rights Act of 1964 and the Voting Rights Act of 1965, the entrance of freedpeople into public life in the 1860s presented an array of legal conundrums in a system that had not made time to inscribe Black humanity into the state and federal statutes. I have attempted to locate sites where Blacks produced space for discourse and organizing by following records of missionaries and activists who observed and participated in early Black political discourse and by observing the geographical factors that eased or complicated communications and organizing. I contend that the production of space to effect political thought and action was a continued necessity from the end of the Civil War into the twentieth century. Quite often the production of space for mass participatory democracy—the typical process among southern Blacks for arriving at community consensus—involved armed defense of the gatherings. Seeing this process through the lens of slavery, Blacks protected their ability to practice thinking out loud.

Enslaved people in the early days of the United States easily apprehended what was otherwise perhaps best known by the founders—that the republic declared in 1776, drawing "just Powers from the Consent of the Governed," was then, and would remain for some time, more idea than fact. Without ending slavery, this nation was an unexecuted idea not only owing to its raw, unconstructed nascency but because the idea of the governed was narrower than reality. People in bondage in the late eighteenth century may not have learned much of European nations ruled more by inheritance than ideals, but like others who lived through the Revolutionary era, they were witnesses to the war here to place "Principles" ahead of "Despotism" and the recipients of rumors about another revolution—one that aimed to free enslaved people in Haiti. Enslaved people were bearers, nurses, and porters of these revolutionary ideas, passing along judgment of both the justice and the romance of the idea of a society honoring rights for all. The thirteen-year bloody siege that declared a nation free of slavery in Saint-Domingue in 1804 (and prompted the end of slavery in the British West Indies) confirmed for many that the inchoate definition of all people being "created equal" and "endowed by their Creator" with unalienable rights in the United States could be elaborated in fact.

The Black Atlantic worldview, informed by news of the Haitian Revolution and antislavery ideologies, was in part articulated by a son of Carolina coastal ports. David Walker was born in Wilmington, North Carolina, among watermen during the long struggle in Haiti, and he spent some years in Charleston as well. His *Appeal to the Colored Citizens of the World, but in Particular, and Very Expressly, to Those of the United States of America* (1829) shows a Black Atlantic outrage shared by many Blacks over the suffering wrought by slavery that was seldom heard by most Americans and reflects connection to republican and antislavery discourse in the Atlantic world. A member of the African Methodist Episcopal (AME) church, which had been formed in resistance to prejudicial treatment in northern white churches, Walker also shares his indignation at the propagation of a distorted Christianity hand in hand with the brutality used to maintain the slave system. He also uses biblical narratives familiar to Black congregations in both the North and the South as ancient parallels to the contemporary slave system told in racialized renderings that also claimed Africanness to be ancient. In the Black Atlantic world, the Bible and the ancient world were Blacker than taught in mainstream society. This deployment of the annals of Moses as non-European history was already part of the eighteenth-century Black Masonic movement initiated by Prince Hall in Boston. Within Walker's four articles are the seeds of Black political argument to come for more than a century from the abolitionists, the Black prophetic ministry, Afrocentrists, nationalists, and radicals advocating self-defense.[15]

The influence of Walker's *Appeal*, delivered to southern ports by various networks including seamen and secret societies, prompted whites to pass laws against the distribution of "incendiary" literature. Walker's call to southern Blacks to take action against their oppression was more threatening to southern planters than his argument that Blacks had built the country and had a claim to rights. His harsh shaming of those who would not resist their condition may have been a part of private discourse among Blacks, but it represents a departure from the conventions of northern abolitionist rhetoric. The proximity of the *Appeal*'s publication and distribution starting in 1829 to Nat Turner's Rebellion in Virginia in 1831, even without any known connection between the pamphlet and Turner, virtually assured that southern legislators would seek legal punishments for the circulation of such ideas. Ideas of freedom were policed as the property of white society in a country that had never had only one ethnicity. Walker's text would have an additional legacy in the emancipation-era black codes with bans on speech by Blacks that were deemed incendiary, punished by prison terms.

Steven Hahn holds that this mid-eighteenth-century work "reflected intellectual and political currents flowing among African Americans, North and South, since the mid-eighteenth century: democratic-republicanism, millennialism, protonationalism, Pan-Africanism." David Kazanjian states that the *Appeal* points to "the paradoxically simultaneous emergence, toward the end of the eighteenth century, of apparently contradictory discursive practice: universal egalitarianism, on the one hand, and the particularistic hierarchies of race and nation, on the other hand."[16] Paul Gilroy adds that "Walker made the problem of black humanity and related issues of rights—political and human—intrinsic to the issue of world citizenship long before [W. E. B.] Du Bois." And more to the point of those fretting planters and lawmakers: "Walker's plea that blacks be recognized as belonging to the 'human family' was combined with the view that their natural rights had been wrongfully confiscated in the condition of slavery, which could, as a result of their exclusion, be justly overthrown."[17]

Walker's rhetorical themes would resonate with Blacks in the North and be elaborated by lettered men who used a form of Black nationalism to consolidate a political base toward unified action in various causes, and they would continue to echo throughout the Black political rhetoric of the nineteenth century. All the strands of political thought identified by Hahn and others as Atlantic currents dating to the eighteenth century, or at least remnants thereof, should be considered part of the world of enslaved people in the ports of the nineteenth-century American slave system and the coastal settlements where fugitives from the slave system took refuge during the Civil War.

Still, it is relevant to look at Cedric Robinson's view of the Black radical tradition making "manifest" a particular consciousness: "It was a consciousness implicated in what Amos Tutuola so many generations later would name 'the bush of ghosts.' . . . the continuing development of a collective consciousness informed by the historical struggles for liberation and motivated by the shared sense of obligation to preserve the collective being, the ontological totality." This is a powerful asset that has created movements needed to speak to innumerable places and times. This collective consciousness strikes me as the womb of the Beloved Community.[18]

Visualizing Political Formation

The data I have assembled on movements in nine southern states from 1868 to 1900 are collected in this book in tables for each state chapter that demonstrate that the durability of political structures built in Reconstruction was often most apparent in very rural places rather than in urban settings. The geography of Black organizing during Reconstruction also troubles the idea that the Black majority population alone was a determinant of success in achieving representation in political institutions. Rural areas offer consideration of the fact that survival depended on solid community building—churches and ministers had to be shared. Congregations moved together, buried each other, and helped each other get to polls. Building cabins was shared work. Family members lived near each other. In South Carolina, I have seen Black family homes arranged in semicircles across a set of lots held in the family since Reconstruction. The families shared arable land and lumber for construction and made collective childcare available for all the households. In some rural counties, political organizing was taken up as a routine facet of church activity—possibly because churches were available gathering places that could be secured and homes to social structures delegating diverse forms of work. Those areas where Blacks engaged in the most diverse forms of community building seem to have had representation with greater staying power as well. The tables and maps in this study show the continuous turns in organizing over time, from electing officials to labor organizing to "Exoduster" movements, especially after loss of the vote within a given area. The maps in the book show that every state had some Black communities engaged in organizing their counties in concert with neighboring counties.[19]

The sustainability or fragility of political organizing in specific places and the systematic effect of violence against those communities is quickly apprehended by their depiction in the maps created for this book (*see plates 1–16*). Mapping is a critical practice because putting organizing in space illuminates scattered evidence not necessarily coherent in narratives that blur specific postwar years and obscure ties between African Americans in various communities. Also, the connections between armed posses creating terror against Blacks and legislators creating laws to suppress Black voting are also clearer if looked at geographically. The terrorists were usually in counties with white majorities that were next door to Black voting centers. There are echoes of this reality in news stories today. Though tools for suppressing the Black vote are still in use, Reconstruction is the era in which an array of voter suppression tactics were created and, over time, refined and perfected (without federal interference) to become increasingly comprehensive in their effect. We can see the gradual success of these tactics across southern counties in mapping. These maps showing Black organizing also specifically or indirectly display the geography of white resistance to Black organizing. This illuminates a reality in the terrain that continues across time, and can chart specific developments at specific times.

Those areas where African Americans did not gain representation obviously were regions in which white electoral power was maintained, but most areas where Blacks won places in constitutional conventions or in the state house were also sites where Black organization was matched with a well-organized white political structure and/or contested by white organizing. Black majorities did not go unopposed simply because the numbers suggested a certain outcome. Just as oppression produced Black organization, the potential of Black power, Black challenges to slavery-era laws and conventions, Black voter organizing, and evidence of separate Black churches and schools (or even the more despised integrated schools) all produced white resistance. Maps of Black representation in Reconstruction in fact show areas that were most heavily contested by whites. Coincidentally, any student of twentieth-century southern movements will recognize many of those places as sites of later engagements won and lost, which speaks to the sustainability or renewability of the palimpsest of Black political thought through the social nature of southern Black culture.

The Emancipation Circuit as Text

After abolition, freedpeople were engaged in a complex process of creating space for freedom—space for autonomous living when possible; for political discourse; for redefining gender roles; for education in citizenship;

for intellectual development; and for privacy, family formation, and spiritual life. Rail construction, a great drive for the increase of production and shipping in the South, itself produced new communities and new space as rural Black workers converged on towns with railroad camps, where they planned and built settlements to avail themselves of the jobs and mobility of the new rail lines. The Emancipation Circuit is an alternative way of seeing the postwar southern terrain. If trains carrying freight stopped at every plantation in a Delta county, so too did the African American men handling the bales, along with the news they carried. Along this circuit, even in times of harsh repression, local associations, entertainers, and Black newspapers produced space for struggle, a spatial imaginary where resistance was at least possible, if also necessitating existential choices.

For outsiders coming south to work with freedpeople, especially Black abolitionists, emancipation and Reconstruction opened an important moment of praxis—Black political theory had to move from abolition to creating freedom in a reality not adequately perceived from afar. Though ideas generated by northern Black abolitionists may have informed Black southerners, the views of northern activists of all stripes were deeply disrupted by going to the South after the war. The small group of activists who worked in the South were jolted out of their preconceptions about what forms of aid were most needed, the breadth of the help needed, and the impossibility of political training without attention to the ideas held by freedpeople and the constant threat of violence toward freedpeople and anyone aiding them in moving from liberation to freedom. Many were radicalized, especially African American ministers, steeped in the abolitionist tradition, whether born in the North or the South. It is in the South that Black prophetic ministry begins and builds its expertise and its storied career in mobilization. Reconstruction puts an abolition-based Black political theory into the massive problem of practicing what was preached. This required realistically envisioning new possible futures and literally building structures that enabled such outcomes.

In the chapters that follow, accounts of episodes and individuals, some of them familiar in the historiography of emancipation and Reconstruction, are arranged with particular attention to place and time. This narrative course—moving from Virginia southward along the Atlantic Coast, across the Gulf Coast, and up the Mississippi River's path to Memphis— replicates much of the chronological order of Black flight made possible by Union forces setting up parameters inside of which fugitives from the slave system expected safety from return to their owners. The overt organizing generally began in each state once the military was at least heard to have arrived and set up camp.

Each chapter of *The Emancipation Circuit* delves into a concept important to understanding Reconstruction. Chapter 1, "Flight: Movement Matters," introduces the flights from the slavery system set off along the Atlantic Coast and the length of the Mississippi River Valley and the camps to which fugitives fled. I contend that their knowledge of where and how to flee—which they continued to use throughout the war—is embodied in the slavery-era use of "rival geography" and word on the "common wind," an oral communication network taking varying patterns in different regions. Central to this geography of Black communication networks are waterways as well as local routes used between plantations or for escape or "laying out" from plantations. The chapter also discusses preexisting political theory concerning affinities among fugitives around blackness as they may have been observed by activists in the camps and in local Black societies that came to aid refugees.[20] Chapter 2, "The Emancipation Circuit: A Road Map," gives a view of the fifteen specific elements in play in the emancipation era and Reconstruction period that allowed the building of multiple and sustained periods of mobilization in certain sites around the former Confederacy. These include various factors providing a measure of safety and, with the arrival of teachers and activists, the onset of literacy instruction; citizenship mentoring; access to news; political organizing connections; and later help on pensions, back pay, and legal matters. Most important perhaps were open sites for worship and community meetings, from which arose a new American politics.

Chapters 3 through 11 recount developments from Virginia south along the Atlantic Coast, west through Gulf Coast states and then in the Mississippi River states, Mississippi and Arkansas. These chapters are organized broadly by the arrivals of Union forces in those areas, which in turn triggered mass movements of the enslaved. Some of these military movements were successful, allowing for occupation; others were fleeting, causing enslaved people to follow US troops toward safety. Chapter 3, "Virginia: Assembly," centers on foundational assemblies of refugees setting out to obtain relief from numerous conditions imposed on fugitives by local white authorities and the military. It details some of the unique facets of these early meetings that also apply to how refugees elsewhere met to think out loud as community. It also emphasizes a pattern of coordinated meetings between communities over months to form regional collective demands with local specifics.

Chapter 4, "North Carolina: Custody," looks at fugitives caught in active war areas through the lens of their attempts to retain control of their own bodies and families in the face of military impressment and "apprenticeship" laws allowing former owners to take custody of African American children. North Carolinians illustrate ways in which fugitives organized themselves and made new iterations of the word *we* that reflected the Black experience of the shared disasters of enslavement. When petitioning the government, these same people reflect or remark on their introduction to being called by collective names based on race, such as *the colored people*. While they were trying to identify a new "we," refugees learned they were being dubbed with a new "they."

Chapter 5, "South Carolina: Majority," shows activists encountering each other during the Port Royal Experiment, as well as the electoral power possible with a widespread Black majority population, and the successful resistance to violence and intimidation in coastal areas that was devastating the up-country. South Carolina shows the social nature of the use of rival geography that is the groundwork of the news and movement on the South Carolina circuit, as well as the social nature of labor organizing, which was open to mass action led by women. It also shows the social nature of the reproduction of political ideology and political formations that is characteristic of the Emancipation Circuit.

Chapter 6, "Georgia: Mobilization," focuses on the state as a site of long-term, inch-by-inch struggle with violent opponents of Black voting. This state epitomizes the effective systematic and geography-based use of terror to defeat Black organizing. Activists in Georgia offer a detailed look at how a few people arriving from the North in the late 1860s and traveling the breadth of the state could organize thousands of people to vote in 1868. Activism in Georgia reveals the methodical teaching and cultivation of a pedagogy on the US Constitution and citizenship rights as it was practiced across much of the South.

Chapter 7, "Florida: Faction," covers the intense use of divisions created by diverse groups with political ambitions contending for the Black vote, some of which were trying to clear the ground for developers seeking cheap labor with which to build their business plans for the state. Gerrymandering in Florida privileged white majority counties as if to flip the advantage of the "three-fifths clause" to reduce the majority Black vote to three-fifths its size. Florida points as well to the lasting impacts of disfranchising those convicted of crimes and of successful Black labor organizing for shorter workdays, wage raises, and other state legislation.

Chapter 8, "Alabama: Redemption," concerns the state with the first Deep South destruction of Reconstruction. Many enslaved people in the state were unable to flee during the war, and yet many others had their enslavement turned into work making munitions and weapons for the Confederacy. With this mix of wartime experience, and the military presence in Selma and Montgomery, the Black Belt became the central byway of activism and political formation across the state. Freedpeople there organized themselves to take advantage of a potential voting majority and became subject to the planter elite deploying race to court Unionist whites away from the radical Republican Party and its support of Black rights. Black Alabamians had at least one lawmaker seek reparations through the legislature and moved quickly into labor organizing and creating farming cooperatives.

Chapter 9, "Louisiana: Societies," focuses on the early organizing taken up by the elite free Black community, which gave an early radical ideology to the meaning of freedom but was superseded over the long term by the persistent labor and political organizing by African Americans in rural areas. Political and labor actions in Louisiana were subject to a stepped-up use of violent repression marked by the use of large military equipment not seen in other southern states up to that time. Louisiana also is instructive on the value of multiple forms of institution building instilling durable organizing skills in communities.

Chapter 10, "Mississippi: Bulldoze," centers on freedpeople organizing in a hostile environment in which the US forces in the state during the Andrew Johnson presidency refused to help people on the ground. Black Mississippians succeeded in gaining representation in government only in a context of secret organizing, policed meeting repression, and constant attempts to disarm Black populations. Still, some in Mississippi, who had been displaced by Union attempts to take control of the Mississippi River, were in autonomous communities and redefined collective organizing under the idea of "We the Colored People." For a short time, the Black majorities in the state did succeed in electing more African American representatives than are serving today, and they kept officeholders for some years after Reconstruction was overthrown.

Chapter 11, "Arkansas: Minority," explores how the devastation of the state and constant displacement of its people forced Blacks into Union centers where they were able to organize and seek medical help and education. Their numbers, however, were much smaller than in neighboring states, and Ku Klux Klan terror forced declarations of martial law. A state whose Black population included a large proportion who had migrated there fleeing hardship elsewhere becomes a site of organizing of the new Pentecostal churches and new migration movements.

....

The tools for struggle available to freedwomen and freedmen, and even later to Black publics following disfranchisement in the 1870s, have to be viewed in terms of a theory of the political rather than purely in terms of inclusion/exclusion from institutional politics, or as if their struggles were the same as those witnessed since the advent of television and the modern documentary. An appropriate theory of the political for the work of southern Blacks in the nineteenth century can only be arrived at by observing their vision of the role of the state through the prism of slavery, and freedom's sudden demands—which became lasting needs. Too often we bring two biases to the task of seeing their efforts: first, that the twentieth-century movements succeeded by unifying around a single goal such as desegregation of bus lines in Montgomery, Alabama, or passage of the Voting Rights Act of 1965; and, second, that success usually meant an effective process that could be repeated. We know, of course, that in some cases southern sheriffs studied the effective twentieth-century methods and functionally counteracted them, and that some other efforts never succeeded. The consciousness that sustains long-term struggle also provides the preservation of successful means and the continuing development of strategies that suit new times. Freedpeople saw the possibilities for the imposition of the terms and conventions of slavery in every facet of society, arenas too numerous to even list, but which placed many of the changes they demanded of the state way ahead of the curve of progressive political thought of their time. We are still doing some of their work.

Autonomy in daily life in fact might rank first among all priorities for freedpeople, but its achievement required much: the right to control one's own body; freedom from random or habitual violence; the tools to produce one's own food and acquire money or property or both; freedom of privacy; freedom of autonomous spiritual practice; freedom from surveillance and arbitrary, racialized policing; participation in governance, including female leadership; access to decent housing; access to health care; access to public space; freedom of expression; freedom of association, privately or publicly and in groups; and many more. The political demands of slavery survivors produced the study of the body as commodity and legislation aimed at protecting the body from covert or cloaked forms of property in human beings, forcible displacement for labor, protection for the integrity of family as defined by the citizen, and protection from the violence of capital and dehumanizing ideologies. These are the foundations of a politics of universal human rights.

1 **FLIGHT**
Movement Matters

Contraband *n* **1 : illegal or prohibited traffic** in goods: smuggling
2 : goods or merchandise whose importation, exportation, or possession is forbidden; *also* smuggled goods **3 :** a Negro slave who during the Civil War escaped to or was brought within Union lines—
contraband *adj*.
—*Webster's Ninth New Collegiate Dictionary* (1986)

Enslaved people were not meant to be moving around. Movement led not
only to freedom but also to knowledge—knowledge developed in meetings and gatherings, and knowledge put toward organizing. Black movement was dangerous. Throughout this book, there are instances in which
local, state, and federal officials endeavor to situate or contain Africans
and African Americans in a particular place. Private businesses after the
Civil War advertised for Black laborers to move to their area, specifying
they must not be troublemakers. A few years later, planters passed local
laws outlawing departure from counties and asked armed forces to keep
Blacks in place, even in the face of natural disaster. For the next five decades, hundreds of thousands would move—small distances and lengthy
migrations—establishing new sites of Black struggle.

But these developments are rooted in the reality that, during the slavery
era, movement and communication across large areas took place all the
time. Knowledge moved. The roots of the Emancipation Circuit were in
the "common wind," the surprisingly effective pattern of communications

among enslaved people that could pass news across plantations, counties, regions, and the oppositional spatial practices McKittrick terms as "alternative patterns that work alongside traditional geographies." As the Emancipation Circuit emerges and develops, it sets up a series of new and alternative practices in traditional geographies and those repurposed by battle. This process began in fugitive camps (also known as contraband camps) and in settlements established by fugitives apart from the grounds of military camps. This chapter looks at the arrival at military installations of hundreds of thousands of fugitives from across the slave system and what life was like where they gathered.[1]

Charles Grandy saw shooting stars, probably in July 1860, while enslaved in Mississippi. His neighbors took the event as a sign of the coming war. "Den de stars commence a shootin' . . . ," Grandy said. "Well, dey's shootin' one right after de other—fast. Den a gra' [great] big star over in de east come right down almos' to de earth. I seed it myself. 'Twas sign o' war alright. Niggers got glad. All dem what could pray 'gin [began] to pray more'n ever. So glad God sendin' de war." Grandy likely saw the Great Comet of 1860, which was visible across the United States in the fall of 1859 and the summer of 1860. He joined his story to the history of nineteenth-century Americans, with a different view perhaps than most printed at the time. Like Grandy, several famous American writers tied the event to a coming war, but they also linked the comet to John Brown's attack at Harpers Ferry in 1859 and to his death in 1860; the comet made its most impressive appearance before Brown's execution. Walt Whitman's "Year of Meteors (1859–1860)" opened with an image of John Brown on the scaffold, and both Henry David Thoreau and Herman Melville used the metaphor of a meteor to describe Brown himself.[2] But the widely documented Great Comet of 1861, which occurred in July 1861, three months after the war's start, was "the war comet," and by the time of its appearance enslaved people were on the move, fleeing plantations across the South. At Fort Monroe, where refugees were given asylum, Edward Lillie Pierce, a Union soldier and Boston lawyer stationed there, also saw the comet. He had been put in charge of fugitives being used as laborers at the fort because so many already had fled there. President Abraham Lincoln, an amateur astronomer, would be forced by these events to free people such as Grandy, and six months after doing so, he visited the US Naval Observatory to study the stars.[3]

Flights from slavery were the first large-scale oppositional practices at the outset of the Civil War. Like Grandy interpreting a meteor through the lens of enslavement, other Black southerners took their own meanings from news of the war. Mary Barbour, born on a plantation in McDowell County in western North Carolina where the slaveowner had sold twelve of her mother Edith's sixteen children when they reached the age of three, was the eldest child when the war stopped the sales. She was awakened one night by her father, the felicitously named Jordan, who was enslaved at a nearby plantation. He dressed her and rushed her, her mother, and the three younger children out into the woods. "I reckon dat I will always 'member dat walk," Barbour recalled, "wid de bushes slappin' my laigs, de win' sighin' in de trees, an' de hoot owls an' whipporwhils hollerin' at each other from de big trees. I wuz half asleep an' skeered stiff, but in a little while we pass de plum thicket an' dar am de mules an' wagin." There was a quilt in the wagon, on which the children lay, and as they rode Mary's father said the Yankees had come to his plantation, set fire to the buildings, and had taken the owner to "down nigh Norfolk." Mary Barbour said that "fer a long time" they traveled by night until they reached the Albemarle Sound. Union troops were there and directed the Barbours to New Bern, where soldiers "puts us on a boat named *Ocean Waves* an' ter Roanoke [Island] we goes. Later I larns dat most o' de reffes [refugees] is put in James City, nigh New Bern, but dar am a pretty good crowd on Roanoke. After a few days dar de *Ocean Waves* comes back an' takes all ober ter New Bern. My pappy wuz a shoemaker, so he makes Yankee boots, an' we gits 'long pretty good." Many left farms in similar circumstances on hearing about the location of Union forces but had more difficult journeys. Clearly, local knowledge informed Jordan of a route across most of the state to Union lines, and as someone who might have spoken with soldiers who showed up at the plantation, he may also have been a source of information for others.[4]

The incidence of a rare blizzard a few years earlier in Virginia gives us a glimpse of another way in which Jordan may have known that US troops were coming, where to take the family, and how to get there. "Cox's Snow" was an example of the common wind at work passing less vital news along the Virginia "grapevine." At least nine slave system survivors interviewed by the Virginia Writers Project spoke of the January 1857 storm named after Dr. Edwin Cox, former mayor of Petersburg, who froze to death trying to get to his farm during the blizzard. Many cited the three-day snow to date their birth by the age they were when it occurred, or used it to date being hired out; several recalled it as one of the most memorable events of their lives, one of whom worked in the household Cox was trying to reach. What is most interesting is that though they may all have seen the blizzard, most of those who recalled Cox's tragedy were at least three counties away from where Cox died, and one was on the other side of the state. Each was, however, located on a river or near a rail line connected to Petersburg. "Sis" Shackelford, who was three years old and nowhere near the event, spoke of the doctor's reported meanness and drinking habits as if she had known him. As she said, "The news that ole Cox was daid went 'roun' like a win.'"[5] On word of Union troop arrivals, many flights like Barbour's began, heading toward a coastline where Union boats might have unloaded troops. This was part of the invisible communications network that fed the flight of enslaved people during the war.

The structure of the Emancipation Circuit was an unintended consequence of Lincoln's orders of April 19 and April 27, 1861—in the first weeks of the Civil War—to blockade thirty-five hundred miles of Confederate coastline from Virginia to Texas. The consequence may not have been desired, but displacement of the enslaved was no surprise. President Lincoln kept on his desk an 1860 map of the enslaved population of the southern states. It was a map sold commercially to raise money to aid sick and wounded Union soldiers; Lincoln used it to determine how many Blacks would be displaced in areas through which his troops moved. He used it so constantly that when Francis Bicknell Carpenter painted his 1864 portrait of Lincoln and the cabinet at the first reading of the Emancipation Proclamation, he placed the map in the scene. The president probably could not have predicted the number of people who actually did move in response to Union soldiers' presence, nor would he have known they would use networks built in slavery to begin mobilizing in those areas, but unlike many, he was aware that he was rearranging the map. For these and other reasons, Black political development after the war has a specific geography.[6]

The naval blockade was meant both to halt the South's trade with Europe, necessary for the survival of its economy, and to prevent any material or military aid reaching the South. Though it took years for the blockade to become truly effective, it caused some enslaved people to hear they would be moved by owners or find themselves being forced away from the coast, hastening questions of flight. A few weeks after the start of the Civil War, a seemingly ordinary event took place at Fort Monroe, the Union's only fort in secessionist Virginia at that time. The escape of three enslaved men provided a powerful encounter for Northern troops entering the South. On May 24, Frank Baker, James Townsend, and Shepard Mallory, who had been hired out by their owner to build Confederate defenses in Norfolk, clearly saw the onset of war as changing their life chances. At night the three rowed a skiff four miles north across rough waters to the fort and asked for asylum. Under the still valid Fugitive Slave Law, such escapees were usually returned to their owners. In this instance, General Benjamin F. Butler decided that given the South had seceded from the Union and its laws, and that the country was at war and workers were valuable resources, the three men could be kept as "contraband of war" and employed like other military resources. Essential to his reasoning was the men's status as property. The armies routinely hauled off the property of other armies. Regardless of arguments in Washington about the salience of Butler's claim, enslaved people took the presence of federal troops exactly as the three men had done: refuge from slavery tantamount to stepping on northern soil. Those who made it to Union lines became known as "contrabands."[7]

If they could, people headed for the Atlantic or the Mississippi. Scenes of arrival were reenacted all along the Eastern Seaboard and the Lower Mississippi Valley and in the wake of US troop movements in Tennessee. The 500,000 who fled to Union lines were literally fugitives until the 1863 Emancipation Proclamation.[8] As troops and naval ships moved south and took control of areas along the Atlantic Coast in what James McPherson has called the "salt-water war," the network of local and regional communications among enslaved people that had long carried raw goods to the Atlantic brought waves of people and information into these contested areas. At the same time, Lincoln's effort to block Confederate use of the Mississippi allowed thousands from Vicksburg to Memphis to escape to Union lines. In their flight toward sanctuary, refugees from slavery put themselves in connection with other enslaved people and with the nation at large. Their names were taken down in military records and some of their experience written up by itinerant reporters from northern papers.[9] The salt-water war in the East went on for four years, but in 1861 Union troops held only Fort Monroe. They then took sites in Key West, Florida; North Carolina's Hatteras Inlet; and Port Royal, South Carolina. The Black political thought and organization that arose in the South after the Civil War emerged from a context that can be characterized as fugitive in every sense of the word—in flight, regarded as outlawed, transient, elusive (especially as to documentation), and vulnerable to repression.

Tom Robinson, born enslaved in North Carolina, was taken to Texas before the war began. He remembered that when the sound of cannon fire was first heard in Cass County, Texas, as Confederates geared up for war, people in his neighborhood made up a song, "Listen to the Home-Made

Thunder." Robinson was like the vast majority of enslaved people who remained where they were during the Civil War, unable to flee or even to move much across their local environs. His case was perhaps unusual as he was the only slave of a couple named Robinson, and in that the slaveholder, Dave Robinson, came and found him milking cows and said he had to read him a document informing him that he was free. The younger man was fifteen or sixteen years old and later ended up in Arkansas. As Hahn notes, "Substantial sections of interior Virginia, North and South Carolina, and Mississippi; almost all of Georgia, Alabama and Florida, and Texas; and sections of Tennessee and Louisiana remained in Confederate hands at least until the war's last months." But the ruptures in the routines of the slavery system that came with the war did create more openings for escape.[10] Some possibilities for escape were chancier than others; many involved considerable distance and terrain that was tough to cross, either naturally so or because of warfare or hostile local forces. Still, an estimated 500,000 men, women, and children moved to Union lines, betting that federal forces could overwhelm the Southern army. This did not mean traveling simply from the countryside to cities. Richmond, for instance, under contest for years, was not a refuge. On the East Coast, urban enslaved people escaped to Atlantic ports.

In 1862, federals took Roanoke Island, New Bern, and Beaufort, North Carolina; then Norfolk, Virginia; followed by the seizure of Fort Pulaski at Savannah and then Jacksonville, St. Augustine, and Pensacola, Florida. News of the capture of these ports triggered more flights by Blacks along the coast, as the ports promised safety and provisions, and the escapes produced the military enlistment of more locals who knew the terrain. In May of that year, Harriet Tubman, born enslaved in 1820 in Maryland and already famous for rescuing hundreds from slavery, was asked by Massachusetts governor John Andrews to go to Beaufort, South Carolina, and assist fugitives arriving at the federal post there. By early 1863 she was building networks of informants among the enslaved in the area. Her task was to get useful information from people native to the area; among her papers were found lists of locals who served her as scouts and pilots.[11] In Florida, where most enslaved people were working cotton fields, saltworks, and fisheries for the South, the Union drew those who took the St. John's River to the Union troops on the coast. All these places became sites on the circuit of emancipation.[12]

Three men who escaped to Savannah from counties in southern Georgia in late May of 1865 gave testimony to a Freedmen's Bureau chaplain. Their stories illuminate the common fact that slavery continued in many places after the Emancipation Proclamation and after end of the war as well, and that thousands of people did not know they were free. They also point to another use of the geography in areas of the South that were still being "developed" for slavery when the war came. Many areas of Georgia and Alabama had enslaved people at work taking down wooded areas to build arable fields. One of the men said people were still held in the slave system "for an hundred miles west of the Altamaha [River]."[13] Though commerce and county lines were redefined by the 1858 arrival of the Atlantic and Gulf Railroad, the tracks proved to be the only defining markers for navigating the area and routes for escape from these isolated areas. The locations where these three men were held were so undeveloped at the time that they described them only by rail flag-stop numbers. All three men used the rail lines to walk north, crossed the Altamaha, and ran into other fugitives on the way. Two were hunted by dogs. All had recently witnessed whippings varying from fifteen blows to seventy-five. A man named Tall Boyd described his point of departure with these words: "I have lived Lowes Co. on the Gulf Rail Road Station Valdoster No 15. I belonged to James Howel. I left Mr. Howel's at the above place a week ago last Thursday arrived in this City last Wednesday." Frank Frazier came at least 160 miles from the sparsely populated Clinch County. His departure point was recorded as follows: "I lived in Clinch Co. Ga at station No. 1, Atlantic and Gulf RR. I belonged to Eli Millett agent of the ware house." George King, who, like many others, was taken at the outset of the war from Savannah two hundred miles away to Brooks County, said: "My place where I lived was Quitman Station No 16 1/2 on the Gulf road about twenty miles from Valdoster. I saw many people on the rail road as I came along . . . all thought they were [still] slaves." Two of the three men were also unaware that they were free. "'I came here,' King said, 'because I heard the Yankees were here.'" He also left due to hunger as the farmhands had been living only on corn for two weeks. Boyd left because the owner vowed to kill him when he went to get fish and honey after being told he was free by the owner's brother. When asked if he thought he could leave his work because he was free, he had said, "Yes, I wanted something to eat."[14]

The war sparked escapes to riverside areas from Memphis to New Orleans. In 1862, as the blockade was taking shape on the Atlantic, the "river war" took place on the Mississippi, highway for the South's great cotton and livestock trade. The Union navy that year took Memphis at the northern end of the Mississippi Valley and New Orleans and Natchez on the southern end and began the siege of Vicksburg in between. When news spread on the river that New Orleans was occupied by the Union, many Black men in the Mississippi Valley set out to enlist. Often the arrival of Union soldiers was a surprise. Ceceil George, then a teen on a plantation in St. Bernard Parish on the Gulf of Mexico, recalled a strange man walking up and following as she and her friends ran to the quarters. He offered hardtack and "wrote on a piece a paper an give it to my uncle, de driver. . . . 'I come from yo' friend Abraham Lincoln,' he say, 'Hold yo' peace.'" The soldier got a map of the parish from someone on the farm and left. "Den my father run off de plantation to de barracks to go to de war. He was killed three months before we knew it."[15]

Camps

Spreading down the Atlantic Coast from Fort Monroe, camps—official and impromptu—were arrayed around the mouth of the James River at port towns, including Hampton and Warwick (now Newport News), and tobacco and navy yard ports such as Norfolk, Portsmouth, and Suffolk. Over the next few years, the populations doubled in Richmond and Norfolk and tripled in Portsmouth. Soon after, other camps and settlements were set up in North Carolina at Roanoke Island; the ports of New Bern, Plymouth, Washington, and Beaufort, where cotton and tobacco shipped; as well as the coastal towns of Beaufort, South Carolina, and Fernandina, Florida, in cotton and rice regions. The populations doubled in Wilmington and Charlotte, North Carolina. Charleston's population grew by more than eight thousand. Union camps simply could not provide shelter for all the refugees and sometimes corralled people in muddy pens like those that held livestock. As a result, people built other encampments near Union positions. There were crude shelters built from the refuse of war such as scrap lumber, barrel staves, and tent materials in places that provided a modicum of autonomy, even if people were going to the army posts for day work, rations, or supplies. These settlements spreading out from "contraband camps" to which people fled or were transported by federal troops, formed the rudiments of a circuit of Black settlements with informal social ties to each other. Maps do not yet convey the density of the improvised communities that developed on the Atlantic, Gulf, and Mississippi shores.[16]

There were camps all across Tennessee and on the Kentucky border: at Memphis (four), Grand Junction, Nashville (three), Clarksville, Hendersonville, Chattanooga, and Knoxville, along with seven smaller sites. The population of Memphis nearly doubled over the next years, and its Black population increased from three thousand in 1860 to twenty thousand in 1870. The populations of Knoxville and Nashville nearly tripled over the next years and that of Chattanooga quadrupled. Enslaved people in Tennessee (and in Kentucky, Missouri, Delaware, and Maryland) were not freed by the Emancipation Proclamation, so although Union troops there facilitated a quasi asylum, these enslaved people could not be deemed "contrabands" and were subject to the Fugitive Slave Law until 1864.[17]

In the Mississippi Valley, camps arose early on in Helena, Pine Bluff, and Little Rock, Arkansas, and doubtless at other spots along the Arkansas River, as numerous cotton workers near the river fled. Little Rock's population would grow four times larger in the next few years. On the Mississippi and for years after the war in the Mississippi Valley where railroads were built, people still fled cotton plantations and made camps. In Mississippi there were camps at Corinth and Holly Springs in the north, at Natchez in the south, and in the middle of the state in Washington County, Vicksburg, and nearby Davis Bend (site of farms run by refugees and leased from the government). The population of Vicksburg grew four times larger. In the Delta, women and children were sent to work on Mississippi Islands 10, 60, 63, 66, 98, 102, and 103; Paw Paw Island, President's Island; and Lake Providence, Louisiana. Other Louisiana camps and farms across the river became sites where women and children, often families of soldiers, were sent to work: DeSoto Landing, Goodrich's Landing, Milliken's Bend, and Young's Point. People left Louisiana sugarcane and rice fields for New Orleans, and that city's population would gain nearly twenty-two thousand people by 1870. In Port Hudson, site of an 1863 siege in which regiments of the US Colored Troops had served heroically and took heavy losses, people referred to the settlements where they spent several years as "citizen camps." In short, the riverside along the Mississippi from Memphis to Vicksburg, including Arkansas and northern Louisiana, became saturated with hastily thrown-up settlements and government work camps where enslaved people assembled in large groups.[18]

Farther south, thousands of people in the sugar parishes found their way to New Orleans. Catherine Cornelius was in her twenties in 1862 and, like everyone in her family, worked on a plantation near Baton Rouge cutting sugarcane. She reported actually speaking with General Butler, who by then was in Louisiana and camped with troops at the plantation. Cornelius and all the other enslaved people there were taken by the owner to Bayou Sara to be hidden, only to be captured by Union troops. "De Yankees brought us hyar [to New Orleans] in a boat," she later recalled. "We was first to de old barracks, dats the first place they took us." Her brother joined the Union army and was killed in the war. Late in the war, the arrival of Union troops in Alabama caused people to flock to Montgomery and Decatur, Alabama, and to Tallahassee, Florida. The National Park Service has thus far located 562 refugee or contraband camps and government farms.[19]

People arriving at any of the camps, especially those with thousands of fugitives present, may have only then had their first inklings of the enormity of the bondage system in which they and their forebears had been trapped. The ten thousand Blacks who eventually gathered at Fort Monroe represented more souls than most slaves could ever have seen in one place, more than the population of many towns on the East Coast. Such sights must have shocked everyone, Black and white, southern and northern, who caught a glimpse of the enormity of the slavery business: for if they saw ten thousand in one town where soldiers landed, they knew there were a dozen towns with similar sights. While the huge increases in African American population came to cities, small towns near federal camps also saw overwhelming change. Before the war, for instance, there were only twenty-six hundred Blacks in Elizabeth City County, Virginia, where Hampton is located (the town nearest to Fort Monroe); by 1865 there were seven thousand Blacks in Hampton alone. Even at that time, people were still waiting for a chance to run. W. L. Bost, enslaved in western North Carolina, said, "There was no fightin' done in Newton. Jes a skirmish or two. Most of the people get everything jes ready to run when the Yankee sojers come through the town. This was toward the las' of the war. 'Cose the n——
—s knew all the fightin' was about, but they didn't say anything." If they had, Bost said, they would have been shot. Some arrived in the company of family, some with most of the members of their neighborhood, and others in all-male groups or groups of women and children, having been separated by the army. Many people fled on rivers, particularly in places like Virginia where Union forces used waterways to move troops. If they were lucky and found US troops, they were put in a convoy of boats for a trip lasting as long as a couple of days, escorted by a gunboat and sometimes under sniper fire.[20]

Black Louisianans like Catherine Cornelius reported similar journeys on federal boats. Maps showing areas occupied by Union troops (as opposed to captured forts) perhaps give a more accurate picture of the swaths of land at the edges of the former Confederacy where many fugitives attempted to provide for themselves and survive. The people of Port Hudson, Louisiana, put the most optimistic claim on their settlements in calling them citizen camps and thereby giving themselves a designation that society had not yet imagined. Perhaps they also honored the dead Black soldiers buried there for a status they had left as a legacy to their survivors. The label *citizen camp* is also a warning that such a term should be an impossible oxymoron, though history tells us otherwise.

Anyone with knowledge of the camps at the time could see that the needs required a diversity of expertise and that the solutions could not be brought by a narrowly conceived politics. People who began to provide leadership in grassroots meetings had to take vexing crises to the political arena, as well as innumerable grievances never before addressed by local commerce, charities, educators, churches, other private institutions, municipal and state governments, or the federal government. The war, as a state of exception, continued to bring new crises. By the second year of the fighting, the army began to use camps to form units of the US Colored Troops, usually with men who had fled to the camps for that purpose. In Virginia, however, a brutal impressment episode involved forcing men out of their settlements and putting them in the army without informing them they had a choice, and in Louisiana, the federals notably ran a larger and more widespread impressment of Black men. Refugee camps were complex centers where food, clothing, and medicine were the most pressing needs for refugees, while for federal authorities the most pressing needs were to make the fugitives useful to the war and to lower the cost of supporting them.[21]

Most striking to those who visited any of the camps were the miserable conditions: crowding, filth, cold, inadequate clothing, and rough housing that, in an irony lost on no one, sometimes included the old slave pens. Jim Downs writes, "In many ways, the contraband camps performed a similar function to antebellum slave pens where auctioneers held people before they were sold on the market." On the Mississippi, "these pens were not torn down or even closed off during the war but were used for emancipated slaves until the federal government could work out plans to establish a labor force to be sent to the Mississippi Valley and the Lower South." J. G. McKee, a member of the Western Freedmen's Aid Commission, wrote of Nashville in 1863, "I conjecture there cannot be less than four thousand contrabands who need help and instruction about this city. I find over 40 crowded into one small house. Sometimes 5 or 6 families in one room without fireplace or chimney." In most of the locations, observers saw firsthand that "forced to live in such unhealthy environments, freedpeople suffered from malnutrition, starvation, and exposure, while others came down with smallpox, dysentery, and yellow fever and died."[22]

At the outset, local African American groups were often the first to organize relief. As a freedman's aid society visitor noticed in Tennessee, regardless of the circumstances, refugees refused his offers to return them to the farms they had fled. Of the situation he wrote:

> In and about Nashville, nobody can tell the number of half-naked contrabands that are crowded into the basements and waste houses, for no white so far as I can learn has taken the trouble to look after them. . . . The colored citizens of Nashville deserve great credit. They organized a "Good Samaritan Society" during last winter to furnish clothing and medicine to the suffering in the colored hospital. Yet of the 1400 contrabands who died here I am credibly informed that at least 700 perished from neglect through hunger, cold, filth and vermin. . . . Since our army arrived several colored schools have sprung up, taught by colored people who have got a little learning somehow.[23]

Though Tennessee and the Virginia/North Carolina coast were early sites where aid from local Black benevolent societies was reported, many such societies rapidly formed across the South.

The experience for refugees was complicated by US troops, many of whom were having their first encounters with Black people. McPherson tells us about Union soldiers in the camps that "only a minority in 1862 felt any interest in fighting for Black freedom. . . . While some Yanks treated contrabands with a degree of equity or benevolence, the more typical response was indifference, contempt, or cruelty."[24] Sheltering in Union camps involved physical cruelty to men and women, theft of supplies for freedpeople, or failure to intervene when local whites brutalized and even murdered Blacks for no reason and without being held to account. Sometimes people who themselves had only just escaped slavery taught others who followed them to the coast. Susie King Taylor, who was enslaved in Savannah and escaped to a boat on the Georgia coast, taught fugitives at Port Royal and soldiers in her husband's unit. She wrote of teaching about forty children in the day, and adults at night.[25]

However, Thavolia Glymph tells us that as more and more Black men got to Union camps and enlisted or were impressed into the service, enslaved women "increasingly found themselves running alone or in the company of other women and children. . . . Leaving slavery was one thing; finding a new home and a source of livelihood within Union lines was another matter altogether. The ever-growing and increasingly female-centered contraband population challenged the resources of commanders in the field."

Amy Murrell Taylor documents several such women, especially Eliza Bogan, who left an Arkansas plantation along with several other women to find her soldier husband in Helena, having heard he was sick, only to see him sent to Louisiana and to be evicted from the tent she shared with him. As the war continued, women like Eliza in many areas were moved to labor sites, as stated earlier, on Mississippi River islands or in the Mississippi Valley.[26]

Over time, returning Blacks to the fields took on a greater centrality in government efforts. In Port Royal, South Carolina, where ten thousand Blacks remained after the flight of planters, the army engaged in an experiment to show the country that slavery survivors would work of their own volition to get the crops out and attend schools. But as William Cohen points out, "The absence of southern whites that made experimentation so easy also created artificial conditions quite unlike those that came to exist in the rest of the South." In fact, each region had its own artificial situations arising from wartime improvisation. In Louisiana, the first labor contract set up by Benjamin Butler to save crops in 1862 was made between the government and planters, and "unlike the annual labor contracts that would emerge later, it was an agreement that Blacks were not parties to."[27] As Downs notes, "Even when labor did not seem to be the preoccupying concern of federal government authorities, it still played an integral role." Life for fugitives arriving to camps began with the military putting men to work, then women, then moving men around to work, and moving women to other outposts to work, as described earlier. But like the people of the self-named citizen camps of Louisiana, freedpeople everywhere taking shelter behind or near Union lines began immediately to build oppositional spatial practices, even on a small scale, as with Susie King Taylor landing at a small outpost and teaching Black soldiers to read. Outsiders—whether the formerly free Blacks who visited the dungeons in Nashville with aid, similar locals in every seaboard town, or Black and white northern activists—brought more substantial and organized assistance for those oppositional practices.[28]

Outsiders

The first northern missionaries to arrive, led by the American Missionary Association (AMA), came during the war to coastal towns in Virginia and the Carolinas, parts of Tennessee, and New Orleans. Societies led by Blacks included the Contraband Relief Association of Washington, the Union Relief Association of the Israel Bethel Church in Washington, the Freedmen's Friend Society in Brooklyn, the African Civilization Society in

New York, the Contraband Aid Association of Cincinnati, and the Contraband Committee of the Mother Bethel AME Church in Philadelphia, the last of which was associated with most of the ministers who appear in these pages. In cooperation with the US Army, missionaries engaged in an array of activities, from assisting with basic needs to organizing prayer meetings and schools to helping people acquire land. They were housed in abandoned homes or at Union forts, and sometimes they lived in the Black community. In 1861 the AMA, which was better equipped to recruit and send people south than some of the newly formed groups, sent missionaries to Hampton, Virginia, as well as to Port Royal and Beaufort, South Carolina. As Du Bois writes, "They extended their work in 1862–63, establishing missions down the Atlantic Coast, in Missouri, and along the Mississippi. By 1864, they had reached the Negroes in nearly all the Southern States." More precisely, Joe Richardson notes, the number of teachers and missionaries rose to "250 in 1864 and to 350 in 1865. By 1868 the AMA had 532 agents in the southern and border states," still a small number to aid four million.[29] Until the formation of the Freedmen's Bureau in 1865, the military officials in Virginia, North Carolina, and South Carolina and the handful of missionaries who traveled there formed the only outside support for the refugees appearing at military lines.[30]

In September 1861, Lewis Lockwood, an AMA minister, was the first missionary to arrive at Fort Monroe. Four months later, Edward Pierce, supervisor of the refugee labor at the fort, was sent to Port Royal, South Carolina, to do similar work. According to Engs, with Pierce's departure, the "makeshift" procedures for care of refugees "collapsed completely." His reassignment also shows the beginnings of the establishment of a circuit along which those charged with aiding fugitives would travel. At the outset, the two places where this was possible were Fort Monroe and Port Royal. By October 1862, Lockwood would be sending letters in preparation for his own move to Port Royal. He had earlier reported having seen refugee David Billops, who told him, "with tears streaming from his eyes, . . . 'I have been laboring faithfully and patiently for government since the troops landed in Hampton—about 5 1/2 months, and I must say that I have fared harder than in slavery.'" He worked on a gang "of about 30," and none of them had received pay or clothing. On January 6, 1862, Lockwood wrote AMA officers in New York pleading for assistance in getting word to New York newspapers and the public about the conditions. He also asked, "Cannot some way be devised to get an investigating Committee appointed in Congress to look into the Contraband affairs at Fortress Monroe?"[31]

Lockwood's letters also are replete with eyewitness accounts of evictions of refugees carried out by soldiers forcing people out of abandoned buildings (and, more than once, Lockwood himself) on empty claims of military need. "The poor and infirm find little or no mercy. This is intended to drag or force men into government service," writes Lockwood. Such reports were typical for him, but Lockwood's letters also capture the ways in which even the incremental changes made possible by officials could be undone on the whim of another.[32]

An important part of missionary work and a mechanism by which conceptions of racialized freedom were dispensed was through the organizing of regular religious gatherings. As refugees routinely initiated religious practice on their own, the meetings sponsored by missionaries tended to instruct the outsiders in southern Black spiritual practice as much as they made refugees familiar with northern ideas of proper services. Lockwood's reports of these events, quoting pages of the refugees' words on Christian teaching, often show him enthralled by the depth of their faith, in his view, *despite* the hardships of their past and immediate situations. At most meetings other community issues were taken up: money raised for particular people in need, or building a cabin for an elderly person. Participants routinely made plans and raised money to build schools or to supply them. At some meetings people gave testimony on their experiences in slavery or soldiers spoke of things they had learned or witnessed. Lockwood was impressed. He wrote, "The meetings are deeply interesting. Thursday evening is to be devoted to an anti-slavery prayer meeting—for prayers & the relation of experiences in slavery."[33]

Prayer meetings were a source of diverse forms of information for refugees as immediate needs of all present were constant. The camps were centers of information even for those who moved to housing outside of the inadequate and crowded Union posts, and they also were an introduction to a haphazard system for wage work and survival outside of plantations. The ideological missions present in the camps early on ranged from preparing Blacks for freedom (including an early Freedmen's Bureau mandate to put abandoned lands in newly free hands) to merely making sure they went back to work with the advice that "freedom means labor." Among Union soldiers there were those who simply wished for refugees to leave their camps and others who befriended them and fought for their often elusive government wages. Some missionaries and some agents of the Freedmen's Bureau preached universal human rights; others urged complying with slaveholder power and southern conventions. But a discourse concerning blackness was also going on in these rare initial opportunities for Black refugees to see themselves as a massive collectivity and to share ideas concerning the possibility of real freedom.[34]

Some of the missionaries arriving early on also viewed the refugees as accruing a debt for assistance given them either by the aid societies or by the government that should be paid with labor and respectability. On abolition, freedom was added to the debt owed. Rebeccah Bechtold points out the conflict that arose: "Unwilling to provide charity but unable to ignore the contrabands' plight, aid societies like the New England Freedmen's Aid Association developed assistance programs with policies implicating contrabands in a type of service economy. Those unable to earn wages through labor were expected to prove their 'right' to freedom in other ways, from their physical maintenance to a proper use of the charitable goods aid societies provided as means of easing their transition to freedom."[35] Bechtold reports that the government forces abetted this kind of thinking with many efforts to offer only minimal aid, usually in the form of rations. "Union officials even deducted 'a portion of the wages paid (or owed) able-bodied black workers as a charge for the support of the sick and disabled.'" This ideology of African American indebtedness with regard to the granting of legal freedom would have a long life in political rhetoric and lasting effects in cultural assumptions.[36]

Contemporary accounts of the self-governance and discourse among freedpeople often used the adjective *secret*, though the gatherings to which such accounts referred may have been meetings in a Black church, and Black public action drew much ire. Blacks had long known that their planning and organizing must be covert and would always be viewed with suspicion because they took place despite policing. One of the most important catalysts for the development of regional rival geographies was the long-standing repression of Black meetings. Beginning in the 1690s, when Virginians began to buy African captives in great numbers, the colonial authorities felt there was more to worry about than the flight of Africans, and Black assemblies became objects of policing. "As soon as Africans arrived in the Chesapeake colonies in large numbers," Allan Kulikoff writes, "government officials began to complain about their clandestine meetings." This pattern of complaint occurred in the midst of a growth in the Black population from about 3 percent in 1650 to 15 percent in 1690 with the onset of direct importation of Africans. In 1687, the Virginia Council was even fretting that masters allowed Blacks to gather in "great Numbers" for funerals. By the mid-nineteenth century, as Christopher Hager writes, "Virginia legislators, with the repetition of the obsessed, used the words *assembly* and *assemblage* eight times in a single section of its 1849 slave code."[37]

In addition, Camp notes, "Between 1748 and 1785 the Virginia Assembly passed a number of laws prohibiting and punishing 'outlying' and 'outlawed' activity. In 1748 Virginia's lawmakers distinguished between outlying runaways (short-term runaways, now called 'truants') and outlawed escapees (now known as 'runaways' or 'fugitives'). Surprisingly, it was not the outlawed that most concerned the legislature, but the outlying." Restricting the movement of enslaved people was a primary concern of slave owners throughout the slavery era, tied to forcing the enslaved to be available at all times for labor and preventing any collective autonomous actions. The policing evolved over time to include passes, curfews, searches of cabins for truants or arms, and the kinds of roll calls and bed checks used by the military and prisons. Thus, the open practice of religion, which alarmed some northerners with its expressive style, and the ability to have sessions of abolitionist prayer and testimony on enslavement experiences such as Lockwood documented were salutary hours for refugees and foundational rites for the young with the futures that the adults began to imagine.[38]

Blackness as Ideology: In Formation or Already Present?

While everyone recognized that food, clothing, and shelter were priorities, and basic education a vital and much-desired asset, there was no unanimity on "messaging" to refugees, even among Blacks arriving to help, as is shown by an October 1862 statement given by AME minister Henry McNeal Turner, while still in the North, in reaction to the preliminary Emancipation Proclamation in September of that year:

> The proclamation of President Lincoln . . . has opened up a new series of obligations, consequences, and results, never known to our honored sires. The great quantity of contrabands (so-called), who have fled from the oppressor's rod, and are now thronging Old Point Comfort, Hilton Head, Washington City, and many other places, and the unnumbered host who shall soon be freed by the President's proclamation, are to materially change their political and social condition. The day of our inactivity, disinterestedness, and irresponsibility, has given place to a day in which our long cherished abilities, and every intellectual fibre of our being, are to be called into a sphere of requisition. The time for

boasting of ancestral genius, and prowling through the dusty pages of an ancient history to find a specimen of negro [sic] intellectuality is over. Such useless noise should now be lulled, while we turn our attention to an engagement with those means which must, and alone can, mould out and develop those religious, literary, and pecuniary resources, adapted to grave expediency now about to be encountered.[39]

Though Turner was a southerner, born free in South Carolina, and would become chaplain to the US Colored Troops and work with the Freedmen's Bureau in Georgia, at this time he promoted a fairly elite view of the means of development for freedpeople. As an AME minister, McNeal would have been very familiar with protonationalist discourse "boasting of ancestral genius" from his pastorate. The church taught "that God had raised up their church 'to minister in holy things: first and foremost, to the Anglo-Africans upon this continent, and then to the colored races of the earth.'" Turner's encounters with his newly freed "flocks" in the South would force him to rely on blackness as a collective concept and find himself leaning toward those ties between the enslaved and "ancestral genius" in Africa in his church rhetoric.[40]

Richard H. Cain, the AME superintendent in South Carolina, viewed this Black denomination as "so eminently qualified" for the work that it had no peer, but like Turner and others, he believed the Black church was "an instrument of God's providence." Cain came to see the success of the African American ministers sent south as due to the fact that "the blacks recognize in our organization the idea of nationality of manhood." Cain's awkward phrase suggests a counterimage of blackness from those created by the slave system, one that exemplifies maturity, masculinity, and the shared attributes then associated with nation, such as common origins, culture, and race as described by euphemisms such as "heritage" or "blood."[41]

A third activist who went south and taught freedpeople about their rights was Martin R. Delany, a well-known author of the very nationalist ideology Cain and others espoused. He was an abolitionist doctor who, for several years, was a coeditor with Frederick Douglass of the *North Star*. By the time of the war, Delany had published a manifesto decrying the condition of the race, exhorting Blacks to form a country in Central or South America or in East Africa. His work echoes the sense of African Americans as a unified group with a global view of their political status found in David Walker's *Appeal*, which refers to African Americans as a "nation within a nation," a phrase that lived on in Black movements for more than a century. It is significant that any such language emerged from Black ministers and/or organizers in the South after abolition, as it reveals the perception of a *preexisting* unity in blackness, and the perceived utility that ideas such as nation had for those introducing political organization to people displaced by the slave system and war, separated even from discrete family units by sale and flight, and systematically closed off from much that constitutes heritage, narratives of origins, and well-preserved customs. Many such activists asserted that in lieu of those lost ties to origins and distinct cultures, blackness could be experienced as community and refuge.[42]

Many African American missionaries found among freedpeople a solidarity already present that they took to be based on blackness. Benjamin Tucker Tanner, founder of the widely read AME periodical the *Christian Recorder* and later an AME bishop and historian of the church, articulated an explanation of how nation or family might be evocative constructs for people whose mutuality consisted of experience with the slave system and ideology that insisted the genetic mark of African heritage was inferiority. Tanner reasoned that "the fires of oppression have melted the Anglo-Africans into one, it has burnt up their wrath and jealousies, and whenever they see each other's face, they see the countenance of a brother." For a southern culture in which trauma made kinfolk of those who shared Middle Passage and necessity made family of those who shared plantation quarters, by choice and by force, Tanner's theory describes quotidian experience. Formerly enslaved people indeed practiced a culture that recognized brothers and sisters in many faces.[43]

Even if many refugees in southern camps encountered people like Turner, who wished to mold them with grave expediency, giving short shrift to teaching specimens of Black intellectuality or any other agenda, it is clear that as the era moved on, freedpeople built a different list of priorities around fair wages, land, and education, and in both their religious practice and private societies found the "useless noise" of "ancient history" helpful for building community solidarity and preserving what they considered useful from communal practices in bondage. The first two AME ministers sent by Bishop Daniel Payne were twenty-four-year-old James D. Lynch and J. D. S. Hall, who went to coastal South Carolina in the spring of 1863, seven months after Turner's speech. Payne discovered through Lynch's and Hall's reports that beyond pastoral gifts, ministering to freedpeople required skills in organizing, politics, and fundraising. Clarence Walker, who studied the work of these ministers who went south, writes: "Above all, these ministers could not be dogmatic or inflexible. To gain converts for their church, they had to accommodate themselves to local customs." Turner, who also went south, became a fierce advocate for southern Blacks and, like his colleagues, not without learning as much as he taught.[44]

There were also many connections between these activists who came as strangers into the new world of refugee camps and settlements. The interactions between activists who were attending conferences and being moved around the emancipation geography offered opportunities to share any ideology of blackness they discovered already present in communities and, further, to elaborate ideas of blackness by using it to teach practical skills such as literacy or political theory they may have expounded. Delany came to his nationalism by learning of family ties to Africa, so his own body carried, so to speak, ties bound by blackness if not the specifics of a particular African culture. Such awareness of ancestral ties, lost or maintained, was common among some Africans still present in the southern populace. These are simple speculations, but they are obscured even in the case of these activists by the fact that the records of their activities are to be found in diverse archives of churches, the military, and aid groups. And there is also loss of other letters and documentation of their lives. In looking across these individual journeys, I have taken notice of sites and times when any of these organizing theorists encountered each other. This, in turn, revealed that an unseemly number of these activists died young—in their thirties and forties—including some murdered for their work. Among those for whom dates are known, most died between the ages of thirty-five and fifty, but an equal number have no known birth dates. Their deaths, which can be used as data because they had at least somewhat documented lives, only hint at the strife suffered by their local counterparts who were not associated with national organizations. What is knowable is that their interconnections on the circuit help us to think about how ideologies may have been shaped along a circuit evolving as quickly as new housing and schools were put up along the displacement routes. Another place to look is at the societies formed by ordinary people in the emancipation era.[45]

Societies on the Ground

With the appearance of fugitives along the Atlantic Coast, extant Black groups began to appear in public. David Cecelski writes of North Carolina that "mutual-aid societies that had existed clandestinely during slavery . . . came out of the shadows to assist the refugees and, at least as important, to serve as foundations for organizing self-help and political groups among the former slaves."[46] Evidence of such organizing, regardless of specific purposes, was viewed by local whites and the press as suspicious, and meetings sometimes were followed by violence. Though the right of assembly is deeply embedded in the American ethos, it was continually challenged, demonized, and policed when practiced by African Americans in the South throughout the nineteenth century and into the twentieth.

As the war disrupted antebellum Black social structures, new sodalities were created wherever refugees assembled. On the Emancipation Circuit, especially the urban centers and the Delta towns, a matrix of benevolent societies shaped a structure for organizing politics, labor, health care, armed self-defense, sport, and social life. Between 1862 and 1880, New Orleans had 226 Black societies. In 1865, Richmond had 30 Black societies, and Norfolk had at least a dozen local groups. Theda Skocpol and Jennifer Lynn Oser write, "From the mid-1800s on, vast and densely rooted networks of fraternal lodges were built and sustained by African Americans—who seem to have embraced to an extraordinary degree this characteristically U.S. form of popular organization." They had to do so; if no fire engine would come, at least a bucket brigade had to be formed.[47]

August Meier wrote in 1964, "As old as the Negro church, and second only to it in importance as a self-help and co-operative institution[,] was the fraternal and mutual benefit society." The oldest benevolent associations in New Orleans were largely charitable and started by free people of color, whereas on the Eastern Seaboard some of the oldest associations, dating back to the early 1800s, were started by free men (women were excluded) to acquire communally owned property for burials.[48] Fraternal groups began attracting Black southerners early in the emancipation period. The southern Black matrix of mutual aid societies, fraternal lodges, and trade associations has traditionally been marked by large numbers of working-class members and a smaller number of elite Blacks, along with overlapping association memberships. William Johnson Jr. was enslaved in Virginia and worked as a butler. In freedom he learned bricklaying and in the 1900s began contracting for himself. In 1937 he said that since the 1870s he had continuously belonged to Richmond's First Baptist Church, the Independent Order of Good Samaritans, the Odd Fellows, the Masons, the Independent Order of St. Luke, and the National Ideal Benefit Society, a mix of national and local Richmond groups. Johnson's account of multiple memberships is similar to listings in many obituaries of both working-class and elite people in southern Black papers in the nineteenth century.

Anna E. Crawford of Petersburg gave this account of her father: "After war mother took in washing and ironing and my father was a cabinet maker. . . . My father after the war, 1865, was past Master Mason of Knights of Pythias and had all the degrees. His name was Isaac C. Washington." These memberships and the offices within them were held in high regard in Black communities. The fact that such groups became so important to slavery survivors, even right after the war, among people who had neither much leisure time nor much disposable income makes it worth asking what the groups were doing.[49]

Black mutual aid societies and fraternal groups in the nineteenth century have been characterized as primarily social without the observation that they evolved over time. Some became primarily social in the twentieth century, but in the years after the Civil War they served to provide specific needs. Many of the earlier scholars of emancipation, especially Black scholars and civic figures, took pains to note the prominence of voluntary associations in African American communities, particularly those that gained wide national membership at the turn of the twentieth century.[50] Aside from the history of mutual aid societies being foundational for durable Black-owned insurance companies and local savings and loan institutions, their pooling of disposable income was foundational for local Black capital formation. Many of the societies active in the early decades of freedom, after those formed to provide food, clothing, and medical help, were formed to aid families and groups in buying land or saving through credit union structures.

These associations are also often said to be imitations of northern white groups. Some groups are what Joe Trotter terms "parallel" groups, like the Odd Fellows, copying exactly the earlier models found in the North, while many others, called "independent orders," have Black origins. What is interesting about all the groups are the ways in which African Americans adapted these association forms (particularly in the South) to serve local community needs and reinterpreted the ideologies to promote living in dignity, which included acknowledgment of ancestral ties to Africa and the Black Atlantic. Benjamin Quarles shows that northern Black societies, which often grew out of white abolitionist groups, were also turned to specific Black (and local) service, like the "direct confrontation" practices of vigilance committees, who boarded ships in northern ports to inform enslaved people brought north by owners that they were free. In the South, however, leaders of the regional associations became powerful presences in their areas. As Harold Forsythe points out, "Local societies capitalized by farmers and tenants were, of necessity, less powerful, but their officers still wielded considerable influence through their ability to invest accumulated proceeds and through their role as masters of ceremonies in the ritual lives within these organizations."[51] Meier, who represents a widely accepted twentieth-century view, says: "It is customary to distinguish between the secret order and the purely mutual benefit society, in that the former stressed ritual and social elements, while the latter emphasized uplift. Actually, there is no sharp dividing line between them. Both were often quasi-religious in outlook, and many societies took religious titles such as the Mosaic Templars of America, the Nazirites, the Galilean Fishermen, the Order of St. Luke, and so forth."[52] I also do not distinguish here between secret orders and mutual benefit societies, but for the contrary reason: both types of groups engaged in programs to assist Blacks in acquiring loans, learning business protocols, and gaining leadership skills, and they encouraged aid toward others in the community. I also see them as part of the palimpsest that is the Emancipation Circuit in that these groups constitute another layer of organizing that taught and reinforced the idea that within racial solidarity there was equality and respect not to be had elsewhere. Black societies and lodges joined community celebrations of Emancipation Day and other political events and considered their activities part of a forward movement for the race. While some used biblical references to explain their origins and path of compassion, others had interesting idiosyncratic and overtly political inspirations. The Grand United Order of Tents, J. R. Giddings and Jolliffe Union was founded in Norfolk in 1867 by two Black women, Annetta M. Lane and Harriet R. Taylor (both enslaved, by most accounts), and may have begun a decade earlier as part of the Underground Railroad (the order's name salutes two abolitionists). The United Brothers of Friendship and Sisters of the Mysterious Ten, founded in Louisville in 1861, called itself "a Negro order" and was begun by enslaved and free men to aid Black soldiers and their families during the war and reorganized itself to respond to freedom. The antislavery statements of the groups' origins contradict the reputation of such groups as distant from the struggles for justice.[53]

Accusations and complaints from whites concerned about Blacks having clandestine meetings run through the documents of the late nineteenth century; these allegations fueled murders, repressive laws, and intricate codes of affront to the customary privileges of whites in the South. Whether these groups adopted the names and rituals of mainstream lodges or had entirely local origins, they would be regarded with suspicion by local whites. As it turned out, they also were distrusted by northern clergy and missionaries, who over the years felt threatened by the popularity of the groups and thought Christians erred by swearing any oath other than to Christ. By the 1880s and 1890s, the groups were assailed from many sides, and their secrecy was taken as an indication of political and/or criminal activity. The fact that mutual aid societies, trade associations, and other sodalities were the inventions of necessity was by then lost on many, but perhaps not their early ties to political organizing, if only because they continued to parade in public for decades longer. As Forsythe points out, "Black churches, benevolent and fraternal orders, plantation associations, and kin and neighborhood networks left faint tracks compared to those of federal and state governments, political parties, plantation owners, and corporations, but these faint tracks may lead to a new understanding of African-American political mobilization and independence."[54]

Even setting aside the content of their civic activity, the existence of ground-level organizations and sodalities as highly structured groups with consensus-driven goals positions them as essential to the community solidarity and mobilization required for shared goals. The existence and persecution of secret societies (through lynchings, hall burnings, and excommunication or exclusion of members from the Catholic, Methodist, and Congregationalist churches) for alleged political activity in Black interests allow us to see the articulation of Black political activism with the profiling of Black groups as criminal. As people charged with ordinary criminal activity were also often accused of belonging to "secret societies," criminals were labeled as organized and part of a secret infrastructure and the infrastructure was labeled as political. The matrix of societies, while providing an infrastructure for community building, is fugitive in the sense of sometimes existing as a set of transient groups unable to withstand mainstream repression, and fugitive in the sense of being labeled as outlaw for practicing Black solidarity out of the mainstream gaze.[55]

Bringing Back the Dead

It also makes sense that groups described as "fraternal" would have strong appeal among people who had been both displaced and separated from blood kin. Reuniting with loved ones was perhaps the most important task chosen in freedom for those who came off plantations. Refugees showing up at camps that housed thousands of others from regional plantations and towns exercised that opportunity to begin the long-term project of trying to find family members. Heather Williams has described these sometimes years-long searches as attempts to "bring back the dead." She shows that freedpeople had "to be strategic, devising targeted appeals for help. When they were able, they sent out missives and messengers who might bring back the dead." Bringing back the dead is an evocative description of all the work facing freedpeople and the mission of circuit organizers who resurrected many dreams, from finding children to becoming literate. These fortunate few who had already rebuilt families and received education brought with them new possible horizons and also must have begun to reimagine possible futures once they were confronted with new realities in the South. This was some of the cultural work of illiterate, often continually displaced persons who kept the dead among the living, preserving old places mythically with storms, stars, and autobiography in the new.[56]

It is hard to imagine slave system survivors viewing any of their crises as outside of their politics both because they were just learning the dimensions of citizenship and because they were confronting the fact that they were not seen as citizens legally or in everyday circumstances. Gaining full citizenship was perhaps the most logical first step beyond food, clothing, shelter, and finding family. Do a noncitizen's efforts to negotiate labor issues stand apart from the political? Does the rape of a woman viewed as former property and not a citizen stand outside of political remedy? Does it make sense that parents born in slavery have no custody rights over their children in freedom? Freedpeople demanded their recognition and developed a politics capacious enough to take on many such issues. Freedpeople were not seen as citizens and, like all stateless, dispossessed populations (and women in most respects), did not exist as acknowledged members of the polity. Political work and goals for freedpeople, whether successful, temporarily achieved, partially won, or utterly failed, would require remaking American politics.

2 THE EMANCIPATION CIRCUIT
A Road Map

> **Circuit** n, **1 a :** a usually circular line encompassing an area, **b :** the
> space enclosed within such a line; **2 a :** a course around a periph-
> ery; . . . **3 a :** a regular tour (as by a traveling judge or preacher)
> around an assigned district or territory; **b :** the route traveled; **c :** a
> group of church congregations ministered to by one pastor; **4 a :** the
> complete path of an electric current including usually the source of
> electric energy; . . . **5 a :** an association of similar groups . . .
> —*Webster's Ninth New Collegiate Dictionary* (1986)

The Emancipation Circuit fits most of the definitions in this chapter's epigraph. It was roughly a horseshoe-shaped route around the periphery of the
South, encompassing internal routes and connections. It was also a series
of routes through terrain served by traveling ministers and activists, as well
as people in search of lost family, church congregations following pastors, or
people migrating for new work. It was a route that connected settlements,
organizations, and pubic outlets for political building and literal community building (later served as well by Freedmen's Bureau agents). It was also
a frontier of independent, often transient or shifting Black encampments
within an active war and a war-damaged landscape. The geography of the

Civil War, evolving as it did during the course of events, impacted civilians at unexpected moments with displacement and chances for the enslaved to take flight. The circuit can be seen as the path of a current of generative human energy responsive to a massive emergency in the wake of war, and also an arena in which groups could coordinate any efforts that seemed of immediate use to freedpeople. The circuit was not everywhere in the South because it comprised a particular mix of community institutions or groups that produced organizing formations that could be expanded and elaborated according to local needs and ideas. This chapter shows the intersections of geography, political developments, institutional political actions, and Black mobilizations that define sites that became part of the Emancipation Circuit. Within that landscape, competing visions of postwar development can be seen. Some of the likely impediments to Black political organizing are also visible when one looks at these same elements of geography, community building, and reactions to political change.

Troop Presence Brought Movement

The Emancipation Circuit is defined by elements common to the history of its locales during the war. Among the shared facets of these locations' histories a number are foundational: 86 percent of the sites on the circuit experienced US troop presence during the Civil War and the construction of refugee camps; both of these factors exposed fugitives to crucial information on citizenship rights and wage work and, often, to local Black activists and missionaries. Federal troop sites were also recruiting points for Black soldiers and spies and drew fugitives who fanned out into the countryside, telling others of Union presence and sometimes literally guiding soldiers who freed people under fire.

In April 1865, when the Confederate States of America surrendered, a breached slave system fully ruptured. Where there had been a well-entrenched legal framework for bondage, laws and conventions became contingent. For those in the South who felt no governance was acceptable that did not exert absolute police control over Blacks, a real crisis was at hand. Existing laws specified applicability to slaves, whites, and free persons of color; freedpeople were not a recognized populace. To many Blacks, who had no standing in the surviving state legal structures, the silence of the law was an opportunity to assume all the rights and privileges enjoyed by anyone else. However, their access to those rights could only be settled by trying to exercise them and going to court, and by rehabilitating state constitutions to remove new white supremacist legislation. For federal officers, whether provisional governors or locally posted troops, there were daily tasks of arbitration as these tests took place. Throughout that year, people employed by the newly established Freedmen's Bureau began to filter into communities and to face these complex negotiations as well. The statutory vacuum presented those vested in the welfare of the newly freed with an opportunity to rethink the role of governance with regard to need before precedent. Some did think this through, but others did not.

The only generalities one can make about the shared goals of southern Blacks come under broad categories such as justice, education, landownership, and an end to violence targeting them. What is so compelling about the situation facing freedpeople at abolition, and their responses to it, is that they constitute the purest definition of political struggle — making themselves heard, recognized as part of the American polity. If the war ended up freeing southern Blacks, it had not begun that way, and no one in the acknowledged bodies politic had planned for inclusion of this population of four million. When the four million began to speak, a challenge was made to every existing institution in society, from political institutions to hospitals, from churches to the military, and from newspapers to businesses, whether large or small or regional or local.

Freedpeople forced the federal government to define its terms of citizenship and forced the federal and state governments to confront challenges to legislated rights and customary behaviors. Though some meetings of Blacks sought not to antagonize local whites, in most public statements they were against any form of racialized freedom. Still, whether Black public iterations of citizenship were conciliatory or aggrieved in tone, their mere existence had sustained power to shock. The fact that southern and northern newspapers made a point to express amazement that freedpeople could hold orderly meetings betrays the shallowness of thought given to the existence of the four million as more than bodies. Black communities attempted to meet this situation of both crisis and opportunity through a wide array of grassroots formations and an expansive conception of the political arena.

Assemblies: Foundational Tools in Freedom

The productive interventions of freedmen and freedwomen in the discourse concerning their futures reflected the understanding that white southerners were primarily concerned with keeping Blacks, as much as possible, in situations of compulsory and unpaid labor in sites from which they could not move. This knowledge amounted to foresight as to directions planters would take in influencing federal officers, agents, and their legislators. Whatever legislative means Blacks pursued to secure the franchise and civil rights, their immediate focus had to be economic survival. Julie Saville's estimation of coastal freedpeople in South Carolina could apply to people across the South: "Making no distinctions between political and economic struggles, South Carolina's agricultural laborers understood the planting of a new social order to be the work of Reconstruction." Importantly, Saville gives evidence that these former enslaved people viewed themselves collectively as a laboring class. People also saw the connection between citizenship rights and economic autonomy not just in the plantation areas but also in cities like Richmond, where men and women were arrested for being in public without "passes" and then leased out for gang labor.[1]

In cities and hamlets, African Americans deployed democratic processes, including gathering testimony concerning treatment by any or all of the contending forces, that produced leadership that was a mix of laboring and elite Blacks (in varying degrees in different locations). They created public venues where women had voice and, as a result, political agendas that were attentive to gendered issues that unsettled friends and foes alike. The testimony enlarged the understanding among freedpeople (and any whites present) of the prevalence of systemic sexual violence on plantations. Significantly, public airing of local plantation abuse in these forums helped to create a collective oral archive of Black experience in the region. At the same time, testimony built documentary incentives for regional resistance to reenslavement measures. Rural communities sometimes pooled resources to send trusted people (with skills for reporting from memory) to distant meetings to bring complete briefings on the proceedings. Finally, it must be said about the first years of freedom that violence was a catalyst for mobilization. Blacks, like people anywhere, were radicalized by violence against them, especially in urban centers where people witnessed it on a nearly daily basis. All of these factors were visibly at work in the early assemblies of freedpeople.

The South's old regime was decidedly disturbed about the silences and gaps in laws and regulations that Blacks were trying to widen between slave system legislation and federal military rule. In the few months after surrender, whites with farms and businesses to run across the South took notice of African Americans having mass meetings, holding protests against police and sheriffs, and shopping their labor among employers. They saw regional migrations, church-building, and attempts to buy lands abandoned but never regarded as given up. People considered very ignorant were writing letters to the president and letters to newspaper editors. Women were getting up in public meetings and describing beatings and rapes and, just by their presence, implicating their known former slaveholders. Such accounts were printed in newspapers near and far. Some of the people gathered were threatening to defend themselves. And some of them were soldiers. Importantly, grassroots meetings and associations coordinated their efforts and walked the fine line of speaking with one voice while allowing for specific protests and demands from localities within their network.

There is little wonder that the most prominent structure of Black political organizing after the Civil War became the mass meeting, which, in its diverse manifestations in fields, in churches, on coastal shores, and at the perimeters of forts across the South, was a public declaration of citizenship. It is easy to imagine the local impact of passing a shaded glen in a Georgia town on a hot day where two thousand Blacks who used to be controlled by whip and rifle were having a meeting with armed Black soldiers present or familiar Black faces standing at the edges of the crowd with their own rifles. This is a sight so taboo in the national mind most Americans have never heard of it. (Such an image still had shock value a hundred years later when some young Blacks showed up at California's capitol displaying what are now called "open-carry" weapons.) Openly carrying arms was legal and ordinary all over the South after the Civil War, except for Blacks. Because the only existing law in 1865 referred to bans on "slaves" owning and carrying weapons, which did not apply to freedpeople, sightings of armed Blacks provoked southern lawmakers to set about trying to make it illegal. Blacks demanding the vote surprised and appalled some, but displaying the right to self-defense and the right to assembly readily mobilized white resistance to Black citizenship.[2]

The mass meeting process in the South after abolition should be described as a foundational tool for Black organizing and mobilization in freedom. As a rupture with the past, these mass meetings rank with any actions of public protest or civil disobedience that have left a mark on our culture, though they have not been described as the change agents and visible enactments of citizenship that they were.

As is shown in the following chapters, the meetings, often witnessed by northern reporters, army staff, and missionaries, were attended by people of all ages, male and female, and often those who could not get into an indoor meeting waited outside for firsthand reports of what went on. The meetings were long and probably boisterous because anyone could speak, and they were open to all forms of speech, including humor and song. The mass meetings were grounded in unique experience. Life in the slave system put people in diverse, sometimes transient plantation structures that undermined hierarchies among the enslaved. As a result, meetings during and after slavery benefited from openness to diverse voices—information, expertise, or wisdom from any members of the community. The mass meeting process of freedpeople of the US South was organic to the wartime events that made any form of news a crowd event in any southern town, massing displaced persons into sites of refuge and putting strangers together who did not share long mutual experiences in one particular setting. Groups relied as standard procedure on oral transmission and memorization of the discourse in meetings. Some participants might be asked later for a rendering of the discussions. Slave system skills and practices clearly facilitated the expansion of political discourse in freedom.[3]

Decisions were made by consensus, usually following the reading of a written rendering of the sense of the meeting. Thus, Black assemblies in several towns could cooperate without trying to alter the resolutions of others, but by augmenting the ideas already voiced. Such allied efforts also gave all of the Black settlements/assemblies involved a sense of momentum and enlarged claims for representation. It would seem, in fact, that the greatest gains of such organizing were often qualitative—creating an engaged, mobilized community and recognition of their numbers as a laboring class rather than achieving specific ends.

In the years before Black men received the franchise, Black meetings were not aimed at achieving representation or operated as traditional representative democracies. And using parliamentary procedure was probably not the norm. The mass meetings were examples of participatory democracy, resistant to efforts by those who attempted to restrict who might participate, and inescapably shaped by elements we may never discover from the decision-making practices on plantations as well as southern Black religious practices of the time. One could say the southern Black mass meetings have some kinship with New England town meetings. But they might be more easily compared to Revolutionary-era meetings, as Emancipation Era assemblies were marked by ongoing crisis, widespread illiteracy, and an underlying society experiencing rupture in which the structures of governance were voided.[4] Still, the mass meetings are most easily differentiated from earlier communal decision-making processes by the size of many of the gatherings and the slave system experience of the people assembled. The size of the meetings provided safety, an important consideration in the South. Though southern Blacks were threatened before and after meetings, and sometimes groups were attacked, breaking up mass meetings required planning and large numbers of armed whites. Southern towns in political battles in the 1860s and 1870s more often saw attacks on specific influential organizers or smaller groups of voters. Fears concerning Blacks having meetings were among the oldest fears in the American South and among the first responses to postwar Black political discourse and organizing. Such fears were deployed as excuses for the repression of African Americans in the South throughout the nineteenth century.

Over time, anxiety about Black meetings outweighed the character of the meetings, whether fraternal lodges or Black labor associations, or even whether they actually took place. In Opelousas, Louisiana, for instance, Litwack reports, "to hold any public meetings or to assemble in large numbers for any reason, blacks needed the mayor's permission, as they also did to 'preach, exhort, or otherwise declaim' to black congregations." The right to assembly for Blacks was contested all over the South from the time of abolition and, with the death of Reconstruction, was for all practical purposes policed for Blacks in all but the biggest cities and Black college towns well into the twentieth century. As Harold Forsythe writes of Virginia: "African-American churches after emancipation operated completely in the open, whereas benevolent societies were private and fraternal orders were for the most part secret. In the southern countryside, even more than in the cities, the political potential of black secular organizations frightened many white men. Building such associations in rural areas was fraught with danger." Black awareness of being monitored in organized behaviors of all kinds has to be considered as much a part of nineteenth-century Black political life in freedom as it was during slavery. Holding meetings was just as dangerous in the 1880s as fifty years earlier, maybe more so.[5]

Southern Black mass participatory democracy influences the organizing process in a particular way by beginning with large meetings, which in turn generate small groups and meetings. Mass movements are frequently built in the opposite way—from the smaller gathering to larger groups—such as often occurred in the twentieth-century southern civil rights movement, in which independent local actions were taken up by neighbors or relatives in nearby towns and were linked by the intention of seizing the opportunity to be seen as regional or expanding. Large groups make open decision-making unwieldy, not to mention lengthy. Consensus requires an expansion of trust, alliances, or representation.

Support for Women Strengthened All

Because Black men and women entered the wage-earning workforce simultaneously, usually expected to do similar or overlapping work, political discourse among freedpeople included gendered occupational hazards, gendered pressures to remake Black households, and the rights of women to speak on these issues. Writing on postwar Richmond, Elsa Barkley Brown details a process that had counterparts around the South: "By the very nature of their participation—the inclusion of women and children, the engagement through prayer, the disregard of formal rules for speakers and audience, the engagement from the galleries in the formal legislative sessions—Afro-Richmonders challenged liberal bourgeois notions of rational discourse. Many white observers considered their unorthodox political engagements to be signs of their unfamiliarity and perhaps unreadiness for politics."[6] In our republic, four score and nine years old at the end of the war, the demos—the "people"—did not yet mean all of the people of the land, and certainly not women and children. Additionally, there was a shock both that an epidemic of sexual assaults on newly free women occurred and that it prompted Black public protests and demands for the protection of females. Given the inability of enslaved people to obtain redress for violence against women over the course of slavery, it is hardly surprising that people would have been mobilized by the suddenly widespread danger of perpetrators, the assaults in response to the appearance of Black women in public spaces, and instances of corrupt use of police power to enable assaults. Mass meetings allowed many to hear of incidents that earlier would have occurred without public notice. Though the grip of concubinage had been loosened, Blacks faced both daily news of assaults on women and pressure from missionaries and Freedmen's Bureau agents to emulate white patriarchy in defining family. At the same time, Black men acted to defend women in their midst. Still, it is difficult to make simple characterizations of the public emergence of the indignant

Black female and male voices testifying to new terrors. Surely some Black men were enacting the patriarchy typical of the moment, some were calling out the strength in numbers that might allow action on abuse that could not be fought in slavery, and doubtless some women and men were displaying leadership roles previously held in plantation communities.

One of the other developments that helped to sustain communities was the assistance to women provided by the Freedmen's Bureau. Women availed themselves of opportunities to file workplace complaints and domestic abuse complaints and sought assistance from the bureau to gain custody of their children, not from partners but from former slaveholders. The bureau was also of assistance to women filing for widow's benefits for Union military service. In the latter cases, as Anthony Kaye has shown, the testimony of women and their neighbors reveals a wealth of information on the control former owners continued to hold over Black family life as well as the extreme care people in community took to support the women's claims. Women openly resisted being disparaged in court for sexual victimization in the slave system and upheld their chosen relationships. Community members stood by women even as testimony had to parse forced relationships from the later consensual ones with men who were soldiers and often shielded local planters who were the fathers of children of enslaved women. They helped to see that a court did not deny a widow's valid claim by assaulting her character for having been a rape victim while enslaved and rendering her one of the many victims who would not receive child support for the children of concubinage.[7]

With the existence of church congregations and a matrix of gendered benevolent societies as a base for building community institutions, both women and men gained organizational skills and established multigenerational organizing practices in their communities. Multigenerational groups nurtured a long life for political knowledge in freed communities. Likewise, slavery traditions of embracing fictive kin had already embedded an expansive conception of family and collective consciousness in enslaved communities.

Goin' to the Law

At the end of 1865 and throughout 1866, all the forces trying to reconfigure southern society worked the breaks in the ruptured system. By the end of 1865, while the Thirteenth Amendment abolishing slavery was in the process of being ratified, southern elites made their first attempt to reestablish near-total control over the labor forces in their states. In the face of abolition, southern state legislatures set out to revise state constitutions, using "black codes" to restore as many important elements of slave system law as possible. For readmission into the Union, states were initially required to rewrite constitutions at least as far as repealing their declarations of secession and accepting the Thirteenth Amendment. The tactics in the black codes for ensuring the availability of the workforce included restricting the ability of Blacks to move, to buy land, or sometimes even to rent a house. Every freedperson had to have written proof of a home and a job, and anyone who quit a contract forfeited wages for work done, usually a year's pay. The codes fined anyone who enticed a worker away from an employer. As Du Bois wrote: "The original codes favored by the Southern legislatures were an astonishing affront to emancipation and dealt with vagrancy, apprenticeship, labor contracts, migration, civil and legal rights. In all cases, there was plain and indisputable attempt on the part of the Southern states to make Negroes slaves in everything but name. They were given certain civil rights: the right to hold property, to sue and be sued. The family relations for the first time were legally recognized. Negroes were no longer real estate."[8] The legislatures gave themselves a great deal of latitude to limit rights after granting them. The vagrancy law in Virginia was so repressive that the provisional governor prohibited its use. The law, including a provision that people declared vagrants should be put to free labor, wearing a ball and chain, was not taken off the books until 1904.[9] The harshest of the codes—in Mississippi and South Carolina—were among the earliest, passed in 1865, along with those of Louisiana and Alabama. With the elaborations of white control of the workforce in the Mississippi code, the state began its terrifying career as a domain synonymous with the violent repression of all rights for African Americans. Blacks were denied Second Amendment rights. Freedpeople outside of the military or not licensed by the county police board would not be allowed to own or carry "fire-arms of any kind, or any ammunition, dirk, or bowie knife." The clause punishing "any freedman, free Negro, or mulatto committing riots, routs, affrays, trespasses, malicious mischief . . . seditious speeches, insulting gestures, language, or acts" also constrained the First Amendment by use of a southern meaning of the word *insulting*.[10]

Insulting language in practice could include any opinions that countered those of whites or speech in defense of one's own rights. Insulting gestures included failure to step off the sidewalk in deference to whites (sometimes resulting in shootings or melees), or even failure to remove one's hat when passing whites on the street, or looking a white person in the eye. So-called insulting language and gestures became a cause for much misery visited on Blacks. On the other hand, insulting language against Blacks was, as freedpeople often observed, daily fare. Also often mentioned by freedmen, the codes kept in place old laws governing crimes by the enslaved to cover offenses by Blacks that were not covered in the new codes, even though slaves no longer existed in the law.[11]

The Mississippi and South Carolina black codes caused such an uproar in the North as obvious attempts to replicate slavery that military officials governing those states voided the legislation. The southern states writing codes in ensuing months feigned compliance with the Civil Rights Act of 1866, which forbade racial distinctions in the law, by simply deleting racial references, though the racialized intent in certain laws was clear. According to Eric Foner, "Florida's code, drawn up by a commission whose report praised slavery as a 'benign' institution deficient only in its inadequate regulation of Black sexual behavior, made disobedience, impudence, and even 'disrespect' to the employer a crime." This code conformed to the others with regard to terms of labor, vagrancy, and firearms. For crimes already on the books, the code added, as Du Bois put it, "the punishment of standing in the pillory for one hour, or whipping, not exceeding thirty-nine stripes on the bare back, or both, at the discretion of the jury." For "exciting an insurrection," the punishment was death.[12]

Radical Reconstruction, which began after the elections of 1866, brought the final demise of most black code language over the next two years by empowering a new electorate to send representatives to state houses to once again rewrite state constitutions. The change in power in Washington also meant that readmission to the Union for former Confederate states required acceptance of the Fourteenth Amendment and the right of African American males to vote. Beyond their brief time as laws, the black codes had significance as inscriptions aimed to restore white property privileges and some "courtesies" that had merely been customarily demanded, such as not looking a white person in the eye. Their major concerns—labor conditions and contracts, vagrancy (and forced labor), civil and legal rights (including jury service and testimony in court), and Black rights to mobility, local housing, and migration—marked the battle terrain for years to come, in some cases, decades. A few years later the raising of Confederate monuments across the South and passage of "Jim Crow" laws would serve as tributes to that same ideal of codified white supremacy. The repeated elaboration of segregation laws and the increased use of unconstitutional devices to repress the Black vote and even entrance to or exit from southern towns, not only served the aim of protecting political control but also made a cultural norm of quotidian unbounded white privilege.[13]

By the spring of 1866, Black political gatherings and Black use of public space, along with the prominent presence of Black troops, caused white anger to boil over around the circuit of federal presence. The passage of the Civil Rights Act in April preceded major violent events in Norfolk, Memphis, and New Orleans, and it contributed directly to the eruption of violence in the first two cities.[14] The bill gave Blacks and whites the same rights and affected people all over the country by outlawing various forms of discrimination. This first real definition of US citizenship, beginning with birth in the United States and excluding consideration of "race and color" and "previous condition of slavery or involuntary servitude," had the rationale of consolidating the Thirteenth Amendment's abolition of slavery with a positive declaration of inclusion. The bill provided freedpeople with the right to make and enforce contracts, to sue and be sued, and to give evidence while extending to them the benefit of all laws serving the security of persons and property, "as is enjoyed by white citizens."[15] It prohibited exactly the kinds of southern racialized laws meant to exclude African Americans from citizenship rights and protections. To most people at the time, the bill must have portended enormous change. Maine senator Lot M. Merrill said at the time, "I admit that this species of legislation is absolutely revolutionary. But are we not in the midst of a revolution?" For white southerners, the phrase "as is enjoyed by white citizens" alone may have suggested revolution.[16]

In Memphis the bill was viewed as worse than undesirable; the conservative *Memphis Argus* said it "may be well described as a bill to destroy the civil rights of white men in the States, and to exalt the negro to superior immunities and privileges."[17] This was not true at all, and the idea that equal protections meant "superior" immunities and privileges is illogical but a prevalent interpretation of Black inclusion in the polity. Black citizenship did, on paper, deprive whites of customary privileges long held by the few rather than the many, such as the "right" to maim or kill Blacks at will—a privilege exercised primarily by those who had owned human chattel. But the Freedmen's Bureau files of "outrages" against Blacks, before and after passage of the Civil Rights Act, detail thousands of incidents by people who expected no penalties whatever to arise for them from such actions. Perhaps the most dangerous and persistent response to legal citizenship for African Americans was systemic immunity for whites for any crime against Blacks. That one portion of the population across an entire region never faced consequences for granting itself immunity for crimes against anyone of another race for at least another century makes Wolin's statement that democratic liberty shields antidemocratic forms of power seem an understatement. Southern impunity in actions against people of color was not shielded in the sense of being obscure. After all, it was not hidden; it was shielded in being known and tolerated.

The 1866 Civil Rights Bill did not provide African Americans with political rights and did not address the right to vote. Most people concerned with freedpeople's rights knew the bill was shortsighted; most black codes had given fair warning that southern state legislators intended to use state authority to bar Blacks from full citizenship. The civil rights bill left it to individuals to go to the courts for enforcement and protection of their rights. This latter outcome of having to go to court for enforcement would remain the onus for individuals, groups, or classes for another century. Even so, the Congress had to overcome two vetoes from President Andrew Johnson to enact the bill and another establishing the Freedmen's Bureau as a government agency.[18]

The passage of the Reconstruction Acts of 1867 divided the South into five military districts, further altering the power relations in the region by inserting military governors at the top of each state's power structure and bringing the federal government into a new set of growing pains as it organized an occupation of the South. The war had already greatly expanded the government itself, and the aftermath of war caused a huge expansion of the missions it undertook and the offices of government required, from rebuilding the economy to taking care of thousands of sick, wounded, and dead.

Circuit Riders

> **Circuit Rider** n. (1837): a clergyman assigned to a circuit esp. in a rural area.
> —*Webster's Ninth New Collegiate Dictionary* (1986)

> **County Circuit Rider:** lawyer following a circuit judge, the most famous of whom was Abraham Lincoln.
> —Guy C. Fraker, "The Real Lincoln Highway: The Forgotten Lincoln Circuit Markers" (2004)

Church Circuit Rider: a traveling preacher.
—African American vernacular

CC Rider: a blues term, early twentieth century.[19]
—Popularized by Ma Rainey, "Rider Blues" (1924)

When the Radical Reconstruction Acts were passed in 1867, providing the vote to Black males, more resources, and a longer tenure for the Freedmen's Bureau and limitations on the old power elite, the South—Black, white, military, civilian, missionary, and political—began an intense period of strategic organization. In some places such as Louisiana and Georgia, reaction to the election of Black representatives was a systematic, county-by-county assault on Black leadership. The one advantage Blacks and those helping them had was keen awareness of the course white reaction might take. The cautions routinely exercised in slavery simply continued.

Among these cautions, the first is that people on the ground knew organizing freedpeople to vote had to be done in person. The Republican Party, which hoped to win over the Black vote in its entry in electoral politics, was accustomed to simply distributing printed materials but quickly realized it needed people to go south as speakers and organizers.[20] To do this work, the Union Republican Congressional Committee (URCC), which had agents in the South from 1867 until sometime in 1868, worked with the Union League (UL), which had begun organizing southern whites in Tennessee during the war and had men across the South from 1867 to 1869. The league first organized, according to Hahn, "chiefly in cities like Richmond, Norfolk, Petersburg, Wilmington, Raleigh, Savannah, Tallahassee, Macon, and Nashville." These sites of initial UL activity were already part of the emerging Emancipation Circuit.[21]

The UL, a predominantly white group, admitted only males over twenty-one years old and operated by way of closed meetings, often in out-of-the-way locations, with guards to deter intrusion or warn of trouble, and it required members to take oaths. (In some places it was known as the Loyal League, and in other places, there were autonomous Black groups, founded earlier, using both names.) Referring to agitation in Alabama and Mississippi over labor conditions resembling slavery, Michael Fitzgerald says that the arriving UL "tapped an existing black political movement, rather than creating one, and this was the key to the organization's rapid growth." A Natchez Freedmen's Bureau agent wrote of the freedpeople there, "There is more method & organization among them than with any other class here."[22]

In Mississippi, where activists could not count on the military or the Freedmen's Bureau for protection, UL organizers had to tap local Black communities for safe passage in their areas. On several occasions in Yazoo City, members of the Black community appeared without being asked and effectively protected the lives of white UL organizers Albert Morgan and his brother Charles, including forming a phalanx around the jail to prevent Charles Morgan from being lynched. In an 1867 investigation of racial violence, a Mississippi conservative testified that leagues were organized as groups called freedmen's aid societies, and accusations that freedmen's benevolent societies were political were common. At the same time, there was also intentional dissembling about the UL's purpose: Benjamin R. Royal, an African American league organizer in Alabama, told a gathering of white planters that the league was a "moral and benevolent society, interfering with no man's political or religious rights." His phrasing is precise: defending the rights of Blacks did not interfere with the rights of whites—literally true but exactly what conservatives viewed as a diminution of their rights. His words implied, of course, that a moral and benevolent society had no concern with rights, which, simply put, was not true.[23]

The existing Black groups discovered by Freedmen's Bureau agents and UL activists arriving in Mississippi included fire companies, fraternal groups, labor associations, educational groups, reading groups where people could have news and literature read aloud, and charitable societies that, as Fitzgerald observes, "often blurred the distinction between political and nonpolitical activities." This diversity and blurring of categories could be said to be true in most regions. Finally, as Hahn has stressed, Blacks in many southern counties had extended kinship ties that were trustworthy units of organization. So, the building of the UL was enhanced by working through several types of existing collectivities from families to societies and labor groups. In the summer of 1867, after the paid UL organizers spread into the South, thousands of people joined the league, but Republican Party leaders who wanted to win the region nonetheless became alarmed that such massive Black participation might force too radical a position on civil rights for the southern whites they were also recruiting to the party. League councils typically met in obscure locations on weekends, and in the cotton belts membership could range from fifty to five hundred. Fitzgerald argues that the league "represented a political movement and an agrarian upsurge. The same quest for land and autonomy visible in other aspects of freedmen's behavior manifested itself through this organization." Over time, he writes, communities insisted on more control and "the leagues became more responsive to wider Black concerns as freedmen became more familiar with politics, and aggressive Black leaders arose who prodded the leagues toward greater militancy." The adjective *wider* is key here, as organizers had to take up issues beyond the Republican Party's primary concern with amassing votes. This insistence from the community also forced organizers to work on issues that aided women and children, who could not vote.[24]

For two short years, the UL endeavored to do work that, like the work of teachers, needed years more time, many more resources, an army of skilled people, and solid political support. Of course, these kinds of resources were sketchy at best and unavailable at worst. Still, before the UL was deactivated in 1869, the Leaguers who came south managed to spread out into many areas and engage freedmen in the mechanics of the electoral process and deployed the literacy necessary to negotiate with employers on contracts or with the political structure. The democratic processes of the league and the Black community consensus process combined to affect a shift to local Black leadership in groups formed by white Leaguers. Union League activists who returned north left behind local Leaguers who were knowledgeable and equipped to carry on innumerable struggles that the Republican Party had not anticipated and likely would not have supported, such as labor organizing, self-defense in the face of Ku Klux Klan assaults, or emigration.[25]

The overlapping work of the UL and the URCC is exemplified by a number of individuals who saw the benefit of ties to multiple northern groups that sponsored activism. James Henry Harris, a UL organizer and one of the Black URCC speakers, was born free in Granville, North Carolina, which became an important political center on that state's circuit, in part due to his work. By the end of the war, he had lived in Ohio, traveled to Canada and to Black American settlements in Sierra Leone and Liberia, and returned to North Carolina, where he served multiple community needs. He was president of the statewide Equal Rights League and chair of the Colored Education Convention. He turned down an appointment as minister to Haiti to stay in his home state and serve as a delegate to the 1868 constitutional convention, as a state representative, and as a state senator, among other posts. He bought a farm outside Raleigh for fourteen Black families to live on and also built a church and school in the area. Many activists found it useful to work for several agencies due to diverse community needs and because the pay and resources offered by each were generally barely sufficient to live on.[26]

By early 1868, the URCC had 118 speakers in the South, a number of whom did double duty as UL organizers, and 83 of whom were Black. Of the Black organizers, 31 were ministers. The men with ties to the UL, the Republican Party, and Black churches proved to be well situated for organizing league chapters, new church congregations, and Black voting precincts. But their effect was not general or evenly distributed throughout the South. Like the UL activists, a number of the URCC speakers found that the work required focus on a variety of efforts beyond the party mission. Virginian John Oliver worked for the American Missionary Association in Newport News teaching during the war but was unable to keep his school open due to white resistance, both local and military. Moving to Richmond, Oliver got involved in political organizing, was a member of the grand jury that indicted Jefferson Davis, and worked for the URCC. But by the early 1870s, having soured on the Republicans as too controlling and reluctant to let Blacks be in charge, he worked as president of the city's Colored National Labor Union. A fellow Virginian URCC speaker, Willis Hodges, was a Norfolk native who, along with his brothers, seems to have been involved in helping enslaved people escape before the war. They moved to New York, where abolitionist Hodges was a suffrage activist and ran a newspaper. He returned to Virginia during the war and served as a naval guide and pilot for Union forces. He and his brothers built political structures, including one of the associations that created the Equal Suffrage movement in Norfolk.[27] He also started a church and a school in the area. He was a delegate to the 1867–68 Constitutional Convention, where he championed the poor and helped to stave off school segregation.[28]

A number of churches sent missionaries, but the AME, which sent seventy-seven ministers south between 1863 and 1870, left the biggest footprint in southern Black organizing, an imprint characterized by its overt articulation of blackness and Christianity and its heritage of separate Black religious practice as a facet of self-definition. The AME built many churches and congregations that would continue in the spirit of their traveling activist founders, who blended the teachings of Christ, self-development, and seeking citizenship rights as part of the attainment of universal brotherhood. The church was slow to warm to participation in the war on the grounds that the Union as it stood in 1861 did not recognize the political and civil rights of free Blacks in the North. The proclamation ending slavery changed minds: church leaders decided the position that the Civil War was a white man's war had been a mistake.[29]

The first AME missionaries in fact discovered that, among freedpeople, withdrawing from segregated planters' churches was taken as a weighty decision and often prompted white terrorism, typically the burning of the Black worship site. According to Clarence Walker, "Most southern blacks rejected the church's ministrations because they wanted to establish a religious life of their own" and feared northern dominance would disparage traditional Black folk practice. This was real as the AME frowned on emotional expressions and "joyous noise" in services. "These differences, though," Walker writes, "did not make them, in most instances, hostile to the A.M.E. Church's political activities." On this point, there is disagreement. James T. Campbell notes that in Bishop Daniel Payne's view, "political involvement, which was inherently worldly and corrupt," was an arena that could "compromise" a minister's commitment. This position would harden during Reconstruction as some of the ministers who worked in the South were elected to office by the freedpeople in their churches. The AME Church, unknown to many people who had been isolated in bondage, was founded in response to northern racial subjugation and exclusion. This fact alone would suggest to many that this Black church had a theology filtered through the prism of blackness, and in that regard, the AME may have seemed a welcome sanctuary to slave system survivors who sought worship without white supervision. Despite conflicts with the Methodist Episcopal Church, North, over southern church buildings, conflicts with Black Baptist preachers who feared loss of their positions, and other hurdles, the sect grew tremendously in the South. Overall AME membership grew from tens of thousands in the Civil War years to hundreds of thousands in the 1870s–80s.[30]

The AME missionaries were foundational to the Emancipation Circuit for their belief in addressing race in both preaching and politics and because they built so many congregations. After three years of work, the *Christian Recorder* claimed, ministers had started churches in "Norfolk, Portsmouth, and Richmond, Virginia; Wilmington, Raleigh, and New Bern, North Carolina; Charleston, Hilton Head, and Beaufort, South Carolina; Savannah, Augusta, Macon, and Atlanta, Georgia; Mobile, Alabama; Vicksburg and Natchez, Mississippi; and in Nashville and Memphis, Tennessee." With the exception of Atlanta, all of these sites were on the state Emancipation Circuits that emerged during and after the war. According to Walker, missionaries also established "circuits" on waterways connecting some of the sites "along the James River [VA]," South Carolina's Combahee, Ashley, and Cooper Rivers, and on the Sea Islands, along the Chattahoochee from near Atlanta to the border of Georgia and Alabama and through Florida to the Gulf. They also worked along the Cumberland through Tennessee and Kentucky, then traveled the length of the Mississippi to the Gulf and preached across the Gulf Coast of Texas.[31]

In their view, the AME ministers' embrace of politics was practical. As Rev. Charles H. Pearce, who organized in Florida and later held office, wrote, "A man in this state cannot do his whole duty as a minister except he looks out for the political interests of his people." Some of the missionaries who later left the church may have done so because of this divide. Nonetheless, those who went South rapidly involved themselves at least in the necessity of helping to assure that Blacks would vote, fearing that otherwise the race would be doomed to reenslavement schemes. They also found that the church's internal organizing structures for proselytizing were helpful in structuring political organizing. And they were of a mind, collectively—perhaps from the prior experience of the many who were born in the South—that they had also to preach cooperation with whites as the future of the South required the races to live and work together. That said, some radicalizing did take place in these missionaries' lives, and like the UL activists, they discovered that the ideologies of the slave system needed direct address. Henry McNeal Turner found himself addressing white supremacist preaching with a sermon entitled "God Is Not White" and, in his district, banning the singing of the hymn "Lord Wash Me and I Shall be Whiter Than Snow." In South Carolina, another minister was publicly criticized for saying that Christ, Mary, and Joseph were Africans "and Black" from the pulpit.[32]

Clearly, the AME developed the church through ties to local ministers, some perhaps ordained after emancipation, who also became effective political activists entrenched in building local sodalities. Though the social gospel strain within the church embracing attention to the material condition of the people was not formalized until late in the nineteenth century, it is easy to see that the AME missionaries transformed their own practices into something resembling or at least anticipating latter-day antiracist social gospel work. James Lynch charged that the AME bishops did not protect ministers who worked in the South, and he criticized them for not traveling to the South to see for themselves the incredible societal changes being attempted by the race's majority. His complaints highlight the distance many activists—Black and white—may have felt from organizational leaders in the North. The AME mission in the South lasted longer than those of the Freedmen's Bureau, the URCC, and the UL, and the churches they built survived to be incubators of the justice-driven gospel created in the Reconstruction period.[33]

All of these groups show the incredible effectiveness and influence that could be achieved by small numbers of activists. Their impact is defined by their systematic education of freedpeople in citizenship rights, voter registration, and the Declaration of Independence and the US Constitution, and in the very capable local organizers living across the South when the northern sponsors withdrew support for the outsiders' work.

Schools Were Central

Another vital factor in the development of sustained organizing was the establishment of schools for freedpeople, which occurred in many locations. The maintenance of these schools was an ongoing struggle, with the eventual withdrawal of funding from agencies like the Freedmen's Bureau and, later, poor funding from states. A marker of Emancipation Circuit sites was the ability to keep schools open with payments made by individual families. These sites often lost some schools over time but were still better equipped to keep the educational link in place for adults seeking new skills and for the next generation than were sites where education was heavily repressed. This served to make educational goals for the next generation durable and renewable. While the value of schools is obvious, their location and connections to community assets were important. Virtually all the Emancipation Circuit locations had AMA or other northern missionary schools by the end of the war. Some of those sites were able to develop schools that became colleges and universities (most backed by the AMA) and some seminaries founded by the AME Church and the Baptists. (See tables 3.1–11.1 for school locations in each state.)

The Freedmen's Schools, as they were known at the time, were built, burned by domestic terrorists, and rebuilt continuously during the emancipation and Reconstruction eras. Many of the historically Black colleges and universities (HBCUs) were started in Reconstruction. Those that developed into seminaries and colleges anchored hubs of the Emancipation Circuit over very long periods of time, and many nurtured the collective consciousness Cedric Robinson defined as mindful of past struggles and instilling a sense of obligation to wholeness of the Black collectivity. The Lincoln School in Marion, Alabama, for instance, established in 1867 by

freedpeople and a Union soldier, was attended seventy-five years later by
Coretta Scott King, as it was the only Black high school near her home. In
the 1950s, the late congressman John Lewis attended the American Baptist
Theological Seminary in Nashville, which began as the Nashville Normal and Theological Institute ninety-two years earlier in 1866. Likewise,
the teachers who were the backbone of such schools—from kindergarten
through college—formed a circuit of connection by serving at multiple
schools. (Those at HBCUs were long barred from jobs at predominantly
white schools.) Black colleges provided a touring circuit for Black authors,
performers, and visiting artists and scientists through the long life of segregation. The HBCUs held the only art exhibits available to most Black artists
and collected their work. They were sites for Black conferences where sizable numbers could meet, and those that stood on privately owned ground
became havens for integrated activities for decades before they were legal
in public spaces in the South. The schools developed a sports circuit that
trained generations of school coaches, as well as amateur and professional
athletes during segregation and since. Thanks to Jim Crow, they were the
only institutions where Blacks could be trained in nursing, journalism,
business, agronomy, and other fields beyond the manual labor training
and domestic service tutelage that were part of their roots. Student activism at these schools became the backbone of young adult participation in
movements for change from early in the twentieth century. In some respects, their very continued existence upheld goals of the movements of
freedpeople.[34]

Blackness as the Culture of Sodalities

Even as activists and ministers were appealing to refugees by centering
Blackness in their renderings of what freedom should mean, benevolent
societies and fraternal orders developing on the circuit were also creating
culture centered on identity. Of the secret societies that began to prolif-
erate and make public processions part of their yearly activities, Taylor
writes: "Secret in principle and benevolent in purpose, these societies afforded unique opportunities for community effort, the promotion of racial
consciousness and the development of leadership. At the time, however,
the whites, believing them political rather than fraternal in practice, opposed their growth."[35] It should first be said that the answer to whether or
not groups were political is not to be found in their incorporation papers
or bylaws. Most fraternal groups and benevolent societies stated chari-

table, educational, and Christian aims. Also, organizers found it a matter of safety to use the "cover" of participating in benevolent or fraternal meetings in order to organize.

Male groups used basically the same rituals as white groups—based on hierarchy and moving ahead by serving the group—but Black female groups, more autonomous than white women's groups, did not emulate the rituals of white female groups, which were based on ideals of Victorian womanhood and the idea of a woman's sphere popular at the time. The Masonic groups conferred "degrees" of accomplishment (ranging from three degrees to thirty-three, depending on the system). Black women's rituals encouraged earning leadership degrees through compassionate work and wisdom, which could be said to reflect "a different set of lived realities" from mainstream groups, according to Bayliss Camp and Orit Kent. They found that Black men's rituals also acknowledged women's equality in ways that white groups did not.[36] Black women's auxiliaries showed a range of messaging on gender from "progressive, even protofeminist" models to more traditional helpmate models.[37] Black groups, male and female, importantly had a larger view of the idea of charity and sometimes espoused good work as "world transforming." Newspaper accounts also show their presence in protests.[38]

Two kinds of African American secret societies arose in the South during the postwar period, groups that were "parallel" to mainstream groups and "distinctive" groups with Black origins. By the 1860s, Freemasonry, which dates to 1733 in North America, had a Black counterpart in the North for nearly a century—the Prince Hall Freemasons (founded in Boston in 1775).[39] At the end of the Civil War a number of distinctive Black lodges founded in the North were expanding their membership.[40] In the 1870s and 1880s, the South had its own important independent fraternal groups founded in at least seven southern states. At least one of these, the Knights and Daughters of Tabor, specifically promoted itself as created in honor of men who escaped slavery and fought for the Union. Though communities everywhere started societies, most of these distinctive groups were founded on the Emancipation Circuit.[41]

Skocpol and Oser, who study African American societies that became regional, found that "African American fraternal groups created more lodges per capita and involved a higher proportion of adults than white fraternals," and within their groups women "played a much more prominent role" than in white groups. Black distinctive groups stand out in particular for more readily developing women's affiliates and having more fully gender-mixed groups. Most of the earlier historians who attempt to give figures for Black society participation have presented very high numbers based on evidence such as bank accounts. In addition to participation in public events, Black fraternal groups are shown to have supported education and community service and provided halls used by other groups, and to have sometimes become involved in "legislative or policy campaigns."[42] The maintenance of halls built by such groups is not to be minimized as a boon to communities, whether the halls in New Orleans where trade groups first met or the Elks Hart Lodge 640 in Greenwood, Mississippi, in which they literally created space for Black public discourse, from politics to music, through the 1960s.[43]

Black Press Mattered

Circuit communities are also marked by the availability of Black newspapers. Such papers, which were begun in fewer places than other assets, were fleeting enterprises, especially the earliest ones; they were hard to sustain on subscriptions but were distributed hand to hand and read aloud among freedpeople. The earliest Black newspapers in the South were two bilingual papers started by Louis Charles Roudanez and serving free Blacks in New Orleans, *L'Union* (1862–63) and the *New Orleans Tribune* (1864–70); *The Colored American* (1865–66), started by J. T. Shuften and James D. Lynch in Augusta, Georgia; three papers started in Charleston between 1865 and 1868; and the widely circulated *Richmond Planet* (1883–1938), started in Virginia by thirteen former enslaved people.[44] At least five others were begun in the 1870s. All these papers carried serious coverage of political developments and labor and business information, as well producing a great deal of regional news by printing letters from people in various towns—a practice continued later by other papers. This communication effort, along with all kinds of organizing, was aided by the postwar construction of rail networks connecting even specific plantations where papers could be dropped.[45]

Population Counted, Especially in the Countryside

The significance of cities for activism can be said to derive as much from being central to the local circuits—sites of frequent regional traffic—as from their size or the presence of a formerly free Black elite. They were often central to *foundational* organizing. It is also important to note that despite the growth of cities like Atlanta and Charleston, in 1870 only 8.8 percent of Black southerners lived in cities. Also, the postwar increase in urban Black populations (sometimes doubling a town's size) did not continue between 1870 and 1880 as it had from 1865 to 1870.[46] At the heart of the circuit in North Carolina, for instance, are a number of counties on the Virginia border with heavily Black populations—later known as the Black Second (Congressional) District—which had no major towns. There was still a sizable population of formerly free Black landowners there, which helped give stability for building schools and institutions at a time when Black laborers were moving around the southern landscape. The Black Second area was linked by railways and waterways and by tobacco shipping between Danville, Petersburg, and Richmond, Virginia, and to Atlantic ports. In times of trouble, both rural and urban areas have been shown to mobilize people from nearby communities by rail, water, and roads.

Capital cities such as Richmond, Virginia, and Columbia, South Carolina, did not sustain Black representation as long as some of the more rural areas in those states. Milledgeville, Georgia, in the middle of the cotton belt and the state capital until 1868, was also in a Black organizing area that elected statewide officials. The new capital, Atlanta, sent no Blacks to the legislature until 1963. The last Black nineteenth-century officials in that state after disfranchisement of African American voters were in rural coastal counties. Black urban population majorities worked as the engines for electoral political achievement in *twentieth-century* politics, a reality from which the entire South, with its early twentieth-century rural majorities, was excluded by voter repression. The nineteenth-century South was different from later political landscapes in that some places had Black majorities that have never been replicated again there or anywhere else. But one of the chief outcomes of those demographics was the development of voter repression techniques such as poll taxes, gerrymandering, and disfranchisement for criminal convictions. As southern white politicians knew in the 1860s, restricting access to the ballot mitigated the power of majorities anywhere. Many of the counties that elected Black officials in Reconstruction were close to a fifty-fifty Black/white split in population; therefore, when Blacks were elected in such counties, certain political skills must have been at work in negotiating the slates and financing and operating campaigns. Also, in some counties where Blacks made up 53 percent of the population, such as Granville County, North Carolina, the difference in actual numbers was very small—a population difference of 1,879 in 1870, and undoubtedly an even smaller difference in voter numbers.[47] In 1935, Du Bois pointed this out in detail, perhaps to help us avoid easy assumptions about the role of population majorities. There are no certainties governing a connection between electoral participation and self-defense, but self-defense has been so obscured that one can only speculate on its effect. The widespread practices of going to the polls in large groups with and without arms had to have been a successful deterrent to violent voter repression to have continued in some places well into the twentieth century. The fact that Blacks physically defended their access to polls in rural and urban settings speaks to their priorities. The practice, now called "souls to the polls" and done without arms, was widely used and widely resisted.[48]

Studying the states by county also affirms Fitzgerald's claim that the primary reason for UL success in rural areas was economic in places like Alabama: "Railroad construction altered the cotton trade to the advantage of plantation belt towns such as Meridian, Selma, and Montgomery." This is an explanation for the fact that some towns that were very important to the *emerging* circuit, such as Vicksburg and Greenville, which thrived on Mississippi River trade, then faded with the rise of the railroad, and cities such as Atlanta and Birmingham emerged as power centers by the 1890s. Populations followed those changes. Cities such as Montgomery and Norfolk, hubs for both forms of transport, produced political motion continuously from the end of the Civil War.[49]

Ties between Communities Enhanced Safety and Political Work

Physical proximity of a Black community to the Emancipation Circuit in a given state is linked to safety and Black political representation. Counties at the outer reaches of a given circuit, even those with a Black majority population, often had no Blacks elected to the constitutional conventions or to Reconstruction state houses and senates, such as one or two Virginia counties with the densest Black populations that were slow to elect Blacks. Some places may have been in areas too remote from military presence for help or may have faced well-organized white resistance, or more likely, both. In Arkansas, Ku Klux Klan dens organized and took shelter in counties at the periphery of the Emancipation Circuit. Though violence was widespread in the South, the locales that lost representation were also often places where activists reported violence, such as the area around Albany, Georgia, the end of a rail line crossing the cotton belt. Vital to sustaining resistance to various threats and the development of the autonomy sought by the newly freed were connections to other organized groups, which included churches tied by denomination or traveling ministers; schools affiliated with northern groups sending teachers. Communities also benefitted from ties that could provide supplies and relay news of their circumstances and connections to neighboring Black farm communities that could be called to march en masse to polling places, courthouses, or jails. Parading and showing the full presence of connected communities in public space, especially with the inclusion of armed veterans, was regularly ridiculed in the white press. But these acts created new representations of Blacks as people who could protect themselves and were less subject to intimidation. When several thousand freedpeople showed up at a rural rally, many with arms and all with grievances, the impact could be read in the alarmed letters from local whites to officials.

Labor Organizing Was Central

Evidence shows a link between labor organizing and effective drives at gaining political representation through voting. Labor organizing, like the building of mutual aid associations, greatly enhanced the ability of communities to mobilize. Labor organizing was often the most prominent form of organizing in rural areas and is consistently evident in sites with sustained political organizing in the Black South. (See tables 3.1 [Virginia], 7.1 [Florida], 9.1 [Louisiana], 10.1 [Mississippi], and 11.1 [Arkansas].) One year after the end of the war, necessity forced Blacks to form assemblies to seek equality in wages as well as citizenship rights, but these struggles also took place in public space—docks and rail yards—where southern politicians and businessmen would take notice. It is estimated that at the end of the Civil War there were 100,000 skilled Black workers, known under the rubric "mechanics," as compared with 20,000 white workers. According to Sterling Spero and Abram Harris, these Blacks included "blacksmiths, gunsmiths, cabinetmakers, plasterers, painters, shipbuilders, stone and brickmasons, pilots, and engineers."[50] As they point out, Blacks competed most successfully in areas in which the labor was conventionally performed by African Americans during the slavery era, such as the building trades and their associated crafts. Blacks also performed heavy work in iron mills and coal mines. Of course, in seaports there was plenty of work that had been performed by enslaved people; when they entered the free labor market, they often dominated manual labor at ports and railroad hubs.

Just as important is the fact that the labor organizing occurred primarily on rail lines that were the spine of the Emancipation circuit in many areas. This allows us to see that rural areas were not "out of the loop" of the information being disseminated in each state. Some of the tiny places that had labor activism but lacked HBCUs or newspapers were on a direct transport line to such resources and sustained political formations. *(See tables 8.1 [Alabama] and 11.1 [Arkansas].)* Labor organizing, which began at abolition on an ad hoc basis and expanded with the arrival of Knights of Labor in the 1880s, also took place in the face of Republican Party pressure to desist.[51]

Places with labor organizing in the nineteenth century tended to be successful in gaining Black electoral representation. Also, the privations deepened by poor crops in 1865–67 must be viewed as a factor that pushed mobilization in rural areas and perhaps created solidarities around changing work conditions that only paid for supplies or produced debt. Most organizers in the South encountered pressure from local freedpeople to deal with labor issues as shown, for example, by Fitzgerald and Saville. In Alabama, all the Black leaders with the UL that I have seen documented were also part of the Alabama Labor Union, a group formed by Black activists. Although this seems completely logical with a population seen almost exclusively as a labor force, and that saw its strength as such, over time the leadership of national groups narrowed priorities to civil rights.[52]

Diverse Organizing Made Any Organizing Renewable

The more kinds of organizing that occurred in a single place, the more evidence there is of institutions being built and of more durable and diverse activism traditions in that site. This was an enormous aid in mobilizing across communities. Cities, of course, had an advantage in meeting places for various types of groups, but the majority of the important sites on the Emancipation Circuit were at best medium-size towns. It would be a mistake to regard Black political organizing in the emancipation era as an urban phenomenon. For instance, while Hahn shows the UL set up councils in the South's major cities, Fitzgerald found the group more successful in rural areas in Mississippi and Alabama, due to the fact that labor issues were pressing. Also, white mob action in cities presented a danger to large numbers of people.[53] Police in the urban mob actions in Memphis and New Orleans were part of the problem and not of help. White mob action occurred in all kinds of locales, but rural police resources were limited, encouraging the formation of armed white squads known as "regulators." Still, in the countryside Black settlements often organized militias or self-defense patrols, and the landscape provided refuge. Stories of voter organizers "laying out" in the woods or cane breaks are common. Activists and officeholders in towns often hired guards. As Hahn writes, "Paramilitary organization had been fundamental to the social and political order of slavery; it remained fundamental to the social and political order of freedom." That reality began, of course, in rural areas where most Blacks lived.[54]

Making Statewide Black Agendas

On August 7, 1865, Blacks of Nashville, Tennessee, hosted a state convention of freedpeople, news of which—covered by Black press—may have influenced organizers in other places. Attended by ninety-five delegates from twenty-two counties, the conclave had the specific aim of acquiring the right to vote. The first speaker, a veteran of the Louisiana US Colored Troops, remarked, "We want two more boxes, beside the cartridge box—the ballot box and the jury box." These three rights of US citizens— military service, the vote, and jury service—were among those most fought for by southern Blacks in the 1860s, while equal pay (with white workers) and safety from violence became daily concerns among the Black populace. All five issues proved enduring.[55]

Pointing to a surprising but perhaps inevitable dilemma—what newly freed people should call themselves—James D. Lynch objected to the *Nashville Dispatch* calling the meeting a "Negro" convention. The young AME minister complained that *Negro* meant "persons of unmixed blood," and therefore recommended *colored*, though he conceded the newspaper editor's likely ignorance of Black concerns with nomenclature. Though *colored* was the prevalent term in Black newspapers and public meetings, Lynch's complaint is notable for anticipating decades of discourse within the race about self-identification. This was already taken up, for example, by the men of Roanoke Island, who related an incident to the president of the United States with the self-reference "the negros as we are Call." Their phrase is so specific as to awaken the reader to the surprise some freedpeople may have had at being newly labeled as a group, and not by former condition but race, and with an old word long ago corrupted into *nigger*. Educated organizers who had lived with labels in the North would certainly have placed emphasis on their own preferred terms for public speech, but it was in no way only a concern among those developing public political speech. Still, in suggesting the use of *colored*, activists like Lynch may have been reaching for an expansive term. Given the diverse African, European, Native American, regional, and experiential backgrounds by then part of the southern African American population (and multiracial ties still part of living memory), it seems a foundational discussion for this group now declaring itself politically as "we" to ponder a capacious term.[56]

The resolutions of the Nashville convention were a priority list for a new Black political agenda in the state and perhaps in other places preparing similar meetings: First, given that Blacks in rural counties were not receiving "just compensation for their labor" and were mistreated by employers, each county delegation would appoint a committee to protect the interests of such people and take grievances to the Freedmen's Bureau. Second, the group resolved to cooperate with the bureau and benevolent societies to set up schools. Third, it voted to make a count of African Americans in every county (including their occupations, property, and taxes paid), adults and children in school, and Black-owned churches, and to publish the data "so that the world may know our true condition."[57]

This emphasis on documenting their "true condition" would also prove to be a necessary tool for decades to come, taken up in the twentieth century by the likes of W. E. B. Du Bois. Again, it is instructive to note that this idea to document and archive began at the onset of political organizing and among farmers, small-business owners, and ministers rather than scholars. James T. Rapier, a twenty-eight-year-old college graduate and suffrage activist who was raising cotton in the area, successfully proposed a study of the number of acres in the state under cultivation by Blacks, "the amount of produce raised, etc.," because "it is generally considered among the whites at the South, and by many at the North, that we are consumers and not producers." He would soon return to his home state of Alabama, where he would be a very successful farmer and activist and would become a US congressman at age thirty-five. Later, in the fall of 1865, a report would show that the federal undertakers in Nashville had, since the Union occupation began, buried 12,631 soldiers, 1,000 other government employees, 8,000 Confederate soldiers, and 10,000 fugitives from slavery.

Clearly people could see the need for more reporting on their condition since flights began during the war. One of the last resolutions of the meeting was to thank the friends of the race in the United States, England, and other nations and to ask for "a continuance of their exertion in our behalf, until we arrive at the fulness of citizenship."[58]

The first public assemblies of Black southerners came to agree on seeking education, the vote, jury service, the right to testify against whites, and other facets of equality before the law. They were all concerned about the passage of any laws that reiterated provisions of slave codes or in any way reproduced slavery. Views diverged in response to federal troop presence, ways in which to create data on their own condition, and degrees of conciliation toward local power elites. An agreement on a single agenda for Blacks across the South was not a practical aim—even though there were areas of broad consensus—and limiting themselves to statewide action should be viewed as both ambitious and a measure of political sophistication. The extent to which African Americans showed agility in organizing and building mechanisms to be responsive to local situations is a measure of practicality and of reciprocal commitments.

The Lens of Enslavement Made for New Politics

The process engaged by freedpeople was the beginning of expansive definitions of political interaction, resistance, and demands for justice. This "big picture" sensibility embraced in any mass meeting the need for decent treatment, fair wages, protection from assaults in settlements and on public streets, freedom from being arrested without notification or probable cause, freedom from being abducted and hired out for forced labor, and the healing exercise of testifying and bearing witness to trauma. The lens of experience with the slave system gave a very farsighted view of the dangers of a racialized quasi citizenship. Authorities of various sorts, from local southern officials to military officers in charge of the federal occupation, were in no way prepared for the exigencies facing four million people trying to rebuild their lives. That the process of seeking protection involved mass meetings of entire neighborhoods or communities in both urban areas and small places affirms Elsa Barkley Brown's observation that Black people "inserted themselves in the preexisting national political traditions and at the same time widened those traditions." The fact that multidimensional organization followed is unsurprising.[59]

The freed politics that began to emerge in the late 1860s would stand at the margins of radical Republican ideology with Pennsylvania congressman Thaddeus Stevens in linking economic opportunity and political equality. And while some Republicans considered getting the ballot a higher priority than getting forty acres of arable land, Blacks knew they needed both. In places where freedpeople thought their children might be well served by Black teachers and integrated classrooms, many who came to aid them would marginalize their analysis to defer to white southern "etiquette." Often African American voices would exhaust Republican patience by claiming the right to self-defense. Such concerns, born of hunger and violence and a desire to thrive in the literate world, would simply be shelved, especially by those who conceived of politics purely as a matter of election victories. African Americans would give Republicans electoral victories, but once they could no longer do that, they would be on their own.[60]

Activism Over Time

It is fruitful to look at communities on the circuit and their engagement in different movements over time. Specific conditions gave sites on the Emancipation Circuit their particular movements, and the experiences of organizers in one campaign or another may have affected which movements arose later. The organizers' *accumulated* experiences in the postwar South should be taken into account in the history of southern Black political theory as they had a broad range of encounters with mass participatory democracy, urban and rural organizing, southern white resistance both political and violent, and confronting institutional racism from a diverse set of prewar backgrounds. Individual organizers also tended to have a broad range of skills and insights due to the varied settings in which they worked. They each carried with them their own evolving political philosophy, their exposure to the ideas of an array of leaders in the North and South, and the creative solutions devised in each region where they worked, all of which lacked for resources and were home to overwhelming numbers of people in need.[61]

Activists' experiences also sometimes informed changes in their work and in the goals of local activism. For instance, interest in emigration to a colony in Liberia waned in the first years of freedom as optimism about autonomous living took root among southern Blacks after the war. But later a number of activists who had disparaged emigration before the war supported Exodusters migrating to Oklahoma, Nebraska, and points west or to Liberia after several years living under the constant threat of violence and privation. Surprisingly, most Black southern activists I tracked for post-Reconstruction activity, people who lived through violence, including attacks on their own homes or persons, actually stayed in the South, many returning to the towns where they were threatened, and there helped organize emigration groups. This suggests strong ties among Reconstruction veterans similar to those made by war veterans. It also points to durable activism experience backing their changing views, for better or worse, in the continuum of activism in those areas.[62]

At the same time, some groups chose to return to fights lost earlier. Communities that had to use extraordinary organization to exercise the vote sometimes returned to fighting for the vote years after disfranchisement at a juncture when it seemed possible to create change or to highlight the denial of the vote, as in Florida in 1920 when the franchise was extended to women.[63] New Orleans had more than one fight for school integration. Streetcar segregation was fought, won, and lost in various southern places from the 1860s into the 1890s and again in the twentieth century, and segregation was fought again over local and interstate buses. Businesses that practiced wage inequality by race helped to keep Black workers organized over time by continuing the discrimination. Black maritime workers deployed strikes over several generations, way into the twentieth century, and in places like Mobile, Alabama, and Newport News, Virginia, shipyard workers and domestics built distinct Black neighborhoods and working-class communities. Black teachers struggled for equal wages through the political system from the 1860s on. Thus, it is important to look at organization over time, within and across communities, rather than solely through rubrics such as civil rights or labor, urban or rural. These rubrics create blind spots that particularly obscure working-class organizing. Working-class organization created institutions with fluid and interdependent campaigns—seats on the streetcars and jobs, voting rights and housing, or sewers, streetlights, and the right to sit on juries. The post–Civil War Black South presents an opportunity to study the development of an ethos of engagement, prompted by a state of crisis intersecting with a widespread immersion in the US Constitution, which was being deeply argued and crucially amended to acknowledge the existence of Black citizens (and others), even as freedpeople young and old began to learn how to read and to vote.[64]

Freedpeople would bring to mass meetings, courts, and governing bodies thousands of new insights and iterations of the arguments of the founders as well as many made by David Walker, Frederick Douglass, and others. They discussed remedies for abuses and dilemmas that society did not readily admit existed, whether concubinage and the abuse of female laborers or unequal pay, violence and systemic terror, the bridling of freedom of speech and movement, or the criminalization of the poor. As lawmakers and elected officials, many Blacks who came to those positions were unprepared for political speech and writing legislation, and unschooled in the diverse forms of chicanery they would meet. Some fell into corrupt schemes; others, late in the century, switched parties in an attempt to save their positions with a "go-along-to-get-along" pragmatism that did not help their neighbors. But as a mass population, freedpeople came into the public sphere with a unique perspective that became foundational to movement building. They brought frank reports on the existence of trauma and the absurdity of racist ideologies as reconciliation papered over all but sentimental renderings of the Black past. Freedpeople came into political life motivated by hunger, literal and spiritual, deeply involved in crash courses in human and citizenship rights, and organized by a dense network of associations created for activism. No other segment of society had been so intensely and cohesively prepared to challenge for the long term the political constructs of the republic only "four score and seven years old" when Lincoln reminded the nation in 1863 how deeply it had been rent.

Every single one of these developments in the first years of legal freedom was absolutely impossible four years earlier, and no one—Black, white, civilian, or military—could guess how far the impossible could go. Some—such as Black southerners who had escaped or been born free and left only to return south knowing that as free men in the North, they did not have full citizenship—knew they would have to reach far and for a long time. Others did not yet see the long-term struggle ahead for them personally because having the chance to decide what to do with one's life required a contemplative investment of its own. It was easier to know what one didn't want. Robert Glenn, enslaved in Kentucky, took his freedom in small steps, having said yes when his former owner asked if he wanted to stay on because he did not know what else to do. One day, after a year of building "air castles," taking time for leisure, even going on trips when he wanted, he was slapped on the head by a boss who wanted him to get out of bed and hitch up the horses. He refused. He was asked what he would do, said he did not know, and walked out the door to be free. Others left right away, also not knowing how it would all go. Felix Haywood of San Antonio recalled, "Nobody took our homes away, but right off colored folks started on the move. They seemed to want to get closer to freedom, so they'd know what it was—like it was a place or a city."[65]

> A British observer "said he attended a concert at the Ebenezer Baptist Church in Richmond, given to raise funds for the erection of a Negro school. 'It was believed that the school would get burned down if erected,' said he, 'but they were disposed to go on with the erection.'"
>
> —Alrutheus A. Taylor, *The Negro in Reconstruction in Virginia* (1926)

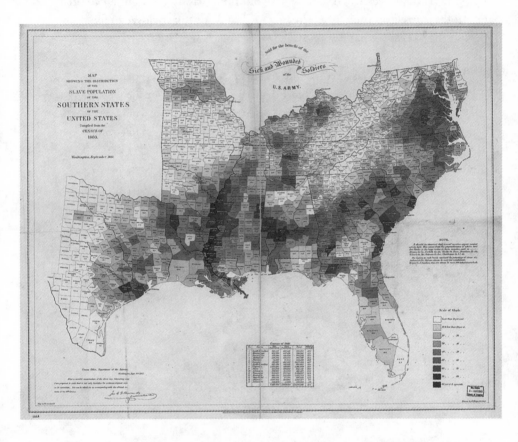

FIGURE 2.1 **Map Showing the Distribution of the Slave Population of the Southern States of the United States Compiled from the Census of 1860.** This map was used by President Abraham Lincoln during the Civil War to estimate the likely displacement of enslaved people that would be caused by the movement of US troops in Southern states. The dark gray and black areas indicate the densest African American populations. The Emancipation Circuit was rooted in these population areas and in the displacement Lincoln rightly anticipated. HENRY S. GRAHAM, CENSUS OFFICE, DEPARTMENT OF THE INTERIOR, WASHINGTON, DC. SEPTEMBER 1861. ACCESSED OCTOBER 29, 2012. HTTPS://WWW.LOC .GOV/RESOURCE/G3861E.CW0013200/.

MAP 2.1 **The Emerging Emancipation Circuit in the 1860s through 1870s**.
The circuit was elaborated in the 1880s by railroad lines crisscrossing the South.
The map shows the importance of waterways (used as shipping routes) to early
Black organizing. In the 1880s and 1890s, more rail lines and the development
of the Florida peninsula and Birmingham, Alabama, and other sites in that
area elaborated the circuit. LIBRARY OF CONGRESS, GEOGRAPHY AND MAP DIVISION,
WASHINGTON, DC. © T. DAVIS AND ALICIA IVERSON, 2021.

3 VIRGINIA
Assembly

NOUNS 1. assemblage . . . 2. assembly (or persons), . . . gathering, foregathering, congregation, congress, convocation, concourse, meeting, . . . convention, . . . caucus . . . 3. company, group, party, band, gang, crew, outfit, pack, cohort, troop, . . . tribe, . . . bunch, mob, crowd, push, shove . . .
—*Roget's International Thesaurus*, 3rd ed. (1965)

From late May 1861, when the Union set up the Department of Virginia to oversee any territory that US forces occupied, fugitives from slavery continued to arrive at Fort Monroe for the duration of the war, especially from areas near the fighting in the state. In 1863 the occupied area came under the jurisdiction of the Department of Virginia and North Carolina, and though the war waged on, teachers began landing in southeastern Virginia, and numerous schools sprang up throughout the area.[1]

Arrivals

In March 1864, twenty-year-old teacher Edmonia G. Highgate, born in upstate New York to parents who had been enslaved, arrived in Norfolk after asking the American Missionary Association to send her south. She described her first months in Norfolk as "the most earnest months of my existence." Her reaction to her first assignment provides one glimpse of the enormous impact of walking among thousands of the people abolitionists had worked to free. It was also typical of the sudden insights gained by activists seeing the enormous scale of the fruition of abolition work in this era:

> I have been able to get so near to so many of my people who have spent most of manhood's and womanhood's freshness in slavery. There are peculiar crushing emotions which, at first, check even my utterance but go away and leave me with such deep compelling motive power to "do with my might whatsoever my hands find to do." . . . [In addition to teaching a class of fifty second-grade pupils,] I have just commenced teaching from four till six at the Rope walk and feel blessed in the effort. . . . Oh how inspiring the thought that these dear souls are "forever free."[2]

Five months after her arrival, the perfect storm of overwhelming circumstances that was liberation after a civil war, exhaustion from trying to meet them, and perhaps the emotional impact of both caused Highgate to be taken home while suffering a breakdown. This experience of sojourners in the overturned slave system is a window on the extremity of the situation. Highgate nevertheless spoke in numerous towns in upstate New York for several months to raise money for southern schools and sent the AMA "$110 and seven boxes and three barrels of clothing."[3]

In April 1865, Robert E. Lee's Army of Northern Virginia surrendered and President Abraham Lincoln was assassinated. Though it was a blow to many who had been emancipated in the South and to Blacks in the North, the end of the conflict meant that some of those who had escaped could go home and do what the formerly enslaved were doing—look for family. George Teamoh (1818–87), who had lived in New England after escaping Norfolk in 1853, went back to find his family, whose sale had caused his flight. Born in Norfolk in 1818, he had been owned by a Portsmouth carpenter at the Gosport Navy Yard and his wife (Gosport was the first US Navy shipyard).[4] Hired out first to a farm and then to a brickyard, Teamoh taught himself to read and sometimes rowed a boat to Norfolk and traveled without a pass to attend meetings. He took chances in order to put himself in direct contact with the political discourse and Black ideology circulating in Atlantic ports in the late 1830s and the 1840s: "I early saw the sad and lamentable condition in which a whole race of mankind had been placed by a power then beyond the reach of their control (slave power). Not being able to weigh this matter intelligently, I took every opportunity to visit church meetings, political gatherings, theaters, etc. with the hope that something might 'leak out' or some revelation [be] made as to the existence of an institution which had already been condemned by the moral sense of the world."[5]

At age twenty-one, Teamoh was working as a ship caulker at the Norfolk Dry Dock and Navy Yard for wages between $1.50 and $1.62 a day (paid to his owner) alongside whites making $2. Working at a US government facility in the 1840s taught him one particular political reality that he explained by citing his government discharge certificates from two terms of service there: "The government had patronized, and given encouragement to Slavery to a far greater extent than the great majority of the country has been aware. It had in its service at the time . . . hundreds, if not thousands of slaves employed on the government works, possibly within a circle of eighteen or twenty miles here abouts in the Norfolk area." This particular education not only taught him that the government engaged in part-time slaveholding but, upon finding that his work might be the same as anyone else's but was paid racialized wages, initiated his lifelong interest in helping other Black workers fight for fair wages and working conditions. The port also gave him a chance to escape. When his wife and three children (who were owned by others) were sold, Teamoh hired on a boat hauling freight to Germany and returning via New York, where he jumped ship.[6] Teamoh found his way to New Bedford, Massachusetts, where he worked in the shipyard when white workers would abide a Black man caulking, then worked as a servant in Providence, Rhode Island, and then as a waiter in Boston. Like other fugitives from slavery, Teamoh encountered the Black abolitionist network in each place he stayed in New England. In Reconstruction, the people of Portsmouth would elect him a delegate to the 1868 constitutional convention and a state senator.

The hiring out of enslaved people was a widespread practice in Virginia, a reality that gave many people like Teamoh access to geographical information and whispers of ways to escape.[7] Being hired out locally put ordinary laborers and children in touch with diverse people and new information. Fannie Berry, born in 1841, probably in Appomattox County, Virginia, was first hired out when she was ten or twelve years old. During 1861, she was brought to Petersburg, a railroad hub, where she was left to sell produce at the train station. She regularly saw slave auctions and people being marched to the train station as they were moved away from the Union troops coming into Virginia. Berry carried the memory of babies being taken from women who had been sold and abandoned on the station platform, and witnessed the recapture of a friend who had escaped a plantation.

Sometime after January 1863, Berry found out that she was free when she was hired to a woman who told her.[8]

Thomas Bayne, who, like Teamoh, would become a Reconstruction leader in Virginia, also landed in New Bedford after his escape. Abraham Galloway, who would become a leader in North Carolina, escaped to Canada and also ended up working with Black abolitionists in Boston. All three men escaped in the 1850s and returned to the South in the 1860s. The two Virginians would come to know each other and may have had mutual acquaintances from New Bedford, while Teamoh and Galloway may have had overlapping acquaintances among Boston abolitionists. These are the kinds of ties by which Black activism in the South gained support in the North.

Teamoh had joined Black activist William Cooper Nell's Adelphic Union and/or his Young Men's Literary Society of Boston, which aided fugitives from slavery, and he also received some education through Nell. About the same age as Teamoh, Nell may well have been one of the more amazing people the ship caulker had then met. Nell housed fugitives as part of the Underground Railroad, published books on African American history, wrote for theater, and was a founder of the Boston Committee on Vigilance, which engaged in direct action to protect people from the Fugitive Slave Law. Another Black activist, tailor Coffin Pitts, trained Teamoh in repairing and cleaning garments, which became his trade while in Boston.[9]

With the war's end, Teamoh sailed to Fort Monroe. He had been back in Portsmouth "but a few weeks when called upon by the freed men to espouse their cause"; however, he chose first to search for his wife, Sallie, and daughter Josephine in Richmond. He learned that a Black minister had taken them in, as he writes, "after being hunted down as they had been by those who owned them." They had been sold twice since he had last seen them, once to a store owner and then to a saloonkeeper who raped Josephine. When Teamoh found them, his daughter had borne a child by the rapist. His two eldest children, John and Jane, had been kidnapped, and their fate was never known. In 1865, the remaining members of the family began their life again in Portsmouth, where he found work as a ship caulker and got involved in politics. Once Union troops had seized the Norfolk-Portsmouth area, it became a hub of in-migration and organizing.[10]

While many freedpeople reported never seeing family members again, others in search of the possibly dead found people in the area. Sister Harrison, who had been enslaved in Norfolk County, saw her two brothers and her mother's niece sold just before the war. When the fighting ended, her brothers and cousin returned to find her and her mother. Her father, who had escaped before the war, sent her fifty dollars to get to his home in Washington, DC. Carolin Hunter, who grew up in Suffolk, said her father was born free but lived with her mother and three brothers. After being beaten because his dog killed a sheep, he left to join the Union army. Her brothers were sold, but after the war she and her mother went to Portsmouth, where they found her father and two of her brothers. The third brother was never seen again.[11]

Still, many just fled to the Norfolk area from the war and destitution. Charles Grandy, who was born in North Carolina, was brought at two months old with his mother to Norfolk and sold to Mississippi. He grew up being moved between the two places. As a child he had had a foot maimed when he was forced to cut corn and also got an arm caught in a cotton gin. He escaped from a farm outside of Portsmouth when Union soldiers were heard to be in the area. Grandy served as a cook in the army for part of the war and then signed up for the US Navy, where he was rowing in a small boat known as a cutter until someone noticed his mangled arm and he was made captain of a cutter. Like many others in Norfolk, he saw the staggering poverty of the fugitives, as is clear from the following description:

> After the war I got a job diggin' out de Norfolk harbor in 1866. Dey paid me $1.25 a day. Nobody owned de niggers; so dey all come to Norfolk, look lak to me. Hundreds hungry an' wid out a house to sleep in was walkin' 'round beggin.' De army fed a lot o' dem, but it couldn' feed all. We use to steal bread an' stuff it in our shirts when we come off duty. . . . We would give it to de hungry women an' babies. Lawd! Dey didn't have no food attall. Women an' chillun use to die two an' three a day f'om bein' hungry.

Many came to Norfolk looking for family members or, like Grandy, because it was a place slavery had brought them before, or hoping for work, or simply for resources that were scarce in the country.[12]

Foundational Assemblies:
Making Consensus

Upriver from Portsmouth and Norfolk, African Americans held a mass meeting on May 31, 1865, in Petersburg and passed a set of resolutions. Petersburg, particularly the Pocahontas Island neighborhood where Blacks had been brought in the 1720s to build a tobacco warehouse, had a long-established African American community. Free Blacks came there to work, and after the American Revolution, numbers of freed Blacks settled there, earning it a reputation as one of the largest free Black communities in the country. As a developed Black community with some institutions already in place, it attracted an even larger population after the Civil War. In the early years of Black electoral participation, Petersburg was the center of Black political power.[13] Attendees at the May mass meeting, citing the service of Black soldiers and the pride taken in local Blacks who were the first Union troops to enter Richmond, refused the idea of being taxed without representation. They held that "our color nor former enslavement is no just cause for our proscription nor disfranchisement, as the word white, nor slave, is not found in the Constitution of the United States." Claiming their relative "ignorance" to be comparable to that of many whites, both native and foreign, they asserted, "We cheerfully submit to any provision [for voting], however rigid, that will apply with equal force to our white fellow-citizens."[14]

On June 5, 1865, the Black community of Norfolk held a mass meeting in response to a number of white mob riots targeting African Americans. Attendees adopted a document addressed both to the nation and to Black Virginians, *Equal Suffrage: Address from the Colored Citizens of Norfolk, Va.*, which proposed "a three-pronged strategy, encouraging Blacks to form political organizations, as well as both labor and land associations." One of its chief authors, Dr. Thomas Bayne (1824–88), who was in New Bedford the year Teamoh got there, is an unusual example of the organic intellectuals, like Teamoh, who were entrusted with leadership by freedpeople. Bayne, who had just returned to Norfolk, had been taught dentistry by a local dentist who was his last slaveholder. He escaped to New England, where he lived for ten years, became literate, and was elected to local office in New Bedford, becoming one of the earliest Black office holders in the country. The other two authors of *Equal Suffrage* were more traditional leaders: Joseph T. Wilson, an author and editor who had a continuing role in politics running local newspapers, and Rev. Jonathan Brown, minister of Norfolk's oldest Black church, St. John's AME. The text warns, "We wish to advise our colored brethren of the State and nation, that the settlement of this question is to a great extent dependent on them, and that supineness on their part will do as much to delay if not defeat the full recognition of their rights as the open opposition of avowed enemies."[15]

Earl Lewis writes that "in both style and content, the *Equal Suffrage* address was a true political sermon, a classic Afro-American jeremiad."[16] As a document of the Black political and rhetorical traditions, it certainly keeps to first principles, upholding foundational ideals and taking the moral high ground. But *Equal Suffrage* also demonstrates—in its authors, the process of its creation, its form, and its content—the essence of the foundations of political thought among the newly emancipated in the South. The authors of the address represent the kind of collaboration between freedpeople, local intellectuals, and known community leaders necessary as African Americans confronted the complex issues presented by freedom. All the organizers involved in the creation of the manifesto took pains to document contact information for groups working on diverse issues in area Black communities to allow for coordination and mutual support. They started working with local groups months in advance to allow for meetings across the area.

The form of the document—a statement adopted by a mass meeting (after a series of earlier mass meetings) in order that it be made public with the knowledge and consent of those to whom it was primarily addressed in Black communities—is also representative of freedpeople's political process. Unlike the resolutions of earlier northern-based "colored conventions," *Equal Suffrage* is an example of a more direct democracy, motivated perhaps by the need to inform a largely illiterate community—but one already aware of shared problems as a laboring class and as a race. If members of the Black elite in the community did not feel affiliation by class and knew only tentative ties by race, they also knew racist violence and white supremacist policing made no such distinctions. The Norfolk meetings, along with others held around the circuit, were open, like church gatherings, to hearing anyone moved to speak.

The content of the *Equal Suffrage* document also speaks to the broad interests of Blacks across the South. The first angle of attack on white supremacist ideology was to take up one of the most lasting rhetorical claims of that ideology: "It is a common assertion, by our enemies, that 'this is a white man's country, settled by white men, its government established by white men, and shall therefore be ruled by white men only.' How far are these statements true and the conclusion reasonable?" After arguing that "every school-boy knows" that Africans labored at Jamestown and afterward in all the other colonies, the Norfolk citizens declare, "Even our enemies and old oppressors, themselves, used to admit, nay, contend for, the urgent necessity of our presence and labor to the national prosperity." They follow with a restatement of the central question, "Again, is it true

that this government owes its existence entirely to white men?" and an iteration of examples of Black roles in the Revolutionary War and the Civil
War, especially the enlistment of 25,000 Black soldiers from Fort Monroe
and the participation of 200,000 Black soldiers overall.[17]

The chief protest made by Norfolk's Black citizens is simply that the
Emancipation Proclamation, "and even the late constitutional amendment
[the Thirteenth Amendment], if duly ratified . . . neither touch, nor can
touch, the slave codes of the various southern States, and the laws respect-
ing free people of color . . . presumed to have lost none of their vitality, but
exist, as a convenient engine of our oppression, until repealed by special
acts of the State Legislatures." The writers list some of the crippling de-
privations of the still extant slave codes such as the prohibitions on Blacks
learning to read, getting married, buying land, making contracts, testifying
in court if a white man was involved in the case, or even walking to work
on city or country roads without a pass. The manifesto cites an incident
of the vengeful deployment of police power in Richmond when, during a
three-day absence of the mayor, eight hundred freedpeople were arrested
for being on the streets without passes. It further protests the election of a
new mayor in Portsmouth based on a campaign to maintain "a white man's
government" and rumors of driving all Blacks from the city. The document
cites as well county meetings in which planters sought to limit Black mobility
by publicly vowing violence against one another for hiring any people they
had not recently owned.[18] Of course, far from repealing the old slave codes,
in fact, state legislatures were crafting new codes to adapt these same pro-
scriptions to a new reality in which a free labor force is presumed to be able
to walk away from onerous conditions. That month, Tennessee led the way
in passing the first elements of a black code.

The central demand of *Equal Suffrage* is offered in one optimistic sentence: "Fellow citizens, the performance of a simple act of justice on your
part will reverse all this; we ask for no expensive aid from military forces,
stationed throughout the South, overbearing State action, and rendering our
government republican only in name; give us the suffrage, and you may rely
upon us to secure justice for ourselves." This theme of self-reliance upon
receiving the vote is often repeated during Black campaigns for suffrage
across the South. This twenty-seven-page document gave a farsighted
warning to northerners who had previously complained about "the slavoc-
racy of the South" about the potential for an even more powerful postwar
southern elite without Black voters. The text notably makes a claim for the
uniqueness of the African American role in achieving abolition: "Among

no other people could such a revolution have taken place without scenes of license and bloodshed, . . . and full information . . . will show that no single disturbance, however slight, has occurred which has not resulted from the unprovoked aggression of white people."[19]

Two years before Black male suffrage was granted for the formation of new constitutional conventions in the South and five years before the Fifteenth Amendment was ratified, Bayne and others knew that, even if won, the vote and political representation would be insufficient tools for overcoming the obstacles facing freedpeople. They urged activism on suffrage, labor problems (wages, access to certain jobs, and improved hours and conditions), and efforts toward landownership. In Virginia, as in South Carolina, the idea of collective landownership was in the mix of approaches to farm acquisition. *Equal Suffrage* recommends the creation of various "associations" focused on suffrage, labor, and land purchase. "Then be up and active, and everywhere let associations be formed having for their object the agitation, discussion and enforcement of your claims of equality before the law, and equal rights of suffrage."[20]

The organizers provided contact information so that any newly formed associations might be connected to others, "to insure uniformity of action," first listing a contact for political associations, then for groups formed to protect "the colored laborer," and a third contact for land purchase associations in order to build a "Union of the Virginian Colored Land Associations."[21] The pattern of coordinated meetings between communities began months, perhaps years, before the first meeting on the manifesto. The printed document of the *Equal Suffrage* address details the process of mass meetings from February 1865, when local whites tried to have civil government restored and get the federal troops removed, until June, and it lists several area Black groups as active in the effort: the Union Monitor Club of Norfolk, formed in February; the Hampton Union League, organized in March; and the Colored Union League of Williamsburg, founded in May. These Union clubs do not seem tied to the national group known as the Union League (UL), but were started locally and run by Blacks, who would build political machines in their areas. Daniel M. Norton, born enslaved in Virginia and later elected to several offices, formed the Hampton group; Willis Hodges was president of the Norfolk club. Born free in Virginia, and a man known for long aiding fugitive slaves in Virginia and New York, Hodges was an acquaintance of abolitionists Gerrit Smith and John Brown. He was later elected to several offices, and he fought school segregation and other issues.[22]

A May meeting at the Bute Street Baptist Church in Norfolk produced a pithier set of resolutions, the third of which states succinctly the common analysis of such meetings, linking citizenship rights to the vital position of Blacks as the South's labor force: "[Resolved] that it is a wretched policy and most unwise statesmanship that would withhold from the laboring population of the country any of the rights of citizenship essential to their well-being and to their advancement and improvement as citizens."[23]

Most notable is the coordination of these and other groups along the James River watershed. Severe hardship and violence, both criminal and racial, forced the formation of defense committees at Black settlements and mass meetings over self-defense, maintaining Blacks' free status, and achieving citizenship rights, particularly in the adjacent peninsula counties of Elizabeth City (Hampton), Warwick, James City, and York. People from each of these communities traveled, likely by boat, to each group's mass meetings, then each locality produced its own document endorsing the Norfolk manifesto and emphasizing particular issues according to their own consensus. Thus, we see the old information highway along the James producing a vetted political statement and additional local concerns from Norfolk, Hampton (and Elizabeth City County), Williamsburg, and Yorktown (plus York and James City Counties). Petersburg also composed a set of resolutions. *Equal Suffrage* lays out in detail both the political process and the demands made in petitions and resolutions that arise later from Black conventions, highlighting regional coordination that may have occurred where possible among other southern communities.[24]

Meetings continued long after the manifesto was produced. For instance, meetings were held in Hampton in August and November in which freedpeople working with two local planters announced the results of a census of Blacks in the town—including the condition of housing on the two largest farms, property held by Blacks, and declarations that better crops were being raised by freedpeople than before. The observation on crops may be due to some crops having suffered in the previous two years due to weather and/or the war (the *New York Times* had reported destruction of wheat by severe weather in 1863 and better crops in 1865; corn in 1865 was one-fourth of the 1860 crop). These freedpeople state a resolve to acquire land and raise crops, and they demand the vote.

Five days after the release of *Equal Suffrage*, five Richmond activists appointed "by a public meeting of the colored people" of the city signed a letter to President Andrew Johnson outlining grievances and evidence of "the persecution of the colored people by the military and the police authorities," a Black population they numbered at twenty thousand people.[25] *The New York Tribune* reproduced the letter, including this affirmation of the Black community's self-reliance in the face of hardship without government assistance: "None of our people are in the alms house and when we were slaves the aged and infirm who were turned away from the homes of hard masters, who had been enriched by their toil, our benevolent societies supported [*sic*] while they lived, and buried when they died, and comparatively few of us have found it necessary to ask for Government rations, which have been so bountifully bestowed upon the unrepentant Rebels of Richmond."[26] The activists remind the president of aid rendered to the "soldiers of Freedom (for which several of our people, of both sexes, have been severely punished by stripes and imprisonment)" during the "Slaveholders' Rebellion." The pointed inclusion of women as having received grievous punishment for aiding the Union echoes the routine protests about the treatment of women in emancipation-era Black political discourse.[27]

Commenting on the same incident of eight hundred arrests mentioned in the Norfolk manifesto, the writers explain that there were often people from outside of Richmond walking the streets making inquiries about lost husbands, wives, and other family members. "Many of these people, who ignorantly supposed the day of passes had passed away with the system which originated them, have been arrested, imprisoned and hired out without their advice or consent."[28] They complain of the reinstatement of a mayor blamed for cruelty to Union prisoners in addition to a history of cruel treatment of Blacks. The letter included a sheaf of fifteen testimonies gathered from locals and visitors, who provided their bona fides by way of either slavery history or professional work, and narrated brutality suffered on Richmond streets. The first and most extreme case involved the severe punishment of a man named Ned Scott accused of attempting to stab two Union soldiers, jailed and put to gang labor after being covered in flour and nearly suffocated to death in a coffin outside his church for defending his wife, who was assaulted, addressed with vulgarities, and pelted with rocks.[29]

The mayor was fired before the Black activists' visit with President Johnson occurred, and on their return to Richmond, according to the *New York Tribune*, "the odious pass system was abolished."[30] Another letter published on June 12, signed by five other activists and "many others," documents mass arrests and decries the mayor and "his former nigger-hunters and whippers," who were "going into people's houses and taking them out and confining them in the City Jail until ... they are marched off by the mounted guard to the bull pen," sometimes seventy-five or eighty at a time. The military, it was charged, used agents to hire out the people for farmwork.[31]

The Fourth of July in 1865 marked the beginning of annual celebrations by freedpeople following the end of the war.[32] On July 6, 1865, in Norfolk, some "southern gentlemen" and members of the New York Thirteenth Artillery began a "reign of terror" by destroying a Black man's vending stand and all his goods. Then, yelling, "Clear out all the niggers," they began three nights of terror in which a group of Black men were shot trying to go to a circus, three others were found hanged, three more shot, and several northern whites attacked. Property was also destroyed. When freedpeople visited the mayor about the violence, he said, "You must fight it out; I can do nothing for you." One local, who said Blacks had been harmed in "every possible way," agreed. "There's nothing left us but to protect ourselves."[33]

Meetings and reports continued in Richmond and other towns through the summer. On August 8 the *Tribune* reported "growing abuse" of Blacks. "Young men, citizens, seem to feel it a duty incumbent upon them to assault and waylay every colored man; while the older heads universally have adopted the plan of fighting our soldiers." Blaming lax law enforcement, the reporter opines, "There is a point beyond which human endurance ceases to be a virtue." A meeting at the Second Baptist Church documented more robberies and assaults "by men in soldiers' dress," noting that the predators were "gobbling up the most likely looking negro women, [who were] thrown into cells, robbed and ravished at the will of the guard." Ed Webster, a man taken from his home on August 2 and jailed "in the next cell could hear the guard abusing and maltreating women. People in the vicinity testify to hearing women scream frightfully almost every night." The petition to the governor drawn up that night listed further incidents and asked for protection "from the proper authorities" or "grant us the privilege of protecting ourselves." The paper also mentioned the formation of a Loyal League "of the colored men" being organized and expected to have thousands of members within a month.[34]

The pattern of abuse in Richmond (and other southern cities) was described as an *escalating* one because abuse had already occurred, even in Union camps, and remained at issue as Blacks later joined electoral politics. Regardless of the diversity in Black responses, it seems fair to say that some common notions of the political were being shaped by the violent reception of freedmen and freedwomen establishing autonomous domestic relationships and access to public space and leisure.[35] Despite the US military presence and sometimes because of it, self-defense was often required of Black communities. The early reports of violence against freedpeople and protests made by Blacks, along with their concerted efforts to get them covered in the northern press, show some shared assumptions: the pass system, forced labor, widespread violence, and the refusal to grant redress marked a return to slavery conditions and worse, and that appeals for relief had to be made locally and nationally. Perhaps the most important information gleaned by freedpeople in the immediate crisis of abolition, regardless of where they were, was that their expectations about freedom—even though many expected continued prejudice—would not be honored and it was necessary for freedpeople to define freedom and make known their demands for its realization.

Out of the Shadows: Emergent Communities

In December the Insurrection Rumor of 1865 that was spreading throughout the South became a subject at Black meetings as a rumor of a local Black insurrection was raised and strenuously rejected by the people present. A local Black paper reported that "a series of resolutions, adopted at a freedmen's meeting in Norfolk, were read and approved, and a Committee appointed to proceed to Washington in connection with Mr. [Calvin] Pepper, to advance the interests of the colored people."[36] Local communities feared the rumor would bring violence against them. That month, various groups sent assembled reports of their meetings and resolutions to the US Quartermaster Department. It was common practice for people across the South to send petitions or complaints to the federal military authorities in the state. A new Norfolk statement warned that "we are a peaceable and law abiding people and that the stories so industriously circulated against us That we are contemplating and preparing for insurrection and riotous and disorderly proceedings are vile falsehoods designed to provoke acts of unlawful violence against us." The Yorktown meeting supported the Norfolk resolutions; added that people in that county were, like those of "Williamsburg, Yorktown and Old Point," pledged to keep the peace; and endorsed "'the proposed National Homestead, Settlement and Labor agency' as approved by the meetings at Norfolk and Hampton."

Portsmouth Blacks joined in support of sending a delegation from the Tidewater area to Washington, and Blacks in Middlesex County wrote the Freedmen's Bureau about being driven off farms without pay after bringing in the crops. The Middlesex letter further stated that their group had been authorized by Blacks in adjoining Essex and King and Queen Counties to speak for them as well.[37]

When the new year of 1866 came, no insurrection occurred. Just as they had remade the Fourth of July, Black people in the South remade New Year's Day—a day often set for sales or leases of the enslaved—by performing a new tradition, the celebration of emancipation. On January 1, four thousand freedpeople of the Hampton area gathered to celebrate the first postwar anniversary of the Emancipation Proclamation.[38] The event was held at the Butler School, a freedmen's school named after the general who specifically made safe escape possible for many in the area. According to a local paper, the day began with a procession from a Black Baptist church led by a band and "the Rising Sons, the Morning Stars, Good Samaritans, Sons of Bethel, Sons of Abraham and Sons of Zion." These benevolent societies, already well known enough that the paper did not list their complete names, were at the heart of local organization. Like others, they performed grassroots uplift built around shared Blackness.[39] Seven speakers gave their thoughts on the importance of the anniversary, including Norfolk's Dr. Thomas Bayne, one of the *Equal Suffrage* authors, and several former enslaved men who had become prominent ministers and community leaders. At the end, the Fort Monroe Brass Band played and the societies marched back through town.[40] As a contemporary observer described the scene, "This march was one of the most interesting we ever saw, old men and women with their gray heads, men and women in the prime of life, boys and girls, mules, horses, wagons and carts all in their order joined in the procession." The reporter for *True Southerner* (a local paper started by a white Union soldier to aid freedpeople and edited by Joseph T. Wilson, a Black veteran and another *Equal Suffrage* author) was impressed as well with the elaborate meal that included turkey, chicken, oysters, and frosted cakes. Later that year a mob destroyed the newspaper's office.[41]

This progressive paper's enthusiasm for a Black celebration was not typical. In the first years after the war, white churlishness about Black use of public space grew, especially for these commemorative spectacles, many of which involved marches by armed Black veterans and others who formed local militias and drilled regularly. The press protested these military displays, as Alrutheus Taylor quotes from a Richmond paper, "fearful lest 'the rougher element of the Negroes might be preparing for a war of the races." In Virginia, freedpeople celebrated April 9 (the anniversary of Robert E. Lee's surrender) and September 22 and January 1 (Emancipation Proclamation days). They later added festivities for ratification of the Fourteenth and Fifteenth Amendments and passage of the Reconstruction Acts and the 1866 Civil Rights Act. "Furthermore," Taylor quips, "the Negroes all but monopolized the celebration of George Washington's birthday and the Fourth of July." As Genevieve Fabre has said, Black celebrations established a whole new calendar.[42] That summer, the *Richmond Enquirer* suggested employers fire anyone who participated in these anniversary events: "If persons in their employ wish to participate in these insulting saturnalia, the employers cannot prevent them from so doing, but they can inform them that their services are no longer needed. Let our citizens refuse to give employment to these participators in these processions, gotten up under the auspices of a handful of fanatics, for the sole purpose of insulting our people."[43] Here is yet another interpretation of the word *insulting*. The assumption by whites that they were the sole object of Black actions as a collective is one of the most common traits of nineteenth-century southern white public discourse and one of the most blinding legacies of slave system culture. The editors promised the celebrations would be seriously hampered if their advice was taken, but the *Enquirer* did not succeed and the public events increased with the constant rise in Black benevolent and fraternal groups late in the century.

It is not surprising that white reaction would erupt in the months following the April enactment of the 1866 Civil Rights Bill, spurred in the first instance by Black celebration of the law. The exact kind of public celebration that provoked angry press notices at New Year's was greeted with violence in Norfolk four months later. Recurring skirmishes were taking place in the streets from the beginning of 1866. "Whites, blacks, soldiers, and former soldiers tangled almost nightly" against a backdrop of carping from the pro-rebel newspaper, the *Day Book*, which complained that there were enough discharged Black troops in Norfolk and Portsmouth "to raise a big corn crop." Trouble was again rumored on April 16, when Blacks began a march in Norfolk in celebration of the passage of the 1866 Civil Rights Act. The local police told the military they were ill-equipped to face the many armed whites planning to attack, so federal soldiers were present when about eight hundred Blacks from Norfolk and Portsmouth paraded. Marchers carried signs that read, "The Ballot Box Free to All,"

"The Rising Sons of Freedom Society," and "The Monitor Union Club" and were escorted by at least eighteen to twenty Black veterans carrying rifles. A fracas broke out at the site of the rally, during which a white man fired a gun into the crowd. Some of those in the parade caught him and killed him. The army escorted Blacks home. Hours later a group of a hundred armed whites in Confederate uniform assembled to attack the Black community. They fired about fifty shots at a Union officer and his orderly, who fled and sent a company after the gunmen, who were not found. Help from the marines was requested from the Norfolk Navy Yard, and ferries were set up for troops from Fort Monroe.[44]

The next day, soldiers heard a white mob was planning to attack the soldiers and "exterminate" the Black community, but with the arrival of two hundred more soldiers and a threat to rioters, the violence stopped. No whites were arrested, but seven Blacks were charged with causing the initial disturbance. Six were released for lack of evidence; the fate of one man is unclear. William Keeling, an African American, was asked in the riot inquiry "if local blacks could get a fair, impartial trial in the courts of Norfolk." He replied, "'I think that is a trick to be tried.'" In 1866, that was a trick still to be tried across the entire South.[45]

George Teamoh was working on the Portsmouth docks in 1866 and had already begun his tutelage in the political needs and possibilities of Black Virginians by attending the 1865 Virginia freedpeople's convention in Alexandria and doubtless numerous meetings prior to that event. Of this time he recalled, "Coming to Portsmouth, my old home, I here tendered my services to the loyal people in what ever form I could accomplish the greatest good for the struggling patriots in a moral warfare to reconstruct the State on a basis of perfect equality before the law, for all men."[46] One of Teamoh's foremost concerns was equal pay for freedpeople. That spring Teamoh worked with the freedwomen vendors of Portsmouth, using his literacy to help them create a protest document. On May 21, 1866, the women held a meeting and aired their grievances over a new municipal tax levied against them on top of existing license fees. Teamoh sent his notes and a letter on behalf of the women to General O. O. Howard, head of the Freedmen's Bureau. His notes, with his corrections penned in, present an extraordinary picture of the women and their process, including questions put to the body and an amen chorus intoning, "True, true." Sarah Nash, the president of this group identified as "the Hucksters (colored) [sic] of this place," explained all the tax and license fees and declared, "'Friends, for the last 30 odd Years, when many of You were children I have been keeping a cook shop, and now I must stop because I ain't (have not) got ($50.00) fifty dollars, to pay into the hands of the collector for one Year's taxes, and I don't make that much in two Years; and now let them break me up, put me in jail or do what they please with me, I say I am done serving them, by the help of God and the U.S. Army.'"[47] Nancy Hodges, vice president, added that she understood the tax money all went to support the Confederate widows, orphans, and invalids, information the others had heard as well. Their discussion informed the general that in the recent election all the local friends of freedpeople had been removed from office. They also reported that their husbands and sons who worked for the city had been fired and their jobs given to whites with rebel sympathies. Freedmen "have no voice" in making city, state, or national government decisions, they said, suggesting they had no recourse for lost jobs other than the bureau. Unionist whites were also having rents raised. After asking for relief to "pursue their legitimate calling," the women signed off "representing hundreds here who huckster for a living" with their good wishes for the bureau leader: "They pray day and night that the Heavenly Father may so surround You by His providential care . . . live the life of the righteous, and live long; and when this painful life endeth, have a Seat in God's Bureau in Heaven."[48]

In towns like Portsmouth, ports and railroads that were moving tobacco, most workers who were not farming the tobacco were processing, packing, or loading it. They were the creators of some of the earliest strikes over wages. In Richmond, on September 18, 1865, men calling themselves "tobacco mechanics" had petitioned tobacco factory owners, saying that as enslaved workers they had been hired to the companies for $12 to $15 a week to the owner, with companies providing room and board. As freedpeople, they were paid $1.50 per hundred pounds of cured, packed tobacco. The authors state that each mechanic, working with a stemmer (who stripped off the stems and wrapped the leaves into "hands"), packed six hundred pounds a week in barrels called "hogsheads," bringing each pair $9 for a week's work. Once the stemmer was paid half, the mechanic took home $4.50 to $5, less than half the slavery-era wage, and with that paid $18 to $20 monthly for rent, "to say nothing about food Clothing medicin Doctor Bills Tax & co." The petition ended: "They say we will starve through laziness that is not so. But it is true we will starve at our present wages. . . . It is impossible to feed ourselves and family—starvation is cirten unless a change is brought about—Tobacco Factory Mechanicks of Richmond and Manchester."[49]

Such strike reports are not just glimpses into the ideas of freedpeople months after the war about their potential as organized workers; they also reveal that in slavery these workers were aware not only of the value of their work but also of variations in that pay. In the case of the Virginia workers, it is also helpful that the mechanics point out they had been hired out for this work, which would have been true of many workers elsewhere. Though packing and stemming tobacco and loading boats were regarded in the labor market as unskilled work, these people were knowledgeable about the value of their experience and skills in this "unskilled" arena.

Of equal importance is the fact that stemmers in Virginia's tobacco industry were always, as far as I have been able to learn, female workers. This makes the mechanics' financial arrangements with the stemmers—splitting the pay equally—worth noting. While the mechanics do not say whether the women demanded these wages, the fact that half was paid them shows an agreement on female workers as equal partners. Owing to the simple fact that the petition signed only by mechanics explains the division of pay, one can speculate that had they received the pay raise, stemmers would have benefited. Even just the process of seeking redress of a grievance by uniting all the mechanics of Richmond and its suburb Manchester five months after war's end would have been instructive to many.

Taylor tells us that right after emancipation, "a few Negroes caught the spirt of organized labor. . . . Strikes for higher wages in the tobacco factories became common." While it is not known if the tobacco mechanics went on strike in 1865, the next year, in late September 1866, Black tobacco workers in Richmond were organizing, and in early October they struck for higher wages. Taylor documents strikes among stevedores and woodcutters from 1867 through 1879 in Petersburg, Richmond, City Point, and Staunton. The skilled trades produced many of the early Black elected representatives, and Black dominance in ports produced early labor organizing. Together they would generate—especially through the work of trade associations—leadership and a base for political mobilization. Black laborers in the 1860s, sometimes acting in awareness of early white worker organizing but chiefly in response to their own needs, did pioneering work by organizing as unskilled workers.[50]

Evidence of Black labor activism, especially tied to the tobacco industry, continued to appear in the press in the 1870s. In May 1872 the *Dispatch* reported:

On Saturday morning the truckmen, twenty-one in number, employed in the freight sheds of the Richmond and Danville Railroad Company's depot, suddenly struck for higher wages. They were all colored men, and some had been employed by this company for a good many years. Since 1866 they have been receiving one dollar a day and ten cents an hour extra for night work. Of late the average wages has been one dollar and sixty cents a day. With a threat, they demanded more. The demand was refused, and they then left the yard, saying that it would be "a long time before them cars are loaded."

The owners replaced the men with others who were inexperienced but in need of work. Many of these strikes were similarly short-lived, but laborers were persistent in walking out throughout the decade and, like these men, were successful in planning their actions and executing them without prior discovery. Later that month there was a strike in a Petersburg tobacco factory, followed by at least two more in 1873.[51] In early summer 1875 there were two strikes in tobacco factories in Richmond and Petersburg, and in August Black laborers held a state convention and formed the Laboring Men's Mechanics Union Association.[52] Strikes and attempts to form unions continued in the 1870s. In Staunton, woodcutters walked out in 1879. They persisted, sometimes using force against uncooperative fellow workers, and despite the governor's claim that there was no "trade unionism and communism" among Blacks.[53]

Arrivals II

In the summer of 1867, as the possibility of registering Black male voters appeared on the horizon for the next year, Rev. John V. Given, a speaker for the Union Republican Congressional Committee (URCC), wrote to the Washington headquarters from Farmville. His account gives a good idea of what the summer and fall of 1867 were like for activists who came south to work with freedpeople and get them registered to vote—especially their surprise at the size of groups coming to hear them. At the time, Farmville was in the middle of a rail line between Lynchburg in the west and Petersburg in the east, and was the western end of a canal system that was the major shipping thoroughfare for tobacco and farm goods. Though Given and his colleagues traveled by various means, they used rail stops as meeting points in farming areas. As Given describes one such encounter, "I met my appointment [at] Nottoway C.H. [Court House] and addressed, at 12 o'clock, a dense mass of men, both white and colored. I spoke from 12 to half past 2. My address was radical. Slaveholders and slavedrivers cried—yes, wept like women—and all vied with each other in treating me friendly."[54] From Nottoway Given rode sixteen miles to Burkeville, where he spoke at 5:00 p.m. "Thousands gathered at Berkeville [sic]. My address was well received. I returned the twelve [sic] miles and preached at Nottoway C.H. Sunday morning." After the service he rode to "the junction," which was likely the junction of the Richmond and Danville Railroad and the Southside Railroad near Burkeville. He preached "that afternoon and evening to a multitude beyond the capacity of any church in the United States to hold. Also organized a Union League council the same day, called the Mount Olive Council of Nottoway county [sic]. I also organized a Republican club. Spoke four times Sunday, July 14. I leave today for Cumberland [County] C.H." Prince Edward County and Cumberland would send delegates to the constitutional convention and elect a healthy number of Black representatives before disfranchisement in 1890. Nottoway would elect Blacks later. The last county Given visited that summer proved even tougher. In his words, "A colored speaker was killed three weeks ago at Lunenburg. I shall go there, and speak where they have cowed the black men so that they dare not even register, and, by the help of God, give them a dose of my radical Republican pills and neutralize the corrosive ascidity [sic] of their negro hate. I want nothing. Congress has made a man of me!" Lunenberg only elected one Black state legislator before the twentieth century, despite a 63 percent Black majority of the population. The violence Given had heard about likely continued, along with the threats to jobs, which was common.[55]

Dr. Henry Jerome Brown, a colleague of Given's, also wrote to the URCC from Farmville that month concerning his work starting Union Leagues: "I am still diligently laboring in the good cause, having held meetings all along the line of the Orange & Alexandria R.R. to this place where I speak today." The distance traveled from Alexandria to Lynchburg on this train line would have been at least 184 miles through nine rural counties with sizable populations. Only two of those counties, Fluvanna and Albemarle, and two others adjoining them elected delegates to the constitutional convention in 1868. But after that, Fluvanna and Albemarle failed to gain representation despite Black majorities, perhaps because their locations were more distant from the circuit hubs in Petersburg and Richmond. But their loss was also likely due to the success of local white organization. In September 1867 the *Charlottesville Chronicle* in Albemarle called for "a white man's party" and asked, "Can we stand together like the blacks? . . . There have been enough negro meetings." It took the locals a while, but by

December the state conservative party became a "white man's party." Three counties on that westernmost route never elected any Black representatives after the constitutional convention until at least 1967.[56]

"Yesterday we had an immense gathering at Lynchburg against which the local press are much exercised," wrote Brown. "Several of the factory hands have been discharged for attending it. . . . The league at that place is eleven hundred strong and was formed by myself the short period of two months ago." From Lynchburg, Brown went to Farmville, putting him on a route through four counties that would become successful in building electoral organizations. Like many organizers, Brown used the rail lines to densely populated agricultural areas, and like many others, he was continually surprised by the number of freedpeople who came to hear him and join the political organizations he was there to build. He likely got used to it, as he worked later on the circuits in North and South Carolina.[57]

Six days after the passage of the first act of Radical Reconstruction in 1865 (the other Reconstruction Acts were passed in 1867), Orlando Brown, assistant commissioner of Virginia's Freedmen's Bureau, sent orders to bureau officers for each to report six names "of the most intelligent of the freedmen belonging to each county, in whom both races have confidence and who have the most influence over their own people," along with the names of at least six respected white men eligible to hold office. Brown's intention to pick leaders for the freedpeople aside, his order also had the effect of requiring that Black meetings be monitored. The influence of this effort on the choice of local leaders depends on who looks at it. The records show the bureau was provided with at least 621 names from ninety-three counties; unaccounted for were seven western counties where Blacks made up 1 percent to 8 percent of the population and two counties on the Emancipation Circuit with Black majorities that struggled for representation. According to Lowe, "Eleven of the eighty-seven black men who served in the state's General Assembly in the nineteenth century were named in the bureau's list," along with three of the twenty-four delegates to the constitutional convention. Most of the Black representatives were clearly chosen by other means, which, I would argue, matched men with local priorities. As Forsythe writes, "Bureau agents failed to foresee that black political leaders in Virginia would arise most often as spokesmen and presiding officials of the institutionalized social networks that were the infrastructure of freed communities."[58]

Making Political Voice

Twenty-four Black men were elected as delegates to the 1867–68 constitutional convention, representing twenty-nine counties and the cities of Richmond and Petersburg.[59] There were no major appointed or elected Black statewide officeholders in Virginia. The leaders who emerged from mass meetings in Virginia's Black communities and went to Richmond as delegates differed from those who met in the 1865 Black convention. The earlier meeting near the end of the Civil War attracted men mostly from the Black elite, born free, literate, and earning stable incomes. Two years later, the men chosen by their neighbors did not so much represent those traditional advantages for leadership but typified instead the characteristics of the most itinerant people on the Emancipation Circuit: little or no traditional education, some past experience of independent income, mobility, and access to information networks not available to most enslaved people. Even given their access to communities beyond their places of birth, Black representatives also shared the markers of family loss, multiple sales and displacements, and witnessing the quotidian violence and cruelty of the slave system.

Most delegates were born in counties lying along the James River and were a generation older than those who appear in the Works Progress Administration's interviews of slavery survivors conducted in the 1930s; many of the most prominent enslavement survivor activists died in the 1870s and 1880s. They were organic intellectuals, in some cases self-taught; in other cases, taught to read by individuals in their midst or in freedpeople's schools. Those who were born free were as likely to be rural people as urban and often eked out a living in farming or a trade such as carpentry; those born in bondage included men who were leased out by their owners. The 29 counties African Americans represented were a minority of the state's 102 counties. Black statewide representation grew to include a total of 38 counties before 1890 and after that shrank to none. For the constitutional convention, most of the counties with Black delegates shared them with another county. This required delegates to report in person in multiple places and be accountable to large numbers of people (crossing counties by horse and/or slow trains). Working for two counties also had its benefits: it facilitated the airing of mutual concerns and finding points of agreement across counties.

Teamoh, the ship caulker from Portsmouth, had become a Union League organizer by 1867 and was elected to represent Portsmouth at the constitutional convention and, later, in the state senate. At the convention he began a long alliance with his fellow Portsmouth delegate, James H. Clements, a white machinist and the town's postmaster. Of his initial experience there, Teamoh wrote:

> We did not have a colored member who could off set a speech of any great length coming from the other side but we have invariably voted right on the proposition from which the arguments were drawn, independent of the many stages of amendments &c through which it may have had to pass. Nor was it to be expected that we—colored,—could by any possibility, at that time have had the most distant knowledge of constitutional reconstruction, as many of us could neither read or write, having gone there as shown by [conservative J. C.] Gibson "from the farm yards" &c. For my part I went . . . a "graduate" from Capt. John Thompson's brick yard, and finished my trade at caulking.[60]

Although Teamoh himself was said to be articulate, one exception to his description of the Black delegates was his more confident and contentious colleague from Norfolk, Thomas Bayne, a practiced and colorful speaker.

Bayne's remarks during the convention ring with the ready humor of someone who enjoyed verbal sport on the floor, and he was probably, as advertised among the jibes from the conservatives, the most able man in the Black caucus for the legislative tasks. The *New York Times* described him as "an eloquent and fiery orator" and as having "a vast amount of general knowledge, a fund of apposite and humorous anecdotes, . . . and withal a good deal of common sense, combined with a smattering of book learning."[61] When white conservatives claimed that "government was the prerogative of white men," Bayne asked one of them:

> Does the gentleman mean that the black men are not to have any rights in this country? Does he mean to set us free today and in fifty or sixty years to come, then to give us the right of suffrage? I want it distinctly understood that the old slaveholders' coach moves too slow for us. . . . They are preaching the danger of a war of races in this hall. They are preaching it in Congress, in the cities and over the country, in the streets, and on the seas, on the steamboats, in the cars, in the taverns, everywhere. This war of races is being preached up constantly, but nobody preaches it up but that side of the House which hates the Republican Party and hates the Federal government.[62]

Bayne was a particular target of the Democratic press, which deployed large-scale front-page cartoons and blackface text against him and other radicals, as if weekly ridicule would stop them. But the mass democratic process produced people like Bayne; these Black delegates did not produce the Black public's impatience with a shackled, racialized, and dangerous freedom. Reconstruction was short-lived in Virginia—1867 to 1873—and did not bring the kinds of political power seen in the Deep South.[63]

The End of Reconstruction

In 1870, the Fifteenth Amendment, which guaranteed the right to vote regardless of race, color, or condition of previous servitude, was ratified nationally but not in Virginia, and over the next six years state legislation was passed to limit Black voter participation by measures such as disfranchisement on conviction for petty theft. In the 1870s, William Henry Scott Sr. wrote about the abusive use of the criminal justice system against Blacks in the state. Born enslaved, he escaped Virginia in 1862 with the help of Union soldiers when he was fourteen years old and became a radical Black activist, a journalist, and a cofounder of the *Boston Guardian* and of the Niagara Movement. Scott charged:

> This is the way we colored people of this State are treated. We are sentenced to the penitentiary for the least offence. They say we vote against their interests. After we are sent there then we are sent to some public works, and under some of the meanest and poorest white men of the State; men who, themselves, have served out their time in the penitentiary, who would rather whip a colored person than do anything else. . . . There is no law which sanctions that after a man has been sent to the penitentiary he can be whipped, under any circumstances whatever.[64]

Black organizing succeeded in making gains in Richmond's large Black community, and in the center of the circuit, especially in counties around Petersburg that were heavily Black and on the Lower Peninsula, where towns had earlier been organizing protests and petitions together. Counties farther from the Petersburg hub and other areas of close cooperation seem to have been more vulnerable to organized pressures. The largest numbers of representatives and longest sustained representation were in the oldest part of the organizing circuit, the greatest number from Petersburg. The elections of the 1870s and 1880s still used mass participatory democracy to achieve consensus, where violence did not disrupt them, and required local precinct organizers who could raise funds needed for running candidates and paying voters' poll taxes to deliver votes. Areas such as Norfolk, where Blacks were not in the majority but elected Blacks, seem to have had organizers able to negotiate with white politicians for spots on the Republican slate and cooperative voter turnout. By the mid-1870s, George Teamoh's political career was finished due to the Democratic takeover, and in his midfifties, he returned to working as a ship caulker. At some point he began to write down his story, *God Made Man, Man Made the Slave*, finishing in 1883 when he was sixty-five, and shortly afterward he disappeared from public records. His colleague Thomas Bayne returned to dentistry after the constitutional convention and held no other office. In 1888, he was admitted to the Central State Lunatic Asylum and died shortly after. According to Eric Foner, the causes of his illness were listed as "religion and politics."[65]

By 1871, there was one sign of the ongoing ties along the Emancipation Circuit in Virginia and along the Atlantic coast: the student body at Hampton Institute, an HBCU founded in 1868. In 1871, the school published a catalog of its progress and listed students for two classes, seniors and the "middle" class. Of the twenty seniors, sixteen were from sites on the circuit, including Charleston, South Carolina; Beaufort and Wilmington, North Carolina; and five Virginia locales, including the Eastern Shore. One of the four from other locations was from Nansemond County, a now extinct county that never elected any Blacks to statewide office but sat near the Norfolk-Portsmouth hub, within a short distance from all the resources of the circuit. Of the thirty-three students in the institute's middle class, thirty were from sites on the Emancipation Circuit, from Wilmington, Raleigh, and Winston (now Winston-Salem), North Carolina, to Charleston, South Carolina, and five Tidewater Virginia counties. Like the other group, the largest number came from Hampton, where the school is located, but the list includes an increased number from the locations of the first group. The students from the Eastern Shore show something of the pattern: six students came from tiny places in that area, most from Northampton County, home of the most well-documented first-generation or "charter" Africans in the 1600s. Despite being separated from the Tidewater section by the Chesapeake Bay, the county was part of the Virginia Circuit, and elected Black representatives to the state legislature.[66]

In Virginia, by 1890, most of the circuit localities had organizers who worked in the Readjuster movement, which for a short time allied yeomen white farmers and Black and white Republican voters. As is shown in table 3.1, Danville, Norfolk, Petersburg, and Richmond had early civil rights movements, and Liberia emigration drives took place in Hampton, Williamsburg, Norfolk, and Lynchburg. It should be emphasized, though, that emigration movements took place as often in counties where Blacks had no representation and were under extreme pressure. By 1891, Virginia had no Black state representation.

In 1894, Virginia passed the Walton Act, said to eliminate voting fraud, but its complex features—including scratching out the names of all candidates one did *not* want elected, and if not eliminating enough names voiding the ballot—required literacy and greatly increased the likelihood of voter error, which resulted in votes being thrown out.[67] In 1900, the Republican Party began to consider excluding Blacks, rebranding itself as "lily white," and did so throughout the first twenty years of the twentieth century. The Virginia Constitution of 1902, designed specifically to eliminate the remaining Black vote, spurred a period of legal challenges; drives to register Blacks who could overcome the law's provisions concerning long-term residence, poll taxes, and literacy. Blacks started doing independent Black slates to make visible the racist intents and outcomes of disfranchising laws. But Black electoral representation was still over from the turn of the century until after passage of the federal Voting Rights Act of 1965.

Looking at Table 3.1

Table 3.1 presents a snapshot of the Virginia circuit, which had numerous institutions present to different extents: most centers were directly linked to railroads (and waterways); most experienced Union troop occupation, which facilitated the arrival of teachers, missionaries, and others who assisted with community building and starting schools. The circuit also had several sites that developed a Black press and were able to continue access to the vote for a period of Black representation in the early 1870s. Importantly, the distances between towns were not great, and people were able to travel and bring together their organizations. A Petersburg reporter writing about an Independence Day celebration in 1873 said that Blacks did most of the celebrating, with train cars of "the Senegambians" arriving from Richmond and Gaston and others taking Petersburg locals to Richmond. Sharing parade practices and showing off lodge and society memberships and bands encouraged connection and the growth of local groups.[68]

TABLE 3.1 Virginia Emancipation Circuit, 1870–90

	Institutions Present							19th Century Activism
	US Troops	RR (1884)	Union League	AMA Schools	Local Black Press	Black Political Reps	Knights of Labor Groups	
DANVILLE ß Pittsylvania County	•	•	•			•	1 M mixed labor 2 M farmers & laborers 2 F mixed labor	Labor
ETTRICK & MANCHESTER Chesterfield County	•	•	•	•	•	•	2 M farmhands & laborers 1 M mixed labor	
FARMVILLE Prince Edward County	•	•	•	Unknown		•		Liberia emigration
HAMPTON ß Elizabeth City County	•	•	•	•	1 1865	•		Readjuster movement Liberia emigration
LYNCHBURG ß Campbell County	•	•	•	Unknown		cc only	2 M mixed labor	Labor Colored Farmers' Alliance (CFA)* Liberia emigration
NEWPORT NEWS Warwick County ß	•	•	Unknown	•	In area	•	1 M carpenters	Labor

Site					KoL assemblies / dates		Knights of Labor	Issues
NORFOLK Norfolk County	+	+	+	+	<u>3</u> 1864 1880 1884	+	1 M laborers 1 M mixed labor 1 M coal trimmers 1 F housekeepers 1 F laundry workers 2 F mixed labor	Labor Civil rights Liberia emigration Colored Farmers' Alliance (CFA)*
PETERSBURG ß Dinwiddie County ß	+	+			3	+	3 M mixed labor 1 F mixed labor	Labor Civil rights Black teacher pay
PORTSMOUTH (then in **Norfolk County**)	+	+				+		Labor Liberia emigration
Prince George County ß	+			Unknown		+	1 M mixed labor	
RICHMOND (independent city)	+	+			<u>2</u> 1877– 1900	+	1 M cigar makers & whip makers 4 M mixed labor 2 F mixed labor 21 KoL assemblies	Voting Tobacco Laborers Union Civil rights

KEY: **Bold** = Site playing multiple roles on the Emancipation Circuit.

ß = Black majority; unless otherwise noted, populations are for 1870.

RR = Rail lines.

Black Political Reps = Black representatives to the 1868 constitutional convention (cc) and/or members of the General Assembly.

Knights of Labor = Black assemblies of the labor organization. Most KoL assemblies were segregated by race and gender: white males, Black males, white females, or Black females. "Mixed labor" is a term from the Garlock data (*see* Table Source Notes) and indicates various forms of work, not mixing by race or gender. **Gender** is indicated here by M or F.

* Appomattox, Dinwiddie, Fluvanna, Isle of Wight, and Mecklenburg Counties also had Colored Farmers' Alliance assemblies.

SOURCES: See Table Source Notes (393–96).

Schools were established in or near those places that achieved some political representation: Petersburg, Hampton, Chesterfield County, Warwick County, Norfolk, Portsmouth, Prince George, and Richmond. As early as 1865, HBCUs were developed in Richmond and Hampton, and later in Lawrenceville, Lynchburg, and Norfolk.

The communities varied widely in size. The countryside offered good sites for labor groups because other forms of organizing already thrived in farming centers where the Black population was dense, voting had been successful, and there were ties to Petersburg, Richmond, and Norfolk. For comparison, the table includes towns that did not then have some of the assets of the multifunction ports of the circuit. Like other circuits in the South, Virginia shows a real range of workers who organized: farm laborers, domestic workers, tobacco specialists such as cigar makers, and dock laborers, including coal trimmers and carpenters. Black dock workers and domestics organized in separate Black assemblies affiliated with a union in Richmond. Women tobacco stemmers, not shown in this table because their union organization was not documented until later, are also part of the labor picture. The high incidence of labor strikes in the 1860s and 1870s illuminates the prominent place this form of organizing had in Black conceptions of freedom and citizenship early on. At the same time, Republican party activists who were there to help mobilize Black voting sometimes were held back by men in Washington unsympathetic to Black labor struggles. Strikes held, for instance, by people in a Black settlement known as Lincolnsville, Virginia (near Portsmouth), prompted the National Council of the Union League to shut down the start of any further league divisions in the area.[69]

4 **NORTH CAROLINA**
Custody

Custody: Protection: NOUNS: **2.** protectorship, guardianship, **care,** charge, . . . auspices, patronage, tutelage, guidance . . . **Imprisonment:** N.: **21.** under arrest, **in custody** . . . in hold.
—*Roget's International Thesaurus*, 3rd ed. (1965)

On March 14, 1862, US troops took the upper coastline of North Carolina and the town of New Bern, prompting a wave of flight from plantations in the area, which became the Department of North Carolina. Camps developed in New Bern, Beaufort, Plymouth Island, Roanoke Island, and other sites. By midsummer, as in Virginia, ten thousand refugees had arrived to this coastal area. North Carolina's freedpeople would henceforth share some of the experiences of battle, resource scarcities, and unpaid labor with people in Virginia, where the military command was based. The next year the occupied areas were named part of the Departments of Virginia and North Carolina, to which sixty-four thousand Blacks had arrived by the end of 1863. The state's developing settlements and activity would begin the creation of an interstate circuit that grew along the Atlantic coast as the Emancipation Circuit. The ties that emerge with Virginia and points north, as well as with Blacks in the state's interior, would prompt mass mobilization.

In Beaufort, North Carolina, fugitives began to perform religious practices in public spaces, especially baptisms and funerals, the emotive expressions of which evidently surprised, even disturbed, Northern soldiers.

People went to the Baptist church established earlier by free people of color, and a second church was formed as well. Communities with churches run by free Blacks may have been few and far between, but wherever they existed, they became foundational for wider development of congregations as in Beaufort.[1]

When Black North Carolinians petitioned for more resources or pay for work done, they were seeking relief from the same sources petitioned by Black Virginians. Freedpeople in northern regions of the state sometimes fled into Virginia, and some others were taken by military from contraband camps into Virginia for work behind military lines. And like people in Virginia, they saw fighting come into the areas where they had taken shelter, causing terror and privation.[2]

African Americans in North Carolina, from leaders to laborers and sailors who fled slavery, show ways in which fugitives organized themselves in groups to deal with common problems and made new iterations of the word *we*. They provide a window into the process by which people spoke for themselves to the public and to military authorities and the US Congress as we, the members of a refugee encampment, we as "contrabands of war," we as conscripted laborers, and increasingly we as a race. *We* as a term denoting race had a greater breadth than *we* as denoting enslaved people, overriding the specific restrictions or privileges of the caste divisions of the slave system. We as a race may have been used by Black folk from different circumstances in the North, but we as a race in the South added four million bodies to the meaning, embracing an immense geography and many complexities of ethnicity and regional cultures. New iterations of the word *we* are foundational to the new knowledge regime built by survivors of the slave system and their allies during and after the Civil War.

North Carolinian freedpeople also showed through their public protests and claims an insistent awareness of the demands made by the rhetoric of military edicts, local newspapers, and missionaries that they not have their hands out for help from society. They often repeated their willingness to wage an inch-by-inch struggle to build lives for themselves, whether as laborers, mothers, or leaders. Blacks in North Carolina, along with other early assemblies such as in Tennessee, set up mechanisms for documenting their condition and, like most early meetings, heard testimony of injustices. They also exploited silences and gaps in law between slave law and the Black codes that did not address the new realities, such as the formation of autonomous Black families. They inserted viable autonomous family life into negotiations which insisted that the military or local judges could break up families to use the labor of one group or another from within the families. While we may assume that autonomous family life is a right, freedpeople began the process of forcing society to conceive of it as a universal human right, rather than a white privilege.

The local organizing already occurring in 1862 among freedpeople when encounters began with military officials, missionaries, and political activists often caught the newly arrived northerners by surprise. Some signs of their community associations went unremarked, as when the military or the Freedmen's Bureau received protests from local Black fire engine companies or an organization of Black women street vendors. To those opposing real freedom, freedpeople's demands could seem outrageous—such as integrating the local police force—and were sometimes characterized as such, but these reactions should not obscure recognition that the demands are indications of self-interest overlooked by others in their midst driving early political demands. A vivid, and theatrical, example is one of the first standoffs created by freedpeople at the refugee camp in New Bern, North Carolina, who were being sought for military enlistment.

In 1862, Abraham Galloway (1837–70), a young man who had escaped North Carolina in 1857 stowed away in a barrel on a ship to Philadelphia, and then got to Canada, was based at Fort Monroe as a spy. He had been sent to General Butler by a Boston abolitionist and began to work for him as a spy, on "special missions" on the Virginia and North Carolina coasts. He is thought to have either enlisted enslaved pilots or gathered information from them on potential Union landing sites. Galloway is said to have had a network of spies working "from thirty to three hundred miles within enemy lines." He also began to work in North Carolina camps, moving between New Bern (which by 1864 would have 8,591 refugees) and Beaufort (refugee population of 2,426), doing basic community building and political education.[3] He was born in Brunswick County, North Carolina, the son of a wealthy planter and an enslaved woman. He was sold in infancy to a Wilmington railroad mechanic and, like Teamoh, was put to work laying bricks but allowed to seek his own work in exchange for fifteen dollars per month. Galloway took up abolitionist work in Ontario and in Boston. As freedmen, he and George Teamoh of Virginia were on Black activist circuits that were connected, and Galloway traveled routinely between the two circuits.[4] Working with Black women organizing relief, especially a group led by local leader Mary Ann Starkey, gave Galloway significant insight into the needs and talents of women who became heads of camp households when men were compelled to work or soldier. These experiences informed his later advocacy as an officeholder on behalf of Black women, and for the vote for all women. Starkey, then in her thirties, ran a school in her home, as well as holding political meetings, and the two activists raised money and supplies for freedpeople.[5]

Taking Custody to Make Demands

In early 1863, as vividly recounted by David Cecelski, when Edward Kinsley, an army recruiting agent, came to New Bern looking for Black men, none would sign up, and people told him to see Galloway. Clearly, some of the men had discussed among themselves and with Galloway the issues enlisting posed for men who may have just been reunited with their families and who reasonably expected capture by Confederates to be a death sentence. If the South was not seen as a separate country by General Benjamin Butler or President Lincoln when contraband status and emancipation for Blacks were deemed possible and advantageous, refugees from the slavery system knew that the South was a different country for them. For those men and their families, statelessness was an issue depriving them of control over their lives, or even the simple protections that freedom would seem to have offered. Despite what may have been an intense desire to fight in the war, it was necessary in negotiations with outsiders to make visible the fugitive aspects of de jure freedom and to shore up the provisional benefits of entry into the war. After a few failed meetings, Kinsley asked to meet Galloway and was given a date to appear at midnight at Starkey's home, where he was blindfolded and led to an upper floor:

> When the blindfold came off, as Kinsley later recounted, "he could see by the dim light of the candle that the room was nearly filled with blacks, and right in front of them stood Abraham Galloway and another huge negro [sic], both armed with revolvers." That night the convocation of liberated slaves did not mince words. If the Union intended to make the war a crusade for black freedom, then Kinsley would find no shortage of recruits in New Bern. If the Federal army planned to use black men like chattel and wage a war merely for the preservation of the Union, that was another story. . . . They bluntly listed their demands: equal pay, provisions for black soldiers' families, schooling for soldiers' children, and assurances that the Union would force the Confederacy

to treat captured blacks as prisoners of war rather than execute them as traitors.[6]

The demands were obviously informed by news on the common wind of the problems Black soldiers suffered with regard to lower pay and the peril of capture. Their demands for their families were plain attempts to protect people in danger of illness and starvation apart from the threat of capture by Confederates. The next day hundreds of men appeared for enlistment, a visible sign of the level of cooperation among the refugees and their trust in the designated negotiators. These are the kinds of tools applied to numerous situations where freedpeople were creating space for deliberations or negotiating relief from various hazards: showing force of numbers and force of arms, reaching consensus in planning, and delegating leaders for petitioning the military or local agencies. With outsiders seeking their cooperation, they sought to arrange for as much control as possible, as in New Bern; policing a meeting was a commonplace practice of nineteenth-century Blackness, before and after abolition. According to Cecelski, "The more than 5,000 African Americans eventually recruited in New Bern, most of them former slaves, became the core of the 35th, 36th, and 37th Regiments, United States Colored Troops, known originally as the African Brigade."[7]

Wartime Labor = Custody = Impressment

In November 1863, some fifty miles south, freedpeople referring to themselves as "Colored Citizens of the town of Beaufort" wrote on behalf of the Black population there to the state military commander, saying the community was being "oppressed by the military authorities in this Vicenity." Their complaint was that people were being "undiscrimatly impressed by the authorities to labor upon the Public works without compensation" and "that in Consequence of this System of fource [sic] labor they Have no means of paying Rents and otherwise Providing for their families." The petitioners offered their wholehearted willingness to aid the "cause of the union," in any way but consistent with their rights. Both of these wartime encounters with demands from these slave system survivors show them organizing themselves to negotiate around issues not only from the standpoint of protecting the right to choose freely to commit one's body to service or labor but also with the goal of feeding and sheltering all members of the community by the use of their worth as able-bodied men. In North

Carolina this organizing would continue through the last days of the war, especially over men being impressed for labor near battlefronts without being honestly informed as to where or why they were being moved at gunpoint.[8]

Six days after the Beaufort citizens posted their letter to Major General Benjamin F. Butler, he issued a long general order prominently announcing that "the recruitment of colored troops has become the settled purpose of the Government." Within the order is one of the primary maxims repeated by those from outside the slave system attempting to guide or aid freedpeople: "Political freedom rightly defined is liberty to work." It then says that no one should enjoy the fruits of another's labor—not as an alert to southerners unwilling to abandon the idea of forcing work from the lash but to inform the entire military occupation apparatus and the public that Black people, who well understood what it was to watch people live on the labor of their generations, would not be permitted to live off the labor of anyone else. Thus, the general warns "no subsistence will be permitted to any negro or his family with whom he lives, who is able to work and does not work." He declares it the duty of the superintendent of Negro affairs to provide work for "all the negroes able to labor . . . and that any negro who refuses to work when able, and neglects his family, will be arrested, and reported to these Head Quarters to be sent to labor on the fortifications, where he will be made to work."[9] These powers, once exercised to force labor from anyone deemed as refusing to work (and sometimes without any such report), caused groups of freedpeople to construct means of collective response to the loss of basic human rights for the duration of the war.

A report from the superintendent of Negro affairs in July 1864 shows the perils presented by the war itself for freedpeople taking shelter on the coast. The Confederates had attacked New Bern in February, forcing all civilians in the area inside the federal lines, and attacked again two months later. Superintendent Horace James reported that during these crises, "the negros came flocking into town for protection, and I was especially busy in feeding, sheltering, and caring for their comfort, as well as in arming and organizing some fifteen hundred of the men to aid in the defence of the city." He was then ordered to construct living space for freedpeople living outside of the town and to move them. A thousand houses were built on one hundred acres, and five thousand people took up residence. He specifies that only one-fourth of that population received rations.[10]

In September, forty-five men, calling themselves "contrabands from Roanoke Island" (North Carolina), wrote to General Butler from Bermuda

Hundred, Virginia, where they had been taken by force. They said that they had spent four weeks in August building breastworks on the island where they lived when told to report to headquarters for their pay. "When we got there, a guard of soldiers was put over us, and we marched on board a steamer, at the point of the bayonet. we were told the paymaster was on board the steamer, to pay us, then we was to go to Fortress Monroe. then told that we was going to Dutch Gap to be paid. true we was on the way to Dutch Gap to work on the canal." In fact, they were pressed into service because General Butler wanted a canal dug at the site.[11]

Most disturbing to the men was the treatment of other members of their community:

> the soldiers broke into the coulored people's house's taken sick men out of bed. men that had sick wives, and men that had large family's of children and no wife or person to cut wood for them or take care of them, were taken, and not asked one question or word about going. had we been asked to go to dutch gap a large number would have gone without causeing the suffering that has been caused. we are willing to go where our labour is wanted . . . and feel it is our duty to help the government all we can.

In closing, the men attest to the veracity of their claims in language that resonates throughout the written protests of freedpeople organizing after abolition: "These thing's are not gess'd at but things that can be prove'd by those that saw them."[12]

Taking Custody of Ideas of Freedom

During the spring of 1864, Abraham Galloway traveled on behalf of the freedpeople of his area. In May, according to Cecelski, he went to Washington as "part of a five-man delegation of black leaders who met with President Lincoln to urge him to endorse suffrage for all African Americans." On May 11, that same delegation visited New York City to promote the suffrage cause, and Galloway spoke that evening at the African Methodist Episcopal Church. Earlier that day the group visited the offices of the militant Black newspaper, the *Anglo-African* (1859–65), run by the brothers Thomas and Robert Hamilton. There he met a fellow North Carolinian, William Gould, who had also escaped slavery—in his case with friends in a rowboat to a Union boat in the Atlantic, on which he became a sailor with the US Navy. From the time of his arrival on the Union boat, Gould kept a diary and occasionally received copies of the *Anglo-African*. His service with Black and white sailors came to shape his interest in the cause of the race. According to Christopher Hager, Gould's diary started first as an accounting of labor performed each day and sometimes referred to everyone on the boat as "we," but in 1864 Gould began to use the plural definer as a Black collective pronoun, only referring to himself and other African Americans as "we." This lone fugitive from the system began to construct his identity as part of a new "we," a people imagining a horizon beyond bondage. Around the time of his visit to the newspaper, he led a drive among his fellow Black sailors to purchase subscriptions to the Hamiltons' paper for Blacks serving in the army. Such encounters among fugitives, which had for decades been been part of network building in the North, continued throughout the war, and after, as part of the recognition of the emergence of a new "we." The significance of a pronoun in one sailor's diary and the efforts of the Hamiltons, Galloway, Gould, and others to create communications among Blacks who were escaping the reach of the Confederacy were a recognition that collective action would be needed to create new possible futures. These veterans of Black life in the North knew that with the death of the noun *slave*, people would have to struggle with two nouns that could reconstitute the old system—*race* and *racism*.[13]

In October 1864, Galloway traveled to Syracuse, New York, for the National Convention of Colored Men, which attempted to imagine African American lives after the end of the slave system. The meeting was the last of a series of conventions spanning more than three decades that grew out of the prewar Black abolitionist movement. The conventions brought together leaders from across the North who had ongoing ties to fugitives from slavery in the South. By 1864, there were participants from the South as well, like Galloway, and including Edmonia Highgate, who worked as a teacher on the Tidewater Virginia circuit and then in Louisiana and Mississippi. Until that year the conventions were named "of colored men" (abolitionist Mary Ann Shadd Cary was the lone woman to have spoken at one), but in 1864 the writer Frances Ellen Watkins Harper spoke, as did Highgate, who was introduced by legendary abolitionist Frederick Douglass.[14] These would have been important voices for Galloway to hear, and among the most progressive female public voices he or most of the men present would have heard at the time.

The convention founded the National Equal Rights League (NERL), looking toward work to be done after the war. It was a meeting where Galloway might have seen people from Boston with whom he had ties, and perhaps might have met Douglass and abolitionists Henry Highland Gar-net and William Wells Brown. But, more important to his work at home, he would have encountered, in addition to Highgate, five organizers from Virginia, three of whom were in the region of his regular travels, as well as nine others organizing in Florida, Louisiana, Mississippi, and Tennessee.[15]

Immediately following the convention, Galloway had the opportunity to get to know James H. Ingraham of Louisiana, who was greeted as a hero for his service with Black troops at Port Hudson. Galloway shared speak-ing engagements with Ingraham after the conference. They were the same age and shared both similar biracial backgrounds and on-the-ground expo-sure to the arrival of fugitives to army and refugee camps. Ingraham would also emerge as a dynamic organizer and leader, especially around the right to vote. Like Galloway, in Reconstruction Ingraham would become a state senator (see chapter 9 on Louisiana). Both men were made vice presidents of the NERL and in that capacity visited several sites in the North to spread the word of the consensus reached at the Syracuse meeting and the found-ing of the league. Once back in North Carolina, Galloway organized five local chapters of the NERL and a statewide chapter. These linked groups, which had specific postwar political agendas such as seeking the right to vote, were part of the process that put Blacks on the coastal waterways in connection with northern and other southern communities also imagining new possible futures as the war collapsed the slave system and as continu-ous pressures threatened horizons still in formation.[16]

In March 1865, the men of Roanoke Island were still fighting to keep the horizon of survival in view despite continuing to find that "those head men [under the superintendent of Negro affairs] have done every thing to us that our masters have done except by [buy] and Sell us and now they are Trying to Starve the woman & children to death cutting off they ration." A new contingent took up the protests as the men taken away earlier had not returned. They wrote several letters dated March 9. The first letter addressed the fact that men were still being conscripted, and among those taken earlier, "Some Got Kill Some died and . . . they taken us just like we had been dum beast." The third letter posed a question regarding other matters: "We want to know from the Secretary of War [if the superinten-dent of Negro affairs] has any wright to take our boy Children from us and from the School and Send them to newbern to work to pay for they ration without they parent Consint." The authors say that there were difficulties with sending children to school, but "rather then they Should Go without learning we thought we would try and doe it." However, they relate that the man in charge of rations had gone to all the white schoolteachers and told them to give the Black boys "orders" to go get rations on a certain day, "so the negros as we are Call are use to the Cesesh plots Suspicion the Game they was Going to play and a Greate many never Sent they Children."[17] The fourth letter of March 9 details the travails of being deceived over pay, though they had not been paid in three years. It stated, "So all we wants is a Chance and we can Get a living like White men. we are praying to God every day for the war to Stop So we wont be beholding to the Government for Something to Eat."[18]

Abraham Galloway spoke on July 4, 1865, at a celebration in Beaufort attended by two thousand people organized by the Salmon P. Chase Equal Rights League. Like his peers elsewhere in the South, he asked for no special treatment but "all equal rights before the law, and nothing more."[19] Little more than a week after the Fourth of July celebrations, the provisional governor of the state received a letter from the mayor of Wilmington warning that "it is generally believed in this community that some insurrectionary movement is contemplated by the colored citizens of this Town," and asking that Black troops be removed because they were believed to be part of the conspiracy. The district commander of Wilmington wrote his headquarters that "no evidence whatever can be discovered of any *secret* organizations among the negroes."[20] The commander's letter is evidence of the Black political organization in place in Wilmington less than three months after the war's end. He reported that the town had several branches of the Equal Rights League, adding that the group's bylaws and membership were open, and "their object is both honest and laudable." He deemed the local Black leaders to be people "of excellent sense." In a separate telegram, he said, "The real danger is to the blacks so soon as military protection shall be withdrawn." A petition was delivered to the mayor from the league chapters and "the colored Fire Engine Companies" asking that Blacks make up half of the local police force. The request was denied.[21]

In August, Galloway appeared as a leader at a mass meeting in New Bern to set a political agenda. It is tempting to surmise that by then Galloway may have had reports of the Nashville convention earlier that month as the rally called for North Carolina to have a freedpeople's convention, and when Galloway called for voting rights and public schools as had the gentlemen in Tennessee, he echoed the veteran who opened that convention, declaring, "If the negro knows how to use the cartridge box, he knows how to use the ballot box." The mass meeting endorsed the need for the franchise and public schools and, in a pattern occurring in other Black state conventions and meetings, took testimony on brutality to freedpeople. The attendees protested the pattern of defrauding farm laborers of their pay, as well as enforcement of the old slave codes that barred Blacks from schools and "deny us the right to control our families, [and] that reject our testimony in courts of justice." The group asked Galloway and two others to call a statewide Black convention.[22]

The dangers of the organizing process became acute in states planning statewide conventions of freedpeople. Following the call for a North Carolina convention, white students from the University of North Carolina attacked a Black meeting in Chapel Hill where people were selecting delegates, and also assaulted the meeting of a Black secret society hearing a speaker from Raleigh. Whites in all the states where Blacks held conventions in 1865 and 1866 went to lengths to discourage, threaten, or prevent people from attending. Black communities took up collections to provide transportation for delegates. Local white actions to sabotage the meetings varied from threats of murder, loss of employment, or the destruction of homes to bribery and boycotts by clients of self-employed people in trades such as carpentry or barbering.[23]

The State Convention of the Colored People of North Carolina was held September 29, 1865, at the Loyal AME Church in Raleigh, bringing together 150 delegates from several dozen counties, with the largest numbers coming from the Union-occupied coast for the simple reason that local threats and transportation problems prevented many in the interior from going. In language closely echoing that of the Tennessee meeting, the convention president listed the aims of the state's Black activists: the right to testify in court, to sit on juries, to act as attorneys in court, and to gain the franchise. But the North Carolina convention produced no resolutions on these aims. The business committee advised freedpeople against "crowding into towns and cities" and declared "the first wants of the colored people to be employment at fair wages, in various branches of industry." Galloway evidently failed to stem the conciliatory tone of the meeting but left an impression: "his power of sarcasm and brutal invective, and the personal influence given him by his fearlessness and audacity, always secured him a hearing."[24] In a pattern beginning across the South, freedpeople had their conventions just as conservative-run constitutional conventions opened in state capitals to draft black codes—laws severely limiting freedpeople's rights. The group notably hailed recent events beneficial to freedpeople and included praise for the 1862 US recognitions of the Independence of Hayti and the Republic of Liberia. The North Carolina convention appointed three people to try to speak to the white convention and seek "favorable legislation," as the Tennessee group had done, efforts all must have known to be hopeless except as an attempt to put Black political speech in the legislative record for the first time.[25]

Custody as Making Autonomous Families

The political organizing of the emancipation era was focused on joining the body politic; the concurrent improvised drive to form autonomous families or reconstitute earlier families in freedom was made by individuals. Families struggled to locate loved ones sold away even during the war, and other families were separated by the war itself, particularly after Black men were able to enlist. The existence and prevalence of concubinage came to light as well during encounters between women and Freedmen's Bureau agents, missionaries, and military superintendents for refugees. By the time of the constitutional conventions in 1867–68, the nascent Black leadership had seen the broad systemic intervention that would be required to help families whose size had been increased by the breeding of children for profit. This would drive some legislative proposals for relief for the poor, elimination of imprisonment for debt, reparations or back wages owed since emancipation, and child support from planters engaged in concubinage. As a subject of legislation, support for the many children living with single female parents died under white reluctance to acknowledge the fact of white paternity of many of the children, and a refusal to seriously confront female-headed households as viable. At the same time there was a parallel insistence from those lawmakers on establishing enforcement for Black paternal support for biological offspring and any other children born to their wives.

Before those debates even took place, however, many women took action. Some would benefit after the war from pensions owed soldiers, which sometimes required women to testify to experiences of concubinage, but often the first step was to seek custody and child support in local and state courts. Innovation in the face of silence in the law regarding Black female custody of children (and difficulties facing any women seeking custody) fell to formerly enslaved women who were willing to pioneer routes to custody, which meant fighting apprenticeship laws designed to maintain the slave system's child labor force.[26]

The apprenticeship laws in the state's 1866 black codes disproportionately affected women with children emerging from slavery because the new legal structure outlined parental obligations but did not fully recognize parental rights. The law was also vague in granting custody to others based on the impression that Black parents "do not habitually employ their time in some honest, industrious occupation."[27] The laws totally neglected the parental rights of unmarried women, Black or white, seriously handicapping victims of concubinage and/or forced breeding practices. While the rights of Black male parents were not yet clear in the law either, the conventions of the day—which discriminated against unmarried mothers of all colors—put freedwomen at a greater disadvantage. That their situation was recognized by Black men after the war, and later as some were elected to office, marks a departure from political norms of the day. Once in office, Black legislators were of course sure to be unsuccessful with legislation for child support from all biological fathers in a society that never accepted the reality that in the South children were bred for profit. Thus, the state courts were forced to face individual crises arising from the denial of the integrity of Black families, many of which were created by the slave system.

The complexity of establishing parental rights is shown in cases the Freedmen's Bureau took to court. When those writing the 1866 black codes simply took out references to race, they left openings for Black parents to assert their rights to their children. According to the codes, the children of freedwomen, freedmen, and unmarried white women were all eligible for "apprenticeship." Black children were usually taken into apprenticeships by their former slaveholders, who made the arrangements with a judge and/ or the Freedmen's Bureau without consulting or even notifying the parents. Karin Zipf, studying women in North Carolina, has shown that numerous people "challenged the indentures. . . . By doing so, freedmen and freedwomen not only questioned apprenticeship law, but they also attacked the very foundation of nineteenth-century citizenship ideals."[28]

In 1866, Lucy Ross set up a household near Wilmington with her brother, William James, and her two daughters, Maria, sixteen years old, and Delia, aged twelve. One night she woke up to find two white men with pistols in the act of abducting her daughters. One of the men was the overseer from her former owner's plantation, and the other was a policeman. When James angrily objected to the abduction, he was arrested. The next day Ross went to Wilmington and found her daughters in jail with other children who had been taken and eventually learned that all the children had been apprenticed to her former slaveholder, Daniel Lindsay Russell Sr., by a judge in his county, quite a distance away. She saw Russell take her daughters off in a wagon.[29]

Even though Russell himself was a judge and had been a delegate to the very constitutional convention that passed the black codes, Ross sought legal remedy. She went to the Freedmen's Bureau, which was sympathetic not only due to her emotional suffering but because the labor of children was essential for most working families to survive, and planters who stole the labor of those children could deny a family its autonomy. Ross made an important intervention by setting out to prove she was head of her household, a status also just then being tested by Black men when it came to child custody. She testified, "I am able and willing to support my children," and stated that her teenage daughters could earn decent wages. A number of men came to court to vouch for Ross's ability to be head of a household; two of her brothers and a neighbor gave depositions attesting that she supported her family independently. Her neighbor testified Ross was "freely able to support her children, having made a good crop during the past season." When the bureau canceled the apprenticeships on the basis that whites were usually notified if their children were indentured and that the Civil Rights Act allowed no differences based on race, Russell simply refused to comply. Her suit served not only to challenge the court to normalize the Black family in the law but also to set a precedent for various iterations of family in contravention of ideals of the era. Though the slavery system had been abolished, and people ignored white paternity, southern society seemed to easily tolerate the idea that Black children be taken from parents by former slaveholders. Ross challenged the convention regarding who could be a head of household as well as discrimination against single mothers. But Ross's lawyers thought granting custody to a single mother was a change no judge would want to author. They chose to fight the apprenticeships with a married couple.[30]

Women in the North often worked outside the home in domestic or factory work, sometimes along with their children. African American women in the North, most of whom did domestic work, had long faced a need for childcare outside the home. Christy Clark-Pujara writes of some such women: "Race-based economic discrimination necessitated the near universal need for black mothers to work outside of the home even while their children were very young. Moreover, in port cities like Providence [Rhode Island] many black households were supported by sailors who were often gone for weeks and months at a time leaving the task of securing childcare to working mothers." The daily absence of one or both parents faced by northern Black women anticipated the common instances of the issue for the much larger population of southern freedpeople. In the case of the Black community in Providence, which numbered about sixteen hundred in 1840, Clark-Pujara found the following: "In the transition from slavery to freedom black Rhode Islanders struggled to maintain and build their families, including using an institution intended to serve orphans as a childcare center and boarding school." Parents there put children in the orphanage and reclaimed them in such a repeated pattern that the institution transformed its mission to aid working mothers.[31]

Even before the end of the war, southern Black organizations also founded orphanages, due to the displacement and separation of children resulting from the slave system and the war. According to Jim Downs, "Over 50 asylums for dependent former slaves were set up in the South [by the Freedmen's Bureau], serving thousands of freedpeople from 1866 to 1870." These institutions served the young, old, and disabled, and as Downs points out were "not adequate to respond to the needs of a population of over four million." The bureau estimated there were "roughly 40 orphanages in operation during Reconstruction." This number seems low as it is easy to find documentation of nearly a dozen orphanages in cities like Charleston and New Orleans. Institutions founded by Blacks in New Orleans, Memphis, Charleston, and other cities became cornerstones for social services that developed over time, lasting long past Reconstruction. But even in the 1860s, some parents were leaving children only temporarily in response to vicissitudes of wage earning or other difficulties. Children placed for short terms were known as *half-orphans*. Jim Downs writes of the development and diverse uses of orphanages, especially in the South, following the war: "Many of these 'half-orphans' had mothers who were temporarily unable to provide for them." If parents got sick, children might also board temporarily. This situation, then, also affords a glimpse into the connection between Black women becoming heads of households in the South, seeking custody in the absence of partners and suing for child support from fathers denying relation to children, and the long-term survival of community-based social services begun by freedpeople.[32]

Though custody was not the issue for many women in the North in Clark-Pujara's study, childcare did play a role for women attempting to secure custody. Southern women like Ross could establish that they were sole providers, particularly if they cited that the children's father had been sold while enslaved, that unique hardship being tantamount to death or divorce as far as maintaining the rights of an absent partner. Those farming could assert that they were also at home to supervise and care for younger children. Even in the remnants of the old regime, which utilized older women to take care of multiple children for women working in the fields, communal or extended family childcare did not require the kinds of monthly costs northern women often took on to place their children in boarding settings for care and school instruction. Freedwomen in the South who were not tending their own cash crops tended to work both in the fields at harvesttime and in domestic work for weekly or monthly cash income. Many sought work outside of the fields both to secure cash for monthly needs because planters paid only once a year and to secure a higher degree of autonomy and safety. Ross was well situated with regard to all these factors.[33]

The bureau lawyers took up a case like Ross's but with Wiley Ambrose and Hepsey Saunders, who had three children abducted, also by Russell, who had also once held that family as property. Saunders, the mother, had twice retrieved the children, once with a bureau order and once without. Russell had threatened to jail both parents. But Ambrose and Saunders's children still technically fell between the cracks of existing law. Russell and the governor felt that Ambrose and Saunders "lacked the unquestioned claims to independence white male citizens possessed."[34] This question of "unquestioned" independence akin to that supposedly possessed by all white males was, of course, a status determined by subjective means, inviting a judge to measure a Black man's freedom by his own and that of his peers. As is clear in the phrasing, such judgments also did not take into consideration the possibility of any females possessing independence. The state supreme court basically did not choose to rule based on the couple's independence but opted instead to decide the case on the fact that the parents and children had not been notified. Again, at a moment when there was no settled law on which to rely, change was possible. The court chose the smallest feasible degree of change and ruled the parents should have been notified of the apprenticeship court proceeding and voided the indentures. But in this moment of contingency, the bureau and parents enlarged the impact of the ruling by canceling or challenging all apprenticeships ordered without parental notification. Single Black women parents objected to apprenticeships and claimed their rights as heads of households due to the fathers having been sold by the slave system or that the fathers were whites who denied paternity. According to Zipf, "Freedmen's Bureau records are replete with letters from freedwomen demanding the return of their children who had been bound out without their permission." The appearance of women in court asking to be named heads of households is a facet of the change in conditions brought by Black women after abolition and one that further empowered drives for autonomy among freedpeople.[35]

Making Political Voice

In 1872, when Democratic lawmakers created the Second Congressional District of North Carolina, which would become known as the Black Second, more than one-fifth of the state's Black population lived in its dozen counties. While these counties had a marked percentage of Black landownership, especially where land was less prized and cheaper, such as in Halifax and Warren, those who were not able to meet the daunting conditions for acquiring land often moved in search of better prospects. Others who stayed fought for more profitable use of their time than had been provided by the routine of the slavery regime. The heart of the Emancipation Circuit in North Carolina on the Virginia border was a rural area where cotton and bright leaf tobacco were produced and moved by waterways to the Atlantic. It was so important to the economy that it regained railway access after the war, and as rails were rebuilt, they facilitated Black connections. This area, like many others in the South, experienced a labor shortage after the war created by the unwillingness of freedpeople to work slavery hours. The shortening of workdays (by about a third) achieved by freedpeople allowed them to build their own lives. According to Eric Anderson, "Across the South, black per capita work hours fell by about one third after the exhausting discipline of the lash was removed, leaving the former masters with a labor shortage." In some cases, Anderson points out, shorter hours or wage increases were won by large numbers acting in concert to threaten to migrate. Farmworkers in Edgecombe County struck in 1870 (asking fifteen dollars per month) and 1874 (for "a dollar a day and board"). After a loss of many workers in that county in 1871, a Tarboro paper reported that "those who remained behind threatened 'to move to Louisiana *en masse*' unless they received a larger share of the harvest." This, of course, is also an indication of the kind of cohesion and mobilization that could be found among freedpeople on labor issues as tensions arose around wage earning, childcare, growing adequate food for survival, and vending for much-needed cash.[36]

Political organizing and resistance to Black political organizing began immediately upon word of the franchise being given to African American males. One of the "circuit rider" organizers who began work in the state was Republican activist James E. O'Hara, who arrived in New Bern during the war once federal forces began occupation in the area. He wrote to the URCC in July 1867 from Goldsboro, an important railroad junction for cotton transport, asking for another organizer to help. "I keep moving but find it a hard task to fill all my appointments as I have to travel a great deal by day and night and very often ten or fifteen miles on foot. I hope the Committee will furnish further aid and enable me to take some one with me in the field for the harvest is truly plentiful but the laborers are few." O'Hara, a native of New York raised in the Virgin Islands, came to North Carolina in 1862 with missionaries, living first in New Bern, then Goldsboro. He became immersed in the emerging Black politics, starting with serving as secretary for the 1866 North Carolina Freedmen's Convention, as president of the Educational Association of the Colored People of North Carolina, and then joining Republican Party politics. In time O'Hara became a US congressman from the Black Second and one of the most powerful African Americans ever elected to office in the state.[37] He worked at the 1868 constitutional convention, studied law at Howard University when its law school opened in 1869, and became a prosperous attorney in North Carolina.

A seemingly minor development in North Carolina points to the resistance arising in opposition to the work of people like O'Hara and the lasting consequences of fear of Black voting. In December 1866, Freedmen's Bureau agent Robert Avery reported to his commander on the practice of civil authorities using or creating criminal records to ensure that Black males could not vote, should they be given that right. Avery wrote that officials had the habit "in various parts of North Carolina, in whipping negroes, ostensibly as a punishment for petty crimes, but in fact with the purpose of disqualifying them in advance from ever exercising the elective franchise . . . should that right be hereafter extended by the law of the land to people of color." They were using "longstanding state laws that made numerous offenses (including petty theft) punishable by whipping and also defined them as infamous crimes, upon conviction for which an offender forfeited his citizenship rights."[38] In the best-case scenario, a person could regain citizenship rights after four years if five "respectable" (likely white) people testified to good behavior. Avery himself heard one state legislator recommending the tactic: "We are licking them in our part of the State and if we keep on we can lick them all by next year, and none of them can vote." Avery wrote that "the assurance comes to me in so many forms, and so frequently on this subject that I cannot resist the conviction that there is a deliberate and a general purpose to seize negroes, procure convictions for petty offenses punishable at the whipping post, and thus disqualify them forever from voting in North Carolina."[39]

The heart of the North Carolina circuit embraces the same waterways worked before the war by the thousands of enslaved watermen. Blacks represented slightly more than a third of the state's population but developed a number of Black majority counties. Like Virginia, North Carolina had no Blacks in major state offices during Reconstruction. The 1868 North Carolina constitutional convention to rewrite the state constitution to regain admission to the Union included fourteen Black delegates.[40] The most enduring structures for political movement were built in the Atlantic counties and in the Black Second area. When mass meetings began on passage of the Reconstruction Acts, a sizable gathering in New Bern (Craven County) was formed by local societies assembling and parading through town. The local paper soon reported meetings in other counties that were relatively nearby (Greene, Jones, Pasquotank) and as far west as Alamance and Person Counties. Heavy opposition also was being built and would result in Ku Klux Klan terror. These early meetings show the geography of political organizing by locals and outsiders. It is important to note, however, that table 4.1 shows Blacks electing delegates to the constitutional convention in three counties with a white population majority (if not a voter registration majority); in fact, Blacks were elected to the convention from four white majority counties and Blacks elected representatives in another white majority county in the 1870s. As Du Bois points out about this state, in 1868, "in [voter] registration, nineteen counties had Negro majorities." That year Black delegates were elected from thirteen counties, and in 1870, Black representatives were elected from sixteen. These are the results of the early organizing in the state.[41]

James H. Harris, of Wake County, who had worked for the Freedmen's Bureau and the Freedmen's Aid Society, became the most highly regarded Black delegate to the constitutional convention. He spoke when some of the conservatives moved to change the wording from the Declaration of Independence; they did not want to include the declaration as we know it but sought to delete "all men are created equal." Harris parsed his reading of the phrase to get the words past those panicked about the idea of "social equality" and into the state constitution: "The Declaration of Independence has only a political and civil meaning. It means that all men are created equally, politically and civilly." By 1872, Harris, who was born free in

North Carolina, had lived in the North, and had been to Liberia and Sierra Leone, had given up his earlier placating tone, saying, "The time had come when the black man demanded and must have perfect social equality for himself and his wife and children" in public places and transport.[42]

Though they proved largely ineffective, the Republicans did get an ordinance in the constitution prohibiting physical and economic voter intimidation, as well as protection for homesteads from involuntary sale for debt. They also blocked a number of attempts to segregate public schools and universities. When conservatives opposed the funding of an office of public instruction, Harris pointed out that conservatives in the last legislature had provided $14,000 to educate the "sons of the aristocracy at Chapel Hill. . . . More had been spent in one year to educate the sons of the gentry, than this Convention proposed to spend on the children of the people for the next ten years."[43]

Abraham Galloway also served as a delegate to the convention, where he argued forcefully for relief for the poor and proposed an amendment for equal rights in conveyances and all business places that died in committee. He served without the ability to read or write. The convention was replete with racial insults from conservatives and the press, such as the *Raleigh Sentinel* saying that "apes and hybrids" were holding a "brutal carnival" in the legislature. This continued when Galloway served in the state senate and he, in turn, apparently routinely reminded his colleagues, especially when others rose to denounce Black men as sexual predators, that white men continued to pursue Black women. He reiterated the facts of his own biracial heritage, specifically that his father was a wealthy planter. This got under the skin of the editors of the *Wilmington Daily Journal*, who took the amusing dodge of calling him the "pugilistic Indian senator" and wrote that he flaunted his "bastardy" in an act of "disgusting vulgarity." Galloway returned home to Wilmington in time to find a KKK terror campaign going on to keep Blacks from voting to ratify the new constitution. He joined a four-night fight that drove out the Klan. Thereafter, he wore a pistol when in town and was elected head of one of Wilmington's several Black militias. Galloway served two years in the senate and survived an assassination attempt before his sudden death at age thirty-three in 1870.[44]

In 1882, James E. O'Hara was elected to Congress on his third try. In the last decades of the century, some men, like John Adams Hyman of Warren County and the Second Congressional District, likely worked with the Democrats to try to gain some offices for Blacks by offering men who were alternatives to more radical Black candidates. In the 1880s, Hyman was seeking conservatives' financial support for an attempt to return to Congress by defeating white Republicans in the Black Second. Democrats wanted to push whites from the Republican Party, but Hyman was an unlikely vehicle for that goal, and he lost. Hyman returned to the Washington area for civil service work. By 1900, a mix of years of gerrymandering (including the creation of five new counties), voter repression laws, and violence ended statewide Black representation for the next sixty-nine years.[45]

Looking at Table 4.1

Table 4.1 shows some of the Emancipation Circuit structure in North Carolina, focusing on rural communities that sent Black elected officials to the capital and developed later movements. The sites with the most documented movement building had developed an array of institutions, including an unusually high presence of Black newspapers. Most of the sites also had labor organizing, though there was less where Black landowners were numerous. The two counties with the highest rates of Black land ownership—Craven County, where by 1900, 51.2 percent of Black farmers owned their land, and Bertie County, where 39.2 percent owned their farms—had no known Knights of Labor groups. Warren and Granville Counties (and later Vance, which was carved out of both) all had Black landowners and also suffered KKK attacks. Edgecombe County, which had the fewest Black landowners in the Black Second District, had more labor organizing. All of these counties except Bertie maintained political organization and representation until 1899. There are doubtless other counties, possibly many, with emigration and self-defense movements beyond those I have found, but ten of the seventeen I looked at had emigration and/or Exoduster movements, which speaks to the fears of the late 1800s in the state. Most Black political circuits grew by organizing the counties adjacent to those where delegates were elected. In North Carolina these were areas easily navigated by rail- or waterways, if horses or wagons were not used. Though Black representation continued to expand, it also met with opposition at the margins of organized areas—margins that would later be redistricted into additional white majority counties, as with Warren and Granville in the heart of the Black Second.[46]

TABLE 4.1 North Carolina Emancipation Circuit, 1870–1900

	Institutions Present							19th Century Activism
	US Troops	RR (1884)	Union League	AMA Schools	Local Black Press	Black Political Reps	Knights of Labor Groups	
Bertie County ß						•		
Caswell County ß		•				•		
CHARLOTTE **Mecklenburg County**		•			4 1880 1882 1884 1890	•	1 M mixed labor	
Chowan County ß	•	•				•		
DURHAM **Durham County (1881)**		•					1 M mixed labor	
FAYETTEVILLE **Cumberland County**					1 1883	•		Kansas exodus
Franklin County ß		•				•		Kansas exodus

NEW BERN Craven County ß	•	<u>6</u> 1867 1868 1879 1885 1886 1890	Voting rights Civil rights Liberia emigration
NORFLEET Halifax County ß	•	<u>2</u> 1884 1888	1 M carpenters & laborers	Civil rights Liberia emigration
OXFORD Granville County ß	•		1 M mixed labor	Election activism Civil rights Black populism
Pasquotank County	•			Liberia emigration
RALEIGH Wake County	•	<u>5</u> 1867 1879 1881 1885 1886	1 M mixed labor	Civil/legal rights Kansas exodus 1 F Temperance group 1 M Temperance group
SALISBURY Rowan County	•	<u>2</u> 1880s 1889		

(Continued)

TABLE 4.1 (*Continued*)

			Institutions Present					19th Century Activism
	US Troops	RR (1884)	Union League	AMA Schools	Local Black Press	Black Political Reps	Knights of Labor Groups	
TARBORO Edgecombe County ß		+	+			+	1 M building trades & shoemakers 1 M & F Black/white, trades unknown	Kansas exodus Farmworker strikes (1870, 1874, 1889, 1900)
Warren County ß		+	+			+		Political hub Civil rights Liberia emigration
WILMINGTON New Hanover County ß	+	+	+	+	<u>2</u> 1883 1890	+	1 M stevedores	Labor Self-defense Anti-KKK Kansas exodus Black populism

SOURCES: *See Table Source Notes* (393–96).

KEY: **Bold** = Site playing multiple roles on the circuit.
ß = Black majority; unless otherwise noted, populations are for 1870.
RR = Rail lines.
Black Political Reps = Black representatives to the 1868 constitutional convention and/or members of the General Assembly.

Knights of Labor = Black assemblies of the labor organization. Most KoL assemblies were segregated by race and gender: white males, Black males, white females, or Black females. "Mixed labor" is a term from the Garlock data (*see* Table Source Notes) and indicates various forms of work, not mixing by race or gender. **Gender** is indicated here by M or F.

SOUTH CAROLINA

Majority

> **Majority:** n. 1 a: a number or percentage equaling more than half of a total; b: the excess of a majority over the remainder of the total: margin; c: **the greater quantity or share;** 2 a: **the age at which full civil rights are accorded;** b: the status of one who has attained this age; 3: the group or political party having the greater number of votes (as in a legislature)
>
> —*Merriam-Webster Online Dictionary* (August 8, 2021)

Due to the fact that perhaps all those who came to South Carolina during the war were preoccupied with putting its huge workforce back in the fields, probably few of them would have been able to predict that the state would develop a Black electorate that would send a Black majority to control the state legislature. The dominant numbers of African Americans in many counties might not have been immediately evident to outsiders staying on the coast. But the military would have been able to look at the same map of the distribution of the enslaved population of the South that Lincoln was consulting and realize that, unlike Virginia and North Carolina, which had numerous western counties with scant Black populations, South Carolina's slavery ports, which brought in Africans by the thousands, had saturated the rice and cotton fields across most of the state with Black laborers.

Union troops came into South Carolina in the late fall of 1861. The coastal area was under the control of the South Carolina Expeditionary

Corps from October 1861 to April 1862. Brigadier General Thomas W. Sherman, commander of the ground forces at Port Royal, South Carolina (no relation to Major General William Tecumseh Sherman), and a man with a low opinion of African Americans, nonetheless did them a favor by writing the War Department in January 1862 asking for teachers for the African Americans in the area. He gave several reasons for his impression that the enslaved people he encountered had not come to offer to work for the army: "1st: They are naturally slothful and indolent, and have always been accustomed to the lash, an aid we do not make use of. 2nd: They appear to be so overjoyed with the change of their condition that their minds are unsettled to any plan." A month later, however, his request for teachers went to Treasury secretary Salmon P. Chase, who would be closely involved in the efforts in South Carolina and elsewhere to bring nongovernmental support for freedpeople for the next several years. Chase saw the need for teachers and missionaries as an opportunity to operate a demonstration case to show the country the gain to be had by offering aid and training to those who had escaped the slave system. And of no small importance, officials wanted the laborers to raise cotton.[1]

South Carolina's journey into and through Reconstruction shows in diverse ways the social nature of the reproduction of political ideology and political formations that is characteristic of the Emancipation Circuit. This chapter also includes an example of the elaborate networks among those still enslaved. African American communities in the state began mobilizing early, taking advantage on the coast of inland waterways linking the enslaved on the Sea Islands and those communities living on land abandoned by the owners. An "experiment" by associates of the occupation in treating refugees of the slave system as capable of independent life also exposed many on the coast to African American and white activists who were themselves defying conventional ideas of womanhood in their sojourns in southern states.

The events that followed the Union occupation in South Carolina began with the military's knowledge from Virginia that its presence would create voluntary displacement of thousands of enslaved people. This simple awareness allowed for commanders to ask the government to build a systematic response. But conditions were not the same as in Virginia, where people toiled on smaller farms, in smaller numbers, raising more diverse crops in the Tidewater area and commercial tobacco in the Piedmont region. South Carolina's massive Black population was held in larger numbers on larger farms than in Virginia, and its work was focused on production of sizable commercial crops of cotton and rice. Also, the way in which people worked on these plantations was different: they operated cooperatively in a mutually understood task system to ensure the survival of their larger communities. Those who had fled to the coast and its islands organized themselves to farm collectivity, eschewed overseers, and in freedom put to use the task work model negotiated in the slave system. Like people in Virginia, coastal folk traveled by boat to share information and to work together on aims. People still trapped on inland farms also worked collectively and had networks within neighborhoods that are shown here to extend hundreds of miles. Outsiders found their dialect strange and their ring shouts in prayer meetings "barbaric," but the absence of owners gave those same outsiders the idea of making coastal South Carolina a test case on freedom.

From the time that Chase decided to raise private aid and send people as employees of the government to train refugees for freedom, a period known as the Port Royal Experiment began to be pieced together. It was dubbed an experiment because most but not all involved thought that freedpeople could become self-sustaining and because many of them, with or without planning and cooperation, set out to prove enslaved people could be "trained" to function in society like whites. By happenstance, abolitionist social networks convened an unusual contingent of actors in Port Royal who aided enslaved people in dismantling the terms on which they had lived in the slave system.[2]

One of those singular persons was Major General David Hunter, commander of the Department of the South. Early on, part of the government's ambivalence about protecting the slave system played out in the area, as it had earlier in Missouri and Virginia. Hunter decided to act on his idea that in a war in which slave states had left the Union, enslaved people under the control of a free country should be free. In April 1862, Hunter conscripted fugitive enslaved men for a Black regiment, which he was then ordered to demobilize. But he did not stop there. In May 1862, he issued General Order No. 11 declaring: "Slavery and martial law in a free country are altogether incompatible; the persons in these three states— Georgia, Florida and South Carolina—heretofore held as slaves, are therefore declared forever free." This did not go over well with President Lincoln, who had already stopped Major General John C. Fremont from the same action in Missouri in 1861. (Hunter had then served under Fremont.) And before that, in May, Major General Benjamin Butler had declared Virginia fugitives as "contraband" not to be returned to owners. Lincoln rescinded

Hunter's order: "Neither General Hunter, nor any other commander, or person, has been authorized by the Government of the United States, to make proclamations declaring the slaves of any State free."[3]

There were other officers in the South who also saw reason to use Black men as soldiers. In compliance with a congressional resolution from border state lawmakers demanding that Hunter answer for continuing to raise troops from among "contrabands," he wrote an unorthodox assessment of his actions: "To the First Question therefore I reply that no regiment of 'Fugitive Slaves' has been, or is being organized in this Department. There is, however, a fine regiment of persons whose late masters are 'Fugitive Rebels,'—men who everywhere fly before the appearance of the National Flag, leaving their servants behind them to shift as best they can for themselves." He described the new soldiers as "working with remarkable industry" to make a successful "pursuit of their fugacious and traitorous proprietors." He denied that anyone who could be described as "fugitive slaves" had been in the area, and held that African Americans had been welcoming and helpful to US forces. In keeping with his inversion of the racialization of fugitivity, Hunter added that he had "clothed, equipped and armed the only loyal regiment yet raised in South Carolina" and that he hoped to have forty-eight to fifty thousand more by the fall.[4]

The War Department finally authorized recruitment of Blacks in August 1862. In fact, in 1863 the famed Massachusetts Fifty-Fourth Regiment would be under Hunter's command in the Second Battle of Fort Wagner. But at this early time, his first impressment of men had not been well received in the refugee community. For many of the men who had fled with their families to the coast, it may have seemed preferable to work in wartime labor, assuming it would allow them to stay with families and not work on Sunday. However, as the men in North Carolina discovered, being a laborer for the military guaranteed neither of these benefits and sometimes did not pay for months. The military was also torn about recruiting men from farms where they were needed if the armed forces were to reestablish agricultural production, even just for local food needs.[5]

Arrivals

In April 1862, the teachers sought by Sherman and Chase began to arrive. Abolitionists in northern cities had formed aid groups, with three organizations most prominently sending teachers to Port Royal during the war: Boston's Educational Commission, New York's Freedmen's Relief

Association, and Philadelphia's Port Royal Relief Association. The Port Royal Relief group sent Laura M. Towne, a thirty-six-year-old white abolitionist, to distribute supplies it had gathered. She became the architect of aid and school development in the area. Trained primarily as a practitioner of homeopathic medicine and having some teaching experience, Towne was situated as housekeeper and secretary to Edward L. Pierce, supervising agent of the Treasury Department for the Department of the South, in charge of freedpeople and the abandoned plantations. (Pierce was chosen because he had been at Fort Monroe dealing with the first "contrabands.") Acting on her own, Towne tended to the sick and began teaching in her residence. She stayed for the rest of her life, nearly forty years, and, along with her friend Ellen Murray, founded the Penn School on St. Helena Island, now known as the Penn Center.[6]

The Boston group had told Black applicant Charlotte Forten that it would not at that time send women, so she went to Philadelphia. In October, the Port Royal Relief Association sent twenty-five-year-old Forten, a young teacher and writer, to South Carolina. When she arrived, Towne and Murray were running a school in the Brick Baptist Church in Frogmore on St. Helena Island. With the local elite having fled, the church had been given to the eight thousand freedpeople in the area, who eagerly welcomed teachers. Forten was born into a Black abolitionist family in Philadelphia, and after the deaths of her mother and grandmother, she was educated by the Massachusetts Black activists Charles Lenox Remond and his wife, Amy Cassey Remond. One of her good friends was William C. Nell, a man twenty years her senior and the Boston activist who mentored Virginian fugitive George Teamoh. She knew a number of the famed abolitionists who spoke in Boston before the war, and she had poetry published in the *Anglo-African* in New York, where North Carolinian fugitives Abraham Galloway and William Gould had ties as well. Forten kept a diary of her experiences in the Port Royal area, and in so doing also documented all the local Black songs she heard, often while being taken by boat between St. Helena and the mainland. Her diary was one of the first memoirs of the time by a Black participant, and her renderings of the local songs were a foundational archive of the music of enslaved African Americans. Forten was fascinated by the landscape and the people on the Carolina coast and stayed until 1864.[7]

Laura Towne also kept journals, and when she brought Forten to live in the house she was using, she recorded the curious reaction that local Black women working in the house had to this northern Black woman. Towne had already noted that the people at the farm, known as The Oaks, acted as though she and other white missionaries were not as genteel as the kind of white people they were used to seeing. Willie Lee Rose writes, "This snobbery of the plantation people was nowhere better demonstrated than at The Oaks when Charlotte Forten arrived." According to Towne, "The people on our place are inclined to question a good deal about 'dat brown gal,' as they call Miss Forten. Aunt Becky required some coaxing to wait upon her and do her room. Aunt Phyllis is especially severe in the tone of her questions. I hope they will respect her. They put on this tone as a kind of reproach to us, I think." However, when Forten, whom Rose describes as "beautiful and delicate," was able to share some of her skills, a second view of her took shape among the Blacks at The Oaks. According to a visitor, "When they heard her *play on the piano*, it quite put them down, and soon all grew fond of her. Miss Towne says 'she is *the* pet and belle of the island.'"[8]

Forten also encountered some of the living legends in the area, one of whom was Robert Smalls, who ran a store serving freedpeople. Smalls, a steamship pilot in slavery, had escaped only months earlier by absconding on a Confederate ship loaded with guns and ammunition, bringing as well his family and families of his crew through Confederate waters to safe harbor with Union forces. The US Congress passed legislation to grant Smalls and his fellow crewmen the prize money for the valuable boat, and in the course of these events, he became quite famous. At Brick Church, Forten heard his story and that he had decided despite making fifty dollars a week [roughly $833 today] as a store owner to give it up in order to enlist. Smalls reportedly said, "How can I expect to keep my freedom if I'm not willing to fight for it?" He actually worked as a civilian for the US Navy and US Army and later became a Reconstruction state representative and one of the first African American members of the US Congress.[9]

Two months after arriving, Forten went to the town of Beaufort on the mainland to meet Harriet Tubman. Tubman, known to many as "Moses" for her work guiding enslaved people to freedom before the war, was another Black abolitionist who came south during the war and in so doing helped to elaborate the development of Emancipation Circuit sites as ports of aid to refugees. At the time of Forten's visit, Tubman was running "an eating house." Forten wrote of being transported by Tubman retelling one of her Underground Railroad journeys and described her eyes tearing up as Tubman sang "the very scraps of jubilant hymns" sung by one man she got to Canada. One month after the war started in 1861, Tubman had trekked from Maryland with General Benjamin Butler's troops to Virginia's Fort Monroe (where Abraham Galloway reported that year as a spy and scout). She worked at the fort in an unofficial capacity, using her experience in working with fugitives and performing domestic work and nursing. Three months after she arrived, one thousand fugitives had taken shelter there. According to Catherine Clinton, "Tubman interpreted flight from the Confederacy as the rising of a race."[10]

Tubman had come to Beaufort in May 1862, seven months before Forten, and worked with the sick and wounded. While in South Carolina she also served as a scout for US forces (though her name was kept secret), essentially tapping into the existing communications networks of locals. From Beaufort, likely in late 1862 or early 1863, Tubman received a request to travel to Fernandina, Florida, to treat patients with dysentery with traditional and herbal remedies, as she had done in South Carolina. When Tubman's scouting work took her back to Florida, it had an impact on Forten's work in ways the teacher may not have known. In March 1863, Forten was also asked to go to Florida, to teach new Black recruits in fighting units there. At the last minute, she was prevented from boarding her ship when informed that the military was evacuating Jacksonville, where she was to land. It happened that early in 1863 Tubman was given the go-ahead to build a network of Black scouts and informants in Florida, and she was listed as commander of the group. Her unit of eight scouts became an "official service of the Department of the South," and that spying operation and the information she provided, according to Clinton, "directly to either General David Hunter or General Rufus Saxton," allowed for the Union forces to plan their attack on Jacksonville March 10–29, which caused Forten's trip to be canceled.[11]

On June 2, 1863, Tubman, back in South Carolina, participated in one of the most famous operations of her life, the Combahee River Raid, during which, according to Tubman, 150 formerly enslaved soldiers were freed, as were more than 756 freedpeople trapped on plantations. The victory ended up exposing Tubman's identity as the prewar liberator "Moses" so despised by slaveholders. This perhaps reminded some northern newspaper readers that African Americans—whether free, formerly enslaved, or fugitives—who went south to help the refugees of slavery took an extra chance with their own lives beyond being exposed to the dangers of war and the diseases then rampant in swampy coastal regions; they could be abducted or killed for assisting escapees. This was also true for the Black soldiers like those of the Massachusetts Fifty-Fourth Regiment, who arrived in Beaufort the day after the Combahee Raid. After serving in other action, they agreed to lead the assault on Fort Wagner on July 18, and that morning Tubman made breakfast for the unit's commanding officer, Colonel Robert Gould Shaw. He was killed that day along with 271 of his men. Wounded white soldiers were sent to a facility on Hilton Head Island, and Black soldiers were brought to Beaufort. According to Clinton, this segregation angered Tubman, whose ire grew upon learning that soldiers were buried in segregated graves. Both Tubman and Forten tended the wounded soldiers, many of whom they knew. Shaw had charmed Forten during several social encounters, and she had prayed for him to be spared even as she heard on July 20 that the battle went badly for the unit. She was devastated four days later on learning his fate and was shocked on a subsequent visit to a friend of Shaw's in the officers' hospital. The wounded major told her that Colonel Shaw had told him that if he was killed he wanted Forten to receive one of the three "very fine spirited" horses he had brought from Massachusetts.[12]

Forten left South Carolina in July 1863 for Philadelphia and later Boston on a doctor's suggestion to overcome the debilitating effects she suffered every summer on the coast. In June 1864, Tubman went to her home in Auburn, New York, suffering her own infirmities and, like Forten, leery of another summer in South Carolina. In March 1865, she returned to Fort Monroe, Virginia, to work with freedpeople and soldiers, and after a July trip to Washington to seek desperately needed help, she was named matron of the Colored Hospital at the fort. By the time of her return, some ten thousand fugitives from slavery had come to the fort, though the assistance she requested did not arrive. Still, the details of the overlapping journeys of these actors in the field of emancipation illustrate ways in which the ground that was laid for local institution building was social in nature. When Fort Monroe's first missionary, Rev. Lewis Lockwood, was departing Virginia, his letters indicate he was asked to go to Beaufort, South Carolina. In this pattern the government itself further elaborated the Emancipation Circuit, deploying private citizens who could set up facilities for distributing goods, building schools and/or hospitals, and putting them in touch with others. In these and other early cases, the aid groups, the government, and the military were sending highly motivated abolitionists who had strong political views and ties to organized groups prepared to help. As they moved, their letters and entreaties for supplies and other hands went to people who endeavored to respond. Contacts such as Tubman and Forten developed also helped to connect ad hoc education in citizenship rights to local Black circuits, not to mention modeling representations of being Black and female that were both iconoclastic modeling empowerment.[13]

A Circuit of Refuge Hundreds of Miles Long

While fugitives who had escaped to the coast of South Carolina waged a struggle for survival and autonomy, many thousands were still living as they always had, trapped on plantations across the rest of the state. The story of the 1864 escape by Union soldier Lieutenant Hannibal A. Johnson and three fellow officers from a Confederate prison camp illustrates the impressive ability of the circuits among enslaved people in South Carolina to communicate and travel across considerable distances, even during the war. The four federal officers, who had been captured in May in Virginia at the Battle of the Wilderness (Johnson, for the second time) and transported to South Carolina, were first imprisoned in Charleston during a federal bombardment, and upon trying to escape from there were shipped to a camp near Columbia. On the night of November 21, after several nights of hearing officers who had escaped being recaptured or shot, the four successfully got out and headed for Union lines at Knoxville, Tennessee, which they guessed to be five hundred miles away. Johnson kept a diary of their travels. They headed in cold weather for a main road, but fortunately for them, they were going in the wrong direction. Moving on foot through unknown woods, on the second night they knocked at a plantation quarters cabin in search of food.

From that cabin, where they were fed and sheltered and warned against the road they had hoped to use, they were guided and handed off from one plantation and guide to another for several weeks, with each guide taking them anywhere from eight to twenty-five miles, leaving them with a new guide and returning the same distance to home. Sometimes three guides would pick them up in the course of one night. People at the Boozier plantation fed them, hid them, and gave them a guide named Frank; people at William Ford's farm fed them and hid and protected them for five nights, having heard General William Tecumseh Sherman might be coming near enough to meet. When that did not pan out, a man named Bob took them a distance, turned them over to George, who kept them three nights and brought along Peter, who turned them over twelve miles away to Joe, who hid them on the Matthews farm. Jim took them eight miles to Arthur, who took them to Vance, after which they followed Charles, David, Hanson, Russel, Dan, Ben, Harrison, Honry, Elijah Waters, Sam Jones, Andrew and another Ned. Russel's community surprised the soldiers with pants, socks, and knit gloves, in addition to food. On December 8 alone, they were guided by Ned, John Wesley, Sandy Latimore, Balus, and Sam Matterson. There are thirty guides mentioned in Johnson's diary, several of whose names have been lost, but it is worth mentioning that the guides took an extra risk in revealing their names. Emmanuel, their last enslaved guide, hid them for three nights before they struck out on their own, got lost, and lucked out on a white Unionist widow, who knew some Unionists hiding in the mountains.[14]

In this fashion they traveled for three weeks along a route headed north and west that was plotted by local Black folk who could connect four soldiers to a town most of the enslaved folk they met would not have visited. They were hidden from hostile eyes and from snow, ice, and rain, and were fed so well and so often they were continually "gaining strength and weight." They traveled the last third of the way with local white Unionist "outliers" through the Appalachian Mountains in freezing and snowy weather over icy trails for two more weeks. Their discreet treks along back trails and through the mountains almost certainly ran up a greater number of miles than the nearly three-hundred-mile distance by today's roads. On the ninth day of this journey, Johnson wrote in his diary: "If such kindness will not make one an abolitionist then his heart must be made of stone." They arrived at a Union camp in the Knoxville area on January 6, 1865.[15]

Johnson's account does not detail the necessary movements invisible to them made by enslaved people who saw to arrangements between plantations before their arrival at the next stop: these would have included a runner (or perhaps a trusted driver) to alert people that they were coming, which in turn spurred the production of four additional dinners, and a trustworthy guide would have to volunteer after an assessment of travel hazards and best routes. Johnson remarked on December 4: "Every mile we advanced toward our journey's end, Tennessee, the stronger was our regard for the poor blacks; for the feeding or assisting an escaping Federal Soldier was the promise of 100 lashes, well laid on. And knowing this would certainly follow, they never failed to meet us with full hands and willing hearts, and even after their hard day's work, they were never too weary to guide us on our journey to places of safety." After the war, Johnson, who had reenlisted, was sent back to the very area through which he had made his trek and was assigned to help make work contracts between freedpeople and planters. He made contracts the planters' said were too favorable to the freedpeople. He also discovered that when he met up with some of the people who had helped him, they did not consider it safe to let on they had ever seen him. Some of them served him dinner as servants in the homes of whites where he had once hidden. He also met up with and aided the widow who took him to the outliers in the mountains. She did not recognize him and handed him a note asking Union officials to help her that he had written the previous year. From her he learned that those white outliers who had turned back because of the harsh conditions had been killed, and though a number had managed to join the Union army, many of those who had survived the war were killed by former Confederates on their return home. Such were the terms of life in northwestern South Carolina, where martial law would later be declared in response to terror against Blacks trying to vote. But Johnson's diary is an archive of local circuits that crossed long distances and provides a glimpse into the proficiency with which these enslaved people who would soon be free could coordinate migration, labor negotiations, or the creation of political formations, and perhaps also how to survive such plans.[16]

Foregatherings

Six days after Johnson and his friends reached safety, on January 12, 1865, Rev. James D. Lynch participated in a meeting in Savannah, Georgia, one hundred miles from Charleston, where he had landed in 1863, to work for the AME Church. The meeting was between Major General Sherman and southern ministers, many of whom had been enslaved until the recent end of Sherman's March to the Sea. Lynch had been sent to the South Carolina Low Country two years earlier, to rebuild the church's presence in the state. The Emmanuel AME Church in Charleston, now known as Mother Emmanuel, was founded by African Americans between 1815 and 1818 and suffered official harassment after ordinances dictated that churches must be majority white. The church was raided, and parishioners arrested and whipped in 1818, 1820, and 1821. The next year, Denmark Vesey, one of the church's founders, was accused of planning a rebellion by enslaved people, with the result that "30 men were executed and others deported from the state," and the church was burned.[17]

Charlotte Forten wrote about hearing Lynch speak at the Brick Baptist Church on St. Helena Island on July 4, 1863, in his first year in the Low Country. By all printed firsthand reports on his work, he was a moving speaker. Colonel Robert Gould Shaw of the Massachusetts Fifty-Fourth wrote of Lynch speaking at the event, with some soldiers from the regiment. In November 1864, he became chaplain of the Fifty-Fourth. The next year he wrote of his work and appealed to other African Americans to come South: "You of the North, perhaps, under-estimate the influence and power that can be wielded by colored men and women of character, intelligence and education." And like others who would follow him, he extolled the power of the work on one's own spirit: "Oh, this work among the freedmen has a charm about it! If there is a soul in you, it is drawn out—any sympathy for your fellow, it is enlarged and made the active instrument of his improvement. God is in the whole work, and in the man whose heart is in it. It has its difficulties, but they may melt away before a cool head and a warm heart." He helped to establish churches and schools in South Carolina and worked in Georgia for several years and also in Mississippi, where he was elected to high office.[18]

The meeting Lynch attended with Sherman proved extraordinary. Lynch was the only northern Black present and one of few who had not been enslaved. His having lived in the North showed in his contrasting positive view on living among whites. Of the twenty Black ministers present, fifteen had been enslaved, and nine of those had been freed by the Union army during the war. The general and the secretary of war, Edwin Stanton, asked the group's spokesman, Baptist minister Garrison Frazier, a sixty-seven-year-old slavery survivor, for his understanding of slavery and freedom. Frazier replied: "Slavery is, receiving by irresistible power the work of another man, and not by his consent. The freedom, as I understand it, promised by the proclamation, is taking us from under the yoke of bondage, and placing us where we could reap the fruit of our own labor, take care of ourselves and assist the Government in maintaining our freedom." When asked if the group thought Blacks in the South had "enough intelligence" among them to sustain themselves and maintain "good and peaceable relations among yourselves and with your neighbors," Frazier said simply, "I think there is sufficient intelligence among us to do so." The men told the general that their main need was land. Several days later, people there learned of the general's Field Order No. 15, promising land to freedpeople in that Atlantic Coast area—forty acres and a mule that were not to come.[19]

A battle over land on the South Carolina coast had already been joined when Sherman issued his field order, setting aside 400,000 coastal acres for use by freedpeople, on January 16. The Sherman Reserve took in arable lands in the areas where fugitives had already fled during the war—the

Atlantic Coast south of Charleston all the way to Jacksonville, Florida, including the South Carolina and Georgia Sea Islands and extending thirty miles inland. Though for some months early in the war Union troops were unable to have a presence over large areas and the order itself would last less than a year before being revoked by President Andrew Johnson, it had several immediate effects as well as a long-term legacy among African Americans. The phrase "forty acres and a mule" lives on today as a term denoting broken promises made to survivors of the country's "original sin."[20]

In South Carolina, people made strenuous efforts to set up self-sustaining farm communities. People who had settled on lands in the Sherman Reserve were seriously aggrieved when the government decided to give the abandoned lands back to former owners. They began to petition authorities stating their refusal to comply with a government that "concluded to befriend its late enemies." A petition from Edisto Island was signed, "In behalf of the people." The organization done on Edisto also took place, according to Hahn and colleagues, "on other islands, and on the mainland, soon constituting a loosely knit network through which freedpeople in the section of the Sherman reserve nearest Charleston exchanged news and information, enforced unity within their ranks, and mobilized for local defense." This "concerted" action also took place in Georgia's reserve areas. The way in which freedpeople began to organize to stay on their homesteads by linking with other settlements is pertinent to the formation of the Emancipation Circuit during the war and after.[21]

The idea built into the origins of the Freedmen's Bureau that resettling Low Country freedpeople on abandoned plantations and perhaps even lending them livestock needed for farming would jump-start an autonomous freedom ignited local vigilantism by Confederate veterans. "It was almost as though the guerilla warfare that some Union officers had expected to erupt in South Carolina in the wake of Sherman's march came to be directed not against armed Union troops but against unarmed slaves," writes Julie Saville. Some people were in fact given forty-acre lots, and the bureau was to see that deeds on the land reflected the changes. Military attempts to manage plantations as part of the order's implementation met with resistance from freedpeople, as did the reversals of the order and its intentions. During the spring of 1865, some forty thousand people who had fled plantations settled on the islands off Charleston alone. Many moved to the islands to avoid military farm management. And some people outside the borders of Sherman's reserve seized plantations as chances allowed, assuming perhaps that the order's principle could or ought to apply there too.[22]

A period of negotiation over Black autonomy occurred along the coast during and after the war, and on the Sea Islands changes were wrought by freedpeople in the amounts of cotton cultivated and how the work was done. In some areas, workers drove off the overseers whom planters had left on the farms to supervise. Though it was not necessarily coordinated, freedpeople in the area arrived at similar demands from similar needs. Their cooperative approach to raising cotton and other labors baffled northern soldiers, observers, and other northerners who were buying land. In one sense, the nature of the resistance in freedpeople's changes in the agricultural work—prioritizing their own survival food among other alterations in the balance of labor—led freedpeople toward political engagement, community organizing, and withholding labor in groups, even if small ones. Such changes were much more dangerous for people inland where owners had not abandoned their lands and kept their labor force trapped by the standard violent methods. There, too, people were cultivating edible crops instead of cotton, which ensured their survival and gave them more time to pursue other means of becoming self-sustaining. Planters responded with "revived patrols, pass systems, and armed scouts."[23]

Of necessity, organizing was taking place and observed in 1865–66. In the Sea Islands area, as in other states, local whites sounded the alarm with military officials both because African Americans were having meetings (often called "secret meetings"). And, because of the war, the federal military presence, and local violence, Blacks had some quasi-military organization and did regular drilling practice with whatever arms or makeshift weapons were at hand. Saville recounts that some locals reported the Blacks were planning for a violent insurrection but suggests that the military affectation among Blacks organizing between plantations was perhaps adopted from earlier encounters with various groups from slave patrols and local militia to Confederate and Union forces. Perhaps more important than the adopted military style is that many of the meetings were about labor action and contemporary reports that Blacks produced unanimity of action and communications across plantations so effectively an outsider might think it "like magic." The intensely organized workers in the rice fields would prove to be a considerable force a decade later when striking for better wages and fighting to maintain Republican power won by Black votes.[24]

One long-term legacy of the experiment was the circulation of the idea among freedpeople throughout the South that they were due "forty acres and a mule" and, later, that the government had reneged on taking this transformational step. While there were various claims of Black rights to land, many centered on the settled view that the land had been made arable only through their toil and that much land had been purchased by the sale of their flesh. As a Virginia freedman put it:

> We was first ordered to pay rent, and we paid de rent; now we has orders to leave, or have our log cabins torn down over our heads. Dey say "de lands has been 'stored to de old owners, and dey must have it. And now where shall we go? Shall we go into the streets, or into de woods, or into de ribber? We has nowhere to go! and we now wants to know what we can do? I is not here to ask de Government to help me nor my family. I has never asked any help from de Government nor from friends, and I never has received any. I has got a living by honest, hard work since I came to the Yankees, and I has saved something besides. I owes no man any thing, but my people cannot all do this. Dey has been bought and sold like horses; dey has been kept in ignorance; dey has been sold for lands, for horses, for carriages, and for every thing their old masters had. I want some gemmen to tell me of one ting that our people hasn't been sold to buy for deir owners.[25]

Henrietta Butler, a Louisiana slavery survivor, said her mother was used by a female slaveholder solely for raising revenue: "They made my Ma have babies all de time, she was sellin' the boys and keepin' the gals."[26] These understandings of forced investment and sacrifice for planter prosperity did not need to be taught to any but young children. Such clarity motivated many, like the large numbers starting over on the Sea Islands, and they began resisting as the government revoked the distribution of land. Whites described such Black views about having earned land with adjectives like "queer" or "extravagant." They charged that Black soldiers "spread seeds of discontent" or were "demoralizing" Blacks with land distribution dreams. It almost goes without saying that missives from the South included reports of "secret" Black meetings.

As occurred in other states, when the old white elites met to rewrite their state constitutions in preparation for being accepted back into the Union, Blacks met to begin carving out an agenda of needs that should be met by the state, and to submit these ideas to the white legislators. As in other states, these submissions were ignored by legislators who were creating black codes to reinstate the powers of the slavery system. In South Carolina, the black codes included white control of the courts and the right of any white to have Blacks arrested, and limiting Black testimony against whites. The codes instituted vagrancy laws, which would be used for decades to conscript Black labor. The new laws also allowed corporal punishment and apprenticing children to planters. Oddly, the codes attempted to define the legitimacy of Black children with the following statement: "Every colored child, heretofore born, is declared to be the legitimate child of his mother, and also of his colored father, if he is acknowledged by such a father."[27]

South Carolina had some especially outrageous features in its codes, including permission for employers to apply "suitable corporal punishment," and "to inflict moderate chastisement and reasonable restraint" on apprenticed children. The state barred Blacks from any work except farming or domestic service unless they paid a yearly license fee ranging from ten to one hundred dollars, the larger figure representing nearly a year's wages for many artisans and craftspeople. The new crimes added to replace slave system law began with the following four in this order: "For a person of color to commit any willful homicide unless in self-defence; for person of color to commit an assault upon a white woman with manifest intent to ravish her; for person of color to have sexual intercourse with white woman by personating her husband; for any person to raise an insurrection or rebellion in this State." South Carolina's code went the extra mile to make white supremacist intentions clear. First, the text defined the races and what they should be called. People who were seven-eighths white would be white, and everyone with fewer than seven white forebears were identified as "persons of color." In the clause permitting Blacks to marry (interracial marriage was barred) and own property, the text stipulates, "Such persons are not entitled to social or political equality." Black employees were to be called "servants," and employers, "masters." Workers were not allowed visitors on farms without employers' consent; "a master could command a servant to aid him in defense of his own person, family or property"; and workers were required to answer a call day or night.[28] According to Saville, "Many small slaveowners thus failed in early contracts to describe the work that they would require of their new employees in terms of specific chores, claiming instead 'there entier servis,' requiring them 'when not engaged in working or gathering the crop to do whatever she [the farm owner] may desire,' or stipulating that a former slave 'do bind herself to obey me as before.'" The rights assigned to employees, which, according to freedpeople, were more honored in the breach, included protection against "unreasonable" demands, attacks on their persons, and insufficient food supplies, as well as specified wages and hours put in writing. The military revoked the codes in January 1866.[29]

"Queer" ideas of autonomy were in fact one immediate response among freedpeople to the passing of the black codes. After meeting to petition the conservative constitutional convention, Blacks began to organize the first colored convention in the state, which took place in November 1865 in Charleston. Those who attended represented a healthy percentage of the future Black leadership in the state but also show an instance of Black activists arriving from the North becoming immersed in the emerging Black political formations. In 1865, Rev. Richard H. Cain, who was born free in Virginia and raised in Ohio, arrived from Brooklyn, New York, where he was minister of the Bridge Street AME Church, the first AME church there. He came to Charleston to become minister of Emmanuel AME. That summer he wrote, "The condition of the freedmen is bad enough, and the destruction among them is very great." He found "many of them are idlers," and yet, he reported to the *Christian Recorder*, "Viewing them generally, I find that there is a disposition to work, and get land, possess property, educate their children, and thus elevate themselves and the race to which they belong." Two months later he was quite impressed with the industry and production of the freedpeople and had found himself with a Charleston congregation that would situate him for political leadership. Many Black southerners were using the choice of their own church as part of establishing autonomy, leaving their former owners' churches for Black churches all over the South. Some found they could only have their own church practice by accepting use of a basement hospitality room in a white church. Others built churches in the countryside, and many city dwellers in Charleston came to Emmanuel. One cannot even calculate the difference it made for many who had been enslaved to be welcomed at the front door of a church, referred to by name with "madam" or "sir," or another prefix of respect, and offered a seat wherever they chose. Many, when enslaved, had been confined to white church balconies. Having left the northern Methodist Episcopal Church due to discrimination, and having been in New York for the 1863 draft riots in which Blacks were killed on Manhattan streets, and for the duration of the war, Cain spoke in masculinist terms about the race coming into its own in freedom. He thought the AME ideology attracted people in the midst of defining freedom: "The blacks recognize in our organization the idea of nationality of manhood. They feel the time has come for the black man to take his place as a free man."[30]

In August 1867, political building was aided by Union Republican Congressional Committee (URCC), organizers sent to help form an electorate ahead of the vote being granted to Black men. An unnamed Republican speaker and Union League (UL) organizer in the state wrote from Charleston of his work meeting freedpeople about their rights: "I have been traveling for some time in this state and have addressed large meetings in 18 or 20 districts. [Counties were called districts in the state until 1868.] Have organized the league in ten districts. The greatest interest exists among the colored men everywhere. They are wide awake. When any person known to be in sympathy with the Republican Party and the North, goes into a neighborhood to speak, the freedmen flock in crowds to hear him." Like the circuit-riding activists in other states, this unnamed speaker had to travel to more than a dozen counties during that summer to perform his share of the instruction in citizenship rights and voting procedures. Michael Fitzgerald reports that organizers themselves were taking note that rural communities dealt with communication of news and organizing ideas without pen and paper: "In councils that had no literate members, freedmen would send individuals to other leagues who would report back on the content of the newspapers. . . . 'Radicals found that many Negroes had photographic memories, for one reading would enable many of the unlettered Negroes to become so familiar with the material that they were able to explain it to other Negroes.' In South Carolina this work done by locals and outsiders was notably successful."[31] At the same time, dockworkers in the coastal cities began successfully organizing to move beyond slavery system wages. According to Eli Poliakoff, "In 1867 local [Charleston] longshoremen walked off the docks to protest low wages, demanding a 50 cents daily increase. Four days later, shipping companies conceded. . . . In January 1868, 200 to 300 longshoremen stopped working and demanded an additional 50 cents a day; after failed efforts to break the strike, shipping companies again increased wages." In 1868, they formed the Longshoremen's Protective Union Association (LPUA), chartered by the state in 1869 and continuing today.[32]

Making Political Voice: The Black Majority Votes

In South Carolina, where Blacks constituted 60 percent of the population by 1870, they had representation in nearly every county in the state for the 1868 constitutional convention, and elected legislators from most counties in the early 1870s. These delegates were able to legislate equal citizenship rights regardless of color; voting rights to all, without any property, literacy, or poll tax requirements; and the establishment of public schools open to all (though the construction of an adequate number of schools was slow to develop) and hospitals for treating the chronically ill and the mentally ill. They established a uniform system for local government, gave the state a divorce law, protected women's property from a husband's debts, ended imprisonment for debt. They voided all contracts left over from slavery, about which one Black delegate said: "It is our duty to destroy all elements of the institution of slavery. If we do not, we recognize the right of property in man." Racial attitudes, however, prevented the implementation of institutions open to all: integration of schools and hospitals remained difficult to achieve for generations. Du Bois points out that a facility to train those with visual, hearing, or speech disabilities opened in 1871 but closed two years later when faculty were "ordered to accept colored students." The state hospital for the mentally ill did open and accepted Blacks, though it seems likely that segregated staffing was used.[33]

Those chosen to go to the constitutional convention made some startling proposals—often suffering opposition from members of their own Black caucus—that would clearly have been transformative for African Americans and the state of South Carolina. For instance, some delegates proposed that the state ask the federal government for $1 million to purchase roughly 500,000 acres of land for freedpeople, giving 20 acres to each family of seven. They succeeded in at least setting up a state commission to buy land for Blacks, funded at first with $200,000 in bonds, later built to $500,000.[34] Some of the far-reaching laws passed, such as relief for the poor, were maintained once conservative rule returned to the state and simply denied to people of color, which along with the public school system aided in the development of a white middle class in the state. Republicans also advocated for back pay for freedpeople dating to the Emancipation Proclamation, an idea that came up in at least one other state. Given that freedpeople had been scrambling for enough wages to support families at least since the war's end, and longer for those near US military forces, a dispensation for those who had worked on farms without pay for the previous eight years may have transformed their ability to stabilize living situations and educate youngsters. Even at $10 per month, such as many farmworkers earned, back pay would have come to nearly $1,000 (equivalent to about $19,133.52 in 2021 dollars), probably enough to buy some amount of land.

Delegate William Whipper (later a state representative) advocated for woman suffrage, joined later by Alonzo Ransier (a delegate, state legislator, lieutenant governor, and US congressman) in numerous attempts with Black suffragists to pass laws and build public discourse on granting women the vote. Ransier also argued for women's right to vote in the US Congress. Needless to say, this was not a purely selfless campaign; in a state with a Black majority population, adding women voters to the electorate would have made likely even larger numbers than Blacks won in the state house and senate but perhaps more statewide and local offices as well. Elsa Barkley Brown and Thomas Holt have shown that Black women were vocal participants in political meetings in the state and were often armed defenders of male voters at the polls. Later, when officeholders were attacked by the violent Red Shirt groups threatening and assaulting Black political participants, women again acted as guards outside the polls. Their impact on the vision of possible futures during this time must have helped to develop some of the progressive proposals that were voiced by Black lawmakers. Brown writes: "African American women's prior history of inclusion, not exclusion, shaped their discourse of womanhood and their construction of gender roles; they did so not in concert with ideas in the larger society but in opposition as white Americans continued to deny African Americans the privileges of manhood or the protections of womanhood, reinforcing the commonality rather than the separateness of men's and women's roles."[35] The seemingly anomalous presence of women in so many aspects of the political life in the state did not go unnoticed. The Democrats trying to reestablish white majority government, according to Brown, believed Black women to be the force behind the Black resistance. Black women would be at the center of the rice strikes to come in 1876 and would consequently be targeted by planters. Brown rightly warns that their broad aspiration would also be met by repression: "Black women's vision of freedom and democracy, like that of black people as a whole, may never have been that expansive again. Yet we must be alert to the persistence of old patterns along with the adoption of new. In the changing political frameworks one might expect to find a continuing thread of women's political participation even at the same time as one finds them more and more fundamentally excluded from both the external and the internal political process."[36] Any perspective on the continuity of Black women's political participation would seem in the current moment to have to concede a stubborn chronicle of activism. The collective ownership of the vote described in Brown's work, which reveals perhaps the social nature of the reproduction of political ideology and formation building in that time, is also a feature of the entire Emancipation Circuit.[37]

Along with Mississippi, South Carolina elected more Black state legislators in Reconstruction than the other southern states. There was a roster of 249 individual legislators (including constitutional convention delegates) elected to 311 seats in South Carolina between 1868 and 1876. Tallies made for this study of all of the representatives in the state for the entire nineteenth century show only 249 *individuals* because those elected in the late 1880s had also been elected earlier. States such as Florida and Arkansas elected a new generation in the 1870s. As Foner points out, "South Carolina was the only state where blacks comprised a majority of the House of Representatives and about half the state Senate between 1872 and 1876." The state also had two African American lieutenant governors, secretaries of state, state commissioners, and speakers of the House, as well as a Black state treasurer and a supreme court judge. South Carolina had the potential to normalize Black officeholding across the state one hundred years before it began to happen anywhere.[38]

Two interesting facets of South Carolina's organizing are visible in table 5.1. First, there is a very high percentage of sites that achieved representation, whether or not those sites had other institutions such as American Missionary Association (AMA) schools or Black press. I have added the numbers to stress the state's difference from most other Reconstruction states. The numbers elected, it should be noted, would be unusual, if not impossible, in most places today as well. For instance, in Beaufort County, where people elected twelve Black people to the constitutional convention and the General Assembly between 1868 and 1873, in 2019 there were two Black representatives in the state house out of six for the county, and one Black state senator out of three. This is also worth looking at as the coastal counties like Beaufort did not suffer the massive organized KKK violence that forced martial law to be imposed elsewhere in the state. Though riots occurred in coastal areas in the 1870s, the targeting of specific officials took place consistently in the northern half of the state. The changes that took place over the more than 150 years since the late nineteenth-century violence against Black voting are due as much to the redistricting and changes in county lines that continued long after the violence subsided. The South Carolina legislature created fifteen new counties between 1868 and 1919, all but one in areas that elected Black officials. (*See the South Carolina maps [plates 14 and 15] for the widespread nature of Black representation in the state and the organized resistance against it through the rest of the century.*)[39]

Second, there is a high percentage of sites where the Union League worked and a low incidence of sites organized by the Knights of Labor

(KoL). According to Saville, most of those who began the education of freedpeople on the rights specified in the Reconstruction Acts were from the state and "veterans of other educational efforts among the freedpeople." And there was local labor organizing going on in the state from emancipation. Strikes on the Charleston docks had led to the formation of the enduring and powerful LPUA; according to Poliakoff, "At its height in the late 1860s and early 1870s, the LPUA's 800–1000 members dominated dock labor, intimidated waterfront businesses, and kept a high profile through media coverage and its leadership of local labor." Later the Colored Farmers' Alliance (CFA) took hold in cotton-growing regions north and west. There was still much labor activism going on in the state when the KoL began organizing Blacks in the South in the 1880s.[40]

In 1871 the Convention of the Colored People to the Southern States in Columbia produced a statement addressed to the people of the United States that gives a sense of how those shaped by representing Black communities analyzed the emancipation era and the beginning of Reconstruction. This statement, which was signed by leaders from seven states, is, as well, an indication of the cooperation among freedpeople from different regions:[41]

> The fruits of the great legal measures that were intended to establish our rights and interests on a common footing with all other citizens of the nation, have, to some extent and in particular locations, been withheld from us by the prejudices and passions left in the hearts of a portion of our fellow-citizens. . . . They have not been content to employ the advantages that capital and experience in public and private affairs confer, but have resorted to *compulsory* means, unsanctioned by the laws of the country, the spirit of American institutions, and the practice of civilized nations.[42]

After recounting the passage of the black codes, the Reconstruction Acts, the Fourteenth and Fifteenth Amendments, they wrote of being offered a choice between "complete political subserviency" and "being deprived of homes and employment." During this time, there was a division of political loyalties building in South Carolina that left African Americans with fewer allies. Du Bois describes the factions among whites as being made up of those "who represented planters and who were willing to accept Negro suffrage as a fact"; others "who proposed to control the Negro vote," in the interests of planters; and those "who wanted to exclude the Negro entirely from the ballot and do this as soon as possible."[43]

This began an uptick in violent attacks on Black electoral networks. Thus, even though Reconstruction was still going on in most states, one sees in the convention address a state of threat to continue for years: "Resort was had to secret organizations, with a view to the control of the masses of the colored people by the murder of the prominent representative men of our class, and by the infliction of bodily pain upon a certain number of their followers.... We have been hunted like beasts by armed and disguised bands. Many, both men and women, have been killed; vast numbers have received severe corporal punishment; and many more found shelter in the swamps."[44] In mapping the crosscurrents of events that influenced the political interests of Black South Carolinians, this narrative is shown at work. South Carolina map 1 (plate 14) shows the areas of Union League influence and the areas especially subject to violence; though Blacks were killed across the South, I have also used representatives who were personally targeted in this state to show where organizing was most dangerous and its systematic nature. (See South Carolina maps [plates 14 and 15].)

In 1871 the federal government had to declare martial law in nine counties in South Carolina, and yet violence persisted in those areas. Planters not averse to Ku Klux Klan repression of Black political organizing also thought measures limiting male suffrage, such as property requirements, were needed to protect white power. The Republicans split in 1872, electing as governor Franklin Moses, a former state house speaker who had organized a Black majority militia to protect Black communities from the KKK and supported integration of the state university. Moses was indicted for corruption while in office, and Republicans supported Daniel Henry Chamberlain, who ran on reforming widespread corruption but began to cozy up to some of those intent on repressing the Black vote and participation in government. That same year Martin R. Delany, and former African emigration organizer who had become the first Black commissioned officer in the Civil War (and is today considered an early Black nationalist author), ran to be the Republican nominee for lieutenant governor. When his bid failed, he ran as nominee for the same post for a party of dissidents from the Republicans and Democrats.

Reactionary forces enraged that Blacks could vote, freely bear arms, and take part in militias that could protect Black communities for the first time in history began to act locally to use force to disarm militias and intimidate Black officeholders. In Edgefield County, where much trouble occurred, Stephen Kantrowitz reports, "Militant planter leadership sought to deny black militiamen land and employment and many Edgefield blacks complained of being driven off lands they had leased or of having their labor contracts broken because they belonged to the state militia or voted Republican." In 1875, after threats from white rifle clubs, a US officer in Edgefield, Colonel Theodore Parmele, naively "believed the rifle clubs would heed the governor's call to disband and opposed stationing U.S. infantry at the Edgefield Courthouse." He tragically ordered "the black militia's weapons, black South Carolinians' only defense, . . . to be locked in the Edgefield jail, from which they were soon stolen." The white terror groups simply stepped up their activities for the next election cycle.[45]

Going After the Black Electorate

In the statewide drive to take back power from Blacks in the election of 1876, several tools were used: Black voter intimidation by paramilitary groups known as Red Shirts and rifle clubs, attempts to raise white voter participation, vote-counting irregularities (along the lines of "stuffing" ballot boxes), and violence, including murder. Most riots occurred in counties where Blacks had a small majority. Sadly, the history of the efforts of South Carolina's conservatives and white supremacists to overthrow the power held by Reconstruction Republicans, known as "the redemption" there and elsewhere, spurred a series of riots in 1876, mostly against Blacks, as elections approached. These incidents, when looked at on a map, also occurred in particular locations.

In July 1876, there was the Hamburg Massacre, in Aiken County, carried out against the Black majority town with Black majority local government, by more than one hundred whites from that county, and violence in Edgefield County (where earlier Black militia were targeted) and in Georgia's Richmond County just across the river. The idea was that if Black leadership figures there were murdered, Democrats could carry the entire county by dint of intimidation or threat. And by this time, many of the militias in the state had been disarmed. However, the attacks on militias put two admired Black leaders into the sights of white rifles: Prince Rivers, a former activist, Union soldier, legislator, and "major general in the state militia," who was by then a local judge; and Dock Adams, also an army veteran, and believed to have been involved in a Black uprising in Georgia, now a militia leader who had refused to disband his group. Adams refused to have his men turn over their weapons after Rivers asked them to do so to settle a dispute whites had lodged against Adams's group for parading in town on July 4, to the annoyance of two prominent whites in a buggy. White rifle clubs continued to arrive, and a five-hour gunfight resulted. Two Blacks were killed during the fight, five were shot after capture, and seven others who had been captured were shot after being told to run. Governor Chamberlain wrote to the president and other officials for help, noting the horror of the massacre as well as the "triviality" of its cause, and warning that whites in the state had adopted the deadly "Mississippi Plan" used to overthrow Reconstruction in that state. Blacks also organized a mass meeting and denounced the massacre as part of a larger electoral strategy. The Democrats pushed a need for polarization, publicly intimidated moderates who condemned violence, and supported Wade Hampton III for governor. Before the war, Hampton was one of the state's largest slaveholders, a lieutenant general in the Confederacy, and a man whose candidacy set off the worst from those after "a white man's country."[46]

On September 6, in Charleston, the King Street riots followed the appearance of one or two Republican dissidents at a Democratic meeting, during a period when the conservatives were trying to recruit Blacks. Blacks attacked the men leaving the meeting and there was fighting in the street. A sizable crowd of Blacks from Charleston's reputedly well-armed Black community appeared, successfully intimidating the smaller numbers of police and Democrats into leaving the area. Looting took place, and some whites were injured. On September 15 in Ellenton, on the border of Aiken and Barnwell Counties (and about ten miles from Hamburg), a Black militia was set upon in a battle that escalated over several days. Some 500 to 1,000 paramilitary men came into the area and killed anywhere from 30 to 100 Blacks, including Simon Coker, a Black state senator. Red Shirts took to attending Black rallies and trying to shout down the speakers. On October 16, in Cainhoy, north of Charleston, a Black political meeting of about 500 people turned into an armed conflict when it was "visited" by 150 white men from Charleston armed with pistols. One of the conflicts that caused this event was over the role of Martin Delany, who was there to speak on behalf of Democrat Hampton in this tumultuous campaign. Blacks had brought and cached their arms, and when whites fired upon them, they discovered they were outgunned. Five whites died, along with one Black, and as many as fifty people were wounded. The next day, up-country in Edgefield when six Red Shirts were attacked by two Black men, one of the whites was killed. Further violence was prevented by two leaders who stepped in, but threats there continued to be severe. The town gained a well-promoted reputation for violence against Republicans, and whites voted with the Red Shirts.[47]

In the fall of that year, strikes going on in the Low Country since the spring, which came to be known as the Combahee Rice Strikes, gained renewed strength. The strikes occurred during a downturn for the rice region that brought severe food shortages for the population. According to Brian Kelly, the problems arose from the long-term damages created by the war, "exacerbated by a depressed rice market, and a series of seasonal, weather-related calamities." When planters tried in the spring to lower the wages they had to pay, strikes began among African American workers who had been struggling for more than a decade to get standard free-labor wages. This campaign, taking place as it did amid the intense drive to put state and local government back solely in the hands of whites, had moments that reflected the violence that had taken place elsewhere in the state. The difference in this case was the overwhelming Black majority of the rice region and the fact that the people who started and built the strikes were women. Other factors at work were the highly organized Black communities described at the beginning of this chapter and the benefit of absent owners. As Kelly and others before him point out, the strikes also created lasting divisions between working-class Blacks, white leaders of the Republican Party, and the more privileged Black men who held office and over time were successfully recruited to work with the Democratic forces to stay in office.[48]

The dispute over wages centered on mostly female hands who lived up-country and came to work in the fields at harvest time. The planters stated an intention to cut wages from fifty cents a day to forty cents. The women struck, but planters were unmoved, so the strike quickly grew: "Almost overnight, the conflict spread north to plantations along the Ashepoo River and expanded to take up grievances of the regular workforce, including their unwillingness to work for 'cat's wages' and resentment against payment in 'checks' or 'scrip' redeemable at plantation stores." The regular workers backed the women's demands and, as Kelly points out, tellingly referred to themselves as "the majority." They were, unsurprisingly, accused of terrorizing the areas and workers unwilling to cooperate. They had, according to contemporary reports, organized a society that required a commitment to uphold the strike. Kelly also enumerates various ways in which observers noted coordination among Blacks and the spread of strike news up and down the coast from Charleston to Beaufort. The "majority" label, a reminder of the electoral reality, also prompted accusations that they were playing politics with the coming elections in mind. In the spring the strike had affected fewer than a dozen plantations on the Combahee River but, according to Kelly, had put "at risk more than 4,000 acres of rice."[49]

In late October, after the violence in these places, the Low Country planters wanted to use force to end the strike and wrote "the Republican Governor with requests that he dispatch federal troops to suppress it." Requesting the help of the federal forces from a Republican governor was not typical, as the US military presence was despised. Blacks and whites had heard by this time of the extraordinary wave of violence in Mississippi the previous year to successfully overthrow or "redeem" Republican control of state government and force Blacks out of office. South Carolina's Republican governor, Daniel H. Chamberlain, tried to placate conservative Democrats and ultimately pleased no one. The Black majority in the Low Country knew he was not their ally and opposed him openly. Once the paramilitary violence took place up-country, Chamberlain's loss in the next election was likely sealed. In a prelude to post-Reconstruction politics to come, a number of Black officials sided with business and steered clear of Black labor actions. Robert Smalls helped both sides, particularly in keeping troops from putting down the strike.[50]

Grant sent twelve hundred federal soldiers to protect the 1876 election, and in December, Wade Hampton III, a former Confederate lieutenant general, was elected governor by a margin of little more than eleven hundred votes. The Red Shirts who helped overthrow Reconstruction and elect Hampton even had reunions in 1908 and 1909. Successive generations of white voters continued the mission of the Red Shirts by contributing to the passage of successive provisions to deny African Americans use of the vote for the next ninety years.

Responses to "Redemption"

Most Black leaders in the state faced local interest in the emigration movements of the late 1870s and early 1880s. As in Virginia, interest in emigration was keen in three types of counties: those outside of the Emancipation Circuit where Blacks lacked support, counties that had lost representation, and counties where gerrymandering divided Black publics to create entities in which whites could run successfully for office (counties of the first two types were often the same places).

The violent end of Reconstruction made people like Harrison Bouey think about leaving the state and the country. After receiving death threats while running for sheriff in Edgefield County, and all that had transpired there, according to Foner, Bouey became "a key organizer of the Liberia Emigration movement." He went to Liberia at least twice and died there in 1909. South Carolinian Henry M. Turner, before expulsion from the Georgia legislature, was like many in having faith that with freedom and the vote Black people could attain some access to power and work with southern whites. He had been quite conciliatory but was enraged by the violence in the 1870s and became an advocate of emigration. Additionally, according to Walker, the failure of a civil rights bill in the US Congress in 1874 further turned the leader toward emigration. In 1875, he wrote, among other remarks in the *Christian Recorder*, "This seems to be the only government on earth that cannot protect its citizens. Every few weeks the cry of insurrection comes from Louisiana, Georgia, Mississippi, etc., and a hecatomb of innocent people must be sacrificed to justify the accursed lie. And yet when you appeal to the government for protection, it is so weak and powerless it cannot give any." Turner would become a leader of the American Colonization Society and make four visits to Liberia. In the 1870s, Aaron Bradley of Georgia, who had one of the most controversial and instructive careers as a Reconstruction activist, left the Georgia Low Country for the South Carolina Low Country, where he worked for the Republican Party in the Beaufort area. By the 1880s, he was working with the Kansas exodus movement in South Carolina.[51]

In 1890, Ben Tillman, one of the most infamous names among the Red Shirts of 1876 and an unrepentant white supremacist, became governor of the state. During his tenure a new constitution was written that successfully disfranchised most African Americans.

In a thoughtful article on a short story by the New England writer Sarah Orne Jewett, Vesna Kuiken examines how Jewett reflected on the Port Royal Experiment in a 1888 narrative based on a trip to Beaufort, South Carolina. Jewett, who usually wrote about her native Maine, was really on her way to Florida and had no practical concern with the first years of freedom for southern Blacks. But in this story she ponders the fitness of various characters, Black and white, for the freedoms the postwar period brought. It voices notable observations about attitudes in the late nineteenth century concerning the provision of degrees of freedom by some Americans to other Americans: "Rather than propose answers or solutions, the story asks . . . whether the *right* to humanity is indeed inalienable. . . . The story's question, finally, reconstructs the world in which the *economic* capacity to participate in the market system is conceived of as the *biological* capacity for independence and freedom." Not only was it a preoccupation of the period, for friend and foe of freedpeople alike, to assume the task of assessing the capability of Blacks but to set an assessment of "competence" as a precondition for the rights already given them in the Constitution. And, beyond that even, Kuiken writes, "As the merging of these two capacities [economic and biological] became the very foundation of political participation, the story shows them to have been inaugurated as a veritable criterion for citizenship and of the humanity of African Americans in [the] postbellum United States."[52]

Looking at Table 5.1

South Carolina was unique in the way in which Black majorities allowed some counties to elect representatives without the array of supportive institutions in at least eight of the seventeen counties I have included. Labor organizing was widespread in the later movements in the state even without a significant presence of the Knights of Labor. It could also be the case that the KoL was not badly needed due to the labor organizing that had long been carried on before the 1880s. Two other factors stand out: wide-ranging Union League work and numerous newspapers. Finally, the numbers of representatives elected in each county are higher than in other states, creating an unusual majority in governance, at least early on.

TABLE 5.1 South Carolina Emancipation Circuit, 1868–1900

| | Institutions Present | | | | | | | 19th Century Activism |
	US Troops	RR (1884)	Union League	AMA Schools	Local Black Press	Black Political Reps	Knights of Labor Groups	
ABBEVILLE **Abbeville County** ß	◆	◆	◆	◆		◆ 10		Labor Colored Farmers' Alliance (CFA) Western exodus
AIKEN (then **Barnwell County** ß)		◆	◆	◆*	2 1865 1873	◆ 9		
BEAUFORT **Beaufort County** ß	◆	◆	◆	◆	3 1862 1860s 1871	◆ 16		Land ownership Rice strikes Liberia emigration
CENTRAL (township) **GREENVILLE** area, Pickens County		◆				◆	1 M renting farmers & laborers	Farm labor
CHARLESTON **Charleston County** ß	◆	◆	◆	◆	5	◆ 40	◆ Number unknown	Vote Liberia emigration Kansas exodus Farm labor

County						Notes
Chester County ß	♦				11	
COLUMBIA Richland County ß	♦	♦		1	10	Labor Liberia emigration
					Number unknown	
Darlington County ß	♦	♦	Unknown		8	Self-defense
Edgefield County ß	♦	♦		$\frac{1}{1865}$	12	Self-defense Liberia emigration Western exodus
Fairfield County ß	♦	♦			11	Liberia emigration
Georgetown County ß		♦	♦	$\frac{1}{1873-75}$	8	
GREENVILLE Greenville County	♦				2	Farm labor
Kershaw County ß		♦			10	
Newberry County ß		♦			7	Liberia emigration

(Continued)

TABLE 5.1 (Continued)

	Institutions Present							19th Century Activism
	US Troops	RR (1884)	Union League	AMA Schools	Local Black Press	Black Political Reps	Knights of Labor Groups	
ORANGEBURG **Orangeburg County** ß	*	*	*		<u>1</u> 1874–76	* 15		Labor Cotton workers strike
ROCK HILL **York County** ß		*	*	*	Possibly in area	* 3		Liberia emigration
Sumter County ß						* 11		Self-defense Labor Colored Workers Alliance

KEY: **Bold** = Site playing multiple roles on the circuit. ß = Black majority; unless otherwise noted, populations are for 1870. RR = Rail lines. **Black Political Reps** = Black representatives to the 1868 constitutional convention and/or members of the General Assembly.

Knights of Labor = Black assemblies of the labor organization. Most KoL assemblies were segregated by race and gender: white males, Black males, white females, or Black females. "Mixed labor" is a term from the Garlock data (*see* Table Source Notes) and indicates various forms of work, not mixing by race or gender. **Union League** was in numerous other counties (*see South Carolina Map 1 [plate 14]*). **Gender** is indicated here by M or F.

*Run by a Quaker, aided by the Freedmen's Bureau and the African Methodist Episcopal Church.

SOURCES: *See* Table Source Notes (393–96).

6 **GEORGIA**
Mobilization

Mobilize: *vt* **1 a :** to put into movement or circulation . . . **b :** to release (something stored in the organism) for bodily use **2 a :** to assemble and make ready for war duty **b :** to marshal (as resources) for action . . .

Demoralize: *vt* **1 :** to corrupt the morals of **2 a :** to weaken the morale of: Discourage. Dispirit **b :** upset or destroy the normal functioning of **c :** to throw into disorder.

—*Webster's Ninth New Collegiate Dictionary* (1986)

Union forces entered Georgia in 1862, landing at Fort Pulaski in Chatham County, and the state was designated, along with South Carolina and Florida, as part of the Department of the South. As a result of federal forces landing on the coast, fugitives from slavery congregated in camps and settlements at Fort Pulaski, Savannah, and Tybee Island (all in Chatham County; Black population in 1860, 15,532), Sapelo Island (pop. ca. 400), St. Simon's Island near Brunswick (pop. ca. 600), and somewhat later in Columbus (Black pop. ca. 8,000) and Atlanta (Black pop. 3,026). Even as people set up housekeeping on the islands, military movements often meant being forced out of new settlements. Coastal planters were vexed by the flight of enslaved people from the plantations and wrote to the Confederate military. In the case of several in Liberty County who wrote to the commander of the Confederate States of America forces, they asked the military to summarily execute any fugitives they found aiding the enemy and "Negroes *taken in the act of absconding*, singly, ~~(or in families)~~ or in parties."[1]

Federal occupations on the coast also shaped how missionaries and activists made their way along the forming Emancipation Circuit because military protection was vital to working on the ground, and because the military itself sent out people like Harriet Tubman and Abraham Galloway to work as scouts. This spurred organizational development in the localities because those arriving unavoidably did community work as well when confronted with the needs. For instance, after organizing in Georgia, the AME ministers also formed a conference of congregations in that state.

African Americans organizing for a fuller freedom beyond the abolition of slavery in Georgia demonstrate "chapter and verse" of how freedpeople forged a new regime of knowledge that would become the core of struggles to more fully realize the meaning of citizenship. This was foundational work engaging freedpeople in not only defining and testing their ideas of freedom but also acting in immediate response to passage of the Thirteenth, Fourteenth, and Fifteenth Amendments, which, after all, their lived experience had necessitated. The Thirteenth Amendment had abolished slavery; therefore, plantations where the routines replicated all the conditions and terms of slavery, including whipping, were essential arenas of struggle to prevent the restoration of the slave system. The Fourteenth Amendment, passed in 1868, as essential to the survival of freedom for all Americans as the Thirteenth, guaranteed equal protection of the law to all citizens for their "life, liberty, and property." The Fifteenth Amendment, granting males the right to vote without regard to "race, color, or previous condition of servitude," would be passed in 1869 and ratified in 1870. Activism practiced in Georgia shows a pedagogy being methodically taught and cultivated across the South on the central tenets of the US Constitution and the new amendments. Invariably, those dispensing the catechism with an aim to making informed voters of rural agricultural workers found their audiences had numerous—and pressing—uses for the right to petition, for the right to peaceful assembly and for the power of a free press to name just three. Freedpeople were experts on the tools that had been used against them, not least of which was language, and on the odd numerical use that had been made of their unfree bodies to increase southern political power. The culture being forged with the blending of the catechism of citizenship and the intrinsic local skills for assembling community and collective action made for many mobilizations.

In Georgia people began with labor organizing and returned to it over time as they persisted in trying to get living wages. But the intense and sustained violence used against the exercise of any of these tools caused freedpeople in the state to forge strategies for dealing with violent opposition, adapting from a diffident early approach toward the holdover Confederate elite to building organizations for schools and community, self-defense, and advocating for real change including enfranchising women, reforming or even abolishing prisons, and ending convict leasing and chain gangs. Their opponents saw that those whom they had kept in well-policed ignorance were indeed not just making "outrageous" demands but building a new regime of knowledge spreading expansive views of freedom that would be derided as "erroneous ideas."

Arrivals

In 1865, as in other states, Georgia saw a rise of activism and a new influx of teachers who shared a personal passion (often rooted in having been enslaved themselves) to nurture the potential of freedpeople. Among the Black activists who arrived that year, and one who would become a leader, was South Carolina–born Aaron Bradley, who came to open a school. He had been enslaved to the wartime governor of South Carolina and trained as a shoemaker before escaping to Boston, where he became a lawyer. Shortly after arriving in Georgia, he got involved with Blacks settled on the land that the Union general William Tecumseh Sherman had declared reserved for freedpeople and urged them on in their refusal to make labor contracts with owners trying to reclaim their plantations. He became such a thorn in the side of the Freedmen's Bureau that he was asked to leave the state a year later. But he returned and did organizing around resisting plantations being handed back to now absentee owners. He was elected a delegate to the constitutional convention and later as a state senator.[2]

Tunis Campbell, an AME Zion minister from New Jersey, would seem the type to get along with Bradley. Campbell proved too militant for the South Carolina Freedmen's Bureau after setting up "the Republic of Saint Catherine's" on one of the Sea Islands and distributing land among Blacks on five of the Sea Islands. He also started a farmers' association and a militia. Having already worked on Georgia's Sapelo Island, after the bureau dismissed him, in 1866 Campbell moved to the Georgia coastal town of Darien. There he built a political machine. He held a number of offices from registrar to state senator. He defended the often-targeted Bradley in the state senate, but then Bradley annoyed him too. Campbell worked in the state's Reconstruction movements on education and labor; in 1876, after conservatives took control of the state government, they set up a board to take control of McIntosh County, which he had run as his own. He was charged with unlawfully arresting a white man and did eleven months of hard labor even though he was justice of the peace at the time.[3]

Malcolm Claiborne, a freedman of South Carolina, came to Burke County in 1865 as a minister and teacher and two years later had what must have been a moving experience registering other Black Carolinians to vote for the first time in history. As a legislator, in 1870, he could do little more than get a bill passed in the state house to end sentencing prisoners to chain gangs that could not pass the senate. During that same year, he was killed by a fellow Black legislator just five years after arriving in the state. His fellow South Carolinian Henry McNeal Turner, who was born free and had left the state in 1859, became a minister at age nineteen. He arrived in 1865 as well, and was based in Macon, having served as the first Black chaplain to US troops. Others came from Virginia, Alabama, and South Carolina. They would all come to know each other as shapers of Black politics in Georgia, collectively working with thousands of freedpeople in the state and having visited the communities of tens of thousands.[4]

In July 1865, Rev. James D. Lynch, who had been sent to build churches in coastal South Carolina, came to Augusta to speak at the first Fourth of July celebration since the war and Abraham Lincoln's death. Lynch was the young minister who sat with General Sherman and a group of other Black ministers six months earlier as Sherman pondered giving freedpeople forty acres and a mule. Lynch's speech declared the holiday "a day of redemption from ignorance, from prejudice and from degradation." John E. Bryant, a former Union soldier and Freedmen's Bureau agent, described the event as "of surpassing interest." Bryant himself was cited in Lynch's speech in connection with a statement thanking northern charities and teachers for making it possible for seventy-five thousand Black children to be then attending schools in the South. Bryant reported in a publication of Lynch's speech that four thousand Black residents had paraded, led by a contingent of US Colored Troops, and that the marchers included "ministers, various societies, persons of the different trades and field laborers, also the children of the schools."[5] This is a glimpse of who was organizing in the area at the end of the war—ministers, benevolent societies, tradespeople, and field workers. The entire audience was estimated at ten thousand.

Lynch asked, "What is the part of the American Republic in the world's drama? What is her mission? Read the Declaration of Independence. . . . That is a doctrine. 'Both pure and sound.' This is a gospel . . . to elevate humanity and to oppose the despotism of the universe." Like many of the other ministers who went south, he saw the war as the inevitable destructive outcome of refusing to honor the republic's moral duty with regard to slavery, and like many others, he positioned Lincoln as an instrument of divine will. "All that my race asks of the white man is justice," said Lynch. In his optimism over the prospects of the day, Lynch misjudged the new president, Andrew Johnson, but also warned that if the country refused to honor its own ideals, it would be relegated to history's roll of failed republics.[6]

Lynch's political rhetoric centered on the republic's ideals was typical of many whose aspiration for freedpeople was inclusion in the body politic. Others advocated for localized self-governance within the parameters of Black-controlled settlements where sustenance crops could be raised and autonomy could be sheltered by geography and protected by the community. The political arena, as most Blacks were beginning to define it, had wages and work conditions as early priorities because workers who were performing jobs they had done as enslaved people not only were contending with the new expenses of rent, medical care, and funding for schools but also commonly faced wages lower than those paid their slaveholders for the same work.

Freedpeople in Georgia would repeatedly turn toward labor organizing when obstacles were put in the path of political empowerment. Over time, a significant number of those who did religious or political work would follow their lead into labor organizing. People working in crews on docks or in packing plants not only were aware of what pay their slaveholders had received when they were in bondage but also were aware of the current disparity in pay compared with that received by white employees doing the same or similar work. Such wage discrimination often led to protests. An example of the kinds of small-scale disruptions that arose occurred on September 4, 1865, in Savannah, when Black stevedores and dockworkers walked out for an increase in wages from $1.50 a day to $2.00. Twenty years earlier George Teamoh had made a better wage—$1.62 a day (for his slaveholders)—caulking ships on the Portsmouth docks and sometimes made slightly more, while at that time whites earned $2.00 or more.[7] To characterize the Savannah wage demand as the local newspaper did as "unjust and unreasonable" was itself exactly that. It is almost certain that white workers made more than these Black stevedores. A local police-man, accompanied by federal troops, arrested the leaders, which broke up the walkout. The paper claimed the strikers threatened to shoot anyone who worked at the current rate. Other than a reference to the men form-ing a "gang," the most telling description of the strikers was the phrase "a crowd of would-be independent negroes [who] concluded not to leave well enough alone."[8] The phrase "would-be independent" used to scoff at the workers aptly captures the intentions of freedpeople in many places with regard to living and working conditions. At the same time, the phrase suggests skepticism that Black self-reliance was possible while inferring objection to the idea. Many workers in the South "concluded not to leave well enough alone."

Mobilization

In January 1866, a state convention of one hundred African Americans met in Augusta at the same time white legislators in the capital were com-pleting the state's black code. Four days before the convention, Augusta's Black newspaper, the *Colored American*, reported on the successful efforts of Blacks to get soldiers stationed in nearby Wilkes County, where planters were forcing people off farms and "bands calling themselves bushwackers, jayhawkers, and regulators, are perpetrating the most shameful outrages—shooting, burning and beating negroes, to get money and for revenge." The paper also complained that the criminals would not be prosecuted, owing to sections of the black code passed a month earlier barring Black testimony against whites: "Their barbarous acts cannot be made known for legal effect except through negro testimony, and therefore cannot be punished."[9]

In some places, African Americans took the law into their own hands in response to a lack of due process for Blacks routinely being arrested in southern towns, or for whites who killed Blacks. In February, in Wilm-ington, North Carolina, Black soldiers "laid siege to the city jail" to halt the whipping of Black prisoners. One of their complaints was exactly the complaint made in Augusta, that in trial Blacks had not been allowed to testify. After this incident, all Black troops were withdrawn from the lower Cape Fear area and replaced with whites, and a freedman described the situation as one in which "if a Negro says anything or does anything that they don't like, [they] take a gun and put a bullet into him."[10] Also that year, armed Blacks in Orangeburg, South Carolina, brought to the jail three whites who had been terrorizing their community to have them charged. These armed reactions—large and small—to the failures of local policing, though exceptional, anticipated Black communities' planned responses a few years later to white vigilantism in small towns and rural locations across the South, particularly in Georgia.[11]

In the run-up to the convention, the paper took up a discussion of *social equality*, a term bandied about by white conservatives as the dreaded outcome of Black freedom. The *Colored American* editors asserted that African Americans wanted political equality but eschewed social equality. The paper was founded in 1865 by J. T. Shuften and the same James Lynch who spoke in Augusta the previous year, and who would address the convention. Invoking some of the exhibition of "fevered minds" among whites no doubt visible during the recent Christmas insurrection scare, Shuften began his editorial, "Equality. Social and Political," with this plaint: "This is the great bugbear of the Southern white man. . . . It is a very common thing for him to declare, in thunder tones, that 'the Negro can never attain unto Social and Political Equality,' yet he is straining every nerve, and not leaving a single stone unturned in order to *prevent* him from attaining unto that giddy distinction." The meaning of *social equality* was clearly understood by Shuften to include intimacy across the color line. On this point, alluding to the rapes and concubinage of the past, he turned ironic: "Is the colored man as anxious to have Social and Political Equality as the white man is not to let him have it? We think the answer to this will be a negative, at least in the case of Social Equality. *He has enough of that without his consent, God knows*."[12] On the past exploitation of women, the editor raised the issue of clauses in the black code requiring Black parents not living together to provide child support for all their children and asserted that justice would require the same for whites. "As it is, they have declared that the father shall support the children of possibly a dozen mothers, which by being sold and transferred from one plantation to another, through the laws of commerce, he was brought in contact with." The paper noted that the wording of the law did not *bar* white fathers being held accountable. "We think it but reasonable and just that the father should support his children," but to ignore white men when the mother was Black was "*unjust and unnatural*." This provision weighing on freedmen who were fathers or accepted that responsibility in marrying women with children could be daunting to men just entering wage work, especially as laborers faced wage cuts and planters who were reluctant to pay at all. Still, many such men raised children of concubinage. But the brunt fell to women, who may or may not have had a partner at emancipation or the means to seek child support. The newspaper editor, however, focused on the earlier harms to women in bondage and the current harms to men.[13]

The Georgia Black convention, which included a number of the activists already organizing in the state and at least six who would later hold office, demanded most of the same political rights as the earlier Black state conventions: some form of voting rights and the right to serve on juries. They called for schools, fair wages, and safe passage on public transport and demanded their assaulters be brought to justice. Safety from violence was the most discussed concern over the days of the convention and in the separate petition addressed to white legislators. The collection of testimony taken from delegates detailed a disturbing array of violent assaults on either the delegates themselves or people known to them. While asserting that "we need the power to represent our interest in every department bearing upon our condition as a people," the Savannah convention did not ask for unfettered suffrage but "at least conditional suffrage." In the final resolutions the language claims only "the same inalienable rights that are other men's." And while demanding "equal justice," they added a resolution stating they had no "desire for social equality beyond the transactions of normal business life." The one hundred delegates founded the Georgia Equal Rights Association (ERA), aiming to have branches in every county "to secure for every citizen, without regard to race, descent or color, equal political rights." It charged each county organization to "secure for all; 1st, equal political rights; 2d, assistance for the destitute; and 3d, the education and elevation of the people."[14]

Demoralization?

The founding of the Georgia ERA at the Augusta meeting had peculiar effects in Dougherty County, which would remain a troubled place throughout Reconstruction. Luckily, no violence resulted from an acute case of fear of a Black meeting in the summer of 1866 when sixty whites, alarmed about rumors concerning a local farm, wrote to the Freedmen's Bureau. The root of suspicions was the fact that the farm was Black-run, "held solely by Colored men, there being no white man upon it." Planters said they had heard a "society" was formed there asking an initiation fee and an oath of secrecy. The rumors involved "ideas of freedom" that included the right to "talk back, decide for themselves when & for what causes they can stay away from work," and the idea that "they are not accountable to the Freedmen's Bureau, or any white men but solely to their own President, or colored men of their own selection." Sixty-one signers made the extraordinary request that the military get the society "broken up" or "do away" with their "erroneous ideas." In this letter, certain "ideas of freedom" were said to be "wholly demoralizing" Blacks. The word *demoralize* is prominent in conservative postwar newspapers and public speech, usually used in a context where one might instead use the word *mobilize* or *mobilizing*. What riled conservative whites was likely not that Blacks might be dispirited or corrupted but that they might be energized.[15]

Incredibly, the former subassistant commissioner had already twice cited the group's president, Lawrence Speed, of the "Equal Rights Society" for "diffusing erroneous ideas among the freedmen." The panic and indignation evident in the neighbors' letter obscure the fact that they had already had several contacts with bureau agents, particularly two from slaveholding families who knew exactly who the group was that was working on the five-hundred-acre farm known as Whitlock. These earlier complaints had likely prompted the bureau's citations against Speed but did not get the farm "broken up."[16]

There are two ironies to the whites forwarding their petition up the chain of command for action from the head of the Georgia Freedmen's Bureau. First, the head of the state bureau was Brigadier General Davis Tillson, who had been the keynote speaker at the convention at which the ERA was formed. The second irony was that Tillson himself had aided this group of freedpeople in obtaining the farm in the first place. Having issued statements that freedpeople must have contracts and work on farms with white supervision *unless* they bought their own land, a branch of the ERA in another county decided to buy a place. Its members raised $7,000 but could not find a seller, and the bureau arranged for them to rent Whitlock from an absentee owner. The farm's inhabitants raised cotton and corn, and according to Lee Formwalt, the farm was "the southwest Georgia headquarters of the state's first Black political action group." The planters in the neighborhood had been told the group was primarily interested in gaining the right to vote, which, even if it was won, would not have changed the political picture in that area.[17]

The real problem was that in a neighborhood where planters barred their workers from having visitors or leaving the farm without permission, the ERA group welcomed and educated workers visiting from around the county. It was well known that it operated in as much secrecy as possible: "Fear of white hostility was a major factor in keeping the meetings closed to all but sworn members who had paid the initiation fee." The ERA group drilled in self-defense on the calculation that it might be attacked. Tillson realized what the agent did not—that "freedpeople have the same undoubted right with white persons to organize & carry on any Society, or Societies of any character whatever so long as such organization does not conflict with the existing laws of the State of which they are citizens." The response sent from the bureau added that the petitioners did not show "in what particular manner the Society is detrimental to the best interests of free labor" and concluded the bureau could not take action.[18]

Within two months of the planters' letter to the bureau, the ERA chapter had allied itself with the Union League, which was then coming into the state. Formwalt writes that the group became known simply as the Dougherty UL. The local planters were bothered with even more demoralization of the mobilizing kind. In 1867 the two groups merged statewide and chose Philip Joiner, formerly enslaved in Dougherty County, to be president. He would be elected as a delegate to the constitutional convention and the legislature, and would be wounded in an assassination attempt in a march into the town of Camilla in the next county.[19]

It speaks to the times that there were southerners who resisted *both* integration and Black separation and autonomy, and that an agent of the government that legalized freedom for enslaved people would issue a citation to freedpeople for disseminating "erroneous" ideas of freedom. While integration was violently resisted for one reason, separate schools for freedpeople were burned down for teaching Blacks at all. Autonomous political organizing was strenuously opposed. But perhaps the marauding white students of New Orleans who fought school integration hold a clue to unite these disparate attacks on the efforts of freedpeople to make their own lives. When the White League students felt the need to search out and eject students "suspected" of being Black in New Orleans in 1874, they situated the postemancipation idea of Blackness as a potentially invisible contaminant. Perhaps the threat posed by a student suspected of being Black was not physical contact or diminution of social status but "ideas of freedom." A threat of ideological contamination unites calls for segregation with a desire for supervision of Blacks and destruction of Black autonomous entities, as well as demands for punishment for "erroneous" private discourse.[20]

Circuit Riders

In Georgia some of the organizers who taught citizenship rights and organized voter registration in 1867 participated in the constitutional conventions and went on to hold office. Georgia elected thirty-seven African American delegates to the 1867–68 constitutional convention, including fifteen ministers, half of whom personally experienced violence between 1866 and 1870. The state had no major Black statewide officeholders (such as state treasurer) during Reconstruction. Not only was organizing in Georgia marked by ministers, but this group of activists contributed a disproportionate share of literature by or about Black organizers' experiences, in part because of their church ties.[21] In Georgia, the AME Church left a particularly enduring footprint; among the thirty-seven Black leaders elected to the state constitutional convention, there were nineteen ministers, eleven of whom were AME ministers (and four of them were also URCC speakers). Georgia stands alone as far as this depth of AME inclusion in its delegation. Like other groups sending organizers to the South, the AME preached industry, thrift, sobriety, and self-reliance, but the church's theology and political ideology perhaps helped nurture the emerging radicalism of southern Blacks. The AME pedagogy also appears complementary to the ideologies of African American fraternal groups expanding in the South, especially the Black Masons. Omar Ali sees the AME as a "staging ground" for Black populism. There were Black Methodists in the South in the early 1800s, notably in New Orleans, Charleston, and Louisville. (As stated earlier, the AME became famous in 1822 when the Denmark Vesey rebellion was exposed in Charleston.) Methodism was the largest Christian denomination in the country. Apart from the AME's Black pedagogy, the denomination was well suited to this southern work, based as it was on forming associations, training in self-governance, group fundraising, and ties to other Methodists. The Black ministers who came south reported being both much inspired by their audiences and inspiring *to* their audiences.[22]

Several letters from Black organizers who worked in Georgia show the methods used to organize freedpeople, and how the common repression in the state shaped priorities: (1) learning from locals the risks involved as far as personal safety; (2) the need to specifically look for local organizers with the courage to persist in a violent environment; (3) the usefulness of urging local organizers and groups to teach largely illiterate audiences to memorize the litany of citizenship rights; and (4) the advisability of making return trips as the passage of voting rights neared. They moved from preaching to teaching rights to setting up groups equipped with people who could follow up later with instruction on how to register to vote. Unmistakable in these letters, as in the words of organizers cited earlier, is the stunning effect on organizers of the size of the audiences that gathered to hear them talk about citizenship. For those men who spent years in the North, just to gaze upon a crowd of thousands of people who had lived in the slave system was transformative and, for many, seemingly motivated years of work long after the Freedmen's Bureau, Union Leagues, and Republican organizations were closed by officials in Washington.

On July 8, 1867, Rev. Henry McNeal Turner wrote to the URCC from Georgia, stating that he had attended the Union Republican State Convention that week and asked the African American delegates from forty counties to remain another day to have a separate meeting. Turner and three other activists trained the delegates in how to inform freedpeople of their citizenship rights and asked them to continue instruction until the people had committed it all to memory. While ministers in other states often got railroad discounts, in Georgia the railroads offered no such amenities and organizers traveled everywhere by horse, often covering more than two hundred miles in a single organizing trip.[23] On July 9, 1867, Turner wrote from Macon about the early days of his organizing efforts, revealing the ways in which activists attempting to register Blacks to vote mobilized the state's Black Belt counties. Activists who could teach rights, he reports, were "sought everywhere":

> A mass meeting was called last night at the Methodist Church to urge upon the people to exert themselves to save their Congressional districts from the wicked designs of men who are trying to prevent our people from registering. After listening to me very patiently, an association was organized to raise money to pay a lecturer to travel through this Congressional district. The ladies fired by a similar goal immediately organized another and each association had the names of fifty subscribers at 10 cents per week. By 12 o'clock we had so organized that we proceeded to elect the person to speak and organize when Lewis Smith of this city was selected. He accepts the position at [$]40 per month and will immediately enter upon the work. Fifteen counties were assigned to him. Mr. Smith is a brave and well informed man and will do much good. I trust the people of Savannah will go and do likewise.[24]

The mention of women forming a separate association, as opposed to joining the group first formed, is in keeping with common practice in the church, fraternal societies, and the Union League. Turner was forming Republican clubs and UL groups and sometimes church congregations on his trips. The emphasis on training males in the Republican clubs and UL was also considered practical because at the time only males would vote. Turner reported that he would follow a similar plan in "all the large places," in hopes of getting communities to choose other lecturers. He included a description of the excited celebration in the church at 1:00 a.m.: "The people shouted, jumped, clapped their hands and cheered till the white people in the vicinity were frightened."[25]

Turner wrote again from Macon on July 23. He traveled to an area that within a year would begin to show violent resistance to Black representation:

> I have just returned from the Southwest portion of the state. Have travelled through that hell-charged section under the garb of a presiding elder, preached at each place, lectured politically and formed Union Leagues, Republican clubs, etc. At Fort Valley, Rev. Isaac Anderson is doing good work. At Americus they have a strong league and the colored people and poor whites are pretty well republicanized. . . . At Albany, I formed a grand league. Was two whole nights drilling them in their duties. The whites are rebs to the pith, but the colored are brave and defiant.
>
> After leaving Albany, I went to Cuthbert where the rebels are very bitter and was advised by the bureau agent not to lecture. But after preaching, I lectured awhile on registration and formed a Union League which I think will save Randolph county. James Jackson of Cuthbert is a fearless fellow and stands up for his race like a hero.[26]

Turner formed "a magnificent league" at Fort Gaines and sent a Reverend Robert Alexander there, writing that "he has revolutionized the whole county. The rebels fear and hate him." In Dawson, Turner reported, "the people were very ignorant about the rights and very indifferent concerning their duties. But I think they are awake now. I was somewhat afraid to organize a league here as confidential men seemed rather scarce. But I have recently sent a preacher named Rev. Wm. Raven, who is a whole-souled fellow and a radical to the back bone." He thought then that the prospect of registering Black voters in the state was "good but not so bright as I would like it." Turner said the whites planned to bribe Blacks not to register to vote and were "without doubt making a desperate effort." Most of the counties he cited were successful early on in electing Blacks, but violence and intimidation were an ongoing issue in all of them for at least ten years.[27]

It is hard to overestimate the value of these ministers' language in describing people they encountered. To simply compliment a Georgia man as "whole-souled" and "radical to the back bone" defies generations of print propaganda on African Americans that Turner himself would have experienced and historical silences that continued from before the war on through the century and beyond. His representations of people who had been enslaved were part of the tiny fraction of documents that would see daylight painting honest assessments of the four million. This nationwide silence on the willingness of Black southerners to resist oppression is one reason these ministers were so startled by their own audiences. The often exuberant letters of Rev. John T. Costin are another example of freedpeople eagerly turning out to hear how to claim more from freedom.[28]

At the same time that Turner was traveling through the southwest counties of Georgia's Black Belt, his colleague Costin, a Virginian and an AME Zion minister, headed in the opposite direction from Macon to Black Belt counties to the northeast. Costin, like two dozen others, would also be elected as a delegate to the constitutional convention and to the legislature, expelled from the legislature, and forced out of his home and county by the Ku Klux Klan. Costin started groups wherever he went, meeting with people in large gatherings but also "in the cabins, sometimes on the plantations and wherever the chance occurred in the churches after preaching," though the URCC described him and the others it hired simply as "colored speakers."[29]

> Left Macon June 6 and proceeded to Jefferson County and held a republican mass meeting at Louisville June 8. It was a grand affair, largely attended by the people of Jefferson as well as surrounding counties. Organized a republican club and a loyal league. Went from there to the help of our friends in Greene County. Here again the mass meeting was a tremendous success. I was met at the depot by about six hundred persons. . . . We proceeded to the grove where there was assembled a vast audience amongst which there were a number of rebels. I felt a little shy to begin with, when I got warmed up, I forgot all about rebs and everything else except my duty.[30]

These counties were at the center of effective Black organizing and increasing armed white resistance. Costin next went to Burke County, about which he had some fear owing to tales he had heard of white hostility in that county. "The first sight that met my eye on arriving at Waynesboro, was a Johnny [Reb] in a one horse buggy, driving at a fast rate with a freedman chained behind him and manacled with an iron collar round his neck. I said to myself this looks rough." Costin saw the local Freedmen's Bureau agent and gave posters for an upcoming mass meeting to "a number of teamsters who had come to the place after corn and provision."[31]

That evening he rode to two farming villages and met people, and later held the Waynesboro mass meeting in a local grove, to which, he said, people had come from as far as twenty-five miles away. "Everything went off peaceable and pleasant. The freedmen declared it to be the first time since their emancipation that they had ever had explained to them their rights before the law. The rebs cursed me terribly, some threatening to shoot me, but the only thing that occurred was being spit upon by a rebel while passing the street. I took no notice of the insult because there were nearly 2000 colored persons in the place and nearly every one had fire-arms." Costin described all these events as barely "a fourth part of my campaign," listing five other towns visited and the formation of "loyal leagues, Union Republican clubs, Educational and Temperance societies in nearly every place of prominence."[32]

Costin's report is startling on several accounts: first, in documenting that freedpeople came armed to mass meetings; second, in detailing what could be accomplished by one tireless organizer; and third, in demonstrating the breadth of organizing undertaken, which spanned numerous community-building needs in any given rural community, from schools to Republican Party organizations, and in his view, groups espousing sobriety. All these revelations speak to the conditions encountered by men and women who had firsthand experience of the postabolition South.[33]

The collective work on voter registration by all the organizers among the freedpeople resulted in an electorate in October 1867 with a white majority of just 1,757 voters in a state of 1 million people. At the same time, Blacks accounted for 90 percent of Republican voters in Georgia. And, across the South, white voters stayed away from the election of constitutional convention delegates. The 37 Blacks were part of a delegation of 165, which shows a paucity of Blacks on ballots. Of Georgia's then 132 counties, Black delegates came from 31 counties, 6 of which would not elect representatives again in the nineteenth century.[34]

Making Political Voice Makes Opposition

The constitutional convention met from December 1867 to March 1868. The new constitution provided for free public education for all and various forms of relief for those faced with foreclosures and tax burdens. It outlawed whipping as a punishment for crime, and imprisonment for debt. It provided "mechanics and laborers" the right to put "liens on property of their employers for labor performed or material furnished" and stipulated that "the social status of the citizen shall never be the subject of legislation." Crucially, as it turned out, in defining citizenship and providing the right to vote to all males born or naturalized in the state, there was disagreement over adding that voters could also hold office. It was argued that the fact that voters could hold office was obvious, and inclusion of such wording was voted down. Delegates Henry McNeal Turner, Tunis G. Campbell Sr., Aaron Bradley, and other Republicans fought for the language. The opposition coalition threatened to vote down the entire constitution, and the Black leaders gave up.[35]

Voting in April 1868 ratified the new constitution, along with the election of a Republican governor, Rufus Bullock, and statewide officeholders. Twenty-three counties elected a total of thirty-two Black legislators—the first African Americans to sit in the state house and assembly—twenty-nine in the House and three in the senate: Aaron Bradley, Tunis Campbell, and George Wallace. Five of the counties sending Blacks to the legislature were previously unable to elect any Blacks to the constitutional convention, suggesting continued political work that bore fruit in those areas. The assembly convened in July 1868 and ratified the Fourteenth Amendment, allowing the state to be readmitted to the Union. Readmission ended the US Congress's control of the state and brought a close to military control.[36]

Several months later, Democrats in the state and in the legislature called into question whether Blacks were eligible to sit in the legislature. Despite Republican majorities in the state house and senate, in mid-September both bodies used the omission of the right-to-hold-office clause to oust Bradley, Campbell, and Wallace from the state senate, and all but three of the twenty-nine African American representatives in the state house. (*See Georgia maps [plates 6 and 7]*.) Though legally still in office, the Black representatives were not allowed to vote on their expulsion. Du Bois later wrote, "This was probably a trick engineered by ex-Governor Brown for election purposes." In the short run it was used to justify unseating nearly every Black officeholder. In the long run, as Du Bois points out, the idea was probably to prevent any other Blacks from ever holding office.[37]

On September 19, 1868, three of the ousted legislators, Henry McNeal Turner, John T. Costin, and James M. Simms, men who had worked as URCC speakers and Republican organizers, wrote in protest to a US senator and to the congressman who headed up the URCC. The three men had been chosen by the expelled officeholders "to lay the case . . . before the Congress of the United States." Turner represented Bibb County and by then had become the most powerful Black leader in the state. Costin, who earlier worked with Turner, represented Talbot County. Simms, who represented Chatham County, had been enslaved in Savannah, had been publicly whipped for teaching other enslaved people to read, and had escaped when the war started. He became a minister and returned to Georgia a year later. Simms worked for the Freedmen's Bureau, was a UL organizer, and had started two newspapers by the time he was elected. Their letter listed the members voted out, adding that the resolutions gave "no reasons for ejection save our being *Free Persons of Color*."[38]

> We therefore Most Respectfully yet earnestly Protest against Said Acts of the General Assembly of the State of Georgia, Also against the admission of the Senators-elect from Georgia to the Senate of the United States Congress, upon the ground that the Reconstruction Measures have not been executed in good Faith by the general Assembly of Georgia as we think we are prepared to Prove, and therefore the State of Georgia is not in that condition for Relations with or in the Union according to the intent and meaning of the Reconstruction Measures of Congress.[39]

One way to understand the Black political work in Georgia is to look at this "class of '68"—the first African American state legislators elected to statewide office in Georgia. Compared with other Black officeholders later in nineteenth-century Georgia, this group suffered the brunt of reaction to change in the political system. Leaving aside the three house members who were not expelled basically because they looked white and refused to admit to being Black, nearly every one of the rest of the group was subjected to violence and intimidation in addition to being expelled. The experiences of the Georgia class of '68 show a daunting pattern: Rev. Thomas Allen: forced out of his county; Eli Barnes: received KKK threats and was visited by armed men; Aaron Bradley: earlier tried by a military commission, had his school closed down; Rev. Tunis G. Campbell: jailed for nearly a year in the 1870s for "improperly" arresting a white man while justice of the peace; Rev. Malcolm Claiborne: KKK threat; George Clower: KKK threat; Rev. Abram Colby: in 1869, taken captive by thirty KKK men and, in the presence of his family, whipped and beaten over a period of hours; Rev. John Costin: KKK threat, forced out of his county; Rev. Monday Floyd: threatened by KKK to not return to office when reinstated; F. H. Fyall (who denied his race): not expelled, but jailed and temporarily run out of his county; William Harrison: KKK threat; James Jackson, arrested for carrying a concealed weapon (though the governor found Jackson needed the weapon and pardoned him); Philip Joiner: wounded in an assassination attempt during the Camilla riot; Rev. Romulus Moore: 1868 KKK threat, home invasion in 1869, threatening him and his wife; Alfred Richardson: two KKK attacks, forced out of his county temporarily, shot, house burned, died in 1872, rumored to have been poisoned; Rev. Henry McNeal Turner: KKK threats, kept armed guards at his home; George Wallace: warrant issued against him.[40]

Twelve members of the class of '68 had no apparent documented threats, but their home counties were all places where real contests were fought over Black representation; in some cases, the most visible leaders in their counties were threatened and others not. The counties on the Atlantic—McIntosh, Liberty, and Chatham—seemed to have fared best in 1868.

Two observations can be made about the violence: the first generation of Black officeholders were the victims of a widespread push to eliminate or intimidate them out of office, and a number of those targeted in 1868–69 who were the first and lone Black representatives of their counties were also the last. This also happened after the 1870 reinstatement of Black legislators in nineteen other counties where there was only one Black legislator. Altogether, after the legislators won reinstatement, twenty-five Georgia counties lost any further Black representation for the rest of the century. Violence was documented against many of those representatives. Even the four counties represented by Blacks who claimed to be white lost Black representation after the reinstatement. Counties that suffered fewer documented violent incidents, probably due to having some of the densest Black majorities in the state, kept representation longer: Liberty, McIntosh, and Camden, sitting on the coast, elected several Black men at the turn of the twentieth century who cooperated with Democrats.[41]

These developments have been spelled out because they suggest patterns linked to violence. As Edmund Drago tells us: "L. N. Trammell, later elected president of the Georgia State Senate, advised a friend in March,

1868: 'the negroes should as far as possible be *kept from the polls*. I think that the organization of the KKK might effect this more than anything else.' The head of the Klan in Oglethorpe County publicly admitted years later that 'the Reconstruction acts and fifteenth amendment put the Southern negroes in politics. The Klan organized to put them out, and it succeeded.'" Blacks in Oglethorpe were unable to elect any Blacks to statewide office beyond the constitutional convention delegates for the rest of the century. Romulus Moore, among those attacked, likened the Klan methods to those of the slave patrols: "There has always been a patrol law in this country; and this is the same, only in worse form."[42]

Making Self-Defense

Table 6.1 shows that contention over representation in the state happened in rural and urban settings, and that the roots of the circuit were on the coast in Savannah, and hubs were in Macon and Augusta in the Black Belt. Black political activity was vigorously contested in Georgia and in some of the sites in table 6.1 that lacked Black press and other institutions that helped other places gain representation despite violence. Dougherty County, home to Albany in southwest Georgia (the area Turner called "hell-charged" in 1867), became a storied place, owing to its Reconstruction history. Dougherty elected two Blacks to the 1867–68 constitutional convention. One was Benjamin Sikes, a farm laborer who had been a voting registrar before the convention. The other was Philip Joiner, born in slavery in Virginia, who also worked in the early Georgia Black labor movement and was elected to the convention and then to the state Assembly, from which he was expelled in 1868 with the other Black legislators. Shortly after the expulsion, on September 19, 1868, Blacks who made a twenty-five-mile march from Albany to a rally just south of Dougherty in one of the few white majority counties in the area became victims of the Camilla Massacre. Joiner was a specific target of the attack and was shot and wounded.

Whites in Mitchell County had threatened African Americans with violence if they held the planned election rally for their candidate for Congress, a white former Union officer. The Camilla sheriff tried to force several hundred headed to the meeting to turn over the guns that many had brought in case of trouble. The Albany Blacks had debated whether to take arms—some did, some did not—and the group had also prepared for trouble by planning safe havens and by arriving in large numbers. When the marchers said their intention was to meet peacefully and refused to surrender their arms, they were fired upon, leaving at least nine dead and dozens wounded. People were chased into the swamps and woods, and a reign of terror against Blacks voting persisted for several weeks.[43]

In Albany the previous day, one minister had advised people to go unarmed. After the shooting, Albany residents discussed organizing a party to try to rescue those still in Camilla. Another minister, AME pastor Robert Crumley, told his church that he had warned those heading to the Camilla meeting to take no fewer than "150 well-armed men, and then suggested traveling there en masse the next day to 'burn the earth about the place.'" A promise from the Freedmen's Bureau agent to call for federal troops and investigate cooled the fury, but no help came.[44]

This particular evidence of debates within a Black community over the need to bear arms for self-defense at an outdoor public meeting reveals one aspect of Black political discourse that is rarely discussed. We do not really know if it was one of the many sudden lessons of abolition for freedpeople that those who had declared civil war and been defeated would then make war on Blacks and become an omnipresent threat. Surely some people expected trouble, but the extent to which it occurred was a new form of shared disaster for freedpeople.

Freedpeople were improvising the groundwork for responding to rural mob violence, urban mob violence, and urban police violence. The conditions for protecting people against any of these were poor. But freedpeople were also shaping a new regime of knowledge for defining citizenship, demanding citizenship, mobilizing forces of change, and asserting rights not yet fully inscribed in law. In many respects this new knowledge regime—that their opponents called "erroneous ideas"—was the cause of much violence and became the legacy protected at the cost of lives in places like southwest Georgia.[45]

In the case of the Camilla Massacre, the people took the threats quite seriously and made preparations both for a fight and for flight. The advice from the first minister, who advocated going unarmed, was not moral advice but tactical thinking—unarmed marchers might not be perceived as a threat and thus might get to the meeting unharmed. The obvious counter to this argument was that they might be shot anyway. What is most telling about Reconstruction is the fact that there was advance tactical debate for a *public* meeting, an exercise in the constitutional right "peaceably to assemble." The rally was not a protest over the ouster of their duly elected officials, though that would make sense, but was intended to allow a white candidate for office to speak. They were armed because they were aware that their right to assembly would be threatened. The idea was for as many people as possible to attend the meeting and survive. If people survived, so might the right of Black citizens to assemble. If they did not try, it would not. It is impressive that at least forty-nine people were killed or injured in defense of the right to hold a meeting, with full knowledge that none of it was likely to result in arrests of assailants.

In the second phase of this episode, the debate about self-defense was not initially about grievance regarding the massacre. It was at first a discussion of how a group of people from one county could go into another county to rescue people who were hurt and hiding and get both rescued and rescuers back alive. Crumley's impassioned advice following the riot to take "150 well-armed men" and to then "burn the earth about the place" is not moral advice any more than that of the first minister but a cry of vengeance and a call perhaps to use retaliatory violence as a warning to Camilla. This is an unsurprising human response. But given the silence of the historiography on Black self-defense, it should be said about these events that the need for self-defense was not questioned, only when and how it should be deployed. This commonsense concern for safety, a quotidian facet of southern Black life, usually survives only in the oral history of a family member who kept a rifle or in the lore of the lone "crazy n——r" who would not cooperate with a facade of docility—a man or woman feared by Blacks and whites alike. Today we can be utterly startled to hear facts in contravention to the silence around Black responses to violence after slavery—even known and expected violence. The southern racial regime so skewed logic that among whites in the nineteenth-century South self-defense by Blacks could be deemed unjustifiable. By the 1890s, Ida B. Wells lists "self-defense" as one of the documented reasons cited for lynchings of Blacks. The behavior of the Camilla sheriff presses home the "logic" of labeling Black self-defense as "crazy"—that any people who had been threatened would refuse to stack their arms on the street to be confiscated as they marched into a hostile town must be crazy, bent on trouble, and criminal, and should be attacked before they could attack first.

Self-defense was surely a much more dangerous act in the slave system, especially given the policing in place to prevent flight and search out hiding places, and was doubtless sometimes engaged by people tired of being afraid, or who were "crazy." Frederick Douglass's act of self-defense with a "slave-breaker" turned out to be sane and, in his case, effective. Freedpeople were often prevented from defending themselves by sheer numbers and in southern civil society also lived inside a wide range of fixed ideas about insanity—usually referred to as defying or deviating from southern "custom." In reality, both ideas concerning Black insanity and the prohibitions of customary practices targeted any display of one's rights of citizenship: unfettered access to public space, the right to gather in public, to bear arms (when it was common on the streets of southern towns), to defend one's home and family with violence if necessary, to demand pay for work done or crops harvested. The willingness of people whose names are not in the public record to take such risks en masse to have a meeting indeed would be crazy if they did not try to survive it. But at the time those were also the terms of going to bed at night in one's own home.[46]

Restoring Political Voice?

Georgia's refusal to ratify the Fifteenth Amendment in March 1869 forewarned citizens that Black voting would be contested on the ground. Congress took up a bill to require the state to ratify the amendment for readmission to the Union. During the debates in December 1869, General Benjamin Butler, by then a Massachusetts congressman, argued against allowing a state legislature that had thrown out its Black representatives to simply resume business. Butler listed disturbing numbers of Black and white legislators who had been murdered since the expulsion, noting that no arrests had been made. He then detailed that more than a dozen others, Black and white, had been "driven from their homes and are to-day refugees from the counties they were elected to represent, driven off by Kuklux [sic] Klans."[47]

Butler ended his account of violence against officeholders with a rhetorical question: "Now, sir, shall we listen to the proposition to wait until the rebel element of Georgia shall elect men in the place of those who have been murdered because they were loyal to the Union? Not much, I think. I think it is a new way in Republican government to change your majorities to murder your opponents, and then ask for time to elect others in the place of those who have been murdered." On December 27, 1869, the US Congress reestablished military rule in Georgia. The African American members of state government were reinstated in 1870 with back pay. On return, they became part of a radical majority, but in the next election the Democrats won majorities in both the state house and the senate. The thirteen Blacks elected in 1871 witnessed the end of Reconstruction Georgia. The legislators who survived had reason for bitterness over the brevity

and terror of the exercise of Blacks' right to vote in Georgia and the consequences thereof, including having a Republican governor who did not
appoint Blacks to office. Edwin Belcher, a class of '68 member who was
not expelled due to his white appearance, protested this absurdity. In an
1868 letter to Butler, Belcher wrote: "Do you think it would be just . . . to
appoint all white men in Georgia when ninety-thousand of the 120,000 republicans in Georgia are colored men?" In an 1870 speech, Henry McNeal
Turner was also blunt: "But for all, what have we got in Georgia, simply the
right to vote and sit in the General Assembly. . . . Not a colored juror or a
colored police in all the State. Two colored magistrates, one colored clerk
of the court, and one or two colored bailiffs. . . . We are forced to pay taxes
to keep up schools and municipalities, and not a dollar is ever extended for
the benefit of colored children." And the governor Blacks had supported,
despite their many efforts to legislate protections and humane treatment
for the incarcerated, had extended the practice of the federal officials of
leasing convicted persons to private entities, putting this inhumane exploitation on the road to legal long-term use. And ironically, as Drago points
out, these Black legislators would also later realize that the very poll tax
they had passed to pay for public schools would be reinstated in 1872 and
used thereafter to repress the Black vote.[48]

Governor Bullock resigned in 1871 and fled the state in fear of corruption charges (of which he was later cleared) and the KKK, which terrorized
the 1870 election. The KKK resented his asking Congress to continue military rule and had an active role in the Democratic victory. The six Black
men who were elected in the 1880s and 1890s, and the two elected in the
early 1900s, were the last elected until 1962.[49]

Freedpeople were also organizing at the time around labor issues. In
November 1869, freedpeople held the Georgia State Colored Convention
in Macon, which brought together 236 delegates from 56 of the state's 132
counties. According to the National Anti-Slavery Standard, the assembly
agreed to form the State Mechanics' and Laborers' Association and to build
a network of "local workingmen's Unions." They chose delegates as well to
attend the Colored National Labor Convention, held in Washington, DC,
in December 1869.[50]

The Macon convention produced a progressive agenda that promoted
the rights of labor, supported the nascent emigration movement in several
resolutions, documented wages and education among freedpeople in the
fifty-six counties, and welcomed Chinese laborers to the United States.
The group agreed to start a newspaper to be run by Henry McNeal Turner.

Matters of further organizing included the recommendations that people create "Cooperative Supply Clubs and associations for the purchase of lands . . . and the forming of clubs among those employed on plantations for material defense." The group also urged women to withdraw from field work when possible, though the *Standard* gives no insight into the reasons for the suggestion. The text enacts a patriarchal masculinity offering protective advice and perhaps promoting traditional gender roles. However, women may have welcomed the chance to raise their children themselves, and staying out of the fields may have been safer as well. Women doubtless also would have been relieved to be able to base such decisions on health, such as pregnancy. Most women likely did not actually just stay home; many did domestic work for badly needed cash and field work during harvests.[51]

The labor group invited detailed testimony on violence and discrimination from every county represented, with the result that there was documentation of more than two dozen murders and numerous additional incidents. Of the twenty-seven murders cited in the article, there were eleven murders in counties on the Georgia Emancipation Circuit as it existed at that time, twelve murders in counties adjacent to the circuit, and murders in four other counties.[52]

Clearly the violence precipitated by the election in 1868 continued. A number of counties maintained the effort and succeeded in electing Blacks in 1870 after the first generation of officials was restored to the legislature. The four counties cited for violence by the labor delegates that were not on the Georgia Emancipation Circuit included some far from the Black Belt, places where the conditions of the slave system were maintained, and one about which delegates testified that people there had never been told they were free.

The convention produced a resolution reading, "We advise our people, to the extent of their power, to defend themselves against any and all of these outrages." The event comports with earlier Black conventions after the Civil War in attempting to create archives documenting the condition of freedpeople. However, it takes a more assertive tone, particularly in response to the expulsion of elected leaders and the right of citizens to defend themselves from violence and terrorism. It also seems to have been one of the early spurs to labor organizing in the state, which continued to the end of the century.[53]

Table 6.1 shows that the hardships of agricultural work resulted in decades of different labor organizing formations alongside political efforts in the Black Belt. While civil rights campaigns in cities may have included desegregation of streetcars, rural agendas remained focused over time on access to the vote, violence, pay, and working conditions, as well as serving on juries and opportunities to own land. Given the numbers of freedpeople who voted, their enthusiasm for the possibilities of change is obvious. Change proved a fugitive goal but allowed these communities to articulate some important interventions that were presented to the legislature, such as barring corporal punishment and proposing to abolish prisons. The limitations and challenges to nineteenth-century federal civil rights acts (and the lack of a federal voting mechanism) required African Americans to fight various forms of discrimination first in southern state courts, and as in the case of *Plessy v. Ferguson* in the Supreme Court, they usually lost. (Boycotts against private companies, even in the nineteenth century, proved more successful.) Though the trajectory of campaigns that could be taken to the courts, such as streetcar segregation, may have engaged the attention of many, these were expensive routes to change, and a final defeat in the courts often ended protests until someone else could again raise funds to take the legal journey. This was a pattern set in Reconstruction that has continued to the present, and Supreme Court decisions from the late twentieth century on have made gaining a discrimination judgment more difficult. Georgia began finding legislative methods of repressing the Black vote in the late nineteenth century. As of 1907, it became impossible to elect an African American to the state legislature. Ironically, more than a century later forces in control of the Georgia state legislature are breaking new ground with efforts to both thwart access to the vote and control judgment of election outcomes.[54]

Due to the persistent lack of safety, organizing in some rural places moved toward emigration strategies in the 1880s and 1890s. These efforts, in turn, sustained local organizing after Reconstruction simply because the process of raising the funds to migrate took years, tended to attract communities that wanted to stay together, and involved multiple generations. Emigration was organized both by the mass participatory democracy process and often in secret, depending on the prevalence of violence. Despite the threat, many emigration groups continued to hold meetings. It is an instructive facet of Black organizing in the South that the unsuccessful movements that arose to get people out of the South would have served to keep people tied to other local Black community organizations and preserved local networks. Alongside emigration societies, other societies thrived late in the century.

In 1895, the *New York Times* published an article on the thousands of "negro societies" in the South and their beneficial effects on African American communities, though citing an "inconvenience and a hardship to the Southern white people, especially housewives," owing to what employers deemed too much time spent at meetings. The article focuses on Macon, Georgia, "with its 12,000 negro inhabitants," of which the reporter guesses that ninety-nine of every hundred people belonged to societies and asserts that some joined as many as six groups, which provided medical and burial benefits. Such press approval was uncommon as by then societies were often demonized by whites in the South and associated with both political and criminal activity, with routine violent consequences. Lynching victims were sometimes accused of being in "societies." At least by 1887, the American Missionary Association and the Catholic Church had started warning Blacks against joining any mutual benefit societies *other than their own*.[55]

The lynching epidemic around the country at the end of the century had well-documented cases in Georgia. There were 138 lynchings in Georgia between 1880 and 1898, and in April 1899 the state gained infamy for the lynching and mutilation of Sam Hose, a Coweta County man accused of killing his employer and, as the story spread, accused of other violent acts as well. The manhunt for him involved hundreds of people and ended in a gruesome lynching witnessed by a mob of two thousand. The Hose murder prompted other violence and widespread outrage, as for many it was the first widely reported spectacle lynching. W. E. B. Du Bois, who was in Atlanta at the time, later described as life-changing the trauma of his proximity to news and evidence of the horror. Between May and November, according to Fitzhugh Brundage, "mobs in Georgia executed nineteen blacks, frequently with blood-curdling savagery."[56]

Black communities continued to respond to protect those they could. One incident took place in McIntosh County, the nearly 75 percent Black county famously organized by Tunis Campbell. By the summer of 1899, Campbell was dead, but the local Black formations lived on. In the town of Darien, in August, a young married white woman accused her well-respected Black neighbor of rape when she gave birth to a biracial child. Henry Delegale turned himself in to the sheriff (perhaps for his own safety), and no one was too worried as the charge was viewed with skepticism by people who knew the accuser. But then the sheriff tried to move him to Savannah. Blacks concerned that Delegale might be killed on the road encircled the jail so that neither the sheriff nor a mob of local whites could get him out of the building. If there was an attempt by anyone to move Delegale, the bell at the First African Baptist Church would ring, summoning Blacks from the area. As it was, men and women came from around the county, including "rural farmers from nearby Sapelo Island, day laborers, sawmill workers, and domestic servants." The sheriff tried to take Delegale out a few more times, "but on each occasion the watchmen rang the bell and hastily gathered crowds of blacks refused to allow the transfer of the prisoner." In response, the sheriff asked the governor for troops, and two hundred state militiamen were sent.[57]

Though not even a fistfight had occurred, the Savannah papers called the Black presence a riot and predicted race war. Delegale was safely taken away by troops as Blacks watched at the train station. Violence did occur, however, when a temporary deputy pulled a gun at the Delegale house, trying to arrest all of his children. One deputy was killed and another wounded. A total of fifty-eight Black men and five Black women were arrested for congregating outside the jail. Two of Delegale's sons were convicted in the deputy's death and sentenced to life, while another brother and a sister were acquitted. Half of the community people were later acquitted, while twenty-three were convicted of rioting "and received fines ranging from two hundred fifty to one thousand dollars and one year prison terms at hard labor." Two women were convicted of rioting and hired out to a sawmill, despite an 1897 law against leasing female prisoners. Henry Delegale was acquitted of the rape charge.[58]

In both the Camilla and Darien mob incidents, the Black people involved made decisions that were tactical, based on the assumption that ad hoc groups of angry whites would use lethal force, that numbers could prevent shootings, and that resistance to mob "justice" was worth the risk regardless of what might happen later in court. The Blacks in Darien did not run. They would have known Sam Hose had been hunted by hundreds over half of the state, and that in the Camilla Massacre thirty-one years earlier, people were chased throughout the county. The people in Albany had tried to do for the people in Camilla what was done in Darien. There was a decision-making process in these situations—largely invisible to us now—by which communities made responses to violence or threats that had become predictable. As Bryan Wagner writes of Du Bois's encounter with the mutilation of Sam Hose, the signs left by these routine acts of war and pathology also "point the way to a new mode of kinship—a kinship that Du Bois would encapsulate in *Dusk of Dawn* not as the continuity of cultural inheritance but as the experience of a common disaster." This kinship, of course, was not new but perhaps was experienced by Du Bois as an awakening shock. Southern Black responses to the mob violence on the rise in the late nineteenth century were born of unrelentingly common, widespread, and shared disaster. And this kinship in freedom embedded itself as part of the new regime of knowledge Black southerners passed on when the details of their experience became obscure. This was a kinship felt even by poor Mr. Berry, a shoemaker in a different county from the Darien incident who was whipped and run out of town for saying that perhaps the married woman in Darien was not above reproach.[59]

Looking at Table 6.1

The most notable characteristic of table 6.1 is the large number of counties that had numerous community institutions, most developed in the later years of the century. The only counties that had such an array in the 1870s were the areas around Savannah and Macon. Greene County, in the heart of the Black Belt, had them early as well—except for local newspapers. The most unusual characteristic is, of course, the short period in which most Blacks had representation in state government. Black populism also developed here, along with some Liberia emigration movements and an unusual prevalence of open organizing against convict leasing and around self-defense.

TABLE 6.1 Georgia Emancipation Circuit, 1870–1900

	US Troops	RR (1884)	Union League	AMA Schools	Local Black Press	Black Political Reps	Knights of Labor Groups	19th Century Activism
				Institutions Present				
ALBANY Dougherty County ß		+		+		+ 1868–70 only		Labor
ATLANTA Fulton County	+	+		+	3 1882 1900	+	2 M mixed labor	Labor Civil rights
AUGUSTA Richmond County	+	+	Possibly	+	7 1865– 1900	+ 1868–70 only	Number unknown, textile workers	Labor Self-defense School access Anti–Jim Crow Liberia emigration
BRUNSWICK Glynn County ß	+	+	Unknown	+		+ 1871–73 only		Anti–convict leasing

(Continued)

TABLE 6.1 (*Continued*)

	US Troops	RR (1884)	Union League	AMA Schools	Local Black Press	Black Political Reps	Knights of Labor Groups	19th Century Activism
					Institutions Present			
COLUMBUS Muscogee County ß	+	+	+	+	$\frac{1}{1900}$	+ 1868–70 only		Liberia emigration
Greene County ß	+	+	+	+	Available in area	+ 1868–70 only		Civil rights Self-defense
MACON Bibb County ß	+	+	+	+	$\frac{1}{1900}$	+ 1868–70 1878–1907		Labor Liberia emigration Black populism Colored Farmers' Alliance (CFA)
McIntosh County ß	+	+	+	+	$\frac{1}{1895}$	+		Land Labor Self-defense

SAVANNAH **Chatham County ß**	•	•		•		•	<u>5</u> 1867 1868 1876 (2) 1888	Liberia emigration
SPARTA **Hancock County ß**	•	In area		Unknown	•	•	1868–70	Liberia emigration
SUMMERTOWN Emanuel County	•	In area		Unknown			1 M / F /Black/white farm workers, RR & mill workers	Labor
WAYNESBORO **Burke County ß**	•	•		In area	•	•	1868–70	Anti–convict leasing

SOURCES: *See* Table Source Notes (393–96).

KEY: **Bold** = Site playing multiple roles on the circuit. **ß** = Black majority; unless otherwise noted, populations are for 1870. **RR** = Rail lines. **Black Political Reps** = Black representatives to the 1868 constitutional convention or members of the General Assembly.

Knights of Labor = Black assemblies of the labor organization. Most KoL assemblies were segregated by race and gender: white males, Black males, white females, or Black females. "Mixed labor" is a term from the Garlock data (*see* Table Source Notes) and indicates various forms of work, not mixing by race or gender. **Gender** is indicated here by M or F.

7 FLORIDA
Faction

Faction: *syn.* party (body of partisans), interest, side, division, sect, wing, splinter group . . .
—*Roget's International Thesaurus,* 3rd ed. (1965)

Carpetbag: *n.* (1830) a traveling bag made of carpet . . . *adj.* (1870) of, relating to, or characteristic of carpetbaggers (a ~government).
Carpetbagger: *n.* (1864) **1 : a** Northerner in the South after the American Civil War usu. seeking private gain under the reconstruction governments . . .
—*Webster's Ninth New Collegiate Dictionary* (1986)

In the fall of 1862, Union forces occupied Jacksonville, though control of the town shifted several times during the rest of the war. Much of the state was still undeveloped, but on hearing of Union ships on the coast, enslaved people there began to move north and east from the peninsula to the Atlantic Coast to take refuge behind Union lines. In October 1861, Union forces had set up camps in what became known as the Department of Florida until 1862, when some sections of the state became part of the military's Department of the South and others became part of the Department of the Gulf. The Union maintained a blockade of all the state's ports throughout the war but only held discrete parts of the state during the war.

Fugitives from slavery appeared at the Atlantic coast military posts as they had farther north. In February 1863, the post commander at Fernandina had reported there were 1,000 refugees at the camp, only 100 of whom were "able-bodied men," and that the post had given rations to 772 Black people. In May, the provost marshal general reported: "The general sanitary condition of the post is excellent. I find at this post some 1050 negro women & children who are provided with quarters & rations by the commissary." However, owing to concerns about overcrowding and the coming of the "sickly season," he recommended "these families be removed to the neighborhood of the station of the regiment to which their protectors [presumably husbands or other male kin] are attached; and that quarters similar to those built at the negro village near Hilton Head, be provided for them." In fact, people were transported from small posts like Fernandina. "Large numbers of unemployed former slaves were simply shipped to Port Royal, [South Carolina,] shifting to another locality the problem of supporting destitute freedpeople whose fathers, husbands, and sons were serving the Union." In fact, aside from earlier movements from North Carolina to Virginia discussed in the preceding chapters, in "July 1865, Colonel Orlando Brown had suggested relocating 'surplus' people from Virginia to public land elsewhere, in order to reduce a glut of labor that was holding down wages. . . . Brown and others advocated their voluntary emigration to Florida, where, with the help of the government, they might acquire homesteads in the public domain." Three months later the same man suggested a similar use of "the large tracts now held by the government in the States of Florida and Texas." This pattern of continually moving people out of a state occurred as well during the war with large numbers on the Mississippi, where families from that state and from Arkansas were put to work on islands on the Mississippi River or delivered to a large contraband camp in St. Louis, Missouri, with no promise of help for them to acquire their own land.[1]

Unlike most other states during the war, Florida had been viewed by planters in neighboring states as a refuge in which they could hide enslaved people from freedom. Surely some of those same enslaved people would have tried to flee to Union lines on the coast. In 1865, J. S. Fullerton, adjutant of the Freedmen's Bureau, wrote to the head of the bureau reporting on a trip to the state: "There are more freedmen now in Florida than there were before the commencement of the war. Many of the planters of Georgia and South Carolina sent their slaves to this state to keep them out of the way of our armies—There will therefore be more suffering amongst them in that state, than in other southern states where there is a greater demand for labor."[2]

Lincoln's assassination on April 15, 1865, days after the Confederate surrender, brought Andrew Johnson to the presidency and the start of the contentious period known as Presidential Reconstruction. Johnson was not concerned with plans to grant citizenship rights to African Americans. The Union took control in Florida in May 1865, and the Emancipation Proclamation was read aloud in Tallahassee. Johnson appointed William Marvin as provisional governor for six months to set up elections for a constitutional convention to write the new constitution needed for the state to get back in the Union. The provisional government allowed no one to vote who had not been able to vote before January 1, 1861; and of course, the legislators meeting in 1865 created yet another southern state constitution with black codes. Johnson expressed no objections to the racially discriminatory laws but rather "congratulated them on a job well done."[3]

Florida's codes created separate courts for freedpeople and still allowed white people to escape ever having testimony made against them by a Black person. They allowed whipping as punishment, which the Freedmen's Bureau had to override. "Cohabitation" by white women and Black men was punishable by a $1,000 fine or three months in jail for each party, but other versions of interracial cohabitation were not mentioned, just as only rapes of white women were to be capital offenses. Joe Richardson theorizes that some of the military occupation regulations, such as "decrees regarding vagrancy and apprenticeships," and the military's willingness to move people and force them to work, as mentioned above, may have given Florida legislators a sense of ample latitude to create racialized laws, and the state's black codes resembled those made by other states. Richardson also aptly points out that the journal of the Florida House cites a comment that Connecticut, Wisconsin, and Minnesota had chosen in 1865 to bar Blacks from voting. Still, the Florida vagrancy law was flagrantly unrestrained, allowing even someone "'wandering or strolling'" to be arrested "on the complaint of any citizen." One of the other remarkable aspects of the racial hostility in the codes was that they contained features such as denying Blacks' Second Amendment right to hold arms that had been in the earlier black codes and widely exposed as unlawful. "Even after Florida's attorney general had declared that the law prohibiting freedmen from owning firearms was unconstitutional, and [the newly elected] Governor Walker had recommended its repeal at the next session, and it had been opposed by the Freedmen's Bureau, the legislators still refused to revoke it." The punishment targeting Blacks for many offenses, or failure to pay fines for them, was labor. Most outrageous perhaps was the stipulation that a person unable to pay a fine could be sold to someone who would pay.[4] A teacher with the American Missionary Association, stationed in Gainesville, wrote of the black codes a few years later in dread expectation of the conservative takeover of state government:

> We know what they *have* done when in power & we have no reason to think they are any better now. It is only a few years since the whipping post was taken from the front of the courthouse in this place. The law—which is down in black & white—is that if a *colored* man steal a chicken he shall be whipped & one who has been whipped shall be disfranchised. In that way they deprive the colored man of his vote. And if a *colored* man could not pay his taxes he would be sold for a year & his children till they were twenty one, &c.[5]

The application of these laws was so brutal that, as in other states, the Freedmen's Bureau had to set up separate courts, and as with the states that did not have the codes overturned by the military, Florida's codes were ended by the Reconstruction Acts of 1867.[6] Even before political organizing heated up, the military had to declare martial law in five counties. According to the *Pensacola Observer*, on June 9, 1866, Major General J. G. Foster declared martial law in Santa Rosa, Escambia, Levy, Madison, and Alachua Counties due to "several murders, attempts to kill and other crimes having been committed upon the persons of loyal citizens and soldiers of the United States" and for which the civil authorities had "failed to bring criminals to justice." Looking at these locations in three different parts of the state (also sites where Unionist whites were attacked) provides an indication of where both political organizing and resistance to Black participation in governing would take place in earnest the next year.[7]

Owing to the disparate areas that were developed in Florida, the Emancipation Circuit was built across the northern third of the state. A railroad line serving the transport of cotton and lumber to ports ran across the northern section from Jacksonville in the east to Pensacola on the western border. A second ran north to south from Tallahassee to St. Marks to move lumber. Another line ran from Fernandina on the Atlantic through counties on the upper peninsula and to Cedar Creek on the Gulf. These three lines and the accompanying roads across the northern tier facilitated ties between Black communities across the developed portion of the state. This was also an asset in times of trouble, when people from neighboring counties could help. Since enslaved people were still clearing tracts of land in the peninsula when the war began, their flight took them north and to the coast. Black organizing took place in the western counties, certain counties in Middle Florida on the Panhandle, and northeastern counties on the Atlantic. It would also take place in the area around Key West, owing to federal presence there at the entrance to the Gulf of Mexico.

Florida in Reconstruction is marked by having been a haven for enslaved people in its earlier history and by becoming a haven after the war for African American Union veterans who dreamed of having their own homes there in freedom. But it is perhaps best known for attracting many others who saw this sizable state with abundant resources and surrounded by watery access to the markets of the world as a sanctuary without a multigenerational old guard—a realm for would-be kings. Not for nothing was Florida accused of having "carpetbag rule." Of the state's six governors between 1865 and the 1880s, only one was born in Florida, and in fact he was the first native-born governor. The state, admitted to the Union in 1845, had in 1860 a tiny population of 140,424, the second smallest of all the states after Delaware and a third smaller than Arkansas, the other least populous state in the South. (Just for emphasis—Dade County, now Miami Dade, then had a population of 83 souls.) In the South there were three states with more than a million people, and most of the nine states discussed in this book had populations between 700,00 and 1 million. In 1865, when a new constitution had to be written, the 34 percent of the population that was made up of allies of slaveholding simply outlawed Black voting, made minimal changes of wording to slave system law, and, expecting the support of President Johnson, planned to carry on as usual. However, one crucial fact came to light when it became apparent that Black men would get to vote that created the faction-ridden new politics of Florida in Reconstruction: the 34 percent would need votes from the 44 percent of the population who had been enslaved.[8]

Arrivals: Five Factions

With the passage of the first Reconstruction Act in 1865, the Freedmen's Bureau sent agents who began to bring assistance to freedpeople. When it became law in 1867 that Black men would be able to vote by 1868, it also became evident that everyone else who came into the state, whether federal officials tied to the Freedmen's Bureau or Black ministers organizing in the newly freed communities, would need Black votes, and most of their votes at that. While the ratios of former enslaved people to allies of slaveholding were similar in other states, the numbers—differing by hundreds of thousands—were crucial. South Carolina, Georgia, and Louisiana had areas of dense Black populations where repression of the vote by brute force was either ineffective or foolhardy. Florida was less lucky.

Du Bois and Canter Brown describe the factions built in Florida in such a way that suggests looking at their geographical dispersal is useful. When the AME expanded in 1867 beyond its original mission in South Carolina, AME organization in the state coincided with the formation of a state Republican Party to begin mobilizing for the onset of Black male voting. A lot of political organizing by Blacks and whites took place in the capital, Tallahassee, and along with agencies like the Freedmen's Bureau or church groups, work fanned out from there. In fact, political formations in the counties surrounding Tallahassee's Leon County (and in the Jacksonville area) would see the most contentious battles and also prove the most resilient. For the same reasons, the slaveholding elite, who were intent on taking control of state government, had groups allied with them in Tallahassee. Finally, corporate interests that wanted to build in the state—varying from railroads to developers who saw Florida as a resort area—were also operating at the capital.

The Black radical faction that emerged in 1867 arose from the arrival of a number of AME ministers. Charles Pearce came to Tallahassee as a missionary in his late forties. Born enslaved in Maryland, he managed to buy his freedom and moved to New England and then Canada, where he became a citizen of the British colony. His colleague Robert Meacham, born enslaved in Gadsden County, Florida, had come to Tallahassee in his thirties and built a church. Pearce took over Meacham's church and sent him to Jefferson County to work on elections. Their statewide AME conference backed the Republican Party, with which they would work. Black political meetings had already started in Leon and Jefferson Counties and in Jacksonville, on the Atlantic coast, where most people first arrived, and in Pensacola at the western state line.[9]

A secret political group known as the Lincoln Brotherhood was started by Thomas Osborn, a former Union colonel from New Jersey and a lawyer who was assistant commissioner of the Freedmen's Bureau in the state. It was to be a moderate Black group led by Osborn and three other whites who had served in the war and had become lawyers. The Freedmen's Bureau worked out of Tallahassee and operated in other Middle Florida counties (Gadsden, Jackson, Jefferson, and Madison), with its connection to the Black community built primarily by enlisting support from Baptist ministers, starting in Tallahassee. Osborn's partners in running the brotherhood were Marcellus Stearns, of Maine, who had been stationed in Gadsden County after suffering war injuries; Captain Charles M. Hamilton of Pennsylvania; and Lieutenant William J. Purman, a Freedmen's Bureau agent, also from Pennsylvania. In 1869, Purman, by then a state senator, would be the victim of an 1869 assassination attempt that ignited the Jackson County War. Regardless of the outcomes for freedpeople, "carpetbagging" worked out very well for all these northerners. All of them except Hamilton were delegates to the 1868 constitutional convention; Stearns would become Florida's eleventh governor; Purman would decline the office of secretary of state and serve several separate terms in the US Senate; and Osborn would also serve a term as a US senator.[10]

Planters and "carpetbaggers" allied with President Johnson consolidated in a conservative group with policy aims that would limit or preclude any Black role in governance. Harrison Reed, of Wisconsin, was sent by President Johnson as postal agent of the state. Reed, former owner and editor of the *Milwaukee Sentinel* several decades earlier and a publisher of the *Wisconsin State Journal* in the years before the war, had most recently worked in the Treasury Department in Washington. He probably put off more than a few freedpeople in 1865 when he wrote in a Jacksonville paper, "Sound policy requires that the freedmen of the South should not be admitted immediately to the right of suffrage." He would become the ninth governor of Florida in 1868 and shepherded the state back into the Union. It seems as though he changed his tactics but not his views.[11]

The early Republican Party, which attracted many of the Union loyalists, was based in the east in Jacksonville, where Union forces first entered in 1862. According to Canter Brown, due to Florida's small numbers, groups such as this small coterie of loyalists had a chance to have a voice in governing if in combination with the potential Black vote: "When combined with several thousand southern Loyalists and 400 to 500 politically active northern whites, majority control seemed assured for Republicans if blacks joined in the coalition." The party was headed by Ossian B. Hart, a Floridian, former slaveholder, and lawmaker who had been against secession and who advocated for Black suffrage after the war. He would become the tenth governor of Florida, after Reed.[12]

The group that was known as the Mule Team was led by two northerners in the Fernandina area: Daniel Richards, an Illinoisan who was head of the Freedmen's Bureau there, and a Unitarian minister who came with him, Liberty Billings of Maine, who was a former lieutenant colonel in the

Union army. Billings had been second in charge of Black troops in South Carolina under Colonel Thomas Wentworth Higginson, another Unitarian minister, but more famously a radical abolitionist and intellectual from Massachusetts. Higginson did not take to Billings and did not think him much of a military man either, an opinion that worsened over time, causing Billings's discharge. Charlotte Forten, a teacher at Port Royal and an acquaintance of Higginson's, also met Billings in South Carolina, at first thinking him genuinely interested in the refugees there, and on a second encounter finding him "somewhat vain." Billings would become a Florida state senator. The faction known as the Mule Team soon gained an effective Black ally in William U. Saunders, another Union veteran. Saunders was born free in Maryland and came south after the war to help build the Republican Party. He was a Union League man and also worked with the Union Republican Congressional Committee (URCC). These three men raised support from Blacks drawn by their demand for full citizenship rights for freedpeople.[13]

These factions all came face-to-face at Florida's first Republican Party convention, in July 1867 in Tallahassee, where Harrison Reed's conservative group had to compete with the moderates in Osborn's Lincoln Brigade for support. When Hart, who had been organizing the party and occupied a space to the left of those two groups, was nominated to be head of the Florida state party, he was attacked by the radical Billings because he was a white southerner (and had Black supporters). In both these rivalries there was something of an attempt to solve the problem of too many factions by sharpening contrasts. In what was perhaps an attempt to forestall polarization, Osborn, the moderate, was elected chair of the Florida Republican Party. The militant Blacks, led by AME leader Pearce, leaned in the direction of the Mule Team. At the same time, it was Saunders who left an impression; a year later the New York Tribune described Saunders as having an eloquence that had "'magnetic influence over a crowd.'"[14]

On July 31, 1867, either Saunders or a colleague working with the URCC wrote from Jacksonville to Washington after the Republican Party convention, which the writer deemed successful. The plan was to "organize Florida on a sound Republican basis and with radical Republican representation. Registration is now in progress and we shall have a large colored majority. Opposition is paralyzed and we expect a victory without asperity of feeling. Crops good and country generally healthy." Organizers did achieve a Black majority of voters, and as in other states, white voters opted to boycott the first election, though the purpose of such an action is still puzzling. And, as elsewhere in the South, resistance to the success of Black voter registration did not gel until after Black voting occurred.[15]

Another new arrival who allied himself early on with the radical Mule Team was Jonathan Gibbs, who was born free in Philadelphia, a Dartmouth graduate, and a Presbyterian minister. He was a delegate to the 1864 colored convention in Syracuse, along with activists mentioned earlier, including Abraham Galloway, Edmonia Highgate, James Ingraham, and Richard Cain. Just as these others returned south after the convention and the formation of the National Equal Rights League, Gibbs came to New Bern, North Carolina (where Galloway was working), care of the American Home Missionary Society. He then moved to Charleston, South Carolina, where he ran a school and got involved in politics. He participated in the 1865 colored convention there protesting that state's black codes. After moving to Jacksonville in 1867, he joined up with the Mule Team. He would become a delegate to the constitutional convention of 1868, where he was nominated by conservatives to run for a seat in the US Congress (but did not win), and later that year he was appointed by Governor Harrison Reed to the position of secretary of state, after bad press coverage over appointing former rebels. His brother, Mifflin Gibbs, often viewed as the most powerful man in Arkansas Reconstruction politics, visited him while he was secretary of state and wrote: "I found him at Tallahassee, the capital, in a well-appointed residence, but his sleeping place in the attic resembled, as I perceived, considerably an arsenal." As someone who opened investigations into the KKK, Jonathan Gibbs was threatened by the group. In the next administration he would become superintendent of public instruction. In both jobs he was the only Black statewide officeholder. Gibbs died suddenly and mysteriously in 1874.[16]

Another African American who joined the radical Mule Team was Josiah T. Walls, formerly enslaved in Virginia and a Union veteran, thanks to having been captured while an enslaved worker for the Confederate army. He was sent north, where he went to school and joined the Union army. He was last stationed in Florida and stayed. When he got involved in politics, he served as delegate to the 1868 constitutional convention from Alachua County and went on to become a state representative, a senator, and the state's first Black US congressman. In the 1870s, he went into law practice with Saunders, owned a newspaper, and ran a successful truck farming business.[17]

Making Political Voice

In June 1867, voter registrars were appointed, and formerly enslaved Floridians were registered for the first time and voted. The Florida constitutional convention of 1868 met in Tallahassee in January 1868. It was known pejoratively as a "Black and Tan" convention, like the nine other southern constitutional conventions that were integrated for the first time. Of the fifty men elected to rewrite the state constitution, most of the white leaders of political factions mentioned earlier were elected as the delegates. Among the nineteen Black delegates were three of the African American leaders mentioned earlier, Pearce and Meacham, of the AME conference, and Saunders, URCC speaker and Mule Team leader. The counties with the largest African American populations had more than one delegate, which also meant that over half of the nineteen Black delegates had to represent more than one county.[18] (See Florida map 1 [plate 4].) Only two of the Black delegates, Emanuel Fortune and Robert Meacham, were born in Florida. The others were from Georgia, North Carolina, Pennsylvania, Maryland, South Carolina, Tennessee, and Virginia. Six of the nineteen Blacks were AME ministers, a number of others were AME members, and the church had a pervasive presence in Black leadership in Florida.[19]

Emmanuel Fortune, born enslaved in Marianna (Jackson County), was one of the two Black delegates to the convention from the county. He was one of those rare people who had learned to read in childhood while enslaved, and he also benefited from having been trained to be a shoemaker and a tanner. In freedom he decided against his owner's name and gave himself, his wife, and his five children the name of his deceased father, an Irishman named Fortune, who was killed in a duel. (One of his children was T. Thomas Fortune, the activist editor and publisher of the New York Age.) He began farming cotton on land owned by a white childhood friend. Among the Union troops arriving in Marianna were two of the Freedmen's Bureau agents mentioned previously, Charles Hamilton and W. J. Purman, who started the Lincoln Brotherhood with Thomas Osborn. According to Thornbrough, these two found in Fortune "an apt political pupil and a loyal ally who also had a flair for public speaking. Even before Emancipation he had acquired a certain leadership among the slaves." In an effort perhaps to win Fortune's backing, Ossian Hart, Republican Party boss and head of voter registration in the state, appointed Fortune voter registrar for Jackson County. As a delegate in the convention, Fortune's votes were allied with those of both Hart and the Lincoln Brotherhood against motions from the radical Mule Team. According to his colleague John Wallace, Fortune "opposed from first to last the conduct of the Billings-Saunders (Mule Team) faction, and but for his unalterable opposition as one of the colored delegates, it is doubtful whether the Purman-Osborn (Lincoln Brotherhood) faction would have succeeded."[20] Black delegate Jonathan Gibbs of the Mule Team was cited by historians and reporters as the most erudite person there. According to Wallace: "He adhered to the Billings faction, but labored hard and honestly to secure a constitution that should protect the property of the State as well as the rights of the freedmen. More than once he arose in the convention and denounced Billings . . . , who would wait until the lobby of the convention would be filled with freedmen, and make that the opportunity for delivering a fiery speech in denunciation of the former slaveholders."[21] The contenders had to go to extreme lengths because at first they were outmaneuvered by the Mule Team. With a slight majority they appointed their allies to important posts along with Blacks such as Pearce and Meacham (of the Black radical group) and Saunders from their own group. Whites reacted with the alarm typical of the times that there would be "Negro Rule." By then, everyone knew that the state had more Black registered voters than white. The moderate Lincoln Brotherhood and conservative planters walked out of the convention—leaving it without a quorum. They left the Black radical group and the Mule Team sitting in the capitol. The insurgents traveled to Monticello, in the next county. There they not only met with Republican Party leader Hart but also got Fortune and two other Blacks to join them and wrote their own constitution. They returned to the capitol, revised qualification rules to eliminate leaders of the Mule Team (with the blessing of the military), and passed their constitution.

The new constitution gave the governor control over all state and county offices, unusual power for that office. But the greatest long-term damage to the new Black majority was a reapportionment plan that produced and guaranteed a white majority by weighting rural counties with small populations over the dense Black majority counties. Florida's infamous law barring ex-felons from voting for life was created in this document. And W. J. Purman (Lincoln Brotherhood) pushed for the ban, later claiming it "kept Florida from becoming 'niggerized.'" Boosting the reapportionment plan was a stipulation that former Confederates could once again vote. Infuriating his colleagues, William Saunders defected from the Mule Team and supported the constitution, and tried to prevail on Blacks to support it. The moderate and conservative bloc carried the election and got its constitution

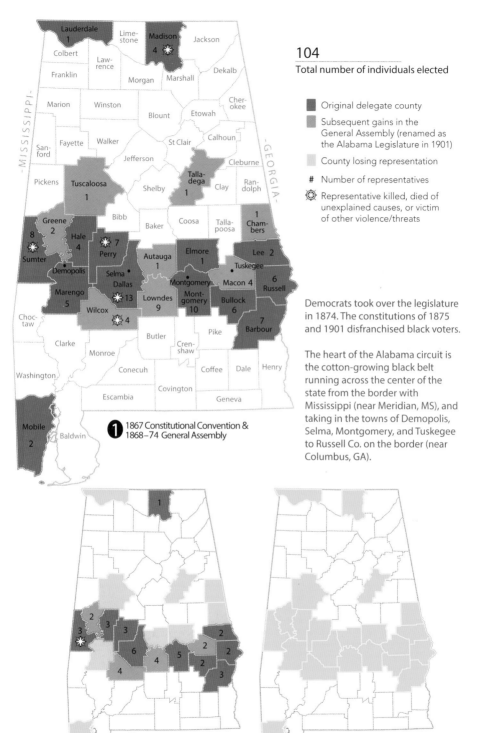

104

Total number of individuals elected

- Original delegate county
- Subsequent gains in the General Assembly (renamed as the Alabama Legislature in 1901)
- County losing representation
- # Number of representatives
- ✸ Representative killed, died of unexplained causes, or victim of other violence/threats

Democrats took over the legislature in 1874. The constitutions of 1875 and 1901 disfranchised black voters.

The heart of the Alabama circuit is the cotton-growing black belt running across the center of the state from the border with Mississippi (near Meridian, MS), and taking in the towns of Demopolis, Selma, Montgomery, and Tuskegee to Russell Co. on the border (near Columbus, GA).

1 1867 Constitutional Convention & 1868–74 General Assembly

2 1875–83 General Assembly

3 1884–1970 Legislature

© T. DAVIS. 2021

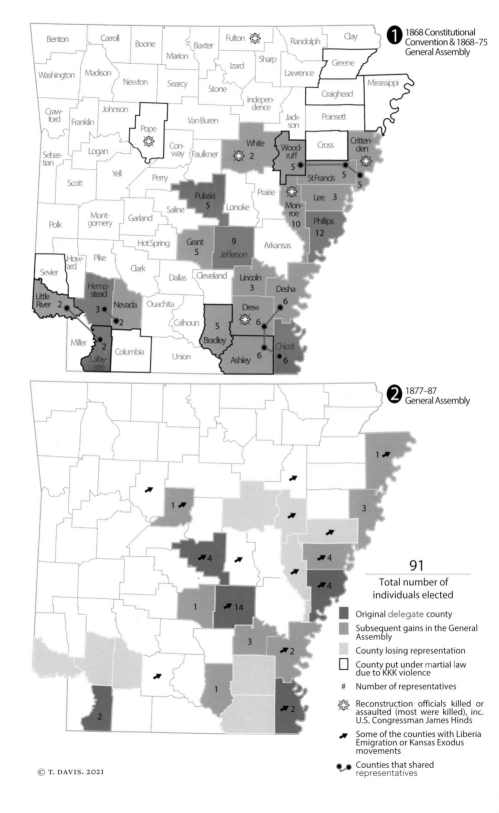

1 1868 Constitutional Convention & 1868–75 General Assembly

2 1877–87 General Assembly

91

Total number of individuals elected

- Original delegate county
- Subsequent gains in the General Assembly
- County losing representation
- County put under martial law due to KKK violence
- # Number of representatives
- Reconstruction officials killed or assaulted (most were killed), inc. U.S. Congressman James Hinds
- Some of the counties with Liberia Emigration or Kansas Exodus movements
- Counties that shared representatives

© T. DAVIS. 2021

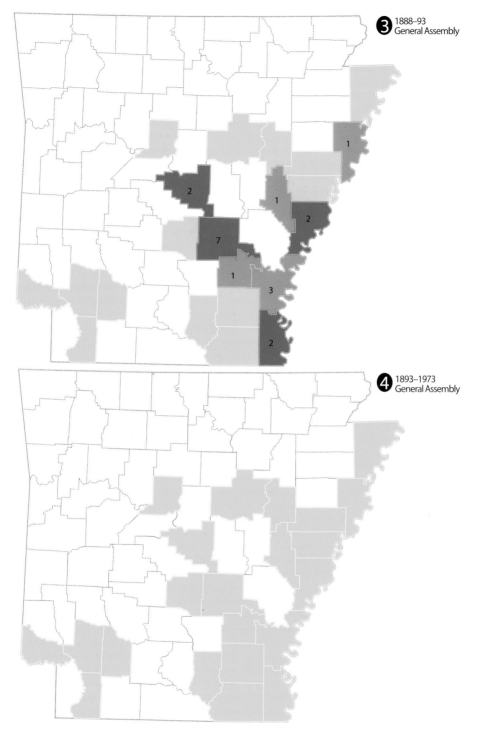

3 1888–93
General Assembly

4 1893–1973
General Assembly

© T. DAVIS. 2021

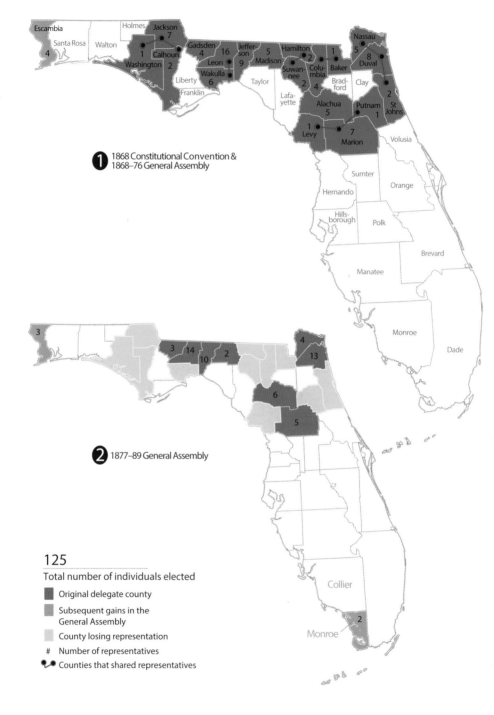

1 1868 Constitutional Convention &
1868–76 General Assembly

2 1877–89 General Assembly

125
Total number of individuals elected

- Original delegate county
- Subsequent gains in the General Assembly
- County losing representation
- \# Number of representatives
- Counties that shared representatives

© T. DAVIS. 2021

3 1890–1968 General Assembly

© T. DAVIS. 2021

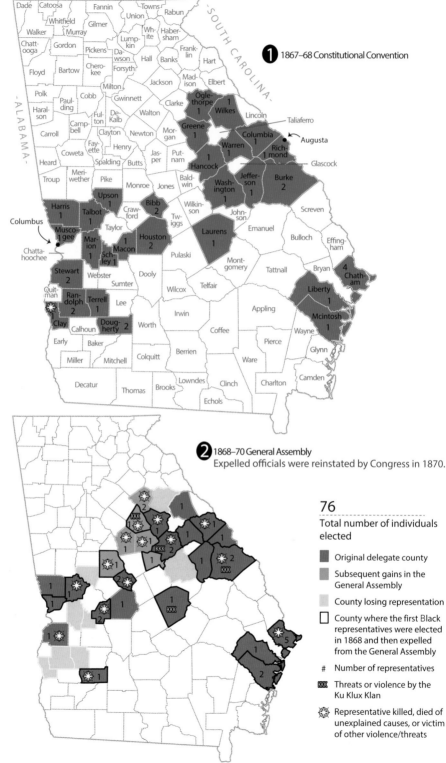

1 1867–68 Constitutional Convention

2 1868–70 General Assembly
Expelled officials were reinstated by Congress in 1870.

76
Total number of individuals elected

- Original delegate county
- Subsequent gains in the General Assembly
- County losing representation
- County where the first Black representatives were elected in 1868 and then expelled from the General Assembly
- # Number of representatives
- KKK Threats or violence by the Ku Klux Klan
- ✷ Representative killed, died of unexplained causes, or victim of other violence/threats

© T. DAVIS. 2021

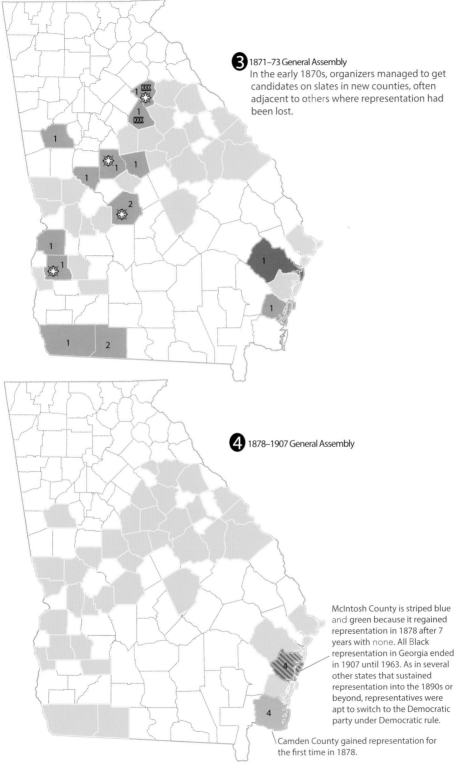

3 1871–73 General Assembly
In the early 1870s, organizers managed to get candidates on slates in new counties, often adjacent to others where representation had been lost.

4 1878–1907 General Assembly

McIntosh County is striped blue and green because it regained representation in 1878 after 7 years with none. All Black representation in Georgia ended in 1907 until 1963. As in several other states that sustained representation into the 1890s or beyond, representatives were apt to switch to the Democratic party under Democratic rule.

Camden County gained representation for the first time in 1878.

© T. DAVIS, 2021

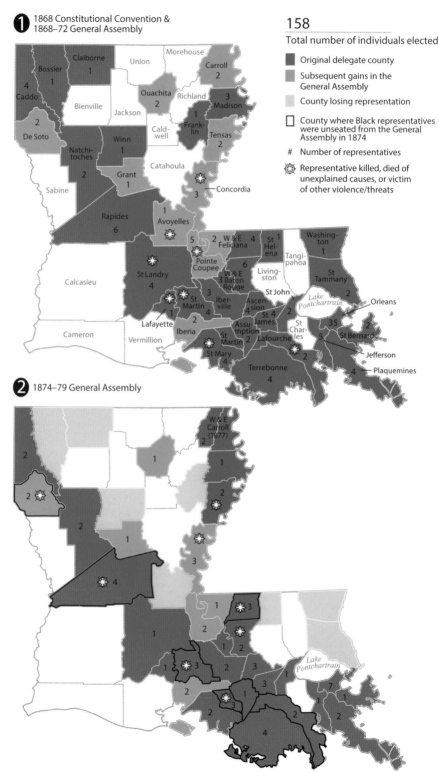

1 1868 Constitutional Convention & 1868–72 General Assembly

158
Total number of individuals elected

■ Original delegate county
■ Subsequent gains in the General Assembly
□ County losing representation
□ County where Black representatives were unseated from the General Assembly in 1874
Number of representatives
✦ Representative killed, died of unexplained causes, or victim of other violence/threats

Claiborne 1
Bossier 1
Caddo 4
Union
Morehouse
Carroll 2
Ouachita 2
Richland
Madison 3
Bienville
Jackson
Caldwell
Franklin 1
Tensas 2
De Soto 2
Natchitoches 2
Winn 1
Catahoula
Grant 1
Concordia 3 ✦
Sabine
Rapides 6
Avoyelles 1 ✦
W & E Feliciana 5 2 4 ✦
St Helena 1
Washington 1
Pointe Coupee ✦
Tangipahoa
Calcasieu
St Landry 4 ✦
W & E Baton Rouge 6 3
Livingston
St Tammany 2
Orleans 35
Cameron
Vermillion
Lafayette 1 ✦
St Martin ✦
Iberville 3
Ascension 4
St John
Lake Pontchartrain
St James 4
St Charles 5
St Bernard 2
Jefferson
Iberia 2
Assumption 2
Lafourche
St Martin 2
St Mary 4 ✦
Terrebonne 4
Plaquemines 4

2 1874–79 General Assembly

2
W & E Carroll (1877) 2
1
2 ✦
2 ✦
2
1
1
3 ✦
4 ✦
1
1 ✦ 3
1 ✦ 3 ✦
2
1 2
1 3 2 3
Lake Pontchartrain
7
1 ✦ 3
2
1
2
1 ✦ 3
2
4
2
1
2

© T. DAVIS. 2021

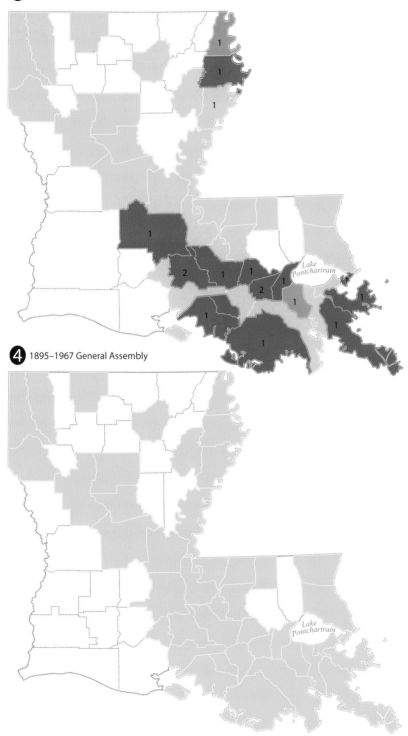

❸ 1880–92 General Assembly

Lake Pontchartrain

❹ 1895–1967 General Assembly

Lake Pontchartrain

© T. DAVIS. 2021

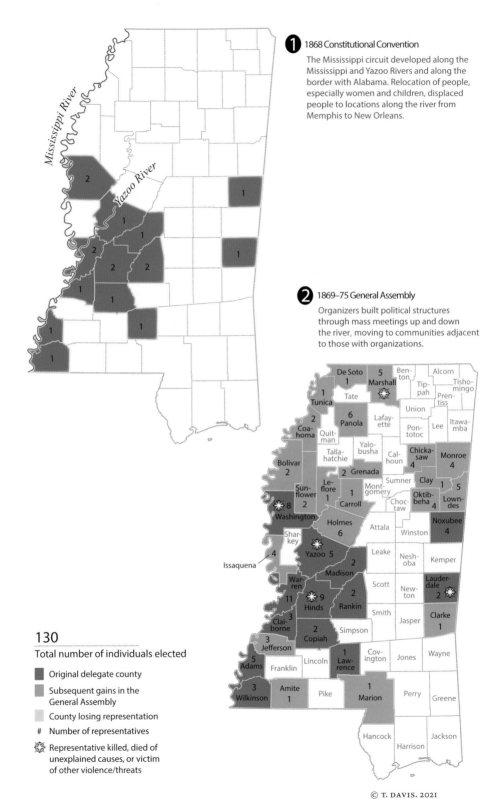

1 1868 Constitutional Convention

The Mississippi circuit developed along the Mississippi and Yazoo Rivers and along the border with Alabama. Relocation of people, especially women and children, displaced people to locations along the river from Memphis to New Orleans.

2 1869–75 General Assembly

Organizers built political structures through mass meetings up and down the river, moving to communities adjacent to those with organizations.

130
Total number of individuals elected

- ■ Original delegate county
- ■ Subsequent gains in the General Assembly
- ■ County losing representation
- # Number of representatives
- ✸ Representative killed, died of unexplained causes, or victim of other violence/threats

© T. DAVIS. 2021

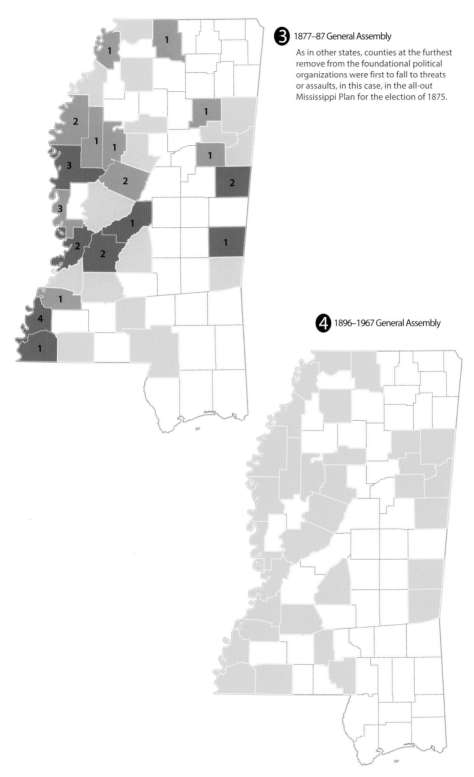

3 1877–87 General Assembly

As in other states, counties at the furthest remove from the foundational political organizations were first to fall to threats or assaults, in this case, in the all-out Mississippi Plan for the election of 1875.

4 1896–1967 General Assembly

© T. DAVIS, 2021

75

Total number of individuals elected

■ County with Black delegates at the 1868 Constitutional Convention and/or representatives elected to the General Assembly

■ Subsequent gains in the General Assembly

☐ County losing representation

☐ County where the governor declared martial law in 1870 after the Ku Klux Klan murder of a white Republican state senator and the lynching of a Black town commissioner, a well-known activist

\# Number of representatives

❶ 1868 Constitutional Convention &
1868–72 General Assembly

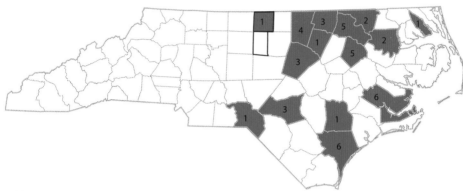

❷ 1873–79 General Assembly

© T. DAVIS. 2021

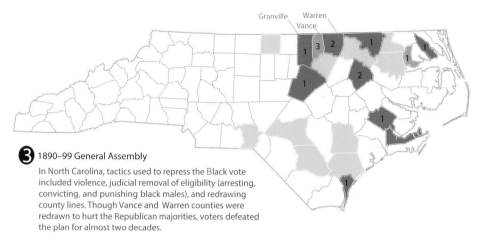

3 1890–99 General Assembly

In North Carolina, tactics used to repress the Black vote included violence, judicial removal of eligibility (arresting, convicting, and punishing black males), and redrawing county lines. Though Vance and Warren counties were redrawn to hurt the Republican majorities, voters defeated the plan for almost two decades.

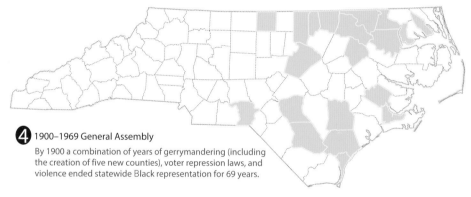

4 1900–1969 General Assembly

By 1900 a combination of years of gerrymandering (including the creation of five new counties), voter repression laws, and violence ended statewide Black representation for 69 years.

© T. DAVIS. 2021

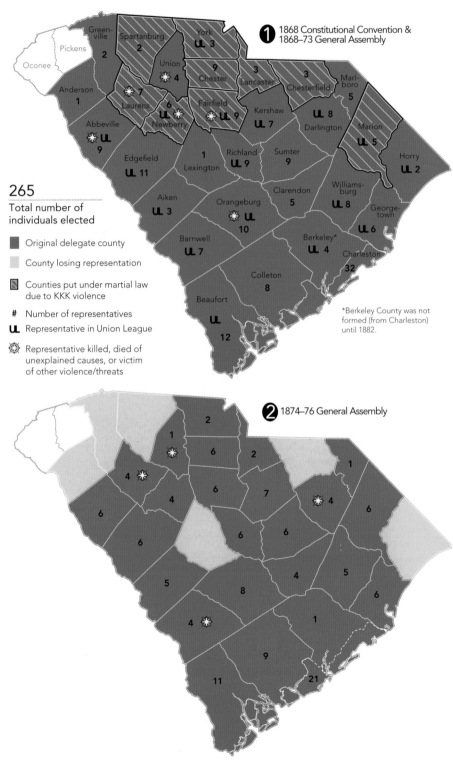

1 1868 Constitutional Convention & 1868–73 General Assembly

Oconee

Pickens

Greenville 2

Spartanburg 2

York UL 3

Union ✷ 4

Chester 9

Lancaster 3

Chesterfield 3

Marl-boro 5

Anderson 1

Abbeville ✷ UL 9

Laurens ✷ 7

Newberry UL 6 ✷

Fairfield ✷ UL 9

Kershaw UL 7

Darlington UL 8

Marion UL 5

Edgefield UL 11

Lexington 1

Richland UL 9

Sumter 9

Williamsburg UL 8

Horry UL 2

Aiken UL 3

Orangeburg ✷ UL 10

Clarendon 5

George-town UL 6

Barnwell UL 7

Berkeley* UL 4

Charleston 32

Colleton 8

Beaufort UL 12

265
Total number of individuals elected

■ Original delegate county

▨ County losing representation

⊠ Counties put under martial law due to KKK violence

\# Number of representatives

UL Representative in Union League

✷ Representative killed, died of unexplained causes, or victim of other violence/threats

*Berkeley County was not formed (from Charleston) until 1882.

2 1874–76 General Assembly

2

1 ✷

4 ✷

6

2

6

7

1

4

6

6

6 ✷

4 ✷

6

1

6

5

8

4

5

6

4 ✷

1

9

11

21

© T. DAVIS. 2021

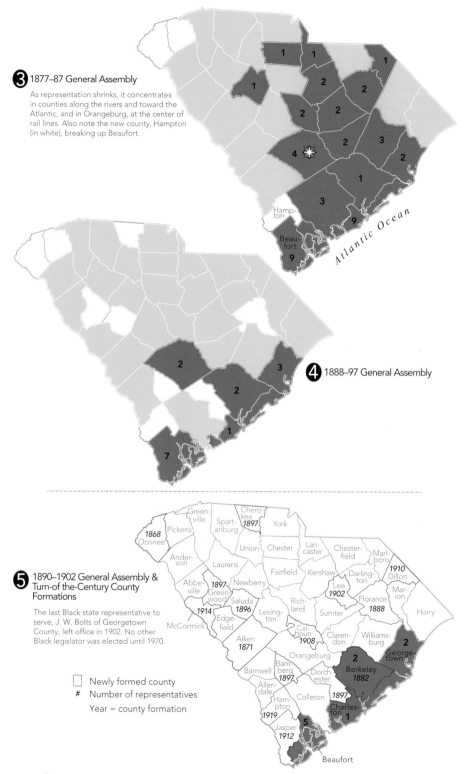

3 1877–87 General Assembly

As representation shrinks, it concentrates in counties along the rivers and toward the Atlantic, and in Orangeburg, at the center of rail lines. Also note the new county, Hampton (in white), breaking up Beaufort.

Atlantic Ocean

Hampton

Beaufort 9

4 1888–97 General Assembly

5 1890–1902 General Assembly & Turn-of the-Century County Formations

The last Black state representative to serve, J. W. Bolts of Georgetown County, left office in 1902. No other Black legislator was elected until 1970.

☐ Newly formed county

\# Number of representatives

Year = county formation

Green-ville
Pickens
Spart-anburg
Chero-kee 1897
York
1868 Oconee
Ander-son
Union
Chester
Lan-caster
Chester-field
Marl-boro
1910 Dillon
Laurens
Fairfield
Kershaw
Darling-ton
Mar-ion
Abbe-ville
1897 Green-wood
Newberry
Rich-land
Lee 1902
Florance 1888
Horry
1914
McCormick
Saluda 1896
Lexing-ton
Sumter
Williams-burg
Edge-field
Cal-houn 1908
Claren-don
2 George-town
Aiken 1871
Orangeburg
2 Berkeley 1882
Barnwell
Bam-berg 1897
Dorch-ester
Allen-dale
Colleton
1897
Ham-pton 1919
Charles-ton 1
5 Jasper 1912
Beaufort

© T. DAVIS. 2021

110

Total number of individuals elected

- Original delegate county
- Subsequent gains in the General Assembly
- County losing representation
- # Number of representatives

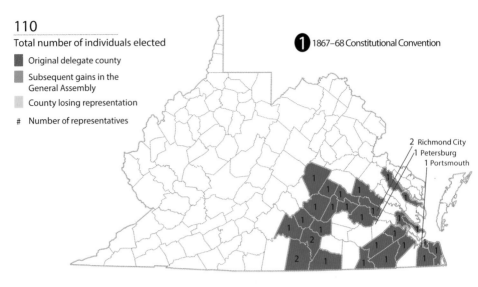

1 1867–68 Constitutional Convention

2 Richmond City
1 Petersburg
1 Portsmouth

COUNTY INDEX

Acc.	Accomack	J.C.	James City	Rap.	Rappahannock
Alb.	Albermarle	K&Q	King & Queen	Rch.	Richmond
Alleg.	Alleghany	K.G.	King George	Shen.	Shenandoah
App.	Appomattox	K.W.	King William	Spot.	Spotsylvania
Buck.	Buckingham	Lun.	Lunenburg	Staff.	Stafford
C.C.	Charles City	Mad.	Madison	War.	Warren
Char.	Charlotte	Mat.	Mathews	Will.	Williamsburg
Chest.	Chesterfield	Mid.	Middlesex		
Cl.	Clarke	Mont.	Montgomery		
Cul.	Culpeper				
Cu.	Cumberland	Nan.	Nansemond		
		N.K.	New Kent		
Din.	Dinwiddie	Norf.	Norfolk		
		N.C.	Norfolk City		
Ess.	Essex	North.	Northampton		
Fluv.	Fluvanna	Not.	Nottoway		
Glo.	Gloucester	Pow.	Powhatan		
Goo.	Goochland	P.E.	Prince Edward		
Gn.	Greene	P.G.	Prince George		
Gre.	Greensville	P.W.	Prince William		
		P.A.	Princess Anne		
Hen.	Henrico				
I.W.	Isle of Wight				

2 1869–90 General Assembly

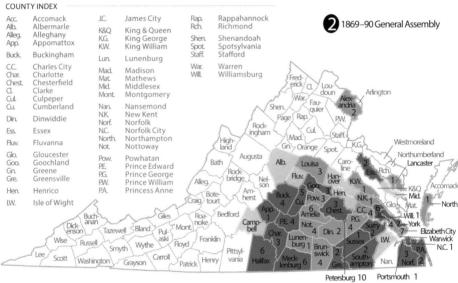

Petersburg 10   Portsmouth 1

3 1891–1967 General Assembly

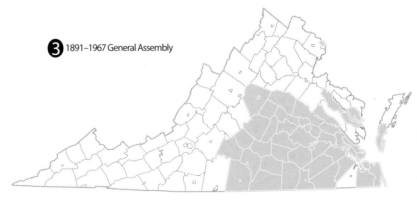

© T. DAVIS. 2021

approved by voters. Harrison Reed of the conservative bloc became the governor. Charles Hamilton of the Lincoln Brotherhood became the US congressman. Of the nearly two dozen Blacks elected to the legislature, Pearce, Meacham, and another AME minister, William Bradwell, became the first Black state senators, and the twenty Black house members included Fortune and Walls. Florida was readmitted to the Union in 1868.[22]

Labor Moves in the Breach of Lost Political Voice

One can get so inured to the idea that southerners did not want African Americans voting and being part of state government that one does not bother to look for other forms of self-interest besides racism that voter repression served. Controlling the labor of the survivors of the slave system was of primary importance. Florida was the least populated southern state because most of it was not developed, and the war also had left this small, poor state with $500 in the government till. According to Foner, "Upon taking office in 1868, Harrison Reed discovered that no account existed of how state monies had been spent between 1840 and 1860 or during Presidential Reconstruction." This fact also points to the common thought at the time that Florida could not be built up into whatever politicians and businessmen dreamt without keeping its labor force the cheapest in the land. When the state issued bonds to raise revenue, they did not sell, and "Northern investors proved unwilling to touch Southern securities until 'political uncertainty' subsided." Black disfranchisement was assumed to make it much easier to keep control of labor's wages, terms, and conditions. Many of the new plans for the state were for "tourism, large farms, and extractive industries (timber, turpentine, and phosphate mining)" and "an end to dependence on cotton." But when the vote was so heavily repressed at the onset of Reconstruction, Black labor took on the issues of wages, terms, and conditions.[23]

Florida dockworkers tried their first strike in October 1868 in Fernandina in Nassau County, which (along with Duval and Escambia Counties) was one of the state's biggest sites for lumber cutting and shipment. Dockworkers in Pensacola (Escambia) struck in December, with hearty local support; in Jacksonville, similar organizing was even supported by city officials. By 1873, according to Jerrell Shofner, Black laborers "on the docks, in the lumber mills, and on the railroads all resorted to collective action of one kind or another." The Pensacola Workingmen's Association—Black longshoremen—had violent encounters with Canadians coming in to take jobs on the docks. The locals used techniques often deployed to force Blacks out of a southern town, such as armed door-to-door searches, and drove the newcomers out of town. There was only one serious injury—to one of the longshoremen—but people were fearful. Authorities were unable to do much and, owing to various complications, were unable to prosecute a case against anyone. The state legislature actually passed a law privileging local residence for a longshoreman's license. In the 1870s, the Jacksonville Labor League, mostly "unskilled" labor at lumber mills, fought for a shorter—ten-hour—workday and a $1.50 minimum daily wage. When negotiations with mill owners failed, workers idled seventeen mills. They were replaced by whites, but when the panic of 1873 struck, many mills had to close, and wages were depressed in the few surviving jobs. Still, in 1875 Florida passed a ten-hour workday law with an overtime provision. The organized agricultural workers helped create a lien favoring laborers on crops they raised; another law gave lumbermen liens on timber and other wood products until they were paid, and in 1875 garnishment of laborers' wages was barred.[24]

Making Political Voice Makes Opposition

Though Union occupation began on the Atlantic coast, the counties with dense Black populations in north-central Florida were best able to sustain their political organization. In most states, the first counties African Americans organized proved the most resilient. Paul Ortiz reports that Democrats failed to gain Black votes for at least two reasons: first, inevitably at Democratic rallies one of the old-time planters would extol the "blessings" of the slave system; second, Black women, who stood guard at polling places against white troublemakers, also enforced punishment of various kinds on any men caving in to employer pressure to vote Democratic. A newcomer writing about the state opined: "It is always something of an astonishment to find how well posted these otherwise ignorant negroes are on political matters, local events or any important occurrence; they seem to have a secret sort of freemasonry by which they learn everything going on." Like many others, the writer was astonished to learn that in Black settlements those who could read provided literacy to the entire community through gatherings where news was read aloud, and that they built schools that served children and adults. Illiteracy may have been enforced by the slave system, but it became a marker of Blackness at this time because the press made such an issue of public men who had been enslaved and served without literacy. It is the most common trait written about Black officeholders other than their free or enslaved status at birth.[25]

Under the new constitution, Emmanuel Fortune was elected to the Florida legislature, where he refused to join the radical Republicans, perhaps out of loyalty to the local Freedmen's Bureau agent, W. J. Purman, and had thus become part of the moderate faction at the constitutional convention. It was written of him at the time that "whenever he believed he was right, neither money nor promises could move him from his position." Still, whites in his county regarded him as dangerous. Local bands of armed men and the newly formed Ku Klux Klan began to intimidate Republicans, Fortune among them, who received death threats. He drilled his family on what to do if "night riders" should come to their home. When Purman was shot and another man killed, followed by Blacks being talked out of destroying the county seat, Marianna, a string of violent attacks on local Black organizers occurred. Blacks engaged in armed conflict with local whites, and more people were killed. Both Purman and Fortune left town.[26]

Fortune's county, Jackson, in north-central Florida, miraculously sent seven Blacks to represent them in the capital between 1868 and 1876, though a heavily former-Confederate KKK engaged in a murderous campaign that became known as the Jackson County War between 1869 and 1872. They murdered at least seventy-five Republicans in the county, nearly all African Americans. When Fortune, by then a member of the state house, was forced out of the county, his wife and children were left for a time to face the threat, with his wife wielding the family shotgun. After many threats, he finally gave up the farm and moved his family to Jacksonville. When someone suggested he return to Jackson County, Fortune asked: "Could I go back there and be a free man as I was when I was there before; . . . use freedom of speech and act in politics as a man would want with his own people—will I be safe to do that?" Charles Pearce, who represented Leon County, famously said of that place, "That is where Satan has his seat; he reigns in Jackson County."[27]

Jefferson County was also dangerous. Robert Meacham had his life threatened in 1867 there and was shot at in 1876. James William Randolph, who became a militant AME minister serving in Crescent City and then Jacksonville (and was the father of later labor and civil rights leader A. Philip Randolph), was born in 1864 in Monticello amid the violence in that county. According to Jervis Anderson, in that early experience, his "public attitudes had also been formed against a background of Black political militancy in Monticello—a period during which Black groups frequently armed themselves to defend their right to vote." Anderson provides an example in a public notice: "One of the armed groups nailed to the front door of the post office: 'We understand that the White People in This Place Say they intend to Kill some of the Colored People in This Place. If such a thing is started Here We Would Not give much for This Place Town and People.'" The battles involving Blacks were about labor; white conservatives stated plainly that it was about control of Blacks, "the only labouring class of any importance" and "our political enemies."[28]

Black legislators had a more specific view of their troubles acquiring land and fair employment practices based on observing the ways in which the state's boosters and lawmakers endeavored to bend every provision toward the convenience of corporations coming to the state. A statement prepared by the Black representatives of Leon County in response to one such piece of legislation reads in part: "Capital needs no legislation in order to provide for its use. Capital is strong enough to take care and provide for itself but corporations are a dangerous power, especially large or consolidated corporations, and the American people fear them with distrust. We want no Tom Scots [sic], Jim Fisks or Vanderbilts in this State to govern us by means of which they would influence legislation tending to advance personal interests."[29] African Americans coming in to freedom had thought the state's large tracts of public domain land held promise for them to own property. Instead, they discovered they had been offered up by state boosters as a cheap labor force. The organized, constant, and no-holds-barred nature of the violence in some of the rural counties may have driven many to urban communities. By 1875, though, President Ulysses S. Grant was weary of making military interventions in southern states like Mississippi, Louisiana, and South Carolina, where groups were also murdering and terrorizing Black political organizers and voters. His view was that in the North, "the days when martial law and military government in the South were deemed acceptable had passed."[30]

The 1876 election between Republican Rutherford B. Hayes and Democrat Samuel J. Tilden ended with a popular vote win for Tilden and a disputed electoral college outcome. The dispute involved Florida's four electoral votes, Louisiana's eight votes, South Carolina's seven votes, and one vote in Oregon. Democrats in Louisiana and South Carolina declared victory and began setting up their state governments. The controversy opened up the wounds of the South's loss of power with the military occupation after the war. It became apparent that the southern states cherished more than other considerations the ability to run their states without interference. This won out as railroads and other businesses were also interested in the matter. Congress set up a commission to decide the issue, and it named Hayes the winner. Republicans in Congress agreed to accept Democrat Wade Hampton III as governor of South Carolina and Democrat Francis T. Nicholls as governor of Louisiana. The declaration of a Democrat's victory in Florida was accepted as well, making George F. Drew, owner of the state's largest sawmill, the new governor. By this time, Drew had been preceded as governor by Ossian Hart and M. L. Stearns, who had been faction leaders in 1868. As part of what became known as the Compromise of 1877, Hayes withdrew the forces guarding the state capitals involved in the dispute, and in so doing signaled the end of any federal enforcement of African Americans' new citizenship rights.

Getting rid of the federal military presence (especially Black soldiers) had been a priority with southern whites since 1865. The commanders of the military districts had nullified black codes, had not disarmed Blacks when southerners reported an insurrection rumor, and had placed workers on abandoned plantations and sometimes let them work on their own. Perhaps worst, they had both intentionally and accidentally informed Blacks of their rights and sometimes assisted in their literacy and in registering soldiers to vote. During Reconstruction, military commanders like Sherman had been issuing orders for such activity, as they did during and after the riots in Norfolk, Memphis, and New Orleans, but as is shown in the Louisiana chapter of this book, once President Johnson was in office, local officials could and did appeal to the president to call off military intervention. In fact, the legacy of federal protection for Blacks entering the polity as voters and officeholders was for southerners to try to make sure it could no longer be provided.[31]

Bradley's study of the military role concludes:

> Among its many duties as the main instrument of the federal government's Reconstruction policy, the Army guarded polling places, patrolled city streets and country roads, and provided posses for U.S. marshals and local sheriffs making arrests. The last function in particular raised the ire of congressional Democrats and led to the passage of the Posse Comitatus Act in June 1878, prohibiting any authority other than the president from summoning federal troops to enforce the law. In effect, military commanders could no longer act on their own responsibility but had to await orders from Washington.[32]

Johnson had already suggested that southern states set up their own posses, in every county, which resulted in a profusion of well-armed ad hoc forces across the South known as "regulators" and by other names.[33]

In the 1880s, Black Republicans in Florida would run people for office in partnership with the Knights of Labor. Fortune, for instance, held a number of local offices after he moved to Jacksonville and helped to create a coalition "of reform-minded Democrats, Republicans, and local assemblies of the Knights of Labor, which won control of the city." But Black representation in the state was under assault, seriously dropped between 1877 and 1889, and ceased to exist after that until 1968. (See the Florida maps [plates 4 and 5].) The violence did not subside; an epidemic of lynching gripped the South, and increasingly, other places to which Blacks fled. "Between 1882 and 1930, African Americans in Florida suffered the highest lynching rate in the United States," reports Ortiz. In fact, the rate of lynchings per capita in Florida was greater than in Mississippi or Louisiana and twice that of Georgia. Black Floridians again took up self-defense, often citing the Fourteenth Amendment and the state's abrogation of provision of equal protection under the law.[34]

Black Floridians sustained movements into the twentieth century, in part by using secrecy to avoid the threats of violence. As Jim Crow advanced at the turn of the twentieth century, organization took place most widely among wage earners, who transformed secret societies into vehicles to advance community organizing. Such sodalities were important to surviving the risks of the dangerous work in the state's developing sawmills, railroad yards, turpentine fields, and docks. At a minimum, the mutual aid groups allowed people to continue a practice made possible by freedom, offering decent burial and respect to family and friends. They also naturally brought together people with the same problems in the workplace, tied in the same ongoing multipronged crisis of economic, racial, and political threats to survival. Benevolent and fraternal society organizing expanded enormously at the end of the nineteenth century, as it did all over the South, and with a difference that separated those groups from their northern and southern white counterparts. Hewitt writes of women in South Florida in the last years of the century, and her comments apply to women elsewhere in the state: "African American women in Tampa pursued social activism with the same zeal as their sisters across the late-nineteenth-century South. A second generation of community builders was coming of age, with sons and daughters following mothers and fathers into local organizations and institutions. Thus, even as electoral rights accrued only to men in the larger civic arena, women remained central to social and political discussion in their own community."[35] The challenges Black Floridians made, like those of many other late nineteenth-century African American campaigns and movements, have remained obscured in the standard narrative of the long arc of the struggle for equal justice in this country in part because they were drives aimed at only one southern state. Many of the structures of inequality were then (and remain) controlled at the state level. Foremost among those discussed here thus far are the controls exercised by the state on voting rights. But education was controlled by the states, as were militias (which could be helpful or harmful to the enforcement of citizenship rights), labor regulation, and access to public accommodations. It would take another hundred years to compel enforcement even of access to federally controlled (interstate) transportation and public accommodations, to mention one area where the federal government could intervene.

In that light, the expansion of local, statewide, or southern regional mutual aid sodalities and fraternal groups in states like Florida was as important as the increased numbers who affiliated with national groups. As the urge to form national Black groups of all kinds arose at the turn of the century, along with the professionalization of those groups and Black churches as well, the allure of a national Black agenda would continue to grow. Black Floridians in wage-earning jobs would continue to need local needs met and could participate in national politics only by fighting for the franchise and participation in governance in the state of Florida.

Looking at Table 7.1

The areas that developed the deepest bench of local institutions in Florida were around Fernandina, Jacksonville, Pensacola, St. Augustine, and Tallahassee. Two of these had Black majority counties, and Fernandina had a Black majority city but its county was not majority Black, nor was St. Johns County, home to St. Augustine. There are other rural Black majority counties that did not have the benefit of rail connections or Union League organizing. What is prevalent throughout the counties in Table 7.1 is a diverse array of labor organizing. Though I did not see it specifically, I would assume Liberia emigration groups were located in port cities as in other states.

TABLE 7.1 Florida Emancipation Circuit, 1870–1900

	Institutions Present							19th Century Activism
	US Troops	RR (1884)	Union League	AMA Schools	Local Black Press	Black Political Reps	Knights of Labor Groups	
Columbia County				+		+		
FERNANDINA ß Nassau County	+	+	+	+		+		Labor Workingmen's Association (docks)
Gadsden County				+		+		
GAINESVILLE ß Alachua County ß			Unknown	+ Freedmen's Bureau	<u>3</u> 1865 1887 1894	+		Labor Colored Farmers Union Farmers Aid Society Liberia emigration
Jackson County ß		+	Unknown	+		+		Labor
JACKSONVILLE ß Duval County ß	+	+		+	<u>5</u> 1870s 1880s 1885 1900 1919	+	1 M laborers	Labor Civil rights Workingmen's Association Labor League Colored Farmers' Alliance (CFA)

Location						Occupations	Organizations
Jefferson County ß					•		
KEY WEST Monroe County	•		•		•		
LEESBURG (then in Sumter County, Lake County as of 1881)	Unknown		•	•	•	1 M farmhands & laborers	
Madison County ß			•		•		
Marion County ß		•	•		•		Lincoln Labor Society (agricultural workers) Liberia emigration Colored Farmers' Alliance (CFA)
PENSACOLA Escambia County	$\underline{1}$ 1900	•	•	•	•	1 M lumbermen, stevedores & laborers 1 F chambermaids & laundresses	Labor Workingmen's Association (docks) Colored Farmers Union
MILL VIEW* PENSACOLA area, Escambia County		•				1 M sawmill hands & carpenters	

(Continued)

TABLE 7.1 (Continued)

	US Troops	RR (1884)	Union League	AMA Schools	Institutions Present — Local Black Press	Black Political Reps	Knights of Labor Groups	19th Century Activism
MILTON* PENSACOLA area, Santa Rosa County		+					1 M sawmill hands	
Putnam County		+				cc only		Colored Farmers Union Colored Farmers' Alliance (CFA)
ST. AUGUSTINE St. Johns County	+	+	+	+	+			
TALLAHASSEE ß Leon County ß	+	+	+	+		+		Labor Civil rights
TAMPA Hillsborough County								Black women's temperance movement

KEY: **Bold** = Site playing multiple roles on the circuit. ß = Black majority; unless otherwise noted, populations are for 1870.
RR = Rail lines.
Black Political Reps = Black representatives to the 1868 constitutional convention (**cc**) or members of the General Assembly.

Knights of Labor = Black assemblies of the labor organization. Most KoL assemblies were segregated by race and gender: white males, Black males, white females, or Black females. "Mixed labor" is a term from the Garlock data (*see* Table Source Notes) and indicates various forms of work, not mixing by race or gender. **Gender** is indicated here by M or F.

* Not on 1870 or 1880 census; in Garlock, *Guide to the Local Assemblies.*
SOURCES: *See* Table Source Notes (393–96).

8 ALABAMA
Redemption

Redemption

NOUN

1   The action of saving or being saved from sin, error, or evil . . .

2   The action of regaining or gaining possession of something
     in exchange for payment, or clearing a debt.

2.1 archaic The action of buying one's freedom.

—lexico.com (August 15, 2021)

Redemption was the process of replacing the radical [Reconstruction] governments with conservative southern white governments. It was a well-organized political effort that also involved economic intimidation, community ostracism, political fraud, and violence. The Ku Klux Klan was the most common group involved in the violence.

—Charles Reagan Wilson and William Ferris, eds., *Encyclopedia of Southern Culture* (1989)

Union troops entered northern Alabama in February 1862 and remained there for the rest of the war. This had a strong impact on the lives of enslaved people near their camps, but the rest of Alabama remained in Confederate hands until shortly after Lee's surrender. Farragut's naval forces won the Battle of Mobile Bay in August 1864, but Mobile was not taken. Selma was finally taken after several attempts in April 1865, followed by

Mobile and Montgomery surrendering days after the April 9 end of the war. Needless to say, for the duration of the Civil War, enslaved people in most of the state were far from places of refuge, and perhaps from news.

Alabama, with its broad strip of cotton-raising counties in the middle of the state, its nascent industrial businesses in the northern section, and its shipping economy in the south, like Florida, had a Black political base that was largely rural and built among agricultural workers. This base was across the middle of the state, a belt of farming counties, worked by African Americans during the slavery period, known as the Black Belt. In the case of Alabama, the name originally signified the region's black soil. The rails crossing the Black Belt after the war would also serve as a corridor for the building of a mobilizing circuit, and later as a route for migration out of the state. Also, like Florida, the state's biggest ports, Mobile and Montgomery, were organized early, and labor remained a primary concern throughout the state. After the Reconstruction Acts were passed, for instance, restaurant waiters in Selma went on strike. But Blacks in Alabama were kept from exerting meaningful power, as in Florida, by strong resistance from the white elite. African Americans held no major statewide offices during the state's short-lived Reconstruction, and their greatest influence was probably in the 1867 constitutional convention.[1]

First Days

No experiment in freedom such as what took place in coastal South Carolina happened in this largely rural, farming state that produced cotton for export. However, during the war, Alabama had an unusual development forced by the exigencies of the Confederate effort to wage war in a region that had few industrial plants making anything but farm tools. It foreshadows the state's later industrial development, particularly in the area around what is now Birmingham. Plants in the Black Belt and nearby counties were reinvented as industrial sites producing for the Confederate military. The embargo of the coastline that created the federal occupations on the Atlantic Coast was effective on the Gulf Coast in blocking global export of cotton and the import of arms and ammunition, so the South had to manufacture its own arms. The Selma Ordnance and Naval Foundry (a former manufacturing plant turned into an ordnance factory), with its one hundred buildings, produced everything from nails and ammunition to the famous "Brooke rifles." These weapons resembling cannon, depending on the model, weighed from ten thousand to fourteen thousand pounds)—and, according to William Still, were "probably the most powerful muzzle-loaded rifled gun used during the Civil War." The naval unit there making ironclad warships became so important during the war that Union forces made three attempts to get to Selma. The site seemed ideal to the Confederate military for the same reason that Selma would later be at the center of the Black Belt's Emancipation Circuit: "[Selma] is now connected by railroad and river with the great arteries of travel from South to North, and . . . is also most fortunately situated with regard to the means of manufacturing iron. The coal beds of Bibb and Shelby [Counties] are only fifty-four miles distant and are immediately upon the Alabama and Tennessee River Railroad." The receipt of iron ore turned out to be more cumbersome than imagined because of the war and deterioration of infrastructure, but some businessmen bought the Selma foundry and then got the Confederate government to share ownership. It is also important to mention here that ironworks across the South owned enslaved people. In Tennessee, for instance, "the overwhelming majority of ironworkers in Stewart County were slaves owned by iron companies or iron company managers or rented from local farmers." This gives another complexity to the Confederacy partnering with the Selma foundry owners.[2]

The Selma plant was only destroyed in April 1865, when General James Wilson occupied the town after the Battle of Selma. On the fifty acres of factories, the works produced "rifles, swords, shot and shell, muskets, pistols and caps, and heavy ordnance," and on site there were "machine shops, car shops, and cotton and woolen mills." According to Richard Stockham, "At the peak of its production the naval foundry employed about three thousand workmen—other war industries in Selma another seven thousand." Studies differ on how many people were in each unit. William Still found that in the Naval Works "by 1865 over four hundred were on the payrolls, of whom at least three hundred were Negroes." He adds that "Negro slaves were usually hired by the year from local planters, and were employed principally in cutting wood for charcoal, and other tasks requiring unskilled labor." This comports with Litwack's report that three-quarters of the workers at the Selma works were enslaved people. And clearly looking across the diverse factories there, enslaved people were likely engaged in numerous forms of work. For instance, in the manufacturing site making small ammunition, clothing, and knapsacks, there was "a large number of women and children." An even more vivid sense of the enslaved experience in Selma is provided in a letter written in 1864 from an officer to Commander Catesby Jones, during one of the severe labor shortages the naval site suffered throughout the war: "Can't start the gun pit while short-handed, work every night in the foundry except Sunday. . . . Twenty-five negroes working over-time in the foundry tonight. Reckon they'll all be dead by the time you return."[3]

As Wilson's army approached Selma, laborers at the naval works were destroying as much of the machinery as possible. Still writes: "Tools and machines that were portable were taken by hand trucks to the river and dumped in. Many of the incomplete cannon at the foundry were also rolled into the river." The city suffered a lot of fires the night before the official army attack, and then Wilson's troops wrecked the site.[4] Smaller than the operations at Selma, the Shelby Iron Works, in the county of the same name, at its peak employed 450 enslaved workers and 100 whites. James Doster found that "turnover was rapid, and a constant battle was waged with Confederate authorities over the conscription of workmen. Many skilled men were detailed from the army to work at Shelby. How-ever, most of the workmen were Negro slaves, of whom about 10 per cent were owned by the company and the rest rented. Some of the Negroes were skilled hands." Those considered skilled hands at Shelby, according to Anne Knowles, were enslaved craftsmen "such as carpenters, shoemakers, tanners, and brick masons." Others in the regular labor category "chopped wood, made charcoal, hauled coal and provisions, built roads, and charged the furnace." Women are assumed to have cooked, done laundry, and kept vegetable gardens. Anne Knowles writes: "A few hired slaves described as 'good furnace hands' may have been experienced forge carpenters and blacksmiths." A study of enslaved workers in the business records of the Shelby works is instructive on several points and in ways that might apply to Selma as well.[5] Robert McKenzie reports that in early 1865, "the Shelby Iron Company employed 303 Negro slaves: 244 adult males, 45 females, and 14 children. Of this number, seventeen males and four females were owned by the company; the remainder had been hired from twenty-nine separate masters." The other enslaved people were from Mississippi, Ten-nessee, and South Carolina.[6]

By the time Union troops came to destroy the Shelby works, there were only those 303 Blacks there. Of the 156 workers whose postwar where-abouts were known, most stayed on as the business tried to reopen. There was insufficient information on another 147 people in the records to deter-mine whether they stayed, left, or were displaced by the company. But the company sent many people back to slaveholders as they were hard-pressed to feed them in April; even after Lee's surrender, they continued to send people back under escort. Robert McKenzie writes that despite an earlier Union raid at the Shelby works, a number of formerly enslaved people were retained and later sent home under escort by company employees: "The managers seem to have realized the fact that the Negroes were free men, but because the company still held open accounts with their former masters and because the managers assumed that former owners had some responsibility and need for their ex-slaves, they began to send the Negroes home 'for safety and want of provisions.'" At that time, the workers came from nearby areas as well as the counties near Selma. By mid-April, when they surely knew of the surrender, the company had sent off "at least one-third" of the enslaved workers and began to hire out the remaining people nearby; others were "put under the care and directions of officials" of the Alabama and Tennessee Rivers Railroad. Again, these workers were free people. Some Blacks returned on their own to their former plantations. Some just left immediately prior to and after the Union raid. Others were released when no word came from a former slaveholder. McKenzie's 1973 theory as to why so many Blacks stayed on as long as possible allowed that we all may have our opinion but asserted that the majority who remained showed "a pattern of lack of individual assertiveness in either childlike abandon or energetic independence." He does admit, however, that the desire for immediate solutions to food, clothing, and shelter could have applied in all the choices made.[7]

The options for workers were complicated by individuals' history and family ties. Returning to one's last plantation could have had the advantage of putting one near family or might have been a prospect the enslaved did not want to face, or both. Remaining in the region as Union troops came through Alabama presented options as well. Staying put on a job, knowing that Union troops might mean protection of their freedom, also has a certain logic. And wages for industrial work (and perhaps proximity to schools) might have seemed a more profitable way of living than agricultural work. Finally, the experience of enslaved people in wartime foundries was to work in a system where the usual violence was not the norm. Knowles found that industrialists learned a lesson to be applied to the enslaved from hiring foreign workers: "Southern industrialists found they had to bargain with men they could not coerce." Still, the Black workers were fortunate in being apprised of the changing order in their state after years of isolation because of the war. It happened that most of Alabama's nearly 440,000 enslaved people gradually learned they were free either by word of the surrender or as troops came through southern regions to the

Black Belt in the middle of the state, and word spread that spring and summer and thereafter.[8]

When troops camped out in Montgomery and Selma, they observed a constant influx of African Americans who had heard of their presence. But judging by the size of the Selma Iron Works, many were already there. If the Shelby example is instructive, people in Selma who had been laboring in making munitions, weapons, and war vessels (some of whom were whole family units living inside the works), and finding the town occupied by the Union army, may have elected not to return to plantations in other states or, if from nearby, moved their families. In 1860, there were 1,809 whites in Selma and 1,368 enslaved people. In 1870, there were 2,824 whites and 3,660 Blacks. The Montgomery newspaper reported the city's newcomers were living in deserted homes, building cabins with discarded lumber, and living under bridges and in riverside caves. It is possible that in-migration increased Selma's white population by 1,015 and its Black population by 2,292, more than twice as much; that would not even be unusual. The in-migration explanation, however, obscures the reality that some of Selma's residents had been owned by a business that worked some of them to death in short order. Still, all who were enslaved there were owned by the war. Another quote from the *Montgomery Daily Advertiser* is evocative of what may have occurred in Selma, where people were seen "living in shanties, old furnaces, boilers, and at the ruins of the arsenals' foundries." The war itself has to be seen as one other explanation for the growth in Black numbers, some perhaps being among the numerous Blacks reported to have followed troops in from rural areas. In any case, the ruin of the Selma foundry seems a likely site for squatters. Even if the people who had worked there had been listed as "unskilled" labor in the ironworks, industrial work prospects after the war in rebuilt foundries may have beckoned.[9]

A short item from the May 1865 New Orleans conference of the newly formed African Methodist Episcopal Zion (AME Zion) churches in Louisiana provides a glimpse as to how Black organizing proceeded from the Gulf Coast to Alabama and other areas occupied by federal troops and accessible by boat and the limited rail lines of the immediate postwar years. The group gave reports showing the pattern of their mission circuit in the Gulf: New Orleans, Terrebonne Parish (west of the city), Mobile, Pensacola, and Key West, all sites of Union troop presence. The missionaries went to Alabama from New Orleans by boat and/or rail northeast to Mobile, and Montgomery, Tuscaloosa, and Elyton (later to become Birmingham).

Crossing the Black Belt in both directions, they stopped at Hayneville and Tuskegee, and then rode the line west to Selma, Demopolis, and Livingston, and then into Mississippi to Meridian, Enterprise, and Jackson. These AME Zion missionaries were creating a blueprint for how the Emancipation Circuit was built across Alabama's Black Belt west into Mississippi (and east into Georgia) and how activists and missionaries built continuous ties to New Orleans.[10] Meridian, Mississippi, only founded in 1860 and a small place, came into existence and got its name thanks to the junction there of a major north-south rail line with the main east-west line, important conduits for cotton and then military supplies. For that reason, General Sherman had destroyed the town in 1864, along with 115 miles of tracks, sixty-one bridges, an arsenal, depots, and sawmills, reputedly prompting him to remark that Meridian no longer existed. The rail tracks were replaced a month later. Selma's naval ordnance plant was in Sherman's sights but escaped due to a change in his orders. And despite his remark, as Reconstruction was brutally put down in the state, Meridian became a refuge for Blacks fleeing violence and onerous contracts in Alabama.[11]

This route became the primary activism circuit in nineteenth-century Alabama and a migration route between Alabama and Mississippi. The presence of US troops allowed for the formation of institutions in the Selma and Montgomery areas (despite commonplace white violence) and between the Black Belt and Gulf cities of Mobile and New Orleans.

Violence against freedwomen in Mobile became a subject of some national attention during the summer of 1865. From July to September, the *New Orleans Tribune* printed letters protesting brutality there against Black women whom local police told to submit to rape or be jailed (which probably ensured assault). These events were also documented by Union general Thomas Kilby Smith. Documentation shows impassioned protests similar to those going on in Richmond, in Natchez, and likely in other places. These assaults, occasioned by the simple fact that women who had been severely confined by the slave system suddenly appeared in public spaces, seem to have had the power to be doubly traumatic events. First, they were violent assaults; second, for others they were assaults on sisters, mothers, wives, and children held in most tender esteem in their communities both for their roles and for their previous suffering; third, they were direct assaults on any ideas of freedom. The fact that many Black women were rounded up in groups, like animals in a herd, and assaulted systematically in a public fashion (invoking spectacle violence to come) simply added to the public message that no Blacks were free. In the slave system, as Hannah Rosen writes: "[Rape] served to exclude enslaved women from legal personhood and to subject them to the public identity and position of will-less subject, of noncitizen to whom the protective powers of the state did not apply, and simultaneously to the position of a woman who was unchaste (by definition, since she could not be legally married) and thus undeserving of state protection against sexual abuse."[12] One of the major problems with these terror incidents in Alabama and elsewhere was that before and after the black codes passed that September, no African American could testify against any white person. In response, Blacks in Mobile formed the National Lincoln Association and petitioned that state constitutional convention for the franchise, legal equality, and protection from violence and abuse in public space, with emphasis on harm done to women and girls. Though these crimes were taking place, President Andrew Johnson wrote the provisional governor, Lewis Parsons (whom he had appointed), and advised him to set up "an armed mounted posse comitatus organization under your militia law" in every county, commenting further that he had done so during the war as military governor of Tennessee. Still, Mobile became a site of organization and mobilizing, typified by mass meetings like other sites. A year later in Selma, African Americans also resisting the law barring Black testimony against whites demanded a white murderer be either brought to justice or turned over to the Black community with the threat of burning the town if nothing was done. The arrival of federal troops simply resulted in the man's escape.[13]

In the winter of 1865–66, Pinckney Benton Stewart spoke to a public gathering in Montgomery decrying the state's black codes and the return of former Confederates to political office in the constitutional convention. A onetime riverboat steward and gambler, Stewart was the son of Eliza Stewart, an enslaved woman, and a planter, Major William Pinchback. He was born in Macon, Georgia, in 1837 and reared near Yazoo City, Mississippi. When Stewart was ten years old, his father, who had married and freed Eliza (which had no legality in Mississippi), sent him and an older brother to school in Cincinnati. A year later his father died, and his mother and siblings fled in fear of being sold. Stewart helped to support his family by working as a hotel porter and as a cabin boy on Ohio riverboats. In the mid-1850s, he began tutelage under riverboat gamblers working the Mississippi, Missouri, and Red Rivers. When war came, Stewart, by then a steamboat steward, maneuvered to Union lines and then to New Orleans. His steamboat work gave him a politician's ease with the elite and a familiarity with carrying a pistol, and his gambler's acumen perhaps gave him a keen eye for moments of advantage.[14] When he spoke in Montgomery, he and his wife, Nina, who had moved there from New Orleans in the summer of 1865, would have been witness to the politics of the state constitution process of that year. The original black codes passed in 1865 were so severe that the governor vetoed most of them, concerned, according to Du Bois, about Northern reaction building against laws replicating the slave system, but there were still "the usual provisions for vagrancy, apprenticeship, enticing labor, etc." And, as Fitzgerald points out, in the black codes as written, "the planters' repressive intentions were manifest to the freedmen." Stewart "exhorted" the community, saying it was "the time when every thinking man must come forward and give his best views to the people."

Stewart, who had recruited several companies of men for the Black Louisiana Native Guard, which became the Corps d'Afrique, said that joining up was "the only time in my life I have felt anything like Patriotism, my Heart is full, my Soul Seams [sic] indeed in arms." But he did not see action in the war because he quit when he discovered his rank of captain was meaningless as the army replaced the African American officers who had formed the units with whites. A man who may have thought early in life that freedom and comfort would come his way, Stewart in 1865 was already a man for whom freedom could never be enough. During this time, he engaged in a bit of code-switching too, taking his planter father's name, Pinchback, as his new last name. He would make the name P. B. S. Pinchback famous, and he chose Black suffrage as his first political work. He also joined the campaign to desegregate New Orleans streetcars, which during the war had begun requiring Blacks to ride in separate cars marked with a star. Pinchback would also look to politics for a comfortable lifestyle. The Pinchbacks stayed in Montgomery two more years, engaged in politics and community building. In 1867, he must have seen a chance in New Orleans to be elected to Louisiana's constitutional convention, and indeed there was.[15]

The politics in Alabama were somewhat unique. Unlike in Florida in 1868, Blacks in Alabama in 1867 would not hold a majority of registered voters, and unlike in most states, an organized group of poor white farmers rose up to keep the old elite from retaking power permanently. These white Alabamans had seen the slaveholders make the 1865 constitution and the black codes, and there was concern about a permanent return of the old guard. Geography plays a role in this situation as well, again in contrast to Florida; for instance, freedpeople and slaveholding lands were in the middle of the state, the Black Belt. The poor white farmers were mostly in the northern section. Why would this matter when Blacks got the vote? They would control a swath of counties in the state's economic engine. The organized white farmers called for a census in 1866, the only such census that exists for a southern state in the middle of that decade of change. They used that census to lobby for reapportionment of the state, giving preference to rural white counties, as Florida would also do to nullify Black votes. Alabamians had already learned what political advantages slaveholders had in counting three-fifths of a person for every enslaved person held. Some of these same planters even brought to the legislature a bill to give the vote to some Blacks, using property or education qualifications. (This, if all Black males between thirty and one hundred years of age qualified and voted with planters—both unlikely to my mind—would have still netted them at best only a few more voters.) Needless to say, the idea did not go far, but it is worth noting as an unusual proposal to grant suffrage before the Reconstruction Acts. Alabama was like Florida in one other rather important detail: it too had a new governor (Robert Patton) declare after the 1865 convention that legislators had restored "a white man's government."[16]

The winter of 1865–66 was bleak for most in the state as food crops were still devastated by both the weather and the contending armies. The thousands of people living in squatter conditions in Alabama's cities also suffered illnesses the state was ill-prepared to treat in such numbers. The Freedmen's Bureau "established regional medical facilities in Mobile, Selma, Garland, Montgomery, Demopolis, Huntsville, and Talladega." As it turned out, crop failures would persist until 1868, and the bureau would have to maintain food relief through those years. Making contracts for the first time in January 1866 proved vexing to planters, as in other places, because workers took their time, hoping some land would be distributed to them. Richard Bailey reports some planters either not informing workers they were free or lying to them about whether a contract was in fact in force. The bureau helped to negotiate contracts that ended up having the same handicaps for workers as contracts throughout the South, creating yearly debts to the landowners that would wipe out earnings, and their children were still subject to being apprehended by former owners for "apprenticeships." The bureau also set up numerous schools and within two years claimed to be serving nearly ten thousand students, but except for one school in Mobile and one in Montgomery, they were in northern Alabama, and not in the big population areas for freedpeople. Whites in the state seemed to take exception to northern white teachers, urged on by political officials who were apt to say African Americans might seek social equality after being fed northern ideas. It was both sad and very common in the South at the time that "planters strongly opposed African Americans observing the first postwar anniversary of the Emancipation Proclamation." As mentioned earlier, whites sometimes took such celebrations as offensive.[17]

Making Political Voice

Freedpeople held colored conventions starting in 1865 in Mobile and again in 1866. The November 1865 gathering was preceded by local meetings in places like Selma. The printed comments from speeches given there seem worded to allay the fears of whites who believed only disfranchisement and black codes, vagrancy laws, and the like would make free Blacks tolerable. The 1866 statewide colored convention had a similar conciliatory tone. But by 1867 much was changing. With passage of the Reconstruction Acts in March, activists like the Union League held a second statewide meeting and had the state's first integrated meeting in April (all in the Unionist northern section). Alabama freedpeople began a complex process of organizing— within the league and outside of it—holding discrete local meetings, learning constitutional rights, and preparing to elect registrars and discuss what goals the Republican Party should stand behind. Mobile, home to a growing African American population of more than eight thousand, held a mass rally reported to have drawn five thousand Blacks and some whites in April 1867, only to have another rally marred a month later by KKK violence in which two people were killed.[18]

The third Alabama convention of freedpeople was held in May 1867 in Mobile. This one was doubtless attended by a number of the leaders of the former free Black community in Mobile, but also dozens of formerly enslaved people from rural communities. An observer who wrote to the *New Orleans Tribune* about the event reported: "Thirty or forty counties were represented by working men who could speak from their eyes, and from the swelling emotions of their souls, though their tongues were unused to the nice points of rhetoric or the utterance of fine grammatical sentences." The reporter characterized the meeting as having "an honesty of purpose, and a simplicity of motive." The group passed a resolution promising community-wide response demanding support from the military and severe legislative action if "employers of colored men carry out their threat to discharge them because of political difference, and to otherwise torment them by the denial of their rights before the law."[19]

They also sponsored a public speech by Thomas W. Conway, a former Freedmen's Bureau official for Alabama and Louisiana. The assembly had been threatened, so Conway spoke in the largest church in the city, with thousands outside as well to hear the speech. The *Tribune* reported that Conway spoke to mass audiences such as the Mobile one in nineteen other southern cities. Conway himself described the Emancipation Circuit in formation in the state when he talked with rural men in Mobile about joining the Union League: "The hands employed on plantations hearing that there is to be a meeting 'in town,' each contribute something toward defraying the expenses of their best man, who is . . . sent off. . . . This person, after learning all he can, returns to the plantation. Soon a meeting is called and the messenger makes his report, which is usually very correct." Within each county, once a UL group was established, Black folk organized their neighbors themselves. Meetings of freedpeople were held in at least the following counties: Autaga, Chambers, Dallas, Lauderdale, Lowndes, Macon, Madison, Mobile, Montgomery, and Morgan.[20]

Fitzgerald notes that the UL organizing among freedpeople was slanted toward conciliation by the league's headquarters: "The leadership hoped to channel the movement toward cautious demands. This outside intervention proved a critical factor in shaping black political activity. On confiscation [of slaveholders' land] and other issues, the wishes of the black community were subordinated to expediency as defined by the National Council of the League and by Republican leaders generally." Over time, this wore thin with freedpeople, who were primarily concerned with issues bearing on their immediate survival and their interest in throwing off both the fetters and the markers of subordination. According to Fitzgerald, "Freedmen reoriented their councils away from the national focus stressed by the League's white leaders. . . . The democratic character of local leagues thus transformed them into a vehicle for black aspirations for autonomy." At the same time, leagues in Unionist areas came to grips with the idea that Black votes would be needed to carry forth their program, and they began to work in counties with larger Black populations.[21]

The system set up by the US Congress for selection of voter registrars required the military to identify two white registrars and one African American for each of the state's newly defined forty-five registration districts. The correspondence listing the virtues of Blacks suggested for these positions must have been something of a new experience for both the writers and the recipients: "has a clear head, quick perceptions, is honest, and has a large influence," "a man of intelligence and undoubted Loyalty," "good man," "first rate man," "bridge builder," "has influence and independence of character." Forty-two Blacks were appointed as registrars, and more than a dozen of them later served as state legislators. Being involved in the registration process was also beneficial for whites interested in political office; the supervisor of registration, William Hugh Smith, for instance, would become the twenty-first governor of the state. There were more Blacks registered than whites, even after the registrars disqualified 405 Black voters and after they added 1,702 whites to create a majority. It turned out not to matter that year because Alabama whites boycotted the vote on a constitutional convention and its delegates. Such boycotts of the elections for authorizing constitutional conventions and choosing delegates and, not incidentally, the first elections in which Blacks participated were the rule rather than the exception in the former Confederacy. Because Alabama, however, had the earliest election date, one could say that it originated the white voter boycott trend. I commented earlier that the boycott in Florida in 1868, for instance, was puzzling; this was because it had been tried in a number states by then with the same undesired results. In Alabama the board of registrars arrived at a white majority, and then the majority stayed home and let the Blacks and Unionist white voters carry the day. Why? The gamble at least for the editor of the *Montgomery Mail* was to persuade whites to stay home on the contention that there would not be a large enough percentage of the registered electorate voting to support a constitutional convention. One reason it did not work was that more than 96 percent of eligible Black voters had been registered. Both the registration rate and a tradition of high voter turnout are legacies of Reconstruction that caused Blacks in Alabama to be the target of voter repression laws and practices for nearly a century, and with unchecked success.[22]

Circuit Riders

Eighteen African Americans were elected as delegates to the constitutional convention, which was held in Montgomery from November 5 to December 6, 1867.[23] These eighteen freedpeople among the one hundred delegates to the convention included twelve from the Black Belt and adjacent counties, two from Mobile County, one each from two counties in the northern Unionist area, and one each from two counties in the Piedmont region. (*See the Alabama maps [plate 1].*) They likely expected to be fairly consistently aligned with their radical Republican allies, at least ten of whom worked with the Freedmen's Bureau and were there to improve the conditions for freedpeople. Although the alliance held in some cases, race and civil rights sometimes left freedpeople on their own, especially when Blacks tried to have racial barriers removed from public accommodations. The discussion of legalizing interracial marriage was a jousting arena for southern Blacks and whites in several constitutional conventions. Apparently, the few outspoken Blacks in the delegation left white Alabamians quite beside themselves simply by speaking frankly. The violence of the slave system and the isolation of the labor force had protected white citizens from hearing what African Americans really thought on almost any subject. Reconstruction politics began their exposure to what was still only *occasional* candor from Black people in public.

While a few of the Black delegates had done earlier organizing for voting registrars and in county meetings, their experiences in life up to that point in some ways differed wildly. Several of the men were circuit riders who organized in various places and were involved early on in building Alabama's Black political formations, quite a few had been born in other states, and some had lived in the North.

Peyton Finley was much like a number of the young activists who came south and ended up in political office. He was born free in Georgia but before the war worked as a doorkeeper in the Alabama legislature, a rare education in the procedures of making laws, especially for a man of color. Finley became a speaker for the URCC, which literally put him on the road speaking and setting up Republican Party groups. He attended the 1867 colored convention and the Republican Party's convention as well. Before coming to the constitutional convention, he was a registrar in Montgomery. He would later hold several political posts.

James K. Green, who was born enslaved in North Carolina, worked as a carpenter and was a Union League activist. He organized in Greene and Hale Counties and agreed to become voter registrar in 1867 in Eutaw after the first registrar was killed. Green was threatened in such a way that the community came out to protect him. As early as 1867 he was said to be interested in Liberia emigration and later advocated sending a group to test migration to Kansas. Green held office in the state house and senate through Reconstruction and, like a number of lifelong activists, later joined the Alabama Labor Union. Benjamin Royal, born enslaved in Alabama, was also a Union League activist and would serve three terms in the state senate. Not long after an incident in his county in which Blacks and whites armed themselves, Royal reported, "Rebels are forming into clubs to prevent the colored people from voting the Radical ticket." Jordan Hatcher, born enslaved in Georgia, worked as a field hand but had become literate and in Selma was a distributor of the radical Black-owned paper the *Mobile Nationalist*. Alfred Strother, who like Hatcher served from Dallas County, was born enslaved in South Carolina, was also literate, and worked as a laborer. He would later serve as a justice of the peace. In the convention, he proposed reparation legislation whereby laborers would be authorized to demand wages unpaid since emancipation.[24]

James T. Rapier was perhaps the most unusual figure among the eighteen, and likely the most educated. He also brought to the convention the experience of having earlier been admitted to the bar in Canada and having attended the 1865 colored convention in Tennessee. Rapier was born free in Alabama to a propertied family funded by his father's barber business. His entire family has an interesting history, partly because his three brothers journeyed to different parts of the country and the Caribbean. He grew up in Nashville and then went to Canada, where he taught and studied law. After the war he farmed successfully in Tennessee before shifting his farming to Alabama. In several years he would win a seat in the US Congress. In his forty-six years he would also publish a newspaper and spend all of his considerable income on numerous causes, including school-building, reform of the convict leasing system, and Kansas migration. The breadth of these delegates' experience contrasted sharply with that of their white counterparts and would deeply inform them as lawmakers on the diverse needs of freedpeople.[25]

Within a year, however, death claimed five of the original delegates, all of whom were newly elected to the state house of representatives. John Carraway was born enslaved in New Bern, North Carolina, to a slaveholder and an enslaved mother; both he and his mother were freed by the father's will, though his mother was still sold to Alabama. He traveled to Brooklyn, New York, where he became a tailor. When the war came and Black men in New York were barred from serving, he traveled to Boston and joined the Fifty-Fourth Massachusetts. When Carraway returned to Alabama to live with his mother, he brought a wealth of experiences and became assistant editor at the *Nationalist* and a regular at Mobile organizing events. He died at age thirty-six in 1870. Ovid Gregory, born free in Mobile, was a well-known Creole community leader and cigar store owner when the war ended; unlike the others, he had seen much of the United States and had been to Latin America. He was routinely characterized as a radical and was about forty-four on his death in 1869. Benjamin Inge, a minister who was born (date unknown) enslaved in Virginia, died in 1869. Columbus Jones was born enslaved in Alabama; little is known about him, including his age at the time of his death in 1869. Thomas Lee, also born enslaved in the state, was a carpenter and laborer, and his age at death in 1869 is also unknown.[26]

Having already been forced to reckon with what it meant to enfranchise Black males in the state as the Reconstruction Acts had done, Alabama's conservatives and its Unionists could not bring themselves to make it state law that Black men could vote. There was much discussion on the issue. On further disfranchisement of former Confederates, beyond the officers and others barred by the Reconstruction Acts, most of the Blacks demurred. Doubtless they didn't push for more punishment both because they had been cautioned to be moderate in their aims, and likely because they would have to live with the reprisals. James T. Rapier basically ended the discussion by offering the following resolution forcing the US Congress to worry about it: "Resolved, that this Convention memorialize Congress, at its next session, to remove all the political disabilities of those citizens of Alabama who have aided in the reconstruction of the State on the plan proposed by Congress; Which was adopted."[27] After proposals passed to support public schools, the whites proved uniformly uncomfortable with requiring them to be integrated. Unwilling to let a requirement for segregation pass, the Blacks used their numbers to table the question. It became necessary to leave the matter unsettled because their northern Republican allies seemed reluctant to reject the position of white Alabamian Unionists. The Unionists, it turned out, were all for the Republican program, except on racial issues. Some southern whites of both stripes refused to vote for the constitution when it was done because racially separate schools were not mandated by law. Of course, segregation of schools was achieved without any legislative demand and later was reaffirmed by Jim Crow laws.

On one of the rare occasions in which Alfred Strother rose to speak, he offered the following resolution: "That the committee on Ordinances be instructed to inquire into the expediency of passing an ordinance empowering the colored people of this State to collect a fair equivalent for their services from those persons who held them in slavery from the 1st day of January, 1863, to the 20th day of May, 1865." The resolution was adopted—yeas 53, nays 31.[28]

If one reckons with an average monthly wage of $10 to $15 for each adult being repaid for a period of twenty-nine months, there would be a sum of

$290 to $435 (approximately $5,263 to $7,895 in 2020 dollars), which could mean a piece of land (especially at the $2 per acre rate cited by a delegate in South Carolina), clothes, and schoolbooks—helpful, even if not real reparations. Though such an outcome would have been transformative, apparently any such requests did not go over well with the planter elite.[29]

Like Black delegates in other states, Ovid Gregory proposed that all laws and regulations be voided that made distinctions based on "caste, color, or former condition of servitude," and this alone proved to be basis on which some whites voted against the constitution or refused to vote. Alternative wording by John Carraway asserted, "The political equality of all men before the law, without regard to race, color, or previous condition, shall be held inviolate, and no Legislature shall have power to deprive, by enactments, any citizen of this right." Once the proposal was read, the "hour of adjournment" was called. On their return in the afternoon, a delegate from Marengo moved that it be tabled, "which was agreed to." This was exactly how it went when Carraway earlier proposed that any male of twenty-one years of age could vote regardless of "race, color, or previous condition"; a man from Monroe County moved that it be tabled, "which was agreed to." Even with additions offered by others, it was tabled once more.[30]

Interracial marriage also became such an unnerving issue that it too was tabled, which upset conservatives who wanted to bar it. The debate included one proposal prohibiting marriage between Blacks and whites, "to the fourth generation," and offering penalties for offenders. Carraway offered a "Modest Proposal" rejoinder: "That any white man intermarrying or cohabiting with colored women [sic], shall be imprisoned for life; which was tabled and ordered printed." Men in several other constitutional conventions would follow suit with similar proposals. Far from striking the white men at these sessions as amusing, these open references to the commonplace facts of life for Black women were likely especially shocking and offensive to men who found many Black opinions offensive, and said so. Rapier, Gregory, and Carraway, who, among the Blacks, were the most apt to speak, got under the skin of some of the die-hards for the old way of life. Carraway called some of the conservatives "just as bitter, just as arrogant, and just as vindictive as they were in 1861." On this Peter Kolchin writes, "Many whites, unused to having their views challenged by blacks, branded such speeches by those three and 'other blacks' to be 'violent and highly inflammatory harangues.'" Not making racial distinctions in marriage laws between races cost the Republicans support of cooperative native whites, and a failure to build schools based on racial separation was also a deal breaker that conservatives saw as tending "to the abasement and degradation of the white population."[31]

Cultural theorist Stuart Hall said once that "race is more like a language than it is like the way in which we are biologically constituted." In the South, race was not only the language of power but one the elite seem to have felt *had* to be deployed literally as language lest their power evaporate. In this case, they held that the constitution couldn't leave out race, period. Even before Black enfranchisement had been legislated, white southerners evidently felt the need for race to be included in all legislated texts in order to maintain Blacks as noncitizens and deprive them of mobility, fair wages, and the right to choose their own partners, own land, rent homes or land, or seek justice in the courts. The Old South ideology held that a society without raced institutions and laws "tended to the abasement and degradation" of whites. In many places Black delegates moved at the outset of constructing constitutions to remove that language, also understanding that without it they at least stood a chance to contest the coercion that accompanied the racialized structure of southern society. Southerners found ways to covertly insert the language of race into all facets of society where it had earlier been served by law and, during Reconstruction and after, simply used violence to prevent Blacks from exercising rights if the language of the law indicated all citizens. At the onset of this battle for control without racialized language, clientelism was also tried—planters assumed Black employees and tradesmen would vote as they were told. Boycotting Black businesses was a threat, and firing people for attending political meetings was common. This was ineffective when the Freedmen's Bureau and the Union League could intervene, but their time in the South was brief and governed by politics in the North. And in 1877, the military also left.[32]

The nineteenth-century usage of words directed at racial issues often contradicts the meanings we now have for these terms, such as *demoralization*, discussed in an earlier chapter as a complaint by whites obscuring a mood of activism among Blacks. Bailey remarks that Democrats charged the Republicans in 1867 with trying to deny the "'rightful' leaders a place in government." In this case, the word *rightful* is a reference to slaveholders who had opted for the wrongful step of making war on the United States that they were now trying to rejoin, bringing about the loss of several hundred thousand lives and the devastation of their own states. The adjective *rightful* implies no wrongful decision in taking four million enslaved humans into war who had no say in the matter, and in 1867 and 1868 claiming those same people were not entitled to vote or pass judgment on who their "rightful" leaders would be. The argument that Blacks should cooperate even superficially leaned on the mutuality of Blacks and whites born in the state and a groundless claim of solidarity and friendship among all from that native ground. The southern elite might even have accurately used kinship as part of the affinity claimed between the races, but no one, not even the Black lawmakers, reminded the whites that many of the opposition had Black kinfolk. Most insupportable was the claim made that Republicans were "dividing the races," when in fact conservative efforts to appeal to Blacks to vote with them had the political goal of keeping the races not only separate in daily life but unjustly divided in power. Everyone in the constitutional convention understood the inverted meanings of Reconstruction vocabulary. [33]

The conservative rhetoric of the day was so self-regarding that inaccurate depictions of others were taken to be common knowledge, not in need of explanation to anyone who similarly saw others as outside the picture. For Blacks to have a celebration, particularly of freedom, was described as "an offense" to whites, betraying a prickliness that could trigger violence but also a blindness to the right of others to celebrate themselves. In common usage, redemption still generally means a spiritual atonement, or turning in reward points from a loyalty card for something that usually costs money. But dictionaries are remiss in not taking note of *Redemption* with a capital *R*. It might be useful for people to know that the word was a cri de coeur, to use another antique term, to assert total white control of their state governments. Redemption was not only not an act of atonement, but a violent series of episodes that involved murders, burnings of communities, and too many sins to name, in which presumably the victims atoned for others losing power after the war. Though the Redemption in Alabama was not the first—those occurred in border states—it was an early Deep South campaign that was emulated elsewhere.

Reparations is also a word with a contemporary meaning quite the opposite of its meaning during the Civil War and its immediate aftermath. A recent article in an online magazine deployed an ironic use of the word in a headline that read "'Reparations' for Confederates?" in a discussion of payments made to the Sons of Confederate Veterans for removing and sheltering the Confederate statue that stood on the campus of the University of North Carolina at Chapel Hill. The trustees had also paid the same group not to display Confederate flags or signage on any of its campuses.

But reparations for Confederates were exactly how it all started. Lincoln had pondered what is now called *compensation* for slaveholders who were going to lose capital with the flight and emancipation of their human property. Some used the term *reparations* for their requests, specifying their financial loss, and thus the term gained its tie to the slavery system. When Lincoln enacted abolition for the District of Columbia's enslaved population in 1862, a small number of slaveholders were in fact paid $300 for each human being's freedom. In Mississippi's first postwar constitutional convention in August 1865, some delegates debated adding a phrase that affirmed their claim for payments. And as Foner writes, "Georgia specified that abolition did not imply the relinquishment of slave owners' claims to compensation." The idea that reparation should be made to those who lost the recognition of their humanity over the long centuries of the slave system is a more recent interpretation.[34]

Mobilizing on the Circuit during the Redemption

The circuit along the rail line in the Black Belt was the lifeline for mobilizations of various kinds during Reconstruction. The state vote to pass the state constitution was nearly sabotaged when another conservative boycott denied the document the required two-thirds majority for acceptance by the US Congress. The Congress had to choose whether to reinstate Alabama for political reasons, varying from needing the state's vote in the next presidential election to business interests wanting to revive industry in the state, or to deny it. Congressional legislators passed an amendment allowing them to make an exception to their own rules and approve the state constitution. This left Republicans in power in Alabama and ignited white resistance to the state government. For African Americans—voters and especially electoral organizers—the intimidation and violence shifted to an organized version from the new terror group, the Ku Klux Klan. Attacks on Blacks elaborated the Emancipation Circuit in the state from its primary role in organizing to an evolving role in self-defense.

As Bailey writes, "Politically active blacks and whites who would participate in the [1870] election of a governor, a legislature, and congressmen were the targets of Klan violence." In June 1870, for instance, when James H. Alston, a state representative (who had earlier organized a four-hundred-member Union League), was shot in Tuskegee, a group of Union League freedmen boarded a train in Montgomery to bring reinforcements, and local white officials came out to stop them. In November, "an unidenti-fied white man approached the Selma and Meridian train and called out for Frank Diggs, a Black postal agent whose train had stopped just in-side the Mississippi line." When Diggs appeared, he was shot dead. It is worth noting that the killer waited to be out of Alabama before shooting Diggs. Many of the Klan assaults that year were never prosecuted on the excuse that the killers were from a different county's Klan and could not be identified.[35]

People in the Black Belt were similarly connected along that same rail line to freedpeople in Mississippi, and they moved along the same route east and west as the AME Zion missionaries did in 1865. Some began to move west to Mississippi. In 1870, when Alabama Klan members abducted workers from Mississippi saying they had fled labor contracts in Alabama, the Union League of Meridian, Mississippi, rode to the rescue. This hap-pened on a larger scale in 1871, tragically leading to the Meridian riot in which the Black political structure of that town was targeted for assas-sination. A white Union League activist from Sumter County, Alabama, had fled to Meridian, where he became a teacher and wrote to his league that "conditions were better across the Mississippi line." Several hundred freedpeople came to Meridian, abandoning some labor contracts in the process. Posses of armed Alabamians, mostly Klan, rode across the bor-der claiming the right to arrest them and return them to Alabama. When one Black Alabamian was seriously wounded in one of these abductions, a league posse captured and beat a Black man aiding the Klan. Meridian whites invited in a throng of Alabama Klansmen, who killed two Black officers and several Black leaders. At a hearing on the trouble, a white man opened fire and a day of rioting ensued in which more than thirty Blacks were killed.[36]

After having gambled on keeping whites from the polls when it came time to ratify the new constitution, and losing when Congress decided to accept the largely Black vote, Alabama's elite developed the strategy for the next election to take control of local voting. They decided on Redemption. An example of this systematic localized drive was the murder of three men who were targeted that year just for working for Rapier's campaign to become Alabama secretary of state, including Guilford Coleman who was killed and thrown in his well in Hale County. White allies also met with the same fate, such as Alexander Boyd, Greene County prosecutor, who had investigated the Klan and, like Coleman, was dragged out of bed and shot. They took over state power in the election of 1873. As Bailey writes:

Whereas Republicans focused on statewide officeholding as a key to power, Democrats perceived early on the value of a local or community power base. Although Republicans didn't unify their forces before the election, Democrats, on the other hand, fully grasped the urgency of defeating Republicans and employed every possible means to guarantee a victory at the polls. . . . Republicans overlooked or minimized the importance of local officeholding. . . . African Americans in Halifax County, North Carolina and in Alabama learned too late that the center of power was not in Raleigh, Montgomery, or Washington—it was in the county seat in Alabama.[37]

On taking power in 1874, the Democrats literally reinscribed race into state laws through a series of voter repression tactics and later Jim Crow laws, though one could argue that southerners had already proved written law was almost unnecessary in the face of local traditions of violence and denying employment. Generations had been taught by violence this language linked to biology by omnipresent, readily accepted vilification. The assault on Black electoral representation from the margins of the Alabama circuit can be seen taking place over the next five years and on the heart of the circuit in the Black Belt over the next six years. (See the Alabama maps [plate 1].)

Just as many of the early protests of freedpeople were over labor, as participation in government came to an early close in Alabama, many activists and officeholders turned their attention to labor formations. Nine of the nineteenth-century lawmakers had been Union League organizers, and that organization had been pushed by freedpeople to be involved in labor negotiations across the state, especially in the Black Belt. Nine of the lawmakers were also involved in the formation of the Alabama Labor Union, founded in 1870 and affiliated with the National Negro Labor Union. Local leaders also made this turn. Allen Alexander helped to found the union, after having been a UL organizer and a member of the Alabama Republican Party's executive committee. He fought for integration of the Mobile police force and became a customs official there. In the 1874 election, he was nearly killed and yet was arrested and charged with inciting to riot after whites had fired on Blacks at a polling site.[38]

As of 1878, the Noble and Holy Order of the Knights of Labor were active among coal miners in Montgomery and Helena (now near Birmingham). In the late 1870s and the 1880s, the Farmers' Alliance had a huge presence all over rural Alabama, and many Blacks joined, but Jim Crow was an issue. Emigration also stayed alive in the state, with freedpeople acting on their own eventually persuading leaders, such as the men who ran the Alabama Labor Union who voted against it, to gradually change their minds. As early as 1868, "emigration agents roamed through" thirteen counties, nine of them just outside the Black Belt, and four in the Black Belt. The largest numbers seemed to have left in 1880 and 1890. Alabama would experience some of the strikes that spread across the South in the 1880s, especially in the mines of Birmingham, and organizing that would influence the next century began in there in 1900.[39]

Looking at Table 8.1

One of the prominent features of Alabama's organizing history is the straight line of mutual access across the Black Belt, where numerous institutions were built from Selma and Perry County to Montgomery and Tuskegee. Birmingham, which was not yet incorporated in the 1860s, had Union League organizers in the area (see the town of Calera, also, in table 8.1) because a mining center was developing there. The rail lines were present to haul ore. During the war, metals used in Selma for munitions and arms were coming from that mining area. Otherwise, the organizing there took off later in the century. In addition to the farmers' movements mentioned earlier, it stands out that in Alabama civil rights activism dates to the nineteenth century. Also not shown here is the development of numerous HBCUs: Alabama A&M (1875) and Oakwood University (1896) in northern Alabama; Miles College (1898) near Birmingham; Talladega College (1865) and Stillman (1876) in the middle of state; and Alabama State University (1867), Selma University (1878), and Tuskegee University (1881) in the Black Belt.

TABLE 8.1 Alabama Emancipation Circuit 1870–1900

		Institutions Present							19th Century Activism
	US Troops	RR (1884)	Union League	AMA Schools	Local Black Press	Black Political Reps	Knights of Labor Groups		
BIRMINGHAM (est. 1871) Then only in Jefferson County		◆	◆	◆	<u>1</u> 1900	◆	2 M coal miners		Labor Colored Farmers' Alliance* (CFA)
CALERA BIRMINGHAM area, Shelby County	◆	◆				◆	1 M mixed labor 1 M limestone, quarry & kiln workers		Colored Farmers' Alliance (CFA)
DEMOPOLIS ß Marengo County ß						◆			
HUNTSVILLE ß Madison County ß	◆	◆	◆	2 (1 Methodist)	<u>2</u> 1877 1879	◆			

Location								
MAYSVILLE HUNTSVILLE area, Madison County ß	•					•	1 M mixed labor	Housing campaign
MOBILE Mobile County	•	•	2 1865 1870	•		•	3 M mixed labor	Labor and housing Colored Farmers' Alliance (CFA)
CITRONELLE Mobile County	•					•	1 M mixed labor	Labor
MONTGOMERY Montgomery County ß	•	•	4 1872 1870s 1880s 1900	•		•	1 M mixed 1 F mixed labor	Civil rights Kansas exodus Colored Farmers' Alliance (CFA)
Perry County ß	•	•	In area	•		•		
SELMA ß Dallas County ß	•	•	1 1886	•	4	•		Civil rights Self-defense
Sumter County ß						•		

(Continued)

TABLE 8.1 (Continued)

| | Institutions Present | | | | | | 19th Century Activism |
	US Troops	RR (1884)	Union League	AMA Schools	Local Black Press	Black Political Reps	Knights of Labor Groups
TALLADEGA ß Talladega County	•	•	•	•		1870–72	
TUSCALOOSA ß Tuscaloosa County			•	Presbyterian		1869–70 only	
TUSKEGEE ß Macon County	•	•	•	•		•	

KEY: **Bold** = Site playing multiple roles on the circuit.
ß = Black majority; unless otherwise noted, populations are for 1870.
RR = Rail lines.
Black Political Reps = Black representatives to the 1868 constitutional convention or members of the General Assembly.

Knights of Labor = Black assemblies of the labor organization. Most KoL assemblies were segregated by race and gender: white males, Black males, white females, or Black females. "Mixed labor" is a term from the Garlock data (*see* Table Source Notes) and indicates various forms of work, not mixing by race or gender. **Gender** is indicated here by M or F.

* The Colored Farmers' Alliance was active in a number of counties not included in this table, including Bullock, Lee, and Monroe.

SOURCES: *See* Table Source Notes (393–96).

9 LOUISIANA
Societies

Society: *n*, **1** : companionship or association with one's fellows . . .
2 : a voluntary association of individuals for common ends; esp. an
organized group working together or periodically meeting because
of common interests, beliefs, or profession; **3 a** : an enduring and
cooperating social group whose members have developed organized
patterns of relationships through interaction with one another . . .
—*Webster's Ninth New Collegiate Dictionary* (1986)

In late 1862, when Louisiana was under occupation, the state became ex-
empt from the Emancipation Proclamation, and enslaved people technically would not be free on the announcement of Lincoln's decree on
January 1. Nevertheless, African Americans in Louisiana took freedom to
be theirs alongside the other millions freed in the South. Just fleeing plantations in Louisiana was contested. Earlier, in February 1862, Louisiana
was made part of the military's Department of the Gulf, and a month
later Major General Benjamin Butler arrived, having left his post at Fort
Monroe. He would not be appreciated by Louisianans, especially citizens
of New Orleans, as he had been by the fugitives who flocked to the fort
in Virginia, but his presence and that of US troops caused thousands of
slaves to run for Union lines in that city, as people had elsewhere. As in
1861, the military was soon overwhelmed by the arrival of ten thousand
fugitives. Butler decided he just could not try to accommodate them all as
he had attempted before, and he revived the slavers' pass system and not

only returned refugees but jailed people in flight who had no passes. Union soldiers, though, freed many. In Louisiana, Butler was an imperious and impolitic administrator who earned the nickname "Beast" by issuing heavy-handed orders that curtailed women's freedom and freedom of speech in the city and shutting down newspapers that printed conservative ideas or even articles he just didn't like. In December he was succeeded by Major General Nathaniel P. Banks, who presented more difficulties for African Americans in the state. Banks also began by returning fugitives to their enslavers.[1]

The history of Reconstruction and its aftermath in Louisiana has two distinct faces. One that was prominent in the historiography was the some-what short-lived leadership asserted by the urbane, elite Black precincts of occupied New Orleans. These elites were people described before emanci-pation as free people of color. During the military occupation, this group was the hub of the Louisiana Emancipation Circuit. The other face of Reconstruction in the state was seen in the agricultural areas where the cir-cuit survived due to Black labor activism that sustained representation and engagement in a shifting political landscape during that period. The people in those areas would maintain local sodalities that later could be turned to work on emigration and western migration (Exoduster) movements. Both the metropolitan areas and the countryside had a high number of Black societies that facilitated mobilization across wards in the city or planta-tions in rural areas. A sample of how this grassroots organization shaped the democratic process of freedpeople can be seen in a comment from Henry Adams, a famed Louisiana organizer, who wrote about planning an 1878 convention in the northern part of the state; Hahn cites Adams's method: "Significantly, they 'Appeal[ed] to the Freedmen without regard to sex religion or politics' to meet within their local groups and choose delegates. The plan gave "any organized Religious body one delegate; any Benevolent Society, one delegate; any Secret Organization, one delegate; any Plantation with 50 persons, one delegate; any organization composed exclusively of Negro people, one delegate."[2]

On December 22, 1862, two men, writing on behalf of a Black group that came to be known as the Union Association (but which earlier may have been the Union Benevolent Association) wrote to Banks for permission for a bona fide New Orleans–style celebration of the expected Emancipa-tion Day, January 1, 1863:

> In obedience To Th High shift an Command of Th Head quarters De-partment of th Gulf Maggor Gen N P Bank WeTh members of Th

union association Desir Th & Respectfully ask of you Th privileges of Salabrating Th first Day of January th 1863 by a Large procession on that Day & We Wish to pass th Head quarters of th union officers High in a authority that is if it Suit your approbation & We also Wish to Give a Grand union Dinner on th Second Day of January that is if it so pleas you & the profit of Th. Dinner Will Go To th poor people in th Camp th Colour Woman & Children.[3]

In Louisiana, in the absence of consistent military assistance and a coherent attempt to assist freedom, a proliferation of citizen-led groups organized both aid and protests. At the beginning of 1863, Banks initiated the creation of labor contracts with planters. Laborers themselves were not party to the contracts for their labor. Banks took the position that the laborers' "presence on an estate constituted 'proof of their assent.'" The blindness to abolition as change indulged by planters and the military caused them to learn the hard way that the labor force thought the terms of the work would now be different. Pay was abominable, a third or less than the average wage, and produced some instances of workers leaving plantations en masse. As in South Carolina, freedpeople were particular about which people were overseers or preferred having none at all. And like people in South Carolina and elsewhere, they constructed gardens for their own survival and had less interest in growing a staple crop—in this case, sugar or cotton—for landowners. One of the most onerous and perhaps silliest restrictions planters tried to implement was to deny Blacks mobility and insist they could not leave plantations. This, of course, produced mobility at will, as well as plantation organizing. Workers realized that group action was the most effective tool for acting in self-interest. Once the Union had won control of the Mississippi River, many rural men found military enlistment preferable to field work and joined new Black units.[4]

That year in New Orleans there were sometimes wholesale arrests of Black folk on the streets either for "vagrancy" or just to be commandeered to labor for the military. The main goal, for Banks, however, was to help rural planters who were losing workers. Banks finally began to take a lot of heat when national attention criticized him for setting up a system that would replicate the slavery system after the military's departure. He had to make a new plan raising wages, forcing planters to provide medical care in addition to the usual shelter and rations, and allowing farmworkers to get a lien against the crop in case of planter failure to pay. He continued to try to restrict mobility for those on farms.[5]

Mass confusion that also mobilized Black workers was brought on when Banks was succeeded in September 1864 by Major General S. A. Hurlbut and Major General E. R. S. Canby, along with a change of administration from the military to the Department of the Treasury. In the currents of turmoil that arose, formerly enslaved men and former free men of color alike began to share the depredations of being conscripted off the street to perform labor. Some fifty-one free men of color wrote to the commander of the Gulf in December 1864 claiming their distinction from "contrabands" and protesting being treated as "the lowest and most degraded class." These men were being picked up from their homes and businesses and thrown in jail. Still, the rough treatment may have been a wake-up call for that community, first, as to what was befalling most Black Louisianans, and second, that the new not-freedom regime made none of the distinctions of class and color that had long insulated them and offered them the privileges of working for themselves and defining their own lives. In March 1865, Lincoln simply restored military control. While the next round of labor regulations gave way to some of the repeated demands of farmworkers, the Black elite, who were also organizing, demanded that everyone have the freedom to make their own work contracts.[6]

In March 1865, former free people of color organized a formal protest of the treatment of African Americans. A letter resulting from resolutions made by a March 17 mass meeting of "colored Citizens of New Orleans" and signed by one of the leaders, Captain James H. Ingraham, a vice president of the National Equal Rights League (NERL) formed at the 1864 National Convention of Colored Men, presented a list of demands, opening with a declaration of the state of affairs as the community saw them:

> Whereas: The labor system established by Maj. General Banks—which does not practically differ from slavery, except by the interdiction from selling and whipping to death, the laborers.[sic] were [sic] only intended by its promoter to be a temporary one. . . .
>
> Whereas: An abridgment of the liberties of the black [sic], will have for effect, the strengthening of the hands, of the enemies of our beloved country, who have been asserting for several years, that the emancipation movement at the North, was a shame, that the United States government was not in earnest, on the abolition question, and did not intend to treat the negro better than the southern slaveocrats do. [sic] thereby damaging before the world, the honor and the social cause of the American Union, and . . .

Whereas: There is no practical liberty for the laborers, without the right of contracting freely, and voluntarily, on the terms of labor.[7]

The group asked for the formation of a "tribunal of Arbitrators composed partly of Freedmen," to handle disputes not satisfactorily resolved by the provost-marshals in the parishes. It also asked for the dismissal of the head of the Bureau of Free Labor in the state. The lengthy but curt response from Major General Hurlbut began by denying that these citizens could say the present circumstances replicated slavery. He followed with a patronizing suggestion: "If instead of assembling in Mass meetings and wasting your time in high sounding Resolutions you would devote Yourselves to assisting in the physical and moral improvement of the Freedmen you would do some practical good." The general then accused them of falsely presenting themselves as freedmen when they were free people of color and there was "bitterness of feeling" between them and those who had been enslaved. He lectured a bit on the technical difference between enslaved persons and freedpeople and gave some advice often heard across the South: "You must wait and work. Not call meetings and pass resolutions but work faithfully and slowly to educate the public mind both of whites and blacks, for the future." Ingraham, to whom the general addressed his response, was in fact born enslaved and had been freed by his white father; by this time he was famous for heroism in the Battle of Port Hudson. He belonged to several groups protesting the labor system and seeking the vote. A month later, on April 15, Lincoln was assassinated and Andrew Johnson became president. The Department of the Gulf ended in May 1865 after the Confederate surrender, but military occupation continued until 1877. Because the military tried to control the labor of refugees, as it had in other places, and many people had not left plantations, problems continued.[8]

Foundational Assemblies

By January 1865, a number of groups had already been formed for political work in New Orleans, most prominently a branch of NERL. In March of that year, Ingraham spoke to the local chapter, remarking: "No system of gradual elevation is needed to make us men. From Red River to the Gulf, we are told by this [Major General Nathaniel P.] Banks oligarchy that we are subject to special rules and regulations in our affairs; we are told that we are not ready to assume the responsibility of citizens of the United States." He reported that on visits to other parishes people complained that Banks's system for policing Black labor was leaving them worse off than they had been in slavery. The Banks command spurred protest by NERL and the *New Orleans Tribune*.[9]

In June 1865, a mixed group of radicals founded the Friends of Universal Suffrage. Jean-Charles Houzeau, managing editor of the *Tribune*, which was allied with the suffrage group, wrote: "The membership . . . consisted of whites and men of African descent. They held a public meeting every week. This was the first time that whites had decided to sit publicly and in a regular manner with blacks. Those who dared to do so were discredited immediately." Some months later, the group merged with the Republican Party.[10]

The Freedmen's Aid Association (FAA) of the City of New Orleans was founded as well that year by a mixed group that shared some leadership with the well-known figures leading NERL. The FAA, which proved to be multifaceted, is now most famous for its tie to the New Orleans "second-line" tradition. The group is credited as a founder of the parade tradition through its early postwar processions in Black neighborhoods to advertise its loan and education programs, and the funeral parades accompanied by bands for its members. In instituting parading as part of its appeal, the FAA built on slavery-era practices that "commemorated outlaws and revolutionaries like Toussaint L'Ouverture and protested the Dred Scott decision." In the antebellum North in the 1850s, Black community celebrations had begun to "favor commemorations of black resistance (crushed or successful), of black heroic deeds and black resilience."[11] The significance of memorializing even the unsuccessful acts of resistance is an indication of Genevieve Fabre's contention that unlike events meant to preserve tradition and the past, "black feasts were primarily concerned with forcing change and inventing a more viable future." According to a study of the New Orleans social and pleasure club traditions, "After the Civil War, associations, benevolent societies, and social clubs were part of a vast network of social groups that gave African Americans a place to analyze and strategize, to organize politically, and to be themselves." After the war, such traditions were used to obscure political activity, as in 1867 in Alabama, where a Black Union League organizer was queried about Black militia drilling in Bullock County and responded that whites had mistaken a funeral commemoration for Union League activity.[12]

Still, the processions in New Orleans were incidental to the FAA's main work and should not obscure the fact that Black politics there was centered on the elite cohort of formerly free *gens de couleur* trying to organize for and with (perhaps in that order) the area's Black workers emerging from the slavery system. The group put out calls for freedpeople seeking work to come to meetings and took pains to interview freedpeople about working conditions. The interviews gave the activists a database for articulating needs and shaping their agenda. In April, they took up the case of a young man jailed for "abuse" for refusing to let a white man take his cart.

Q. Have you any white friend, in your parish, who will support your claim or take your defense?

A. We have no white friends there.

Q. Have you any colored friend who could do so?

A. No colored man has anything to say; none has any influence.

Q. Is not the Provost Marshall a protector for your people?

A. Whenever a new Provost Marshall comes he gives us justice for a fortnight or so; then he becomes acquainted with planters, takes dinners with them, receives presents; and then we no longer have any rights, or very little.[13]

The Louisiana black code of 1865, not repealed until 1868, required freedpeople to have work contracts and said those contracts bound all their children as well to ten-hour workdays in summer, nine hours in winter. If a worker failed to work for more than three days, he or she could be sentenced to forced labor on public works. Of particular interest in this code is its bar on Blacks having meetings and congregations after sunset and daytime meetings without written permission of the police board. (The police board or police jury is the governing body in parishes in the state.) First Amendment rights were further negated by the code: "No negro shall be permitted to preach, exhort, or otherwise declaim to congregations of colored people, without a special permission in writing from the president of the police jury."[14]

The FAA was part of an ambitious vision promoted by the group's backers, the Black-owned *New Orleans Tribune* and its owner, J. B. Roudanez. The association helped people to lease farms and get supplies and by 1866 was also tied to the Louisiana Homestead Association, which assisted people seeking land under the Southern Homestead Act of 1866. The paper published its vision of Black landownership in several issues in the spring and summer of 1865:

The solution . . . was to "let the land go into the hands of actual laborers," for one cannot expect "complete and perfect freedom for working men, so long as they remain the tools of capital, and are deprived of the legitimate product of the sweat of their brow." . . . The planter class would be replaced by the mass of workers who, since "capital is created by labor," would themselves raise the capital to operate the plantations. The freedmen would purchase small shares in "self-help" banks, which would in turn buy land and factories and rent them to voluntary associations of workers. A portion of the profits from each enterprise would be returned to the banks to expand their ownership of land and factories, and the rest would be divided among the workers.[15]

The FAA raised money through dues to do its work but could not finance a bank. It did rent several plantations and made loans by putting liens on freedpeople's crops and sought donations of funds and equipment from various groups. Donors included French intellectuals like writer Victor Hugo, socialist Louis Blanc, abolitionist Victor Schoelcher, and statesman Adolphe Cremieux. In January 1865, even as the Thirteenth Amendment abolishing slavery was passed, local activists like the *Tribune* editors and the FAA officers were worried about the reimposition of slave system terms and conditions.[16] The *Tribune* kept up a drumbeat on the southern view of "free" labor, including laws preventing a freedperson from seeking work "to his best advantages" at the end of a contract; laws requiring Blacks to have passes to seek work even one or two miles away, while "emigrants [*sic*] or American white mechanics, not being classified 'free laborers,' are *free* to go everywhere *without* a pass"; and planters refusing to pay more than ten dollars a month because "they know the workers can't leave the Parish." The paper campaigned for Blacks to have the vote and ran notices of benefits for an "orphans industrial and education home for the children of freedmen." It also reported on schools opened by the National Freedman's Relief Association on "the Atlantic Coast and Gulf of Mexico and both banks of the Mississippi at St. Louis, Cairo, etc." In this way, the paper made New Orleanians aware that they were connected to people making similar efforts upriver, across the Gulf, and in points north—in short, part of a circuit.[17]

Encounters: Black Women Teachers and Black Women Refugees

In April 1865, Edmonia Highgate, by then teaching in rural Maryland after serving in Norfolk, Virginia, learned that her soldier brother had been severely wounded in the taking of Petersburg, Virginia. She asked her mother to replace her and went to Virginia. When her brother died, she accepted a position in New Orleans, becoming principal of the Frederick Douglass School and its eight hundred students. In early 1866, she wrote to her former pastor, "It may perhaps amuse you to know that the building in which I teach was formerly a slave pen but now conveniently fitted up as a graded school."[18] The retooling of a brick slave pen, which also happened in other places, points to the rupture of the slave market system in towns like New Orleans, if not of the policing and incarceration habits in the South. Highgate's journey from Virginia to Maryland and Louisiana, and her mother's movement from upstate New York to Maryland are only the first legs of their postwar travels to work with freedpeople. Highgate's two sisters would also come south and teach in Mississippi. These women's journeys demonstrate how the Emancipation Circuit was elaborated by people continually opening new schools and bringing new tools to one community after another. They show how the influx of information from communities outside the South was continuously diversified and elaborated by the mobility, race, and gender of these teachers and activists, whose impact often remained in place when they left for the next location. They lived in the Black communities, counseled families, and ordered the books and tools needed in the schoolrooms.

The women missionaries and teachers, usually single young women or women whose children were grown, had had their options defined by reproduction and marital status but in no way to the extent that women in the slave system had suffered lives severely controlled by the ability to produce children. The teachers, whose very independence and education allowed them to travel to the war zones where conflict did not cease at the end the war, came face-to-face with the role reproduction played in determining the specific hardships of female enslavement. In the slave system, as these women learned, reproduction often determined the forms of labor women performed and the stages of life when they were tasked with the heaviest work. Manda Cooper, of New Orleans, was born in North Carolina but sold away from her mother and siblings to a man who brought her to Louisiana. She reported: "My maw never worked in the fields she had a baby every year she had twins one time, so the old Master taken care of her she brought him more money having children than she could working in the field. None of us had the same father. . . . When I got old enough to Breed and never could have no children I stayed in the field."[19] Cooper worked in rice and sugarcane fields most of her life. Women like her mother, who had five other daughters with her in 1865, faced freedom with quite a large family. Deborah Gray White has speculated that for enslaved women like Cooper's mother, the heaviest work years came in middle age, after the childbearing years. Henrietta Butler, of Gretna, Louisiana, was born in Lafourche Parish, Louisiana, and said her enslaver there, a woman, "made me have a baby by one of dem mens on de plantation. De ole devil! I gets mad every' time I think about it. Den dey took de man to war." Butler's baby died, so the enslaver made her serve as wet nurse for her child. Butler entered freedom alone, with few skills for wage work, and earned a living by cleaning shrimp and doing laundry. Many women, like Cooper and her mother, who had few wage-earning skills, could not earn enough for children to go to school.[20]

Women like Cooper's mother and their children were a specific concern for Highgate as principal of the Douglass School. In February 1866, she wrote an AMA official to ask for assistance for the school, which was still governed by the Freedmen's Bureau, though the bureau had withdrawn all its financial support. General O. O. Howard, head of the bureau, had implemented a fee schedule of $1.50 per month for each student, and the enrollment had dropped from 800 to 127. Highgate reported that "nearly 3000 children have been shut out of our schools because their widowed mothers are 'too poor to pay,' their fathers being among the numbers 'who made way for Liberty and died.'" The bureau was behind in paying teachers, and her 150 teachers had fallen to 28. The fees of the remaining students would not cover pay even for the remaining instructors. As a Black teacher, Highgate was a rare figure in the postemancipation South. The AMA, for which Highgate and her mother and sisters worked as teachers, was slow to integrate the ranks of those it sent to newly freed communities. Joe Richardson finds that Black teachers were a small proportion of those who went south: "During the 1866–67 school year there were only 28. The number increased to 100 in 1868–69 and to 105 in 1869–70. In the latter school year Blacks made up about one-fifth of the AMA's southern personnel." In 1866, Highgate became a witness to the incendiary power struggle between Republicans hopeful of change and the stubborn local support of antidemocratic forms of power.[21]

The Fires of the Fourteenth

In Louisiana the connections between legislation ensuring citizenship to freedpeople and mob violence were very direct. In the summer of 1866, there was no need to look deeply for the resentments at the appearance of

Black autonomy in public space, as in the April white mob riot in Norfolk, or hostility over public access and toward Black soldiers that drove the May riot in Memphis, which destroyed that city's entire Black neighborhood. The June 13 passage of the Fourteenth Amendment (then yet to be ratified) and its affirmations of the Civil Rights Act of 1866 were directly tied to actions taken against Blacks and other Republicans in New Orleans on July 30.[22]

The amendment guaranteed equality before the law, barring states from abridging "the privileges or immunities of citizens," depriving "any person of life, liberty, or property, without due process of law," or denying any person within its jurisdiction "the equal protection of the laws." The second clause, meant to discourage disfranchisement of Blacks, warned that if any state denied the vote to any voting-age male citizens, the size of its congressional delegation would be reduced in proportion to the size of the entire population of those denied the vote. Having already lost the advantage of counting three-fifths of the enslaved population as constituents, the South was going to lose a lot of seats if it did not let Blacks vote. With the Black male vote, the South would hold an even larger share of the US Congress than before—which self-interest, some thought, would sway the South toward letting Blacks vote. Despite some who said that southerners would rather be left to run their region as they pleased than have more power in Washington, Republicans in Congress decided to gamble on southerners doing the right thing. Depending on the state, this gamble cost Blacks the vote from fifty-six to eighty-six years in the South. The third provision of the amendment was expected by many to eviscerate the South's old regime. It said that no one could hold office as a US senator or representative, be an "elector of President or Vice President or hold any office, civil or military," or of any state, who had taken an oath to uphold the US Constitution and then "engaged in insurrection or rebellion" against the same. Southern conservatives sought to move this guardrail too.[23]

After the passage of the amendment, Louisiana Republicans thought they could lay the groundwork for taking power by adopting it, which would remove the old elite from office, allow Black suffrage, and give Republicans control of the legislature. This was possible, as they saw it, because when the Louisiana constitutional convention had met in 1864 to rewrite the constitution for readmission to the Union, the meeting had left a provision that allowed for reconvening on a call from the legislature or a presiding officer.[24] The Republicans elected a friendly judge as the new president pro tempore of the convention, and he called it back into session to revise the constitution and "consider the adoption of the XIV Amendment," on July 30 at the Mechanics Institute (the temporary capitol in New Orleans). On the night of July 27, the "Friends of Freedom" had a rally, including calls for universal suffrage. In this case, people on all sides saw the same outcome if the twenty-five delegates made new law in the convention: Black voters and radical control of Louisiana.[25]

By all accounts, the man most against Republicans reopening the constitutional convention was the ex-Confederate mayor of New Orleans, John T. Monroe. He wrote to the federal commander, Major General Absalom Baird, to tell him that he would stop the meeting, using a local variation on a "no-Black-meetings" regulation (barring "all assemblies calculated to disturb the public peace"), and to let the commander know his help would *not* be needed. Baird informed the mayor that anyone could have a meeting, even one that brought change. He put it more elegantly:

> If these persons assemble . . . I presume, in virtue of the universally conceded right of all loyal citizens of the U.S. to meet peaceably and discuss freely questions concerning their civil government—a right which is not restricted by the fact that the movement proposed might terminate in a change of existing institutions. If the assemblage in question has the legal right to remodel the state government, it should be protected in so doing; if it has not then its labors must be looked on as a piece of harmless pleasantry to which no one should object.[26]

Baird's position, when it came to the constitutional convention reassembling, gave him two duties. The first was not to interfere unless help was requested by local authorities. The second was created by General Grant's Order 44 of July 6, which directed commanders to arrest people committing crimes against any citizens (or officers) in cases "where the civil authorities have failed, neglected, or are unable to arrest and bring such parties to trial." Grant made this order after the murders of officers in Grenada, Mississippi, and Thomasville, Georgia, but of course it also seems a logical response to the Memphis massacre. Baird informed the mayor that if a "riotous attack" on the assembly was expected, the military would be there. On July 28, the mayor again saw Baird to ask him not to intervene, to no avail. But the mayor was backed by President Johnson, who telegraphed the state attorney general: "Sustain the civil authority in suppressing all illegal or unlawful assemblies. . . . Usurpation will not be tolerated." No copy of the message was sent to Baird, who telegraphed Secretary of War Edwin Stanton for the president's instructions. No answer came. Baird put both Black and white troops on alert and arranged for a steamer to deliver troopers, planning to have them a few blocks away an hour before the meeting. Yet he got the time wrong.[27]

On July 30, at the Mechanics Institute, Monroe's ex-rebel police force met some two hundred Blacks, mostly former soldiers, who made a New Orleans–style procession with horns and drums in support of the convention. Some attacks occurred as the procession neared the hall, but the real fighting broke out when the soldiers took shelter in the hall with the delegates, and the police attacked. The unarmed delegates used chairs to defend themselves, and some were hunted down as they escaped through windows and into the streets. Other Blacks in the path of the mob were also killed. The report of the Select Committee on the New Orleans Riot supplied much gruesome detail on the brutality against various individuals caught in the riot. The troops arrived at least two hours late, and "the army's surgeons later reported that 38 people, mostly blacks, were killed and 147 wounded." Among the several whites killed was the convention's leader, Dr. Anthony Dostie, and the former governor was wounded. General Philip Sheridan, commander of the Division of the Gulf, who was away that day, wrote to General Grant on August 2, perhaps the most famous description of the event: "It was no riot; it was an absolute massacre by the police which was not excelled in murderous cruelty by that of Ft. Pillow."[28]

President Johnson was angered that Baird's troops had intervened at all, and that Baird had declared martial law. A grand jury exonerated the local government of any wrongdoing. Baird had to release those rioters he had arrested and then had to arrest surviving members of the convention. After hearing the facts, Grant ordered the continuation of martial law. Johnson seemed to think that delegates bent on "usurpation" were to blame.[29]

Ulysses Grant, if no one else, was very clear about lessons learned. By November 22, when he had received letters saying some of the president's proclamations had voided his General Order No. 44, Grant wrote to Secretary Stanton arguing its validity: "It is evident to my mind that the provisions of the Civil Rights Bill cannot properly be enforced without the aid of Order No. 44 or a similar one." Grant's assessment had been and appears to have remained that federal forces had to be an option where local authorities failed to protect citizens. In this case, the withdrawal of troops would set the local population back into a long-term process of forcing change on the ground and seeking more lasting legal remedies in a climate of dangerous intimidation. In this way, the realism of a general accustomed to sudden exigencies and ruptures engendered by military presence ran into the unrelenting will of conservative political forces that protected and preserved antidemocratic forms of power.[30]

Six months after the mob action, in December 1866, Edmonia Highgate found herself in a Louisiana hamlet engaged in the slow process of seeking change without the protection Grant saw as a necessity. Highgate, who had been in New Orleans during the riot and, having already suffered one nervous breakdown after leaving Norfolk, had fled New Orleans for her health after the mob action. She ran a day school, a night school, and "a glorious Sabbath School of near one hundred scholars." She wrote to her former pastor from Lafayette Parish, west of Baton Rouge, where she was teaching under the auspices of the Freedmen's Bureau.

> After the horrible riot in New Orleans in July I found my health getting impaired from hospital visiting and excitement so I came here to do what I could and to get stronger corporally. . . . The majority of my pupils come from plantations, three, four, and even eight miles distant. So anxious are they to learn that they walk these distances so early in the morning as never to be tardy. They, with but few exceptions are [Black] French Creoles. My little knowledge of French is put in constant use in order to instruct them in our language.[31]

Highgate learned that because the corn, cotton, and sugar crops had been good that year, the people, who were generally working on one-year contracts for "their former so called masters," were able to survive, and most were trying to buy a home. Few, she reported, belonged to or went to a church because they worked their own gardens on Sundays. She found some of the distances hard to travel because she was seldom able to find a horse to rent. Highgate was also startled by the fact that many couples that she got to know saw no need to be married: "They are given greatly to the sin of adultery. Out of three hundred I found but three couple[s] legally married. This fault was largely the masters and it has grown upon the people till they cease to see the wickedness of it." In the world from which Highgate came in upstate New York, a pregnancy from such a relationship would be ruinous, not just in the religious community in which she traveled but also something that would end a career for a woman teacher. In fact, finding any work involving clients, such as sewing in the home or other work that involved dealing with "polite" folk like herself, often led women to change their place of residence or to claim to be widowed. Meeting an entire community of people who had been forced by enslavement to reconstitute definitions of family was apparently challenging. Finally, Highgate reported that whites in the area were hostile to the schools, and given that she was two hundred miles from military help in New Orleans, she had been fortunate. She ended with mention of the threat under which she worked: "There has been much opposition to the School. Twice I have been shot at in my room. My night scholars have been shot but none killed. The rebels here threatened to burn down the school and house in which I board before the first month was passed yet they have not materially harmed us."[32]

This was not unusual. During the mob riot in Memphis that year, which left "at least forty-eight African Americans dead and wounded between seventy and eighty," teachers and schools from Highgate's organization were attacked. Rosen reports of the Memphis riot, "They set fire to 91 houses and cabins, 4 African American churches, and all 12 schools that served African Americans in the city."[33]

Highgate would return to New Orleans sometime that year to become the only woman officer of the Louisiana Education Relief Association, which was founded in response to the withdrawal of Freedmen's Bureau support for the schools for Black children. When the New Orleans school board announced plans to segregate public schools—the first integrated public schools in the South—she threatened to quit if her schools were put under school board jurisdiction. Segregation prevailed. The schools would be desegregated again in 1871. White mob violence erupted in 1874 over integration of the Upper Girls High School, and "Members of the White League promoted 'well-orchestrated violence,' and for a full week, the high school students who followed the White League vandalized integrated schools, terrorized teachers, and 'removed suspected black students' from the buildings." The end of Reconstruction would install segregation for more than eight decades.[34]

Making Political Voice

At a Republican meeting in New Orleans in 1867 to choose delegates to that state's constitutional convention, P. B. S. Pinchback saw that the onset of Black political participation considerably raised the stakes for African Americans and for coexistence among the contending forces in the South: "There is a sense of security displayed by our people that is really alarming. They seem to think that all is done, the Great Battle has been fought and the victory won. Gentlemen, this is a fallacy. The Great Contest has just begun."[35] Pinchback, the steamboat steward who had had the good fortune to be spirited out of the slavery system in Mississippi, had found his calling. New Orleans proved the perfect place for a man who felt at home among the elite and had the self-possession for the local gentleman's sports of gambling with one's fortune in new ventures or with one's life in dueling. He also survived facing down the contempt of the planter elite and a mob trying to force the door of the constitutional convention. Even after quitting the army, he had continued to wear the uniform that garnered respect from many on New Orleans streets and began a political career that would be marked by similar self-interest. Pinchback was one of those outsize figures as unique to the mid-nineteenth-century South as any of the adventurers, rakes, or self-made men who still *laissent les bon temps rouler* in literature and film, except he was born in an epoch that had no Black leading characters in popular culture, except Harriet Beecher Stowe's Uncle Tom.[36]

The Republicans agreed that half of their delegation to the convention would be African Americans and the other half whites. The Blacks among them were dominated by men from New Orleans—members of the Black Creole class, people who owned businesses or farmland. In 1860, New Orleans was home to "four-fifths of the region's 14,000 free blacks." Most of them lived apart from the sugarcane fields to the south and west or the cotton fields to the north where most Blacks toiled—in 1860, "nine-tenths of the region's 117,000 slaves."[37] Organizers did a massive job to establish representation throughout the southeast and southwest areas around New Orleans, in the middle of the state branching out from Alexandria, in the northwest around Shreveport and along the Mississippi River. In the next elections they expanded to counties that had ties throughout the organizing circuit.[38] (*See Louisiana map 1 [plate 8].*)

Organizing by freedpeople was heavily rural, concentrated on labor, particularly in the 1870s (*see the Louisiana maps [plates 8 and 9]*). The access rural areas had to newspapers (see table 9.1) may have been helpful in areas where access to other institutions may not have been local. Most of the sugar parishes, for instance, sent students for higher education to Straight University in New Orleans. Loss of the Black militias in that area during the fight to crush Reconstruction meant sending to New Orleans for assistance, which did not always work out. Still, while the maps also show Black representation being knocked down in the 1870s and wiped out by 1881 in the parishes where New Orleans, Shreveport, and Alexandria are located, rural parishes held on.

At the constitutional convention of 1867–68, James H. Ingraham, representing Caddo Parish in the north of the state, proposed one free public school in every parish run on an integrated basis, and he helped to write the constitution's bill of rights. David Wilson of Orleans Parish put up an amendment also giving the state power to educate the young, but the two men only achieved passage of a provision that there would be no separate schools established for any race—language that did *not* prevent school segregation in Louisiana. Ingraham and others proposed several amendments to provide for recognition of marriage between people who had been barred from that legal status by the slavery system. This never got out of committee and into state law until the next year, when Pinchback went into the state senate. Ideas promoted by the *Tribune* for redistribution of state-held land to citizens at low prices did not make it into the constitution. The old labor laws were scratched, but planters succeeded in avoiding regulation of labor or fixed wages. Imprisonment for debt was ended. Another Black delegate proposed state-regulated "institutions for the support of the insane, the education and support of the blind and the deaf and dumb." Pinchback led the successful drive for inclusion of a civil rights clause in the constitution, giving Blacks equal access to public accommodations, business, and entertainment, later vetoed by the Republican Party's own governor, Henry Clay Warmoth. A number of these achievements by the Black framers of the constitution, of which many Republicans, Black and white, were quite proud, proved to be battlegrounds almost immediately, even with the man they supported for governor.[39]

Following the convention, the Republicans chose twenty-six-year-old former Union officer Warmoth as their gubernatorial candidate; as their candidate for lieutenant governor they chose African American Oscar James Dunn, enslaved at birth, an advocate for the full range of rights for freedpeople, and a man who had a hand in every Black sodality in New Orleans. The rest of the party's slate included some who proved to be opportunists, and the whole array caused Louis Charles Roudanez, the Black Creole founder and principal financier of the radical *Tribune*, to bolt from the carefully crafted unity of the Republican Party. Roudanez sponsored an independent ticket joining a wealthy white Unionist planter and former slaveholder, James Govan Taliaferro, with a wealthy and educated Black Frenchman, Francis Ernest Dumas, who had held even more enslaved people than Taliaferro. Roudanez's decision to promote Franco-African leadership cost him support from the African American community at large, allies outside the Black Creole inner circles, and the *Tribune*'s editor, Jean-Charles Houzeau. The Roudanez ticket lost, and his paper, one of the foremost voices of Black political vision, went under. It seems entirely in keeping with the New Orleans Black elite's earlier efforts in the political arena that they would have supported their own for the most powerful elective offices to maintain leadership among African Americans. The fact that Pinchback, Ingraham, and John W. Menard, a local newspaper publisher (and later a Florida leader and publisher), stuck with Warmoth suggests they too were disaffected by the idea of slaveholder leadership.[40]

But they all lost. To the great disappointment of his supporters, Warmoth did not honor the delegates' work on behalf of freedpeople. This was particularly galling as, according to Charles Vincent, "Warmoth carried thirty 'black parishes' and only three parishes where a majority of registered voters were whites." As Houzeau writes: "During his tenure as governor, Warmoth vetoed two civil rights bills, resisted integration of the public schools, refused to enforce the equal accommodations provision of the state constitution, and presided over one of the most corrupt administrations in the history of a notably corrupt state. In fact, Warmoth's excesses provoked Roudanez to revive the *Tribune* and to continue publishing it until 1871."[41] In November 1871, lieutenant governor Oscar Dunn died suddenly, and as Senate president pro tem, P. B. S. Pinchback became lieutenant governor. A year later, when the legislature initiated impeachment proceedings against Warmoth over a disputed election, he was required to take a suspension for the remaining six weeks of the administration's term, and for that period the thirty-five-year-old Pinchback served as governor of Louisiana, the first African American to do so in this country. (It would be 120 years before L. Douglas Wilder was inaugurated in Virginia.) The Louisiana Emancipation Circuit came under threat in 1874 when Black legislators were thrown out of the General Assembly and as violence and intimidation were used against Black political work through the end of the century. Voter repression was effective in the state until 1967.

Association, Fellowship, Alliance, Assembly

The end of Reconstruction came in Louisiana in 1876 and with it a new constitution that removed the equal rights language guaranteeing civil, political, and public rights that freedmen like Pinchback had put in the constitution. As Rebecca Scott writes, state power "could now be exercised directly against the interests of former slaves and their descendants." But two responses emerged among African Americans: to make appeals to the federal government, and to rely on each other. In doing the latter, "communication up and down the river and the bayous was of great importance and families in towns like Donaldsonville and Thibodeaux who had easy access to New Orleans could use strategies not open to those living on scattered cotton farms in isolated parishes to the north."[42]

The Louisiana maps (*plates 8 and 9*) show that many sites in southern Louisiana were tied into a circuit easily navigated by waterways, railroads, and close-knit ties across plantations lining the waterfront. Most of these parishes sent representatives to state government in the late 1870s and through the 1880s. Voter repression laws in the 1880s and 1890s ended Black representation. The end of Reconstruction prompted a flurry of expansions of Black activism. Several Black newspapers appeared in the 1870s, and labor organizing was widespread. Strikes on the New Orleans docks continued in the 1870s. Interracial dockworkers' unions continued to make progress, and as Eric Arnesen shows, Black union members continued to build their agendas and encourage the development of other municipal unions through the matrix of local aid associations they had formed and other sodalities to which they belonged. Early in the next century, for instance, led by Ella Peete, "wife of freight handlers' union president Sylvester Peete, Black women organized a Domestic Workers Union in July 1918."[43] Another of those who typify the New Orleans version of carrying on after the loss of power through sodalities was Rodolphe Lucien Desdunes, who would write a history of Black Creoles. He was a son of Haitian and Cuban parents, trained as a lawyer, and ran a tobacco shop. After the end of Reconstruction, he edited a Black newspaper and was part of the anti–Jim Crow movement. According to Scott, he "was an active Mason who took a broad view of the struggle, which he saw as encompassing the principles of the French and Haitian revolutions, the Louisiana Constitution of 1868, and the history of the fight for equal rights across the Caribbean. As Reconstruction was rolled back, he labored to sustain a radical interpretation of the Republican Party's commitments."

In an 1876 speech, P. B. S. Pinchback gave a compelling summary of the southern meaning of redemption and unknowingly warned of events still to come from labor organizing in the sugar-growing parishes: "Gentlemen, as disagreeable as it may be to you to hear and as unpleasant as it is, there is no denying the fact that the bloody shirt is no mythical garment . . . to-day, in that vast area of country lying south of Mason and Dixon's line . . . neither free speech, free press, peaceable assembly, not the right to keep and bear arms, or security for persons and property, are enjoyed by Republicans."[44]

For a northern audience he raised a list of place-names that Black southerners would know: "New Orleans, Colfax, Coushatta, Vicksburg, Clinton, Yazoo, East Feliciana and Hamburg," informing the audience that Blacks in those places knew if they engaged a "war of the races," extermination would be the result, and they knew with "certainty that their murderers will be regarded as heroes instead of criminals." These place-names were a shorthand list of violent attacks on African Americans and their allies and are well known as follows: the 1874 New Orleans Battle of Liberty Place, the 1873 Colfax Massacre (Louisiana), the 1874 Coushatta Massacre (Louisiana), the 1874 Vicksburg riot (Mississippi), the 1875 Clinton riot (Mississippi), the 1875 Yazoo City riot (Mississippi), the 1876 East Feliciana riot (Louisiana), and the 1876 Hamburg Massacre (South Carolina). Many of the events—some directly attacking Black voting activists—signaled the end of Reconstruction in those places, all of which were on the Emancipation Circuit.[45]

The Colfax Massacre, the worst of the group, not only took the lives of one hundred to two hundred Black people in Grant Parish (most of whom had surrendered) but resulted in the legal case *United States v. Cruikshank*, which condemned many more African Americans to the depredations of paramilitary groups like the Ku Klux Klan, Louisiana's White Camelias, and the Red Shirts of North and South Carolina by blocking the federal government from protecting their rights of due process and equal protection under the Fourteenth Amendment. The 1876 Supreme Court ruling found the white mob members faultless in interfering in the Blacks' First Amendment right to assembly and Second Amendment right to keep and bear arms, saying only *states*, not *persons*, could hinder those rights. This somewhat confounding ruling had the disastrous effect of preventing federal enforcement of the rights of Blacks across the South until 1966.[46]

Not surprisingly, the Democratic takeover alarmed Blacks with the possibility that their situations could get even worse, threatening a return to bondage in all but name. For these and other reasons, the Kansas exodus of 1879 had some momentum in Louisiana. In March of that year, Pinchback, who had earlier opposed emigration, visited Delta, a town on the Mississippi, and one of the staging areas for people leaving the state. He wrote in his newspaper, the *Louisianian*, of his "surprise, on nearing the Delta ferry landing to find the banks of the river literally covered with colored people and their little store of worldly goods." He reported that the new constitution being written by the Democrats gave some Black residents "an apprehension of undefined danger," and others feared the reinstitution of slavery.

"They religiously believe that the [next] constitutional convention bodes them no good; that it has been called for the express purpose of abridging their rights and liberties. . . . They are absolutely panic stricken."[47]

In April of 1887, pages of New Orleans's newest Black newspaper, the *Weekly Pelican*, listed announcements for the "Colored State Fair," a temperance convention, a benefit promoted by the Ladies Aid Union Longshoremen's Circle, a concert for the Justice Educational Fund, and a ball for the Rising Sons of Liberty (a venerable Black "souls to the polls" society with the same name as a Revolutionary-era group). One group was hosting "a sparring match" in the Pythian Hall (run by the Knights of Pythias). A column on news from the Algiers neighborhood reported that "there is plenty of work for the laboring people, consequently all are happy." The paper had a regular column called "Secret Societies." Though benevolent association listings outnumbered all others at this time, whether church or trade events, the Knights of Labor (KoL) began to appear in the pages. In August the Teamsters and Loaders Association of Mobile was hosting an excursion, and the KoL was having a parade and banquet, alongside events being hosted by eleven other societies and benevolent associations. But in late fall, the Knights came out of the social listings of the Trade Assembly parade, the Good Intent Fire Company excursion, and the Creole Social Circle "fancy dress and calico ball," and on to the news pages. The paper began to cover a massive KoL strike begun on November 1 at the onset of sugarcane grinding season in Lafourche, Terrebone, and St. Mary Parishes. On November 5, the paper reported that "many planters acceded to the demands of labor but a majority of them refused . . . [and] last Tuesday the strike was inaugurated. In all of these proceedings there were no warlike preparations on the part of the laborers, but many planters fearing trouble made application to Governor Samuel D. McEnery for protection, and he, without investigation of any kind, immediately ordering troops to the supposed scene of the trouble." The strike involved thousands of workers (90 percent of whom were said to be Black), and cooperation between Black and white and male and female KoL assemblies. The strike was a "cross-class alliance between field laborers, most of whom were themselves former slaves or the descendants of slaves, and men and women based in town . . . artisans, teachers, urban laborers, and organizers." The sheer numbers of workers in sugar fields eased the organizing of mobilizations. In the bayou parishes ministers and teachers had been involved in mobilizations before, and some writers simply described the area, especially Thibodaux, as "militant."[48] The paper immediately pleaded for keeping troops and bloodshed out of the area. Planters who had faced two earlier strikes and who railed against the KoL as a secret, oath-bound association (which it was) demanded the governor send troops. Two companies of militia and a Gatling gun arrived in Houma to evict workers from plantations. Many fled twenty-six miles upriver to Thibodaux, where locals tried to accommodate them, and disastrously, a "Peace and Order Committee" composed of both Democratic and Republican planters sealed off the town. The governor declared the problem solved and removed his troops, except for a unit from Shreveport. Blacks trapped in the town were reported to have moved on the streets armed and still sometimes displaying defiance. On November 22, a planned assault began, now known as the Thibodaux Massacre, and ended in the murder of at least fifty people, including three strike leaders. One of the remarkable features of this retribution is that planters had workers killed who lived on their own plantations, some of whom had been there before abolition twenty-two years earlier. Unlike urban mob riots and the incident in Camilla, Georgia, assailants in Thibodaux attacked people they knew well.[49]

Blacks in the area still had representation despite voter suppression and continued the effort to get as many votes in as possible. In writing of Thibodaux, Scott provides a specific window into how sites on the circuit maintained a broad sense of the political and ready units of organization through the proliferation of sodalities that provided services within each community: "Both by design and as a result of overlapping leadership, large-scale rural mobilization had become intertwined with associational and electoral politics in town. Each new initiative thus threatened elements of white supremacy on two fronts: the workplace and the public sphere. Although the black and interracial militias of the 1870s had been destroyed, there were still black fire companies and mutual-aid associations that drew members from town and country and displayed their numbers publicly."[50] Scott recounts a visit of the Vigilance Fire Company and Pride of Iberia Hook and Ladder Company to Thibodaux that brought more than five hundred people for festivities.

The discrepancy between activism in the city and countryside was sharp. New Orleans protests famously gave rise to the 1892 *Plessy v. Ferguson* case upholding streetcar segregation. The political elite of New Orleans had pushed for equal access on public transportation since the end of the war. Though organization had been occurring on the city docks and among workers in related trades, events such as at Thibodaux isolated rural workers from support from outside. Following the segregation of schools and public conveyances and disfranchisement that came in 1890, there was a flurry of new and old associations working in New Orleans, specifically fighting the new laws. Even had the New Orleans efforts succeeded in ending segregation on public transportation, in opera houses, or in the schools, such rulings would have affected little in the countryside.

> My uncle told me told me that the family tradition in Tangipahoa Parish was [for the mother and father] to sleep back-to-back with a gun on the floor on each side of the bed.

—Mercedes Franklin, telephone interview with the author (2011)

Looking at Table 9.1

The cities in Louisiana have all the assets that one might expect, but Louisiana is unusual in that a number of parishes with very few of the assets I looked for still elected representatives. Whereas nearly every place experienced the presence of US troops, St. Martin Parish, which had none of these assets—but a Black majority—still elected officials. Pointe Coupée, also lacking many documented schools or outside organizers, sits on the Mississippi River, which brought US troops and likely a wealth of information from the entire area. But labor organizing was conducted nearly everywhere, and Liberia or western emigration were in sites on the rivers and the Gulf of Mexico.

The table gives a glimpse of the divide between the urban seats of elite Blacks and the rural communities where the Knights of Labor activism would later help sustain organization. Nineteenth-century Louisiana was well served by Black newspapers and, in some places, Black militia. It was pretty well served in terms of schools, but many rural Blacks sent their children for a high school education to New Orleans. Blacks in the state were ill-served by the friendly ties planters had with their peers (or kinfolk) in Mississippi who sent men and large arms to crush political actions and strikes. While rural areas had representation longer, Orleans Parish was able to continue drives for civil rights and against Jim Crow as their middle-class communities could support court suits. Finally, table 9.1 is unable to show some forms of rural resistance such as the numbers of schools rebuilt after being burned in the name of segregation and denial of tax dollars to educate Black children. Schoolhouses were commitments kept for decades.[51]

TABLE 9.1 Louisana Emancipation Circuit, 1870–1900

		Institutions Present						19th Century Activism
	US Troops	RR (1884)	Union League	AMA Schools	Local Black Press	Black Political Reps	Knights of Labor Groups	
DARROW (then DARROWVILLE) **Ascension Parish** ß	•				$\underline{1}$ 1877	•	1 M plantation hands	Liberia emigration
BATON ROUGE **E. Baton Rouge Parish** ß	•	•	•	•	$\underline{2}$ 1871 1900	•		Liberia emigration Western exodus
Concordia Parish ß	•	•			$\underline{1}$ 1873	•		Kansas exodus
FRANKLIN **St. Mary Parish** ß	•	•				•	1 M plantation hands	Labor
Jefferson Parish ß	•	•			1	•		
MONROE **Ouachita Parish** ß		•				•	1 M unknown occupations	

Location / Parish					Freedmen's Bureau		No. / Dates		Occupations	Issues / Causes
MORGAN CITY St. Mary Parish ß		•				•			1 M RR workers 1 F mixed labor	Labor Liberia emigration
NEW ORLEANS Orleans Parish	•	•		3		•	$\underline{11}$ 1856–1900		1 occupations unknown	Labor Civil rights Kansas exodus Anti–Jim Crow
Plaquemines Parish ß		•				•	$\underline{1}$ 1876			Labor
Pointe Coupée Parish ß		•				•	$\underline{1}$ 1873			
Rapides Parish ß		•				•			•	Colored Farmers' Alliance (CFA)
Saint Bernard Parish ß		•				•				Labor
Saint John the Baptist Parish ß		•				•				Labor
SHREVEPORT Caddo Parish ß		•		• Freedmen's Bureau		•	$\underline{3}$ 1890s			Labor Liberia emigration Kansas exodus

(Continued)

TABLE 9.1 (*Continued*)

	Institutions Present							19th Century Activism
	US Troops	RR (1884)	Union League	AMA Schools	Local Black Press	Black Political Reps	Knights of Labor Groups	
Saint Martin Parish ß								Labor
HOUMA		+		+		+	1 M/F plantation hands, mechanics & laundry workers	Labor
LITTLE CAILLOU							1 M/F mixed labor	
SCHRIEVER							1 M plantation hands	
TERREBONNE							1 M plantation hands	
Terrebonne Parish ß								
THIBODAUX	+			+	<u>1</u> 1860s	+	1 M plantation hands	Labor
Lafourche Parish ß								Sugar worker strikes

SOURCES: *See* Table Source Notes (393–96).

KEY: **Bold** = Site playing multiple roles on the circuit. ß = Black majority; unless otherwise noted, populations are for 1870.

RR = Rail lines.

Black Political Reps = Black representatives to the 1868 constitutional convention or members of the General Assembly.

Knights of Labor = Black assemblies of the labor organization. Most KoL assemblies were segregated by race and gender: white males, Black males, white females, or Black females (*see* Table Source Notes) and indicates various forms of work, not mixing by race or gender. **Gender** is indicated here by M or F.

MISSISSIPPI
Bulldoze

Bull-dose, doze, . . . *sb.* and *v. U.S. colloq.* [According to US newspapers, f. BULL + Dose] *sb.* . . . **A.** A severe dose (of flogging). **B.** *v. a.* To flog severely. b. To coerce by violence, intimidate. Hence **Bull-dozer, a.** one who 'bull-dozes.' . . . **1876** *American Newspr.*, If a negro is invited to join it [a society called The Stop] and refuses, he is taken to the woods and whipped . . . for the purpose of making Tilden voters. . . . **1881** *Sat. Rev.* 9 July 40/2 To 'bull-dose' a negro in the Southern States means to flog him to death, or nearly to death.
—*The Compact Oxford English Dictionary* (1971)

The machine known as a bulldozer was not invented until 1923.
—According to "History of the Bulldozer" (2020)

Union troops were engaged in several regions in Mississippi from as early as 1861, when they occupied Ship Island off the Gulf Coast and had skirmishes at Mississippi City, Biloxi, and Pass Christian. A more important presence began in 1862 with the siege of Corinth, at the northern end of the state, which resulted in long-term changes for enslaved people who were in the area and, over time, others who were able to make their way there. The Union took Natchez in September 1862, and by 1863 Blacks began to move there and take advantage of resources becoming available. The Battle of Port Gibson took place on May 1, 1863, and the Union victory allowed local people to gain information concerning emancipation and the leeway to assemble, organize schools, and seek autonomy. The Union success at Jackson two weeks later had a similar impact. And of course, the July 1863 end of the siege of Vicksburg near these two other towns allowed for African Americans from all these areas to build community ties, share resources, and build political formations. Mississippi became part of the Military Division of the Mississippi from 1863 until the end of the war and Military District Number Five from 1867 until readmission to the Union in 1870. But the new development that would transform Mississippi from a refuge for freedpeople escaping "Redemption" in Alabama into the Mississippi known for its violent abuse of its Black residents was the right to vote. This cruel culture of suppression would, in turn, create a restorative Black culture through new musical and spiritual practices adept at acknowledging and transforming trauma. Contrary to the intent of their foes, the Mississippi Delta would also give rise to generations of fearless organizers, most of whom are unknown in popular culture.

Forgatherings

Assaults on newly free Black women like those in Richmond, Mobile, and elsewhere had a similar radicalizing effect in Mississippi, especially in Mississippi ports where people had taken to moving from the countryside. In June 1865, a Natchez freedman wrote to the AME *Christian Recorder* reporting that Black men in the area had witnessed the "forcible violation of the virtue of their wives and daughters by white guards and [Union] soldiers" and protested that "the Emancipation *seems* only to have been a ruse."[1] In June, a mass meeting was held in Vicksburg to work on "the question of civil rights of the colored citizens of Mississippi, and take measures to secure them." Resolutions were composed and "adopted with no dissenting voice." They protested the provisional government and the convening of a constitutional convention made up of the old elite and asked that the state not be restored to the Union without giving freedpeople the right to vote. Finally, they called for the founding of a newspaper "that shall fearlessly and faithfully defend the rights of the colored citizens."[2]

That fall, Vicksburg freedpeople held another mass meeting in response to the 1865 state constitution, which included the state's version of black codes and was written by members of the old regime to reestablish complete control of the Mississippi labor force. The written protest issued from the mass meeting expressed realistic alarm that if the state was returned to the Union with that constitution, the legislature would go further and "pass such proscriptive class laws against the freedmen as will result in their expatriation from the State or their practical reenslavement." Soon after their protest, they found "open meetings no longer possible," and a committee was set up to petition the US Congress, which was done. The right to assembly was already being shut down in Mississippi, and the black codes being passed aimed to codify that deprivation in law.[3] The Mississippi code also outlined broad conditions for custody of Black children to be taken by planters under "apprenticeship" language that explicitly gave terms of "indenture" of the children until age twenty-one for males and eighteen for females. The Mississippi vagrancy law contained eight sections of particulars leading to arrest and forced labor of adults. The codes threw a tight net around emancipation and set up a broad and diverse terrain for freedpeople to contest, both openly and with discreet behaviors.[4]

One reason the people of Vicksburg found it no longer safe to hold public meetings may have been the growing unrest among whites around the idea that Blacks were going to rise up against them. Looked at from so many years later, the Christmas Insurrection Scare of 1865, a widespread fear of a Black rising that afflicted whites all over the South, seems hard to credit but also fortuitous for all those southern elites creating black codes to shackle the potential power of the region's major labor force. Among other things, the insurrection scare produced a direct assault on the right of freedpeople to bear arms. The rumor that spread around the South in the fall of 1865 was that Black soldiers were informing freedpeople that abandoned land would be divided up and given to them, and that when they found out that in fact abandoned lands were being returned to former owners, they would rise up against whites. Though most of the land held by the government was in the lower Mississippi Valley, and on the lower Eastern Seaboard, the insurrection rumor knew no boundaries. Word had it that the promised division of land would occur around January 1, 1866, and noticeable numbers of Blacks were refusing to sign work contracts until that date in case it was true.[5]

While historians occasionally have tried to explain the great emotional disturbance wrought among white southerners by abolition, accompanied as it was by the damage and material ruin of war, often the tremendous numbers of violent incidents against Blacks is not part of the context. Hahn is an exception as he does write about the prevalence of armed conflicts and the patterns of where such battles took place. As to placing white violence in the context of abolition distress, he gestures toward "a peculiarly irrational psychology." Planters' diaries and testimony from people who had been enslaved give ample evidence of deeply suffered distress, but the patterns of group hysteria and the arming episodes in white communities throughout the emancipation and Reconstruction periods are insufficiently explained, and their prevalence is observed by few who have written on the South as a whole. Hahn theorizes that in the absence of real power for so many former Confederates early in the postwar years, "much of day-to-day life there became politicized." This, however, actually suggests that perhaps the question is not so much which grievances were most difficult or widespread but what has nurtured them for so long—a question perhaps beyond the work of historians. Still, historians run across the traces of disturbing rationales along with the evidence of disturbing events. Litwack describes the state of white southerners in the fall and winter of 1865 as a case of "fevered minds" that "fanned the flames of the conflagration they had largely created themselves," which must have been partly the case. Among the many trivial false sightings of Black insurrection planning, Litwack cites the sound of normal singing. A South Carolina plantation mistress heard song coming from the quarters and found it ominous "as only they could sing in these times," a condition that she further assumed could be prelude to "a horde pouring into our houses to cut our throats." Albert Morgan heard suspicions raised because someone "saw them [Black people] talkin' together in groups." He reports being swayed by the fears, which he found genuine, even though he knew many of the Black organizers in Yazoo, where he lived, and even though he wrote that he saw no evidence of trouble brewing and didn't think a rising would make any sense.[6]

In reality, for any planter without the sure knowledge of the power of local and state violence over Black labor, merely looking out the window at a field full of peacefully employed workers could bring home the reality that there were large numbers of people around them with serious grievances and the human potential for vengeance. Yet it was seldom put that way. Causes for vengeance were not acknowledged. Clearly, people who had held laborers prisoner, beaten and killed them, sold their families, and waged war to maintain that system knew someone might harbor resentment even if planters were simultaneously convinced that African Americans were wholly ignorant and that slavery was benign.[7]

Sometimes planters were told. Fanny Cannady of North Carolina remembered the day the master's son, Gregory Moss, whom she thought was so mean "twould take more den a bullet to kill," came home on furlough from the war. He seemed rather taken with himself "wid his sword clankin' and his boots shinin'" while "struttin' 'roun' de yard," but his father took exception when he heard Leonard Allen, an enslaved man, say, "Look at dat God damn sojer. He fightin' to keep us n——s from bein' free." When the father dared Allen to repeat what he said, Allen stared at him, repeated his words exactly, and was shot dead.[8]

In the absence of any consensus regarding the source of white hysteria, it is easy to countenance the opinion of some federal officials who thought political motives lay behind the spreading of rebellion rumors. Clearly, fear of violence could be real among those who had only discovered during the war that the loyalty they assumed from enslaved people was illusory, and just as plain is the fact that some who had held power had ideas about how to reclaim it. Finally, the end of 1865 was the time for the first annual wages to be paid to the formerly enslaved workers, as well as the point when they might leave farms. For everyone involved, it was a moment when they could be certain the next year would be nothing like the last.

In the Christmas Insurrection Scare, though, the protests made by whites to provisional governors and other officials had the logic of demanding the removal of the US Colored Troops, divesting Blacks of arms, forming white militias, and terrorizing freedpeople who might form groups of any kind, whether meetings, assemblies, crowds, or mobs. Their solutions were not "fevered" but calculated. Just as in July in Wilmington, North Carolina, the requests for help prioritized Black troop removal, and the multiple requests may have given force to opinion in Washington that Black military presence could make for unstable towns. "Respectable citizens" of Monroe, Louisiana, charged that "the colored troops, so far from affording protection, are the most dangerous element in our midst." Freedmen's Bureau commissioner Howard was told by Mississippi's provisional governor William L. Sharkey that there were "many reasons to believe" a revolt was "contemplated" if land was not awarded. One of the first claims Sharkey made, after saying a revolt was expected and that Black soldiers would lead it, was that "most of the negroes in the country have arms," adding the more questionable assertion, "procured from soldiers or officers, which it is supposed they are providing for carrying out their diabolical scheme." The removal of Black soldiers was advised. In many of these missives about the scare, white protesters asked for arms and ammunition. As Samuel Thomas, Howard's assistant commissioner for Mississippi, told him after dismissing the rumor, "People who talk so much of insurrections, and idleness, and vagrancy among the freedmen, have an ulterior motive. . . . If they can once get free of all [federal] control, they know they can do as they please with the negro." Thomas claimed that the white criticism of the bureau was part of an effort to get rid of it as well, stating, "This is the whole secret of the insurrection-stories."[9]

As Hahn has observed, whites were most likely to make such requests "in states where Blacks formed clear or near population majorities, and where some federal officials, together with newly installed post-Confederate officeholders, were regarded as sympathetic to their concerns—Mississippi, Louisiana, Alabama, Georgia, and South Carolina being the prime examples." Louisiana officials wrote of an expected rising in Terrebone Parish due to "ill minded white men" coming to the area. And they were frank in desiring to create forces large enough to "overawe the colored population." These requests, which were sometimes forwarded to President Johnson, caused wrangling among federal officials, with many who were on the ground in the South expressing their skepticism about a rising and the requests for arms. Sadly, Johnson had already allowed militias to be formed and advised it for Alabama as well.[10]

Freedpeople were in fact the only people in danger. As Litwack writes, freedpeople knew such panics produced "the inevitable floggings, beatings, and assassinations." Some Blacks, "unaware of conspiracies in their midst, . . . concluded—logically enough—that the fear of insurrection served only the purposes of their former masters, providing them with the opportunity to invade their homes, to seize their weapons, to make assaulted examples of their leaders, and to otherwise terrorize and harass them until they revised their notions of the perquisites of freedom." At mass meetings in various sites freedpeople reacted to the imposition of black codes and publicly denied any conspiracies to rise against whites. For three more years the Democratic newspapers in the South would continue to promote the idea that Republicans were still promising freedpeople land and that freedpeople were still waiting for it.[11]

Making Political Voice

In Port Gibson, an 1865 assembly whose members called themselves "the Colored People of Mississippi" wrote to the governor and made clear the threat of the recent white mobilization in the legislature and on the ground:

> Mississippi has abolished—Slavery does She mean it or is it a pollicy for The present we fear the late acts of the Legeslature that she will not treat us as free . . . your honor is it just that wee all shoulde come under the stringent Laws the legeslature has past. we are to holde no

contract it is left intirely to our imployer he [holds?] the writing and one of his white [neighbo]rs holde the duplicate and if we shoulde leave from eny cruel treatement we are to be caught and brought by force to our employer and the niger-runner is to hav a fee of five dollars or ten cents a mill to be paid out of our wages. we are to well acquainted with the yelping of bloodhounds and the tareing of our fellow servents To pisces when we were slaves and now we are free we do not want to be hunted by negro-runners and thair hounds unless we are guilty of a criminal crime.[12]

The documents of Black assemblies in 1865 also show a keen sensitivity to how people were being portrayed in the local and statewide press. The Port Gibson petition reports: "Our faults are dayley published by Editors, not a statement will you ever see in our favour thair is Shureley Some a mong us that is honest, trutheful, and indestrious, and Some of us are working and making our superiours comferttable who finde so much fault of our freedom."[13] As people who were having such charges against them read at mass meetings, they began to confront their image in society as an untrust-worthy mass and the need to make concerted public self-representation.

An Old South that had never disarmed had the perilous effects of en-couraging vigilantism and providing the military-style structure for the organized violence that would crush Radical Reconstruction. The local militias could be used for the first wave of repression aimed at Black gatherings. As Hahn writes, "Any black assembly, any sign of economic independence, any attempt to ignore or reject the conventions of racial subordination became an invitation to harassment or summary punish-ment." The Freedmen's Bureau gave support to the whites' attempt to reas-sert control with a concerted effort to inform freedpeople there would be no land given to them, advising them to sign contracts and warning them that refusing to work would not be tolerated. White southerners continued to agitate for removal of all federal supervision, especially by Black soldiers. Freedpeople continued to delay contract negotiation, look for other places to work, and explore ways to buy land. The federal government, for its part, continued to give back the land it held. If Blacks were disappointed that planters' abandoned lands were being returned to them, the black codes were also fair warning that the southern elite wanted to keep them work-ing for bare subsistence on their land. Owning land and property was for Blacks—the majority of whom were agricultural workers—the quickest and most preferred route to autonomy.[14]

The freedpeople of Port Gibson had an assessment of the crisis of late 1865 worth considering: "We pray you do not believe the falsehood our enimies has got up for some purpose that we intend an insurrection. we have [no] [s]uch thought now we are free what [would?] we rise for we no that we hav good white friends and we depend on them by the help of god to see us righted and we do not want our rights by murdering." To say they did not want to gain their rights by murder probably represented the views of many, people already traumatized by war and its privations, and now well aware of the arms that would be raised against them.[15]

The Union presence in all the sites on the Emancipation Circuit also meant women could work as individual proprietors doing laundry, tailoring, dressmaking, and domestic work. Over time, laundry workers, who in various towns often worked together in a neighborhood, would organize their labor. They sometimes organized around other issues as well, and they were later followed by waiters and hotel workers in cities, notably in Galveston and Atlanta. On June 20, 1866, Black women laundry workers in Jackson released a letter to the mayor following a meeting at which they had decided to "join in charging a uniform rate for our labor." Philip Foner and Ronald Lewis called this the "first collective action of black women workers." The women stated they had joined in asking $1.50 per day, $15 a month for family washing, and $10 a month for individuals, "under the influence of the present high prices of all the necessaries of life, and the attendant high rates of rent, while our wages remain very much reduced, we, the washerwomen of the city of Jackson, . . . [are] thinking it impossible to live uprightly and honestly in laboring for the present daily and monthly recompense, and hoping to meet with the support of all good citizens." Uniform rates proved an effective tool for such proprietors.[16]

Circuit Riders

In 1867, John Mercer Langston, a Republican organizer, came to Mississippi. He was a former Underground Railroad activist and a trained lawyer who would later be one of the last African Americans in the US Congress in the nineteenth century, among other accomplishments. In Ohio, where he was educated, he had recruited Black soldiers during the war. He came to Mississippi for the Republicans after his appointment as inspector general of the Freedmen's Bureau, and while serving as president of the National Equal Rights League (NERL).[17] He wrote from Jackson to the URCC on July 7, 1867, that "the work goes bravely in this State. I have spoken to three of the largest meetings within ten days you ever saw. Two in this city and one at Vicksburg." Like the organizers in Virginia and Georgia, he was surprised at the turnout on word that someone had come to talk to people about their rights.[18] That same week, activist Rev. James Lynch wrote to the URCC from Jackson. Over the previous two years he had spent time organizing in South Carolina and Georgia and in Philadelphia editing the *Christian Recorder*. He was now twenty-eight years old. He had been in the state "about ten days," had spoken several times, and formed some Union League groups. His assembly in Jackson had been "immense" and enthusiastic. While he reported there were no established Republican groups, he found the town of Vicksburg politically well organized. His overview was as follows:

> Of the 434,000 colored people in the state of Mississippi not 60,000 live in cities and towns. They mostly reside on the farms and plantations. The rebels hope to carry the localities distant from prominent towns along the lines of railway. When such men as Gov. Sharkey will tell colored men in the highway that "every one of them who registers [to vote] will have to go into the army and fight Indians" you may know how vigorously they are at work. The colored people seem very dependent but they have much spirit and it seems as if when instructed in the *least degree* as regards their political situation, they comprehended the whole.[19]

John Langston and James Lynch, who were good friends, worked different counties in Mississippi just as Henry McNeal Turner and John Costin had in Georgia. They covered a lot of ground in a matter of three weeks.

Langston wrote again on July 21, this time from Corinth, 240 miles north of Jackson, having spoken in Meridian, Jackson, Canton, Holly Springs, and Corinth "to immense and attentive audiences of white and colored persons." He reported that he was treated with respect in all those places and that both Union Leagues and Republican clubs were being organized "in many parts of the state." In the coming days, he would organize in Columbus, Macon, and Aberdeen on the eastern side of the state. He had met up with Lynch in Canton and, praising Lynch's speaking skill, wrote, "He wins many friends wherever he goes." Langston's note to the URCC was followed by that of an army major who wrote from Meridian to ask for more resources for Lynch, whom he found effective with Black and white audiences alike. "I conceive," he wrote, "that one lecture, such as he delivered to a large assembly of freemen and others at this place on Saturday . . . accomplishes more good for the cause of Reconstruction than the combined efforts of the Military Authorities and the Freedmen's Bureau can accomplish in a month."[20]

Building Political Formations Is Multifaceted

It would seem to be testimony to the climate of Mississippi in 1867 that the state's military commander, General Edward O. C. Ord, issued General Order No. 5, forbidding "assemblies of any armed organizations under any pretense whatever." While the Ku Klux Klan and other armed organizations attacking Republicans might be assumed to be the targets of the order, it may have been aimed at the Union League and its Black members, who often carried arms to meetings, as the order also gratuitously advised freedpeople to work rather than going to political meetings. Ord had a dim view of Union League organizers and warned General Grant of an impending race war, implying Union League activism was at fault, and then issued an order "that seemed to call upon the leagues to disband," according to Michael Fitzgerald. Grant saw this as overreach, and Ord resigned. His successor, General Alvan C. Gillem, turned out to be worse. The Republican Party had a hard time gaining ground in Mississippi in part because its activists were not protected by the military, and under Gillem they felt no support for their political rights, and found the Freedmen's Bureau helpless as well.[21]

Black voter registration proceeded slowly in the state in 1867 and was opposed by landowners who complained as if to imply their only unhappiness was that workers were absent from the fields. In 1867 and 1868, the Freedmen's Bureau received complaints from Louisville in eastern Mississippi and Magnolia at the southern end of the state that employers were "discharging men and women for attending public meetings."[22] Still, seventeen African Americans were chosen as delegates to the constitutional convention, denigrated locally as the "Black and Tan Convention," and coarser labels.[23] Assessments of the men vary, but there is agreement that Charles Caldwell of the Jackson area (Hinds County), J. Aaron Moore of Meridian (Lauderdale County), and Thomas W. Stringer of Vicksburg (Warren County) were the strongest forces among the Blacks and wielded considerable influence. (See the Mississippi maps [plates 10 and 11].)

Caldwell, who had been a blacksmith while enslaved and was regarded as utterly fearless by people who knew him, was a powerful organizer.

Radical carpetbagger Albert T. Morgan, a white delegate from Yazoo, described Caldwell, armed with a pistol, defending him at the convention from an armed Democrat and wrote that Caldwell headed the Black militia that tried to keep the peace during the deadly days before the 1875 election. An armed mob that attacked a rally in Clinton in 1875 during the violent end of Mississippi Reconstruction went after Caldwell, but he escaped. He was murdered several months later when lured to have a drink with a "friend."

Aaron Moore was a minister and one of those building a power base in Meridian who became more militant in response to Klan violence. He was hunted for assassination during the Meridian riot of 1871, in which his home was burned, but escaped and lived on in Jackson. One of the extraordinary stories of the convention centers on Moore's white counterpart, delegate R. C. Merryman. Once at the convention, Merryman evidently allied himself with the conservatives and disparaged the Meridian Union League activists. According to the proceedings, he was also censured for repeated drunkenness and unbecoming behavior. The Blacks of Meridian deposed him "in absentia," writes Fitzgerald, "and they allegedly wrote him not to return to town because they did not want to have to hang" a delegate.[24]

Thomas Stringer, an AME minister who came to Mississippi from Ohio in 1865 and became a Union League activist and later a Freedmen's Bureau agent, was often cited as an able man for the task of making a constitution, though he was viewed as too conservative by others from his area. But Stringer is still esteemed locally today as much for having been a powerfully talented organizer of church congregations, and as the founder of the Mississippi Prince Hall Masons in 1867 and Black lodges of the Knights of Pythias fraternal organization in 1880, which lived long after him. (The Mississippi Prince Hall Masons have a long history tied to the twentieth-century civil rights movement.) At the turn of the twentieth century, the Stringer Knights branched out into an array of publishing efforts run by William A. Scott, who also became the publisher for the new Black Holiness church sects that arose in the Mississippi and Arkansas deltas. These links begun in Vicksburg and Jackson and spreading throughout the delta should not be overlooked in the continuation of Black activism in the late nineteenth century.[25]

Table 10.1 shows that Stringer came into an environment where Blacks worked valiantly to sustain newspapers from 1865 when a Vicksburg mass meeting called for a paper that would "fearlessly" defend the right of "colored citizens." In the early days, the heart of the Emanicpation Circuit was along the Mississippi River. The boats working the river made many stops, and labor, voting, and emigration mobilizations came to those sites as well. Organizing moved north to counties near Memphis and south along the river to Louisiana. On the eastern border along the rail lines from the Black Belt of Alabama, organizing took place and moved to counties adjacent to Lauderdale and Noxubee. As on the East Coast, the federal troop presence helped secure community building in places large and small on the waterways. In the wake of the tremendous numbers of people who risked their lives to vote or to watch polls, and the numerous people who gave their lives for Black voting, pervasive activism on labor issues and emigration work ensued, as shown in table 10.1.

At the end of October 1868, Edmonia Highgate, who had been teaching in rural Louisiana, wrote to the *American Freedman* from Enterprise, Mississippi, just south of Meridian, where she was teaching sixty-eight students. By the next spring her mother, Hannah, and two sisters, Carrie and Wilella, were teaching in Jackson. "White Democrats" had already forced Highgate's host to put her out of the home in which she had stayed. To keep the school open, the community paid a collective sum between eight and fifteen dollars every month, and bought its own books. Highgate asked people in the North for donations of teaching materials such as maps, charts, and a globe. Teachers, she wrote, needed a fund for medicines for very sick children. "Some children are yet 'held to service' and brutally used, and, when really very ill, are wantonly neglected and left to die." Sometimes, she reported, the Freedmen's Bureau was able to intervene successfully. A year later she returned to New York physically and mentally exhausted and in 1870 died at twenty-six years of age in a tragic incident involving a pregnancy. In the six years since she went south from New York State in 1864, she had taught freedpeople in Virginia, Maryland, Louisiana, and Mississippi.

Making Political Voice Makes Opposition

John Roy Lynch, only several years younger than Highgate, had been born enslaved in Louisiana and escaped a Mississippi plantation in 1863 when US troops occupied Natchez. In 1865–66, he learned the photography business while working in a local shop in the day and attending a freedmen's school at night. In 1869, at age twenty-one, he was appointed a justice of the peace in Natchez. By 1873, the twenty-six-year-old Lynch was in the US Congress, where he served until 1877. In the run-up to the election campaign of 1875, Democrats taking action against Republican power armed themselves. According to Lynch, then running for reelection: "Nearly all the Democratic clubs in the state were converted into armed military companies. Funds with which to purchase arms were believed to have been contributed by the national Democratic organization. . . . To enable the Democrats to carry the state a Republican majority of between twenty and thirty thousand had to be overcome."[26] The targets of mob action are worth examining: the mobs specifically went after Black elected officials and demanded they resign or ran them out of their counties, apparently not for being Republican but for being in office while Black. They disrupted as much as possible the ability of African Americans to hold meetings. Lynch, who wrote one of the earliest of the few accounts of Reconstruction by a Black participant, recalled: "Nearly every Republican meeting was attended by one or more of those [armed Democratic] clubs or companies, the members of which were distinguished by red shirts indicative of blood." Lynch found himself trying to make stump speeches in increasingly dangerous situations. The violent election of 1875 was the end of Reconstruction in Mississippi. Talk of taking the state back by any means began in 1874. In Hinds County the plan included an armed attack on a rally of three thousand Republicans that spread around the county and left several whites and several dozen Blacks dead. The strategy being deployed against people like Lynch, which made the state famous for its ruthless approach to Black political power, was known as "the Mississippi Plan" and its successful execution was known as the Redemption.[27]

The Mississippi Democrats had laid out their strategy in January 1874 at a "Taxpayers Convention" in Jackson and published it in the press in the fall of 1875. The secretary of the Hinds County Democratic campaign, W. Calvin Wells, recalled in his account of the election (including his presence at the Clinton riot) the plan used by the Democratic "taxpayers" clubs he organized. Among the tactics were intimidating any Blacks who could not be persuaded to vote Democratic, which included telling them they would be on a "dead list." Wells outlined the Mississippi Plan that was printed in local papers:

1   A solidly organized Democratic front;
2   Individual effort with negroes, persuasive, but if necessary, intimidation;
3   And if these failed, then stuff the ballot box by putting in Democratic votes after the election . . . ;

4   Destruction of Republican tickets when they could be
    gotten;

5   Substitution of Democratic for Republican tickets in the
    hands of negroes by inserting "Republican" at the top of
    Democratic tickets and have the names of Democrats below
    the word "Republican";

6   As a dernier resort, if these plans did not carry, then the
    Republicans were to be counted out and the Democrats
    counted in.[28]

Wells denied ballot stuffing or recounting actually took place, claiming they were unnecessary, but admitted to the rest, as well as bribing a vote counter. He assumed the reader of his article who had not lived through "that terrible ordeal" would "lift up his hands in horror and say that those were corrupt practices. And I am not prepared to deny it. . . . We were forced to a choice between the evils of negro rule and the evils of the questionable practices to overthrow it. We chose what we thought was the lesser evil, and it is now not to be regretted." The Mississippi Plan was adopted by forces in South Carolina who used these methods to unseat Black office-holders and begin the disfranchisement of Black voters.[29]

In a tragic but telling episode, dozens of Blacks going to register for the upcoming election were trapped in the village of Satartia heading to the registrar. They were caught between a posse of riflemen on horses who came by road from Yazoo City, and men with rifles who jumped aboard a boat downtown and came to the riverside site to prevent escape by water. One witness said there was a rumor that the would-be voters were going to murder people in the village. One man who testified, local chancery clerk James Dixon, a freedman, said there had been an incident the previous day in which whites went to start a fight in the area, and once they fired on the Black folk, the Blacks fired back, wounding one or two whites. The next day, according to S. G. Bedwell, "a party of colored men came over from Brannon Ewing's plantation, and wanted to register . . . and they were driven back." Driven back is an understatement, as he explains: "[They] drove them into the river, and there is no telling how many were killed. I heard one man, who was wounded there, and who is now dead, say that from the number of cries and groans that came from the damned niggers, they must have got a bushel of them. . . . They disappeared anyway, and were never seen or heard afterwards."

Bedwell, who was interviewed in a US Senate investigation of the election, was asked how many people had been killed in Yazoo County prior to the election. He responded:

A: I should suppose there were some six, eight, or ten. Every
few days while I was away I would read notices in the paper
of darkies being hung here and there and elsewhere, and
some disappearing. I could not state how many. It was variously estimated at from five to fifteen.
Q: That does not include those killed at the time they were
driven into the river?
A: No, sir.[30]

The violent "electioneering" of the Democrats in the 1875 election was successful in attacking Black representation in more than a dozen counties. Between 1877 and 1887, only eight of the original thirteen counties still had representation. (See the Mississippi maps [plates 10 and 11].)

Albert Morgan wrote with anger and grief about the loss of friends and allies he had seen defeated, and those who stood up and were killed, using the metaphor of a single human bulldozer to represent the violent posses and assassins:

Some of the survivors of the campaign of 1875 the bull-dozer has silenced by cajolery, some he has bribed to silence, some he has silenced by threats and some he has killed. But such as he could neither cajole, bribe, intimidate, nor kill, he has pursued with a malice, a cunning, and a persistency that has driven them from their homes and scattered them to the four corners of the earth.

Chisholm [the white Republican Kemper County sheriff] refused to surrender or run, and the bull-dozer killed his daughter that he might make surer work of him. Gilmer [a white Republican storekeeper running for office] refused, and he "filled him full of lead." Charles Caldwell [Hinds County Republican leader] refused, and he "shot him all to pieces," and wantonly slew him and all his children, from the elder son to the baby in the cradle. But why continue the list? I could add a hundred names to it.[31]

It is difficult to imagine Black childhoods in this kind of environment, but the life of the crusading journalist Ida B. Wells provides a glimpse of the ongoing need for safety, secrecy, and the continuation of the community practices of Reconstruction even after its violent end. Born in Mississippi in 1862, Wells recalled learning to read as a child at a local school and reading the newspaper at an early age for her father and his friends, and her mother's anxiety over her father's habit of attending political meetings at night. When her parents and an infant brother died in a yellow fever epidemic in 1878, and Wells was left at age sixteen as the head of a household of five younger siblings, she recalled that the Black Masonic group to which her father belonged came to their home and decided "what to do with us." For a time, she actually kept the children with her. The group had enlisted help from households that could take in one or two of the children. After becoming a teacher and moving to Memphis in 1882, Wells joined the AME Church, where she heard Henry McNeal Turner, who had organized in Georgia and had become the first southern AME bishop in 1880. She also enrolled in a "lyceum" where teachers read aloud essays and other literature, a group also attended by many other citizens who, in the 1880s, were still coming to hear public readings of the latest news.[32]

It should surprise no one that migration was one of the responses among African Americans to the violence, the unrelenting poverty, and the subversion of every element of an open democratic process. In the Mississippi Delta in the 1870s through 1890s, migration movements took several forms, sometimes rising and falling in sequence: Liberia emigration, Kansas exodus, and Oklahoma exodus. In 1892, after the lynching of three of her friends, Wells, then a newspaper editor in Memphis, was persuaded by Oklahoma Exodusters to go see the West for herself, and she became an advocate of "Exodusting." Some Blacks moved into Arkansas, which, they learned, did not offer an improved political climate but did hold out a chance of acquiring land.[33]

Blacks who were being hired to build railroad lines in the Mississippi Delta became aware of railroad plans to expand along the Arkansas River and built towns near the planned railroad lines, going to the rail companies and asking for money to build churches.[34] The migration patterns were influenced by railroad work and rail access, and were made possible by the news along the existing Emancipation Circuit while at the same time expanding the circuit. B. F. Watson explained this when he testified before the Senate Select Committee investigating the Black exodus phenomenon.

Q. And the news spreads among them rapidly?

A. Yes, sir.

Q. So the news of the bulldozing in Louisiana spreads to Mississippi and causes a stampede there?

A. Yes, sir: and those of them there who know of it and who are seeking to get away have to be pretty mute on the subject.[35]

The interviewee also alludes here to the fact that these early migrants had to depart their Mississippi locations in secret, usually at night, or face violence or intimidation. Documentation of the spread of both news of violence and Exoduster ideas along the Mississippi River affirms the existence of interstate communication along the traditional routes of commerce, but the rail lines would in effect create an inland highway for word-of-mouth information and copies of newspapers from Mississippi and elsewhere.

In 1890 the state created a new constitution that required a poll tax for voting, a literacy test, as well as proof that two years of taxes had been paid, and reapportioned the number of representatives for every county. This crushed the Black vote and hampered the poor white vote. The constitution also dictated separate schools for Blacks and whites and permitted use of the Christian Bible in classrooms. As John Roy Lynch wrote in his account of Reconstruction, "My own state, Mississippi, was the first to give legal effect to the practical nullification of the Fifteenth Amendment." In fact, the delegates added a provision advising the federal government to repeal the Fifteenth Amendment giving Black males the right to vote. The only Black delegate at the 1890 constitutional convention was Isaiah Montgomery, founder and mayor of the all-Black town Mound Bayou. Montgomery's participation in the convention that disfranchised Blacks was villified, especially because he not only voted for the measures that would virtually eliminate the votes of tens of thousands of Black citizens but, more controversially, he spoke in favor of the measures, saying that he hoped they would improve race relations. Others have surmised he was trying to protect his own power in Bolivar County. Regardless of his motive, his cooperation with the disfranchisement enraged Frederick Douglass, who denounced it publicly more than once, and it also angered *New York Age* editor T. Thomas Fortune, who wrote that African Americans would only lose in this "bargain" Montgomery tried to strike: "Can a thief be just to the man he has robbed?"[36]

John Roy Lynch, by then a former US congressman, was a peer of Montgomery's who had known him well "for many years." He described how the president of the 1890 convention, Judge S. S. Calhoun of the state supreme court, had openly said that the convention had been called "for the purpose of ensuring the ascendancy of the white race or the Democratic Party" in the government by some means other than the bulldozing that had taken place. Calhoun threatened that if they did not establish this envisioned white rule that "the blood of every Negro that will be killed in an election riot" would be on their hands. But perhaps the most extraordinary idea shared by the man was that the violence had been corrupting whites and that if Blacks were disfranchised, the corruption of the public would end. As Lynch explained Calhoun's logic, whites would be better behaved because "there would be no occasion to suppress their [Black]votes by violence because they would have no votes to suppress; and, having no votes in the ballot boxes, there would be no occasion to commit fraud in the count or perjury in the returns, as heretofore." Lynch reported himself surprised at Montgomery's actions in support of Black disfranchisement, saying they "will continue to be an inexplicable mystery." On the other hand, the outcome of the new constitution's provisions was not a mystery: Black representation in elected office in Mississippi was eliminated by 1896, and no Black person was elected to statewide office again until 1967.[37] (See the Mississippi maps [plates 10 and 11].)

Blues and Holiness Riding the Rails

The last decades of the century were still marked by an epidemic of lynchings, and Black newspapers reported on numerous assaults on African Americans in the state, especially on women in public spaces. Spectacle lynchings were advertised in advance in newspapers. At the same time, the Mississippi Delta was experiencing a sudden proliferation of rail lines connecting plantations and the human beings living on them, and aiding out-migration. The cultural wave that began to ripple out from those farms would be more important than anyone at the time could imagine. The trains themselves lit the imaginations of whole communities who poured out to stations to see trains come in. The Pea Vine Branch of the Yazoo and Mississippi Valley Railroad met the Memphis-to-Vicksburg line at a tiny place named Boyle, Mississippi, home to the Dockery Plantation, now famous as the home of twentieth-century bluesmen Charlie Patton, Robert Johnson, and Howlin' Wolf. Farm owner Will Dockery had used gangs of his employees to clear the land for him to build a train line that wound its way northwest to Rosedale on the Mississippi and back southeast to Cleveland. During most of the year, when the cotton harvest was not being shipped, the line was reportedly crowded with migrating local Blacks, some of whom had to leave in the middle of the night from a station in another town from where they lived. Beginning in 1890, this little "dog" of a rail line provided "reliable transportation for bluesmen among the plantations of the Mississippi Delta" to Cleveland, Mississippi. As John M. Giggie has shown: "The representation of the railroad among blacks gathered in complexity and public visibility and ultimately developed as a modern crossroads where black hopes and ambitions for a better life intersected with social customs and legislation that would constrain them. Beginning in the late 1890s, for example, Delta blacks hosted prayer meetings at depots and depicted individual spiritual journeys as train journeys. They evangelized and constructed new churches near railroad stations." This phenomenon made sense given that camps housing workers building the new rail lines created communities to be served, but it is also perhaps an example of what Katherine McKittrick discusses as "oppositional spatial practices." In an era when Jim Crow was redrawing the lines of politics and railcars, and public access of all kinds, the new grassroots congregations repurposed spaces constructed for commerce and control. Simultaneously, this was the beginning of the routes of those Paul Oliver called the "songsters of the road shows"—such as the Delta's most popular show, the Rabbit Foot Minstrels, which featured Ma Rainey, Ida Cox, Bessie Smith, and later artists like Ethel Waters who performed in Black vaudeville. The railroads redefined their transportation and the locations of tent shows. At the same time, the tent shows themselves were repurposed from the usual religious revivals (which continued), to discourse centered on Blackness as expressed in blues culture. The events also served no small purpose in producing space for public discourse. In an area in which local Black newspapers were burned for printing political or labor news, tent shows offered joyous human contact, images and rhetoric of autonomy, especially for women, and a glamorous view of new possible futures.[38]

Oliver called others who used this rail circuit "the saints of the sanctified churches." One of the late-century movements aided by the new rail lines along the fluid Mississippi-Arkansas circuits was the birth of the Black "holiness" or "sanctified" churches (now often termed Pentecostal), specifically, the Church of the Living God (founded in Arkansas, 1889, now known as the CTLGWFF); the Church of God in Christ (Mississippi,

1897, now COGIC); and the Church of God in Christ Holiness (Mississippi, 1907, now COCHUSA), three groups developed by sharecroppers and farmers who sometimes experienced their spiritual practice as a specific response to the disastrous political Redemption. This development is part of the shared history of Mississippi and Arkansas. These churches began as protests against changes in the Black Baptist and Methodist churches: over the institutional churches' condemnations of fraternal groups, the commercialization of churches and promotion of Christian products, and new hierarchal structures of the churches into large regional bodies and the threat that that change posed to local autonomy in "doctrine, liturgy, and worship." The Holiness founders held the democratizing belief that God sometimes acts directly on individuals through the personal experience of "sanctification," which washes one of sin and confers salvation on that believer. This movement can perhaps most easily be seen as the radical change agent it was taken to be by institutional churches in the fact that its founders did not feel ministers had to have any formal education, adopt the new liturgical reforms, or be men; they only had to be sanctified.[39]

The modernizers of the established churches thought of themselves as Progressives but the Pentecostal-Holiness movement is a fascinating combination of what could be viewed as progressive and conservative teachings, as well as respect for the Afrocentric ideas and practices widely embraced through fraternal groups. Some of the progressive values included fostering ways in which to care for members of the community, as well as empowering the uneducated and female regarded as accomplished in Christian living. The new congregations drew large numbers of women who had roles in church work. Some of the conservative practices such as bans on smoking, drinking, dancing, swearing, and owning expensive material goods came with other practices that preserved traditional Black religious practice in a way that one might view as a progressive response to local desire to honor Black culture rather than imitating mainstream hierarchal and material practices that would disempower and marginalize the poor and uneducated in the church, especially women. Women in the Holiness churches rode the rails and started up study groups known as "bands" in rural areas along the Emancipation Circuit.

The new churches also claimed the validity of dreams and visions among believers, and some also accepted "speaking in tongues" (surprisingly, a new phenomenon encountered elsewhere by the founding ministers) as part of the experience of spirit—opposing the modern view that such occurrences should be shunned as holdovers of the slave system. (They were *not* necessarily all remnants of Black practices in the slavery era.) This is interesting for its value as an affirmation of the internal life of parishioners. These communities were unique in American history, having experienced the severe traumas of generations spanning nineteenth-century slavery, the Civil War, and the harsh realities of abolition, not to mention the violence of Reconstruction and its aftermath. Their collective acceptance of processing the unfathomable and, for many, the inexpressible through an open spiritual practice seems a boon to survival with sanity. In this regard the Holiness churches seem to have been sensitive to the present moment rather than simply conserving and reiterating past practices for their own sake. For this perspective, Clyde Woods's blues epistemology is very helpful, describing as it does how communities adapt (if not immediately reorganizing) and respond to horizon collapses. This observation about blues culture also seems to apply to the rise of Holiness church practices after the collapse of the possible futures offered by Reconstruction.[40]

The sects were also viewed as conservative at the time because they feared that the new Baptist and Methodist professionalizing "religious culture dangerously insulated men and women from the workings of the Holy Spirit." Perhaps one of the most disturbing generosities of the Holiness churches for the modernizers was the innovation of allowing local popular music—early blues—in the liturgical service. Giggie tells us of foundational practices in the new churches: "Holiness men and women were free to respond to . . . God's grace by pounding their feet on the floor, spinning around, beating their chests, and singing at the top of their lungs. . . . Blues notes and slurry rhythms, guitars, horns, and drums, when used with the proper intention of glorifying God and exciting the congregation to worship ever more energetically, were perfectly acceptable."[41]

By the 1900s, the churches were "the fastest growing form of organized Black religion in the nation." Some of the churches even tried to revive a Liberia emigration movement. As McKittrick writes, "Social practices create landscapes and contribute to how we organize, build, and imagine our surroundings. Black subjects are not indifferent to these practices and landscapes; rather they are connected to them due to crude racial-sexual hierarchies *and* due to their (often unacknowledged) status as geographic beings who have a stake in the production of space." The Mississippi Delta Holiness movement was an elaboration of the Black church born out of the struggles of the first mass movement after abolition and speaks to experience with and a continuation of mass participatory democracy, the sustained social production of space for expression and discourse, and the intention to retain forums open to all voices. It also gives one an inkling as to how the mass movement of freedpeople that began as political—a broadly inclusive sense of the political—helped to form the populist gears of a southern Black cultural engine that would generate the blues (including borrowings from country music), gospel music, jazz, and rhythm and blues. The cultural engine of freedpeople would redefine the culture of the country as one born in America.[42]

Looking at Table 10.1

Mississippi was empowered by organizing, institution building, and "circuit riders" (both locals and outsiders). Voters there elected hundreds of Black officials, exceeded only by Louisiana and South Carolina. (They have still not elected as many in recent years.) Early calls by citizens for Black newspapers resulted in many taking up publication, though they ended up being severely repressed by local terrorism after Reconstruction. Mississippi's geography and its cotton business created many routes for ties between communities and the circulation of ideas and culture by river and rail, and through church circuit riders and itinerant blues musicians as it emerged. Labor organizing seems to have been widespread, as were emigration movements. Most of the emigration movements I have tracked were on river ports, and we know from memoirs and testimony on western emigration that many escaped their counties by rail as well as by river. Politicians early on tried to prevent migration by outlawing leaving one's county. Due to the very fact that the Mississippi Valley became such a conduit for people and ideas over the centuries, we can feel sure also that the practices and experiences shown in counties on this table went north and west with the Great Migrations of the early and mid-twentieth century.

TABLE 10.1 Mississippi Emancipation Circuit, 1870–1900

	Institutions Present							19th Century Activism
	US Troops	RR (1884)	Union League	AMA Schools	Local Black Press	Black Political Reps	Knights of Labor Groups	
BILOXI Harrison County	•		•	• (non-AMA)		•	1 M/F packers & shippers	Labor
BRANDON Rankin County ß	•	•	•			•		
CANTON Madison County ß	•	•	•			•		Kansas emigration
CLEVELAND Bolivar County (est. 1886) ß	•	•	•		<u>2</u> 1870	•		Labor Liberia emigration Kansas exodus
GREENWOOD LeFlore County (est. 1871)		•				•		Vote Labor

(Continued)

TABLE 10.1 (*Continued*)

	Institutions Present						Knights of Labor Groups	19th Century Activism
	US Troops	RR (1884)	Union League	AMA Schools	Local Black Press	Black Political Reps		
GREENVILLE Washington County ß	•	•		•	<u>1</u> 1895	•		Vote Labor Kansas exodus
GULFPORT Harrison County (est. 1898)	•	•						
JACKSON Hinds County ß	•	•	•	•	<u>6</u> 1860s–90s	•	1 F mixed labor	Labor Antilynching
Lowndes County				•	<u>1</u> 1880s			
MERIDIAN Lauderdale County		•	•	•		•	1 M mixed labor	Labor Vote
Monroe County ß			•			•		Liberia emigration

NATCHEZ Adams County ß	•	•	•	<u>3</u> 1860s 1880 1890	•	2 M mixed labor · Kansas exodus
PORT GIBSON Claiborne County ß	•	•	Available in area	<u>1</u> 1870s & 1890s	•	· Kansas exodus
SUMMIT MCCOMB area, Pike County	•				•	1 M mixed labor · Labor
VICKSBURG Warren County ß	•	•	•	<u>3</u> 1860 1900	•	1 M laborers · Labor Kansas exodus
WATER VALLEY OXFORD area, Yalobusha County ß	•		•		•	1 M mixed labor ·

KEY: **Bold** = Site playing multiple roles on the circuit. ß = Black majority; unless otherwise noted, populations are for 1870. RR = Rail lines. **Black Political Reps** = Black representatives to the 1868 constitutional convention or members of the General Assembly.

Knights of Labor = Black assemblies of the labor organization. Most KoL assemblies were segregated by race and gender: white males, Black males, white females, or Black females. "Mixed labor" is a term from the Garlock data (*see* Table Source Notes) and indicates various forms of work, not mixing by race or gender. **Gender** is indicated here by M or F.

SOURCES: *See* Table Source Notes (393–96).

11 **ARKANSAS**
Minority

Minority: *n* . . . **1 a :** the period before attainment of majority . . . **2 :**
the smaller in number of two groups constituting a whole; *specif* :
a group having less than the number of votes necessary for control
3 a : a part of the population differing from others in some characteristics and often subjected to differential treatment **b** : a member
of a minority group.
—*Webster's Ninth New Collegiate Dictionary* (1986)

The Civil War divided the state of Arkansas in such a way that the chance
to flee plantations was determined by the scattered locations where US
troops were able to hold ground. For these reasons, the Emancipation Circuit in the state would get its start in three regions fairly distant from one
another: predictably on the Mississippi River, with its constant contact
locally and intermittently with river traffic, including US forces; along the
Arkansas River in Little Rock, Pine Bluff, and other sites; and in southwest
counties near Louisiana and Texas. The circuit would expand to connect
most of these places while still leaving counties on the margins vulnerable to threat. Thanks to documentation left by a former governor of the
period, it is possible to situate Ku Klux Klan organizations next door to
these vulnerable areas. As a result of federal struggles to take the state, as in
Virginia, many slave system survivors who had been in flight had to move
several times.

The Union army, under Major General Samuel R. Curtis, first came into Arkansas from Missouri in March 1862 to defeat Confederate forces in the Battle of Pea Ridge, near Fayetteville. Federal troops occupied a portion of the northwestern section of the state. Arkansas had a consequential number of Unionists in the central and northern counties, farmers who for the most part were not able to own enslaved people and did not raise cotton, like large landholders in counties along the Mississippi. When the first convention to consider secession was held in March 1861, voters had elected a Unionist majority, which blocked any decision to secede. Lincoln's request for state militia troops after the attack on Fort Sumter triggered a successful secession vote in May.

When war began, the geographical divisions remained apparent. Adeline Blakeley, born enslaved in Tennessee, had been brought to a farm near Prairie Grove, Arkansas, with her mother and other family members. As she later recalled in an interview, "Mr. Parks [the owner] didn't believe in seceding. He held out as long as it was safe to do so. If you didn't go with the popular side they called you 'abolitionist' or maybe 'submissionist.' But when Arkansas did go over he was loyal. He had two sons and a son-in-law in the Confederate army. One fought at Richmond and one was killed at Gettysburg." Blakeley was near troops for at least two years, whether at the farm or at a home in Fayetteville owned by Parks's daughter (to whom she was given as a wedding present). As Blakeley recalled, "Even the little children were taught listen to for bugle calls and know what they meant. We had to know . . . how to act when we heard them." Both the Battle of Pea Ridge and the Battle of Prairie Grove were nearby, and soldiers came in the door at both places where she lived: "Fayetteville suffered all through the war. You see we were not very far from the dividing line and both armies were here a lot. The Federals were in charge most of the time." Except for a few months, the Union occupied the area from late 1862 until spring 1865.[1]

The fighting during 1862, with two armies living off the land, devastated property and resources for Arkansans of all classes and caused displacement of many people in some sections. As occurred elsewhere in the region, slaveholders who were able to do so attempted to move their enslaved people farther south and west, often to Texas, to prevent their loss to Union forces. Tom Robinson, an Arkansas resident born enslaved in North Carolina, had been sold at a young age to a man who soon sold him to another. He later told a Works Progress Administration interviewer: "But pretty soon after he bought me old man Dave Robinson moved to

Texas. We was there when the war started. We stayed there all during the war. I was set free there." And, in Arkansas as on the Eastern Seaboard, many enslaved people fled when Union troops neared their area.[2]

Departures and Arrivals

Throughout General Curtis's movement deeper into central Arkansas, whites and Blacks fled their homes to follow his forces. In early 1862, Curtis began granting freedom to fugitives who made it to his lines and setting up refugee camps, and he attempted to form Black army units before the government had sanctioned them, enlisting more than fifty-five hundred men. In August 1862, when Curtis was replaced by General Frederick Steele, "a conservative Democrat with far less interest in emancipation," the granting of free status to refugees ceased and Black troop formation was halted. According to Amy Murrell Taylor, Steele also forced all freedpeople, including five hundred women and children, out of the town of Helena on the Mississippi, excepting those (presumably men) who were "working on the defenses." Only after the Emancipation Proclamation of January 1, 1863, were African Americans in Arkansas again allowed to enlist.[3]

Boston Blackwell, who specified that Blackwell was his "freed name," had been sold to a plantation owner in Jefferson County before the Civil War. He heard about the Emancipation Proclamation in 1863, and in October of that year, at about age twenty-three, he and another young man fled the slave system for Union lines at Pine Bluff. They were hunted by dogs and yet succeeded in finding a Union camp after two cold days and nights of tramping through woods. At the camp they were fed, and he saw what he thought could have been "hundreds" of other refugees. "When I got to Pine Bluff I stayed contraband." He got a job as a driver. "They told me I was free when I gets to the Yankee camp, but I couldn't go outside much." On the battlefield he carried water to protect cotton bale breastworks that were set ablaze by weapon fire. Later, in Little Rock, he enlisted. "I was swored in. . . . Year of '64."[4]

After the war in the northwest region, Adeline Blakeley and her family lived off Union soldiers' rations. As she recalled, "They had good rations which were issued uncooked. They could get them prepared anywhere they liked. We were good cooks so that is the way we got our food—preparing it for soldiers and eating it with them." In the same way Blakeley learned that she was free and that soldiers were making sure people knew they were free: "After the war they came to Mrs. Blakeley, the soldiers did, and accused her of keeping me against my will. I told them that I stayed because I wanted to, the Blakeleys were my people. They let me alone, the whites did, but the Negroes didn't like it. They tried to fight me and called me names." She reports that Union soldiers "stayed on for a long time. Fences were down, houses were burned, stock was gone, but we got along somehow."[5]

The Emancipation Proclamation issued January 1, 1863, as Taylor writes, "came and went that day with little change in the region." In her study of the lives of a number of freedpeople in Virginia, Arkansas, and Kentucky during the war, Taylor shows that unenlightened attitudes among members of federal forces were an issue. This was particularly crucial as the US government began to assemble a Unionist state government in Arkansas, and in Helena, where thousands of Black people arrived on their own or were brought by Union troops. In July, Union forces prevailed at Helena, and in September they took both Fort Smith on the western border and the capital, Little Rock. The Union's success prompted the arrival of more fugitives where troops camped. According to Carl Moneyhon, by a year later, "there were large slave settlements at Van Buren, Fort Smith, Little Rock, and Pine Bluff." Flights also occurred across the river in the Mississippi Valley—thousands in Memphis and at Corinth, Mississippi, and other sites—from whence some came to Arkansas. Even as this occurred, Steele's command failed to pay laborers working for the military and neglected to supply provisions necessary for survival and medical care. Freedpeople in the area, whom Taylor documented through the war and beyond, appear to have continued to try to take shelter with the Union forces (and some signed up to fight) because they saw the armed forces as "mobilized to combat their owners."[6]

In March of 1863, three months after emancipation, the overwhelmed military started simply shipping refugees elsewhere, mainly to the Midwest. They did so without concern that in border states, where the Emancipation Proclamation had no force, they put freedpeople in danger of being reenslaved. The editors of *Freedom: A Documentary History of Emancipation 1861–1867* point out that "commanders of the Department of the Missouri established no government farms or other federally sponsored agricultural operations," as were set up in the Mississippi Valley and on islands in the Mississippi. "They organized one contraband camp, at St. Louis, and it originated not to feed and shelter fugitive slaves from Missouri, but to care for refugees from Arkansas." The origin of the camp was unlike the organic development of settlements around army operation bases in most other places. In mid-March five hundred freedpeople were shipped from the overcrowded camp at Helena to St. Louis, Missouri, with Chaplain Samuel W. Sawyer in charge. The Union commander in St. Louis, Major General Samuel R. Curtis—the same Curtis who had been "freeing" refugees in Arkansas the year before—had not been notified of the human cargo. Sawyer reported on the refugees' arrival in St. Louis in a letter to Brigadier General Benjamin Prentiss, Commander of the District of Eastern Arkansas:

> Towards midnight Saturday we reached St. Louis & [sic] Sabbath handed our dispatches to Maj. Gen. Curtis—"*Five hundred contrabands! What in the world shall I do with them!*" exclaimed the General. . . . While consulting on this matter some of the prominent citizens, called, & urged the General not to suffer the contrabands to land because Missouri being a slave state still their personal liberty might possibly be endangered again, but to ship them round to Cincinnati or on to Keokuk [Iowa].[7]

The general decided to unload the freedpeople in St. Louis, where they would be housed in an abandoned hotel that could house a thousand people. Sawyer reported that "Monday evening the whole city nearly turned out to see the contrabands disembark & pack & load their baggage & strike a line for the Missouri Hotel." Sawyer found work for these refugees and those who continued to be shipped there (increasingly from Mississippi as well as Arkansas) "in St. Louis, or in Iowa, Illinois, and Kansas." By midsummer of that year the government had shipped "an estimated 2,500 freedpeople" to free states. As with other slavery-era ruptures, African Americans caught up in these shipments suffered random separations, many permanent. Some enslaved people from Missouri who had been transported by a woman slaveholder to Mississippi to escape Union troops, and were then captured by Union troops en route to Texas, were placed in Helena's refugee camp and then shipped to the St. Louis camp. Two of them later wrote letters to their former enslavers looking for friends and kin after being separated from them in the St. Louis site and then shipped out. One woman wrote from Ottomwa, Iowa, citing a man named Ab who had returned from Iowa to St. Louis looking unsuccessfully for a friend of theirs named Ellen from whom they had been separated there. When shipping people north was halted in October, "General Napoleon B. Buford, the commander at Helena, moved hundreds of freedpeople to Islands 63 and 66, in the Mississippi River, where the men cut wood and the women and children corded it."[8]

The American Missionary Association (AMA) began to arrive in Arkansas in 1863, followed soon by the Friends Freedmen Association and freedmen's schools formed "at Helena [Phillips County], Little Rock [Pulaski], Pine Bluff [Jefferson], . . . Island No. 63, White River Island and De Valls Bluff [Prairie]." By 1867–68, AMA schools had also been started, mostly on plantations, in Fayetteville (Washington County); Fort Smith (Sebastian); Hot Springs (Garland); Lewisville (Lafayette); Arkadelphia (Clarke); Washington (Hempstead); and in Little River, Sevier, and Desha Counties.[9]

One issue that prevented these slave system fugitives from getting a foothold on freedom was the military's preference for preserving large-scale plantations rather than breaking the farms up into smaller units that Black families could farm on their own. "As a result, the system inaugurated in 1864," writes Moneyhon, "was the one in place at the end of the war and was taken over by . . . the Freedmen's Bureau . . . in May, 1865." Blacks who were able to lease land rather than farm for wages were able to make a living for themselves and save some as well, whereas others continued to live at subsistence levels. Many Blacks attempted to lease land for farming, but, as occurred in some other states, the Freedmen's Bureau, aware that sharecropping put Black farmers at the mercy of planters for supplies, often costing them all the year's income, still urged the wage contracts on freedpeople.[10] Henry Blake, who was born in Little Rock at the end of the war, recalled how his family lived: "After freedom, we worked shares a while. Then we rented. When we worked shares, we couldn't make nothing—just overalls and something to eat. . . . A man who didn't know how to count would always lose. He might lose anyhow. They didn't give no itemized statement. No, you just had to take their word. They just say you owe so much. No matter how good account you kept, you had to go by their account."[11] Another consequence of the war for both farming and politics was a serious drop in the population—white and Black—caused by displacement, people going into the army and not returning, and casualties of the conflict. Many counties showed a loss of half of their populations by 1866. This, too, made trying to preserve the old system problematic.[12]

The arrival of Union troops provided security for many of the white citizens but not for African Americans seeking shelter and employment with the federal units. The military gave housing and took it away when it was needed for troops. As Taylor shows, Blacks in Helena were subject to insecure housing, Confederate guerrilla raids, and privation for the rest of the war. In the camps, the risk of serious illness was high. Rhonda Kohl writes of Union forces, "When supply considerations necessitated the army's occupation of Helena, Arkansas, in July 1862, the army became an ineffective force in fighting not only the Confederates but also the disease-ridden Helena environment. Sickness did not abate over the three and a half years of Federal occupation as Helena became known as one of the most insalubrious locations in the Union." The primary illnesses Kohl identifies were dysentery, malaria, typhoid, and typhus. As in many other locations, most freedpeople arriving in Helena seem to have received tents without flooring. As Jim Downs explains about all the refugee camps, "Forced to live in such unhealthy environments, freedpeople suffered from malnutrition, starvation, and exposure, while others came down with smallpox, dysentery, and yellow fever and died. Contraband camps and former slave pens sadly represented for many refugees their first encounter with 'freedom.'" However, for African Americans in Union locations, there was at least a temporary acknowledgment of the Emancipation Proclamation, and the new provisional Unionist state government in Arkansas formed in 1864 ended slavery during the war (unlike southern sites exempted from the Emancipation Proclamation). Unfortunately, this new governing body did allow for apprenticeship, the system by which many Blacks elsewhere lost custody of their children under black codes. The new and, as it happened, temporary constitution did not grant African Americans citizens rights with their freedom, the denial of which would be a catalyst for organizing in Black communities. These were bitter pills given that the dangers that accompanied flights to Union lines often landed them in a place where they faced other deadly consequences. In December 1865, the US Congress passed the Thirteenth Amendment abolishing slavery. Freedom, however, lacked few real options for survival.[13]

For freedpeople, the tasks were myriad: food, clothing, shelter, and medical help to assist the survival of infants, children, and adults, many of whom had chronic conditions from sustained harsh conditions. Autonomy was much sought after and often only approximated by exercising the ability to move from one farm to another. People were also well aware of the need for literacy to better negotiate a living wage and possible credit. At the same time, the work of activists and missionaries in the emancipation era did accomplish the important task of mass education in citizenship rights and, for thousands, varying degrees of literacy. Beyond these lifelong struggles on which freedpeople were now embarked, they desired justice—the citizenship tools with which to seek restitution or accountability from those who wronged them and the vote to choose officials and law enforce- ment. By the time they would begin to vote, people were being made aware that they had helped create changes in the country's constitution—the Thirteenth, Fourteenth, and Fifteenth Amendments—that gave freed- people those rights they had seen others enjoy. Their attempts to test these rights were hampered by the fact that state laws specifically addressed and limited rights by race through slave system statutes that had not been re- vised and would not be rewritten until 1868. While the old laws did not apply to the current moment, it went a long way with whites that slave system laws had come to seem reasonable to their communities. The Thir- teenth Amendment would not be enough to stop laws meant to maintain the established treatment of Blacks by exchanging the word *slave* for the term *colored person*.

Foundational Assembly

When the Arkansas Convention of Colored Citizens met in Little Rock from November 30 to December 2, 1865, with only twenty delegates repre- senting five counties, it drafted a number of appeals to the legislature. First, the delegates' petition asked that lawmakers "clothe us with the power of self-protection, by giving us equality before the law and the right of suf- frage, so we may become bona fide citizens of the State." Second, they argued, given that "we are taxed to support the Government of the State of Arkansas, we respectfully claim the right to be represented in the Gov- ernment of the State." Third, they affirmed that the state needed educated labor and asked for schools for their children. The fourth appeal was quite simple: "As we are subject to law, we should be protected by law." Lastly, they requested redress of a regional problem: "Believing, as we do, that we are destined in the future, as in the past, to cultivate your cotton fields, we claim for Arkansas the first [*sic*] to deal justly and equitably for her labor- ers." Leading the South in just treatment of laborers was a goal for which there was no competition.[14]

William H. Grey, a businessman new to the state, spoke to a change among freedpeople on realizing their freedom—abandoning dissembling for whites—and anticipating a figure of speech foundational to postslavery Black literature, most notably in Paul Laurence Dunbar's poem "We Wear the Mask" (1896): "True, they had always been accustomed to hear their ad- vice received respectfully, in short monosyllables—yes, sir, massa; or no, sir, massa. They never once dreamed that under this seeming respect there was a human soul, with a will and a purpose of its own. We have now thrown off the mask, hereafter to do our own talking and to use all legitimate means to get and enjoy our political privileges. We don't want anybody to swear for us or to vote for us; we want to exercise those privileges for ourselves." Grey also struck an evocative note from the discourse of Delta political activism, a response to the "go back where you came from" rhetoric of conservatives who saw no use for African Americans who wanted more than to serve as a supine labor force: "Here we have lived, suffered, fought, bled and many have died. We will not leave the graves of our fathers, but here we will raise our children; here we will educate them to a higher destiny; here, where we have been degraded, will we be exalted—*Americans in America, one and indivisible.*" Many did stay. Yet ten years later many of the unprotected, terrorized rural Black Arkansans would be meeting locally and with organizers in New Orleans about how to migrate west or to Africa. By the late 1870s, many would travel west with all their portable belongings as part of a sizable Exoduster movement or east to the Mississippi River in Liberia emigration movements. Many more would try to leave without success in that period.[15]

How Much Freedom for Them Is Good for Us?

In stark contrast to freedpeople who sought to be in charge of their lives for the first time, whites of various classes took the position that *they* should be able to decide which of these ordinary rights should be held by freedpeople. Many who had held enslaved people, and some who feared having Blacks as equals even at the bottom of their agrarian society, could not accept that Blacks were now citizens and therefore should have the right to live free from violence in a workplace; free from impulsive violence for exercising the First Amendment freedom of speech; free from violence for using the First Amendment right to assembly; and free from being fired and evicted for petitioning the government for redress of grievances. There was openly aired concern that freedpeople were using the Second Amendment right to have arms and operated as if they should be able, according to the Fourth Amendment, to keep rifles in their homes free from nighttime raids in which unlawful search and seizure were used to take arms kept for hunting and self-defense. The idea that Black people had a right to live without their "persons, houses, papers and effects" being harmed or stolen was a new thought.[16]

More alarming to many were assumptions in the US Constitution that persons of color could expect to be able to testify against whites who had done them harm, or that they could testify against whites whom they had witnessed harming others. They also held that Black people had the right to serve on juries or to sue whites in civil court. And worst, with the vote, Black Arkansans might choose the state's leaders and seek and obtain office themselves. Indeed, these were points of alarm across the white South.

Many scholars have cited documents in official records and local newspapers detailing prevailing stereotypes and racist jargon concerning Blacks being lazy, unmotivated to improve their circumstances, immoral, disrespectful, and even savage as reasons that planters fought to keep the right to whip workers and others fought against Black children attending the same plantation schools with white children. Moneyhon, for instance, lists contemporary prejudices followed by a comment: "These racial attitudes created the framework within which whites developed their own beliefs about what freedom should mean for the freedmen." The phrase "what freedom should mean for the freedmen" eliminates the assumption that it *would* mean what it meant for most people in their time. The phrase "for the freedmen" becomes the new iteration of identifying different forms of citizenship among American citizens, elaborating difference named earlier in federal law by gender and property; the new phrase cited free citizens as people of a given race. While Moneyhon's statement is true, it fails to examine the southern preoccupation with the idea that only whites *should* decide the parameters of Black freedom. Freedpeople were seen by mainstream southern culture primarily in terms of their usefulness to others, not themselves. Beyond the stipulation of white privilege in a slave system society, the focus on white prejudicial language obscures the fear of the powers of citizenship rights that should have come to Blacks with abolition: the real exercise of citizenship rights quite obviously would upend the historically unchallenged exploitation of the African American population. Since it was not in fact the job of white society to limit the rights of citizens who were not white, they sought other (not explicitly racial) legislative language with which to exercise that extraconstitutional control. Sadly, this is a tactic that still has currency in some quarters.[17]

Federal officer General James Brisbin reported the following to the Thirty-Ninth Session of Congress: "I think many of the people entertain the belief that if the State was once more in operation under a State government . . . they could then regulate the black population by a system of vagrant laws amounting to slavery." Arkansas and many southern states did exactly that. Powell Clayton (governor from 1868 to 1871) later recalled that in 1866 the planter elite had a plan to run the state as they pleased under control of the provisional Unionist government headed by Isaac Murphy. They aimed to placate the Republicans in the US Congress with a policy of electing senators and congressmen who were reliable secessionists but not well known as such. They succeeded in dominating the elections, and yet to get their congressional choices accepted by the US Congress, the members of the legislative commission who went to Washington had to plead with state leaders on their return not to allow violence by white mobs like the riots that took place that year in Memphis and New Orleans. The argument against allowing a white mob riot was not for human decency or even public order but politics: "A Memphis or New Orleans riot would vitalize their [the Republicans'] party and prolong its existence." These men had good reason to be worried about attention-getting mob violence against Blacks. That year Arkansas went down in history as the site of one of the worst lynchings in US history. In May 1866, near Pine Bluff, unknown parties burned a Black settlement and hanged twenty-four men, women, and children in the trees around their burned homes. The incident remains remarkable for the fact that no one learned what triggered the massacre. But the commission's chief concern was that Norfolk had had an anti-Black riot in April; a mob in Memphis had burned an entire neighborhood in May, and New Orleans had a riot in July in which nearly fifty people were killed and another hundred wounded.[18]

In 1867, the US Congress passed the Fourteenth Amendment precisely because the dilemma of racism could not be waved away and because of the difficulties that southerners were displaying in imagining a southern world in which Blacks could assume the freedoms in the Bill of Rights and the Thirteenth Amendment and were deploying violence not being contained by the occupying federal troops. The more lasting and corrosive effect of the fear of full Black citizenship may have been the idea that members of one racial group, whether officials or ordinary voters, or ad hoc posses and nightriders, should determine how much freedom members of another race should have, despite any stipulations of law.

While owning and exploiting Black bodies had been a white privilege, it was a classed one. For those who had not owned human chattel, finding freedpeople eating, drinking, and dancing in the same saloons or dance halls exposed them to changes in working-class white privilege. The public leisure enjoyed by freedpeople was only one marker of change that sparked violence—there were armed Black soldiers with the victorious

Union troops occupying the South; missionaries and schools were educating Black children while poor white children had long gone without schooling (which had to be paid for), among many other changes. But now those Black bodies were not worth such amounts of money that a white man might get charged and fined for harming a planter's property. This change also quickly made white votes more important than ever before, both to their self-interest and to conservative elites who had likely long controlled their votes through clientalism. In 1867, with the passage of the Reconstruction Acts, the feds declared Arkansas's provisional government and constitution illegal, and the state became part of Military District 4, along with Mississippi. Only when required by federal law for readmission to the Union to grant citizenship rights to freedpeople did Arkansans rewrite their constitution in 1868.

Making Political Voice

The Emancipation Circuit in Arkansas developed along the Mississippi and Arkansas Rivers and in the southwestern corner along the Red River, a major thoroughfare between Texas and Louisiana. (*See the Arkansas maps [plates 2 and 3].*) While the Union League did not create the same kind of presence it had in places like South Carolina and Alabama, it was able to organize among Blacks in Little Rock and Pine Bluff enough to become a thorn in the side of the conservatives and white supremacist groups. "The conservatives charged that the Union League had extensive power, but Freedmen's Bureau agents found that it was only thoroughly organized around Little Rock," writes Moneyhon, adding that planters held sway in the countryside. But planters complained that many workers left work to attend a state Republican convention. "S. R. Cockrill of Pine Bluff complained to President Johnson that Republican efforts were preventing restoration of order in the work force. He concluded: 'The idea of *voting*, has had a most demoralizing influence.'" As in cases mentioned earlier, *demoralizing influence* probably should be read as *mobilizing influence*. *Demoralized* may have been a more accurate description of the planters' state. A Freedmen's Bureau agent said Blacks were "becoming quite enthusiastic and are getting rather over zealous in attending barbecues and political meetings . . . to the detriment of their crops."[19]

In 1867, African American males were able to vote for delegates to rewrite the constitution so that the state might rejoin the Union. As a result, 21,696 Black men registered to vote, and many participated in the vote for the constitutional convention. During Reconstruction the state had only one African American in statewide office—superintendent of public instruction Joseph C. Corbin (a former journalist with a graduate degree from Ohio University)—and managed to send only eight Blacks to the convention: two from the Helena area; two from Little Rock; and one each from Pine Bluff, Texarkana, Hope, and Lake Village in the Delta.[20]

The longest wrangles in the 1868 constitutional convention, both in debate and in maneuvers to shelve proposals, were over giving Blacks the vote and legalizing interracial marriage. Unlike some other southern states, conservatives in Arkansas did not have to fear a Black majority or the dreaded "Negro Rule." The African American vote in the state did not threaten them politically as much as it disturbed white supremacist thinking. Republicans were successful with Black enfranchisement—unsurprising since Black male enfranchisement was soon to be federal law. The debate still brought out their most eloquent statements while eliciting the most bigoted responses from conservatives. Interracial marriage was not only one of the first subjects to arise but also caused one of the first rifts within the Republican delegation because early on a white Republican delegate introduced a motion to prohibit it. The discussion prompted some to bitterly refer to the history of rape's prevalence in the slavery system and others to openly joke about white male slaveholders as fathers of biracial people. William H. Grey, who had worked riverboats and was an AME minister in Helena, opposed the measure with a facetious approach, after saying the prohibition was pointless: "I know that such provisions have heretofore more or less obtained; but while the contract has been kept on our part, it has not been kept on the part of our friends; and I propose, if such an enactment is inserted in the Constitution, to insist, also that if any white man shall be found cohabiting with a negro woman, the penalty shall be death." Amid the laughter, Grey's Republican colleague who had moved for the ban asked if the law was unnecessary: "Why in the name of God, do you object to having a line established . . . ?" Grey, a biracial person himself, couldn't resist saying the state would have to set up a board of "physicians or professors of anatomy" to determine the race of Arkansans to decide who was breaking the law. On another objection to interracial marriage, Rev. James White, who became a prominent Black leader during the period, weighed in: "When I look around I see an innumerable company of mulattoes, not one of them the heir of a white woman." A biracial person himself, White continued, "Gentlemen, the shoe pinches on the other foot . . . the white men of the South have been for years indulging in illicit intercourse with colored women, and in the dark days of slavery this intercourse was largely forced upon the innocent victims, and I think the time has come when such a course should end." The kind of rhetoric used by these two men, including the Black humor, was also part of the African American delegates' approach to this topic in other state constitutional conventions and later in legislative debates in several states.[21] Grey also engaged a bit of David Walker–style rhetoric on the subject of whether a conservative (who thought Blacks should never vote) might refer to Blacks as Negroes: "Grey . . . said he took no objection to the appellation; his race was closely allied to the race which built the great pyramids of Egypt, where slept the remains of those whose learning had taught Solon and Lycurgus to frame the systems of their laws, and to whom the present ages are indebted for the hints of art and knowledge."[22]

On the subject of Black suffrage and invoking military service at the birth of the Republic and the service of African Americans in the Civil War, Grey said citizenship belonged to Blacks: "It is ours, because from the Revolution down to and through the rebellion, we have stood unswervingly by our country and the flag. We fought for liberty. That liberty cannot be secured to us without the right of suffrage. The government owes the debt, acknowledges it, and apportions it out among the several states. We are here, sir, to receive the amount due us from the State of Arkansas."[23] Once voting became a reality for Black males in the state, Black Arkansans greeted the franchise with enthusiasm. Boston Blackwell, who worked for the Union army during the war and settled in Little Rock afterward, recalled "army men come around and registered you before voting time." In 1938 he looked back on voting for Ulysses S. Grant in 1868: "It wasn't no trouble to vote them days; white and black all voted together. . . . Gol 'er mighty. They was colored men in office, plenty. Colored legislators, and colored circuit clerks, and colored county clerks. They sure was some big officers colored in them times. They was all my friends. This here used to be a good county. I think it's wrong—exactly wrong that we can't vote now. The Jim Crow law, it put us out. The Constitution of the United States, it gave us the right to vote; it made us citizens, it did."[24]

The impact of voting had a broader reach than state officeholders, as Moses Jeffries attests, but like other survivors of the period, his recollections of voting were tied to the voter repression he saw. "The ex-slave voted like fire directly after the war," said Jeffries, who lived in Arkansas and New Orleans during slavery. Decades later he could list the names of all the Black men elected during Reconstruction, starting with education superintendent Corbin, and local officials from coroner, to chief of police, to every alderman in Little Rock, where he himself was an alderman. He named officeholders in other counties, ending his list with how a "grand-father law" restricted voting and crushed the Black vote. "Negroes were intimidated by the Ku Klux. They were counted out. Ballot boxes were burned and ballots destroyed."[25]

"I have voted," said William H. Harrison, of Forrest City, who, when en-slaved in Virginia, grew up with the William Harrison who became presi-dent because his slaveholder was a Harrison cousin. The enslaved Harrison was sent to war with the Confederacy as servant to his owner's son. By luck he was captured by Union soldiers, and spent three and a half years in the federal army, in which he also received some education. "I voted a Republi-can ticket because it hope [sic] [helped?] the party out that freed my race. Some white men told me they burnt up a lot of our votes. I never seen it done. I can't see to fool with voting." Absolom Jenkins, of Helena, said, "I voted a long time. The voting has caused trouble all along." Arkansan Frank Greene, who earlier lived through the Red Shirt violence over voting in South Carolina, especially during the Hayes-Tilden election, said, "I used to vote—the Republican ticket. We ain't nothin' now, we can't vote."[26]

In September 1868, the new Republican governor of Arkansas, Powell Clayton, first heard the odd name of a new organization showing itself through mysterious postings for meetings, strange costumes, and deadly intents. The Ku Klux Klan was founded across the river in Tennessee in 1865 by a small group of former Confederates. Nathan Bedford Forrest, the notorious former Confederate general, who was commander at the Fort Pillow Massacre, became the group's first Grand Wizard in 1867. Clayton, who was governor from 1868 to 1871, was a northerner and by war's end a Union brigadier general. He had led units at Wilson's Creek, Missouri, in the Battle of Helena, Arkansas, and defeated Marmaduke in the Battle of Pine Bluff. At the end of the war, he made his home in the state. Still, he was quite taken aback by what he began to hear of the KKK. In his memoir Clayton quoted a 1911 *Arkansas Gazette* article claiming the initial name of the group was "the Order of the White Man," and that the purpose of the "purely military" group was "taking law in their own hands for the preser-vation of a government by the whites."[27] In anticipation of the effects of the Reconstruction Acts, there was much violence in 1868, particularly against Black members of the Reconstruction political machinery.

Clayton was moved to declare martial law in November 1868 in five counties that were part of the Emancipation Circuit and in six that were adjacent to the circuit. *(See the Arkansas maps [plates 2 and 3].)* He had realized Klan members were not just "Democratic devices to intimidate the negroes and prevent them from registering and voting," but criminals committing "assassinations and outrages perpetrated upon Republicans alone, and in most cases State officials." The most famous cases among the latter were two white men: James Hinds, a US congressman who was killed in 1868, and Joseph Brooks, a state representative who was wounded in the same incident. Clayton organized a state militia and declared martial law in ten counties, a number that grew to include operations in a total of fourteen counties. He accused the white supremacist group of "assassinations, robberies, threats, and intimidations." In addressing the public on his decision, he enumerated roughly thirty-seven violent episodes of "recent months" in thirteen counties, from murders to running voter registrars out of town, that would have involved at the very least some sixty victims. One of the distressing elements in trying to piece together the harm done to Black people in southern states during this time (usually over voting or election organizing or as intimidation to prevent voting) was the habit of those who documented it, such as Clayton's sources and informants, to treat Black victims solely as bodies, in contrast to the obligation to account for every known detail in relation to the murder or wounding of white people.[28]

Clayton quotes, for instance, a detailed affidavit of several pages from a Klan member of the assaults and murders he committed or knew about, including plans to murder individuals (and death threats against members who did not carry out murders). But a report the arrested man gave of "raids" on what could have been dozens of freedpeople is worded as follows:

> I was in one raid just before the election in White County—ten or fifteen were in the party. The party went out about two miles, had masques on, pistols, etc. I think Russell was in command of this raid. We went to Bob Jones', called Coburn's black people and old man Holt's—we frightened them and told them they must vote the Democratic ticket and use their influence for it or they would be killed. One raid was made to Ed Robbins'. I was not along. William Sewell broke the door down with a rail, took pistols and guns from the negroes.

Though the larger number of the victims in his deposition were described as still belonging to or controlled by landowners—"Coburn's black people" and "old man Holt's"—they were visited for the same reason whites were killed or wounded: being regarded as willing to act on their own in an election. Yet documenting the history of Black struggle in the South after abolition is obscured by the continued postwar reference to belonging to a planter as the identifier of farmworkers. The difference made by abolition, of course, was that a posse could have a free hand to wield violence against the landowners' labor force, damage their homes, and seize their property. This is another reason it is not possible to count the victims in many of these reports.[29]

Clayton was able to provide names and details on the deaths of a number of African Americans, though usually these were incidents about which articles circulated the spurious claim that other Blacks had killed political organizers in their own communities. Black assassination victims such as Ban Humphries, Captain E. G. Barker, and Captain Simpson Mason, for instance, were named in local papers and accused of having been distrusted by other Blacks. Humphries was allegedly killed by Blacks for past duty as an enslaved servant with Confederate forces and possibly only pretending to be with the radical Republicans. Clayton quotes a Klansman's affidavit that Humphries was in fact killed "because he was a leading and influential radical colored man in the county." Barker, a Union soldier and a Freedmen's Bureau agent, was reported to have been killed because "he had the quality of making himself hated," and Mason because "he was a man of bad character, and we have no doubt the radical press and party will attribute his death to political causes." More relevant perhaps is that Mason worked with the Freedmen's Bureau and was voter registrar of Fulton County. (Voter registrars were prime targets in a number of states.) In these last three cases, Black people were charged with the crimes.[30]

The last case cited, the "assassination of Major Andrews, Lieutenant Willis and an unknown colored man," provided the following detail from an army colonel: "I found that P. J. Andrews, H. R. Willis, and one negro, name unknown, had been murdered. A coroner had held an inquest over the bodies of Andrews and Willis, but no inquest was held over the body of the negro." Both Andrews and Willis worked with the Freedmen's Bureau, and Hiram Willis had threatened local planters with a tax as compensation for damages from all the violence.[31]

Some remembered even more vividly the violence of the 1870s. Rev. Ellis Jefson of Hazen, who was brought to the state by his enslavers when he was six, along with his mother and sisters, remembered: "We had rebellions at Helena in 1875. The white folks put the Negroes out of office. They put J. T. White in the river at Helena but I think he got out. Several was killed. James White was a colored sheriff in Phillips County. In Lee County it was the same way. The Republican party would 'lect them and the Democratic party roust them out of office." White was indeed a sheriff that year and, in addition to having been a delegate to the 1868 constitutional convention, served twice as a state senator, was commissioner of public works, and was one of the few Black delegates to the 1874 constitutional convention the year before the incident. The violence of which Jefson spoke did not go away.[32]

Unlike some other states, which had their largest numbers of Black state officeholders in 1874, Arkansas's forces of repression stepped up their attacks at that time. In Arkansas, Black representation hit its high mark in 1873 when eighteen African Americans sat in the state legislature, fourteen in the house, and four in the senate. (See the Arkansas maps [plates 2 and 3].) In 1874, after a two-year period of chaos, Democrats took control of state government in the wake of a standoff known as the Brooks-Baxter War, in which two men claimed the governorship. In 1872, several splits had developed in the Republican Party, with the result that some activists were ready to make concessions to conservatives. There were the "regular" Republicans, known colloquially as "the minstrels," who did not put forward a candidate for Arkansas governor. Then there was a more radical group, known as the "Brindletail" Republicans, initially supported by Blacks and led by Joseph Brooks, a minister from Ohio and a former Methodist circuit rider in Virginia and Iowa, who became an abolitionist and served as chaplain with Black troops in the war. He was one of the wounded listed by Clayton in 1868, as he was shot during the assassination of Congressman James Hinds. The Brindletails decided to support the ticket of the national Liberal Republican Party and, calling themselves the Reform Republicans, put Brooks up as candidate for governor. Finally, there were the Liberal Republicans, begun by Republicans who wanted to make concessions with conservatives on issues like the right to vote for former Confederates. Their Republican candidate was a compromise figure, Elisha Baxter, a former slaveholder, Union veteran, and a judge at the time. The Democrats threw in with the Liberals reinstating the vote to former Confederates who had been disfranchised and ended up supporting Brooks. In the long run, that was probably the most important decision for retaking power in the state.

Brooks turned out to be someone who conceded too much to the Democrats. In a dramatic scene after Baxter was declared the winner, the Republicans repudiated their own governor and both sides literally set up camp, with militias. An amendment was passed to allow former Confederates the franchise, and the legislature came under conservative control. After two years of warring factions ended, in May 1874 President Grant recognized Baxter as governor, and the state came under conservative control for over ninety years.[33]

Despite the violence of 1875, ten African American men were elected to the state legislature, nine in the house and one seat in the senate, held first by John W. Williams, who died in office and was replaced by William Grey. Violence continued into the 1880s. Rev. Frank T. Boone of Little Rock compared those times to another state. He was born in Virginia and moved to South Carolina around the end of Reconstruction, where he did voter work, spoke at rallies, and carried Republican ballots to polls. He survived the Red Shirt violence there, which began in 1875 and continued through the elections of 1900.

> When I first went to South Carolina, them n——s was bad. They organized. They used to have an association known as the Union Laborers, I think. [The Union League, which had organized in at least seventeen counties in South Carolina, spawned several other similar groups when it left the state, including by 1875 a group known as the Laboring Union.] . . . I don't know's they ever had any trouble but they were always in readiness to protect themselves if any conflict arose. . . . It was a secret order carried on just like any other fraternal order. They had distress calls. Every member has an old horn which he blew in time of trouble. I think that same kind of organization or something like it was active here when I came.[34]

Violence attended the elections in the 1870s and 1880s. One reason for the renewed violence was that some counties that had had small Black populations were becoming Black majority due to the arrival of newcomers from elsewhere in the South. People were fleeing places like South Carolina as Boone did, only to find their increasing numbers triggering the same kind of violence they had fled. His observation that African Americans in his county perhaps had a defense group only points to the likelihood of sustained threats to Blacks in the state. At the same time, the new numbers allowed Arkansas to elect Black legislators surprisingly late in the century. African Americans had difficulties in working with white members of the Republican Party throughout the last half of the century, due to the turn-of-the-century "lily white" fever that struck the Arkansas Republican Party, and few Blacks could get on any slates. The party broke into formally segregated groups, with Blacks being the first to exit. Unlike Virginia, North Carolina, and Alabama, for example, Black Arkansans were able to continue to elect Black legislators in the 1880s and 1890s, with eight serving in 1887, ten in 1889, twelve in 1891, and five in 1893, the last year for Black representation in the state. Four of those elected in 1879 ran on the Greenback ticket, an effect of the farm populism movement growing among white and Black farmers, some of whom used the Greenback ticket to run people for office. The electoral wins may also indicate candidates' work to appeal to some of the unrepentant working-class conservatives; two men ran as Democrats (in 1879 and 1891). As the movement known as the Agricultural Wheel (founded in 1882) grew, Blacks joined, such that Kenneth Barnes reports that, in 1877, "Arkansas's Agricultural Wheel had become a biracial organization of the rural poor, and the organization grew rapidly in the state. By 1888, the Wheel claimed more than 75,000 members in Arkansas and had spread to neighboring states, swelling to a total membership of half a million. Two hundred of the nearly two thousand local Wheels in Arkansas were black."[35] But the African Americans who were elected in 1890 and served in 1891 saw the end of Black voting as that very legislature passed a law that would wipe out most of the Black vote by use of literacy requirements.

The Not So Sunnyside Delta Labor Site

At the 1868 constitutional convention there was one Black delegate, James Mason (later a state senator) of Chicot County on the Mississippi River, who sometimes voted with the conservatives. His story and that of his home are novel even for the South, but they suggest what happened in Arkansas over the course of the century. Mason was the recognized son of Sunnyside Plantation's second owner. Elisha Worthington, a white planter, maintained a long-term relationship with a Black woman, a bond that probably ended his marriage after six months when his wife left over unspecified "adultery." Worthington raised Mason and his sister, Martha, and sent them to Oberlin College, and also sent James to study in France. In the prewar period, Sunnyside was "the largest and most prosperous" operation in the cotton district, and Worthington increased its size, worth, and productivity; by 1860, the twelve-thousand-acre site had 543 enslaved laborers. Sunnyside produced seventeen hundred bales of cotton per year. When the Civil War fighting neared his county, Worthington took most of his enslaved workers and his livestock to Texas and left James and Martha in charge.[36]

Late in the war, both Union and Confederate forces plundered the plantations. When Worthington returned, his laborers were free, the price of cotton was sinking, and his lands—considered abandoned—were in the control of the Freedmen's Bureau. The place was converted to wage labor supervised by the bureau, but crops were bad in 1866 and 1867, and an ailing Worthington sold Sunnyside. When he died without a will, James and Martha went to court, along with the creditors. The plantation's successive owners let ideology get in the way of economics. The first owner after Worthington so ignored the bureau's management rules that the agent threatened to send in troops.[37]

During this time, the reputedly charismatic James Mason became Republican "boss" of the overwhelmingly Black county. He became postmaster in 1867, the first documented African American postmaster in the country, and was elected to the Arkansas senate in 1868. However, when Mason's appointment to county probate judge was countermanded in April 1871, he assumed office anyway. He assembled a militia and forced his replacement out of the county, as well as the new county assessor, a Black colleague of Mason's from the legislature. Trouble ensued for a year. He was accused of inspiring an incident called the Chicot Massacre in which three whites deemed responsible for the murder of a Black lawyer and friend of Mason were taken out of the jail and shot. Hundreds of Blacks then reportedly looted the town of Lake Village and terrorized people such that many whites fled the county. Mason remained a power in the county, becoming sheriff in 1872, but died in 1874. Martha succeeded in being named an heir to her father's land. Blacks controlled offices in the county until 1883, a time in which the Emancipation Circuit was being reduced by violence and intimidation to its riverside counties.[38]

Along the Arkansas River, African Americans were moving into the state from places as near as Mississippi and as far as Edgefield County, South Carolina, and setting up Black settlements, still in search of autonomy. Starting with the fall of Reconstruction in 1877, not only did African Americans move from farther south to Arkansas but others began to take interest in emigration to Liberia. In the late 1870s and the 1880s, the emigration movements for both Kansas and Liberia took hold in the state. According to Kenneth Barnes, "8,000 black migrants actually moved to Kansas in 1879 and 1880." Calling the figure "modest," Barnes says the numbers likely attest to the poverty of people who may have wanted to go and could not, rather than modest interest in emigrating. One possible explanation for the relatively close proximity in time of migration to Arkansas and the movements to leave the state is that the latter may have included people, particularly younger generations of a family, who had only moved to Arkansas a few years earlier and then opted to leave the state or leave the country.[39] Barnes reports that no state had more emigrants than Arkansas: "More than a third of all known black American emigrants to Africa [left] in the years from 1879 to 1899—despite the fact that Arkansas's black population was smaller than that of any of its southern neighbors. And for each one of the approximately 600 who left Arkansas for Africa, hundreds more applied unsuccessfully to go."[40] The counties people left from were near the cities of Little Rock and Pine Bluff and in more remote counties where drought, followed by heavy rain, and dropping cotton prices were real hazards, along with violence and intimidation.

By 1890, all but one of the counties on the Mississippi River were 75 percent or more Black (the exception was 50 to 75 percent Black); ten other counties bordering the river counties, and on the Texas and Louisiana borders, had 50 to 75 percent Black populations, and sixteen others had Black populations between 25 and 49 percent. According to Barnes, letters to the American Colonization Society in 1891 came from all the counties along the Arkansas River and a surprising number of counties where Blacks were in the majority.[41] During the same time, the new owners of Sunnyside made a series of novel and counterproductive economic decisions about farming. They bought it as part of a scheme for "colonizing negroes . . . to work plantation lands on the cooperative basis." When they came into Arkansas, two grandsons of John C. Calhoun got eastern backers because of plans for railroads. Trains were no small matter; according to John Giggie, until 1871, "people traveling from Little Rock to Memphis took a combination of stagecoach, riverboat, and train in a trip that collectively lasted up to thirty-two hours" (a two-hour drive today). But, of course, cotton, not passengers, was the priority for rail lines. Due to downturns in the economy in the 1870s, any number of rail ventures collapsed and no new tracks were laid in the state before 1875. John Calhoun explained his farming system to newspapers and an 1883 Senate committee on education and labor. He described his plantations as "independent and self-sustaining" communities with their own churches and schools but under financially centralized operation. (The Calhoun company in fact used sharecropping, rental deals, and wage contracts.) The "so-called negro question" was not a problem, he maintained; planters needed to urge Blacks to give up their idleness and work for necessities. He opined that African Americans "would not be able to compete with the Caucasian" for generations. But none of it worked;

cotton production was low, and in the early 1880s the railroads still had not gotten near the Sunnyside properties. By 1884, Calhoun was living in New York and making a name on Wall Street.[42]

In 1893, J. C. Coovert, a photographer born during the Civil War, came to Sunnyside and made a collection of photographs that would represent the Old South (and literally named such) long into the next century, despite the fact that the people photographed were freed thirty years earlier and the slave system had looked quite different in antebellum times and in various places. Most of the images show Blacks producing cotton. But images of enslaved African Americans had long been subject to the stasis that occurred when names, places, and dates were not attached to visuals, and this reality simply continued for freedpeople. At around the time of Coovert's visit, Blacks at Sunnyside refused to work for the next owner, New Yorker Austin Corbin, and left the area. In 1894, Corbin made a deal with the state to have prisoners farm the land through the convict leasing system. An average of 251 prisoners worked for the state labor camp at Sunnyside. A year later, the New York Times announced that Corbin had made arrangements to bring Italian immigrants to farm his land, an "agricultural experiment" that made the plantation famous. While the railroads and chambers of commerce wanted immigrants, many southerners were less welcoming, and newspapers even outside the state disparaged southern Italians, questioned the legality of the contracts, and exercised the habit of public epithets concerning difference. Corbin died in the midst of all this, and his creditors turned elsewhere, primarily concerned with progress on rail lines. Both of these experiments to keep Sunnyside alive had their origins in federal experiments described earlier to place freedpeople back on plantations rather than on small, autonomous farms, and, of course, convict leasing had been tried as well to serve the same kinds of large cotton enterprises. The idea to bring in Italians was also fraught with race-based ideologies both from people who advocated it and from people against it. The two sides only agreed that the much-vaunted white Anglo-Protestant roots of the American colonial settlers were superior.[43]

The second group of Italian immigrants to arrive became more disaffected than the first, and Corbin's heirs sold the land to famed Mississippi planter and future senator Leroy Percy, who was convinced Italians were superior to Blacks, and the experiment continued to fail. This time the Italians just moved out. By 1910, Black sharecroppers were working the land. Twentieth-century ownership of Sunnyside brought a long list of corporations, removal of rail lines, and a fire destroying many of the buildings, and the former plantation became a property of the New Deal Resettlement Administration. If one looks today for information on Sunnyside Plantation, there are many items to read—novels, histories, genealogies—as well as rescued sites, a local museum, and photographs, but only concerning the Italian immigrant story that began there in 1895. Despite its colorful, well-documented history, even the Lake Village historical marker that is all that remains of the actual plantation simply celebrates the place for the introduction of Italian immigrants into Arkansas life. Given that the place became a plantation in the 1830s, and was bought by Worthington in the 1840s as a farm of "2,215 acres and forty-two slaves," it would seem that sixty years of history and four or five generations of Black lives have held no interest even to the local residents who approved a historical marker.

Other than a wide shot of people picking cotton, later printed with the title "Dixie Land" written across it, for me, one of the most compelling of Coovert's photographs of this plantation is labeled "Sunnyside store, office and engine house." When enlarged it shows a train engine and one flatbed car with no walls, on which are standing what looks like a whole church congregation of Black folks, dressed up, women in crisp white skirts, and packed so closely together one would have to pray the train never moved. More information about what the image might represent simply makes it worse. At the beginning of twentieth-century, railroads offered cheaper fares "exclusive to blacks," as John Giggie writes, "usually on Sundays," and the trains were "often no more than an open-air platform" and "very popular." He uses the photograph as an example, renaming it as a photo of an excursion train. This was the beginning of "excursion" fares on trains. Imagining the figures in the photo traveling any distance on the flatbed as photographed is daunting. The photo, identified by the buildings it captures, is illustrative of the incidental inclusion of Black folks in peril in the landscape and, as well, an apt metaphor for the marginal place of slave system survivors in American memory. Toni Morrison has written eloquently and incisively about the noticeably reiterated presence of Blacks in the speechless, dimly lit precincts of our literature: "To enforce its invisibility through silence is to allow the black body a shadowless participation in the dominant cultural body."[44]

The Emancipation Circuit in Arkansas held on to Black legislative representation until 1893, and thereafter total disfranchisement kept Blacks out of statewide office for eighty years, until 1973. In the early twentieth century, Black folk who had not moved west began to move north.[45]

My great-grandfather lived in Arkansas and he was one of those "crazy n———s" who wore a gun all the time. Black people and white people were scared of him. In a picture he had, he and his wife looked like people from Pancho Villa's army, with the straps of bullets across their chests. The white people kept trying to take his land. When a group of men came to take his farm by force, he shot them all. That's how we ended up in Chicago.

—Henry Threadgill, interview with the author, New York, 2011

Looking at Table 11.1

Blacks in Arkansas were a minority throughout the state except in Jefferson County, where they made up 80 percent of the population. They were half the population of the city of Helena due to the wartime influx described earlier in the chapter. The state's diverse resources meant diverse forms of agricultural and industrial labor, from raising cotton and lumber to mining ores, raising livestock, and servicing tourism. So, it is unsurprising that the state had consistent labor activism and farmer populism. As shown earlier, it also produced many emigration movements, mostly along the water routes to the Mississippi. Here again, HBCUs were salutary developments from early freedpeople's schools.

TABLE 11.1 Arkansas Emancipation Circuit, 1870–1900

	Institutions Present							19th Century Activism
	US Troops	RR (1884)	Union League	AMA Schools	Local Black Press	Black Political Reps	Knights of Labor Groups⁺	
ARGENTA (NORTH LITTLE ROCK) GALLOWAY (LITTLE ROCK area) HENSLEY (LITTLE ROCK area) Pulaski County	+	+		+		+	1 M farmers 1 F mixed labor 1 F mixed labor 1 M mixed labor	Liberia emigration
Chicot County	+					+		Kansas exodus
Desha County	+			+		+		Kansas exodus
FORT SMITH Sebastian County	+	+		+			1 M mixed labor	
HELENA/ELAINE Phillips County	+	+	+	+	<u>1</u> 1900	+	1 M sawmill hands & cotton compressors	Labor Populism Liberia emigration
HOT SPRINGS (then in Hot Springs County) Garland County		+		+			1 M mixed labor	

(Continued)

TABLE 11.1 (Continued)

	Institutions Present							19th Century Activism
	US Troops	RR (1884)	Union League	AMA Schools	Local Black Press	Black Political Reps	Knights of Labor Groups+	
LITTLE ROCK Pulaski County	+	+		+	4* 1868 1869 1883 1900	+	3 M mixed labor 2 F mixed labor 2 M farmers & farmhands	Labor Anti–Jim Crow Populism Liberia emigration
Monroe County	+							Liberia emigration
PINE BLUFF Jefferson County ß	+	+	+	+	1 1900	+	2 M farmers & laborers	Labor Populism Liberia emigration

KEY: **Bold** = Site playing multiple roles on the circuit. ß = Black majority; unless otherwise noted, populations are for 1870.

RR = Rail lines.

Black Political Reps = Black representatives to the 1868 constitutional convention or members of the General Assembly.

Knights of Labor = Black assemblies of the labor organization. Most KoL assemblies were segregated by race and gender: white males, Black males, white females, or Black females. "Mixed labor" is a term from the Garlock data (see Table Source Notes) and indicates various forms of work, not mixing by race or gender. **Gender** is indicated here by M or F.

* Includes one Black Democratic newspaper.

+ There were also KoL associations in Jackson County and in Greer (Jefferson County).

SOURCES: See Table Source Notes (393–96).

CONCLUSION

What Lives On Is Black Political Thought

Biela's Comet . . . created quite a stir back in 1877, when some astronomers predicted that one of the pieces of the split comet would hit the Earth—nothing happened.
—Steve Katz, "Witness the Potential Return of a 19th Century Meteor Shower" (2018)

When Reconstruction was abruptly brought to its end in a political deal that assured the presidency for Republican Rutherford B. Hayes and conservative control of the former Confederacy, it brought the death of government defense and protection of Black citizenship rights. Those rights went across the horizon like Biela's Comet, with no fiery blow striking earth, no sudden, mysterious, biblical fires across cities and wilderness as attributed to Biela fragments in 1871. No popular imaginings of the omens or meanings. The disaster that occurred that year seemed only to affect Black southerners and the larger society moved on as if there were no consequences for the rest of the country. The bitter irony for the unfortunates then was that the dispute over the election returns in 1876 centered on the three states that still had federally enforced Reconstruction going on and an active Black electorate: Florida, South Carolina, and Louisiana. The tragic reality for the country now is that the disfranchisement models are being refashioned at this moment on a scale that takes in states across the country. The states once in rebellion had managed in many places where there was a Black majority to completely repress that vote. All the measures it took to accomplish the silencing of the African American electorate—from violence and intimidation to literacy tests, poll taxes, and grandfather clauses—would be held unconstitutional over time but the resulting disfranchisement remained.

Why? Southern conservatives had decades to continue wielding the silencing advantage of redistricting their legislatures and creating new counties to divide Black constituencies. Southern politicians started creating new counties and, in many cases, dividing those with dense Black populations from the time Black men began to vote. Mississippi created one county named after Robert E. Lee in 1866 and made eighteen more new counties by 1918. Arkansas created seventeen between 1867 and 1883; Louisiana created twenty-seven new parishes between 1868 and the early twentieth century; South Carolina named fifteen counties between 1868 and 1919; and Georgia made three new counties in the 1870s and twenty-four in the early twentieth century. A second wave of new counties were created during Jim Crow and as white supremacist politics were promulgated late in the century.

Why was that needed? The development of the Emancipation Circuit shows how dense political organizing, especially work done to register and mobilize hundreds of thousands of new Black voters, saturated rural and urban areas of the South where Blacks lived in significant numbers. How else might we describe a transformation in the southern electorate that resulted in the same year in which Black males got the franchise: Black majorities of registered voters in South Carolina, Alabama, Florida, Louisiana, Mississippi; over 45 percent of voters in Virginia and Georgia; 41 percent in North Carolina; and 35 percent in Arkansas? The percentage of Black males who were eligible to register and did so was over 90 percent in every state except Mississippi, where it was about 83 percent. These are extraordinary numbers for any American electorate.[1]

Looking across the second half of the nineteenth century, it is evident that the more kinds of organizing that occurred, and the more institutions built in a single community, the more lasting and diverse the activism traditions in that site. It is also clear that railroad construction played an important role in building Black political circuits, uniting rural and urban areas, facilitating communication and repeated mobilizations. Labor organizing is shown over time to be the most prominent form of organizing in rural areas, linked to political organizing and at the core of the most consistent organizing in the Black South. Labor organizing, which begins at abolition on an ad hoc basis and expands with the arrival of Knights of Labor organizers in the 1880s, also took place despite Republican Party pressure to desist. Due to these factors, rural areas have to be considered as vital to the progression of the southern electorate as urban ones.

The rise and decline of circuits in most states also demonstrate that some combination of factors at work in the geographical origins of the state circuits sustained their political structures when sites at the margins of the circuit came under assault. To survive, the last of the local leaders had to maintain some form of visibility and relationships with both national Republican Party people and conservative actors in the local political structure. Some who could not get elected otherwise switched to the Democratic Party. Most of the Black men who had held offices in their states and municipalities returned to their former work after Reconstruction if they were in a trade. If they were professionals who relied on local clientele, they often migrated elsewhere. Many died poor. Some had ties to people in the federal government and got wage work in federal institutions. Women lost standing in many of the churches that professionalized their ministries, and thus they participated in keeping labor organizations and benevolent associations alive and joined other movements that rose and waned, such as the emigration drives.

The idea of a national civil rights agenda akin to those pursued in the second half of the twentieth century seems to have taken root with the birth of northern-based national organizations such as the National Equal Rights League (1864–1915), which began as an abolitionist assembly in 1843; the first National Labor Convention of the Colored Men of the United States (1869); the Colored National Labor Union (1869–74); the National Association of Colored Women (1896–present), a merger of three metropolitan organizations; the National Association for the Advancement of Colored People (1909–present); and the National Urban League (1911–present), which also arose from the merger of three northern groups. Only the last three still exist. There were others such as the National Afro-American League (1890–ca. 1894), which became the National Afro-American Council (1898–ca. 1908), and the National Afro-American Press Association (1890–ca. 1909), which was formed by activist newspaper publishers and lives on today as the National Newspaper Publishers Association (1909–present). The impact of the *desire* to form a national agenda is more interesting than the specific contents of any put forward, though it is obvious that creating nationwide agendas limited their missions. It is worth considering a comparison of what national groups thought possible and what freedpeople tried to accomplish in their states—it is something like the difference between doable political realities and possible futures. A great deal of the thinking among freedpeople in the South—regarding issues such as legalizing female custody of children, legalizing interracial marriage, eight-hour workdays, punishing domestic abuse, reimagining legal punishment, or prison abolition—took a long time to seep into mainstream movements. Some of their ideas still prompt debate.

What were African Americans hoping to do with participation in governance in the South? Accounts of the destruction of Reconstruction have charted the rise of "lily white" fever among politicians and newspaper rhetoric about an apocalypse called "Negro Rule," as well as alliances between planters and poor whites to wage campaigns of violence to take control of the former Confederacy from those who might "Africanize" it. A white delegate to the Arkansas constitutional convention of 1868 objected to giving Blacks the vote, saying the change would bring an end to the "white man's government of our fathers, and an erection of an Africanized government in its stead."[2] As Du Bois relates, when Reconstruction was crushed in Louisiana in 1874, the state Democratic convention addressed a public that was by then a Black majority population as "we, the white people of Louisiana." Du Bois was at pains to explain not only that Negro Rule failed to arise but that it was not possible. Negro Rule or "black domination," as it was also called, was conjured as a strange mix of horrifying revenge fantasy and incompetent mayhem. But were the goals of freedpeople's constitutional amendments, proposed amendments, and proposed laws or actual legislation obscured by the fear of domination by the Africanizing imaginary? Maybe, but some of the laws passed stayed on the books long enough to prove beneficial to white publics, and these were maintained. Others were perhaps too farsighted by being too fair. Assembled in the following pages are some examples of attempts to make law that reflect priorities shown by African American lawmakers and their radical Republican allies. The number of instances and the people mentioned do not represent the full picture, as some of the debates are lost and other issues tended to get the attention of reporters' covering the legislatures. Still, we have clues as to the priorities and of the duration of some struggles, such as protecting the Black vote or ending the cruelty and misuse of the prison system.[3]

Removing Race from Citizenship

The actions of those elected men who tried to make or change law in the South are at least a clue to the nature of discussions in Black communities about changes that would most benefit the formerly enslaved and their children and descendants. The most foundational proposal made by the Black Republicans who sat in constitutional conventions was the removal of race from the states' legislation. In Alabama's 1868 constitutional convention, Ovid Gregory proposed repeal of any laws and regulations that used racial distinctions.[4] The Black delegates' opponents sometimes tried to substitute other qualifiers for voting and officeholding that would eliminate most African Americans, such as property and education requirements, and fought mightily to insert direct reference to race even in regulations governing the seating plan for men in the legislature. Though the African Americans' aim was surely to eliminate legislated discrimination, the approach was simply to remove race as a descriptor in the laws. Thomas Bayne, of Virginia, was like many delegates in these conventions in stating that he had pledged to the "people of his section that he would endeavor to aid in making a constitution that would not have the word black or the word white anywhere in it." If this was done without further elaboration, it would make everyone subject to laws on the books. The opponents of such ideas preferred explicit markers for the despised, sometimes suggesting language purporting to give reasons for public prejudice. Simply removing textual reference to race was only a start. James W. B. Bland, a delegate to the 1867–68 Virginia constitutional convention (and later a state senator), was thinking along the same lines with regard to gender. He suggested new wording for the preamble to the constitution that would declare in part "all men are endowed by nature equally free and independent, and have certain inherent rights." Bland said that as he recalled, "men" had previously meant only white men and suggested "mankind," which he said included women and children as well. Though the idea was rejected by some whites, his additional text "irrespective of race or color" drew objections from other Blacks, who feared using any ethnic referent was dangerous. The new wording was voted down. This issue of officials wanting to explicitly name those they wished to exclude from the polity or even from entering the borders of the country is today still a marker of a perceived political need to openly discriminate that speaks of their desire to shrink the American electorate to adherents of one ideology or another.[5]

Textual marking was even an issue personally for the delegates, as in most places both the records of the convention and the newspapers initiated a practice of printing a Black delegate's name followed by "(Negro)" or "(colored)"—a practice that persisted in daily papers for nearly a hundred more years. When this came up in the Mississippi convention, delegate James Lynch moved that the record also include delegates' hair color, jokingly suggesting a nonracial physical descriptor, and pointing to the mainstream view of whiteness as universal and not requiring markers. Whiteness was treated as the norm and was not noted in public documents. Even though the words *colored* and *Negro* were new usages triggered by freedom, they served the southern habit of letting no descendant of Africa go unmarked. Freedpeople understood the power of centering and normalizing whiteness and the dangers of being marked in person or on paper.[6]

In 1868 South Carolina delegate Benjamin Randolph, who was killed by the Klan months later, introduced a bill specifically outlawing racial discrimination, which passed. But many of the delegates across the South believed that removing the dreaded textual markers of race (and sometimes the phrase "condition of former servitude") was foundational to a universal citizenship. It was a position that left to individuals the daily battles for equal treatment and attempts to remove the structural supports of the slave system. In fact the delegates were, in many cases, fighting for unraced law but *not* for integration. Bailey writes of Alabama, for instance, that even "in the absence of antebellum slave codes, postbellum Black Codes, or late nineteenth-century Jim Crow laws, African Americans . . . saw their lives governed by a 'separate but equal doctrine' because too few lawmakers pushed for integration." He says that Blacks had been building their own institutions under the assumption that there would be no white support, adding that "they too had no appetite for integration." Bailey remarks that white legislators were already saying separate did not mean unequal and argues that Blacks were shortsighted in not seeing "they would be in no position to enforce the equality of the separateness." Hindsight tells us this was quite true, especially given the disfranchisement of Black voters, but it could also be argued that Blacks did not expect separate and equal and perhaps hoped their own institutions would do a better job, for instance, in educating their children. Still, Bailey's inference that intimidation in the fight for integration was the decisive factor may have been the case.[7]

When in South Carolina the problem of unpaid contracts for pre-1865 purchases of human chattel came up, the freedmen voted to void any such contracts. Delegate Jonathan Wright said, "It is our duty to destroy all elements of the institution of slavery. If we do not, we recognize the right of property in man." This is the unique prism through which freedpeople saw the diverse instruments of government, laws, contracts, and forms of debt that would interact with their vision of taxpayer-sponsored education for all youth, relief for the poor, hospitals for those with disabilities, and state militias to keep the peace. To achieve this complex of goals, freedpeople and their Republican allies felt they had to argue for the repeal of distinctions among citizens and, just as important, persuade the conventions to increase the size and complexity of government itself to serve all the citizenry. In order to prevent codification of Blacks as second-class citizens, radical lawmakers had to make an analysis of how to break the hold of a small white elite and raise a structural tide that could float all boats. This principle underlies the other areas in which they tried to make law, or make change through the courts.[8]

Land

People in different states came at the restructuring of the vestiges of the slave system from various angles. When the proposition for distribution of land to freedpeople was in the air, people in many places withheld services and agreement to yearly contracts in hopes of acquiring their own land. Some organizers, particularly in the area of Sherman's Reserve, like Aaron Bradley and Tunis Campbell in Georgia, organized resistance to the restoration of Low Country land to planters and northerners. In the reserve area, 485,000 acres had been distributed to forty thousand Blacks, who were driven off those same properties when the government decided to restore land to its prewar owners. The idea among organizers in a number of states was to find ways in which to break the stranglehold of large plantations and the few elite families who owned them by making land available in smaller lots and protecting average landowners from losing land or being jailed for ordinary debts. This obviously would aid poor whites as well. Blacks argued for land parceling on behalf of the poor of their states and the economic welfare of the states. To the extent that they succeeded in passing laws that protected family farms and ended jail time for debt, white southerners did in fact benefit. The administration of these changes just did not help African Americans to the same extent, as acquiring land remained difficult.[9]

By the time the constitutional conventions began in 1867 and 1868, most people had been informed that no land redistribution was forthcoming.

But both the idea of unclaimed land being held in various states and the realization that the government had at least *contemplated* land distribution remained in organizers' minds as a strategy to which they would return. In Louisiana, a state-run land distribution idea supported by Blacks did not make it into the constitution. In South Carolina, delegates proposed that Congress "be petitioned to lend the state one million dollars to be used in the purchase of land for colored people." And one delegate argued that one-quarter of the population of the state could be rescued from starvation by the purchase of 500,000 acres at two dollars an acre with the one million dollars. Such an arrangement would give 20 acres to families averaging seven members. As Du Bois reports, Francis Cardozo, South Carolina's Black secretary of state, did not believe in confiscation but avowed that the death of the slave system had arrived and "the plantation system must go with it." The South Carolina convention did set up a state commission to buy land and sell it to freedpeople, which Cardozo managed to accomplish to some degree.[10]

Nearly ten years later, while James T. Rapier represented Alabama in the US Congress from 1873 to 1875, he proposed Congress set up a bureau to make land in the West available to African Americans. He told the National Labor Convention of the Colored Men of the United States in 1869 that if Black laborers could "obtain the wild lands of Kansas or other new States, they can live and thrive there without paying tribute." In 1876, as the Exoduster movement was beginning to gain adherents, John H. Williamson, a member of the North Carolina General Assembly and a Black newspaper publisher, argued that the depth of racial hostility was grounds for a petition to Congress to set aside land in the West for African Americans. Had any of these ideas taken hold across the South, a foundation would have been laid for an expanding Black middle class. In fact, the changes that were made likely helped more poor whites to hold on to land simply because more of them already owned land, and laws were passed that ended imprisonment for debt.[11]

Labor

Freedmen's Bureau complaints constituted a continued regional protest against violent assaults on workers, denial of wages, and harsh work conditions, as well as any situation that could be construed as a reimposition of any slave system conditions. Those complaints are also the plainest evidence that most people running farms just tried to operate them as they had when slavery was legal. In the constitutional conventions, Black delegates fought for labor regulations and fixed minimum wages that did not pass. Again, the introduction of minimum wages for unskilled labor would have aided all of the poor, mitigating the severely uneven economy in southern states. Black legislators in Florida made tireless attempts over several sessions to get bills passed to protect laborers, primarily from employers failing to comply with labor contracts. At least one such bill was countered by a bill to deduct a month's pay for a worker missing a single day of work. One or two weakened bills were passed. After the first of these, workers complained so bitterly that legislators started over with new proposed bills. In Georgia, state senators Aaron Bradley and Henry McNeal Turner advocated for an eight-hour workday, and in North Carolina, Abraham Galloway, as a state senator, helped try to get a ten-hour workday passed. As shown earlier, workers in Florida on their own actually succeeded in getting a ten-hour workday. Peter O'Neal, also of Georgia, proposed a bill in 1870 to "ensure payment of wages due agricultural workers." Radicals in Virginia put forward legislation to ban the firing of any employee for his or her political opinions, no doubt a reaction to the firing of 150 iron mine workers for voting Republican in the first elections that included Black voters.[12]

Cyrus Myers moved in the 1868 constitutional convention in Mississippi to provide pensions for slavery survivors, a lifesaving idea that did not pass. The previous year Alfred Strother of Alabama had proposed payment of back wages for all people in the state emancipated on January 1, 1863. It was agreed that employees could only ask for them. Delegates in South Carolina also asked for back wages from emancipation and, in the case of tenant farmers, the award of an extra one-half crop. Any structure for compensation for labor since 1863 would have created more landowners, more proprietors of business, and an educated younger generation, as putting up cash stakes made land purchase easier and could provide supplies for farms or businesses, as well as school fees. As reparations were first conceived as payment to planters for lost property in humans dating to emancipation, it would have made sense in the 1860s to compensate the primary victims of the slave system for the loss of the few years when they might have begun earning wages. People likely would have accepted a smaller investment rather than holding a sustained argument of the race's investment in the entire building of the country's economy. The arguments about the enslaved investment in the southern economies were, in fact, made by many ordinary people, especially in mass meetings. Freedpeople readily reeled off the facts concerning the sale of their children to purchase land or pay debts. When these claims were heard in mainstream society, they were ridiculed in the Democratic press. In the 1870s, when it appeared that the Georgia legislature would not act on behalf of labor, Jefferson Long and Turner tried to build a state Black labor union to force changes.[13]

Women

The aims of Black delegates and legislators also included the striking presence of legislative cases made for female suffrage, support for children of concubinage, raising the age of consent, legalizing interracial marriage, and inheritance across racial lines to protect women who had been concubines and might be beneficiaries of homes or funds. Custody cases also reveal male testimonial support in cases where women sought child custody and head-of-household status. As discussed earlier, freedwomen also addressed the state for justice in cases of politically motivated sexual violence and to honor partnerships with soldiers through claims to the government for widow's relief benefits, and many of the latter cases were successful. Freedmen's Bureau complaints also constituted a continued protest from women against any abuses in workplaces or in domestic life.

Henry McNeal Turner of Georgia introduced a bill during his tenure in the General Assembly (1868–70) to give women the right to vote. During the same two years, Galloway also supported woman suffrage in North Carolina. Advocating for woman suffrage was a logical position for men like Galloway who had worked with abolitionists and feminists, and yet their ability to serve in this capacity due to the granting of Black male franchise had caused a split among their one-time white feminist allies. Black male voting had divided suffragists, some of whom argued that woman suffrage should come first. Neither change, nationally or in southern states, would have enfranchised southern Black women once repression of the Black vote began. The split that occurred in suffragist meetings starting in 1868 brought to the surface both promoters of educational qualifications for voting (which would have also disadvantaged Black women), and revealed the promoters of Black inferiority among suffragists, which had a devastating effect on many Black activists. So Turner and Galloway's support of universal female suffrage speaks well of their attention to the logical argument that the reasons for enfranchising men applied to women, and to their intention to make the effort on behalf of freedpeople, however futile. Had they been successful, of course, the political import in their states would have been enormous, in the short term doubling the Black vote and putting pressure to expand the electorate elsewhere. One can imagine other gains as well, but surely they knew they were simply arguing the meaning of equality.[14]

Turner also introduced legislation intended to protect married women from domestic violence. One of the documented revelations of the early efforts of outsiders to encourage marriage and promote filing complaints with the Freedmen's Bureau about violence was that the bureau received many complaints of domestic violence. Legislators like Turner were perhaps aware that Black family relations were not regarded as deserving equal treatment as white relations (though the law was not good for white women, either). The first time a court in this country denied the right of a man to beat his wife was in Alabama in 1871, in the *Fulgham v. State* case, brought by a Black woman. As Margo Mahan writes, "A few months later, Massachusetts did the same. However, the Supreme Court of North Carolina undermined that ruling. And it was not until 1882 that any state outlawed domestic violence, when Maryland made it punishable by forty lashes or a year in jail." Mahan argues that the commonly held narrative that domestic violence laws were prompted by the northern women's movement obscures the southern origins of the first rulings validating women's charges but also elides the role of race in the court decisions and applications of such law. "The problem with assuming that early wife-beating laws originated from feminist agitation is that any inquiry at the intersection of race, class, and gender in the nineteenth century necessitates close consideration of regional variation."[15] What possessed Turner beyond the awareness that violence against women went on in his midst? Again, I can only conjecture that he saw violence against women in freedom through the lens of the unchecked violence of the slave system, as a tool to crush human will.[16]

In 1867, delegates in the Alabama constitutional convention barred the seizure of a married woman's property for a husband's debts; the following year the South Carolina constitutional convention passed similar legislation, as well as providing the state with its first divorce law. After the Civil War, roughly 5 percent of the US population was divorced. Again, divorce was a right embraced by early feminists and some in the abolitionist community because marriage at the time gave men such extensive rights over a woman's body, labor, property, and personal agency. It is easy to imagine Black southern support for the ability to dissolve marriages created by the slave system. Both Black women and men had good reason to support accepting state-sanctioned unions and for supporting a means to sever those ties as well. Newly freed women who were capable and determined to be self-sufficient heads of households were being pushed toward marital ties by missionaries and others, and some also found themselves in partnerships arranged by enslavers only to realize the possibility of reuniting with partners and children from earlier years, or meeting others. Both state and government agencies such as the Freedmen's Bureau tried to force men into patriarchal financial responsibilities despite whatever number of families the slave system may have forced them to form. One can surmise that permitting divorce may have helped to end the iron grip of patriarchy over the marital connections that had ensured ownership of land and human chattel. As such, it was a blow to the structural hold the old system had on huge parcels of land in the South.[17]

In 1877, Willis Dunn, a representative in the North Carolina House, tried unsuccessfully "to amend state law to prevent young black women from being apprenticed" to former enslavers. Some form of compulsory apprenticeships lived on in North Carolina until the twentieth century. This attempt to free young Black women to stay with their families was a much needed reparation for the health of the affectionate life of African American families, for the number of hands on a Black family's farm, and probably of most importance to the lawmaker, to protect daughters of Black families from sexual exploitation and other forms of violence still prevalent on southern plantations.[18] In the 1880s, James O'Hara, a US congressman representing the Black majority counties in north-central North Carolina, endeavored to get relief for dependent parents of deceased Black Civil War soldiers. He also introduced a federal bill barring any form of discrimination based on gender. This was crucial to all women seeking industrial work and Black women in particular, who were kept out of many factories—which paid better than farm labor—except for occasional janitorial types of work. Woman suffrage was again raised in the South, this time in the 1895 South Carolina constitutional convention, supported by Thomas Miller, who had served in the South Carolina House and Senate and in the US Congress in 1889. These actions are a logical extension of the early attempts by Black legislators to have an unmarked citizenry, and aiming for universal rights continually pushed them toward progressive proposals. If one looks at the fact that it took some eighty years for a bill like O'Hara's to become federal law, and how much longer equal pay provisions have been fought (especially considering the 1938 Fair Labor Standards Act did not cover agricultural workers and domestic workers), one can see the significance of the vision provided by wanting to rid society of the remnants of the worldview ingrained by the country's slave system. One can even regard the fixes that came with the Civil Rights Act of 1964 and the Voting Rights Act of 1965 to nondiscrimination law such as the 1963 Equal Pay Act (and perhaps even the Lilly Ledbetter Fair Pay Act of 2009) as legacies of people who knew the slave system and knew women workers to be equals in that work.[19]

Self-defense

Black communities all across the South seem to have maintained their right to defend their homes from the time of flight from plantations during the war. It is not possible to document the numbers of officials who, under threat, lived with guards or arms in their homes, but evidence indicates that many had to do so. Some organized resistance to KKK terror, such as Aaron Bradley of Georgia and the people of Wilmington, North Carolina, who did so successfully in the period after Blacks gained the vote. In 1869, Abram Colby, a former Freedmen's Bureau agent and a Georgia state representative, was stripped and beaten by thirty Klansmen at his home in front of his family for going to the new capital in Atlanta to seek protection for Blacks from such terror. He testified to the congressional committee investigating Klan terror campaigns that he was most disturbed that a gun was pointed at the head of his young daughter for begging them not to take him away, and reported that she never recovered from the trauma. Many other officials also testified before the Klan violence investigation, as did numerous ordinary citizens who testified on violence in the late 1870s in hearings on Black flight to Kansas and other states.[20]

In Alabama, people in the Black Belt organized as well, but early on. Even during the Union military occupation in Montgomery, they were subject to roving bands randomly shooting freedpeople. A radical white delegate to the Alabama constitutional convention in fact tried to add to the federally imposed restrictions on voting rights for former Confederates a proscription from voting or holding office for those who had killed Black people in the two years since the end of the war and requiring them to accept by oath the "civil and political equality" of all citizens. This was a salutary gesture that envisioned a politics in which open murder of the formerly enslaved should bar participation from governing but one that could only be regulated by accepting testimony from Blacks, which itself was a change freedpeople had to make throughout the South. In fact, Blacks testifying against whites (and Black lawyers recognized in courts) did not really begin in the South until the mid-twentieth century. So, the idea of disfranchising people who killed African Americans was an innovative move given that in 1868 Blacks in Alabama had no other recourse for holding people accountable for the murder of African Americans. Freedpeople continually addressed the state and federal government for protection from and punishment for the violence owing to their helplessness in seeking justice at the local level.[21]

Securing, Expanding, or Saving the Black Vote

Often the first discussions at the constitutional conventions concerned defining the new electorate, a topic that caused many a southerner to vent about allowing Blacks to vote (though they had no choice because federal law required it). They held that Black voters would rain destruction down on white people or, in some cases, what they termed the *white state*. In Georgia, Black delegates were probably tricked as they tried to ensure an end to discrimination in general and specifically in the right to vote. When nearly every Black who had won a seat in the legislature was later expelled from that body, it was done on the excuse that the constitution did not grant Blacks the right to hold office. Though the excuse for exclusion was absurd, it took two years and action from Washington for these legislators to regain their seats, and several of them died before the issue was resolved.[22]

In Florida, a split in the convention among whites competing for control resulted in the production of an 1868 constitution that gave the governor extraordinary powers and skewed the district lines to minimize Black representation and produce a government controlled by planters and rural white voters. The damage done to Black representation was, in a sense, permanent. After that year, the state only made new constitutions in 1885 and 1968, and major changes—negative and positive—to Black access to the vote occurred in both cases. In 1885, Blacks attempted to amend a formula favoring white majority counties and were rewarded with poll taxes that disfranchised the majority of Black voters. Three years later, new provisions were legislated to further tighten the snare for the few Black voters managing to vote, and Black voting ended along with voting by many poor whites. In 1968, legislators had to come to grips with the 1965 Voting Rights Act. Battles over the district lines and the Black vote simply continued.[23]

Galloway, as a member of the judiciary committee and the commit-tee on local government at the North Carolina constitutional convention, tried to see that judges were elected rather than appointed by the governor. In Florida's constitution, which was completed three months earlier, the governor's extraordinary powers included naming judges. Given the gen-tleman in the job in Florida, Galloway may have thought his state would fare better with voting for judges. At least electing judges provided public recourse for getting a harmful judge removed. This discussion occurred elsewhere as well and marks the preference many freedpeople seemed to have to battle discrimination in the courts in the public eye, even with the risk of failure, rather than create a system of a few men with a debt to the governor. In the case of North Carolina, where state legislators had long schemed to use the criminal justice system to disfranchise Black men, Gal-loway was responding to charges that some judges were alleged to have imprisoned Black men purely to keep them from voting. In Mississippi in 1868, Matthew Newsom, delegate to the constitutional convention and later a state representative, anticipated tactics to limit the Black vote and proposed a bar on poll taxes. As mentioned previously, Thomas Miller of South Carolina, one of the last remaining Black representatives in the South, supported woman suffrage in the 1895 constitutional convention and also fought (unsuccessfully) the disfranchisement of Blacks, which moves in that context would seem to have been complementary efforts to save representation of a vast swath of the state population.[24]

Criminal Justice

In one of the first mass meetings in Georgia after passage of the Recon-struction Acts, Blacks petitioned for an end to corporal punishment. Though this was surely meant for any situation, employment as well as criminal punishment, it shows an early intent to seek legislation to end another of the foundations of the slave system. Black legislators also had an abiding interest in reforming the prison system. Because jails were being used to create forced labor, there was a demand from conservatives for more of them in the 1870s, as Du Bois put it, "beyond the natural demand due to the rise of crime." The legislature voted to approve a convict leasing contract made by Governor Rufus Bullock in 1869, which started the state-wide system that allowed the state and private companies to profit from the convictions of Black people for at least the next twenty-eight years, and—as shown in chapter 6, on Georgia—Black women were leased for at least two years after the state outlawed subjecting women to the convict leasing system. James Rapier of Alabama worked on the state and federal level to end convict leasing, as did James Blue in the Georgia House in the late 1870s. Peter O'Neal, of Baldwin County, in Georgia's Black Belt, one of the original legislators expelled in 1868, introduced a bill in 1870 to abolish the prison system. James Simms led the efforts of the Black delegation to get better treatment for prisoners and obtain more pardons. Turner introduced bills to establish a state police, as the state militias were often composed of many who participated in terror campaigns against African Americans, and he moved to provide chaplains for convicts, which would also have allowed ties between prisoners and community.[25]

In the 1870s, Stewart Ellison, a state representative of North Carolina, introduced a bill to end the whipping of prisoners. The bill failed to pass. This practice did not finally end until the 1968 case of *Jackson v. Bishop*, involving the Arkansas State Penitentiary. As shown earlier, freedpeople had been staging impromptu protests over the whipping of prisoners since the end of the Civil War and as a regular routine had assembled at local jails in an attempt to prevent extralegal violence against Blacks who were jailed, especially under inflammatory charges.[26]

Civil Rights

African Americans fought for civil rights bills more or less continuously from abolition. Some bills were passed during the Reconstruction period, including one passed by the US Congress, and generally they were later repealed. Those who worked on the federal Civil Rights Act of 1875, which was greatly watered down in efforts to get it passed, included Congressman Rapier of Alabama and Congressman John R. Lynch of Mississippi. In 1883, it was voided by the Supreme Court. Congressman James O'Hara of North Carolina moved to revive it with an amendment to overturn the court's decision that was unsuccessful. (The federal Civil Rights Act of 1866, however, does still play a role in civil rights litigation today, though, as mentioned earlier, it requires individuals to find the wherewithal to pursue their rights through the courts.) What *civil rights* included in most cases in the late nineteenth century was simply freedom from discrimination in the exercise of citizenship rights, but such bills inevitably specified equal access to public accommodations. Aaron Bradley fought for similar rights in Georgia, and he wrote the declaration of rights in the state's constitution that provided for "equal protection" of the laws. Representatives from urban centers fought for unfettered access to streetcars and places of public entertainment, and people in most states tried to end segregated cars on trains crossing larger areas. Still, for rural people, civil rights needed to include very basic assumptions for most citizens: the right to raise one's own children, testify in court, serve on juries, hold meetings in public space, and other issues not routinely associated with the twentieth-century idea of civil rights even though these rights were still at times under contest in certain places. In Louisiana, Blacks called for equal political rights, reapportionment for greater representation in the legislature, and return of children to parents who had been turned over to planters by judges in the black code "apprenticeship" clause.[27]

Mississippi barred discrimination specifically on means of transportation, and Republicans unsuccessfully introduced a bill to prohibit segregation in other public accommodations. In the legislature, then state representative Hannibal Carter led a drive for a civil rights act in the 1870s. (The former URCC speaker was later Mississippi secretary of state.) In Louisiana, P. B. S. Pinchback led the drive for a civil rights bill several times in the constitutional convention and in the legislature, finally getting it passed only to see the governor he and the other Black Republicans had supported refuse to sign it. In Georgia's constitutional convention, Turner was lead advocate for civil rights.[28]

The right to marry across racial lines was usually hotly contested by conservatives. In the Alabama House, John Carraway spoke against the existing ban on interracial marriage. His approach showed clearly that past practice was to punish only Black people for violating the law; to drive home the point, he suggested penalties for whites, including imprisonment. He pushed another law compelling any white man identified as living with a Black woman to marry her. The convention decided it was unnecessary to make law on the issue at that time. (Interracial marriage was outlawed again after Reconstruction, and in fact, despite federal law, Alabama was the last state to remove its ban, which occurred in 2000.)[29] But Mississippi passed an amendment legalizing interracial marriage and also barred racial distinctions in the possession or inheritance of property. In the black code in that state, African Americans had been prohibited from owning homes in urban areas, and Republican "carpetbagger" Albert Morgan, who took advantage of the interracial marriage law himself, viewed the inheritance law as a possible boon for women who had been trapped in concubinage. Apart from the short-lived legality of interracial marriage during Reconstruction, it was not truly legal across the country until the US Supreme Court's decision in *Loving v. Virginia* in 1967.[30]

Education

A striking note concerning one of the first mass meetings in Georgia after the passage of the Reconstruction Acts was that the freedpeople there petitioned for the government to ensure the education of the "whole people" of the state. This was one of many iterations of the Black argument for public schools: that the education of the vast majority of citizens of the state would serve the best interests of the state. African Americans knew there was resistance among the elite even to educating poor whites and that their education would also help bring about the destruction of the old system. Blacks at the time also believed, like many after them, that racism was a product of ignorance. Some pointed out that Black and white children commonly played together as children, and to sit beside one another in a classroom would not be as uncomfortable for them as for adults. Once public schools were approved in the Arkansas constitution, Black delegate James White said, among other remarks, "That is the only way that these Southern people can be elevated. Were they properly educated they would not be led from any prejudice to oppress other men." A segregated system was authorized in 1873.[31]

Mississippi passed a provision for mixed public schools in the constitution. Louisiana authorized a public school in every parish, enrollment not based on race or sex, as well as a public university and a lottery to support education and relief for the poor. In Alabama a public system was provided by the constitutional convention, with integration or segregation decisions pushed off to the Board of Education. In Virginia, Bland introduced a bill ensuring equal opportunity for admission to any educational institution. But segregation was established in schools across the South, and though it was broken in the civil rights era, its vestiges are widespread. As a sign of the times, James Rapier, the US congressman, seeing the Democrats trying to take down the school system after they gained control of the state, proposed in 1872 that the federal government set up government-run schools with the words *United States* on every school and "a national series of textbooks." Again, a doomed proposal tells us something about Rapier's analysis of the conservative desire in the state to reinsert discrimination in functions run by the state. His proposal for federal schools brings to mind many of the other ideas from southern Black legislators that were meant to circumvent the overlap of white supremacist influence in various spheres of state service, whether the militias or contracting infrastructure construction. And it is significant that so early on Rapier realized the state-produced textbooks might be deficient in fair representation, a problem that still arises.[32]

Access to Health Care

In the late nineteenth century, African Americans continued to have to rely on their benevolent and trade associations for routine medical care. Some constitutional conventions did fund state-run hospitals for chronic illnesses. But with the closure of freedmen's hospitals set up by the Freedmen's Bureau, local people began a long struggle all over the South to get African Americans admitted to the few existing hospitals, especially those for mental illness. They were successful in some places, though care for mental illness seems to have been poor in most places. The South Carolina legislature founded an institution for people with sight, hearing, or speech disabilities in 1871 and also a hospital for mental illness, though it failed when white doctors would not treat Blacks in the institution mandated as integrated. The quality of these hospitals was likely very poor given the impoverishment of most state budgets and the minimal commitment to these innovative institutions, but the intention to include hospitalization and chronic care among government functions was important in assuring help for the entire population. One might also view this intervention from legislators who knew the slave system as a recognition not just of dire health conditions in postwar communities but of trauma. Virginia set up the Central Lunatic Asylum, a hospital for Blacks of "unsound mind," in a former Confederate hospital in 1869, and the state took over running it in 1870. "Colored asylums" were institutions called for and created by people who had seen the violent treatment of enslaved people with mental illness (Solomon Northup's memoir gives examples of this) who had experienced trauma in the slave system. Freedpeople spoke of trauma in testimony before senate hearings on postwar violence, some wrote about it in memoirs or autobiographies, and hundreds of slave system survivors documented it in Works Progress Administration interviews. But every community of survivors lived with past and present trauma in the home, at work, in church, and in funerals for those who died of the innumerable causes of death in the postwar environment.[33]

State Provision of Charity and Benevolent Group Aid

Radical delegates to conventions in most southern states fought for relief for the poor and at some points succeeded, even if the aid was short-lived. In Georgia, Tunis Campbell argued for such help for the poor, and Turner got land for an orphans home. South Carolina established a similar safe haven for orphans in 1869 and relief for the poor in 1870. Blacks in the postbellum period set up countless privately financed institutions for orphans, childcare, and education, some of which still exist. But the determination to secure such services with taxpayer funding was novel. In Alabama, John Carraway succeeded in getting an ordinance passed to turn over church property that had been used by Blacks when enslaved to those parishioners after their efforts with national church headquarters failed. Turner also advocated unsuccessfully for infrastructure improvements in Georgia to be made by the state rather than by private companies—what we would call today not only a job creation measure but one that he doubtless hoped would secure a hiring process freer of discrimination than the corporate process.[34]

Building Black Public Voice

Attempts in the 1890s and 1900s to build movements with national aspirations by first creating a national vehicle (with or without a mass democratic process) and then forging small meetings far removed from the founding vanguard brought increasingly mixed results over time, owing perhaps to the distance in time, place, and experience between those regional or national leaders and local voices. Southern members of these groups could only be active by way of the US mail; there were southern places where holding open chapter meetings of national Black groups with radical agendas was dangerous. Such groups, built on centralized, northern elite leadership, often failed to create grassroots structures after an initial representative-based gathering, which may have included some southerners. T. Thomas Fortune's National Afro-American League (1890–93) and its distinguished revival as the National Afro-American Council (1898–1907) are examples of two of the first attempts at national groups. Some used local chapters for financial maintenance without building mechanisms for the adoption of national goals with endorsements of local initiatives. Organizations that arose by merging regional groups, such as with the late nineteenth-century women's club movement, were more successful in sustaining themselves, the National Association of Colored Women's Clubs (1896–present) being a prominent example.[35]

Freedpeople did not merely create a Black public in the South, which did occur; they created a *mobilized* public. They did not merely create a public voice for Black people, which was necessary; they attempted immediate actions. The shared experience of the oppression of the slave system and creating a unified but heterogeneous Black culture within the slave system had already made possible an open space for the expression of an admixture of practices and traditions. It made for a participatory process that assumed mutual respect, publicly recognized suffering, and trusted in testimony about events not witnessed by everyone in the deliberative body. These are the foundations of the movement process as developed, sustained, and disseminated over the long arc of Black movement building.

The laws and provisions that freedpeople and their allies wrote into their state constitutions, passed in the legislatures, or tried to pass reflect the lessons learned from the slave system regarding the innumerable harms to human beings wrought by treating them as disposable property. Without necessarily being aware of the conditions in which other people toiled in the North, freedpeople and their allies assisted this society in coming to understand that people should not be physically assaulted in the workplace, beaten in their own homes, or deprived of humane work hours or leave for illness. They attempted to make changes so that women would have the right to be heads of households and have custody of their children, dissolve a problematic partnership, speak in public, participate in governance, own property, earn equal wages, and, along with all others, have equal protection under the law. They could see that such decisions were sought or acted on every day. Freedpeople saw that state and federal governments needed to expand their missions not only to help build infrastructure but also to aid in matters of public health, the enormous problem of sick and orphaned children following the war, and educating all the citizens for the sake of a more enlightened society.

These and other ideas articulated by the few people who had the opportunity to address them as possible legislative norms arose from a unique experience in which the four million freed by abolition, several generations in the South, experienced a deep immersion in the founding documents of this country and the rights of citizens over a short period of several years following the war. They benefited from discussions and debates regarding what the country should and could be in groups never before assembled—mass meetings of the formerly enslaved, classrooms of fifty to one hundred students of all ages, literacy groups in which newspapers were read to whole church congregations, small gatherings in remote sites in the woods that once held hush harbors. This immersion was accompanied by a sense of urgency that rarely sweeps across broad swaths of society except in times of war, epidemics, famine, or other disasters. These proposals arose from envisioning survival and better lives for children, new possible futures in a landscape of violent resistance.

The Emancipation Circuit was a regional movement embracing the South through which the four million emancipated from the slave system there sought to define freedom as a state in complete opposition to what became known politely as their "previous condition of servitude." It was an achievement in that it conceived of freedom requiring systemic changes of the hundreds of laws, rules, and customs and the commonly accepted discrimination that would continue as vestiges of the slavery system's legacy in this country. These people took into account all that they knew of the habits of mind of those who treated them as property. This circuit of communication and political formation was an achievement that emerged as a product of displacement during the Civil War and emancipation, created by people defined by overt fugitive status and characterized by the understandings people had that displacement and fugitive status provoked policing and resistance. In other words, the circuit was shaped by seeing freedom through the prism of enslavement, flight from slavery, and the new conditions of displacement and the statelessness that were the first realities of abolition. In this regard, these American forebears continue to inform a society in which displacement and disfranchisement mark whole populations, and statelessness recurs.

The construction of a circuit of political, social, and cultural action is also important in that the circuit proved both durable and renewable. The organizing knowledge acquired persisted in labor struggles, churches, and benevolent and fraternal associations that built systems for medical care, landownership loans, childcare for working families, and labor associations in a context of racism. In an era when freedpeople were being told to work hard and emulate mainstream culture without asking for "handouts" or becoming "dependent," they built institutions to help each other, to do on a larger scale that which had been done for fictive kin on agricultural labor sites across the South. As a result, the mobilization process adopted by freedpeople struggled to remain egalitarian and continue hearing all voices and testimony.

In community organizing among freedpeople social reproduction took place in the creation of institutions supporting autonomous families, and in the processes of creating institutions in an environment of policing and opposition that elided differences between the political and criminal, or action regarded as "offensive" in southern culture. Out of necessity, these are elements that proved durable and renewable in later political and cultural development. The means by which the people on the Emancipation Circuit struggled for citizenship and justice also immediately affected others coming into the country, immigrants who may have known nothing of the history of these four million whose experience forced the making of the Thirteenth, Fourteenth, and Fifteenth Amendments but that they would learn in order to become citizens. Organizing in the early twentieth century continued to involve whole communities and maintained the cautions of the past, as the dangers did not disappear. Survivors of Reconstruction nurtured the widespread teaching that one person's efforts matter and are part of what we now call long-term struggle.

Biela's Comet, which failed in 1877 to mark the loss of freedom, has not been traced in recent decades. The Great Comet of 1861 is not due to come by again for two centuries. And the Great Comet of 1860 is now understood to be a "procession" of things to watch out for—"earth-grazing comets." But the Leonids are different. During the war, Abraham Lincoln recalled his reaction as young man seeing the 1833 Leonid showers with people who thought the world was ending. He saw that the stars usually seen at night remained in their stations as the meteors fell and said thirty years later that was how he saw the Union surviving the war. A teenage Frederick Douglass, who saw the Leonids at daybreak, a time when many enslaved people might have seen them, writes of the meteors in his second autobiography as a "gorgeous spectacle." No fear inhabits his memory that "the air seemed filled with bright, descending messengers from the sky," as he took the sight as "the harbinger of the coming of the Son of Man; and, in my then state of mind, I was prepared to hail Him as my friend and deliverer." Harriet Tubman, who was about thirteen then, witnessed the Leonids and remembered that some people would not step outside to watch and that "everyone" thought it was the end of world. Because it was not, perhaps she cataloged the event as among the many unusual experiences she had from which others shied away. These people were incredible optimists, and though each struggled repeatedly with the darkness of collapsed horizons, their persistence marked the whole society.

Biblical fires are still with us, as well as floods and tornadoes, but they are no longer mysteries, are no longer seen as caused by stars falling from space. Our Old Testament–like disasters—simultaneous hurricanes rushing into the Gulf of Mexico, followed by others lining up from the old slave coast of Africa to cross the Atlantic, fires the size of major metropolitan areas—could be interpreted as generations past might have seen them. Epidemics are now pandemics, and only the cures baffle, not the causes. These disasters occur in many a week. The Leonids those generations saw are still with us; they remain visible in November every year. We have choices as to whether or not to take them with fear or motivation, demoralization or mobilization.[36]

> We do not know
> If any have reached that Canaan
> We have received no word
> —Sterling Brown, "Crossing" (1980)

NOTES

Introduction. Black Political Thought as Shaped in the South

1. King, *Why We Can't Wait*, 106.

2. Baldwin, *Fire Next Time*, 138–39.

3. "Malcolm X warns, 'It shall be the ballot or the bullet,' Washington Heights, NY, March 29, 1964," Malcolm X's Audubon address from archive.org, accessed August 27, 2020, http://www.vlib.us/amdocs/texts/malcolmx0364.html.

4. It is hard to convey the hunger that existed then for information, history, and art on various aspects of human experience such as the Black experience in the United States, and the Americas, the African diaspora, Asian American experience, sexuality (especially homosexuality), and a host of other subjects.

5. Davis, "Reflections on the Black Woman's Role," 81–100.

6. At the same time, I want to also alert the reader that I find the "long civil rights movement" can obscure the phases of the long-term struggle for universal human rights, of which many Black movements have played a part. I think specific terms—such as the 1880s streetcar integration campaigns—that do not limit the inclusion of regional campaigns can help to avoid the misapprehension that there have been long periods of uncontested stasis. The pendulum perhaps swings from the national campaigns such as the effort to get Black soldiers in the Civil War, or the drive for the Black vote, to the urgent and local or statewide concerns, such as asking Homer Plessy in 1892 to take a seat in a whites-only streetcar in New Orleans. He was backed by people who had tried the same thing decades earlier without getting a case to the Supreme Court. Two years before Plessy, Black women organized a streetcar boycott in Atlanta and beat Jim Crow there for a decade. When Ida B. Wells sat in a whites-only train car in Memphis in 1884, she was following on the heels of several other women she knew who had defied the law. Her case got as far as the Tennessee Supreme Court before she was denied justice. Before all of them, Sojourner Truth sued a horse-drawn streetcar company in Washington, DC, for throwing her off a car during the Civil War and she won. It was a battle fought intermittently all over for nearly thirty years before *Plessy v. Ferguson* gave us sixty-four years of Jim Crow streetcars and bus lines. The long arc to Rosa Parks starts in 1865 with Ms. Truth.

7. "By the middle of 1864, as Abraham Lincoln pessimistically contemplated his reelection prospects, nearly 400,000 slaves had rebelled against their masters and

gained a presumptive freedom within Union lines. Their numbers were greatest in the border South and Mississippi Valley states where northern armies had long been conducting operations, and, to a lesser extent, along the Atlantic coast. . . . Substantial sections of interior Virginia, North and South Carolina, and Mississippi; almost all of Georgia, Alabama, Florida and Texas; and sections of Tennessee and Louisiana remained in Confederate hands at least until the war's last months." Hahn, *Nation under Our Feet*, 82–83.

8. Camp, *Closer to Freedom*, 7.

9. McKittrick, *Demonic Grounds*, xiv; see also 9 and 1–35.

10. Foner, *Second Founding*, xxv–xxvi; Fifteenth Amendment to the United States Constitution, Constitution Annotated, accessed May 24, 2017, https://constitution.congress.gov/constitution/amendment-15/.

11. Wolin, "Fugitive Democracy," 43, 41.

12. Thanks to Emily Kristin Hartwig for telling me what I was saying.

13. While the agendas are more similar than dissimilar, I intentionally describe them in the plural, so as to avoid inferring that there was a single Black political agenda, in the sense of a unified southern or national agenda.

14. The term *matrix* here is used to mean "something within which something else originates, develops, or takes form," as well as "an array of circuit elements for performing a specific function as interconnected," per *Webster's*. My usage is meant to suggest both foundational tissue, or template, and a network conducive to organizing.

15. Walker, *David Walker's Appeal*.

16. Hahn, *Political Worlds of Slavery and Freedom*, 45; Kazanjian, *Colonizing Trick*, 2.

17. Gilroy, *Darker Than Blue*, 60–61.

18. Robinson, *Black Marxism*, 170. The Tutuola reference is to his 1954 novel, *My Life in the Bush of Ghosts*, the story of a young boy abandoned in a slave raid and left in a forest of spirits for many years before returning to the world of the living. The text was widely read in the 1960s by members of Black cultural nationalist movements.

19. The term *Exoduster movement* is used today to denote several migratory patterns starting in 1879, with thousands of Blacks moving from the South, especially Mississippi, Louisiana, Texas, and Tennessee, to Kansas. People also later moved to Oklahoma. Arkansas, which was at one time a destination, also had Exodusters leave the state.

20. On terminology with regard to those who fled to Union lines, I use both *fugitive* and *refugee*. The vast numbers of government and private documents referring to these enslaved people who were able to flee refer to them as *contrabands*. Occasionally, I do use the term *contraband camp* to distinguish those sites from

settlements or neighborhoods built in the same region by fugitives from slavery. I am aware of the objections posed by historians to replication of the term, which are obvious in its original use for property such as ordnance and even livestock. But historians are also discussing the word because a lot of people use it today. At a conference I attended on the "contrabands," I met only one descendant of those fugitives who eschewed the term. As a descendant myself, I regularly hear from people researching their families from the early date of entering military records afforded by fleeing to government lines. It has a specificity now that did not exist before due to a general lack of attention to freedpeople as central actors in their own freedom, which many descendants claim as a useful specific.

Chapter 1. Flight: Movement Matters

1. See Scott, "Common Wind"; McKittrick, *Demonic Ground*, xiv.

2. Perdue, *Weevils in the Wheat*, 115. On Whitman and the meteor: Kahn, "Solving Walt Whitman's Meteor Mystery"; Zielinski, "Rare Meteor Event." On Whitman, Thoreau, Melville, and the poem: Kent Ljungquist, "'Meteor of the War.'"

3. Goodheart, *1861*, 350. On Abraham Lincoln: John Kelly, "Solving Walt Whitman's Meteor Mystery," *Washington Post*, May 27, 2014. It was Walt Whitman who documented Lincoln having recalled during the war his sighting of the 1833 Leonid meteor shower: Donald W. Olson and Laurie E. Jasinski, "Abe Lincoln and the Leonids," *Sky and Telescope*, November 1999.

4. Mary Barbour interview, "Born in Slavery: Slave Narratives from the Federal Writers' Project, 1936 to 1938," North Carolina Narratives, vol. 11, pt. 1, 79–81, accessed June 5, 2013, https://www.loc.gov/item/mesn111/.

5. Perdue, *Weevils in the Wheat*, 50, 63, 74, 142, 199, 205, 213, 218, 250–52. Shackelford's name in census records is Keziah. *Grapevine* is a common African American term, dating to the slavery era, for the common wind among Blacks; a variation was the *grapevine telegraph*.

6. Susan Schulten, "Visualizing Slavery," Opinionator, *New York Times*, December 9, 2010.

7. Engs, *Freedom's First Generation*, 14–15; Berlin et al., *Free at Last*, 9–11; Goodheart, *1861*, 296–303, 312–15, 317–18. Thavolia Glymph has argued that these people should really be referred to as "contrabandists, active participants in the war and in their own fate, rather than as contraband, passive prizes of war." Glymph, "'This Species of Property,'" 58. The term has endured and is often embraced by their descendants, as they have told me, because it is well known. Glymph's term, *contrabandists*, is useful.

8. Those from states not in the Confederacy were technically still fugitives until state laws changed, or until passage of the Thirteenth Amendment abolishing slavery. Maryland ended slavery in 1864 and Kentucky, Missouri, and Tennessee in 1865.

9. McPherson, *Battle Cry*, 369.

10. Tom Robinson interview, Federal Writers' Project: Slave Narrative Project, vol. 2, Arkansas, pt. 6, Quinn-Tuttle, 61–68, accessed August 8, 2019, https://www.loc .gov/resource/mesn.026/?sp=66; Hahn, *Nation under Our Feet*, 83.

11. Clinton, *Harriet Tubman*, 152, 155–67.

12. McPherson, *Battle Cry*, 372–73, 377; Catton, *American Heritage New History of the Civil War*, 165; Rivers, "Florida's Culture of Slavery," n.p.; Ortiz, *Emancipation Betrayed*, 5–7;

13. Hahn et al., *Freedom*, 90–91.

14. Hahn et al., *Freedom*, 90–94.

15. McPherson, *Battle Cry*, 392, 418; Berlin, Glymph, et al. *Freedom*, 621–27; Pound, "Slave to the Ex-Slave Narratives," 168–69.

16. Hahn, *Nation under Our Feet*, 70, 73, 119; Cecelski, *Waterman's Song*, 44; Litwack, *Been in the Storm So Long*, 52; Ninth Census of the United States, accessed January 10, 2022, https://www2.census.gov/library/publications/decennial/1870/ population/1870a-04.pdf.

17. Hahn, *Nation under Our Feet*, 118–20; Hahn et al., *Freedom*, 625; Ninth Census of the United States, accessed January 10, 2022, https://www2.census.gov/library/ publications/decennial/1870/population/1870a-04.pdf.

18. Hahn, *Nation under Our Feet*, 72, 73, 75, 106–7, 119; Berlin, Glymph, et al. *Freedom*, 625–50; Hahn et al., *Freedom*, 396, 745; Bercaw, *Gendered Freedoms*, 42–43; Litwack, *Been in the Storm So Long*, 52; Frankel, *Freedom's Women*, 38; Taylor, *Embattled Freedom*, 87–89; Ninth Census of the United States, accessed January 10, 2022, https://www2.census.gov/library/publications/decennial/1870/ population/1870a-04.pdf.

19. Pound, "Slave to the Ex-Slave Narratives," 95, 97–98. Interviewers with the Louisiana Writers' Project, like some others in the Federal Writers' Project, commonly made judgments on the appearance, homes, demeanor, and attitude of interviewees. In this case, the interviewer commented that Cornelius "has apparently led a quiet and sane life, and strange to say, not in the least superstitious, having no belief in voodoo, not even being familiar with the name of Marie Laveau" (95). This seems very peculiar, both for judging her "sane" life and that it was odd she was not superstitious. Hahn et al., *Freedom*, 646–47; Ortiz, *Emancipation Betrayed*, 6; Hahn, *Nation under Our Feet*, 119; Ninth Census of the United States, https://www.census.gov/population/www/documentation/twps0027/tab09.txt; NPS Heritage Documentation Program's Cultural Resources Geographic Information Systems, http://www.nps.gov/history/hdp/exhibits/african/contraband.htm.

20. Engs, *Freedom's First Generation*, 67, 32, 52; W. L. Bost interview, "Born in Slavery: Slave Narratives from the Federal Writers' Project, 1936–1938," North

Carolina Narratives, vol. 2, pt. 1, 144, accessed June 5, 2013, https://www.loc.gov/item/mesn111/.

21. Engs, *Freedom's First Generation*, 30–31.

22. Downs, *Sick from Freedom*, 47; McPherson, *Negro's Civil War*, 143; Downs, *Sick from Freedom*, 47.

23. McPherson, *Negro's Civil War*, 142–43.

24. McPherson, *Battle Cry*, 497.

25. Taylor, *Black Woman's Civil War*, 37–38.

26. Glymph, "'This Species of Property,'" 61; Taylor, *Embattled Freedom*, 101–5, 119–20.

27. Cohen, *At Freedom's Edge*, 8, 9; Blassingame, *Black New Orleans*, 30–32.

28. Downs, *Sick from Freedom*, 47.

29. Others providing aid included "the National Freedmen's Relief Association, the New England Freedmen's Aid Society, and the Western Freedmen's Aid Commission"; McPherson, *Battle Cry*, 709–10. McPherson, *Negro's Civil War*, 137; Du Bois, *Black Reconstruction in America*, 77; Richardson, *Christian Reconstruction*, viii.

30. Establishment of the Freedmen's Bureau: Library of Congress, A Century of Lawmaking: U.S. Congressional Documents and Debates, 1774–1875, Statutes at Large, Thirty-Eighth Congress, Sess. II, Ch. 89, 90, 1865, 507–9, accessed May 24, 2017, http://memory.loc.gov/cgi-bin/ampage.

31. Engs, *Freedom's First Generation*, 21; Rose, *Rehearsal for Reconstruction*, 21–23; Lewis Lockwood, Letters to the American Missionary Association, October 10, 1862 (H1-4563); October 28, 1862 (H1-4575); January 6, 1862 (H1-4357), American Missionary Association Collection, Amistad Research Center, Tulane University.

32. Lockwood, Letters, AMA, January 6, 1862 (H1-4357). Amy Murrell Taylor, who documents the lives of a Black couple enslaved nearby, also shows her subjects often being evicted by the military from whatever lodgings they had found or made; Taylor, *Embattled Freedom*, 19–82.

33. Lockwood, Letters to the AMA, March 18, 1862 (H1-4400).

34. McPherson, *Battle Cry*, 497; Taylor, *Black Woman's Civil War*, 37–38.

35. Bechtold, "'Human Longing for Redress,'" 100, 103. For a related discussion of this legacy, see Saidiya Hartman's *Scenes of Subjection*, 121–24, 125–63. Hartman shows continuities between slavery and racialized freedom that act powerfully against genuine agency and will, deftly using "freedom manuals" dispensed by white groups in an effort to teach Blacks freedom as responsibility.

36. Bechtold, "'Human Longing for Redress,'" 103.

37. Kulikoff, *Tobacco and Slaves*, 329, 319, 329; Hager, *Word by Word*, 114.

38. Camp, *Closer to Freedom*, 12–16. As Bryan Wagner has pointed out, these southern plantation policing mechanisms not only were centralized and systematized, but after abolition they were publicly supported. See Wagner, *Disturbing the Peace*.

39. McPherson, *Negro's Civil War*, 135–36.

40. Walker, *Rock in a Weary Land*, 15, 129.

41. Walker, *Rock in a Weary Land*, 51; Campbell, *Songs of Zion*, 49–51; Jones, *All Bound Up*, chap. 5. One could probably write an essay on the broad adoption of the word *heritage* as a marker of "southern" culture (which in fact continues to be used to mean white southern culture), having been in part premised on the widespread idea that African Americans had no heritage.

42. Jones, *All Bound Up*, 63–65; Delany, *Condition, Elevation, Emigration and Destiny*, 221. By the beginning of the war Delany also had published a novel in serial form that focused, as Floyd J. Miller writes, on "the 'practicality' of militant slave revolution, and, most importantly, the psychological liberation possible through collective action." See Delany, *Blake or the Huts of America*, xxi.

43. Walker, *Rock in a Weary Land*, 63.

44. Walker, *Rock in a Weary Land*, 64.

45. Examples include James W. B. Bland (VA), age ca. 26–32 years; Joseph Cox (VA), 47; Robert Cromwell (LA), 50; Abraham Galloway (NC), 33; William H. W. Gray (SC), 58; Edmonia Highgate (VA, LA, MS), 34; James Ingraham (LA), 44; Griffin Johnson (SC), 40; Samuel Johnson (SC), 46; James D. Lynch (MS), 33; Benjamin Randolph (SC), 31; Mitchell Raymond (LA), ca. 40; Alfred Richardson (GA), 35 (possibly murdered).

Examples of the assassinated: Charles Caldwell (MS), 44; Simon Coker (SC), 29; William H. Foote (MS), 40 (lynched); Alexander Francois (LA), 49; Wade Perrin (SC), 50. Others killed who were likely of the same generation killed: Lee Nance, d. 1868; Alfred Rush (SC), d. 1876. Foner, *Freedom's Lawmakers*; Sterling, *We Are Your Sisters*, 294–305.

46. Cecelski, *Waterman's Song*, 169.

47. Skocpol and Oser, "Organization Despite Adversity," 370.

48. Meier, *Negro Thought in America*, 136–37; Virginia Writers Project, *Negro in Virginia*, 292; K. Martin, "Community and Place," 40–41.

49. Blassingame, *Black New Orleans*, 147; Virginia Writers Project, *Negro in Virginia*, 29; Lewis, *In Their Own Interests*, 72; Perdue, *Weevils in the Wheat*, 165, 170; Cecelski, *Waterman's Song*, 192.

50. Du Bois, *Co-operation among Negro Americans*; Odum, "Social and Mental Traits"; Jacobs, "Benevolent Societies of New Orleans Blacks," 21–33; St. Clair Drake, "Churches and Voluntary Associations in the Chicago Negro Community," mimeograph (Chicago: Work Progress Administration, 1940); E. Palmer, "Negro Secret Societies," 207–12.

51. See E. Palmer, "Negro Secret Societies"; Rael, *Black Identity and Black Protest*; Trotter, "African American Fraternal Associations," 355–66; Ortiz, *Emancipation Betrayed*, 106–10; Quarles, *Black Abolitionists*, 14, 150–56; Forsythe, "'But My Friends Are Poor,'" 429.

52. Meier, *Negro Thought in America*, 136–37.

53. Joshua Reed Giddings was an Ohio congressman known for arguing in 1841 after a successful slave revolt aboard the ship *Creole* that the federal government must not intercede on behalf of slave owners who wanted payment or the return of their human property. Joliffe seems to refer to John Joliffe, a lawyer who routinely defended fugitive slaves. Biographical Dictionary of the United States Congress, accessed July 27, 2014, http://bioguide.congress.gov/scripts/biodisplay .pl?index=G000167; Common Pleas Court of Clermont County, Ohio, History, accessed July 27, 2014, http://www.clermontcommonpleas.com/history4.aspx; Glenn Smith, "Order of Tents True to Christian Code," *Charleston Post and Courier*, November 16, 2008; Gibson, *History of the United Brothers*. Joliffe most notably defended Margaret Garner, a slavery fugitive who murdered one of her children in an attempt to kill herself and her children just before recapture.

54. Forsythe, "'But My Friends Are Poor,'" 436.

55. My use of the word *outlawed* and the use of *outlaw* elsewhere in the text are prompted in part by lines in Wagner's *Disturbing the Peace*: "Once outlawed, a slave could be slain without fault. If the outlaw were killed, the person responsible would never be tried for murder nor compelled to compensate the owner for destruction of property. As far as the law was concerned, the outlaw did not exist" (70–71). Though Wagner points out that outlawing individuals was used infrequently in the nineteenth century, I use the term as a reminder of the existential stakes for freedpeople as the practice of regarding Black autonomy and collective action as outlaw behavior was prevalent after abolition.

56. Williams, *Help Me to Find My People*, 123.

Chapter 2. The Emancipation Circuit: A Road Map

1. Saville, *Work of Reconstruction*, 4.

2. On objection to the idea of Blacks (and women) voting, there is much contemporary material; for example, see Brown, "To Catch the Vision"; Kolchin, *First Freedom*; Williams, *They Left Great Marks on Me*, 28–34. On resistance to Blacks appearing armed at their meetings, see Fitzgerald, *Union League*, 47.

3. Fitzgerald, *Union League*, 58, 61.

4. Brown, "To Catch the Vision," esp. 80–84.

5. Litwack, *Been in the Storm So Long*, 368; Forsythe, "But My Friends," 429.

6. Brown, "Negotiating and Transforming," 70.

7. Kaye, *Joining Places*, 55, 80–81.

8. Du Bois, *Black Reconstruction in America*, 167.

9. Foner, *Reconstruction*, 155.

10. Act to Punish Certain Offenses Therein Named & for Other Purposes, Laws of the State of Mississippi, Passed at a Regular Session of the Mississippi Legislature, held in Jackson, October, November and December, 1865, Jackson, 1866. Commager, *Documents in American History*, item 246, "Black Code of Mississippi," 2: 2–5.

11. Morgan, *Yazoo*: on whites carrying arms, 48; on being arrested for lending a pistol to his driver, 114–16; on Blacks in 1866 Mississippi expected to stay off the sidewalk and walk in the street with "other cattle," 113; on Blacks "sassing" by refusing to answer a planter on where they "belonged," 57. On sidewalk "insults" causing the 1883 Danville riot, see Dailey, "Deference and Violence," 553–90.

12. Du Bois, *Black Reconstruction in America*, 172; Foner, *Reconstruction*, 200.

13. Emancipation brought on a host of local provisions as to where Black people could live, and as time wore on, provisions against Black migration out of towns that needed their labor, or even visitation in certain all-white towns (known as "sundown towns"), which in turn were followed by restrictive covenants barring Black people and others from communities all over the United States.

14. For detailed accounts of the mob actions in Norfolk and New Orleans, see chapter 3 on Virginia and chapter 9 on Louisiana. On the Memphis riot, see Rosen, *Terror in the Heart of Freedom*.

15. *An Act to protect all Persons in the United States in their Civil Rights, and furnish the Means of their Vindication*, Thirty-Ninth Congress. Sess. I. Ch. 31. 1866," 27–30, accessed February 6, 2021, https://www.loc.gov/item/llsl-v14/.

16. "An Act to protect all Persons," 27–28; Foner, *Reconstruction*, 245.

17. Rosen, *Terror in the Heart of Freedom*, 39–40.

18. Du Bois, *Black Reconstruction*, 271–84; Foner, *Reconstruction*, 243–45. The Civil Rights Act of 1866 is still in force, and subsequent legislation and court cases have increased its effectiveness.

19. *Circuit rider*: Though I once thought this was a novel term for activists, I was reminded on revisiting his work that Jeffrey Kerr-Ritchie's *Freedpeople in the Tobacco South* refers in passing to outside activists in Virginia as circuit riders. *Church circuit rider*: possibly a reference to early Methodist circuit riders, to whom the earliest dictionary meanings are ascribed. cc *rider*: There are many definitions and guesses as to what is meant by the term, many referring to events, places, or slang developed way after the term's first use in popular music by Ma Rainey; most of those suggest an intimate partner, not implied here.

20. The question of literacy was first asked in the 1870 US Census; at that time 11.5 percent of whites nationwide were illiterate as were 79.9 percent of African Americans; "120 Years of Literacy: Literacy from 1870–1979," National Center for Education Statistics, accessed July 22, 2020, https://nces.ed.gov/naal/lit_history .asp.

21. Abbott, "Black Ministers," 1; Fitzgerald, *Union League*, 2, 58, 61; Hahn, *Nation under Our Feet*, 177. In a comment echoing observations of the ability of the rebels in the 1841 Creole uprising to create conceptual maps, league activists at meetings in South Carolina where printed materials were read aloud at length to illiterate members remarked that people were able to recall what they heard exactly and in the order presented.

22. Fitzgerald, *Union League*, 26, 31, 32–33, 47, 58–59.

23. Fitzgerald, *Union League*, 47, 58–59, 155; Morgan, *Yazoo*, 164, 168, 181, 188–93, 244–46.

24. Fitzgerald, *Union League*, 2, 6, 26, 32, 37, 58–59; Hahn, *Nation under Our Feet*, 183.

25. Foner, *Reconstruction*, 283; Hahn, *Nation under Our Feet*, 177.

26. Foner, *Freedom's Lawmakers*, 96–97.

27. On the equal suffrage movement, see chapter 3 on Virginia.

28. Hodges, *Autobiography*; Taylor, *Negro in Reconstruction in Virginia*, 1–7, 227, 228, 231, 233; Foner, *Freedom's Lawmakers*, 105–6.

29. Walker, *Rock in a Weary Land*, 50.

30. Walker, *Rock in a Weary Land*, 109, 50, 91; Campbell, *Songs of Zion*, 59–60.

31. Walker, *Rock in a Weary Land*, 74.

32. Walker, *Rock in a Weary Land*, 108, 126–28; Campbell, *Songs of Zion*, 60.

33. Angell and Pinn, *Social Protest Thought*, 310–11; Walker, *Rock in a Weary Land*, 79.

34. Many HBCUs were in rural areas off the beaten track of what would become the early Emancipation Circuit (such as those developed later in Huntsville and Birmingham, Alabama, or in sites in Texas), and some benefited from proximity to it, such as Wiley College and Prairie View in Texas.

35. Taylor, *Negro in Reconstruction in Virginia*, 64.

36. Camp and Kent, "'What a Mighty Power We Can Be,'" 439–83.

37. Camp and Kent, "What a Mighty Power We Can Be," 461–62, 464–65, 473. "Progressive, even protofeminist" models: Prince Hall Eastern Star (Black Masons) and the Daughters of the Improved Benevolent and Protective Order of Elks of the World (IBPOEW) (Black Elks); more traditional helpmate models: the

Grand United Order of Odd Fellows (GUOFF)'s female auxiliary (the Household of Ruth) and the Courts of Calanthe, female affiliate of the Black chapters of the Knights of Pythias.

38. Camp and Kent, "What a Mighty Power We Can Be," 453, 474.

39. Other well-known Black parallel groups: Grand United Order of Odd Fellows (GUOFF), started in 1843, based rituals on those of the exclusively white and male Independent Order of Odd Fellows (IOOF), formed in 1819; the Knights of Pythias of North and South America, Europe, Asia, Africa and Australia (also known as the Stringer Knights after the founder Thomas Stringer) (1880) was patterned after the Knights of Pythias (1864); and the Improved Benevolent and Protective Order of Elks of the World (IBPOEW) (1898) was modeled on the Benevolent Protective Order of Elks (BPOE) (1866).

40. Among expanding northern groups were the Good Samaritans and Daughters of Samaria, which began as integrated groups and became all Black. Independent groups formed during and shortly after the Civil War that were at least regionally popular included the United Brothers of Friendship (UBF) and its affiliate, the Sisters of the Mysterious Ten (1861), begun in Louisville by young Black men, enslaved and free; Baltimore's Grand United Order of Nazarites (1863); Norfolk's Grand United Order of Tents of J. R. Giddings and Jolliffe Union (1866), founded by two enslaved women, named after abolitionists; and the Independent Order of St. Luke (1867), started in Baltimore and a strong economic institution in Virginia based in Richmond. Most of these groups still exist. Skocpol and Oser, "Organization Despite Adversity," 392, 398, 393, 394 (see also the tables following p. 375); Gibson, *History of the United Brothers*, iii; Smith, "Order of Tents True to Christian Code," *Charleston Post and Courier*, November 16, 2008.

41. Skocpol, Liazos, and Ganz, *What a Mighty Power We Can Be*, 398.

42. Skocpol, Liazos, and Ganz, *What a Mighty Power We Can Be*, 370–72, 411–17, 402.

43. Due to Jim Crow, the Greenwood Elks Hall has a long history into the twentieth century as a concert site for many artists including B. B. King, Lightnin' Hopkins, Muddy Waters, and James Brown. Also part of its legacy is having become a meeting site for the Student Nonviolent Coordinating Committee in the 1960s. Owing to the hall's significance for popular culture, it is part of the Mississippi Blues Trail: see "Elks Hart Lodge No. 640—Greenwood," Mississippi Blues Commission, accessed August 8, 2021, www.msbluestrail.org/blues-trail-markers/elks -lodge. See Payne, *I've Got the Light of Freedom*, 132–79.

44. *L'Union*, accessed August 22, 2020, https://chroniclingamerica.loc.gov/lccn /sn83026401/; *New Orleans Tribune*, accessed August 22, 2020, https://www .congress.gov/congressional-record/2014/07/23/extensions-of-remarks-section /article/E1207-3; *Colored American*, accessed August 22, 2020, https://www.loc .gov/item/sn82014351/ (the Augusta *Colored American* should not be confused

with the earlier New York paper of the same name); *Richmond Planet*, accessed August 22, 2020, https://chroniclingamerica.loc.gov/lccn/sn84025841/.

45. Giggie, *After Redemption*, 31, 33.

46. Goldin, "Female Labor Force Participation," 87–108.

47. US Census Bureau, manuscript, Ninth Census of the United States, accessed January 10, 2022, https://www2.census.gov/library/publications/decennial/1870/population/1870a-04.pdf.

48. *Mississippi in 1875*, 1649–51; Brown, "Negotiating and Transforming the Public Sphere," 78–79; on "The Mississippi Plan," stipulating use of intimidation against voters, see Davis, *My Confederate Kinfolk*, 33. It is worth mentioning that state laws targeting the legacy practice of Sunday "souls to the polls" are a continuation of Black voter repression today and are not confined to the South.

49. Fitzgerald, *Union League*, 192. On that page Fitzgerald also cites Howard N. Rabinowitz on the rise of railroads: "'In the postbellum period it was the railroad rather than a choice water location' that brought economic success."

50. Spero and Harris, *Black Worker*, 16–17.

51. On Republican pressure, see Fitzgerald, *Union League*, 16.

52. Fitzgerald, *Union League*, 28, 168–69; Meier, *Negro Thought in America*, 9.

53. Hahn, *Nation under Our Feet*, 118; Fitzgerald, *Union League*, esp. chap. 5, "Land, Labor and the Loyal League."

54. On Memphis, see Rosen, *Terror in the Heart of Freedom*, chap. 5; on New Orleans, see chapter 9 of this book; Hahn, *Nation under Our Feet*, 266.

55. *Proceedings of the State Convention of Colored Men of the State of Tennessee*, 16.

56. "State Convention of the Colored Men of Tennessee, Nashville, August 7, 1865," in Foner and Walker, *Proceedings of the Black National and State Conventions*, 112–29; on Lynch: Foner, *Freedom's Lawmakers*, 137–38.

57. *Proceedings of the State Convention of Colored Men of the State of Tennessee*, 18–19.

58. Franklin and Schweninger, *In Search of the Promised Land*, 17, 19; Nashville item: *Liberator* 35, no. 40 (October 6, 1865): 159, http://fair-use.org/the-liberator/1865/10/06/the-liberator-35-40.pdf.

59. Brown, "Negotiating and Transforming the Public Sphere," 73.

60. On Stevens and uneven wealth and land distribution, see Foner, *Reconstruction*, 236.

61. Foner, *Freedom's Lawmakers*, 7, 137–38; Sterling, *We Are Your Sisters*, 294–302.

62. See in Foner, *Freedom's Lawmakers*: Raiford Blunt (LA), Harrison N. Bouey (SC), John M. Brown (MS), Richard H. Cain (SC), Alfred Fairfax (LA), and James K. Green (AL). A similar transition would later occur to Ida B. Wells after violence in Mississippi. This is only a sample group; there are quite a few more.

63. On Florida, see Ortiz, *Emancipation*.

64. Mansfield, "'A Slide, a Swing and an Oak Tree.'" The development of the Black shipyard community in Newport News is evident in articles on diverse strikes and job actions in the 1880s, 1890s, 1903, 1919, and during World War II. These job actions resulted in a tract of housing in 1941.

65. Berlin, Favreau, and Miller, *Remembering Slavery*, 271–75, 266.

Chapter 3. Virginia: Assembly

1. Records of United States Army Continental Commands, 1821–1920, 393.4, Records of Named Departments, 1821–1920, National Archives, accessed June 17, 2018, https://www.archives.gov/research/guide-fed-records/groups/393.html; Newby-Alexander, *African American History of the Civil War*, 56.

2. Sterling, *We Are Your Sisters*, 295–96. The Rope Walk in Norfolk was the area where new arrivals from the countryside gathered.

3. Sterling, *We Are Your Sisters*, 295–300; Richardson, *Christian Reconstruction*, 97.

4. Teamoh, *God Made Man*, 7–8. According to the Naval Sea Systems Command, Gosport, built in 1767, became a navy port in the 1790s and was renamed Norfolk Navy Yard in 1862; Naval Sea Systems Command, "Norfolk, History, Roots," accessed January 27, 2014, https://www.navsea.navy.mil/Home/Shipyards/Norfolk/About-Us/History/Roots/; "Norfolk Naval Shipyard-History," accessed August 5, 2021, https://www.navsea.navy.mil/Home/Shipyards/Norfolk/About-Us/History/.

5. Teamoh, *God Made Man*, 70

6. Teamoh, *God Made Man*, 7–9, 83.

7. See Hughes, "Elizabeth City County, Virginia"; Hughes, "Slaves for Hire," 260–86.

8. Perdue, *Weevils in the Wheat*, 30–50.

9. Teamoh, *God Made Man*, 8–18, 105–15, 188nn81–82; Smith, "William Cooper Nell," 182–99; Quarles, *Black Abolitionists*, 103–4; Cecelski, "Abraham H. Galloway," 42.

10. Teamoh, *God Made Man*, 8–18.

11. Perdue, *Weevils in the Wheat*, 134–35, 149–51.

12. Perdue, *Weevils in the Wheat*, 111–19.

13. Smith and Dance, *History and Legend*, 3–8.

14. "The Intelligence of the Colored Citizens of the South," *Liberator*, June 30, 1865, 102.

15. Lewis, *In Their Own Interests*, 11; Foner, *Freedom's Lawmakers*, 13–14. Bayne went on to serve any number of progressive campaigns among freedpeople, some of which appear below. In 1867–68 he became, according to Foner, "the most important black leader" in the Virginia constitutional convention; *Equal Suffrage*, 7–9.

16. Lewis, *In Their Own Interests*, 11.

17. *Equal Suffrage*, 1–2.

18. *Equal Suffrage*, 2–3.

19. *Equal Suffrage*, 5–7 (italics in original).

20. *Equal Suffrage*, 7.

21. *Equal Suffrage*, 7–8.

22. *Equal Suffrage*, 9–16, 27; Foner, *Freedom's Lawmakers*, 105–6, 162.

23. Aptheker, *To Be Free*, 139.

24. "Committee Representing Virginia Freedpeople to the Quartermaster General, Enclosing the Proceedings of Two Mass Meetings," in Hahn et al., *Freedom*, 455–59; Engs, *Freedom's First Generation*, 64, 67–72.

25. "Richmond Freedmen: Their Visit to the President," *New York Tribune*, June 17, 1865, 1, accessed July 14, 2017, https://chroniclingamerica.loc.gov/lccn/sn83030213 /1865-06-17/ed-1/.

26. On "Richmond Freedmen": The signers were Richard Wells (1827–after 1876), minister of Richmond's Ebenezer Baptist Church, who was sold away from his mother at age eight, hired out at eleven, and sold again at thirteen. He was a shoemaker, called to preach as a young man, and became literate after the war. Peter Woolfolk (1820–95), born enslaved, was a Confederate prisoner in the war and later became a teacher and cofounder of Virginia's first Black newspaper, the *Virginia Star*. Fields Cook (1817–97), minister of the First Baptist Church, born in slavery, is presumed to have hired himself out as of 1834 and bought his family out of slavery. Also listed were physician Walter Snead (1824–77) and Nelson Hamilton, about whom I have found no information except mentions in other articles as organizers. See Pegues, *Our Baptist Ministers*, 523–25; Green, "Educational Reconstruction"; "Black History Month Now Becomes Personal," PRSAY, February 13, 2013, accessed July 14, 2017, http://prsay.prsa.org/index.php/2013/02 /13/black-history-month-now-becomes-personal/; Library of Virginia, "Trailblazers," accessed July 14, 2017, http://www.lva.virginia.gov/public/trailblazers /2008/index.htm?id=2; 1870 US Census, accessed July 14, 2017, https://www. census.gov; Virginia Deaths and Burials Index, 1853–1912, accessed January 10, 2022, Virginia Deaths and Burials Index, 1853–1912 https://www.familysearch. org/search/collection/1708697.

27. "Richmond Freedmen."

28. "Richmond Freedmen."

29. "Richmond Freedmen."

30. "Richmond Freedmen"; "Treatment of Negroes in Richmond," *Liberator*, June 30, 1865, 1, accessed February 7, 2021, http://fair-use.org/the-liberator/1865/06/30/the-liberator-35-26.pdf.

31. "Virginia: The Civil Government—Getting to Work," *New York Daily Tribune*, June 12, 1865, 8, accessed July 14, 2017, https://chroniclingamerica.loc.gov/lccn/sn83030213/1865-06-12/ed-1/seq-8/.

32. Many communities chose to celebrate July 4, the September 22 preliminary Emancipation Proclamation, the January 1 final proclamation, and Decoration Day in May (now Memorial Day).

33. "The Reign of Terror in Norfolk," *New York Tribune*, July 11, 1865, accessed July 14, 2017, https://chroniclingamerica.loc.gov/lccn/sn83030213/1865-07-11/ed-1/seq-4/.

34. "From Richmond: Fresh Abuse of the Blacks," *New York Tribune*, August 8, 1865, accessed July 14, 2017, https://chroniclingamerica.loc.gov/lccn/sn83030213/1865-08-08/ed-1/seq-1/.

35. For an insightful study of attacks in response to autonomous domestic relationships, access to public space and leisure, and the lengths freedwomen took in seeking justice, see Rosen, *Terror in the Heart of Freedom*.

36. "Can the Freedmen Take Care of Themselves? Interesting Facts," *True Southerner*, November 30, 1865; "Meeting of Freedmen," *True Southerner*, December 7, 1865. Pepper, a white northerner and lawyer, led several delegations to Washington and was much trusted by local freedpeople until he began to become elusive after using veterans' discharge papers to expedite payments owed them, and he was eventually arrested for defrauding people of their investments in an agency to acquire land. On crops: "The Crops in Virginia," *New York Times*, March 26, 1864, accessed March 12, 2017, http://www.nytimes.com/1864/03/26/news/the-crops-in-virginia.html; "The Crops of Virginia," *New York Times*, June 20, 1865, accessed March 12, 2017, http://www.nytimes.com/1865/06/20/news/the-crops-in-virginia.html; "The Corn Crop in Virginia," *New York Times*, August 7, 1865, accessed March 12, 2017, http://www.nytimes.com/1865/08/07/news/the-corn-crop-in-virginia.html.

37. Hahn et al., *Freedom*, 457–58, 774. This agency, a short-lived land project of Massachusetts governor John Andrews, was designed to purchase large tracts of land and facilitate the sale of small parcels to Black and white farmers in the South; Aptheker, *To Be Free*, 162.

38. *True Southerner*, January 4, 1866, 2. In 1870 the town's population would be only three thousand, so this large number of celebrants must represent part of the ten thousand people who had escaped to Fort Monroe and stayed in the area.

39. The term *uplift* is commonly associated with a turn-of-the-century movement, led by middle-class Blacks, to stimulate social mobility by promoting moral, educational, sexual, and health "improvement" among working-class Blacks through programs instructing people in behavioral change (even dissemblance) in comportment with "respectability" and standard mainstream (and Victorian) ideals. My use of the term is shorthand for the many shared goals of groups such as fraternal associations that promoted social mobility through moral, spiritual, and educational improvement along with the development of social and procedural skills for business, as well as commonsense financial instruction.

40. All but one of these groups seem to be local, though the Rising Sons could be the Rising Sons and Daughters of Liberty. According to Theda Skocpol and Jennifer Lynn Oser, the Independent Order of Good Samaritans and Daughters of Samaria was organized in New York in 1847. See Skocpol and Oser, "Organization Despite Adversity," 367–437. The Sons of Bethel may be a local reminder of the Battle of Big Bethel, in which a local runaway led Union troops to Confederate forces. The Sons of Zion may be associated with the Daughters of Zion, founded by the area's first Black teacher, Mary Peake, in Norfolk during the war. See Lockwood, *Mary S. Peake*, 14.

41. "Celebration," *True Southerner*, January 4, 1866, 2. Joseph T. Wilson, veteran of the Massachusetts Fifty-Fourth and a former Union spy, went on to start the *Union Republican* in Petersburg in 1867 and two Norfolk papers in the 1880s. See Foner, *Freedom's Lawmakers*, 233–34.

42. Taylor, *Negro in Reconstruction in Virginia*, 62–63. On Fabre, on the proliferation of nineteenth century Black celebrations, 72–73; also see chapter 9 on Louisiana in this volume.

43. Taylor, *Negro in Reconstruction in Virginia*, 63.

44. Moore, "Norfolk Riot," 155–64; Coakley, *Role of Federal Military Forces*, 273–74; Moore, "Norfolk Riot," 157.

45. Moore, "Norfolk Riot," 163–64.

46. Teamoh, *God Made Man*, 116; Virginia House of Delegates and the Senate of Virginia, Joint Resolution No. 89, *Recognizing the African American Members Elected to the Virginia General Assembly during Reconstruction*.

47. "Letter from Nancy Hodges et al. to Major General O. O. Howard (May 21, 1866), enclosed in letter from Geo. Teamoh to Major General O. O. Howard (May 21?, 1866)," in Miller et al., "Between Emancipation and Enfranchisement," 1070.

48. Miller et al., "Between Emancipation and Enfranchisement," 1070–71.

49. Aptheker, *To Be Free*, 154–55.

50. Taylor, *Negro in Reconstruction in Virginia*, 120nn52, 53; *Richmond Enquirer*, September 26, 1866; *Enquirer*, October 9, 1866.

51. *Richmond Dispatch*, May 6, 1872, 2; *Richmond Enquirer*, May 21, 1872; *The Whig*, March 25, 1873; *The Whig*, March 28, 1873.

52. *Richmond Dispatch*, June 12, 1875; August 21, 22, 1875. *Richmond Enquirer*, June 25, 1875; August 21, 22, 1875.

53. Taylor, *Negro in Reconstruction in Virginia*, 119–20.

54. John V. Given, transcript of a letter, July 23, 1867, Robert C. Schenck Papers, Correspondence of Thomas Tullock.

55. Given, transcript of a letter, July 23, 1867.

56. H. J. Brown, transcript of a letter, July 23, 1867, Robert C. Schenck Papers, Correspondence of Thomas Tullock; Forsythe, "'But My Friends Are Poor,'" 433; *Richmond Enquirer*, September 11, 1867; Kerr-Ritchie, *Freedpeople in the Tobacco South*, 76–77.

57. Brown, transcript of a letter, July 23, 1867.

58. Lowe, "Local Black Leaders during Reconstruction," 181–206; Forsythe, "'But My Friends Are Poor,'" 412–13. The General Assembly of Virginia consists of the House of Delegates and the state senate.

59. African American delegates to the 1867–68 Virginia constitutional convention: 1. William H. Andrews (Isle of Wight and Surry Counties); 2. James D. Barrett (Fluvanna); 3. Thomas Bayne (Norfolk); 4. James William D. Bland (Prince Edward and Appomattox); 5. William Breedlove (Middlesex and Essex); 6. John Brown (Southampton); 7. David Canada (Halifax); 8. James B. Carter (Chesterfield and Powhatan); 9. Joseph Cox (Richmond); 10. Willis A. Hodges (Princess Anne); 11. Joseph R. Holmes (Charlotte and Halifax); 12. Peter K. Jones (Greenville and Sussex); 13. Samuel F. Kelso (Campbell); 14. Lewis Lindsay (Richmond); Peter G. Morgan (Petersburg); 16. William P. Moseley (Goochland); 17. Francis "Frank" Moss (Buckingham); 18. Edward Nelson (Charlotte); 19. Daniel M. Norton (James City and York); 20. John Robinson (Cumberland); 21. James T. S. Taylor (Albemarle); 22. George Teamoh (Portsmouth); 23. Burwell Toler (Hanover and Henrico); 24. John Watson (Mecklenburg). Sources: Commonwealth of Virginia, Dr. Martin Luther King Jr. Memorial Commission, "African American Legislators in Virginia"; Hume, "Membership of the Virginia Constitutional Convention of 1867–1868," 461–84; *Journal of the Constitutional Convention of the State of Virginia, convened in the city of Richmond, December 3, 1867, and an order of General Schofield, dated Nov. 2, 1867, in pursuance of the act of Congress of March 23, 1867* (Richmond, VA: Office of the New Nation, 1867), 7–9; Foner, *Freedom's Lawmakers*, by name.

60. Teamoh, *God Made Man*, 20–21, 118. Gibson, a former Confederate officer and delegate to the constitutional convention, criticized the inclusion of freedmen.

61. Teamoh, *God Made Man*, 117; Foner, *Freedom's Lawmakers*, 13–14; Du Bois, *Black Reconstruction in America*, 541–46; *Debates and Proceedings of the Constitutional Convention of the State of Virginia, 1867–1868*.

62. Bayne, quoted in Du Bois, *Black Reconstruction in America*, 542–43.

63. See in particular the *Southern Opinion*, December 28, 1867, to April 4, 1868. *Blackface text* is my term for language that re-creates in prose the grotesqueries earlier known primarily through visual media such as cartoons. Bayne and others elected to office were subjected to such language passed off as reporting.

64. William Henry Scott Sr. (1848–1910), untitled article in scrapbook, William H. Scott, Sr. Papers, William H. Scott Family Papers, Stuart A. Rose Manuscript, Archive and Rare Book Library, Emory University, Atlanta, GA, BV2 Scrapbook, 1874–1880. Scott was correct in identifying the whipping of prisoners as a violation, and Reconstruction lawmakers tried to end the practice, which did not come to a complete halt until 1968. See the conclusion of this book.

65. For an account of one of the Black political bosses in tobacco country, Mecklenburg's Ross Hamilton, see; Foner, *Freedom's Lawmakers*, 14; Forsythe, "'But My Friends Are Poor'"; Teamoh, *God Made Man*, 25–26.

66. Hampton Normal and Agricultural Institute, *Catalogue of the Hampton Normal and Agricultural Institute, Hampton, VA for the Academical Year 1870–71* (Boston: T. B. Marvin and Son, 1871), 7–9, accessed November 12, 2015, https://babel.hathitrust.org/cgi/pt?id=emu.010002408647; Heywood and Thornton, *Central Africans, Atlantic Creoles, and the Foundation of the Americas*, 246.

67. On the Walton Act: University of Virginia, Virginia Center for Digital History, "1894 Walton Act," accessed April 17, 2014, http://www2.vcdh.virginia.edu/afam/politics/legislation.html#walton.

68. Taylor, *Negro in Reconstruction in Virginia*, 63–64.

69. Foner, *Reconstruction*, 281; Fitzgerald, *Union League*, 15; "The Negro Strike," *Richmond Enquirer*, February 22, 1867; "Stevedores' Row," *Richmond Enquirer*, May 4, 1867; "The Negroes Employed in the Tobacco," *Richmond Enquirer*, May 15, 1867.

Chapter 4. North Carolina: Custody

1. Berlin, Miller, et al., *Freedom*, 90–91; Cecelski, *Waterman's Song*, 169.

2. Records of United States Army Continental Commands, 1821–1920, 393.4, Records of Named Departments, 1821–1920, National Archives, accessed June 17, 2018, https://www.archives.gov/research/guide-fed-records/groups/393.html; Newby-Alexander, *African American History of the Civil War*, 56.

3. McPherson, *Battle Cry*, 369–71; Cecelski, "Abraham H. Galloway," 43–44.

4. Cecelski, "Abraham H. Galloway," 37–67.

5. Cecelski, "Abraham H. Galloway," 44.

6. Cecelski, "Abraham H. Galloway," 38.

7. Cecelski, "Abraham H. Galloway," 39.

8. "North Carolina Freedmen to the Commander of the Department of Virginia and North Carolina, [Beaufort, NC, November 20, 1863]," in Berlin, Miller, et al., *Freedom*, 166.

9. "Order by the Commander of the Department of Virginia and North Carolina, [Fort Monroe, VA, December 5, 1863]," in Berlin, Miller, et al., *Freedom*, 168–74.

10. "Report by the Superintendent of Negro Affairs in the 3rd District of the Department of Virginia and North Carolina, [New Berne, NC, July 1864]," in Berlin et al., *Freedom*, 199–201.

11. "North Carolina Freedmen to the Commander of the Department of Virginia and North Carolina [Bermuda Hundred, VA, September 1864]," in Berlin, Miller, et al., *Freedom*, 202.

12. "North Carolina Freedmen to the Commander of the Department of Virginia and North Carolina [Bermuda Hundred, VA, September 1864]," Berlin, Miller, et al., *Freedom*, 202–3.

13. Cecelski, "Abraham H. Galloway," 48; Hager, *Word by Word*, 108, 118–19, 132, 134; Jackson, "'Cultural Stronghold,'" 331–57. Gould's diary: William Benjamin Gould, *Diary of a Contraband: The Civil War Passage of a Black Sailor*, ed. William B. Gould IV (Stanford, CA: Stanford University Press, 2002). The church where Galloway spoke was likely First AME Bethel, then in lower Manhattan but still in New York City.

14. Sterling, *We Are Your Sisters*, 296; Howard H. Bell, "Proceedings of the National Convention of Colored Men Held in the City of Syracuse, N.Y., October 4, 5, 6, & 7, 1864," in *Minutes of the Proceedings of the National Negro Conventions*, 15, 25.

15. Bell, "Proceedings of the National Convention of Colored Men," 3–6; Foner, *Freedom's Lawmakers*, 100, 199; Cimprich, *Slavery's End in Tennessee*, 110; Harvey, *Freedom's Coming*, 16; Jenkins, *Race, Representation and Photography*, 109–33; Ash, *Massacre in Memphis*, 143; "First Baptist Church, Memphis, U.S. National Register of Historic Places," accessed August 7, 2021, http://www.waymarking.com/waymarks/WMT59E_First_Baptist_Church_Memphis_TN.

16. Foner, *Freedom's Lawmakers*, 113–14; Cecelski, *Fire of Freedom*, 155; Bell, "Proceedings of the National Convention of Colored Men," 29; Cecelski, "Abraham H. Galloway," 48.

17. "North Carolina Freedmen to the President and to the Secretary of War [Roanoke Island, March 9, 1865]," in Berlin, Miller, et al. *Freedom*, 231–33.

18. Berlin, Miller, et al., *Freedom*, 233–34.

19. Cecelski, "Abraham H. Galloway," 49.

20. "Mayor and City Commissioners of Wilmington, NC to the Provisional Governor of NC," in Hahn et al., *Freedom*, 131–35.

21. Hahn et al., *Freedom*, 135n1 (telegram of July 16, 1865).

22. Cecelski, "Abraham H. Galloway," 49–50. Cecelski says Galloway used the "box" phrase two years earlier; perhaps it was a common expression among Black veterans like James Ingraham, also of Louisiana, whom he heard in 1864. The Nashville church was also known as the Lincoln Church.

23. Foner, *Reconstruction*, 120; Litwack, *Been in the Storm So Long*, 507–8.

24. Foner and Walker, *Proceedings of the Black National and State Conventions*, 179–181; Cecelski, "Abraham H. Galloway," 50–51.

25. Foner and Walker, *Proceedings*, 181.

26. For more on testimony regarding concubinage, see Kaye, *Joining Places*, ch. 2.

27. Zipf, "Reconstructing 'Free Woman,'" 9.

28. Zipf, "Reconstructing 'Free Woman,'" 18.

29. Zipf, "Reconstructing 'Free Woman,'" 17.

30. Zipf, "Reconstructing 'Free Woman,'" 18–19.

31. Clark-Pujara, "In Need of Childcare," 297.

32. Downs, *Sick from Freedom*, 140. Orphanages serving southern Blacks (and founded by or with Blacks) that had lasting influence include: *1860s*: the National Home for Destitute Colored Women and Children, Washington, DC (as of 1930, the Meriwether Home for Children); Soule House Colored Orphans Home (as of 1867, Providence Asylum), created by Louisiana Assoc. for the Benefit of Colored Orphans, New Orleans; Colored Orphan Asylum, Memphis (founded by Martha Canfield); Friends Asylum for Colored Orphans, Richmond, now Friends' Assoc. for Children (founded by Lucy Goode Brooks and others); *1880s*: Carrie Steele Home, Atlanta, now Carrie Steele Pitts Home; *1890s*: Janie Porter Barrett Locust Street Social Settlement, Hampton, Virginia, now exists as the state-run Barrett Learning Center.

33. Glymph, "'A Makeshift Kind of Life': Free Women and Free Homes," in *Out of the House of Bondage*, 167–203.

34. Zipf, "Reconstructing 'Free Woman,'" 22.

35. Zipf, "Reconstructing 'Free Woman,'" 24.

36. Anderson, *Race and Politics in North Carolina*, 4, 16–17, 22–25, 29.

37. James E. O'Hara, transcript of a letter by John E. O'Hara, July 19, 1867, in Robert C. Schenck Papers, Correspondence of Thomas Tullock. This letter is likely mislabeled as being from a John E. O'Hara; the North Carolina activist who

worked with the URCC, and was elected to the US Congress in 1882, was James E. O'Hara. Foner, *Freedom's Lawmakers*; Anderson, *Race and Politics in North Carolina*, 62–73; Benjamin R. Justesen, "James Edward O'Hara (1844–1905)," North Carolina History Project, accessed May 28, 217, http://northcarolinahistory.org /encyclopedia/james-edward-ohara-1844-1905/. "Minutes of the Freedmen's Convention, Held in the City of Raleigh, on the 2nd, 3rd, 4th and 5th of October, 1866: Electronic Edition. Freedmen's Convention (1866: Raleigh, N.C.)," accessed August 7, 2021, http://docsouth.unc.edu/nc/freedmen/freedmen.html.

38. *Longstanding* in this case means that this particular tactic became policy and is still alive and well. Restoring voting rights to ex-offenders is still being fought in some states; see the ACLU's map "Felony Disfranchisement Laws" on the millions of Americans still disfranchised, accessed August 7, 2021, http://www.aclu.org /maps/map-state-felony-disfranchisement-laws.

39. Miller et al., "Between Emancipation and Enfranchisement," 1074–75.

40. African American delegates to the 1868 North Carolina Constitutional Convention: 1. Wilson Carey (Caswell County); 2. Henry Cherry (Edgecombe); 3. Henry Eppes (Halifax); 4. Abraham Galloway (New Hanover); 5. James Henry Harris (Wake); 6. W. T. J. Hayes (Halifax); 7. Samuel Highsmith (Duplin); 8. Bryant Lee (Bertie); 9. Rev. (later Bishop) James Walker Hood (Cumberland); 10. John Adams Hyman (Warren); 11. Cuffie Mayo (Granville); 12. Clinton D. Pierson (Craven); 13. Parker David Robbins (Bertie); 14. John Hendrick Williamson (Franklin). Bernstein, "Participation of Negro Delegates," 391–409; Foner, *Freedom's Lawmakers*; General Assembly of North Carolina, Session 2013 Ratified Bill, Resolution 2013-7 Senate Joint Resolution 133; *Journal of the Constitutional Convention of the State of North-Carolina*.

41. Hahn, *Nation under Our Feet*, 201; Du Bois, *Black Reconstruction in America*, 529.

42. Bernstein, "Participation of Negro Delegates," 404, 394; Foner, *Freedom's Lawmakers*, 109.

43. Bernstein, "Participation of Negro Delegates," 398.

44. Cecelski, "Abraham H. Galloway," 54, 55–56.

45. Anderson, *Race and Politics in North Carolina*, 87–88, 143–45; Foner, *Freedom's Lawmakers*, 113.

46. Anderson, *Race and Politics in North Carolina*, 23–24.

Chapter 5. South Carolina: Majority

1. Berlin, Glymph, et al., *Freedom*, 118–19, 87–101; Forten, *Journal*, 27–30.

2. Berlin, Glymph, et al., *Freedom*, 87–88; Forten, *Journal*, 29.

3. Berlin et al., *Free at Last*, xxix, 9–11, 46–48; McPherson, *Battle Cry*, 352–53, 355–56; Berlin, Glymph, et al., *Freedom*, 18–19, 97–98.

4. Berlin et al., *Free at Last*, 56–59.

5. Berlin, Glymph, et al., *Freedom*, 98–101.

6. Forten, *Journal*, 30, 138; Rose, *Rehearsal for Reconstruction*, 76–78. On Towne and Murray founding the Penn School: Sterling, *We Are Your Sisters*, 278n; Burton, *Penn Center*, 4. The Port Royal Relief Association later became the Pennsylvania Freedmen's Relief Association. Edward Pierce's original mission was "to assist in reorganizing Florida on the basis of equal suffrage for Negroes," but that never occurred because of the fighting in South Carolina. He was also "attending to the commercial interests of the government in the occupied portions of South Carolina, Georgia, and Florida, until September, 1863." See Forten, *Journal*, 275n58.

7. Forten, *Journal*, 2–26, 114, 138, 257n44; Smith, "William Cooper Nell," 182–99. Nell also wrote for the *Anglo-African*. James Forten, Forten's grandfather, founded the famed Vigilance Committee of Philadelphia, which may have also given her a link to Nell, a founder of the Boston Committee of Vigilance after passage of the Fugitive Slave Law in 1850. Brick Baptist Church history, accessed August 10, 2021, http://brickbaptist.com/history.html.

8. Rose, *Rehearsal for Reconstruction*, 161–62.

9. Rose, *Rehearsal for Reconstruction*, 149–50; Forten, *Journal*, 155.

10. Forten, *Journal*, 180; Clinton, *Harriet Tubman*, 147–50.

11. Sterling, *We Are Your Sisters*, 258–59; Cecelski, "Abraham H. Galloway," 49; Clinton, *Harriet Tubman*, 163–64.

12. Clinton, *Harriet Tubman*, 167, 173, 177; Sterling, *We Are Your Sisters*, 260; Forten, *Journal*, 214–17.

13. Forten, *Journal*, 218; Clinton, *Harriet Tubman*, 180–81, 186–87.

14. Johnson, *Sword of Honor*, 152–55.

15. Johnson, *Sword of Honor*, 30, 34.

16. Johnson, *Sword of Honor*, 32–33, 48–52; McPherson, *Negro's Civil War*, 152–55.

17. Mother Emanuel AME Church history, accessed January 10, 2020. https://motheremanuel.com/our-story.

18. Forten, *Journal*, 212. According to Forten, another speaker that day was Edward L. Pierce, supervising agent in the area, who had been at Fort Monroe. Emilio, *History of the Fifty-Fourth Regiment*, 49–50, 232; McPherson, *Negro's Civil War*, 136–37. For more on Lynch, see McPherson, *Negro's Civil War*, chaps. 5 and 11.

19. Berlin et al., *Free at Last*, 310–18.

20. Saville, *Work of Reconstruction*, 71–75; Foner, *Reconstruction*, 70–71; Special Order 15 text, accessed January 10, 2022. http://www.freedmen.umd.edu/sfo15.htm.

21. Hahn et al., *Freedom*, 408, 440–41.

22. Saville, *Work of Reconstruction*, 14, 73, 75; Foner, *Reconstruction*, 69–70.

23. Saville, *Work of Reconstruction*, 13, 20–21, 23.

24. Saville, *Work of Reconstruction*, 146–48.

25. "Report of a Speech by a Virginia Freedman [Philadelphia, PA, late December 1866] [published by Friends' Association of Philadelphia and its vicinity for the Relief of Colored Freedmen. Office, No. 501 Cherry Street, Philadelphia]," Freedmen and Southern Society Project, University of Maryland, accessed February 6, 2021, http://www.freedmen.umd.edu/Wyat.html.

26. Pound, "Slave to the Ex-Slave Narratives," 84–85.

27. Foner, *Reconstruction*, 104–5, 200; Hahn, *Nation under Our Feet*, 133–35; Du Bois, *Black Reconstruction in America*, 167–72, 175–76; Holt, *Black over White*, 20, 23; *Statute at Large of South Carolina Vol. XII*, 269–85.

28. *Statute at Large of South Carolina Vol. XII*, 272, 279, 274–76, 278; "An Act to Amend the Criminal Law. No. 4731," in *Acts of the General Assembly of the State of South Carolina, Passed at the Session of 1864–1865*, 271–78; "An Act Preliminary to the Legislation Induced by the Emancipation of Slaves. A.D. 1865, No. 4730," in *Acts of the General Assembly of the State of South Carolina, Passed at the Session of 1864–1865*, 271.

29. Saville, *Work of Reconstruction*, 23; *Statute at Large of South Carolina Vol. XII*, 278; Du Bois, *Black Reconstruction in America*, 169–71.

30. "CAIN, Richard Harvey," US House of Representatives, History, Art and Archives, accessed August 20, 2021, http://history.house.gov/People/Detail/10470?ret=True. Bridge Street AME Church, Brooklyn, was a haven on the Underground Railroad and a site where Harriet Tubman spoke. "Bridge Street AWME Church," Mapping the African American Past, Columbia Center for New Media Teaching and Learning, accessed September 38, 2018, http://maap.columbia.edu/place/11.html; Walker, *Rock in a Weary Land*, 55, 63; *Proceedings of the Colored People's Convention of the State of South Carolina, Held in Zion Church*, 7; Foner, *Freedom's Lawmakers*, 35–36.

31. "A colored speaker and organizer in South Carolina," transcript of a letter by a URCC speaker (unnamed), August 2, 1867, in Robert C. Schenck Papers, Correspondence of Thomas Tullock; Fitzgerald, *Union League*, 61.

32. The union continues today. Poliakoff, "Charleston's Longshoremen," 247–48.

33. Du Bois, *Black Reconstruction in America*, 393–94, 413.

34. Du Bois, *Black Reconstruction in America*, 394–95, 406.

35. Brown, "Negotiating and Transforming," 108; Holt, *Black over White*, 34–35; Kelly, "Black Laborers," 375–414.

36. Brown, "To Catch the Vision of Freedom," 80.

37. Brown, "To Catch the Vision of Freedom," 82; Kelly, "Black Laborers," 408–9.

38. African American delegates to the 1868 South Carolina constitutional convention: 1. Purvis Alexander (Chester County), 2. Martin F. Becker (Berkeley), 3. John Bonum (Edgefield), 4. Isaac P. Brockenton (Darlington), 5. Barney Burton (Chester), 6. Benjamin Byas (Berkeley), 7. Edward J. Cain (Orangeburg), 8. Richard H. Cain (Charleston), 9. Francis L. Cardozo (Charleston), 10. John A. Chestnut (Kershaw), 11. Frederick Albert Clinton (Lancaster), 12. Wilson Cooke (Greenville), 13. William Darrington (Williamsburg), 14. Nelson Davis (Laurens), 15. Robert C. DeLarge (Charleston), 16. Abram Dogan (Union), 17. William A. Driffle (Colleton), 18. Harvey D. Edwards (Fairfield), 19. Robert B. Elliott (Edgefield), 20. Rice Foster (Spartanburg), 21. William H. W. Gray (Berkeley), 22. David Harris (Edgefield), 23. Charles D. Hayne (Barnwell), 24. Henry E. Hayne (Marion), 25. James N. Hayne (Barnwell), 26. James A. Henderson (Newberry), 27. Richard H. Humbert (Darlington), 28. Henry Jacobs (Fairfield), 29. George Jackson (Marlboro), 30. William R. Jervay (Berkeley), 31. John W. Johnson (Marion), 32. Samuel Johnson (Anderson), 33. William E. Johnson (Sumter), 34. W. Nelson Joiner (Abbeville), 35. Charles L. Jones (Lancaster), 36. Henry W. Jones (Horry), 37. Jordan Lang (Darlington), 38. Landon S. Langley (Beaufort), 39. George H. Lee (Charleston), 40. Samuel Lee (Sumter), 41. Hutson J. Lomax (Abbeville), 42. Julius Mayer (Barnwell), 43. Harry McDaniels (Lauren), 44. Whitefield J. McKinlay (Orangeburg), 45. William McKinlay (Charleston), 46. John W. Meade (York), 47. Abram Middleton (Barnwell), 48. Lee A. Nance (Newberry), 49. William Beverly Nash (Richland), 50. William Nelson (Clarendon), 51. Samuel Nuckles (Union), 52. Joseph H. Rainey (Georgetown), 53. Benjamin F. Randolph (Orangeburg), 54. Alonzo J. Ransier (Charleston), 55. Prince R. Rivers (Edgefield), 56. Thaddeus K. Sasportas (Orangeburg), 57. Sancho Saunders (Chester), 58. Henry L. Shrewsbury (Chesterfield), 59. Robert Smalls (Beaufort), 60. Calvin Stubbs (Marlboro), 61. Stephen A. Swails (Williamsburg), 62. William M. Thomas (Colleton), 63. Augustus R. Thompson (Horry), 64. Benjamin A. Thompson (Marion), 65. Samuel B. Thompson (Richland), 66. William M. Viney (Colleton), 67. William James Whipper (Beaufort), 68. John H. White (York), 69. Charles M. Wilder (Richland), 70. Thomas M. Williamson (Abbeville), 71. Coy Wingo (Spartanburg), 72. Jonathan J. Wright (Beaufort). Sources: Burke, "All We Ask Is Equal Rights"; Foner, *Freedom's Lawmakers*, xiii, xvi; *Proceedings of the Constitutional Convention of South Carolina Held in Charleston, S.C.*; *H*3695 Concurrent Resolution*; Holt, *Black over White*, table 5.

39. South Carolina Legislature, County Delegation Information, accessed November 26, 2019, https://www.scstatehouse.gov/countydelegationinfo/cntymast.php; Du Bois, *Black Reconstruction*, 683; "Special Dispatch to the *New York Times*," "The KuKlux. Proclamation of Martial Law in South Carolina,'" 1.

40. Saville, *Work of Reconstruction*, 161–62; Poliakoff, "Charleston's Longshoremen," 248; Du Bois, *Black Reconstruction in America*, 417.

41. Signers of the "Address of the Southern States Convention in Columbia to the People of the United States": Robert Elliott, Speaker of the South Carolina House and, two years later, a member of the US Congress; James M. Simms, Georgia state representative who had worked with the Freedmen's Bureau and the Union League; Richard Nelson, a newspaper publisher and organizer of the 1869 Texas Colored Labor Convention; Josiah T. Walls, a Union army veteran, Florida's only African American in the US Congress, and a former member in the state senate and house; Isaac Myers of Baltimore, founder and president of the Colored National Labor Union; B. A. Bosemon, a South Carolina state representative; Felix C. Antoine, a Louisiana state representative; John F. Quarles, a Georgia lawyer and civil rights activist; and F. G. Barbadoes, a California equal rights organizer.

42. "The Colored People: Address of the Southern States Convention in Columbia to the People of the United States," *New York Times*, October 26, 1871.

43. Du Bois, *Black Reconstruction in America*, 412.

44. "The Colored People."

45. Kantrowitz, *Ben Tillman*, 60, 62–63, 165.

46. Hahn, *Nation under Our Feet*, 305–7; Foner, *Reconstruction*, 570–71; Holt, *Black Over White*, 199–201; Kantrowitz, *Ben Tillman*, 66–69.

47. Hahn, *Nation under Our Feet*, 307–8; Foner, *Reconstruction*, 574; Kantrowitz, *Ben Tillman*, 74–75; Foner, *Freedom's Lawmakers*, 59–60.

48. Kelly, "Black Laborers," 375–414. Kelly provides helpful detail on the pressures on Black officials coming from workers and from Democrats. For other studies that note defections of Black officeholders toward Democrats during the 1876 election, see Hahn, *Nation under Our Feet*, 308–9; Foner, *Reconstruction*, 572.

49. Kelly, "Black Laborers," 384–86, 389.

50. Kelly, "Black Laborers," 390, 394–95, 400.

51. Foner, *Freedom's Lawmakers*, 22, 23–24, 215–16; Walker, *Rock in a Weary Land*, 135–36.

52. Kuiken, "'Fit to Be Free,'" 241.

Chapter 6. Georgia: Mobilization

1. US Census Bureau, manuscript, Eighth Census of the United States, 1860; Berlin et al., *Free at Last*, 61–66 (emphasis in the original).

2. Foner, *Freedom's Lawmakers*, 23; Drago, *Black Politicians*, 41–43; Hahn et al., *Freedom*, 52.

3. Foner, *Freedom's Lawmakers*, 37–38; Drago, *Black Politicians*, 82–84; Hahn, *Nation under Our Feet*, 239–41.

4. Foner, *Freedom's Lawmakers*, 46, 215–16; Drago, *Black Politicians*, 12–13, 24.

5. *The Mission of the United States Republic, an Oration Delivered by Rev. James Lynch, at the Parade Ground, Augusta, GA, July 4, 1865* (Augusta, 1865), 2, accessed June 19, 2017, https://archive.org/stream/22466289.3809.emory.edu/22466289 _3809_djvu.txt.

6. *The Mission of the United States Republic*, 7, 8, 14, accessed January 10, 2022 https://archive.org/details/22466289.3809.emory.edu.

7. Teamoh, *God Made Man*, 8.

8. "Strike among the Negro Laborers," *Liberator*, October 6, 1865, 159.

9. *Colored American*, Augusta, January 6, 1866. The *Colored American* was one the first African American papers to begin publication in the South after the war and one of four or five that came into existence in 1865 but did not survive past 1866.

10. Cecelski, "Abraham H. Galloway," 53; Litwack, *Been in the Storm So Long*, 289.

11. Foner, *Reconstruction*, 121.

12. *Colored American*, Augusta, January 6, 1866 (italics in the original). "Fevered minds" is the perfect term Litwack gave to those disturbed by the December rumor of a Black rising. Litwack, *Been in the Storm So Long*, 426; on Lynch, see I. Garland Penn, *The Afro-American Press and Its Editors*, 101–4; Foner, *Freedom's Lawmakers*, 137–38.

13. *Colored American*, Augusta, January 6, 1866.

14. "State Convention of the Colored People of Georgia, Augusta, January 10, 1866," in Foner and Walker, *Proceedings of the Black National and State Conventions, 1865–1900*, 230, 232; *Proceedings of the Freedmen's Convention of Georgia, Assembled at August, January 10, 1866* (Augusta: The Loyal Georgian, 1866), 13, 30, 32, 36, accessed July 26, 2018, http://coloredconventions.org/files/original/75cc9ef ba86a2ae725b9eba305586742.pdf.

15. Miller et al., "Between Emancipation and Enfranchisement," 1072–74.

16. Miller et al., "Between Emancipation and Enfranchisement," 1074; Formwalt, "Origins of African-American Politics," 211–22.

17. *Proceedings of the Freedmen's Convention of Georgia, Assembled at August, January 10, 1866*, 36; Formwalt, "Origins of African-American Politics," 212.

18. Formwalt, "Origins of African-American Politics," 212–17; Miller et al., "Between Emancipation and Enfranchisement," 1074.

19. Formwalt, "Origins of African-American Politics," 218–19.

20. Miller et al., "Between Emancipation and Enfranchisement," 1073; see chapter 9 on Louisiana for specifics on student rioting over integration of New Orleans high schools.

21. Texts, including memoirs by activists, were published in the nineteenth century by Tunis Campbell, Edward R. Carter, John Wesley Gaines, Willis A. Hodges, James Walker Hood, Emanuel King Love, James D. Lynch, Charles Henry Phillips, James Meriles Simms, Benjamin Tucker Tanner, Susie King Taylor, Edgar Garfield Thomas, Alexander Walker Wayman, and George Washington Williams, as well as the Convention of the Equal Rights and Educational Association of Georgia, the Council of the Georgia Equal Rights Association, and the Freedmen's Convention of Georgia. Early twentieth-century volumes: "Colloquy with Colored Ministers: A Civil War Document," *Journal of Negro History* 16 (January 1931): 88–94; Mungo Melanchthon Ponton, *Life and Times of Henry M. Turner* (Atlanta, GA: A. B. Caldwell, 1917); and others. On class and the experience of Black officeholders, see Drago, *Black Politicians*, 35–40.

22. Angell and Pinn, *Social Protest Thought in the African Methodist Episcopal Church*, 1; Ali, *In the Lion's Mouth*, 24. The church, rebuilt twice, is widely known as Mother Emanuel; Mother Emanuel AME Church, accessed January 10, 2020. https://motheremanuel.com/our-story emanuelamechurch.org; Walker, *Rock in a Weary Land*, 7.

23. Henry McNeal Turner, transcript of letter of July 8, 1867, Robert C. Schenck Papers; on railroad travel: Walker, *Rock in a Weary Land*, 67.

24. Henry McNeal Turner, transcript of a letter of July 9, 1867, Robert C. Schenck Papers.

25. Henry McNeal Turner, transcript of a letter of July 9, 1867.

26. Henry McNeal Turner, transcript of a letter July 23, 1867, Robert C. Schenck Papers.

27. Henry McNeal Turner, transcript of a letter July 23, 1867.

28. This lacuna is the reason I have quoted the activists' letters at some length. Some of these same letters have been cited before in excellent works without description of the state of freedpeople attending the organizing rallies, the size of the crowds, or the emotional impact of the encounters.

29. John T. Costin, transcript of a letter of July 25, 1867, Robert C. Schenck Papers.

30. John T. Costin, transcript of a letter of July 25, 1867.

31. John T. Costin, transcript of a letter of July 25, 1867. Costin used only the word *Johnny*, which probably refers to the nickname "Johnny Reb," a commonly used personification of Confederate soldiers during the Civil War.

32. John T. Costin, transcript of a letter of July 25, 1867.

33. John T. Costin, transcript of a letter of July 25, 1867; US Census Bureau, manuscript, Eighth Census of the United States, 1860.

34. Du Bois, *Black Reconstruction in America*, 498; Drago, *Black Politicians*, 35.

35. African American delegates to the Georgia 1867–68 Georgia constitutional convention: 1. Robert Alexander (Clay County), 2. Isaac H. Anderson (Houston), 3. Simeon Beard (Richmond), 4. John R. Bell (Oglethorpe), 5. Moses H. Bentley (Chatham), 6. Aaron A. Bradley (Savannah), 7. Tunis G. Campbell Sr. (McIntosh), 8. James C. Casey (Marion), 9. George W. Chatters (Stewart), 10. Malcolm Claiborne (Burke), 11. Samuel A. Cobb (Houston), 12. John T. Costin (Talbot), 13. Thomas Crayton (Stewart), 14. Robert Crumley (Warren), 15. Jesse Dinkins (Schley), 16. William A. Golding (Liberty), 17. William A. Guilford (Upson), 18. William H. Harrison (Hancock), 19. James A. Jackson (Randolph), 20. Philip Joiner (Dougherty), 21. Van Jones (Muscogee), 22. George Linder (Laurens), 23. Robert Lumpkin (Macon), 24. Romulus Moore (Columbia), 25. William H. Noble (Randolph), 26. Daniel Palmer (Washington), 27. Lewis Pope (Wilkes), 28. W. H. D. Reynolds (Chatham), 29. Benjamin Sikes (Dougherty), 30. James Stewart (Chatham), 31. Alexander Stone (Jefferson), 32. Henry Strickland (Greene), 33. Henry M. Turner (Bibb), 34. George Wallace (Bibb), 35. John Whitaker (Terrell), 36. Robert Whitehead (Burke), 37. Samuel Williams (Harris). Sources: Drago, *Black Politicians*, appendix A: Black Legislators and Convention Delegates, 1867–1872; Foner, *Freedom's Lawmakers*; Grant, *Way It Was*; Legare, *Darien Journal*, 138n170; *Journal of the Proceedings of the Constitutional Convention of the People of Georgia*; Work, "Some Negro Members of Reconstruction Conventions," 63–119.

36. Drago, *Black Politicians*, appendix A: Black Legislators and Convention Delegates, 1867–1872; Du Bois, *Black Reconstruction in America*, 498, Hester, *Enduring Legacy*, 60–66. The four kept in office seem to have survived owing to declarations that they were white (though they were biracial) and despite the strange efforts on the part of white legislators to determine their race. See Wight, "Negroes in the Georgia Legislature," 85–97.

37. 1868 Georgia Constitution, accessed August 1, 2017, https://georgiainfo.galileo.usg.edu (website no longer active); Du Bois, *Black Reconstruction in America*, 498, 500–2; Drago, *Black Politicians*, 40–52.

38. Henry McNeal Turner, transcript of a letter of September 19, 1868, to Senator E. L. Morgan (likely Edwin D. Morgan), and Congressman Robert C. Schenck, Robert C. Schenck Papers, Box 4.3 21A-F-5c, Special Collections, Miami University, Ohio.

39. Henry McNeal Turner, transcript of a letter of September 19, 1868.

40. Drago, *Black Politicians*; 42, 67, 90, 146–47, 152, 153; Foner, *Freedom's Lawmakers*, 6, 12, 37–38, 46, 47–48, 50, 76, 80, 98, 115, 120, 153, 182, 215–16, 221–22; Hahn

et al., *Freedom*, 470–76; Hester, *Enduring Legacy*, 125–210; Wight, "Negroes in the Georgia Legislature," 85–97.

41. Counties unable to elect Blacks after the 1868 constitutional convention: Clay, Marion, Oglethorpe, Schley, Terrell, and Washington; counties unable to elect Blacks after 1870: Baldwin, Burke, Chatham, Clarke, Columbia, Dougherty, Greene, Hancock, Harris, Jasper, Jefferson, Laurens, Macon, Muscogee, Putnam, Richmond, Talbot, Warren, and Wilkes. (*See the Georgia maps [plates 6 and 7].*)

42. Drago, *Black Politicians*, 152–53.

43. Hahn, *Nation under Our Feet*, 289–92.

44. Hahn, *Nation under Our Feet*, 289–92.

45. This knowledge regime was successfully repressed in some places, particularly after the death of the last generation of slavery survivors. Excavating traceable remnants of the nineteenth-century knowledge regime around organizing access to citizenship rights would be helpful. We have living civil rights movement veterans today who were unaware in the 1950s and 1960s of the fact that Black southerners had voted in certain areas in the previous century. The history taught on this period outside of graduate studies still seems to be meager.

46. For related thoughts on the defense of the home as a repository of the personal histories of trauma among slavery survivors, see an episode on the gathering of oral history from slavery survivors in Davis, "Recovering Fugitive Freedoms," 61–67.

47. Butler, *Speech of Hon. Benjamin F. Butler*, 4. Butler included whites among the unnamed victims, making it more difficult to try to verify his numbers, as Black victims have been documented in more sources.

48. Butler, *Speech of Hon. Benjamin F. Butler*, 3–4; Drago, *Black Politicians*, 59, 63–64, 148–49.

49. Butler, *Speech of Hon. Benjamin F. Butler*, 3–4; Du Bois, *Black Reconstruction in America*, 504, 511; Drago, *Black Politicians*, 65.

50. *National Anti-Slavery Standard*, coverage of the *Georgia State Colored Convention*, Macon, GA, November 1869, 412.

51. *Georgia State Colored Convention*, Macon, GA, November 6, 1869, 412.

52. *Georgia State Colored Convention*, Macon, GA, November 13, 1869, 413–14.

53. *Georgia State Colored Convention*, Macon, GA, November 13, 1869, 413.

53. In the twentieth and twenty-first centuries such cases have been further complicated by having to prove discriminatory intent, which in turn has been made

more difficult. For further information, see two articles on the ongoing effects of the 1976 case *Washington v. Davis*: Strauss, "Discriminatory Intent Eyer, "Ideological Drift." On voter repression in the present moment—and with the caveat that it will be some time before it is known if new bills will become settled law—see the dozens of voter issues in GA s.b.202: Nick Corasaniti and Reid J. Epstein, "What Georgia's Voting Law Really Does," *New York Times*, published April 2, 2021, updated August 18, 2021, accessed August 19, 2021, https://www.nytimes.com/2021 /04/02/us/politics/georgia-voting-law-annotated.html.

54. "Mutual Benefit Clubs: They Are Many and Popular among the Southern Negroes," *New York Times*, June 9, 1895; "How to Organize and Conduct a Ladies' Missionary Society—Secret Societies Among the Colored People," *American Missionary* 4, no. 4 (1887): 120–22; "The Colored Catholics," *New York Times*, January 4, 1889.

55. Du Bois, *Dusk of Dawn*, 67–68. Du Bois writes of Hose's alleged crime as he heard of it at the time—the murder of his employer's wife, though it was the employer who was killed. Brundage, "Darien 'Insurrection' of 1899," 236.

56. Brundage, "Darien 'Insurrection' of 1899," 237–39.

57. Brundage, "Darien 'Insurrection' of 1899," 244–45, 247; "Georgia Riot Cases," *Los Angeles Herald*, no. 341, September 6, 1899, accessed May 31, 2014, https://cdnc.ucr.edu/cgi-bin/cdnc?a=d&d=LAH18990906.2.73#; Legare, *Darien Journal*, 16. By 1908, when the state had abandoned convict leasing for chain gangs, the state "formally defined 'woman' as a category constituted by whiteness" (and a category spared from chain gangs), while "females" (read Black women) could be put on gangs. For more on this, see Haley, "'Like I Was a Man,'" 53–77.

58. Wagner, "Disturbing the Peace," 183; "Negro Whipped in Dublin. He Made Remarks Reflecting on White Women," *Atlanta Constitution*, September 14, 1899.

Chapter 7. Florida: Faction

1. Berlin, Glymph, et al., *Freedom*, 225–26, 100; Hahn et al., *Freedom*, 410, 435.

2. Hahn et al., *Freedom*, 147.

3. J. M. Richardson, "Florida Black Codes," 369.

4. J. M. Richardson, "Florida Black Codes," 373–74, 370, 371, 372, 375; Thornbrough, *T. Thomas Fortune*, 10.

5. J. M. Richardson, "'We Are Truly Doing Missionary Work,'" 194.

6. Foner, *Second Founding*, 66.

7. "Martial Law in Florida," *Pensacola Observer*, June 21, 1866, reprinted in the *New York Times*, July 4, 1866, accessed December 11, 2019, https://timesmachine .nytimes.com/timesmachine/1866/07/04/79809780.html?pageNumber=2.

8. US Census Bureau, manuscript, Eighth Census of the United States, 1860.

9. Brown, *Florida's Black Public Officials*, 4–5; Foner, *Freedom's Lawmakers*, 147, 168.

10. Thornbrough, *T. Thomas Fortune*, 15; Hume, "Membership of the Florida Constitutional Convention of 1868," 1–21; Florida Department of State, "Marcellus Lovejoy Stearns, accessed January 10, 2022, https://dos.myflorida.com/florida -facts/florida-history/florida-governors/marcellus-lovejoy-stearns/.

11. Brown, *Florida's Black Public Officials*, 2–3, 6–9; Du Bois, *Black Reconstruction in America*, 511–23; Wallace, *Carpetbag Rule*, 72, 75; US Census Bureau, manu-script, Eighth Census of the United States, 1860; simpler source for counties: US Census Bureau, "Census Bulletin," no. 16, November 20, 1900, accessed Decem-ber 9, 2019, https://www2.census.gov/library/publications/decennial/1900 /bulletins/demographic/16-population-fl.pdf; Florida Department of State, "Harrison Reed," accessed December 9, 2019, https://dos.myflorida.com/florida -facts/florida-history/florida-governors/harrison-reed/. There were two impeach-ment attempts against Reed while he was governor.

12. Brown, *Florida's Black Public Officials,* 6; Florida Department of State, "Ossian Bingley Hart," accessed December 9, 2019, https://dos.myflorida.com/florida -facts/florida-history/florida-governors/ossian-bingley-hart/.

13. Brown, *Florida's Black Public Officials*, 7–11; Asarch, "Liberty Billings"; Forten, *Journal*, 173; Foner, *Freedom's Lawmakers*, 189–90; Higginson, *Army Life in a Black Regiment*; Hume, "Membership of the Florida Constitutional Convention of 1868," 4n12.

Recent articles on Billings being honored in Florida and on the preservation of his Fernandina home assert that he was an African American. I found no men-tion of his being a person of color in any of the sources on Black officeholders in Reconstruction or those above, including those from people who knew him, with the exception of John Wallace, who recounts an upset among Blacks at the 1867 Republican Party convention over his placement on their ticket, that was resolved by having a Blacks-only meeting to which he was denied admission; see Wallace, *Carpetbag Rule in Florida*, 57–58; Osborn, "Letters of a Carpetbagger in Florida," 239–85. Also Daniel Richards, who came with Billings to Florida, lists his group's proposed ticket as "all white men" and includes Billings.

14. Brown, *Florida's Black Public Officials*, 8.

15. Transcript of a letter by "An efficient laborer in the Cause," July 8 and 9, 1867, Robert C. Schenck Papers, Correspondence of Thomas Tullock.

16. Du Bois, *Black Reconstruction in America*, 521; Gibbs, *Shadow and Light*; Brown, *Florida's Black Public Officials*, 16; Wallace, *Carpetbag Rule*, 55.

17. Foner, *Freedom's Lawmakers*, 222–23.

18. The ten "Black and Tan" conventions were held in the states discussed in this book and in Texas. White leaders mentioned above who were in the convention were Osborn, Stearns, Purnam, Hart, Richards, and Billings.

19. African American delegates to the 1868 Florida constitutional convention: 1. O. B. Armstrong (Leon and Wakulla Counties); 2. William Bradwell (Nassau, Duval, and Saint John); 3. Homer Bryan (Washington, Calhoun, and Jackson); 4. Alonzo Chandler (Putnam, Marion, and Levy); 5. Green Davidson (Leon and Wakulla); 6. Auburn Erwin (Columbia and Baker); 7. Emanuel Fortune (Washington, Calhoun, and Jackson); 8. Jonathan Gibbs (Nassau, Duval, and Saint John); 9. Frederick Hill (Gadsden); 10. Major Johnson (Madison); 11. Robert Meacham (Jefferson); 12. Anthony Mills (Jefferson); 13. Joseph E. Oates (Leon and Wakulla); Charles H. Pearce (Leon); 15. William Saunders (Gadsden); 16. Thomas Urquhart (Hamilton and Suwanee); 17. Josiah T. Walls (Alachua); 18. Richard Wells (Leon); 19. John W. Wyatt (Leon). Sources: Brown, *Florida's Black Public Officials*; Foner, *Freedom's Lawmakers*; *Journal of the Proceedings of the Constitutional Convention of the State of Florida*; Rivers and Brown, "African Americans in South Florida."

20. Thornbrough, *T. Thomas Fortune*, 3–7, quotation on 12; Wallace, *Carpetbag Rule*, 55.

21. Brown, *Florida's Black Public Officials*, 10; Wallace, *Carpetbag Rule*, 55, 70.

22. Shofner, "Constitution of 1868," 374; Mary Ellen Klas, "Florida Has a History of Making It Harder for Black Citizens to Vote," *Miami Herald*, August 12, 2016. The Florida law, which was only recently repealed, is still a source of controversy as the state attempted to make new penalties that would have a disfranchising effect on ex-felons. On July 17, 2020, the US Supreme Court ruled to leave in place requirements that they pay "all fees, fines, and restitution," which will keep many from voting. Nina Totenberg, "Supreme Court Deals Major Blow to Felons' Right to Vote in Florida," NPR, July 17, 2020, accessed August 13, 2021, https://www.npr .org/2020/07/17/892105780/supreme-court-deals-major-blow-to-ex-felons-right -to-vote-in-florida. On Saunders: Osborn, "Letters of a Carpetbagger in Florida," 239–85; Foner, *Freedom's Lawmakers*, 189–90.

AME officeholders: Josiah Armstrong, William Bradwell, Noah Graham, Henry Harmon, Thomas W. Long, Robert Meacham, Charles Pearce, John R. Scott, William G. Stewart, and John W. Wyatt. For examples of leaders who were also builders of the AME Church in Florida, see Rivers, and Brown, "African Americans in South Florida," 5–23.

23. Du Bois, *Black Reconstruction in America*, 514; Foner, *Reconstruction*, 383; Ortiz, *Emancipation*, 12.

24. Shofner, "Militant Negro Laborers in Reconstruction Florida," 397–408.

25. Ortiz, *Emancipation*, 22–23.

26. Thornbrough, *T. Thomas Fortune*, 13–16; Wallace, *Carpetbag Rule*, 64.

27. Thornbrough, *T. Thomas Fortune*, 17–19; Foner, *Freedom's Lawmakers*, 168; J. Richardson, *Negro in the Reconstruction of Florida*, 171–72.

28. J. Anderson, *A. Philip Randolph*, 29; Ortiz, *Emancipation*, 18.

29. Scott, Fisk, and Vanderbilt were Gilded Age businessmen, all of whom were involved in railroads. Scott was also involved in the Compromise of 1877 that ended federal troop presence and therefore Reconstruction in the South. The reference here is specifically also aimed at the men's reputation for buying legislative cooperation.

30. Bradley, *Army and Reconstruction*, 68.

31. Foner, *Reconstruction*, 575–82.

32. Bradley, *Army and Reconstruction*, 71–72.

33. Hahn, *Nation under Our Feet*, 149, 151. An exception to the Posse Comitatus Act was used by President Dwight D. Eisenhower in 1957 to send troops to protect nine children attempting to attend Central High School in Little Rock, Arkansas. I mention this only to say that in the twentieth and twenty-first centuries, the law has experienced many renewed debates.

34. Foner, *Freedom's Lawmakers*, 77–78; Ortiz, *Emancipation*, 61, 270n3. Though voter repression has returned as an issue in 2021, the eventual resolution is likely some time off, given that new Florida laws will be contested. To get details on the new laws echoing and elaborating the state's nineteenth-century assault on Black voting, see Eliza Sweren-Becker, "Florida Enacts Sweeping Suppression Law," April 30, 2021, updated May 6, 2021, https://www.brennancenter.org/our-work/analysis-opinion/florida-enacts-sweeping-voter-suppression-law.

35. Hewitt, *Southern Discomfort*, 53.

Chapter 8. Alabama: Redemption

1. Foner, *Reconstruction*, 281.

2. Stockham, "Alabama Iron for the Confederacy," 163; Still, "Selma and the Confederate States Navy," 23; Knowles, "Labor, Race, and Technology."

3. Still, "Selma and the Confederate States Navy," 26, 27, 29; Stockham, "Alabama Iron for the Confederacy," 166, 171; Litwack, *Been in the Storm So Long*, 37.

4. Still, "Selma and the Confederate States Navy," 29, 32, 36.

5. Doster, "Shelby Iron Works Collection," 14; Knowles, "Labor, Race, and Technology," 20–21.

6. McKenzie, "Shelby Iron Company," 343.

7. McKenzie, "Shelby Iron Company," 344, 345–46, 347.

8. Bailey, *Neither Carpetbaggers nor Scalawags*, 1; Knowles, "Labor, Race, and Technology," 26.

9. US Census Bureau, manuscript, Eighth Census of the United States, 1860; US Census Bureau, manuscript, Ninth Census of the United States, 1870; Bailey, *Neither Carpetbaggers nor Scalawags*, 2.

10. "Proceedings of the Louisiana Conference of the African Methodist Episcopal Zion Church, New Orleans, May 17, 1865," in Foner and Walker, *Proceedings of the Black State Conventions, 1865–1900*, 76–79. These would have been lengthy trips then: at the common speed of fifteen to twenty miles per hour, the ride could take more than eleven hours; Montgomery to Meridian took at least six and a half hours; Montgomery to Jackson, at least ten hours.

11. Katcher, *Battle History of the Civil War*, 106–7; Kevin Dougherty, "Sherman's Meridian Campaign: A Practice Run for the March to the Sea," *Mississippi History Now*, April 2007, http://www.mshistorynow.mdah.ms.gov/articles/2/shermans-meridian-campaign-a-practice-run-for-the-march-to-the-sea; History, City of Meridian, accessed December 24, 2019, http://www.meridianms.org/index.cfm/residents/history/.

12. Rosen, *Terror in the Heart of Freedom*, 10.

13. Gutman, *Black Family in Slavery and Freedom*, 387–88; Litwack, *Been in the Storm So Long*, 289; Hahn, *Nation under Our Feet*, 151.

14. Dray, *Capitol Men*, 103–4; Foner, *Freedom's Lawmakers*, 13, 171.

15. Dray, *Capitol Men*, 104–6; Foner, *Freedom's Lawmakers*, 171–72; Blassingame, *Black New Orleans*, 35–36; Fitzgerald, *Union League*, 29. Pinchback and his family had used the name earlier in Cincinnati when he was thirteen, and he, his mother, and his sisters gave the name for the 1850 census.

16. Du Bois, *Black Reconstruction in America*, 488–89; Bailey, *Neither Carpetbaggers nor Scalawags*, 12–13, 14, 15.

17. Bailey, *Neither Carpetbaggers nor Scalawags*, 3–5, 7–10.

18. Bailey, *Neither Carpetbaggers nor Scalawags*, 17–18; Kolchin, *First Freedom*, 152–53; Schweninger, "Alabama Blacks and the Congressional Reconstruction Acts," 182–92.

19. "State Convention of the Colored Men of Alabama."

20. "State Convention of the Colored Men of Alabama"; Fitzgerald, *Union League*, 58.

21. Fitzgerald, *Union League*, 16, 37–38.

22. Bailey, *Neither Carpetbaggers nor Scalawags*, 31–33, 36; Fitzgerald, *Union League*, 43. Voter registration drives by 1960s activists produced renewed intimi-

dation of several kinds until the passage of the Voting Rights Act of 1965, which reanimated the state's high Black voter turnout. Voter repression attempts continued in the twenty-first century with a voter ID law and attempts to close thirty-one motor vehicle department agencies across the Black Belt and in neighboring counties. The voter ID law was still being contested in 2020. Kyle Whitemire, "As It Turns Out . . . Bentley's Driver's License Closures Were Racial, after All," *AL .com*, January 5, 2017, updated March 6, 2019, https://www.al.com/opinion/2017 /01/as_it_turns_out_bentleys_drive.html. As of July 2021, Alabama joined dozens of other states in passing laws that restrict voting access, specifically two bills: ALHB 538, which will "shorten the window to apply for a mail ballot," and HB285, which will "increase barriers for voters with disabilities." "Voting Laws Roundup: July 2021," July 22, 2021, https://www.brennancenter.org/our-work/research -reports/voting-laws-roundup-july-2021.

23. African American delegates to the 1867 Alabama constitutional convention: 1. Benjamin F. Alexander (Greene County); 2. Samuel Blandon (Lee); 3. John Carraway (Mobile); 4. Thomas Diggs (Barbour); 5. Peyton Finley (Montgomery); 6. James K. Greene (Hale); 7. Ovid Gregory (Mobile); 8. Jordan Hatcher (Dallas); 9. Benjamin Inge (Sumter); 10. Washington Johnson (Russell); 11. Columbus Jones (Madison); 12. L. S. Latham (Bullock); 13. Thomas Lee (Perry); 14. J. Wright McLeod (Marengo); 15. James T. Rapier (Lauderdale); 16. Lafayette Robinson (Madison); 17. Benjamin F. Royal (Bullock); 18. Alfred Strother (Dallas). Sources: Bailey, *Neither Carpetbaggers nor Scalawags*; Du Bois, *Black Reconstruction in America*; Foner, *Freedom's Lawmakers*; *Official Journal of the Constitutional Convention of the State of Alabama*; Richard Bailey and Beth Thacker, Unpublished Roster of Alabama House Members, 1997, accessed February 11, 2019, https://archives .alabama.gov/afro/AfricanAmerican%20Legislators%20in%20Reconstruction%20 Alabama1867.pdf.

24. Foner, *Freedom's Lawmakers*, 75, 90–91, 187; Bailey, *Neither Carpetbaggers nor Scalawags*, 38–40, 103, 241; Fitzgerald, *Union League*, 79, 155–56, 214.

25. Bailey, *Neither Carpetbaggers nor Scalawags*, 66–67; Foner, *Freedom's Lawmakers*, 177–78; Schweninger, "Alabama Blacks and the Congressional Reconstruction Acts," 182.

26. Bailey, *Neither Carpetbaggers nor Scalawags*, 39, 40, 66, 69–70; Foner, *Freedom's Lawmakers*, 41, 91, 113, 121, 131; Schweninger, "Alabama Blacks and the Congressional Reconstruction Acts," 194.

27. *Official Journal of the Constitutional Convention of the State of Alabama*, 8.

28. *Official Journal of the Constitutional Convention of the State of Alabama*, 61.

29. Du Bois, *Black Reconstruction in America*, 394.

30. *Official Journal of the Constitutional Convention of the State of Alabama*, 141, 93; Schweninger, "Alabama Blacks and the Congressional Reconstruction Acts," 189; Kolchin, *First Freedom*, 171.

31. *Official Journal of the Constitutional Convention of the State of Alabama*, 15, 189; Du Bois, *Black Reconstruction in America*, 492; Kolchin, *First Freedom*, 169.

32. William Yardley, "Stuart Hall, Trailblazing British Scholar of Multicultural Influences, Is Dead at 82," *New York Times*, February 17, 20014.

33. Bailey, *Neither Carpetbaggers nor Scalawags*, 37.

34. Anne Branigin, "'Reparations' for Confederates? UNC System Trustees Face Backlash after Paying More Than $2.5 Million to Confederate Group to House 'Silent Sam,'" *The Root*, December 18, 2019, https://www.theroot.com /reparations-for-confederates-unc-system-trustees-fac-1840517913; Foner, *Reconstruction*, 6, 194.

35. Bailey, *Neither Carpetbaggers nor Scalawags*, 169–70; Fitzgerald, *Union League*, 193; Schweninger, "Alabama Blacks and the Congressional Reconstruction Acts," 186.

36. Fitzgerald, *Union League*, 197; Dray, *Capitol Men*, 180–82; Foner, *Reconstruction*, 428.

37. Bailey, *Neither Carpetbaggers nor Scalawags*, 169, 170, 205–6.

38. Bailey, *Neither Carpetbaggers nor Scalawags*, 208; Foner, *Freedom's Lawmakers*, 3.

39. Bailey, *Neither Carpetbaggers nor Scalawags*, 146–47; Foner, *Freedom's Lawmakers*, 3; Bailey, *Neither Carpetbaggers nor Scalawags*, 208. On Birmingham, see Kelly, "Beyond the 'Talented Tenth.'"

Chapter 9. Louisiana: Societies

1. McPherson, *Battle Cry*, 551–52; Berlin, Glymph, et al., *Freedom*, 348–54; Du Bois, *Black Reconstruction in America*, 67–69; Both Butler and Banks were politicians (and, in fact, former political rivals in Massachusetts), with no training for military command who proved disastrous leaders in military operations. Even as politicians they both had the habit of irritating foes and allies by acting out of expediency more often than conviction.

2. Blassingame, *Black New Orleans*, 28–34; Scott, *Degrees of Freedom*, 30–37; Hahn, *Nation under Our Feet*, 317–18.

3. Signed by "J. M. Marshall, President of the Union Association," and "Henry Clay, Superintendent of the Dinner"; Berlin et al., *Free at Last*, 85.

4. Berlin, Glymph, et al., *Freedom*, 355, 356–57, 361.

5. Berlin, Glymph, et al., *Freedom*, 360, 364.

6. Berlin, Glymph, et al., *Freedom*, 373, 374–75, 570–71.

7. Berlin, Glymph, et al., *Freedom*, 594–98.

8. Berlin, Glymph, et al., *Freedom*, 594–98; Vincent, *Black Legislators in Louisiana*, 17–22; Blassingame, *Black New Orleans*, 168; Foner, *Freedom's Lawmakers*, 113–14.

9. McPherson, *Negro's Civil War*, 132.

10. Howard H. Bell, ed., "Proceedings of the National Convention of Colored Men, Held in the City of Syracuse, N.Y., October 4, 5, 6, and 7, 1864, with the Bill of Wrongs and Rights, and the Address to the American People," in *Minutes of the Proceedings of the National Negro Conventions*, n.p., last item; "National Equal Rights League," *New Orleans Tribune*, January 3, 1865; Houzeau, *My Passage*, 110–11.

11. Vincent, *Black Legislators in Louisiana*, 38. The Freedmen's Aid Association (FAA), a local organization, should not be confused with the northern-based Freedmen's Aid Society, a national group, begun by the AMA; Regis, "Social and Pleasure Clubs," 126–31; Regis, "Second Lines," 472–504.

12. Fabre, "African-American Commemorative Celebrations," 72–91; Regis, "Social and Pleasure Clubs," 128. While Regis is adapting to New Orleans the events related to the Haitian Revolution and Dred Scott, her source, Fabre, is actually discussing Black public events in the North. Fabre, who shows the development of an antebellum Black calendar of commemorations, does suggest to this reader that the August 1, 1834, British West Indies emancipation, celebrated in 1859 in fifty-seven locations, may have also had celebrants in Louisiana and other southern sites. On drilling in Alabama: Fitzgerald, *Union League*, 153.

13. "Freedmen's Aid Association," *New Orleans Tribune*, March 28, 1865; "Freedmen's Aid Association," *New Orleans Tribune*, April 11, 1865.

14. Du Bois, *Black Reconstruction in America*, 168–69.

15. Houzeau, *My Passage*, 37.

16. Houzeau, *My Passage*, 33; Blassingame, *Black New Orleans*, 57.

17. *New Orleans Tribune*, April 9, 1865; April 4, 1865; see also issues from April 2 to 14, 1865.

18. Sterling, *We Are Your Sisters*, 298.

19. Pound, "Slave to the Ex-Slave Narratives," 93–94. Cooper's name is given as Manda Cooper Col on the transcription. Col may have been Cole or an abbreviation (Col) for "colored," so I have used Manda Cooper.

20. Pound, "Slave to the Ex-Slave Narratives," 94, 84–85; White, *Ar'n't I a Woman?*, 114.

21. Sterling, *We Are Your Sisters*, 297–98; Richardson, *Christian Reconstruction*, 191.

22. On the Norfolk riot, see chapter 3 on Virginia. On Memphis: Rosen, *Terror in the Heart*. On all of the riots: Coakley, *Role of Federal Military Forces in Domestic Disorders*.

23. *The Declaration of Independence and the Constitution of the United States,* 37–38, U.S. Citizenship and Immigration Services, accessed August 18, 2021. https://www.uscis.gov/sites/default/files/document/guides/M-654.pdf; Foner, *Reconstruction,* 254–60.

24. Coakley, *Role of Federal Military Forces,* 280–81; Foner, *Reconstruction,* 263.

25. The tortured construction of this amendment and the compromise final version that inserted the word *male* into the clause on representation chagrined and radicalized many feminists in the abolitionist movement, who began a movement in search of another constitutional rupture for winning female suffrage. See Foner, *Reconstruction,* 255–60. For "Friends of Freedom," see Coakley, *Role of Federal Military Forces,* 282.

26. Coakley, *Role of Federal Military Forces,* 281; Dray, *Capitol Men,* 29.

27. Coakley, *Role of Federal Military Forces,* 282–83; Dray, *Capitol Men,* 29–30; Grant, *Papers of Ulysses S. Grant,* vol. 16, *1866,* 228.

28. Dray, *Capitol Men,* 28–32; Coakley, *Role of Federal Military Forces,* 281–85; Foner, *Reconstruction,* 263. The Battle of Fort Pillow, which took place April 12, 1864, became infamous when Confederate forces under Lieutenant General Nathan Bedford Forrest massacred hundreds of US Colored troops who had surrendered, an event covered in the papers as a scene of savagery.

29. Coakley, *Role of Military Federal Forces,* 285–86.

30. Grant, *Papers of Ulysses S. Grant,* 390.

31. Sterling, *We Are Your Sisters,* 298.

32. Sterling, *We Are Your Sisters,* 299.

33. Rosen, *Terror in the Heart of Freedom,* 62; Richardson, *Christian Reconstruction,* 219.

34. Sterling, *We Are Your Sisters,* 298–300; Al Kennedy, "The History of Public Education in New Orleans Still Matters" (2016), History Faculty Publications, Paper 5, accessed July 9, 2016, http://scholarworks.uno.edu/hist_facpubs/5.

35. Dray, *Capitol Men,* 106.

36. Dray, *Capitol Men,* 104–6; Du Bois, *Black Reconstruction in America,* 488; Foner, *Freedom's Lawmakers,* 13, 171–72; Arnesen, *Waterfront Workers of New Orleans,* 15; Terry L. Jones, "The Free Men of Color Go to War," *New York Times,* October 19, 2012.

37. Berlin, Glymph, et al., *Freedom,* 348.

38. African American delegates at the 1867–68 Louisiana constitutional convention: 1. Caesar C. Antoine (Caddo Parish); 2. Arnold Bertonneau (New Orleans); 3. Ovide Blandin (New Orleans); 4. Emile Bonnefoi (West Baton Rouge); 5. Henry Bonseigneur (New Orleans); 6. William G. Brown (Iberville); 7. Dennis

Burrell (Saint John the Baptist); 8. William Butler (Saint Helena); 9. Robert I. Cromwell (New Orleans); 10. Samuel E. Cuney (Rapides); 11. Pierre G. Deslonde (Iberville); 12. Auguste Donato Jr. (Saint Landry); 13. Gustave Dupart (Saint Tammany); 14. Ulgar Dupart (Terrebonne); 15. John B. Esnard (Saint Mary); 16. Louis Francois (E. Baton Rouge); 17. John Gair (E. Feliciana); 18. R. G. Gardner (Jefferson); 19. Ovide C. Glandin (New Orleans); 20. Leopold Guichard (Saint Bernard); 21. James Ingraham (Caddo); 22. Robert H. Isabelle (New Orleans); 23. Thomas H. Isabelle (New Orleans); 24. George H. Jackson (Saint Landry); 25. George Y. Kelso (Rapides); 26. Victor M. Lange (Baton Rouge); 27. Charles Leroy (Natchitoches); 28. Richard Lewis (E. Feliciana); 29. Theophile Mahier (W. Baton Rouge); 30. Thomas N. Martin (Jefferson); 31. Jules A. Massicot (Orleans); 32. William R. Meadows (Claiborne); 33. Milton Morris (Ascension); 34. Solomon R. Moses (New Orleans); 35. William Murrell (Lafourche); 36. Joseph C. Oliver (Saint James); 37. John Pierce (Bossier); 38. P. B. S. Pinchback (New Orleans); 39. Robert Poindexter (Assumption); 40. Curtis Pollard (Madison); 41. Fortune Riard (Lafayette); 42. Daniel D. Riggs (Washington); 43. J. H. A. Roberts (Jefferson); 44. Lazard A. Rodriguez (New Orleans); 45. John Scott (Winn); 46. Sosthene L. Snaer (Saint Martin); 47. Charles A. Thibaut (Plaquemines); 48. Edward Tinchaut (New Orleans); 49. P. F. Valfroit (Ascension); 50. Henderson Williams (Madison); 51. David Wilson (New Orleans). Sources: Foner, *Freedom's Lawmakers*; Hume and Gough, *Blacks, Carpetbaggers, and Scalawags*; *Official Journal of the Proceedings of the Convention: For Framing a Constitution for the State of Louisiana*; Rankin, "Origins of Black Leadership," 417–40; Vincent, "Negro Leadership and Programs," 339–51; Vincent, *Black Legislators in Louisiana*, 226–27.

39. Vincent, "Negro Leadership and Programs," 339–51; Houzeau, *My Passage*, 46–56; Vincent, *Black Legislators in Louisiana*, 69.

40. Houzeau, *My Passage*, 47–53, 149–52; Blassingame, *Black New Orleans*, 152–53, 212–13; Foner, *Reconstruction*, 331–32; Bell, *Revolution, Romanticism*, 268–75.

41. Vincent, *Black Legislators in Louisiana*, 68; Houzeau, *My Passage*, 56.

42. Scott, *Degrees of Freedom*, 71–72.

43. For an interesting analysis of why voter repression laws were successful in Louisiana, and the connection between the highly effective Understanding Clause in that state and contemporary repressive laws, see Keele, Cubbison, and White, "Suppressing Black Votes." For those curious about the most recent bills in Louisiana, see Mark Ballard, "Louisiana 2021 Voting Bills Not as Harsh as Other States: Here's Why," June 5, 2021, https://www.theadvocate.com/baton_rouge/news/politics/legislature/article_334d74bc-c62c-11eb-be02-ff61ecdccf39.html; Arnesen, *Waterfront Workers of New Orleans*, 74–75, 84–89, 229.

44. Lemann, *Redemption*, 197.

45. Lemann, *Redemption*, 197.

46. Dray, *Capitol Men*, 144–50.

47. Dray, *Capitol Men*, 285–86.

48. "Labor World," *Weekly Pelican*, April 2, 1887; "Rakings," "Angiers Angling," and "Secret Societies," *Weekly Pelican*, April 23, 1887; "Rakings," *Weekly Pelican*, August 13, 1887; "Sugar Laborer's Strike," *Weekly Pelican*, November 5, 1887; Scott, *Degrees of Freedom*, 81; Hahn, *Nation under Our Feet*, 420–21. Scott cautions that the most-often-cited number of strikers—ten thousand, used in all the papers and ending up in the historiography—is hard to document and that various parties had reason to use a large number.

49. Scott, *Degrees of Freedom*, 80–87; Hahn, *Nation under Our Feet*, 420–21. An example of this familiarity is that a descendant of one of the Black families that survived the massacre told me that her ancestors had been owned by the Minor family in Mississippi and were brought to their Southdown and Hollywood plantations in Terrebonne, and also worked at their Rienzi plantation in Thibodaux.

50. Scott, *Degrees of Freedom*, 82–83. For a detailed examination of how both the enormous strike and political activism were organized in the bayou parishes, see Scott, "'Stubborn and Disposed to Stand Their Ground,'" 103–26.

51. Scott, *Degrees of Freedom*, 75.

Chapter 10. Mississippi: Bulldoze

Epigraph: "History of the Bulldozer," August 14, 2020, https://youtu.be/O9kaGueXHqY.

1. Gutman, *Black Family in Slavery and Freedom*, 387.

2. Aptheker, *To Be Free*, 148.

3. Aptheker, *To Be Free*, 148–49, 156.

4. *Act to Punish Certain Offenses Therein Named & for Other Purposes*, Laws of the State of Mississippi; *An Act to Regulate the Relation of Master and Apprentice as Relates to Freedmen, Free Negroes and Mulattoes*, Laws of the State of Mississippi.

5. Hahn, *Nation under Our Feet*, 130, 148–51.

6. Hahn, *Nation under Our Feet*, 146–47; on politicization of daily encounters: Hahn, *Nation under Our Feet*, 128; Litwack, *Been in the Storm So Long*, 426; Morgan, *Yazoo*, 57, 60.

7. Litwack, *Been in the Storm So Long*, 430. Litwack grants a justification not part of the hysteria of the time: "It was not as though the blacks had no reason to revolt. Even as they persisted in testing their freedom, they had not succeeded in breaking the bonds that tied them to the farms and plantations as agricultural laborers."

8. Fanny Cannady interview, "Born in Slavery: Slave Narratives from the Federal Writers' Project, 1936 to 1938." North Carolina Narratives, vol. 11, pt. 1, 159–164, accessed June 5, 2013, https://www.loc.gov/resource/mesn.111/?sp=2.

9. "White Louisianans to the Governor of Louisiana, October 13, 1865," in Hahn et al., *Freedom*, 820–21; "Mississippi Freedmen's Bureau Assistant Commissioner to the Freedmen's Bureau Commissioner, November 2, 1865," in Hahn et al., *Freedom*, 816–17; Hahn, *Nation under Our Feet*, 148–53.

10. Hahn, *Nation under Our Feet*, 149, 151; "Duncan S. Cage, et al to His Excellency J. Madison Wells, December 15, 1865," in Hahn et al., *Freedom*, 874.

11. Litwack, *Been in the Storm So Long*, 428; Fitzgerald, *Union League*, 117–18.

12. "We the Colorede [*sic*] People to the Governer of Mississippi," letter from freedpeople of Claiborne County, MS, December 3, 1865, in Hahn et al., *Freedom*, 856–58. Bracketed additions are the editors' attempts to replace characters presumed lost to damage to the document.

13. "We the Colorede [*sic*] People to the Governer of Mississippi," 856–58.

14. Hahn, *Nation under Our Feet*, 151.

15. Hahn et al., *Freedom*, 857.

16. Foner and Lewis, *Black Workers*, 142; Sterling, *We Are Your Sisters*, 355–57; Hunter, *To 'Joy My Freedom*, 75–76.

17. Foner, *Freedom's Lawmakers*, 127–28; Bell, "1864 Convention," in *Minutes of the Proceedings of the National Negro Conventions*, 29.

18. John M. Langston, transcript of a letter of July 7, 1867, Robert C. Schenck Papers.

19. James D. Lynch, transcript of a letter of July 9, 1867, Robert C. Schenck Papers. Lynch's figure for the Black population is close to the actual number, which was 436,631, and perhaps larger by the time he was there. Amber Periona, "Which U.S. States Had the Most Slaves at the Start of the Civil War?," WorldAtlas, September 28, 2018, accessed February 14, 2021, https://www.worldatlas.com/articles /which-u-s-states-had-the-most-slaves-at-the-start-of-the-civil-war.html.

20. John M. Langston, transcript of a letter of July 21, 1867, Robert C. Schenck Papers; Major Thomas L. Norton, U.S. Army, July 30, 1867, Robert C. Schenck Papers.

21. Fitzgerald, *Union League*, 46–49.

22. Frankel, *Freedom's Women*, 166.

23. African American delegates to the 1868 Mississippi constitutional convention: 1. John C. Brinson (Rankin County); 2. Charles Caldwell (Hinds); 3. William T. Combash (Washington); 4. Amos Draine (Madison); 5. Charles W. Fitzhugh (Wilkinson); 6. Emanuel Handy (Copiah); 7. Henry P. Jacobs

(Adams); 8. Albert Johnson (Warren); 9. Wesley Lawson (Lawrence); 10. William Leonard (Yazoo); 11. Henry Mayson (Hinds); 12. J. Aaron Moore (Lauderdale); 13. Cyrus Myers (Rankin); 14. Matthew T. Newsom (Claiborne); 15. Isham Stewart (Noxubee); 16. Doctor Stites (Washington); 17. Thomas W. Stringer (Warren). Sources: Foner, *Freedom's Lawmakers*; *Journal of the Proceedings in the Constitutional Convention of the State of Mississippi, 1868*; Wharton, *Negro in Mississippi*.

24. Morgan, *Yazoo*, 168, 481; Wharton, *Negro in Mississippi*, 146–51; Dray, *Capitol Men*, 180–82, 188; Foner, *Freedom's Lawmakers*, 36–37, 152–53, 206; Fitzgerald, *Union League*, 63, 198–99; *Journal of the Proceedings in the Constitutional Convention of the State of Mississippi, 1868*, 250–52, 302, 308.

25. Sewell and Dwight, *Mississippi Black History Makers*, 49–51. For those interested in continuity with twentieth-century movements: The Mississippi Prince Hall Masons are well known for their ties to the southern movement after 1955 include associations with Thurgood Marshall and Medgar Evers and serving the meetings of the NAACP, Council of Federated Organizations (COFO), Mississippi Freedom Democratic Party (MFDP), and Mississippi Teachers Association. See also Alferdteen, *History of the Most Worshipful*.

William Scott's sons would in turn operate the Scott Newspaper Syndicate, a Black-owned chain of *Daily World* papers in Atlanta, Birmingham, and Memphis. See Sewell and Dwight, *Mississippi Black History Makers*, 273–77; Thompson, *Black Press in Mississippi*, 16. The *Atlanta Daily World* still exists.

26. Lynch, *Reminiscences*, 166.

27. Lynch, *Reminiscences*, 166.

28. Wells, "Reconstruction and Its Destruction in Hinds County," 85–108.

29. Wells, "Reconstruction and Its Destruction in Hinds County," 104–5.

30. Davis, *My Confederate Kinfolk*, 234–35.

31. Morgan, *Yazoo*, 505.

32. Wells, *Crusade for Justice*, 9, 16, 22–23. The experience with these local publications was Wells's introduction to a life in journalism.

33. Wells, *Crusade for Justice*, 47–52, 55–58.

34. Giggie, *After Redemption*, 34–35.

35. *Report and Testimony of the Select Committee*, 351.

36. Thornbrough, *T. Thomas Fortune*, 148; Lynch, *Reminiscences*, 340; *Journal of the Proceedings in the Constitutional Convention of the State of Mississippi*. Frederick Douglass et al. and the race problem: "The Race Problem. Great Speech of Frederick Douglass, delivered before the Bethel Literary and Historical Association, in the Metropolitan A.M.E. Church, Washington, D.C." [October 21, 1890], accessed November 7, 2019, www.loc.gov/item/74171961/.

37. Lynch, *Reminiscences*, 418, 341–42, 343.

38. R. Palmer, *Deep Blues*, 52–53; "Peavine," Mississippi Blues Trail, accessed November 12, 2019, http://www.msbluestrail.org/blues-trail-markers/peavine; Oliver, *Songsters and Saints*, 78; McKittrick, *Demonic Grounds*, xiv; Giggie, *After Redemption*, 24–25, 26.

39. Oliver, *Songsters and Saints*, 172–95; Giggie, *After Redemption*, 168–69.

40. Woods, *Development Arrested*.

41. Giggie, *After Redemption*, 165, 167–69, 174, 175, 181–82, 187. The innovation of blues music became a big part of the development of gospel music and the practice of the Church of God in Christ, in particular. Its musical ministries, now under its International Department of Music, are today justly famous.

42. Giggie, *After Redemption*, 169, 187; McKittrick, *Demonic Grounds*, xiv.

Chapter 11. Arkansas: Minority

1. Adeline Blakeley interview, Federal Writers' Project: Slave Narrative Project, vol. 2, Arkansas, pt. 1, Abbott-Byrd, 180–83, accessed August 8, 2019, https://www.loc.gov/resource/mesn.021/?sp=185. These interviews were often conducted by individuals who were primarily interested in the former enslaved people's recollections of African American folklore, and often the interviewees went to some lengths to recite their family origins as far back as they knew, to mark permanent separations from parents and siblings, and to recount interesting facts concerning places they had been taken by their owners, people known to them by virtue of bondage, and pressing needs concerning their immediate survival as older citizens.

2. Moneyhon, *Impact of the Civil War*, 127–36; Tom Robinson interview, Federal Writers' Project: Slave Narrative Project, vol. 2, Arkansas, pt. 6, Quinn-Tuttle, 61–68, accessed August 8, 2019, https://www.loc.gov/resource/mesn.026/?sp=66.

3. Moneyhon, *Impact of the Civil War*, 94–97, 132–33, 138; Taylor, *Embattled Freedom*, 106–8.

4. Boston Blackwell interview, Federal Writers' Project, Slave Narrative Project, vol. 2, Arkansas, pt. 1, Abbott-Byrd, 168–74, accessed August 8, 2019, https://www.loc.gov/item/mesn021/. One of the interesting facets of Blackwell's interview was his continued apparent surprise that after he explained an episode of his life, the interviewer would ask him what he did next. At one point, he exclaims, "I ain't never been axed about myself in my *whole* life!" This points to the possible subjective significance mass meetings may have held for freedpeople, given the frequency of personal testimony at such meetings. It shines a disturbing light on the cultural damage of a population whose members not only were systematically told they had no history but in which individuals were inured to the idea that society had no interest in their personal experience.

5. Blakeley interview, Federal Writers' Project, 189, 190.

6. Berlin, Miller, et al., *Freedom*, 38–39; Moneyhon, *Impact of the Civil War*, 137–38; Taylor, *Embattled Freedom*, 108–9.

7. Berlin, Miller, et al., *Freedom*, 551, 555–56.

8. Berlin, Miller, et al., *Freedom*, 556, 565; Berlin, Glymph, et al., *Freedom*, 637, 699; Davis, *My Confederate Kinfolk*, 186–87.

9. Moneyhon, *Impact of the Civil War*, 151; Richardson, *Christian Reconstruction*, 48; Pearce, "American Missionary Association," 242–59; Friends Freedmen's Association records (mc.950.075), Quaker and Special Collections, Haverford College, Haverford. See also table 11.1 at the end of chapter 11.

10. Moneyhon, *Impact of the Civil War*, 150; Berlin, Glymph, et al., *Freedom*, 646–47.

11. Henry Blake interview, "Born in Slavery: Slave Narratives from the Federal Writers' Project, 1936 to 1938," Arkansas narratives, vol. 2, pt. 1, Abbott-Byrd, 177–79, accessed August 8, 2019, https://www.loc.gov/resource/mesn.021/?sp =180; Moneyhon, *Impact of the Civil War*, 178; Berlin, Glymph, et al., *Freedom*, 646–47.

12. Moneyhon, *Impact of the Civil War*, 178; Berlin, Glymph, et al., *Freedom*, 646–47.

13. Kohl, "'This Godforsaken Town,'" 109–44; Du Bois, *Black Reconstruction in America*, 547; Downs, *Sick from Freedom*, 47; Moneyhon, *Impact of the Civil War*, 138–40, 161, 164, 219; Taylor, *Embattled Freedom*, 106–39, 140–44, 179.

14. *Proceedings of the Convention of Colored Citizens of the State of Arkansas*.

15. "Proceedings of the Convention of Colored Citizens of the State of Arkansas, Held in Little Rock, Thursday, Friday and Saturday, Nov. 30, and Dec. 1, and 2, 1865," in Foner and Walker, *Proceedings of the Black State Conventions, 1865–1890*, 192, 193. On Exodusters from Arkansas, see *Report and Testimony of the Select Committee*. On Africa emigration from Arkansas, see Barnes, *Journey of Hope*.

16. Fourth Amendment to the US Constitution, Constitution Annotated, accessed January 10, 2022, https://constitution.congress.gov/constitution /amendment-4/.

17. Moneyhon, *Impact of the Civil War*, 209.

18. Foner, *Reconstruction*, 119; Moneyhon, *Impact of the Civil War*, 210, 138–40; Clayton, *Aftermath of the Civil War*, 30–31, 33; Taylor, *Embattled Freedom*, 106–39, 140–44. Regarding the riots in which there were serious failures of the military to protect freedpeople against domestic terror in Norfolk, Memphis, and New Orleans, these episodes followed the April passage of the Civil Rights Act of 1866. For detailed information, see Moore, "Norfolk Riot," 155–64; Coakley, *Role of Federal Military Forces*; Rosen, *Terror in the Heart of Freedom*.

19. Moneyhon, *Impact of the Civil War*, 244–45.

20. Delegates to the 1868 constitutional convention: 1. William H. Grey (Phillips County [Helena]); 2. Monroe Hawkins (Lafayette [Texarkana]); 3. Thomas P. Johnson (Pulaski [Little Rock]); 4. James W. Mason (Chicot); 5. William Murphy (Jefferson [Pine Bluff]); 6. Henry Rector (Pulaski); 7. Richard Samuels (Hempstead [Hope]); 8. James T. White (Phillips). Sources: *Debates and Proceedings of the Convention Which Assembled at Little Rock*; Dillard, "To the Back of the Elephant," 3–15; Foner, *Freedom's Lawmakers*; St. Hilaire, "Negro Delegates in the Arkansas Constitutional Convention," 38–69; Wintory, "African-American Legislators," 385–434.

21. St. Hilaire, "Negro Delegates in the Arkansas Constitutional Convention," 53.

22. Du Bois, *Black Reconstruction in America*, 549, 548. Grey became a grand master of his lodge in 1873. On his Masonic membership: "Arkansas Black Lawyers," August 15, 2019, http://arkansasblacklawyers.uark.edu/lawyers/whgrey.html.

23. Du Bois, *Black Reconstruction in America*, 548–50; St. Hilaire, "Negro Delegates in the Arkansas Constitutional Convention," 45.

24. Blackwell interview, Federal Writers' Project, 172.

25. Moses Jeffries interview, Federal Writers' Project: Slave Narrative Project, vol. 2, Arkansas, pt. 4, Jackson-Lynch, 38–42, accessed September 7, 2019, https://www.loc.gov/resource/mesn.024/?sp=41. The "grandfather law" Jeffries cites is what was known as a "grandfather clause," inserted in some southern state constitutions in 1865, that had the effect of only allowing voting by people whose grandfather could vote prior to the Civil War.

26. William H. Harrison interview, Federal Writers' Project: Slave Narrative Project, vol. 2, Arkansas, pt. 3, Gadson-Isom, 185–89, accessed September 7, 2019, https://www.loc.gov/resource/mesn.023/?sp=186. Harrison, who said he was owned by a cousin of Benjamin Harrison, and knew him as a child, also said he wrote President Harrison, who sent for him twice to play fiddle (which a former owner had forced him to learn) at the White House.

Ab Jenkins interview, Federal Writers' Project: Slave Narrative Project, vol. 2, Arkansas, pt. 4, Jackson-Lynch, accessed August 8, 2019, https://www.loc.gov/resource/mesn.024/?sp=51; Frank Greene interview, Federal Writers' Project: Slave Narrative Project, vol. 2, Arkansas, pt. 3, Gadson-Isom, accessed August 8, 2019, https://www.loc.gov/resource/mesn.023/?sp=103.

27. Clayton, *Aftermath of the Civil War in Arkansas*, 58–59. The Fort Pillow Massacre occurred on April 12, 1864, in Tennessee, resulting in the deaths of about three hundred Black soldiers, most of whom had surrendered.

28. Clayton, *Aftermath of the Civil War in Arkansas*, 61, 63, 68, 69–70, 111–63; Moneyhon, *Impact of the Civil War and Reconstruction*, 251.

29. Clayton, *Aftermath of the Civil War in Arkansas*, 76–84.

30. Clayton, *Aftermath of the Civil War in Arkansas*, 51, 70, 88–91, 135–37.

31. Clayton, *Aftermath of the Civil War in Arkansas*, 99–100, 102; Finley, *From Slavery to Uncertain Freedom*, 146, 152.

32. Ellis Jefson interview, Federal Writers' Project: Slave Narrative Project, vol. 2, Arkansas, pt. 4, Jackson-Lynch, 43–46, accessed August 10, 2019, https://www.loc .gov/resource/mesn.024/?sp=47.

33. Moneyhon, *Impact of the Civil War and Reconstruction*, 256–63; Clayton, *Aftermath of the Civil War in Arkansas*, 70, 86, 96, 347; Foner, *Reconstruction*, 528; Atkinson, "Arkansas Gubernatorial Campaign and Election of 1872," 307–21; Woodward, "Brooks and Baxter War in Arkansas," 315–36. The word *brindletail* means striped like a tiger, but Atkinson reports that the nickname came from a Black man who disparaged Brooks's voice by comparing it to a brindletail bull whose bellow "scared all the cattle."

34. Frank Boone interview, Federal Writers' Project: Slave Narrative Project, vol. 2, Arkansas, pt. 1, Abbott-Byrd, 202–9, accessed August 10, 2019, https://www.loc .gov/resource/mesn.021/?sp=207; Foner, *Reconstruction*, 344.

35. On conflict with the party: Dillard, "To the Back of the Elephant," 3–15; Barnes, *Journey of Hope*, 41.

36. Gatewood, "Sunnyside," 5–29.

37. Gatewood, "Sunnyside," 11–13, Foner, *Freedom's Lawmakers*, 142.

38. Gatewood, "Sunnyside," 5–13; Foner, *Freedom's Lawmakers*, 142; "The Arkansas Troubles," *New York Times*, December 27, 1871, 1 (letter from James W. Mason); "The Chicot County (Arkansas) Affair," *New York Times*, December 28, 1871, 5; "The Arkansas Troubles: Emphatic Denial by the Governor, A Singular Narrative of Events by an Eye-Witness," *New York Times*, December 29, 1871, 2; "Chicot," *Memphis Daily Appeal*, March 2, 1871, 2; "Murder and Pillage by Armed Negroes," *Edgefield Advertiser*, December 28, 1871, 2; "Chicot County Race War of 1871," Encyclopedia of Arkansas, accessed August 11, 2019, http://www .encyclopediaofarkansas.net/encyclopedia/entry-detail.aspx?entryID=7615.

39. Barnes, *Journey of Hope*, 12.

40. Barnes, *Journey of Hope*, 2.

41. Barnes, *Journey of Hope*, 36, 60.

42. Gatewood, "Sunnyside," 14–22; Giggie, *After Redemption*, 28–29.

43. Gatewood, "Sunnyside," 13–26; "J. C. Coovert," accessed August 12, 2019, www .jccoovert.com/sunnyside/sunnyside_gallery.html.

44. Gatewood, "Sunnyside," 7; Giggie, *After Redemption*, 36–37; Morrison, *Playing in the Dark*, 10.

45. Gatewood, "Sunnyside," 26–28; National New Deal Preservation Association, https://web.archive.org/web/20160303214424/http://newdeallegacy.org/table _communities.html (no longer available).

Conclusion. What Lives on Is Black Political Thought

1. Hahn, *Nation under Our Feet*, 199, 525n60. For comparison, in 2020—a banner year for registration—the rate was 73 percent of voting-age Americans registered. Jennifer Cheeseman Day and Thom File, "What Recent Elections Tell Us about the American Voter Today," US Census Bureau, October 5, 2020, accessed August 22, 2021, https://www.census.gov/library/stories/2020/10/what-can-recent -elections-tell-us-about-the-american-voter-today.html. Participation improved quite a bit in 2020. See Jacob Fabina, "Record High Turnout in 2020 General Election: Despite Pandemic Challenges, 2020 Election Had Largest Increase in Voting Between Presidential Elections on Record," April 29, 2021, accessed August 22, 2021, https://www.census.gov/library/stories/2021/04/record-high -turnout-in-2020-general-election.html.

2. St. Hilaire, "Negro Delegates in the Arkansas Constitutional Convention of 1868," 49.

3. Du Bois, *Black Reconstruction in America*, 483.

4. Kolchin, *First Freedom*, 170; Foner, *Freedom's Lawmakers*, 91.

5. Du Bois, *Black Reconstruction in America*, 542; Taylor, *Negro in Reconstruction in Virginia*, 229.

6. Du Bois, *Black Reconstruction in America*, 395, 436; Foner, *Freedom's Lawmakers*, 176.

7. Bailey, *Neither Carpetbaggers nor Scalawags*, 51.

8. Du Bois, *Black Reconstruction in America*, 394.

9. Drago, *Black Politicians*, 42; Foner, *Reconstruction*, 163–64; Foner, *Freedom's Lawmakers*, 38.

10. Du Bois, *Black Reconstruction in America*, 393, 395.

11. Foner, *Freedom's Lawmakers*, 177, 233; Foner and Lewis, *Black Workers*, 177.

12. Drago, *Black Politicians*, 87; Foner, *Freedom's Lawmakers*, 23–24, 82, 163; Du Bois, *Black Reconstruction in America*, 544; Taylor, *Negro in Reconstruction in Virginia*, 223.

13. Holt, *Black over White*, 155–62; Foner, *Freedom's Lawmakers*, 157; *Official Journal of the Constitutional Convention of the State of Alabama*, 61; Du Bois, *Black Reconstruction in America*, 399.

14. Du Bois, *Black Reconstruction in America*, 505; Foner, *Freedom's Lawmakers*, 82; Gordon, *African American Women and the Vote*, 2, 15–16, 49–51. Though females

gained the franchise in 1920, the majority of southern Black women did not get to vote until after the Voting Rights Act of 1965.

15. Mahan, "Racial Origins of U. S. Domestic Violence Law," 1, n5, 4. See also "Domestic Violence: Best Practices for Law Enforcement Response," North Carolina Governor's Crime Commission Violence Against Women Committee, January 1998, ii, accessed September 25, 2021, https://files.nc.gov/ncdps/documents/files/dvproto.pdf.

16. Foner, *Freedom's Lawmakers*, 82; on complaints to the Freedmen's Bureau: Schwalm, *Hard Fight for We*, 254–68; on domestic violence law: Mahan, "Racial Origins of U. S. Domestic Violence Law," 1, 1n5.

17. Du Bois, *Black Reconstruction in America*, 396; Bailey, *Neither Carpetbaggers nor Scalawags*, 47; Furstenberg, "History and Current Status of Divorce," 30.

18. Foner, *Freedom's Lawmakers*, 31.

19. Reid, "Four in Black," 229–43; Foner, *Freedom's Lawmakers*, 164. On the Equal Pay Act and Lilly Ledbetter Act, see "Equal Pay Act of 1963 and Lilly Ledbetter Fair Pay Act of 2009," US Equal Employment Opportunity Commission, accessed August 22, 2021, https://www.eeoc.gov/laws/guidance/equal-pay-act-1963-and-lilly-ledbetter-fair-pay-act-2009.

20. Drago, *Black Politicians*, 146; Foner, *Freedom's Lawmakers*, 47–48.

21. Du Bois, *Black Reconstruction in America*, 491. On violence against Blacks observed by Union troops, see Davis, *My Confederate Kinfolk*, 164–65, 167–69 (entries from the diary of Elijah Evan Edwards, a Methodist Chaplain, 7th Minnesota Volunteer Infantry).

22. Drago, *Black Politicians*, 40, 48–49; Du Bois, *Black Reconstruction in America*, 500–503.

23. DuBois, *Black Reconstruction in America*, 515; "The 1885 Florida Constitution," Constitutional Revision Florida, accessed January 10, 2022, http://library.law.fsu.edu/Digital-Collections/CRC/CRC-1998/conhist/1885con.html. The constitution used today is the one completed in 1968, though revisions were made in 1977 and 1997. A ruling on July 12, 2014, by a Leon County judge regarding the redistricting in that county and neighboring counties—the very counties most contested by Black leaders in nineteenth-century Florida—threw out a new map, charging that Republicans made a "mockery" of a new transparent redistricting process mandated by law in 2010. One of the plaintiffs, the League of Women Voters, has been fighting the skewing of districts since its foundation in 1942, and the ruling represents its first breakthrough for voters. David Zucchino, "Florida Redistricting Illegally Favors Republicans, Judge Rules," *Los Angeles Times*, July 10, 2014.

24. Cecelski, "Abraham H. Galloway," 53–54; Foner, *Freedom's Lawmakers*, 160, 150.

25. Du Bois, *Black Reconstruction in America*, 497, 505–7.

26. Foner, *Freedom's Lawmakers*, 70–71; University of Michigan Law School, Civil Rights Clearinghouse, Case Profile, Jackson v. Bishop, accessed July 14, 2014, http://www.clearinghouse.net/detail.php?id=554.

27. Du Bois, *Black Reconstruction in America*, 468–69; "Rapier, James Thomas, Biography," History, Art and Archives, US House of Representatives, accessed August 23, 2021, https://history.house.gov/People/Detail/20161; "Lynch, John Roy, Biography," History, Art and Archives, US House of Representatives, accessed August 23, 2021, https://history.house.gov/People/Detail/17259; Drago, *Black Politicians*, 44; Vincent, *Black Legislators in Louisiana*, 61–62.

28. Du Bois, *Black Reconstruction in America*, 437, 472–73; Dray, *Capitol Men*, 108–9; Foner, *Freedom's Lawmakers*, 164.

29. Bailey, *Neither Carpetbaggers nor Scalawags*, 44–45.

30. Bailey, *Neither Carpetbaggers nor Scalawags*, 44–45; Du Bois, *Black Reconstruction in America*, 437; Morgan, *Yazoo*, 204–6, 211–13.

31. Du Bois, *Black Reconstruction in America*, 497, 550–51.

32. Lowe, "Virginia's Reconstruction Convention," 345, 357; Foner, *Freedom's Lawmakers*, 19; Bailey, *Neither Carpetbaggers nor Scalawags*, 46; Du Bois, *Black Reconstruction in America*, 437, 468; Foner, *Reconstruction*, 452.

33. Downs, *Sick from Freedom*, 146–61; Du Bois, *Black Reconstruction in America*, 413; Northup, *Twelve Years a Slave*. What is now known as Central State Hospital still exists: "History behind Central State Hospital," accessed August 23, 2021, http://www.csh.dbhds.virginia.gov/about.html.

34. Du Bois, *Black Reconstruction in America*, 413, 499.

35. On the National Afro-American League: Thornbrough, *T. Thomas Fortune*, 105–16; on the National Afro-American Council: Thornbrough, *T. Thomas Fortune*, 174–86, 191–92, 273–74; Giddings, *When and Where I Enter*, 93.

36. On Biela: Kazuo Kinoshita, "3D/Biela: Past, Present, and Future Orbits," Gary W. Kronk's Cometography, accessed August 26, 2020, https://cometography.com/pcomets/003d.html; Great Comet of 1861: "c/1861 J1 (Great Comet of 1861)," accessed August 26, 2020, https://cometography.com/lcomets/1861j1.html; Great Comet of 1860: Zoe McIntosh, "It Turns Out Walt Whitman Was Right about Those Giant Meteors," *Christian Science Monitor*, June 7, 2010; Leonids: Donald W. Olson and Laurie E. Jasinski, "Abe Lincoln and the Leonids," *Sky and Telescope*, November 1999; Joe Rao, "The Leonid Meteor Shower Revealed: Shooting Star Show's Brilliant History," Space.com, November 12, 2010, https://shar.es/1lo2WC; Douglass, *My Bondage and My Freedom*; Humez, *Harriet Tubman*, 180, 212.

TABLE SOURCE NOTES

Sources

Tables 3.1–11.1

Ali, Omar. *In the Lion's Mouth: Black Populism in the New South, 1886–1900.* Jackson: University Press of Mississippi, 2010.

Catton, Bruce. *The American Heritage New History of the Civil War.* Edited by James M. McPherson. New York: MetroBooks, 2001.

Chronicling America. Historic American Newspapers Database. Library of Congress, Washington, DC.

Fitzgerald, Michael W. *The Union League Movement in the Deep South: Politics and Agricultural Change during Reconstruction.* Baton Rouge: Louisiana State University Press, 1989.

Foner, Eric. *Freedom's Lawmakers: A Directory of Black Officeholders during Reconstruction.* Rev. ed. Baton Rouge: Louisiana State University Press, 1996.

Foner, Eric. *Reconstruction: America's Unfinished Revolution, 1863–1877.* New York: Harper and Row, 1988.

Garlock, Jonathan. *Guide to the Local Assemblies of the Knights of Labor.* Westport, CT: Greenwood Press, 1982.

Hahn, Steven. *A Nation under Our Feet: Black Political Struggles in the Rural South from Slavery to the Great Migration.* Cambridge, MA: Harvard University Press, 2003.

Kann, Kenneth. "The Knights of Labor and the Southern Black Worker." *Labor History* 18, no. 1 (1977): 49–70.

Katcher, Philip. *Battle History of the Civil War, 1861–1865.* New York: Barnes and Noble, 2000.

Litwack, Leon F. *Been in the Storm So Long: The Aftermath of Slavery.* New York: Vintage, 1980.

McPherson, James M. *Battle Cry of Freedom: The Civil War Era.* New York: Ballantine, 1989.

Richardson, Joe M. *Christian Reconstruction: The American Missionary Association and Southern Blacks, 1861–1890.* Tuscaloosa: University of Alabama Press, 1986.

US Census Bureau. Manuscript. Eighth Census of the United States, 1860; Ninth Census of the United States, 1870; Tenth Census of the United States, 1880.

Additional Sources

Table 3.1

Letters of Dr. H. J. Brown and Rev. John V. Given, July 23, 1867. Robert C. Schenck Papers. Correspondence of Thomas Tullock, Secretary of the Union Republican Congressional Committee (July 1867). Special Collections, Miami University, Oxford, OH.

Newby-Alexander, Cassandra L. *An African American History of the Civil War in Hampton Roads*. Charleston, SC: History Press, 2010.

Richardson, Alfred M. *Map of the Southern Express Company*. Charleston, SC: Walker, Evans and Cogswell, ca. 1884. Library of Congress. Accessed January 10, 2022. https://www.loc.gov/item/gm71000842/.

Spriggs, William Edward. "The Virginia Colored Farmers' Alliance: A Case Study of Race and Class Identity." *Journal of Negro History* 64, no. 3 (1979): 191–204.

Table 4.1

Anderson, Eric. *Race and Politics in North Carolina, 1872–1901: The Black Second*. Baton Rouge: Louisiana State University Press, 1981.

University of North Carolina Libraries. African American Newspapers in North Carolina. Accessed May 28, 2017. http://www2.lib.unc.edu/ncc/ref/study/africanamericannewspapers.html.

Table 5.1

Kessler, Sidney H. "The Organization of Negroes in the Knights of Labor." *Journal of Negro History* 37, no. 3 (1952): 248–76.

Table 6.1

Mitchell, Michele. *Righteous Propagation: African Americans and the Politics of Racial Destiny after Reconstruction*. Chapel Hill: University of North Carolina, 2004.

Table 7.1

Hewitt, Nancy A. *Southern Discomfort: Women's Activism in Tampa, Florida, 1880s–1920s*. Urbana: University of Illinois Press, 2001.

Mitchell, Michele. *Righteous Propagation: African Americans and the Politics of Racial Destiny after Reconstruction*. Chapel Hill: University of North Carolina Press, 2004.

Ortiz, Paul. *Emancipation Betrayed: The Hidden History of Black Organizing and White Violence in Florida from Reconstruction to the Bloody Election of 1920*. Berkeley: University of California Press, 2005.

Richardson, Joe M. "'We Are Truly Doing Missionary Work': Letters from American Missionary Association Teachers in Florida, 1864–1874." *Florida Historical Quarterly* 54, no. 2 (1975): 178–95.

Shofner, Jerrell H. "Militant Negro Laborers in Reconstruction Florida." *Journal of Southern History* 39, no. 3 (1973): 397–408.

Table 8.1

Bailey, Richard. *Neither Carpetbaggers nor Scalawags: Black Officeholders during the Reconstruction of Alabama, 1867–1878*. 2nd ed. Montgomery, AL: Richard Bailey Publishers, 1993.

Mansfield, Michael W. "'A Slide, a Swing and an Oak Tree': Maysville, Alabama, and the Birth of an African American Community." PhD diss., University of Alabama, 2005.

Mitchell, Michele. *Righteous Propagation: African Americans and the Politics of Racial Destiny after Reconstruction*. Chapel Hill: University of North Carolina Press, 2004.

Richardson, Alfred M. *Map of the Southern Express Company*. Charleston, SC: Walker, Evans and Cogswell, ca. 1884. Library of Congress. Accessed January 10, 2022. https://www.loc.gov/item/gm71000842/.

Rogers, William Warren. "The Farmers' Alliance in Alabama." *Alabama Review* 15, no. 1 (1962): 5–18.

Rogers, William Warren. "The Negro Alliance in Alabama." *Journal of Negro History* 45, no. 1 (1960): 38–44.

Table 9.1

Blassingame, John W. *Black New Orleans, 1860–1880*. Chicago: University of Chicago Press, 1973.

Dray, Philip. *Capitol Men: The Epic Story of Reconstruction through the Lives of the First Black Congressmen*. Boston: Houghton Mifflin, 2008.

Mitchell, Michele. *Righteous Propagation: African Americans and the Politics of Racial Destiny after Reconstruction*. Chapel Hill: University of North Carolina Press, 2004.

Report and Testimony of the Select Committee of the United States Senate to Investigate the Causes of the Removal of the Negroes from the Southern States to the

Northern States. S. Rep. No. 693, 46th Cong., 2d Sess. Washington, DC: Government Printing Office, 1880.

Scott, Rebecca J. *Degrees of Freedom: Louisiana and Cuba after Slavery.* Cambridge, MA: Harvard University Press, 2005.

Table 10.1

Mitchell, Michele. *Righteous Propagation: African Americans and the Politics of Racial Destiny after Reconstruction.* Chapel Hill: University of North Carolina Press, 2004.

Report and Testimony of the Select Committee of the United States Senate to Investigate the Causes of the Removal of the Negroes from the Southern States to the Northern States. S. Rep. No. 693, 46th Cong., 2d Sess. Washington, DC: Government Printing Office, 1880.

Wharton, Vernon Lane. *The Negro in Mississippi, 1865–1890.* New York: Harper and Row, 1965.

Willis, John C. *Forgotten Time: The Yazoo-Mississippi Delta after the Civil War.* Charlottesville: University of Virginia Press, 2000.

Table 11.1

Barnes, Kenneth C. *Journey of Hope: The Back to Africa Movement in Arkansas in the Late 1800s.* Chapel Hill: University of North Carolina Press, 2004.

Dillard, Tom. "To the Back of the Elephant: Racial Conflict in the Arkansas Republican Party." *Arkansas Historical Quarterly* 33, no. 1 (1974): 3–15.

Mitchell, Michele. *Righteous Propagation: African Americans and the Politics of Racial Destiny after Reconstruction.* Chapel Hill: University of North Carolina Press, 2004.

Report and Testimony of the Select Committee of the United States Senate to Investigate the Causes of the Removal of the Negroes from the Southern States to the Northern States. S. Rep. No. 693, 46th Cong., 2d Sess. Washington, DC: Government Printing Office, 1880.

BIBLIOGRAPHY

Collections

Alabama Department of Archives and History, Montgomery, AL. https://digital
.archives.alabama.gov/

Tulane University, New Orleans, LA

Amistad Research Center, American Missionary Association Collection, Archives
and Special Collections

Arkansas Digital Archives. https://digitalheritage.arkansas.gov/

Columbia University Rare Book and Manuscript Library, New York, NY

Emory University, Stuart A. Rose Manuscript, Archive and Rare Book Library,
Atlanta, GA

William H. Scott, Sr. Papers, William Henry Scott, Sr. (1848–1910). BV2
Scrapbook 1874–1880

Georgia Archives. https://www.georgiaarchives.org/research

Library of Congress, Washington, DC

Chronicling America. Historic American Newspapers Database.

Federal Writers' Project. "Born in Slavery: Slave Narratives from the Federal
Writers' Project, 1936 to 1938." https://www.loc.gov/collections/slave
-narratives-from-the-federal-writers-project-1936-to-1938/about-this
-collection/.

Library of Virginia, Richmond

Virginia Writers Project Oral Histories

Virginia African American Newspapers Collection

Louisiana State Archives, Baton Rouge. https://www.sos.la.gov
/HistoricalResources/ResearchHistoricalRecords/LocateHistoricalRecords
/Pages/default.aspx.

Louisiana State University, Baton Rouge

Louisiana Newspapers. https://www.lib.lsu.edu/special/CC/louisiana
-newspapers.

Miami University Libraries, Walter Havighurst Special Collections, Oxford, OH

Robert C. Schenck Papers, Correspondence of Thomas Tullock, Secretary of the
Union Republican Congressional Committee

Mississippi Department of Archives and History, Jackson

Journal of Proceedings. Grand Lodge, Knights of Pythias, State of Mississippi,
1882

Mississippi State University Libraries Digital Collections. https://www.library
.msstate.edu/digitalcollections.
National Archives, Washington, DC
Records of the Freedman's Savings and Trust Company
New Orleans Public Library, New Orleans, LA
African American Collections
South Carolina Department of Archives and History, Columbia.
https://scdah.sc.gov/.

Newspapers and Periodicals

Afro-American Churchman (Virginia; 1886)
American Eagle (Virginia)
Atlanta Constitution (national)
Baltimore Afro-American (national)
Chicago Defender
Chicago Tribune
Christian Recorder (national)
Colored American (Georgia), 1865–66
Danville Register
Danville Times
Free State (Mississippi)
Golden Rule (Mississippi)
Jackson Advocate
Jackson Daily News
Jackson Headlight
Light (Mississippi; 1891)
The Louisianian (issues from 1870–72, 1872–78, 1879–82)
L'Union (Lousiana; 1862–64)
Lynchburg Opportunity (1915)
Midland Express (Virginia; 1893)
Monthly Advocate (Virginia; 1896)
National Baptist World
National Pilot (Virginia; 1890)
New Orleans Tribune (1864–69)
Newport News Star (1931–35)
New York Age
New York Daily Tribune
New York Times
Norfolk Journal and Guide (1916–27)
People's Advocate (Virginia; 1876–86)
Petersburg Lancet (1882–86)

Pittsburgh Courier
Richmond Daily Dispatch (1850–84)
Richmond Daily Enquirer
Richmond Planet (1883–1938)
Richmond Reformer (1897–1905)
Richmond Times
Roanoke Weekly Press (1892)
Southern News (Virginia; 1892)
Southern Opinion (Virginia; 1867–69)
Southwestern Christian Advocate (Louisiana; 1877–1929)
Staunton Tribune (Virginia; 1927)
True Southerner (Virginia; 1866)
Virginia Star (1877–82)
Weekly Pelican (1886–89)
Whig (Virginia)

Published Primary Sources

An Act to protect all Persons in the United States in their Civil Rights and liberties and furnish the Means of their Vindication, Thirty-Ninth Congress, Sess. I. Ch. 31. 1866. [April 9, 1866]. Accessed February 5, 2021. https://www.loc.gov/item/llsl-v14/.

Acts of the General Assembly of the State of South Carolina, Passed at the Session of 1864–65. Columbia, SC: Julian A. Selby, Printer to the State, 1866. Accessed July 18, 2018. https://www.carolana.com/SC/Legislators/Documents/Acts_of_the_General_Assembly_of_the_State_of_South_Carolina_1864_1865.pdf.

American Missionary Association. *History of the American Missionary Association with Illustrative Facts and Anecdotes.* New York: AMA Bible House, 1891.

Baldwin, James, *The Fire Next Time.* New York: Dell, 1963.

Bell, Howard H., ed. *Minutes of the Proceedings of the National Negro Conventions.* New York: Arno Press and the New York Times, 1969.

Berlin, Ira, Barbara J. Fields, Steven F. Miller, Joseph P. Reidy, and Leslie S. Rowland, eds. *Free at Last: A Documentary History of Slavery, Freedom, and the Civil War.* New York: New Press, 1992.

Berlin, Ira, Thavolia Glymph, Steven F. Miller, Joseph P. Reidy, Leslie S. Rowland, and Julie Saville, eds. *Freedom: A Documentary History of Emancipation, 1861–1867,* series 3, vol. 1, *The Wartime Genesis of Free Labour: The Lower South.* Cambridge: Cambridge University Press, 2012.

Berlin, Ira, Marc Favreau, and Steven F. Miller, eds. *Remembering Slavery: African Americans Talk about Their Personal Experiences of Slavery and Emancipation.* New York: New Press, 2011.

Berlin, Ira, Steven F. Miller, Joseph P. Reidy, and Leslie S. Rowland, eds. *Freedom: A Documentary History of Emancipation, 1861–1867*, series 1, vol. 2, *The Wartime Genesis of Free Labor: The Upper South*. Cambridge: Cambridge University Press, 1993.

Bien, Julius. *Map of United States Rail Roads, Showing the Rail Roads Operated during the War from 1862–1866, as Military Lines; under the Direction of Bvt. Big. Gen. D. C. McCallum, Director and General Manager*. New York: n.p., 1866. Library of Congress Geography and Map Division, Washington, DC. Accessed May 30, 2013. http://www.loc.gov/item/98688412.

Blassingame, John W., ed. *Slave Testimony: Two Centuries of Letters, Speeches, Interviews, and Autobiographies*. Baton Rouge: Louisiana State University Press, 1977.

Butler, Benjamin. *Speech of Hon. Benjamin F. Butler, of Massachusetts, Delivered in the House of Representatives, December 20 and 21, 1869*. Washington, DC: F. J. Rives & Geo. A Bailey, Reporters and Printers of the Debates of Congress, 1869. Reprinted, Washington, DC: Library of Congress, 2017.

Clayton, Powell. *The Aftermath of the Civil War in Arkansas*. New York: Neale Publishing, 1915. Reprint, London: FB&C, 2015.

Commager, Henry Steele. *Documents in American History*, vol. 2 of 2. 9th ed. New York: Appleton-Century-Crofts, 1973.

Debates and Proceedings of the Convention Which Assembled at Little Rock, January 7th, 1868 under the Provision of the Act of Congress of March 24, 1867, and the Acts of March 23rd and July 19th, 1867, Supplementary Thereto, to Form a Constitution for the State of Arkansas. Little Rock: J. G. Price, Printer to the Convention, 1868. Accessed July 8, 2013. http://onlinebooks.library.upenn.edu/webbin/book/lookupname?key=Arkansas%20Constitutional%20Convention%20.

Delany, Martin R. *Blake or the Huts of America*. Edited by Floyd J. Miller. Boston: Beacon, 1970.

Delany, Martin R. *The Condition, Elevation, Emigration and Destiny of the Colored People of the United States*. Philadelphia, PA: by the author, 1852. Accessed June 14, 2016. https://www.gutenberg.org/files/17154/17154-h/17154-h.htm.

Douglass, Frederick. *My Bondage and My Freedom*. New York: Miller, Orton and Mulligan, 1855.

Douglass, Frederick. *Narrative of the Life of Frederick Douglass, An American Slave, Written by Himself*. Edited by Benjamin Quarles. Cambridge, MA: Belknap/Harvard University Press, 1973.

Douglass, Frederick. *Selected Speeches and Writings*. Edited by Philip S. Foner. Chicago: Lawrence Hill Books, 1999.

Du Bois, W. E. B. *Dusk of Dawn: An Essay toward an Autobiography of a Race Concept*. New York: Schocken Books, 1968.

Du Bois, W. E. B., ed. *Some Efforts of American Negroes for Their Own Social Betterment: Report of an Investigation under the Direction of Atlanta University;*

Together with the Proceedings of the Third Conference for the Study of the Negro Problems, Held at Atlanta University, May 25–26, 1898. Atlanta: Atlanta University Press, 1898. Accessed January 11, 2022. https://citeseerx.ist.psu.edu/viewdoc/download?doi=10.1.1.1063.9578&rep=rep1&type=pdf.

Equal Rights and Educational Association of Georgia. *Proceedings of the Convention of the Equal Rights and Educational Association of Georgia, Assembled at Macon, October 29th, 1866; Containing the Annual Address of the President, Captain J. E. Bryant.* Augusta, GA: The Loyal Georgian, 1866.

Equal Suffrage: Address from the Colored Citizens of Norfolk, Va., to the People of the United States: Also an Account of the Agitation among the Colored People of Virginia for Equal Rights, with an Appendix Concerning the Rights of Colored Citizens before the State Courts. New Bedford, MA: E. Anthony and Sons, Printers, 1865. Accessed August 9, 2021. https://www.loc.gov/item/09032794/#:~:text=(1865)%20Equal%20suffrage%3A%20address,witnesses%20before%20the%20state%20courts%20.

Foner, Philip S., and Ronald L. Lewis, eds. *The Black Worker: A Documentary History from Colonial Times to the Present.* Vol. 3, *The Black Worker during the Era of the Knights of Labor.* Philadelphia: Temple University Press, 1978.

Foner, Philip S., and Ronald L. Lewis, eds. *Black Workers: A Documentary History from Colonial Times to the Present.* Philadelphia: Temple University Press, 1989.

Foner, Philip S., and George E. Walker, eds. *Proceedings of the Black State Conventions, 1840–1865.* Vol. 1, *New York, Pennsylvania, Indiana, Michigan, Ohio.* Philadelphia: Temple University Press, 1979.

Foner, Philip S., and George E. Walker, eds. *Proceedings of the Black State Conventions, 1865–1900.* Vol. 1. Philadelphia: Temple University Press, 1986.

Forten, Charlotte L. *The Journal of Charlotte L. Forten: A Free Negro in the Slave Era.* Edited by Ray A. Billington. New York: W. W. Norton, 1953.

Fortune, T. Thomas. *After War Times: An African American Childhood in Reconstruction-Era Florida.* Edited by Daniel R. Weinfeld. Tuscaloosa: University of Alabama Press, 2014.

Georgia State Colored Convention (Macon, GA, 1869). In *Proceedings of the Black National and State Conventions 1865–1900,* edited by Phillip S. Foner and George E. Walker, 412–14. Philadelphia: Temple University Press, 1986.

Gibbs, Mifflin Wistar. *Shadow and Light: An Autobiography.* Lincoln: University of Nebraska Press, 1995.

Grant, Ulysses S. *The Papers of Ulysses S. Grant.* Vol. 16, *1866.* Edited by John Y. Simon. Carbondale: Southern Illinois University Press, 1988. Accessed January 11, 2022. https://msstate.contentdm.oclc.org/digital/collection/USG_volume/id/9071 of Ulysses S. Grant%2C Volume 16: 1866%2C page 228/field/title/mode/exact/conn/and.

Hahn, Steven, Steven F. Miller, Susan E. O'Donovan, John C. Rodrigue, and Leslie S. Rowland, eds. *Freedom: A Documentary History of Emancipation,*

1861–1867, Selected from the Holdings of the National Archives of the United States, series 3, vol. 1, Land and Labor, 1865. Chapel Hill: University of North Carolina Press, 2008.

Hodges, Willis. The Autobiography of Willis Augustus Hodges, a Free Man of Color. In Free Man of Color: The Autobiography of Willis Augustus Hodges, edited by Willard B. Gatewood Jr. Knoxville: University of Tennessee Press, 1982.

Houzeau, Jean-Charles. My Passage at the New Orleans Tribune: A Memoir of the Civil War Era. Baton Rouge: Louisiana State University Press, 1984.

Johnson, Hannibal A. The Sword of Honor: A Story of the Civil War. Hallowell, ME: Register Printing House, 1906.

Journal of the Constitutional Convention of the State of North-Carolina, at Its Session 1868. Raleigh: Joseph W. Holden, Convention Printer, 1868. Accessed July 8, 2013. http://docsouth.unc.edu/nc/conv1868/conv1868.html.

Journal of the Constitutional Convention of the State of Virginia, Convened in the City of Richmond, December 3, 1867, and an Order of General Schofield, Dated Nov. 2, 1867, in Pursuance of the Act of Congress of March 23, 1867. Richmond, VA: Office of the New Nation, 1867. Accessed August 5, 2021. https://babel.hathitrust .org/cgi/pt?id=umn.319510024615024&view=1up&seq=13&skin=2021.

Journal of the House of Representatives of the State of South Carolina Being the Regular Session of 1870–71. Columbia, SC: Republican Printing Co., 1871. Accessed March 4, 2020. https://www.carolana.com/SC/Legislators/Documents /Journal_of_the_House_of_Representatives_of_the_State_of_South _Carolina_1870_1871.pdf.

Journal of the House of Representatives of the State of South Carolina Being the Regular Session of 1871–72. Columbia, SC: Republican Printing Co., 1872. Accessed March 4, 2020. https://www.carolana.com/SC/Legislators/Documents /Journal_of_the_House_of_Representatives_of_the_State_of_South _Carolina_1871_1872.pdf.

Journal of the House of Representatives of the State of South Carolina Being the Regular Session of 1872–73. Columbia, SC: Republican Printing Co., 1873. Accessed March 4, 2020. https://www.carolana.com/SC/Legislators/Documents /Journal_of_the_House_of_Representatives_of_the_State_of_South _Carolina_1872_1873.pdf.

Journal of the Proceedings of the Constitutional Convention of the People of Georgia Held in the City of Atlanta in the Months of December, 1867, and January, February and March, 1868. And Ordinances and Resolutions Adopted. Published by Order of the Convention. Augusta, GA: E. H. Pughe, Book and Job, Printer, 1868. Accessed July 8, 2013. http://dlg.galileo.usg.edu/meta/html/dlg /zlgb/meta_dlg_zlgb_gb0086.html?Welcome.

Journal of the Proceedings of the Constitutional Convention of the State of Florida: Begun and Held at the Capitol, at Tallahassee, on Monday, January 20th, 1868. Tallahassee, FL: Edward M. Cheney, Printer, 1868. Accessed January 11, 2022. https:// babel.hathitrust.org/cgi/pt?id=mdp.35112105447702&view=1up&seq=1.

Journal of the Proceedings in the Constitutional Convention of the State of Missis-sippi. Jackson, MS: E. L. Martin, 1890. Accessed July 11, 2019. https://catalog .hathitrust.org/Record/100200913/Home.

Journal of the Proceedings in the Constitutional Convention of the State of Mississippi, 1868. Jackson: E. Stafford, Printer, 1871. Accessed July 8, 2013. https://catalog .hathitrust.org/Record/010423330.

Journal of the Senate of the State of Georgia, 1870, 8–13; 137–38. Accessed January 11, 2022. https://books.google.com/books?id=Du5AAQAAMAAJ&pg=PA137 #v=onepage&q&f=false.

Journal of the Senate, State of Georgia in the General Assembly, 11–1–1871. Accessed January 11, 2022. https://books.google.com/books?id=Du5AAQAAMAAJ& pg=PA137#v=onepage&q&f=false.

Journal of the Senate of the State of South Carolina Being the Regular Session, Commencing November 22, 1870. Columbia, SC: John W. Denny, Printer to the State, 1870. Accessed August 15, 2013. https://www.carolana.com/SC /Legislators/Documents/Journal_of_the_Senate_of_the_State_of_South _Carolina_1870_1871.pdf.

King Martin L., Jr. *Why We Can't Wait.* New York: Signet Classics, 2000.

Laws of the State of Mississippi, Passed at a Regular Session of the Mississippi Legis-lature, Held in Jackson, October, November and December, 1865, Jackson, 1866. In Hahn et. al, *Freedom,* 56–59, 57 n 126.

An Act to Amend the Vagrant Laws of the State.

An Act to Confer Civil Rights on Freedmen, and for Other Purposes.

Act to Punish Certain Offenses Therein Named & for Other Purposes.

An Act to Regulate the Relation of Master and Apprentice as Relates to Freedmen, Free Negroes and Mulattoes.

Legare, John Girardeau. *The Darien Journal of John Girardeau Legare, Ricegrower.* Athens: University of Georgia Press, 2012.

Lockwood, Lewis. *Mary S. Peake: The Colored Teacher at Fortress Monroe.* Boston: American Tract Society, 1862.

Lynch, John Roy. *Reminiscences of an Active Life: The Autobiography of John Roy Lynch.* Edited by John Hope Franklin. Chicago: University of Chicago Press, 1970.

Mellon, James, ed. *Bullwhip Days: The Slaves Remember, An Oral History.* New York: Avon Books, 1990.

Mississippi in 1875. Report of the Select Committee to Inquire into the Mississippi Election of 1875, with the Testimony and Documentary Evidence. In Two Vol-umes. 44th Cong., 1st Sess., Rep. No. 527. Washington, DC: Government Printing Office, 1876. Accessed July 12, 2013. https://babel.hathitrust.org/cgi /pt?id=uc1.c025383545&view=1up&seq=7&skin=2021.

Morgan, Albert T. *Yazoo; or, On the Picket Line of Freedom in the South: A Personal Narrative.* Columbia: University of South Carolina Press, 2000.

Northup, Solomon. *Twelve Years a Slave: Narrative of Solomon Northup, a Citizen of New York, Kidnapped in Washington City in 1841, and Rescued in 1853 from*

a Cotton Plantation Near the Red River in Louisiana. Auburn, NY: Derby
and Miller, 1853. Accessed January 17, 2018. http://docsouth.unc.edu/fpn
/northup/northup.html.

*Official Journal of the Constitutional Convention of the State of Alabama: Held
in the City of Montgomery, Commencing on Tuesday, November 5th, A.D.
1867*. Montgomery: Barrett and Brown, Book and Job Printers and Binders,
1868. Accessed July 8, 2019. https://catalog.hathitrust.org/Record/011618221.

*Official Journal of the Proceedings of the Convention: For Framing a Constitution for
the State of Louisiana*. New Orleans: J. B. Roudanez and Co., Official Printers, 1867–68. Accessed July 8, 2013. https://catalog.hathitrust.org/Record
/001143968.

Perdue, Charles L., Jr., ed. *Weevils in the Wheat: Interviews with Virginia Ex-Slaves*.
Charlottesville: University of Virginia Press, 1994.

Pierce, Edward Lillie. "The Contrabands of Fortress Monroe." *Atlantic Monthly*,
November 1861, 626–40.

Pound, DaNean Olene. "Slave to the Ex-Slave Narratives." Master's thesis, Northwestern State University of Louisiana, 2005.

*Proceedings of the Colored People's Convention of the State of South Carolina, Held
in Zion Church, Charleston, November, 1865. Together with the Declaration of
Rights and Wrongs; An Address to the People; A Petition to the Legislature, and
a Memorial to Congress*. Charleston: South Carolina Leader Office, 1865. Accessed September 28, 2018. http://coloredconventions.org/items/show/570.

*Proceedings of the Constitutional Convention of South Carolina Held in Charleston,
S.C., beginning January 14th and ending March 17th, 1868, including the Debates
and Proceedings*, vol. 1. Charleston: Denny and Perry, 1868. Accessed July 8,
2013. http://archive.org/details/proceedingscons00carogoog.

*Proceedings of the Convention of Colored Citizens of the State of Arkansas, Held in
Little Rock, Thursday, Friday and Saturday, Nov. 30, Dec. 1 and 2, 1865*. Colored
Conventions Project. Accessed August 4, 2019. http://coloredconventions.org
/items/show/559.

*Proceedings of the State Convention of Colored Men of the State of Tennessee, with
the Addresses of the Convention to the White Loyal Citizens of Tennessee, and
the Colored Citizens of Tennessee.: Held at Nashville, Tenn., August 7th, 8th,
9th and 10th, 1865*. Nashville: Daily Press and Times Job Office, 1865. http://
coloredconventions.org/items/show/522.

*Report and Testimony of the Select Committee of the United States Senate to Inves-
tigate the Causes of the Removal of the Negroes from the Southern States to the
Northern States*. S. Rep. No. 693, 46th Cong., 2d Sess. Washington, DC:
Government Printing Office, 1880.

*Resolution 133, A Joint Resolution Honoring the Life and Memory of Dr. Joy Joseph
Johnson, Fred D. Alexander, Richard C. Erwin, John W. Winters, Sr, Dr. Alfreda Johnson Webb, Jeanne Hopkins Lucas and Other Pioneer African American Members of the General Assembly, in Observance of African American His-*

tory Month. Accessed April 17, 2014. http://www.ncga.state.nc.us/Sessions
/2013/Bills/Senate/PDF/S133v2.pdf.

Richardson, Alfred M. *Map of the Southern Express Company.* Charleston, SC:
Walker, Evans and Cogswell, ca. 1884. Library of Congress. Accessed January
10, 2022. https://www.loc.gov/item/gm71000842/.

*Senate Journal of the Proceedings of the Senate of the State of Florida at the Thirteenth
Session of the Legislature. Begun and Held at the Capitol, in the City of Tallahassee, on Tuesday, January 6, 1885.* Tallahassee: Charles E. Dyke, State Printer,
1885. Accessed October 15, 2019. https://hdl.handle.net/2027/chi.096238112
?urlappend=%3Bseq=13.

"State Convention of the Colored Men of Alabama, Mobile, May 4, 1867." *New
Orleans Tribune,* May 7, 1867. Colored Conventions Project. Accessed December 25, 2019. https://omeka.coloredconventions.org/items/show/565.

*Statute at Large of South Carolina Vol. XII containing the Acts from December 1861
to December 1866. An Act to Establish and Regulate the Domestic Relations of
Persons of Color and to Amend the Law in Relation to Paupers and Vagrancy,
Act No. 4733. General Assembly, 19 December 1865.* Columbia, SC: Republican
Printing Corp., 1875. University of South Carolina Law Library, Statutes
at Large 1682-1866. Accessed January 11, 2022. https://archive.org/details/
statutesatlarge013repu/page/268/mode/2up.

Taylor, Susie King. *A Black Woman's Civil War Memoirs: Reminiscences of My Life
in Camp with the 33rd U.S. Colored Troops, Late 1st South Carolina Volunteers.*
Princeton, NJ: Markus Wiener, 1997.

Teamoh, George. *God Made Man, Man Made the Slave: The Autobiography of
George Teamoh.* Edited by F. N. Boney, Richard L. Hume, and Rafia Zafar.
Macon, GA: Mercer University Press, 1990.

*Thirteenth Session, 1885. The Acts and Resolutions Adopted by the Legislature of
Florida, at its Thirteenth Session, under the Constitution of 1868, Together with
an Appendix Containing a Statement of Receipts and Expenditures for 1883–84,
as Required by the Constitution.* Tallahassee: Charles E. Dyke, State Printer,
1885.

US Census Bureau. Manuscript. Eighth Census of the United States, 1860;
Ninth Census of the United States, 1870; Tenth Census of the United
States, 1880.

US Congress. Senate. *Mississippi in 1875: Report of the Select Committee to Inquire
into the Mississippi Election of 1875.* 2 vols. 44th Cong., 1st Sess., Rep. No. 527.

Walker, David. *David Walker's Appeal: To the Coloured Citizens of the World, but
in Particular, and Very Expressly, to Those of the United States of America.*
Boston: David Walker, 1830. Accessed September 21, 2011. http://docsouth
.unc.edu/nc/walker/menu.html.

Wallace, John. *Carpetbag Rule in Florida.* Jacksonville, FL: Da Costa Printing and
Publishing House, 1888. Accessed February 2, 2019. http://hdl.handle.net
/2027/mdp.39015032045307.

Washington, Booker T. *The Booker T. Washington Papers.* Vol. 5, *1899–1900*. Edited by Louis R. Harlan and Raymond W. Smock. Urbana: University of Illinois Press, 1976.

Wells, Calvin W. "Reconstruction and Its Destruction in Hinds County." In *Publications of the Mississippi Historical Society*, vol. 9, edited by Franklin L. Riley, 85–108. Oxford, MS: Mississippi Historical Society, 1906.

Wells, Ida B. *Crusade for Justice: The Autobiography of Ida B. Wells.* Edited by Alfreda M. Duster. Chicago: University of Chicago Press, 1970.

Wells, Ida B. *Southern Horrors and Other Writings: The Anti-lynching Campaign of Ida B. Wells, 1892–1900.* Edited by Jacqueline Jones Royster. Boston: Bedford/St. Martin's, 1997.

Secondary Sources

Abbott, Richard. "Black Ministers and the Organization of the Republican Party in the South in 1867: Letters from the Field." *Hayes Historical Journal* 6, no. 1 (1986). Accessed July 22, 2013. http://www.rbhayes.org/research/hayes -historical-journal-black-ministers-and-the-republican-party/.

Adams, Jessica. *Wounds of Returning: Race, Memory, and Property on the Postslavery Plantation.* Chapel Hill: University of North Carolina Press, 2007.

Alferdteen, Harrison. *A History of the Most Worshipful Stringer Grand Lodge: Our Heritage Is Our Challenge.* Jackson, MS: Most Worshipful Grand Stringer Lodge, 1977.

Ali, Omar H. *In the Lion's Mouth: Black Populism in the New South, 1886–1900.* Jackson: University Press of Mississippi, 2010.

Anderson, Benedict. *Imagined Communities: Reflections on the Origin and Spread of Nationalism.* Rev. ed. New York: Verso, 1991.

Anderson, Eric. *Race and Politics in North Carolina, 1872–1901: The Black Second.* Baton Rouge: Louisiana State University Press, 1981.

Anderson, Jervis. *A. Philip Randolph: A Biographical Portrait.* Berkeley: University of California Press, 1986.

Angell, Stephen W., and Anthony B. Pinn. *Social Protest Thought in the African Methodist Episcopal Church, 1862–1939.* Knoxville: University of Tennessee Press, 2000.

Aptheker, Herbert. *To Be Free: Pioneering Studies in Afro-American History.* 1948. New York: Citadel Press, 1991.

Arnesen, Eric. "Following the Color Line of Labor: Black Workers and the Labor Movement before 1930." *Radical History Review* 55 (1993): 53–87.

Arnesen, Eric. *Waterfront Workers of New Orleans: Race, Class and Politics, 1863–1923.* New York: Oxford University Press, 1991.

Asarch, Rhonda V. "Liberty Billings, Florida's Forgotten Radical Republican." Master's thesis. Florida Atlantic University, 2012. Accessed August 2, 2020.

https://fau.digital.flvc.org/islandora/object/fau%3A3991/datastream
/OBJ/view/Liberty_Billings__Florida_s_forgotten_radical_Republican
.pdf.

Ash, Stephen V. *A Massacre in Memphis: The Race Riot That Shook the Nation One Year after the Civil War.* New York: Hill and Wang, 2013.

Atkinson, James H. "The Arkansas Gubernatorial Campaign and Election of 1872." *Arkansas Historical Quarterly* 1, no. 4 (1942): 307–21.

Ayers, Edward L. *The Promise of the New South: Life after Reconstruction.* New York: Oxford University Press, 2007.

Bailey, Richard. *Neither Carpetbaggers nor Scalawags: Black Officeholders during the Reconstruction of Alabama, 1867–1878.* 2nd ed. Montgomery, AL: Richard Bailey Publishers, 1993.

Baptist, Edward. "'Cuffy,' 'Fancy Maids,' and 'One-Eyed Men'": Rape, Commodification, and the Domestic Slave Trade in the United States." In *The Chattel Principle: Internal Slave Trades in America*, edited by Walter Johnson, 165–202. New Haven, CT: Yale University Press, 2004.

Barnes, Kenneth C. *Journey of Hope: The Back to Africa Movement in Arkansas in the Late 1800s.* Chapel Hill: University of North Carolina Press, 2004.

Barnes, Kenneth C. *Who Killed John M. Clayton? Political Violence and the Emergence of the New South, 1861–1893.* Durham, NC: Duke University Press, 1998.

Bechtold, Rebecca. "'A Human Longing for Redress': Contrabands and the Language of Debt in Louisa May Alcott's Civil War Literature." *J19: The Journal of Nineteenth-Century Americanists* 4, no. 1 (2016): 99–123.

Behrend, Justin J. *Reconstructing Democracy: Grassroots Black Politics in the Deep South after the Civil War.* Athens: University of Georgia Press, 2015.

Bell, Caryn Cosse. *Revolution, Romanticism, and the Afro-Creole Protest Tradition in Louisiana, 1718–1868.* Baton Rouge: Louisiana State University Press, 1997.

Bennett, Lerone. *Before the Mayflower: A History of the Negro in America, 1619–1962.* Chicago: Johnson, 1962.

Bercaw, Nancy D. *Gendered Freedoms: Race, Rights, and the Politics of Household in the Delta, 1861–1875.* Gainesville: University of Florida Press, 2003.

Berlin, Ira. *Generations of Captivity: A History of African American Slaves.* Cambridge, MA: Harvard University Press, 2003.

Berlin, Ira. *Slaves without Masters: The Free Negro in the Antebellum South.* New York: New Press, 1974.

Berlin, Ira, Barbara J. Fields, Steven F. Miller, Joseph P. Reidy, and Leslie S. Rowland. *Slaves No More: Three Essays on Emancipation and the Civil War.* Cambridge: Cambridge University Press, 1992.

Bernstein, Leonard. "The Participation of Negro Delegates in the Constitutional Convention of 1868 in North Carolina." *Journal of Negro History* 34, no. 4 (1949): 391–409.

Blackmon, Douglas A. *Slavery by Another Name: The Re-enslavement of Black People in America from the Civil War to World War II*. New York: Doubleday, 2008.

Blassingame, John W. "Before the Ghetto: The Making of the Black Community in Savannah, Georgia, 1865–1880." *Journal of Social History* 6, no. 4 (1973): 463–88.

Blassingame, John W. *Black New Orleans, 1860–1880*. Chicago: University of Chicago Press, 1973.

Blevins, Brooks. "Reconstruction in the Ozarks: Simpson Mason, William Monks, and the War That Refused to End." *Arkansas Historical Quarterly* 77, no. 3 (2018): 175–207.

Blight, David W. *Frederick Douglass and Abraham Lincoln: A Relationship in Language, Politics, and Memory*. Milwaukee: Marquette University Press, 2001.

Blight, David W. *Frederick Douglass' Civil War: Keeping Faith in Jubilee*. Baton Rouge: Louisiana State University Press, 1989.

Blight, David W. *Race and Reunion: The Civil War in American Memory*. Cambridge, MA: Harvard University Press, 2001.

Blight, David W. *A Slave No More: Two Men Who Escaped Freedom, Including Their Own Narratives of Emancipation*. Boston: Mariner Books, Houghton Mifflin Harcourt, 2007.

Blight, David W., and Jim Downs, eds. *Beyond Freedom: Disrupting the History of Emancipation*. Athens: University of Georgia Press, 2017.

Boyd, Willis Dolmond. "Negro Colonization in the Reconstruction Era 1865–1870." *Georgia Historical Quarterly*, 40, no. 4 (1956): 360–82.

Bradley, Mark L. *The Army and Reconstruction, 1865–1877*. Washington, DC: Center of Military History United States Army, 2015. Accessed January 11, 2022. https://history.army.mil/html/books/075/75-18/index.html.

Branam, Chris W. "'The Africans Have Taken Arkansas': Political Activities of African Americans in the Reconstruction Legislature." *Arkansas Historical Quarterly* 83, no. 3 (2014): 233–67.

Brown, Canter, Jr. *Florida's Black Public Officials, 1867–1924*. Tuscaloosa: University of Alabama Press, 1998.

Brown, Elsa Barkley. "Negotiating and Transforming the Public Sphere: African American Political Life in the Transition from Slavery to Freedom." In *Time Longer Than Rope: A Century of African American Activism, 1850–1950*, edited by Charles M. Payne and Adam Green, 68–110. New York: New York University Press, 2003.

Brown, Elsa Barkley. "To Catch the Vision of Freedom: Reconstructing Black Women's Political History, 1865–1880." In *African American Women and the Vote, 1837–1965*, edited by Ann D. Gordon, 66–99. Amherst: University of Massachusetts Press, 1997.

Brown, Sterling A. *The Collected Poems of Sterling A. Brown*. New York: Harper and Row, 1980.

Brown, Sterling A. "Negro Character as Seen by White Authors." In *A Son's Return: Selected Essays of Sterling A. Brown*, edited by Mark A. Sanders, 149–83. Boston: Northeastern University Press, 1996.

Brown, Vincent. "Social Death and Political Life in the Study of Slavery." *American Historical Review* 114, no. 5 (2009): 1231–49.

Bruce, Dickson D., Jr. *Black American Writing from the Nadir: The Evolution of a Literary Tradition, 1877–1915*. Baton Rouge: Louisiana State University Press, 1989.

Brundage, W. Fitzhugh. "The Darien 'Insurrection' of 1899: Black Protest during the Nadir of Race Relations." *Georgia Historical Quarterly* 74, no. 2 (1990): 234–253.

Buchanan, Thomas C. *Black Life on the Mississippi: Slaves, Free Blacks, and the Western Steamboat World*. Chapel Hill, University of North Carolina Press, 2004.

Burke, W. Lewis. "All We Ask Is Equal Rights: African American Congressmen, Judges and Lawmakers in South Carolina." University of South Carolina Law School. Accessed March 9, 2014. http://law.sc.edu/equal_rights/4b1 -chronological_19c.shtml.

Burton, Orville Vernon. *Penn Center: A History Preserved*. Athens: University of Georgia Press, 2014.

Camp, Bayliss J., and Orit Kent. "'What a Mighty Power We Can Be': Individual and Collective Identity in African American and White Fraternal Initiation Rituals." *Social Science History* 28, no. 3 (2004): 439–83.

Camp, Stephanie M. H. *Closer to Freedom: Enslaved Women and Everyday Resistance in the Plantation South*. Chapel Hill: University of North Carolina Press, 2004.

Campbell, James T. *Songs of Zion: The African Methodist Episcopal Church in the United States and South Africa*. Chapel Hill: University of North Carolina Press, 1998.

Carby, Hazel V. "'On the Threshold of Woman's Era': Lynching, Empire, and Sexuality in Black Feminist Theory." *Critical Inquiry* 12, no. 1 (1985): 262–77.

Carby, Hazel V. *Reconstructing Womanhood: The Emergence of the Afro-American Woman Novelist*. New York: Oxford University Press, 1987.

Carey, Hampton D. "New Voices in the Old Dominion: Black Politics in the Virginia Southside Region and the City of Richmond, 1867–1902." PhD diss., Columbia University, 2000.

Catton, Bruce. *The American Heritage New History of the Civil War*. Edited by James M. McPherson. New York: MetroBooks, 2001.

Cecelski, David S. *The Fire of Freedom: Abraham Galloway and the Slaves' Civil War*. Chapel Hill: University of North Carolina Press, 2015.

Cecelski, David S. "Abraham H. Galloway: Wilmington's Lost Prophet and the Rise of Black Radicalism in the American South." In *Time Longer Than Rope: A Century of African American Activism, 1850–1950*, edited by

Charles M. Payne and Adam Green, 37–67. New York: New York University Press, 2003.

Cecelski, David S. *The Waterman's Song: Slavery and Freedom in Maritime North Carolina*. Chapel Hill: University of North Carolina Press, 2001.

Cimprich, John. *Slavery's End in Tennessee*. Tuscaloosa: University of Alabama Press, 1985.

Clarke, Erskine. *Dwelling Place: A Plantation Epic*. New Haven, CT: Yale University Press, 2005.

Clark-Pujara, Christy. *Dark Work: The Business of Slavery in Rhode Island*. New York: New York University Press, 2016.

Clark-Pujara, Christy. "In Need of Childcare: African American Families Transform the Providence Association for the Benefit of Colored Orphans in the Aftermath of Slavery, 1839–1845." *Journal of Family History* 45, no. 3 (2020): 295–314.

Clinton, Catherine. *Harriet Tubman: The Road to Freedom*. New York: Little, Brown, 2004.

Coakley, Robert W. *The Role of the Federal Military Forces in Domestic Disorders, 1789–1878*. Washington, DC: Center of Military History, United States Army, 2011.

Cohen, William. *At Freedom's Edge: Black Mobility and the Southern White Quest for Racial Control, 1861–1915*. Baton Rouge: Louisiana State University Press, 1991.

Commonwealth of Virginia, Dr. Martin Luther King Jr. Memorial Commission. "African American Legislators in Virginia: Virginia Constitutional Convention of 1867–1868." Division of Legislative Services, Legislative Information System, Virginia General Constitutional Convention Assembly. Accessed October 17, 2012. http://mlkcommission.dls.virginia.gov/lincoln/african_americans.html#.

Cooper, Frederick, Thomas Holt, and Rebecca Jarvis Scott. *Beyond Slavery: Explorations of Race, Labor, and Citizenship in Postemancipation Societies*. Chapel Hill: University of North Carolina Press, 2000.

Crouch, Barry A. "Self-Determination and Local Black Leaders in Texas." *Phylon* 39, no. 4 (1978): 344–55.

Dailey, Jane. "Deference and Violence in the Postbellum Urban South: Manners and Massacres in Danville, Virginia." *Journal of Southern History* 63, no. 3 (1997): 553–90.

Davis, Angela. "Reflections on the Black Woman's Role in the Community of Slaves." *Massachusetts Review* 13, nos. 1/2 (1972): 81–100.

Davis, Thulani. *My Confederate Kinfolk: A Twenty-First Century Freedwoman Discovers Her Roots*. New York: Basic Civitas Books, 2006.

Davis, Thulani. "Recovering Fugitive Freedoms." *Social Text* 33, no. 4 (125) (2015): 61–67.

Dawson, Michael. *Black Visions: The Roots of Contemporary African-American Political Ideologies*. Chicago: University of Chicago Press, 2003.

Decaro, Louis A., Jr. *"Fire from the Midst of You": A Religious Life of John Brown.* New York: New York University Press, 2005.

Desdunes, Rodolphe Lucien. *Our People and Our History: Fifty Creole Portraits.* 1964. Translated and edited by Sister Dorothea Olga McCants. Baton Rouge: Louisiana State University Press, 2001.

Dillard, Tom. "To the Back of the Elephant: Racial Conflict in the Arkansas Republican Party." *Arkansas Historical Quarterly* 33, no. 1 (1974): 3–15.

Doster, James F. "The Shelby Iron Works Collection in the University of Alabama Library." *Bulletin of the Business Historical Society* 26, no. 4 (1952): 214–17

Downs, Jim. *Sick from Freedom: African-American Illness and Suffering during the Civil War and Reconstruction.* New York: Oxford University Press, 2012.

Drago, Edmund. *Black Politicians and Reconstruction in Georgia: A Splendid Failure.* Athens: University of Georgia Press, 1992.

Dray, Philip. *Capitol Men: The Epic Story of Reconstruction through the Lives of the First Black Congressmen.* Boston: Houghton Mifflin, 2008.

Dubois, Laurent, and Julius S. Scott, eds. *Origins of the Black Atlantic.* New York: Routledge, 2010.

Du Bois, W. E. B. *Black Reconstruction in America, 1860–1880.* Cleveland: World Publishing, 1968.

Du Bois, W. E. B, ed. *Co-operation among Negro Americans: Report of a Social Study Made by Atlanta University, under the Patronage of the Carnegie Institution of Washington, D.C., Together with the Proceedings of the 12th Conference for the Study of the Negro Problems, Held at Atlanta University, on Tuesday, May 28, 1907.* Atlanta: Atlanta University Press, 1907.

Du Bois, W. E. B. *The Correspondence of W. E. B. Du Bois.* Vol. 1, *Selections, 1877–1934.* Amherst: University of Massachusetts Press, 1973.

Du Bois, W. E. B. "The Negroes of Farmville, Virginia: A Social Study." In *Contributions by W. E. B. Du Bois in Government Publications and Proceedings,* edited by Herbert Aptheker, 5–44. Millwood, NY: Kraus-Thomson, 1980.

Du Bois, W. E. B. *Newspaper Columns by W. E. B. Du Bois.* Vol. 1, *1883–1944.* Edited by Herbert Aptheker. White Plains, NY: Kraus-Thomson, 1986.

Du Bois, W. E. B. *The Souls of Black Folk.* New York: Fawcett, 1961.

Dunlap, Leslie K. "The Reform of Rape Law and the Problem of White Men: Age of Consent Campaigns in the South, 1885–1910." In *Sex, Love, Race: Crossing Boundaries in North American History,* edited by Martha Hodes, 352–72. New York: New York University Press, 1999.

Edwards, Laura F. *Gendered Strife and Confusion: The Political Culture of Reconstruction.* Urbana: University of Illinois Press, 1997.

Emilio, Luis F. *History of the Fifty-Fourth Regiment of Massachusetts Volunteer Infantry, 1863–1865.* Boston: Boston Book Co., 1894.

Engs, Robert F. *Freedom's First Generation: Black Hampton, Virginia, 1861–1890.* New York: Fordham University Press, 2004.

Eyer, Katie R. "Ideological Drift and the Forgotten History of Intent." *Harvard Civil Rights–Civil Liberties Law Review* 51, no. 1 (2016): 1–74.

Fabre, Genevieve. "African-American Commemorative Celebrations in the Nineteenth Century." In *History and Memory in African-American Culture*, edited by Genevieve Fabre and Robert O'Meally, 72–91. New York: Oxford University Press, 1994.

Fausette, Risa. "Race, Migration and Port City Radicalism: New York's Black Longshoremen and the Politics of Maritime Protest, 1900–1920." PhD diss., State University of New York, Binghamton, 2002.

Finley, Randy. *From Slavery to Uncertain Freedom: The Freedmen's Bureau in Arkansas 1865–1869*. Fayetteville: University of Arkansas Press, 1996.

Fitzgerald, Michael W. *The Union League Movement in the Deep South: Politics and Agricultural Change during Reconstruction*. Baton Rouge: Louisiana State University Press, 1989.

Foner, Eric. *Freedom's Lawmakers: A Directory of Black Officeholders during Reconstruction*. Rev. ed. Baton Rouge: Louisiana State University Press, 1996.

Foner, Eric. *Reconstruction: America's Unfinished Revolution, 1863–1877*. New York: Harper and Row, 1988.

Foner, Eric. *The Second Founding: How the Civil War and Reconstruction Remade the Constitution*. New York: W. W. Norton, 2019.

Foner, Philip S., and Robert James Branham, eds. *Lift Every Voice: African American Oratory, 1787–1900*. Tuscaloosa: University of Alabama Press, 1998.

Formwalt, Lee W. "The Origins of African-American Politics in Southwest Georgia: A Case Study of Black Political Organization during Presidential Reconstruction, 1865–1867." *Journal of Negro History* 77, no. 4 (1992): 211–22.

Forsythe, Harold S. "'But My Friends Are Poor': Ross Hamilton and Freedpeople's Politics in Mecklenburg County, Virginia, 1869–1901." *Virginia Magazine of History and Biography* 105, no. 4 (1997): 409–38.

Foucault, Michel. *Discipline and Punish: The Birth of the Prison*. New York: Vintage, 1995.

Fraker, Guy C. "The Real Lincoln Highway: The Forgotten Lincoln Circuit Markers." *Journal of the Abraham Lincoln Association* 25, no. 1 (Winter 2004): 76–97.

Frankel, Noralee. *Freedom's Women: Black Women and Families in Civil War Era Mississippi*. Bloomington: Indiana University Press, 1999.

Franklin, John Hope. "A Century of Civil War Observance." *Journal of Negro History* 47, no. 2 (1962): 97–107.

Franklin, John Hope. *Reconstruction after the Civil War*. 2nd ed. Chicago: University of Chicago Press, 1994.

Franklin, John Hope, and Loren Schweninger. *In Search of the Promised Land: A Slave Family in the Old South*. New York: Oxford University Press, 2006.

Furstenberg, Frank F., Jr. "History and Current Status of Divorce in the United States." Special issue, *Children and Divorce: The Future of Children* 4, no. 1 (1994): 19–43.

Garlock, Jonathan. *Guide to the Local Assemblies of the Knights of Labor*. Westport, CT: Greenwood Press, 1982.

Garlock, Jonathan. "A Structural Analysis of the Knights of Labor: A Prolegomenon to the History of the Producing Classes." PhD diss., University of Rochester, 1974.

Gatewood, Willard B., Jr. "Sunnyside: The Evolution of an Arkansas Plantation, 1840–1945." *Arkansas Historical Quarterly* 50, no. 1 (1991): 5–29.

Genovese, Eugene D. *Roll, Jordan, Roll: The World the Slaves Made*. New York: Pantheon Books, 1974.

Gibson, W. H., Sr. *History of the United Brothers of Friendship and Sisters of the Mysterious Ten in Two Parts. A Negro Order. Organized August 1, 1861, in the City of Louisville, KY*. Louisville: Bradley and Gilbert Company, 1897. Accessed July 22, 2013. http://archive.org/details/brofriendsismystoogibsrich.

Giddings, Paula. *When and Where I Enter: The Impact of Black Women on Race and Sex in America*. New York: William Morrow, 1984.

Giggie, John M. *After Redemption: Jim Crow and the Transformation of African American Religion in the Delta, 1875–1915*. New York: Oxford University Press, 2008.

Gilmore, Glenda. *Gender and Jim Crow: Women and the Politics of White Supremacy in North Carolina, 1896–1920*. Chapel Hill: University of North Carolina Press, 1996.

Gilroy, Paul. *The Black Atlantic: Modernity and Double Consciousness*. Cambridge, MA: Harvard University Press, 1993.

Gilroy, Paul. *Darker Than Blue: On the Moral Economies of Black Atlantic Culture*. Cambridge, MA: Harvard University Press, 2010.

Glymph, Thavolia, ed. *Essays on the Postbellum Southern Economy*. College Station: Texas A&M University Press, 1985.

Glymph, Thavolia. "'Liberty Dearly Bought': The Making of Civil War Memory in Afro-American Communities in the South." In *Time Longer Than Rope: A Century of African American Activism, 1850–1950*, edited by Charles M. Payne and Adam Green, 111–39. New York: New York University Press, 2003.

Glymph, Thavolia. *Out of the House of Bondage: The Transformation of the Plantation Household*. Cambridge: Cambridge University Press, 2008.

Glymph, Thavolia. "'This Species of Property': Female Slave Contrabands in the Civil War." In *A Woman's War: Southern Women, Civil War and the Confederate Legacy*, edited by Edward D. C. Campbell, Jr., and Kym S. Rice, 55–73. Richmond: Museum of the Confederacy; Charlottesville: University Press of Virginia, 1996.

Goldin, Claudia. "Female Labor Force Participation: The Origin of Black and White Differences, 1870 and 1880." *Journal of Economic History* 37, no. 1 (1977): 87–108.

Goodheart, Adam. *1861: The Civil War Awakening*. New York: Vintage, 2011.

Gordon, Ann, ed. *African American Women and the Vote, 1837–1965*. Amherst: University of Massachusetts Press, 1997.

Gramsci, Antonio. "The Intellectuals." In *Selections from the Prison Notebooks of Antonio Gramsci*, edited and translated by Quintin Hoare and Geoffrey Nowell-Smith, 3–23. New York: International Publishers, 1971.

Gramsci, Antonio. "Some Aspects of the Southern Question." In *Selections from Political Writings (1921–1926)*, edited by Quintin Hoare, 441–507. Minneapolis: University of Minnesota Press, 1990.

Grant, Donald L. *The Way It Was: The Black Experience in Georgia*. Athens: University of Georgia Press, 1993.

Green, Hilary. "Educational Reconstruction: African American Education in the Urban South, 1865–1890." PhD diss., University of North Carolina, 2010.

Gutman, Herbert G. *The Black Family in Slavery and Freedom, 1750–1925*. New York: Pantheon Books, 1976.

*H*3695 Concurrent Resolution, Govan, Sellers, Brantley, Hodges, Scott, Rutherford, J. H. Neal, Anderson, R. Brown, Clyburn, Cobb-Hunter, Hart, Hosey, Jefferson, Kennedy, Mitchell, Weeks, Whipper and Williams, A Concurrent Resolution to Honor and Recognize the African-American Members of the South Carolina Executive, Legislative, and Judicial Branches of Government and the Members of the State's Congressional Delegation who Heroically Served the People of this State following the Civil War until the Early Twentieth Century*. Accessed January 10, 2022. https://www.scstatehouse.gov/query.php?search=DOC&searchtext=Edward%25&category=LEGISLATION&session=0&conid=6902064&result_pos=150&keyval=1173695&numrows=50.

Hager, Christopher. *Word by Word: Emancipation and the Act of Writing*. Cambridge, MA: Harvard University Press, 2013.

Hahn, Steven. *A Nation under Our Feet: Black Political Struggles in the Rural South from Slavery to the Great Migration*. Cambridge, MA: Harvard University Press, 2003.

Hahn, Steven. *The Political Worlds of Slavery and Freedom*. Cambridge, MA: Harvard University, 2009.

Haley, Sarah. "'Like I Was a Man': Chain Gangs, Gender, and the Domestic Carceral Sphere in Jim Crow Georgia." *Signs* 39, no. 1 (2013): 53–77.

Hall, Jacqueline Dowd. "'The Mind That Burns in Each Body': Women, Rape, and Racial Violence." In *Powers of Desire: The Powers of Sexuality*, edited by Ann Snitow, Christine Stansell, and Sharon Thompson, 328–49. New York: Monthly Review Press, 1983.

Hall, Stephen G. *A Faithful Account of the Race: African American Historical Writing in Nineteenth-Century America*. Chapel Hill: University of North Carolina Press, 2009.

Hall, Stuart. "Gramsci's Relevance for the Study of Race and Ethnicity." *Journal of Communication Inquiry* 10 (1986): 5–27.

Harris, William H. *The Harder We Run: Black Workers since the Civil War*. New York: Oxford University Press, 1982.

Hartman, Saidiya V. *Scenes of Subjection: Terror, Slavery, and Self-Making in Nineteenth Century America*. New York: Oxford University, 1997.

Harvey, Paul. *Freedom's Coming: Religious Culture and the Shaping of the South from the Civil War through the Civil Rights Era*. Chapel Hill: University of North Carolina Press, 2012.

Hester, Al. *Enduring Legacy: Clarke County, Georgia's Ex-Slave Legislators, Madison Davis and Alfred Richardson*. Athens, GA: Green Berry Press, 2010.

Hewitt, Nancy A. *Southern Discomfort: Women's Activism in Tampa, Florida, 1880s–1920s*. Urbana: University of Illinois Press, 2001.

Heywood, Linda M., and John K. Thornton. *Central Africans, Atlantic Creoles, and the Foundation of the Americas, 1585–1660*. Cambridge: Cambridge University Press, 2007.

Higginson, Thomas Wentworth. *Army Life in a Black Regiment*. Boston: Fields, Osgood and Co., 1870. Accessed December 9, 2019. https://www.gutenberg .org/files/6764/6764-h/6764-h.htm.

Hine, Darlene Clark. "Rape and the Inner Lives of Black Women: Preliminary Thoughts on the Culture of Dissemblance." *Signs* 14 (1989): 912–20.

Hodes, Martha, ed. *Sex, Love, Race: Crossing Boundaries in North American History*. New York: New York University Press, 1999.

Hodes, Martha. *White Women, Black Men: Illicit Sex in the Nineteenth-Century South*. New Haven, CT: Yale University Press, 1997.

Holt, Thomas. *Black over White: Negro Political Leadership in South Carolina during Reconstruction*. Urbana: University of Illinois Press, 1979.

Holt, Thomas. *The Problem of Freedom: Race, Labor, and Politics in Jamaica and Britain, 1832–1938*. Baltimore: Johns Hopkins University Press, 1992.

Holton, Woody. "Rebel against Rebel: Enslaved Virginians and the Coming of the American Revolution." *Virginia Magazine of History and Biography* 105, no. 2 (1997): 157–92.

Honey, Michael. "The Power of Remembering: Black Factory Workers and Union Organizing in the Jim Crow Era." In *Time Longer Than Rope: A Century of African American Activism, 1850–1950*, edited by Charles M. Payne and Adam Green, 302–35. New York: New York University Press, 2003.

Hughes, Sarah Shaver. "Elizabeth City County, Virginia, 1782–1810: The Economic and Social Structure of a Tidewater County in the Early National Years." PhD diss., College of William and Mary, 1975.

Hughes, Sarah Shaver. "Slaves for Hire: The Allocation of Black Labor in Elizabeth City County, Virginia, 1782 to 1810." *William and Mary Quarterly*, 3rd ser., 35, no. 2 (1978): 260–86.

Hume, Richard L. "Membership of the Florida Constitutional Convention of 1868: A Case Study of Republican Factionalism in the Reconstruction South." *Florida Historical Quarterly* 51, no. 1 (1972): 1–21.

Hume, Richard L. "The Membership of the Virginia Constitutional Convention of 1867–1868: A Study of the Beginnings of Congressional Reconstruction in the Upper South." *Virginia Magazine of History and Biography* 86, no. 4 (1978): 461–84.

Hume, Richard L., and Jerry B. Gough. *Blacks, Carpetbaggers, and Scalawags: The Constitutional Conventions of Radical Reconstruction*. Baton Rouge: Louisiana State University Press, 2008.

Humez, Jean M. *Harriet Tubman: The Life and Life Stories*. Madison: University of Wisconsin Press, 2004.

Hunter, Tera. *To 'Joy My Freedom: Southern Black Women's Lives and Labors after the Civil War*. Cambridge, MA: Harvard University Press, 1997.

Jackson, Debra. "'A Cultural Stronghold': The 'Anglo-African' Newspaper and the Black Community of New York." *New York History* 85, no. 4 (2004): 331–57.

Jacobs, Claude F. "Benevolent Societies of New Orleans Blacks during the Late Nineteenth and Early Twentieth Centuries." *Louisiana History: The Journal of the Louisiana Historical Association* 29, no. 1 (1988): 21–33.

Jacobson, Matthew Frye. *Whiteness of a Different Color: European Immigrants and the Alchemy of Race*. Cambridge, MA: Harvard University Press, 1999.

James, Winston. "Being Red and Black in Jim Crow America: On the Ideology and Travails of Afro-America's Socialist Pioneers, 1877–1930." In *Time Longer Than Rope: A Century of African American Activism, 1850–1950*, edited by Charles M. Payne and Adam Green, 336–400. New York: New York University Press, 2003.

Jenkins, Earnestine Lovelle. *Race, Representation and Photography in 19th Century Memphis: From Slavery to Jim Crow*. New York: Routledge, 2016.

Johnson, Walter, ed. *The Chattel Principle: Internal Slave Trades in America*. New Haven, CT: Yale University Press, 2004.

Johnson, Walter. *Soul by Soul: Life Inside the Antebellum Slave Market*. Cambridge, MA: Harvard University Press, 1999.

Jones, Jacqueline. *Labor of Love, Labor of Sorrow: Black Women, Work, and the Family, from Slavery to the Present*. New York: Vintage, 1995.

Jones, Martha S. *All Bound Up Together: The Woman Question in African American Public Culture, 1830–1900*. Chapel Hill: University of North Carolina Press, 2007.

Jung, Moon-Ho. *Coolies and Cane: Race, Labor, and Sugar in the Age of Emancipation*. Baltimore: Johns Hopkins University Press, 2006.

Kahn, Amina. "Solving Walt Whitman's Meteor Mystery, *Los Angeles Times*, June 5, 2010.

Kann, Kenneth. "The Knights of Labor and the Southern Black Worker." *Labor History* 18, no. 1 (1977): 49–70.

Kantrowitz, Stephen. *Ben Tillman and the Reconstruction of White Supremacy*. Chapel Hill: University of North Carolina Press, 2000.

Kaslow, Andrew Jonathan. "Oppression and Adaptation: The Social Organization and Expressive Culture of an Afro-American Community in New Orleans, Louisiana." PhD diss., Columbia University, 1981.

Katcher, Philip. *Battle History of the Civil War, 1861–1865*. New York: Barnes and Noble, 2000.

Kates, Steve. "Witness the Potential Return of a 19th Century Meteor Shower." Dr. Sky Blog, November 29, 2018. https://ktar.com/story/2327342/witness -the-potential-return-of-a-19th-century-meteor-shower/

Kaye, Anthony E. *Joining Places: Slave Neighborhoods in the Old South*. Chapel Hill: University of North Carolina Press, 2007.

Kazanjian, David. *The Colonizing Trick: National Culture and Imperial Citizenship in Early America*. Minneapolis: University of Minnesota Press, 2003.

Keele, Luke, William Cubbison, and Ismail White. "Suppressing Black Votes: A Historical Case Study of Voting Restrictions in Louisiana." *American Political Science Review* 115, no. 2 (2021): 694–700. Accessed August 19, 2021. https://www-cambridge-org.ezproxy.library.wisc.edu/core/journals/american -political-science-review/article/suppressing-black-votes-a-historical-case -study-of-voting-restrictions-in-louisiana/662970B089BC99495ADC2F6E3 CBF61FD.

Kelly, Brian. "Beyond the 'Talented Tenth': Black Elites, Black Workers, and the Limits of Accommodation in Industrial Birmingham, 1900–1921." In *Time Longer Than Rope: A Century of African American Activism, 1850–1950*, edited by Charles M. Payne and Adam Green, 276–301. New York: New York University Press, 2003.

Kelly, Brian. "Black Laborers, the Republican Party, and the Crisis of Reconstruction in Lowcountry South Carolina." *International Review of Social History* 51, no. 3 (2006): 375–414.

Kerr-Ritchie, Jeffrey R. *Freedpeople in the Tobacco South: Virginia, 1860–1900*. Chapel Hill: University of North Carolina Press, 1999.

Kessler, Sidney H. "The Organization of Negroes in the Knights of Labor." *Journal of Negro History* 37, no. 3 (1952): 248–76.

King, Desmond, and Stephen Tuck. "De-centering the South: America's Nationwide White Supremacist Order after Reconstruction." *Past and Present*, no. 194 (2007): 213–53.

Klas, Mary Ellen. "Florida Has a History of Making It Harder for Black Citizens to Vote." *Miami Herald*, August 12, 2016.

Knowles, Anne Kelly. "Labor, Race, and Technology in the Confederate Iron Industry." *Technology and Culture* 42, no. 1 (2001): 1–26.

Kohl, Rhonda M. "'This Godforsaken Town': Death and Disease at Helena, Arkansas, 1862–63." *Civil War History* 50, no. 2 (2004): 109–44.

Kolchin, Peter. *First Freedom: The Responses of Alabama's Blacks to Emancipation and Reconstruction*. Tuscaloosa: University of Alabama Press, 2008.

Kremm, Thomas W., and Diane Neal. "Clandestine Black Labor Societies and White Fear: Hiram F. Hoover and the 'Cooperative Workers of America' in the South." *Labor History* 19, no. 2 (1978): 226–37.

Kuiken, Vesna. "'Fit to Be Free': From Race to Capacity in Jewett's 'Mistress of Sydenham Plantation.'" *J19: The Journal of Nineteenth-Century Americanists* 5, no. 2 (Fall 2017): 239–66.

Kulikoff, Allan. *Tobacco and Slaves: The Development of Southern Cultures in the Chesapeake, 1680–1800.* Chapel Hill: University of North Carolina Press, 1986.

Lemann, Nicholas. *Redemption: The Last Battle of the Civil War.* New York: Farrar, Straus and Giroux, 2006.

Lewis, Earl. *In Their Own Interests: Race, Class, and Power in Twentieth-Century Norfolk, Virginia.* Berkeley: University of California Press, 1991.

Lewis, Ronald W. *The House of Dance and Feathers.* New Orleans: University of New Orleans Press, 2009.

Lipsitz, George. "The Racialization of Space and the Spatialization of Race: Theorizing the Hidden Architecture of Landscape." *Landscape Journal* 26, no. 1 (2007): 10–23.

Litwack, Leon F. *Been in the Storm So Long: The Aftermath of Slavery.* New York: Vintage, 1980.

Litwack, Leon F. *Trouble in Mind: Black Southerners in the Age of Jim Crow.* New York: Vintage, 1999.

Ljungquist, Kent. "'Meteor of the War': Melville, Thoreau, and Whitman Respond to John Brown." *American Literature* 61, no. 4 (December 1989): 674–80.

Logan, Rayford. *The Negro in American Life and Thought: The Nadir, 1877–1901.* New York: Dial Press, 1954.

Lowe, Richard. "The Freedmen's Bureau and Local Black Leadership." *Journal of American History* 80, no. 3 (1993): 989–98.

Lowe, Richard. "Local Black Leaders during Reconstruction in Virginia." *Virginia Magazine of History and Biography* 103, no. 2 (1995): 181–206.

Lowe, Richard. "Virginia's Reconstruction Convention: General Schofield Rates the Delegates." *Virginia Magazine of History and Biography* 80 (1972): 341–60.

Mahan, Margo. "The Racial Origins of U. S. Domestic Violence Law." PhD diss., University of California, Berkeley, 2017. Accessed August 23, 2021. https://escholarship.org/uc/item/0zs890k1.

Mann, Susan A. "Slavery, Sharecropping, and Sexual Inequality." *Signs* 14, no. 4 (1989): 774–98.

Mansfield, Michael W. "'A Slide, a Swing and an Oak Tree': Maysville, Alabama and the Birth of an African American Community." PhD diss., University of Alabama, 2005.

Martin, Kimberly. "Community and Place: A Study of Four African American Benevolent Societies and Their Cemeteries." Master's thesis, Clemson University and College of Charleston, 2010.

McGuire, Danielle. "'It Was Like All of Us Had Been Raped': Sexual Violence, Community Mobilization and the African American Freedom Struggle." *Journal of American History* 91, no. 3 (2004): 906–31.

McKenzie, Robert H. "The Shelby Iron Company: A Note on Slave Personality after the Civil War." *Journal of Negro History* 58, no. 3 (1973): 341–48.

McKittrick, Katherine. *Demonic Grounds: Black Women and the Cartographies of Struggle*. Minneapolis: University of Minnesota Press, 2006.

McKittrick, Katherine, and Clyde Woods, eds. *Black Geographies and the Politics of Place*. Cambridge, MA: South End Press, 2007.

McPherson, James M. *Battle Cry of Freedom: The Civil War Era*. New York: Ballantine, 1989.

McPherson, James M. *The Negro's Civil War: How American Blacks Felt and Acted During the War for the Union*. New York: Ballantine, 1991.

Meier, August. "Negroes in the First and Second Reconstructions of the South." *Civil War History* 13, no. 2 (1967): 114–30.

Meier, August. *Negro Thought in America, 1880–1915: Racial Ideologies in the Age of Booker T. Washington*. Ann Arbor: University of Michigan Press, 1964.

Miller, Steven F., Susan E. O'Donovan, John C. Rodrigue, and Leslie S. Rowland. "Between Emancipation and Enfranchisement: Law and Political Mobilization of Black Southerners during Presidential Reconstruction, 1865–1867." *Chicago-Kent Law Review* 70 (1994–95): 1059–77.

Mitchell, Michele. *Righteous Propagation: African Americans and the Politics of Racial Destiny after Reconstruction*. Chapel Hill: University of North Carolina Press, 2004.

Moneyhon, Carl H. *The Impact of the Civil War and Reconstruction on Arkansas: Persistence in the Midst of Ruin*. Baton Rouge: Louisiana State University Press, 1994.

Moore, James T. "Black Militancy in Readjuster Virginia, 1879–1883." *Journal of Southern History* 41, no. 2 (1975): 167–86.

Moore, John Hammond. "The Norfolk Riot: April 16, 1866." *Virginia Magazine of History and Biography* 90, no. 2 (1982): 155–64.

Moore, John Hebron. "Simon Gray, Riverman: A Slave Who Was Almost Free." *Mississippi Valley Historical Review* 49, no. 3 (1962): 472–84.

Morgan, Jennifer L. *Laboring Women: Reproduction and Gender in New World Slavery*. Philadelphia: University of Pennsylvania Press, 2004.

Morrison, Toni. *Playing in the Dark: Whiteness and the Literary Imagination*. Cambridge, MA: Harvard University Press, 1992.

Moses, Wilson Jeremiah. *The Golden Age of Black Nationalism, 1850–1925*. New York: Oxford University Press, 1978.

Muhammad, Khalil Gibran. *The Condemnation of Blackness: Ideas about Race and Crime in the Making of Modern Urban America*. Cambridge, MA: Harvard University Press, 2010.

Newby-Alexander, Cassandra L. *An African American History of the Civil War in Hampton Roads*. Charleston, SC: History Press, 2010.

Odum, Howard W. "Social and Mental Traits of the Negro: Research into the Conditions of the Negro." PhD diss., Columbia University, 1910.

Oliver, Paul. *Songsters and Saints: Vocal Traditions on Race Records*. New York: Cambridge University Press, 1984.

Omi, Michael, and Howard Winant. *Racial Formation in the United States, from the 1960s to the 1990s*. 2nd ed. New York: Routledge, 1994.

Ortiz, Paul. "'Eat Your Bread without Butter, but Pay Your Poll Tax!': Roots of the African American Voter Registration Movement in Florida, 1919–1920." In *Time Longer Than Rope: A Century of African American Activism, 1850–1950*, edited by Charles M. Payne and Adam Green, 196–229. New York: New York University Press, 2003.

Ortiz, Paul. *Emancipation Betrayed: The Hidden History of Black Organizing and White Violence in Florida from Reconstruction to the Bloody Election of 1920*. Berkeley: University of California Press, 2005.

Osborn, George C. "Letters of a Carpetbagger in Florida." *Florida Historical Quarterly* 36, no. 3 (1958): 239–85.

Oshinsky, David. *"Worse Than Slavery": Parchman Farm and the Ordeal of Jim Crow Justice*. New York: Free Press, 1997.

Painter, Nell Irvin. *Exodusters: Black Migration to Kansas after Reconstruction*. New York: W. W. Norton, 1992.

Painter, Nell Irvin. *Standing at Armageddon: The United States, 1877–1919*. New York: W. W. Norton, 2008.

Palmer, Edward Nelson. "Negro Secret Societies." *Social Forces* 23, no. 2 (1944): 207–12.

Palmer, Robert. *Deep Blues*. New York: Penguin Books, 1982.

Pascoe, Peggy. *What Comes Naturally: Miscegenation Law and the Making of Race in America*. New York: Oxford University Press, 2010.

Paton, Diana. *No Bonds but the Law: Punishment, Race, and Gender in Jamaican State Formation, 1780–1870*. Durham, NC: Duke University Press, 2004.

Payne, Charles M. *I've Got the Light of Freedom: The Organizing Tradition and the Mississippi Freedom Struggle*. Berkeley: University of California Press, 2007.

Payne, Charles M., and Adam Green, eds. *Time Longer Than Rope: A Century of African American Activism, 1850–1950*. New York: New York University Press, 2003.

Pearce, Larry Wesley, "The American Missionary Association and the Freedmen's Bureau in Arkansas, 1866–1868." *Arkansas Historical Quarterly* 30 (1971): 242–59.

Pegues, A. W. *Our Baptist Ministers and Schools*. Springfield, MA: Willey, 1892.

Poliakoff, Eli A. "Charleston's Longshoremen: Organized Labor in the Anti-union Palmetto State." *South Carolina Historical Magazine* 103, no. 3 (2002): 247–64.

Quarles, Benjamin. *Black Abolitionists*. New York: Da Capo, 1969.

Rachleff, Peter. *Black Labor in the South: Richmond, Virginia, 1865–1890*. Philadelphia: Temple University Press, 1984.

Rael, Patrick. *Black Identity and Black Protest in the Antebellum North*. Chapel Hill: University of North Carolina Press, 2002.

Rancière, Jacques. *Disagreement: Politics and Philosophy*. Minneapolis: University of Minnesota, 1999.

Rankin, David C. "The Origins of Black Leadership in New Orleans during Reconstruction." *Journal of Southern History* 40, no. 3 (1974): 417–40.

Regis, Helen A. "Second Lines, Minstrelsy, and the Contested Landscapes of New Orleans Afro-Creole Festivals." *Cultural Anthropology* 14, no. 4 (1999): 472–504.

Regis, Helen A. "Social and Pleasure Clubs." In *The House of Dance and Feathers*, edited by Ronald W. Lewis, 126–31. New Orleans: The Neighborhood Story Project, University of New Orleans Press, 2009.

Reid, George W. "Four in Black: North Carolina's Black Congressmen, 1874–1901." *Journal of Negro History* 64, no. 3 (1979): 229–43.

Richardson, Heather Cox. *The Death of Reconstruction: Race, Labor, and Politics in the Post–Civil War North, 1865–1901*. Cambridge, MA: Harvard University Press, 2001.

Richardson, Joe M. *Christian Reconstruction: The American Missionary Association and Southern Blacks, 1861–1890*. Tuscaloosa: University of Alabama Press, 1986.

Richardson, Joe M. "Florida Black Codes." *Florida Historical Quarterly* 47, no. 4 (April 1969): 365–79.

Richardson, Joe M. *The Negro in the Reconstruction of Florida*. Tallahassee: Florida State University, 1965.

Richardson, Joe M. "'We Are Truly Doing Missionary Work': Letters from American Missionary Association Teachers in Florida, 1864–1874." *Florida Historical Quarterly* 54, no. 2 (1975): 178–95.

Richings, G. F. *Evidence of Progress among Colored People*. Philadelphia: George S. Ferguson, 1896.

Ricks, Markeshia. "Tradition of Excellence: Historians Highlight First Black Legislative Caucus." *Montgomery Advertiser*, February 28, 2009.

Rivers, Larry E., and Canter Brown Jr. "African Americans in South Florida: A Home and a Haven for Reconstruction-Era Leaders." *Tequesta*, no. 56 (1996): 5–23.

Rivers, Larry Eugene. "Florida's Culture of Slavery." *Florida Humanities*, February 24, 2020. https://floridahumanities.org/floridas-culture-of-slavery/. Originally published in *The Forum* 24, no. 1 (Spring 2010).

Robinson, Cedric. *Black Marxism: The Making of the Black Radical Tradition*. Chapel Hill: University of North Carolina Press, 2000.

Roediger, David R. *The Wages of Whiteness: Race and the Making of the American Working Class*. Rev. ed. London: Verso, 2002.

Rogers, William Warren. "The Farmers' Alliance in Alabama." *Alabama Review* 15, no. 1 (1962): 5–18.

Rogers, William Warren. "The Negro Alliance in Alabama." *Journal of Negro History* 45, no. 1 (1960): 38–44.

Rogers, William Warren. "Negro Knights of Labor in Arkansas: A Case Study of the 'Miscellaneous Strike.'" *Labor History* 10, no. 3 (1969): 498–505.

Rose, Willie Lee. *Rehearsal for Reconstruction: The Port Royal Experiment*. Athens: University of Georgia Press, 1964.

Rosen, Hannah. *Terror in the Heart of Freedom: Citizenship, Sexual Violence, and the Meaning of Race in the Postemancipation South*. Chapel Hill: University of North Carolina Press, 2009.

Saville, Julie. "Rites and Power: Reflections on Slavery, Freedom and Political Ritual." *Slavery and Abolition: A Journal of Slave and Post-slave Studies* 20, no. 1 (1999): 81–102.

Saville, Julie. *The Work of Reconstruction: From Slave to Wage Labor in South Carolina, 1860–1870*. Cambridge: Cambridge University Press, 1994.

Saxon, Lyle, Edward Dreyer, and Robert Tallant, eds. *Gumbo Ya-Ya: A Collection of Louisiana Folk Tales*. Gretna, LA: Pelican Publishing, 1987.

Schwalm, Leslie A. *Emancipation's Diaspora: Race and Reconstruction in the Upper Midwest*. Chapel Hill: University of North Carolina Press, 2009.

Schwalm, Leslie A. *A Hard Fight for We: Women's Transition from Slavery to Freedom in South Carolina*. Champaign: University of Illinois Press, 1997.

Schwalm, Leslie A. "'Overrun with Free Negroes': Emancipation and Wartime Migration in the Upper Midwest. *Civil War History* 50, no. 2 (2004): 145–74.

Schweninger, Loren. "Alabama Blacks and the Congressional Reconstruction Acts of 1867." *Alabama Review* 31 (July 1978): 182–92.

Scott, David. *Conscripts of Modernity: The Tragedy of Colonial Enlightenment*. Durham, NC: Duke University Press, 2004.

Scott, Julius S. "The Common Wind: Currents of Afro-American Communication in the Era of the Haitian Revolution." PhD diss., Duke University, 1986.

Scott, Rebecca J. *Degrees of Freedom: Louisiana and Cuba after Slavery*. Cambridge, MA: Harvard University Press, 2005.

Scott, Rebecca J. "'Stubborn and Disposed to Stand Their Ground': Black Militia, Sugar Workers and the Dynamics of Collective Action in the Louisiana Sugar Bowl, 1863–87." *Slavery and Abolition: A Journal of Slave and Post-slave Studies* 20, no. 1 (1999): 103–26.

Sewell, George A., and Margaret L. Dwight. *Mississippi Black History Makers*. Jackson: University Press of Mississippi, 1984.

Shofner, Jerrell H. "The Constitution of 1868." *Florida Historical Quarterly* 41, no. 4 (1963): 356–74.

Shofner, Jerrell H. "Militant Negro Laborers in Reconstruction Florida." *Journal of Southern History* 39, no. 3 (1973): 397–408.

Sidbury, James. "Saint Domingue in Virginia: Ideology, Local Meanings, and Resistance to Slavery, 1790–1800." *Journal of Southern History* 63, no. 3 (1997): 531–52.

Singh, Nikhil Pal. *Black Is a Country: Race and the Unfinished Struggle for Democracy.* Cambridge, MA: Harvard University Press, 2004.

Skocpol, Theda, Ariane Liazos, and Marshall Ganz. *What a Mighty Power We Can Be: African American Fraternal Groups and the Struggle for Racial Equality.* Princeton, NJ: Princeton University Press, 2006.

Skocpol, Theda, and Jennifer Lynn Oser. "Organization Despite Adversity: The Origins and Development of African American Fraternal Associations." *Social Science History* 28, no. 3 (2004): 367–437.

Smith, James Wesley, and Martha S. Dance. *The History and Legend of Pocahontas Island.* Petersburg, VA: Plummer, 1981.

Smith, Neil. *Uneven Development: Nature, Capital and the Production of Space.* Oxford: Basil Blackwell, 1984.

Smith, Robert P. "William Cooper Nell: Crusading Abolitionist." *Journal of Negro History* 55, no. 3 (1970): 182–99.

Soley, James Russell. *The Navy in the Civil War,* vol. 1 of 3. New York: Charles Scribner's Sons, 1883.

Somers, Margaret R. *Genealogies of Citizenship: Markets, Statelessness, and the Right to Have Rights.* Cambridge: Cambridge University Press, 2010.

"Special Dispatch to the *New York Times,* 'The KuKlux. Proclamation of Martial Law in South Carolina.'" *New York Times,* October 18, 1871.

Spero, Sterling D., and Abram L. Harris. *The Black Worker: The Negro and the Labor Movement.* 1931. Reprint, New York: Atheneum, 1969.

Spivak, Gayatri Chakravorty. "Can the Subaltern Speak?" In *The Post-colonial Reader,* edited by Bill Ashcroft, Gareth Griffiths, and Helen Tiffin, 28–37. London: Routledge, 2006.

Spriggs, William Edward. "The Virginia Colored Farmers' Alliance: A Case Study of Race and Class Identity." *Journal of Negro History* 64, no. 3 (1979): 191–204.

Sproat, John G. "Blueprint for Radical Reconstruction." *Journal of Southern History* 23, no. 1 (1957): 25–44.

Sterling, Dorothy. *We Are Your Sisters: Black Women in the Nineteenth Century.* New York: Norton, 1984.

St. Hilaire, Joseph M. "The Negro Delegates in the Arkansas Constitutional Convention of 1868: A Group Profile." *Arkansas Historical Quarterly* 33, no. 1 (1974): 38–69.

Still, William N. "Selma and the Confederate States Navy." *Alabama Review* 15 (1962): 19–37.

Stockham, Richard J. "Alabama Iron for the Confederacy: The Selma Works." *Alabama Review* 21 (1968): 163–72.

Strauss, David A. "Discriminatory Intent and the Taming of Brown." *University Chicago Law Review* 56, no. 3 (1989): 935–1015.

Summers, Martin. *Manliness and Its Discontents: The Black Middle Class and the Transformation of Masculinity, 1900–1930*. Chapel Hill: University of North Carolina Press, 2004.

Taylor, Alrutheus A. *The Negro in Reconstruction in Virginia*. New York: Russell and Russell, 1926.

Taylor, Amy Murrell. *Embattled Freedom: Journeys through the Civil War's Slave Refugee Camps*. Chapel Hill: University of North Carolina Press, 2018.

Taylor, Joseph H. "Populism and Disfranchisement in Alabama." *Journal of Negro History* 34, no. 4 (1949): 410–27.

Thompson, Julius E. *The Black Press in Mississippi, 1865–1985*. Gainesville: University Press of Florida, 1993.

Thornbrough, Emma Lou. *T. Thomas Fortune: Militant Journalist*. Chicago: University of Chicago Press, 1972.

Thornton, John. "The African Experience of the '20. and Odd Negroes' Arriving in Virginia in 1619." *William and Mary Quarterly* 55, no. 3 (1998): 421–34.

Trelease, Allen W. "Republican Reconstruction in North Carolina: A Roll-Call Analysis of the State House of Representatives, 1868–1870." *Journal of Southern History* 42, no. 3 (1976): 319–44.

Trotter Joe W. "African American Fraternal Associations in American History: An Introduction." *Social Science History* 28, no. 3 (2004): 355–66.

Trotter Joe W., W. Earl Lewis, and Tera W. Hunter, eds. *The African American Urban Experience: Perspectives from the Colonial Period to the Present*. New York: Palgrave Macmillan, 2004.

Troutman, Phillip. "Grapevine in the Slave Market: African American Geopolitical Literacy and the 1841 *Creole* Revolt." In *The Chattel Principle: Internal Slave Trades in America*, edited by Walter Johnson, 203–33. New Haven, CT: Yale University Press, 2004.

Vincent, Charles. *Black Legislators in Louisiana during Reconstruction*. Carbondale: Southern Illinois University Press, 2011.

Vincent, Charles. "Negro Leadership and Programs in the Louisiana Constitutional Convention of 1868." *Louisiana History: The Journal of the Louisiana Historical Association* 10, no. 4 (1969): 339–51.

Virginia House of Delegates and the Senate of Virginia. Joint Resolution No. 89. *Recognizing the African American Members Elected to the Virginia General Assembly during Reconstruction*. January 11, 2012, Session, Legislation. Accessed October 15, 2012. http://leg1.state.va.us/cgi-bin/legp504.exe?121+ful+SJ89.

Virginia Writers Project. *The Negro in Virginia*. New York: Hastings House, 1940.

Wagner, Bryan. *Disturbing the Peace: Black Culture and the Police Power after Slavery*. Cambridge, MA: Harvard University Press, 2009.

Walker, Clarence E. *A Rock in a Weary Land: The African Methodist Episcopal Church during the Civil War and Reconstruction*. Baton Rouge: Louisiana State University Press, 1982.

Walker, David. *David Walker's Appeal: To the Coloured Citizens of the World, but in Particular, and Very Expressly, to Those of the United States of America.* Boston: David Walker, 1830. Accessed September 21, 2011. http://docsouth .unc.edu/nc/walker/menu.html.

Walker, Harry J. "Negro Benevolent Societies in New Orleans: A Study of Their Structure, Function, and Membership." Master's thesis, Fisk University, 1937.

Waselkov, Gregory, ed. *Powhatan's Mantle: Indians in the Colonial Southeast.* Revised and expanded edition. Lincoln: University of Nebraska Press, 2006.

Wharton, Vernon Lane. *The Negro in Mississippi, 1865–1890.* New York: Harper and Row, 1965.

White, Deborah Gray. *Ar'n't I a Woman? Female Slaves in the Plantation South.* New York: W. W. Norton, 1999.

Wight, Willard E. "Negroes in the Georgia Legislature: The Case of F. H. Fyall of Macon County." *Georgia Historical Quarterly* 44, no. 1 (1960): 85–97.

Williams, Heather Andrea. *Help Me to Find My People: The African American Search for Family Lost in Slavery.* Chapel Hill: University of North Carolina Press, 2012.

Williams, Kidada E. *They Left Great Marks on Me: African-American Testimonies of Racial Violence from Emancipation to World War I.* New York: New York University Press, 2012.

Willis, John C. *Forgotten Time: The Yazoo-Mississippi Delta after the Civil War.* Charlottesville: University of Virginia Press, 2000.

Wintory, Blake J. "African-American Legislators in the Arkansas General Assembly, 1868–1893." *Arkansas Historical Quarterly* 65, no. 4 (2006): 385–434.

Wintory, Blake J. "William Hines Furbush: African-American Carpetbagger, Republican, Fusionist, and Democrat." *Arkansas Historical Quarterly* 63, no. 2 (2004): 107–65.

Wolin, Sheldon S. "Fugitive Democracy." In *Democracy and Difference: Contesting the Boundaries of the Political,* edited by Sela Benhabib, 31–45. Princeton, NJ: Princeton University Press, 1996.

Wood, Peter H. *Black Majority: Negroes in Colonial South Carolina from 1670 through the Stono Rebellion.* New York: W. W. Norton, 1974.

Wood, Peter H. "The Changing Population of the Colonial South: An Overview by Race and Region, 1685–1790." In *Powhatan's Mantle: Indians in the Colonial Southeast,* edited by Gregory A. Waselkov, Peter H. Wood, and Tom Hatley, 57–132. Lincoln: University of Nebraska Press, 2006.

Woodruff, Nan Elizabeth. *American Congo: The African American Freedom Struggle in the Delta.* Cambridge, MA: Harvard University Press, 2003.

Woodruff, Nan Elizabeth. "The New Negro in the American Congo: World War I and the Elaine, Arkansas Massacre of 1919." In *Time Longer Than Rope: A Century of African American Activism, 1850–1950,* edited by Charles M. Payne and Adam Green, 150–78. New York: New York University Press, 2003.

Woods, Clyde. *Development Arrested: The Blues and Plantation Power in the Mississippi Delta*. London: Verso Books, 1998.

Woods, Clyde. *Development Drowned and Reborn: The Blues and Bourbon Restorations in Post-Katrina New Orleans*. Edited by Jordan T. Camp and Laura Pulido. Athens: University of Georgia Press, 2017.

Woodward, C. Vann. *The Origins of the New South: 1877–1913*. Baton Rouge: Louisiana State University Press, 1971.

Woodward, C. Vann. *The Strange Career of Jim Crow*. New York: Oxford University Press, 1955.

Woodward, Earl F. "The Brooks and Baxter War in Arkansas, 1872–1874." *Arkansas Historical Quarterly* 30, no. 4 (1971): 315–36.

Work, Monroe N., Thomas S. Staples, H. A. Wallace, Kelly Miller, Whitefield McKinlay, Samuel E. Lacy, R. L. Smith, and H. R. McIlwaine. "Some Negro Members of Reconstruction Conventions and Legislatures and of Congress." *Journal of Negro History* 5, no. 1 (January 1920): 63–119.

Zielinski, Sarah. "Rare Meteor Event Inspired Walt Whitman." *Smithsonian Magazine*, June 7, 2010. https://www.smithsonianmag.com/science-nature/rare-meteor-event-inspired-walt-whitman-29643165/.

Zipf, Karin L. "Reconstructing 'Free Woman': African-American Women, Apprenticeship, and Custody Rights during Reconstruction." *Journal of Women's History* 12, no. 1 (2000): 8–31.

INDEX

Note: Page numbers followed by *t* indicate tables.

collective identity, 33–34, 110, 116

collective names, race-based, 15; as in "colored," 71, 72, 274–75

Colored American, The (newspaper), 66, 170–71

Colored Education Convention, 59

Colored Farmers' Alliance (CFA), 154

Colored National Labor Convention, 187

Colored National Labor Union, 60, 323

Colored Union League of Williamsburg, 88

Columbia, South Carolina, 141

Columbus, Georgia, 165

Columbus, Mississippi, 277

Combahee Rice Strikes, 158–59

Combahee River Raid, 139–40

"common wind," 14, 19, 21

communication, 19–20, 342; alternative patterns of, 20; complications of, 8, geography of, 14; interstate, 285; networks, 21–22, 23, 116, 322;

communities: burning of, 235; emergent, 92–98; ties between, 68–69

community building, 3, 7–8, 11, 44, 105, 111

community institutions. *See tables for each state*

community organizing, 3–7, 11, 16–17, 146, 158, 166, 167; geographical factors, 8; social reproduction through, 343; violence against communities, 11–12

complaints, to Freedmen's Bureau, 331

conceptual maps, 353n21

concubinage, 119, 121; inheritance laws and, 337; paternity and, 119, 122, 128, 148, 171–72; support for children of, 330

Confederate monuments, 54

Confederate states, requirements for readmission to Union, 54

Confederate veterans, vigilantism of, 145–46

consensus: making, 84–92; mass participatory democracy and, 103–4

constitutional conventions, 60, 119, 122, 327–28; in Alabama, 218, 224, 229–36, 325, 338; in Arkansas, 305–13, 324; defining the new electorate, 334–35; in Florida, 203–7, in Georgia, 174, 175, 179, 180, 183, 337; in Louisiana, 253–54, 257–59, 263, 337; access to medical treatment and, 339; in Mississippi, 236, 270, 278, 279, 285–86, 326, 335; in North Carolina, 335; in South Carolina, 147–49, 150, 326, 328; in Virginia, 101–3, 104

Contraband Aid Association, 32

"contraband camps," 23–32, 346–47n19; complexity of, 29; conditions in, 29, 32; female-centered, 30–31; information at, 33–34; missionaries in, 31–35; in Missouri, 297–98; overcrowded, 297–98. *See also* fugitive settlements

Contraband Committee of the Mother Bethel AME Church, Philadelphia, 32

contrabandists, as a term, 347n7

Contraband Relief Association of Washington, 31

"contrabands." *See* fugitives

convict leasing, 167, 192, 316, 335–36; in Alabama, 336; in Georgia, 336

Cook, Fields, 357n26

Cooper, Manda, 251–52

Coovert, J. C., 316, 317

Corbin, Austin, 316

Corbin, Joseph C., 306, 308

Corinth, Mississippi, 27, 269, 277, 297

Cornelius, Catherine, 27–28, 348n19

corporal punishment, 148, 335, 336

Corps d'Afrique, 225

cotton, 218, 290, 315–16

Coushatta, Louisiana, massacre in, 262

Cox, Edwin, 21–22

Cox, Ida, 287

"Cox's Snow," 21–22

Crawford, Anna E., 40

credit unions, 40

Cremieux, Adolphe, 250

criminal conviction: black codes and, 148–49; disenfranchisement and, 16, 103, 206, 335, 375n22;

Crumley, Robert, Rev., 184, 185

Curtis, Samuel R., Gen., 295, 296, 298

custody, 15, 109–32, 271, 300, 324, 330, 337; impressment and, 113–15; as making autonomous families, 120–25; taking custody of ideas of freedom, 115–20; using custody to make demands, 112–13

Cuthbert, Georgia, 177

Danville, Virginia, early civil rights movement in, 105

Darien, Georgia, 190; mob incident in, 191

Davis, Jefferson, 60

Davis, Angela, 2

Davis Bend, Mississippi, 27

Dawson, Georgia, 177

Decatur, Alabama, 28

Declaration of Independence, 63, 127–28, 169

Delany, Martin R., 36–37, 38, 155, 157

Delegale, Henry, 190–91

Delta, Mississippi, 262–63

democracy, 6; mass participatory, 7, 8, 84–92

Democratic Party, 104, 128–29, 152, 156, 157, 182, 234, 274, 323; in Alabama, 238; in Arkansas, 311; electioneering by, 283; in Louisiana, 262–63; in Mississippi, 281–82, 283

Demopolis, Alabama, 223

Desdunes, Rodolphe Lucien, 261

Diggs, Frank, 237

"direct confrontation" practices, 40

discrimination, 189, 340; on means of transportation, 337; testimony on, 188

disfranchisement, 17, 67, 75, 321–22, 326, 334–35, 335, 342; in Alabama, 228; in Arkansas, 317; for criminal conviction, 103, 375n22; criminal conviction and, 16; criminal justice system used for, 335; in Florida, 375n22; in Georgia, 189; in Louisiana, 253; in North Carolina, 129; in Mississippi, 285–86; in South Carolina, 160; in state functions, 338–39; through state legislation, 105; in Virginia, 103. *See also* voter repression

displacement, 4–5, 16–17, 22, 43, 101, 123, 134–35, 342

District of Columbia, compensation of slaveholders in, 236

Dixon, James, 282

Dockery, Will, 286–87

Dockery Plantation, 286

dock labor, 108, 169, 207–08, 261, 263

domestic service, 108, 188, 261, 276

domestic violence, legislation on, 331

Domestic Workers Union, 261

Doster, James, 220

Dostie, Anthony, 255

Douglass, Frederick, 36, 76, 116, 117, 185, 285, 343

Downs, Jim, 29, 31, 123, 300

Drago, Edmund, 182–83, 187

Dred Scott opinion, 248, 380n12

Du Bois, W. E. B., 1–2, 10, 32, 53, 68, 72, 127, 151, 154, 180–81, 190–92, 225, 324, 328, 335

Dumas, Francis Ernest, 259

Dunbar, Paul Laurence, 301–2

Dunn, Oscar James, 259, 260

Dunn, Willis, 332

East Feliciana, Louisiana, riot in, 262

Edisto Island, 145

education, 14, 15, 17, 37, 46, 63–64, 111, 166, 168, 175, 187, 258–59, 265, 300, 338–39; citizenship and, 12; on citizenship rights, 140–41; public, 180; in Alabama, 338; in Virginia, 338. *See also* HBCUS (historically Black colleges and universities), schools

Educational Association of the Colored People of North Carolina, 126

Eisenhower, Dwight D., 376n33

Ellenton, South Carolina, 157

Ellison, Stewart, 336

Elyton (later Birmingham), Alabama, 222

emancipation, 13; celebrations of, 41, 93–94; displacement and, 5. *See also* abolition

Emancipation Circuit, 5–7, 19–20, 44–77, 79; as alternative way of seeing postwar southern terrain, 13; description of, 3–5; elements defining, 45–79; ongoing ties on Atlantic Coast, 104; as regional movement in the South, 342; rise and decline of circuits in most states, 323; sites on, 24. *See also specific states and maps*

Emancipation Proclamation, 22, 23, 27, 87, 296–97, 300; celebrations of, and other holidays, 93–94, 94–95, 248; Louisiana exempted from, 243; responses to, 35–36; slave system continued after, 24–25

emigration movements, 159–60, 187, 189, 239, 290, 317–18; Exoduster movement, 11, 74–75, 129, 244, 262–63, 265, 284–85, 302, 314–15, 317, 328, 346n19; Liberia emigration drives, 105, 159–60, 230, 284, 289, 302, 314; in each state, *See state tables*

Emanuel AME Church (Mother Emanuel), Charleston, South Carolina, 143, 149

enslaved people: burial of, 8; citizenship rights and, 8–9; displacement of, 22; hiring out of, 82–83; mass movements of, 14

Engs, Robert F., 32

Enterprise, Mississippi, 223, 280

equal access to public accommodation, 336–37

equality, 333; before the law, 333–34; voting rights and, 331

Equal Pay Act of 1963, 332–33

equal protection under the law, 333–34, 337

Equal Rights League, 59, 116, 117, 246–48, 276

Equal Suffrage: Address from the Colored Citizens of Norfolk, Va., 85–89, 93; movement, 60

Exoduster movement, 11, 74–75, 129, 244, 262–63, 265, 284–85, 302, 314–15, 317, 328, 346n19

Fabre, Genevieve, 94, 248, 380n12

family/families, 13, 119; autonomy and, 110–11, 119, 120–25; definition of family, 51; expansive conception of, 52; family life as a right, 110–11; family loss, 83–84, 101, 122–25, 298; formation of, 13, 51, 110–11, 119; integrity of, 121; proximity to members, 11; rebuilding, 42–43, 119; search for family members, 83–84; separation of, 122–25, 298

Farmers' Alliance, 238

farming, 148; farm collectives, 135; farming centers, 108; farming cooperatives, 16; self-sustaining farm communities, 145. *See also* agricultural labor

Farmville, Virginia, 98–99, 100

Federal Writers' Project, 348n19, 386n1

Fernandina, Florida, 26, 139, 213

Field Order No. 15, 144–45

Fifteenth Amendment, 6, 88, 94, 103, 154, 166, 183, 186, 285, 301, 343

Finley, Peyton, 230

First Amendment rights, 10, 53–54, 249, 262, 302

Fitzgerald, Michael, 57–59, 68, 70, 150, 225, 228, 278, 279

Florida, 15–16, 24, 135, 139, 196–216, 229; African American majorities in, 322; African American political representation in, 153, 205–7; appointment of judges in, 335; black codes in, 54; boycotts of elections in, 229; constitutional convention in, 334; disfranchisement in, 375n22; election of 1876 and, 321–22; five factions in, 201–4; institution building in, 214, 215–16t; labor laws in, 329; labor movement in, 207–13; legislation in, 329; politics in, 225, 226; redistricting in, 334, 391n23; state constitution of, 334, 391n23; St. Johns County, 213; voter repression in, 376n34; woman suffrage in, 75

Floyd, Monday, Rev.,182

Foner, Eric, 54, 104, 153, 160, 236

Foner, Philip, 276

Formwalt, Lee, 173

Forrest, Nathan Bedford, Gen., 308, 381n28

Forten, Charlotte, 137–38, 139, 140–41, 143–44

Forten, James, 365n7

Fort Gaines, Georgia, 177

Fort Monroe, Virginia, 20, 22–23, 26, 28, 32, 80, 83, 87, 93, 95, 111–12, 115, 137, 139–40

Fort Pillow Massacre, 308

Fort Pulaski, Georgia, 24, 165–66

Fort Smith, Arkansas, 297, 299

Fort Sumter, South Carolina, 295

Fortune, T. Thomas, 285, 340

Fort Valley, Georgia, 177

Fort Wagner, South Carolina, 136, 140

"forty acres and a mule," 144–47

Fourteenth Amendment, 6, 54, 94, 154, 166, 180, 252–57, 262, 301, 343; mob violence in response to, 252–53; passage of, 304

Franklin, Mercedes, 265

fraternal orders, 39, 40, 42, 50, 64–66, 94, 175

Frazier, Frank, 25

Frazier, Garrison, 144

Frederick Douglass School, New Orleans, 251, 252

Freedmen's Aid Association (FAA), 248–50

Freedmen's Aid Society, 29–30, 127

Freedmen's Bureau, 8, 32–33, 36, 44, 46, 55, 58, 63, 339; abandoned land and, 314; agents of, 310; in Alabama, 226–27, 230, 234–35; in Arkansas, 299, 305; Camilla Massacre and, 184; complaints to, 72, 328–32; education and, 63–64; established as government agency, 56; freedmen's hospital closures, 339; in Georgia, 167, 172–73, 176–77, 179, 181; grievances to, 72; in Louisiana, 256, 261; in Mississippi, 275–76, 278–80; in North Carolina, 111, 119, 122, 124, 127; parental rights cases and, 121; paternity and, 332; in South Carolina, 145; testimony to, 24–25; in Virginia, 93, 95, 100; white criticism of, 273–74; women and, 52

Freedmen's Friend Society, Brooklyn, New York, 31

Freedmen's Relief Association, 136–37

Freedmen's Schools, 63–64

freedom, 6, 17–18, 33, 144, 145, 160–61, 342; conceptions of, 108, 167, 172–73, 174, 223; demands of, 17; expectations about, 91; ideas of, 10, 115–20; loss of, 343; possibility of real, 34; production of space for, 12–13; white privilege and, 302–5

freedpeople, 3, 13, 17; in Alabama, 16; celebrations of emancipation and other events, 93–94, 94–95, 248; citizenship and, 6–7; citizenship rights and, 45–46; discourse and, 34; legal framework and, 45–46; "memory of the political" and, 7; methods used to organize, 175–76; not recognized in the South, 45–46; portrayal in the press, 275; production of space for freedom, 12–13; self-governance and, 34; survival needs of, 299–301; tools for struggle available to, 17; unique perspective on public sphere, 76. *See also* African Americans

Freemasonry, 39, 40, 65, 175, 279, 284, 385n25

Fremont, John C., Gen., 135

French Revolution, 261

Friends Freedmen Association, 299

"Friends of Freedom," Louisiana, 254

Friends of Universal Suffrage, New Orleans, 248

fugitives, 14–15, 20–24, 27, 30, 34–35, 114–15, 135–37, 346–47n20, 347n8; aid to, 83, 88, 134; as capable of independent life, 134; collective identity and, 110, 116; collective self-organization by, 110; Black women teachers and Black mothers, 250–52; housing needs of, 299–300; "messaging" to, 35–36; returned to owners by Union, 243–44; sent elsewhere by Union forces, 297–98 fugitive settlements, 4–5, 13, 17, 20, 26–31, 38, 44–45, 109–12; poor conditions in, 299–300. *See also* each state

Fugitive Slave Law, 23, 27, 83

Fulgham v. State, 331

Fyall, F. H., 182

Galilean Fishermen (Grand United Order of Galilean Fishermen, 1856), 41

Galloway, Abraham, 83, 111–12, 115–19, 128, 137, 139, 166, 329, 330–31, 335

Galveston, Texas, 276

Garnet, Henry Highland, 117

Garvey, Marcus, 4

General Order No. 5, 278

General Order No. 11, 135

George, Ceceil, 26

Georgia, 15, 24, 24–25, 135, 160, 165–95, 193–95t, 277, 334; African American population in, 322; Bibb County, 181; Black Belt counties in, 176, 178, 183, 189–90, 192; black codes in, 170; Black mass meetings in, 176–79, 183; Burke County, 168, 178–79; Camden County, 182; Chatham County, 165, 181; civil rights in, 336–37; coastal planters in, 165–66; colored conventions in, 170–71, 187–88; community institutions in, 192, 193–95t; compensation of slaveholders in, 236; conference of congregations in, 166; constitutional convention in, 174, 175, 179, 180, 183, 337; contention over representation in, 181–83; convict leasing in, 336; Dougherty County, 172–73, 174, 183; Edgecombe County, 125, 129; education in, 338; election of 1868 in, 188; Greene County, 178, 192; Jefferson County, 178, 318; labor laws in, 329, 330; labor movement in, 183; legislation in, 329, 330; Liberty County, 165–66, 182; lynching in, 190; McIntosh County, 168, 182, 190–91; military rule reestablished in, 186–87; Mitchell County, 183–86; redistricting in, 322; Oglethorpe County, 183; orphanages in, 340; Randolph County, 177; refusal to ratify Fifteenth Amendment, 186; relief for the poor in, 340; repression in, 175–76; Richmond County, 156, state constitution of, 180, 334; state legislature, 180–83, 186–87, 189, 330; Talbot County, 181; Union forces in, 165–66; unseating of African American legislators in, 180–82; violence against Black political activists, 181–83, 186–87; Wilkes County, 170; woman suffrage in, 330

Georgia Equal Rights Association (ERA), 172, 173–74

Georgia Sea Islands, 62, 134, 145, 146, 147

gerrymandering, 15–16, 67, 129, 159. *See also* redistricting

Giddings, Joshua Reed, 351n53

Giggie, John M., 287, 289, 315, 317

Gillem, Alvan C., Gen., 278

Gilroy, Paul, 10

Given, John V., Rev., 98–99

Glenn, Robert, 76–77

Glymph, Thavolia, 30–31, 347n7

Goldsboro, North Carolina, 126

Gould, William, 115–16, 137

Grand Junction, Tennessee, camps in, 26

Grand United Order of Tents, J. R. Giddings and Jolliffe Union, 41

Grandy, Charles, 20–21, 84

Grant, Ulysses S., 159, 255–56, 278, 307, 312; Order 44, 254, 255

Great Comet of 1859, 20

Great Comet of 1860, 343

Great Comet of 1861, 20, 343

Green, James K., 230

Greenback Party, 313

Greene, Frank, 308

Greenville, Mississippi, 68

Greenwood Hall, Mississippi, 354n43

Gregory, Ovid, 231–32, 233, 325

Grenada, Mississippi, 254

Grey, William H., 301–2, 306–7, 312

Gulf Coast, 13, 14, 62

Hager, Christopher, 34–35, 116

Hahn, Steven, 10, 24, 57, 70, 71, 145, 244, 271, 272, 274

Haiti, US recognition of independence of, 9, 119, 261

Haitian Revolution, 9, 261

Hall, J. D. S., Rev., 37

Hall, Stuart, 234

Hamburg Massacre, 156

Hamilton, Nelson, 357n26

Hamilton, Robert, 115, 116

Hamilton, Thomas, 115, 116

Hampton, Virginia, 26, 28, 32, 88, 89, 92, 93; HBCU in, 108; Liberia emigration drives in, 105; schools in, 108

Hampton, Wade, III, 157, 159

Hampton Institute, 104

Hampton Union League, 88

Harper, Frances Ellen Watkins, 116

Harpers Ferry, 20

Harris, Abram, 69

Harris, James Henry, 59–60, 127–28

Harrison, Sister, 83–84
Harrison, William, 182
Harrison, William H., 308
Hartman, Saidiya, 349n35
Hatcher, Jordan, 231
Hayes, Rutherford B., 321
Hayes-Tilden election, 308
Hayneville, Alabama, 223
Haywood, Felix, 77
HBCUS (historically Black colleges and universities), 63–64, 104, 108, 239, 318, 353n34
health care, access to, 8, 17, 245, 339 (see also hospitals)
Helena, Alabama, 238
Helena, Arkansas, 31, 297–98, 299–300, 306, 308, 318; camps in, 27; violence in, 310–11
Hendersonville, Tennessee, camps in, 26
Higginson, Thomas Wentworth, 203
Highgate, Carrie, 280
Highgate, Edmonia G., 80–81, 116, 250–51, 252, 256–57, 280
Highgate, Hannah, 280
Highgate, Wilella, 280
Hilton Head, South Carolina, 61
Hinds, James, 309, 311
Hodges, Nancy, 96
Hodges, Willis, 60, 88
Holiness churches, 287–89
Holly Springs, Mississippi, 27, 277
Holt, Thomas, 152
Hope, Arkansas, 306
Hose, Sam, 190, 191
hospitals, 140, 151, 339
Hot Springs, Arkansas, 299
Houzeau, Jean-Charles, 248, 259, 260
Howard, O. (Oliver) O., Gen., 95, 252, 273
Howel, James, 25
Howlin' Wolf, 286
Hugo, Victor, 250
human rights, universal, 18, 33
Humphries, Ban, 310
Hunter, Carolin, 84
Hunter, David, Gen.,135–36, 139
Hurlbut, S. (Stephen) A., Gen., 246, 247
Hyman, John Adams, 128–29

illiteracy, 43, 50, 175
immigrants, 343; Chinese laborers, 187; Italian, 5–6, 316–17
impressment, 15, 30–31, 136; custody and, 113–15
"incendiary" literature during slavery, 9–10

indebtedness, fugitives from slavery charged with, 34
Independent Order of Good Samaritans, 39
Independent Order of St. Luke, 39
"independent orders," 39, 40
information, 49, 69, 285; actionable, 5; at camps, 33–34; dissemination of, 5; movement of, 23; at prayer meetings, 33–34
Inge, Benjamin, Rev., 232
Ingraham, James H., 117, 246–48, 258–59, 260
inheritance, 337; across racial lines, 330; concubinage and, 337
"insulting" language, 53–54, 94
Insurrection Rumor of 1865, 92–93, 271–74
interracial marriage, 230, 233–34, 306–7, 324, 330, 337–38

Jackson, James, 177, 182
Jackson, Mississippi, 223, 270, 276, 277, 279, 281–82
Jackson v. Bishop, 336
Jacksonville, Florida, 24, 139, 145, 213
James, Delia, 121
James, Horace, 114
James, Maria, 121
James, William, 121
James City, Virginia, 89
James River watershed, 89
Jeffries, Moses, 307–8
Jefson, Ellis, Rev., 310–11
Jenkins, Absolom, 308
Jewett, Sarah Orne, 160–61
Jim Crow, 54–55, 64, 232, 238–39, 265, 287, 307, 322, 334, 345n6
Johnson, Andrew, 16, 56, 90, 145, 169, 224, 247, 254, 274, 286, 305
Johnson, Hannibal A., Lt., 141–43
Johnson, Robert, 286
Johnson, William, Jr., 39–40
Joiner, Philip, 174, 182, 183
Jones, Catesby, Cdr., 219–20
Jones, Columbus, 232
Jones, Sam, 142
juries, right to sit on, 172, 190, 303, 337
justice, 5, 46, 168, 172, 300–301, 330, 343; demands for, 73; difficulties obtaining, 309–10; equality before the law, 302–3, 333–34

Kansas exodus movement, 129, 160, 230–31, 244, 262–63, 265, 284, 314–15, 328
Kantrowitz, Stephen, 155–56
Katz, Steve, 321

Kaye, Anthony, 52

Kazanjian, David, 10

Keeling, William, 95

Kelly, Brian, 158–59

Kent, Orit, 65

Kentucky, 27, 62; camps in, 26; end of slavery in, 347n8

Kerr-Ritchie, Jeffrey, 352n19

Key West, Florida, 222

King, Coretta Scott, 64

King, George, 25

King, Martin Luther, Jr., 1, 2, 3

King Street riots, in Charleston, South Carolina, 157

kinship ties, 58

Kinsley, Edward, 112

Knights and Daughters of Tabor, 65

Knights of Labor (KoL), 70, 129, 153–54, 161, 238–39, 263–65, 323

Knights of Pythias, 279

knowledge: knowledge regimes, 7, 166, 167, 184, 342, 372n45; movement of, 19–20. *See also* information

Knowles, Anne, 220, 221

Knoxville, Tennessee, 141, 142; camps in, 26, 27

Kohl, Rhonda M., 300

Kolchin, Peter, 233

Kuiken, Vesna, 160–61

Ku Klux Klan (KKK), 17, 68, 294, 333; in Alabama, 228, 236–37; in Arkansas, 308–9; founding of, 308; in Georgia, 178, 181–83, 186–87; in Louisiana, 262; in Mississippi, 278–79; in North Carolina, 127–29; in South Carolina, 153, 155

Kulikoff, Allan, 34

labor, 7, 47, 114, 168, 328–30; Blacks as South's labor force, 89; centrality of labor organizing, 69–70, 244; complaints to Freedmen's Bureau, 328–32; compulsory, 47, 54, 243–48, 249, 271, 275, 335–36; contracts, 31, 54, 275, 326–27; forced, 54; gender and, 51; labor laws, 259, 329, 330; policing of, 243–48, 270–71; shortages of, 124, 219; in South Carolina, 133–34; in South Carolina's black codes, 148–49; strikes, 96–98; unpaid, 47; wage work, 33, 45, 125; wartime, 113–15; white control of, 53; women and, 188; workers' demands, 7; working-class organization, 75; working conditions, 169, 170, 190, 328–29

Laboring Men's Mechanics Union Association, Virginia, 98

labor organization, 11, 16, 75, 318, 330; in Alabama, 238; in Black Belt, 188–89; centrality of, 69–70, 244; of domestic workers, 276; in Florida, 207–13; in Georgia, 167, 169–70, 183, 187–89; in Louisiana, 245–46, 261, 263–64, 265; in Mississippi, 290; in New Orleans, Louisiana, 248–49; in North Carolina, 129; political representation and, 69–70; in rural areas vs. cities, 322–23; social nature of, 15; in South Carolina, 146, 150, 154, 161; in Virginia, 88, 96–98, 108; women in, 323

Lake Village, Arkansas, 306, 314, 317

land, 37, 284, 327–28; abandoned, 134, 144–46, 167, 271, 275, 314; distribution of, 151, 167, 259, 271, 274, 275, 327–28; leasing of, 299; preservation of plantations, 299; sharing of, 11

landownership, 46, 89, 125, 129; autonomy and, 275; collective, 88, 188; opportunities for, 190; promise of, 144–47, 249–50. *See also* "forty acres and a mule"

Lane, Annetta M., 41

Langston, John Mercer, 276–78

language, 166; legislative, 303, 325–27; prejudicial, 303; race and, 234–35, 238, 325–27; white privilege and, 303

Latimore, Sandy, 142

laundry workers, 276

Lawrenceville, Virginia, HBCU in, 108

Lee, Robert E., Gen., 322; surrender of, 81, 94, 220

Lee, Thomas, 232

legislation/law, 14, 52–56, 87, 119, 127–28, 154, 228, 324, 330, 332; African American officeholders and, 325–41; to bar gender discrimination, 332; child labor and, 119–20; civil rights legislation, 336; disfranchisement through, 105; on domestic violence, 331; freedpeople and, 45–46; labor laws, 328–29; legal rights, 54; need to inscribe Black humanity in, 8; prejudicial language of, 303; race and, 238, 325–27; replicating the slave system, 225, 301; silences and gaps in, 110–11; white supremacist, 46, 148–49, 156, 322; on woman suffrage, 330–31. *See also* black codes; constitutional conventions; Jim Crow; segregation; slave codes; *specific legislation and states*

Leonid meteor showers, 343–44

Lewis, Earl, 86

Lewis, John, 64

Lewis, Ronald, 276

Liberal Republican Party, 311

Liberia, US recognition of, 119

Liberia emigration, 74–75, 105, 159–60, 230, 265, 284, 289, 302, 314

Merryman, R. C., 279

meteors, 20–21; Leonids, 343–44

Methodism, 175

Methodist Episcopal Church, 61, 149, 288. *See also* African Methodist Episcopal (AME) Church

migration, 5–6, 17, 19–43, 284–87, 290, 302, 317. *See also specific movements and state tables*

Miles College, 239

militias, 71, 146, 155–57, 273, 274, 275, 279, 309, 336

Milledgeville, Georgia, 67

Miller, Thomas, 332, 335

Millett, Eli, 25

ministers, 11, 13, 60, 62–63, 167, 168, 175, 178

missionaries, 31–35, 45, 60–62, 134, 138, 222–23, 305; deaths of, 38; military protection and, 166; records of, 8; women, 251–52

Mississippi, 14, 16, 24, 58, 223, 237, 269–93, 298, 329; African American political representation in, 153, 274–76, 285, 290; African American population in, 322; African American press in, 290; assembly in, 270–71, 274–75; black codes in, 53–54, 270–71, 275, 337; blues and, 286–90; camps in, 27; circuit riders in, 276–78, 290; civil rights in, 337; compensation of slaveholders in, 236; constitutional convention in, 236, 270, 278, 279, 285–86, 326, 335; constitution of, 285; discrimination on means of transportation in, 337; emigration movements in, 290; forgatherings in, 270–74; Hinds County, Mississippi, 281, 283; inheritance laws in, 337; institution building in, 290, 291–93*t*; interracial marriage in, 337; labor organization in, 290; multifaceted building of political formations in, 278–80; new counties created in, 322; poll taxes in, 285; public schools in, 338; railroads in, 286–90, 287; Union forces in, 269–70; violence against political organizers in, 159, 278, 281–83; Washington County, Mississippi, 27

Mississippi City, Mississippi, 269

Mississippi Plan, 157, 281–82

Mississippi Prince Hall Masons, 279

Mississippi River Valley, 13–14, 25–26, 280, 297; camps in, 27; labor sites in, 31

Missouri, 27, 295; camps in, 297–98; end of slavery in, 347n8

Mobile, Alabama, 61, 217, 218, 222, 223, 224, 226–27, 229

Mobile Nationalist (newspaper), 231

mobilization, 13–15, 42, 44, 108, 125, 244, 305, 322; in Alabama, 236–39; Black prophetic ministry and, 13; creation of a mobilized public, 341; vs. demoralization, 344; egalitarianism and, 342;

in Georgia, 165–95; tools for, 7; trade associations and, 97; triggered by Union forces, 22–24, 45–46, 134–35, 243, 269, 296

Moneyhon, Carl, 297, 299, 303, 305

Monroe, John T., 254, 255

Monroe, Louisiana, 273

Montgomery, Alabama, 16–17, 28, 68, 218, 222–27, 230, 236–39

Montgomery, Isaiah, 285–86

Montgomery Daily Advertiser (newspaper), 222

Montgomery Mail (newspaper), 229

Moore, Aaron, Rev., 279

Moore, J. Aaron, 278

Moore, Romulus, 182, 183

Morgan, Albert T., 58, 272, 279, 283, 337

Morgan, Charles, 58

Morrison, Toni, 317

Mosaic Templars of America, 41

Moses, Franklin, Gov., 155

Moss, Gregory, 272

Mound Bayou, Mississippi, 285

murder, 30, 38, 41, 119, 188, 309–10, 314; accountability for, 333–34; of African American leaders, 155–56, 186, 279; of African American political organizers, 209–10, 237, 264; lynchings, 190, 286; of officers, 254; *redemption* and, 235

Murphy, Isaac, Gov., 304

Murray, Ellen, 137

mutual aid societies, 8, 38–42, 58, 190

Myers, Cyrus, 329

Nash, Sarah, 95–96

Nashville, Tennessee, 31, 71; camps in, 26, 27, 29, 30; state convention of freedpeople in, 71–73, 118

Nashville Dispatch (newspaper), 71

Nashville Normal and Theological Institute, 64

Natchez, Mississippi, 57, 61, 223, 269, 270, 280; camps in, 27; occupied by Union forces, 25–26

National Afro-American Council, 323, 340

National Afro-American League, 340

National Afro-American Press Association, 323

National Anti-Slavery Standard (newspaper), 187, 188

National Association for the Advancement of Colored People (NAACP), 323

National Association of Colored Women, 323

National Association of Colored Women's Clubs (NACWC), 341

National Convention of Colored Men, Syracuse, New York, 116, 117, 246–47

Peete, Sylvester, 261

Penn School, St. Helena Island (now Penn Center), South Carolina, 137

Pensacola, Florida, 24, 213, 222

Pentecostal-Holiness movement, 17, 287

Pepper, Calvin, 92, 358n36

Percy, Leroy, 316–17

Petersburg, Virginia, 21–22, 84–85, 97–98, 99, 103, 105, 108, 250–51

Pierce, Edward Lillie, 20, 32, 137

Pinchback, P. B. S., 225, 257–63, 337. *See also* Stewart, Pinkney Benton

Pinchback, William, 224, 225

Pine Bluff, Arkansas, 27, 294, 296, 304, 305, 306, 308, 315

Pitts, Coffin, 83

plantations, 134–35; organizing on, 245; replication of slave system in, 166; seizure of abandoned, 144–46

planters, 16; insurrection hysteria of, 271–72; labor contracts with, 245; reparations for, 235–36, 329

Plessy, Homer, 345n6

Plessy v. Ferguson, 189, 264, 345n6

Plymouth, North Carolina, 26

Plymouth Island, North Carolina, 109, 110

Pocahontas Island neighborhood, 84–85

Pointe Coupée, Louisiana, 265

Poliakoff, Eli, 150, 154

police/policing, 5, 71, 87, 336

political equality vs. social equality, 171

political formation(s), 15, 16, 149–50, 278–80, 342; social nature of reproduction of, 134; visualizing, 11–12

political ideology, reproduction of, 15, 134

political interactions, new definitions of, 73

poll taxes, 67, 105, 187, 285, 334, 335

populism, 175, 290, 313, 318

Port Gibson, Mississippi, 274–75, 276

Port Hudson, Louisiana, 27, 28–29, 117

Port Royal Experiment, 15, 135, 160–61

Port Royal Relief Association, 136–37

Port Royal, South Carolina, 30, 31, 32, 134, 135, 136–37

Portsmouth, Virginia, 26, 61, 83, 84, 87, 93, 101–2, 108; celebrations in, 94–95; freedwomen vendors in, 95–96; as hub of in-migration and organizing, 83; schools in, 108; strikes in, 96–97

Prairie Grove, Arkansas, 295

prayer meetings, among slavery fugitives, 33–34

Prentiss, Benjamin, Gen., 298

press, the, 46–49, 93–94, 127; Black press, 66, 93–94, 103, 105, 115, 129, 137, 149, 160, 161,

170–72, 190, 192, 227, 231, 248, 249, 250, 259, 262, 263, 265, 270, 279, 285, 286; conservative postwar, 173; Democratic, 103, 330; importance for gaining representation, 183, 270, 290; in Mississippi, 290; northern, 23, 90–91, 102, 103, 139, 187, 280, 316; power of free press, 166; terror against, 290; southern conservative white, 69, 94, 97, 99, 99–100, 103, 128, 169, 173, 191, 222, 229, 275, 310, 330. *See also specific publications*

Prince George, Virginia, schools in, 108

Prince Hall Free Masons, 65, 385n25

prison camps, Confederate, 141

prison reform, 167, 335, 336

protests, 47–49, 110–11, 117–18, 169–70, 238, 245–48, 287

Providence, Rhode Island, 122–23

public accommodations: equal access to, 336–37; segregation of, 337

public space, 93–94, 128, 253; religious practices in, 109–10

public universities, 338

Quarles, Benjamin, 40

Rabbit Foot Minstrels, 287

race, 116; language and, 234–35, 238; legislation and, 238, 325–27; removing from citizenship, 325–27; textual marking of, 325–27

Radical Reconstruction, 54–57; end of, 275

Radical Reconstruction Act of 1865, 100

railway, 25, 70, 105, 125, 129, 284–85, 287–88, 316–17, 322; in Alabama, 236, 237, 239; in Arkansas, 315–16; in Louisiana, 261; in Mississippi, 286–90, 287; railroad camps, 13; railroad construction, 13, 68

Rainey, Ma, 4, 287, 352n19

Raleigh, North Carolina, 61, 119

Raleigh Sentinel, The (newspaper), 128

rallies, 94–95, 228, 254

Randolph, Benjamin, 326

Ransier, Alonzo, 151–52

rape, 51–52, 223–24, 306. *See also* sexual violence

Rapier, James T., 72–73, 231–33, 237–28, 336, 338–39

rations, 117–18, 296–97

Raven, William. Rev., 177

Readjuster movement, 104–5

Reconstruction, 6, 13, 63, 155, 189; durability of political structures built in, 11; end of, 16, 103–5, 159–60, 186–87, 260–61, 279, 314, 324; HBCUs started in, 63–64; historiography of, 5; literature of, 2–3; Red Shirts violence in

segregation, I, 54–55, 64, 128, 151, 232, 326, 338, 345n6; in military hospitals and graves, 140; persistence of, 338; of public accommodations, 337; public schools and, 338; of public transport, 189, 264–65; of schools, 12, 233, 234, 259, 264, 285, 303, 338. *See also* Jim Crow

self-defense, 89, 91, 148, 156, 167, 179, 183–86, 188, 236, 278, 279, 333–34; making, 183–86; right to, 48, 53, 68; self-defense movements, 129; self-defense patrols, 71; in slave system, 185–86

self-governance, 34

Selma, Alabama, 16, 68, 217–18, 220–23, 228, 237, 239

Selma Ordnance and Naval Foundry, 218–19, 223, 239

Selma University, 239

"separate but equal doctrine," 326

sexual violence, 332; politically motivated, 330; sexual exploitation, 332; testimony of, 47. *See also* African American women

Shabazz, Malcolm (Malcolm X), 2

Shackelford, "Sis," 22

sharecropping, 288, 299, 315, 316–17

Sharkey, William L., Gov. (provisional) 273, 277

Shaw, Robert Gould, 140, 144

Shelby Iron Works, 220–21, 222

Sheridan, Philip, 255

Sherman, Thomas W., Gen., 134, 136

Sherman, William Tecumseh, Gen., 141, 143, 144–45, 167, 168, 223

Sherman Reserve, 144–46, 167, 327

Sherman's March to the Sea, 143

Shuften, J. T., 66, 171

Sikes, Benjamin, 183

Simms, James M., 181, 336

slave codes, 87, 110–11. *See also* specific states

Slave Narrative Project, 386n1

slave patrols, 146

slave population, distribution compiled from Census of 1860, 78

slave system, 7, 10, 144; challenges to slavery-era laws, 12; Christianity and, 9; continued after Emancipation Proclamation, 24–25; corporal punishment and, 335; experience from, 49–50; flight from, 13–14, 19–43; laws reinforcing, 301; markers of, 101; marriages created by, 331–32; patriarchy and, 332; rape in, 48, 52, 306; remnants of, 333; replication of, 166, 225, 245, 328–32; resistance to, 2–4; rupture of, 45–46, 52–53; self-defense in, 185–86; the state and, 17; violence of, 230. *See also* concubinage

Smalls, Robert, 138, 159

Smith, Bessie, 4, 287

Smith, Gerrit, 88

Smith, Lewis, 176

Smith, Thomas Kilby, Gen., 223

Smith, William Hugh, Gen., 229

Snead, Walter, 357n26

societies, 7–8, 16, 38, 41, 105, 179, 189–90, 243–68. *See also* specific societies

sodalities, 39, 64–66, 244, 259; and community solidarity, 42

Sons of Confederate Veterans, 235–36

"souls to the polls," 68

South Carolina, 11, 15, 24, 31, 32, 36, 47, 133–64, 331; access to medical care in, 339; African American political representation in, 133–64; African American population in, 322; Aiken County, 157; Barnwell County, 157; Beaufort County, SC, 153; black codes in, 53, 54, 147–49; constitutional convention in, 147–49, 150, 326, 328; Edgefield County, 155–56, 159–60, 314; election of 1876 and, 321–22; farming in, 134–35; first colored convention in, 149; legislation in, 329; legislature of, 153; local circuits in, 141–43; martial law in, 155; new counties created in, 322; organizing in, 153; plantations in, 134–35; problem of unpaid contracts in, 326–27; rice region, 158; riots of 1876, 156; state constitution of, 160; teachers in, 136–37; Union forces in, 133–35; use of Mississippi Plan in, 282; white supremacist legislation in, 148–49; woman suffrage in, 332

South Carolina Expeditionary Corps, 133–34

southern customary conventions, 33

Southern Homestead Act, 249–50

space: "oppositional spatial practices," 287; oppositional spatial practices, 4–5, 31, 285, 287; production of, 8, 12–13, 289–90. *See also* public space

Speed, Lawrence, 173

Spero, Sterling, 69

Stanton, Edwin, Gen., 144, 254–55

Starkey, Mary Ann, 111–12

State Convention of the Colored People of North Carolina, 119–20

State Mechanics' and Laborers' Association, Georgia, 187

state services, white supremacist influence on, 338–39

statewide conventions, dangers of organizing, 119

St. Augustine, Florida, 24, 213

Staunton, Virginia, 97, 98

Steele, Frederick, Gen., 296, 297

stevedores, 97–98, 169, 170

Stevens, Thaddeus, 74

Stewart, Eliza, 224

Stewart, Nina, 225

Stewart, Pinckney Benton, 224–25. *See also* Pinchback, P. B. S

St. Helena Island, South Carolina, 137, 143–44

Still, William, 219

Stillman College, 239

St. John's AME, Norfolk, 85

St. Louis, Missouri, 297–98

Stockham, Richard, 219

Straight University, 258

strikes, 96–98, 146, 158–59, 170, 218, 239, 263–64; in Charleston, South Carolina, 154; in Louisiana, 261; organized by women, 158; in Virginia, 108. *See also* labor organization

Stringer, Thomas W., 278, 279–80

Strother, Alfred, 231, 232–33, 329

St. Simon's Island, Georgia, 165

Suffolk, Virginia, 26

suffrage movement, 60, 88, 115, 253–54; Equal Suffrage movement, 60; universal suffrage, 254; woman suffrage, 151–52, 167, 330–31, 332, 335, 381n25. *See also* enfranchisement; voting rights

Sunnyside Plantation, Arkansas, 313–18

Supreme Court of North Carolina, 331

Taliaferro, James Govan, 259

Talladega College, 239

Tallahassee, Florida, 28

Tanner, Benjamin Tucker, 37

task work model, 135

"Taxpayers Convention," 281–82

Taylor, Alrutheus, 94

Taylor, Amy Murrell, 31, 64, 296, 297, 299–300

Taylor, Harriet R., 41

Taylor, Susie King, 30

teachers, 14, 30–32, 59, 75; in Alabama, 226–27; encounters between Black women refugees and Black women teachers, 250–52; in Georgia, 167–68; in Louisiana, 256; in Mississippi, 280, 284; in North Carolina, 105; in South Carolina, 134, 136–37; in Virginia, 80

Teamoh, George, 81–83, 85, 95–96, 101–2, 104, 111, 137, 169

Teamoh, Jane, 83

Teamoh, John, 83

Teamoh, Josephine, 83

Teamoh, Sallie, 83

Teamsters and Loaders Association of Mobile, 263

temperance societies, 179

tenant farmers, 329. *See also* sharecropping

Tennessee, 23, 24, 27, 62, 110, 142, 345n6; benevolent societies in, 30; camps in, 26; end of slavery in, 347n8; missionaries in, 31; state convention of freedpeople in, 71–73, 119

terror, 12, 15, 17, 91, 127–28, 143, 153, 156, 183–88, 223–24, 273, 290, 333, 336. *See also* Ku Klux Klan (KKK); violence

testimony, 47, 48, 52, 90, 148, 172, 188, 337, 342; barring of black against white, 170, 224, 303, 333–34; of brutality, 119; of injustices, 110

Texarkana, Arkansas, 306

Texas, 23–24, 295–96

Thibodaux, Louisiana, massacre in, 263–64

Thirteenth Amendment, 6, 52–53, 55, 87, 166, 250, 300–301, 343, 347n8

Thomas, Samuel, 273–74

Thomasville, Georgia, 254

Thoreau, Henry David, 20

Threadgill, Henry, 318

"three-fifths clause," 15–16, 226, 253

Tidewater Virginia, 93

Tillman, Ben, 160

Tillson, Davis, Gen., 173

tobacco industry, 96–98, 98, 108, 125

Towne, Laura M., 136–38

Townsend, James, 22–23

trade associations, 7, 39, 42, 97, 98, 108, 339. *See also specific associations*

trade unions, 108, 261

Trammell, L. N., 182–83

trauma, acknowledgment and transformation of, 270

Trotter, Joe, 40

True Southerner, The (newspaper), 93–94

Truth, Sojourner, 345n6

Tubman, Harriet, 24, 138–41, 166, 343

Turner, Henry McNeal, Rev., 35–36, 62, 160, 168, 176–78, 180–82, 187, 277, 284, 329, 330–31, 336, 340

Turner, Nat, 10

Tuscaloosa, Alabama, 222

Tuskegee, Alabama, 223, 236–37, 239

Tuskegee University, 239

Tutuola, Amos, 11

Tybee Island, Georgia, 165

Underground Railroad, 4, 7, 41, 83, 138, 276

Union [Benevolent] Association, New Orleans, 244–45

voter intimidation, 156, 156–59, 183, 281–82

voter registration, 12, 63, 127, 168, 175–78, 230, 278, 282, 305–8, 322; collective work on, 179; drives for, 378n43; instruction on, 176–77; US Congress and, 228–29

voter repression, 6, 12, 67, 322; in Alabama, 229, 238, 378n23; in Arkansas, 307–9; in Florida, 376n34; in Georgia, 180, 182–83; 186–87; in Louisiana, 260–61, 261, 264; in Mississippi, 270; in North Carolina, 129; in South Carolina, 143, 152–54; violence and, 153, 157; Virginia, 105

voting rights, 47–48, 54, 57, 71, 75, 253–54, 324, 334–35, 381n25; for African American men, 305–8, 330; African American women and, 330; in Alabama, 226, 232, 378n23; of Black men, 305–6, 322, 324; contested in Georgia, 186; in Georgia, 166, 172, 176, 180, 190; impact of, 307–8; literacy tests and, 105; in Louisiana, 253–54; in Mississippi, 270, 280, 285; in North Carolina, 115, 118, 125–26; poll taxes and, 105; residence requirements and, 105; in South Carolina, 150–52, 154; in Virginia, 89, 103; voting rights activism, 6; Voting Rights Act of 1965, 8, 17, 105, 333, 334, 377–78n22; white reaction to, 155–56; women and, 330–31

Voting Rights Act of 1965, 8, 17, 105, 333, 334, 377–78n22

wages, 37, 151, 167, 172, 187, 245, 273, 329; back wages, 14, 186, 190, 329; disparity in, 169–70; disputes about, 158–59; unpaid, 297, 326–27; wage discrimination, 169–70; wage inequality, 75

Wagner, Bryan, 191, 351n55

Walker, Clarence, 37–38, 61–62, 76, 160

Walker, David, 9–10, 36–37, 307

Wallace, George, 180–81, 182

Wallace, John, 374n13

Walton Act, 105

War Department, 134, 136

Warmoth, Henry Clay, Gov., 259, 260

Warwick (Newport News), Virginia, 26, 89

Washington, Arkansas, 299

Washington, D.C., 93

Washington, George, 94

Washington, Isaac C., 40

Washington, North Carolina, 26

Waters, Elijah, 142,

Waters, Ethel, 287

Watson, B. F., 284

we, new iterations of the concept, 16, 110, 116

Weekly Pelican, The (newspaper), 263–64

Wells, Ida B., 283–84, 345n6

Wells, Richard, 357n26

Wells, W. Calvin, 281–82

Wesley, John, 142

Western Freedmen's Aid Commission, 29

Whipper, William, 151–52

White, James (J. T.), 306, 310–11, 388n20

White Camelias (Mississippi), 262

whiteness, treated as norm, 326

white privilege, 54–55; citizenship rights and, 302–5; elite vs. working class, 304–5; freedom and, 302–5; systemic immunity for crime against Blacks, 55–56; vs. universal human rights, 111. See also testimony

white supremacism, 62, 306, 322; white supremacists, 160, 305, 309; influence on state services, 338–39; legislation, 54–55, 148–49, 156. See also Jim Crow

white voter boycotts (1868), 203–4, 229

Whitlock farm, 173

Whitman, Walt, 20

Wilder, L. Douglas, 260

Williams, Heather, 43

Williams, John W., 312

Williamsburg, Virginia, 88, 92; Liberia emigration drives in, 105

Williamson, John H., 328

Willis, H. R., 310

Wilmington, North Carolina, 26, 61, 118, 121, 128, 170, 273, 333

Wilmington Daily Journal, The (newspaper), 128

Wilson, David, 259

Wilson, James, 219–20

Wilson, Joseph T., 85–89, 93

Wilson's Creek, Missouri, 308

Wolin, Sheldon, 6, 56

woman suffrage, 151–52, 167, 330–31, 332, 335, 381n25

women's club movement, 341

women tobacco stemmers, 108

Woods, Clyde, 289

Woolfolk, Peter, 357n26

Works Progress Administration, 101, 295–96

Worthington, Elisha, 313–14, 317

Wright, Jonathan, 326–27

Yazoo City, Mississippi, 58, 272, 282–83; riot in, 262, 282–83

Yorktown, Virginia, 92

Young Men's Literary Society of Boston, 83

Zipf, Karen, 121, 124

MORE PRAISE FOR THULANI DAVIS

Praise for *Nothing but the Music*

"*Nothing but the Music* dares the reader to take it all in, to meditate, and then act (react), whether a dance, a cry, or an amen of acknowledgement and remembrance. Yes, each poem here rocks steady, carrying the natural freight of confrontation and jubilation."—YUSEF KOMUNYAKAA

"If the immense sound heard in these poems strikes you as its own cosmic event horizon, then yes, you have learned the coded labyrinth that is Thulani Davis's intricate, soulful, and playful mind. . . . *Nothing but the Music* transports us and attunes our ears to a profound era that sought to invent our future and then more future."—MAJOR JACKSON

Praise for *1959*

"*1959* is an engaging, richly textured story of collective political action and everyday heroism."—*Boston Herald*

"*1959* is not merely the story of one girl's loss of innocence; rather, it is the story of an entire community's coming of age. It is the story of private lives colliding with politics and history, the story of the civil rights struggle and how it affected one small town in the South. . . . [Davis] is able to show the consequences of integration on a single family and community with insight, sympathy, and grace."—*The New York Times*

"*1959* evokes the cool echoing voice of a storyteller within a story. . . . Davis's novel has an uncanny capacity to enthrall the reader, a power that derives from her impeccable control of horror and response to horror."—*Los Angeles Times*

"Exceptional."—*The Times Literary Supplement*

"Davis poetically renders the tiny dots that make up the larger, dramatic picture of the civil rights movement. She also provides a complex and compelling portrait of a solid African American community—something all too rare in contemporary fiction."—*Orlando Sentinel*